Case Law in Health Care Administration
Second Edition

George D. Pozgar, MBA
President
Gp Health Care Consulting, International
Arlington, Virginia
Field Representative
Joint Commission on Accreditation of Healthcare Organizations
Oakbrook Terrace, Illinois

with

Nina S. Pozgar, JD

This publication is designed to provide accurate and authoritative information in regard to the Subject Matter covered. It is sold with the understanding that the publisher is not engaged in rendering legal, accounting, or other professional service. If legal advice or other expert assistance is required, the service of a competent professional person should be sought. (From a Declaration of Principles jointly adopted by a Committee of the American Bar Association and a Committee of Publishers and Associations.)

Library of Congress Cataloging-in-Publication Data

Pozgar, George D.
Case law in health care administration/
George D. Pozgar with Nina S. Pozgar.—2nd ed.
p. cm.
Includes bibliographical references and index.
ISBN 0-8342-1204-8
1. Medical care—Law and legislation—
United States—Cases. 2. Medical personnel—
Malpractice—United States—Cases.
I. Pozgar, Nina S. II. Title.
KF3821.A7P69 1999
344.73'0321—dc21
98-44120
CIP

Aspen Publishers, Inc., grants permission for photocopying for limited personal or internal use.
This consent does not extend to other kinds of copying, such as copying for general distribution,
for advertising or promotional purposes, for creating new collective works, or for resale.
For information, address Aspen Publishers, Inc., Permissions Department,
200 Orchard Ridge Drive, Suite 200, Gaithersburg, Maryland 20878.

Orders: (800) 638-8437
Customer Service: (800) 234-1660

About Aspen Publishers • For more than 35 years, Aspen has been a leading professional publisher in a variety of disciplines. Aspen's vast information resources are available in both print and electronic formats. We are committed to providing the highest quality information available in the most appropriate format for our customers. Visit Aspen's Internet site for more information resources, directories, articles, and a searchable version of Aspen's full catalog, including the most recent publications: **http://www.aspenpublishers.com**
Aspen Publishers, Inc. • The hallmark of quality in publishing
Member of the worldwide Wolters Kluwer group.

Editorial Services: Jane Colilla
Library of Congress Catalog C

*This casebook is dedicated to
Louis Angelo Santucci
who was right when he said
Knowledge is Power.*

Table of Contents

Preface

This second edition of *Case Law in Health Care Administration* is a unique companion guide to a wide variety of texts utilized in the study of health care administration, such as *Legal Aspects of Health Care Administration, Seventh Edition*. Moreover, it is an independent compendium of more than 200 case studies from a wide array of jurisdictions covering important legal issues.

The text is designed for use by both students and practicing health care professionals. It is written using terminology focused on the layperson and provides health care professionals with the necessary knowledge to become conversant in legal issues pertinent to their jobs.

Every effort has been made to ensure that the material in this text is current. The information contained in this casebook relies on current statutory and decisional authority, as well as the author's specialized knowledge gained through extensive experience in the health care field.

In a litigious environment such as exists in the United States, where malpractice and negligence suits are increasing at an alarming rate, it is imperative that all professionals who deal with patients know their rights and responsibilities under the law of their jurisdiction, and the possible legal ramifications of their actions.

An in-depth review of more than 200 cases decided in the 1990s has revealed that the same or similar negligent acts have been repeatedly committed by health care professionals. The passage of time has only changed the names of the litigants. This guide presents the most recent cases in a format that informs and enlightens the reader about important medical and legal issues. After reading each fact pattern, decision, and reasoning by the court, readers are presented with discussion questions. The questions are intended to allow readers to demonstrate their understanding of, and ability to, explain the issues. Moreover, readers will be able to apply what they learn to their professional problem solving. Each case, and subsequent decisions presented, have had an effect on the health care system. Therefore, readers should understand and apply political, social, and economic factors when analyzing the cases. The cases selected have relevance to, and are reflective of, case law from the majority of states.

CASES

The general format of each case reviewed is as follows:

- **Title.** Each case is given a title that signals the type of case about to be reviewed.
- **Citation.** Students may wish to research cases cited in this text to gain a deeper understanding of the topics covered. A case citation describes the identity of the parties in the case, the text in which the case can be found, and the year in which the case was decided. For example: *Bouvia v. Superior Court (Glenchur)*, 225 Cal. Rptr. 297 (Cal. Ct. App. 1986)
  - *Bouvia v. Superior Court (Glenchur)*—Identifies the basic parties involved in the lawsuit.
  - 225 Cal. Rptr. 297—Identifies the case as being reported in volume 225 of the California Reporter at page 297.
  - Cal. Ct. App. 1986—Identifies the case as being decided in the California Court of Appeal in 1986.

Students who decide to research a specific case should visit a law library, which will contain various federal, state, and regional reporters. To assist the reader in understanding the important aspects of each case, they are presented in the following manner:

- **Facts.** A review of the facts of the case.
- **Issue.** The issues discussed in any given case are selected for review on the basis of medical and legal pertinence to the health care professional. Although any one case in this text may have multiple issues, emphasis was placed on selecting those issues considered to be most relevant for the reader.
- **Holding.** The court's ruling based on the facts, issues, and applicable laws pertaining to a case.
- **Reason.** The rationale as to how the court arrived at its decision based on the facts, issues, and relevant laws surrounding a case. There are several cases explained in the text that require students to analyze the case themselves and determine the facts, issue, holding, and reason for that case.
- **Discussion.** Discussion questions, although prompted by a particular case, may not necessarily be germane to the facts of the case. For example, in the *Bramer v. Dotson* case described in Chapter IV, one of the discussion questions asks, "What instructions should the physician have provided to the patient for continuing care?" The fact that this question was asked does not mean to imply that the physician provided or failed to provide instructions for continuing care. The questions are merely presented as opportunities for discussion and in no way add to the facts of a specific case. For some cases, students are asked to develop their own discussion questions for class review.

SELF-TEST

For review and reinforcement of case issues, a self-administered test is provided at the end of the text. An attempt has been made to make the multiple-choice questions a learning tool for both beginning and intermediate students, as well as for seasoned professionals.

Each of the questions or incomplete sentences is followed by four to six suggested answers. Although two or more answers may be or appear to be correct, be sure to select the best alternative answer.

The questions have been designed to provide an opportunity for further discussion of the instant case, as well as to provide a springboard for discussion of what lessons can be gleaned and transferred to one's own work environment. The multiple choice questions test the student's

- **Knowledge.** Students are required to recognize or recall specific legal facts, terminology, classifications, principles, and theories (answers to these questions do not require reasoning, only remembering the material involved).
- **Comprehension.** Students are required to demonstrate not only their knowledge about the law but also a degree of understanding of the material issues involved in each case. This is accomplished with questions that have been designed to have more than one right answer, thus requiring the student to select the best answer.

ANSWERS

The answers to the self-tests are provided at the end of the text.

SUMMARY NOTES

Included at the end of the case book are three charts that contain summary notes pertaining to physicians, nurses, and pharmacists. These notes should prove helpful to the practitioner in understanding the case law presented in this text.

New to this edition is the section Assessing the Quality of Care in Health Care Organizations: Self-Evaluation and Redundancy in Systems. This self-assessment tool should generate lively discussion and provide innovative insight into the cases reviewed in this and similar texts.

Tort Law

1. NEGLIGENCE/PREMATURE DISCHARGE/ PREGNANCY

Citation: *Somoza v. St. Vincent's Hosp.*, 596 N.Y.S.2d 789 (N.Y. App. Div. 1993)

Facts

The plaintiff was admitted to the hospital on December 12, 1982, in the 29th week of her pregnancy under the care of her private attending physician, defendant Dr. Svesko. She presented herself to the hospital with complaints of severe abdominal pain. Upon her admission to the hospital, the plaintiff was examined by Dr. Gutwein (a resident physician at the hospital), who, according to the notations she made on the plaintiff's chart, independently formed the impression that the plaintiff might be suffering from either left pyelonephritis, premature labor, or polyhydramnios. Dr. Gutwein recorded a written plan and orders requiring that the plaintiff be hooked up to a fetal monitor. She was also to undergo a number of diagnostic tests, including a renal pelvic sonogram. The results of the sonogram were abnormal and the radiologist recommended a follow-up sonogram. However, no follow-up was ordered by the attending physician. Despite the abnormal sonogram and various findings on the physical examinations, Dr. Svesko decided to release the plaintiff from the hospital because her pain had subsided. He orally conveyed this order to Dr. Gutwein. According to Dr. Gutwein, she did not formulate an opinion as to the correctness of the decision to discharge since "[i]t wasn't my place to say one way or the other." Instead, pursuant to Dr. Svesko's instruction, on her early morning rounds, Dr. Gutwein simply signed an order discharging the plaintiff from the hospital.

Four days later, the plaintiff returned to the hospital suffering severe pain and soon thereafter delivered twin girls. The twins were diagnosed as suffering from cerebral palsy resulting from their premature birth. The plaintiff brought a medical malpractice action against the hospital and Dr. Svesko arising out of the premature birth of the twins.

The New York Supreme Court, Appellate Division, denied the defendants' motion for summary judgment, and the defendants appealed.

Issue

Were there material issues of fact precluding summary judgment for the defendants?

Holding

The supreme court held that there were material issues of fact as to whether the mother's symptoms exhibited during her physical assessment contraindicated her release from the hospital and that ordinary prudence required further inquiry by the resident physician, Dr. Gutwein.

Reason

The plaintiffs presented an affidavit by expert witness Dr. Sherman, who stated that "the failure of the hospital staff to discharge without another physical examination, in my opinion, with a reasonable degree of medical certainty, is a departure from good and accepted medical practice. The resident clearly had an obligation to examine even a private patient in the face of a changing cervix and not just to discharge her pursuant to some attending physician's order." *Id.* at 791. It is well established that, "[i]n the absence of an employment relationship, a hospital cannot be held legally responsible for the actions of a private physician attending his private patient so long as the hospital staff properly carries out the physician's orders" (*Hicks v. Ronald Fraser Clinic*, 169 A.D.2d 558, 559; 565 N.Y.S.2d 484). However, even where the action at issue has been ordered by a private physician, a hospital whose staff carries out that order may nevertheless be held responsible where the hospital staff knows, or should know, that a physician's orders are so clearly contraindicated by normal practice that ordinary prudence requires inquiry into the correctness of the orders. In this case, the plaintiff's release from the hospital was so clearly contraindicated by normal practice that ordinary prudence required further inquiry by Dr. Gutwein into the correctness of the discharge order.

Discussion

1. What further steps could the resident have taken to prevent the premature discharge of the patient?
2. What options do nurses have available to them when they are concerned about the premature discharge of a patient?
3. What process changes are needed in order to help prevent similar instances from occurring in the future?

2. NEGLIGENCE/FAILURE TO OVERRIDE THEORY/DEATH OF NEWBORN

Citation: *Greer v. Bryant*, 621 A.2d 999 (Pa. Super. Ct. 1993)

Facts

Mrs. Greer, while at the Philadelphia College of Osteopathic Medicine (PCOM) and under the care of her physician, Dr. Bryant, was diagnosed with "pre-eclampsia," a condition characterized by high blood pressure in the mother that poses a risk to the unborn child. On September 20, the patient suffered symptoms of fetal distress and was examined by the hospital's interns and residents. Tests ordered at the time of her visit revealed that the fetus was suffering from "decelerations," a periodic lowering of the heartbeat. Following her examination, Mrs. Greer was instructed to return to the hospital on September 23. During that visit, it was noted that the fetus was experiencing "poor beat to beat variability." Mrs. Greer was once again sent home with instructions to return to the hospital on September 27. However, on September 26, Mrs. Greer, experiencing severe pains, called the hospital emergency department. She was

told to wait until her scheduled appointment the following day. Her appointment was subsequently canceled because of inclement weather. Upon the insistence of her sister, Mrs. Greer went to the hospital on September 27, where she delivered her child. The infant, suffering from "severe meconium aspiration" (inhalation by the fetus of its own fecal matter while in utero), died several days later.

The plaintiff alleged that the hospital, through its negligence, had contributed to her child's death. Mrs. Greer sued Dr. Bryant and PCOM separately. She alleged that based on the prenatal test results during her September 23 visit to PCOM, she should have been delivered on that date by Dr. Bryant. Questions were raised as to whether Dr. Bryant was aware of the test results. The plaintiff argued that, even if the test results had been communicated to Dr. Bryant and he decided to send her home, the residents should have recognized the serious condition of the fetus and, if necessary, sought approval from their superiors to keep the child at the hospital.

Dr. Bryant made an offer to settle and the plaintiff accepted. The Court of Common Pleas, upon jury verdict, entered judgment for the mother, finding PCOM 41 percent liable to the plaintiff. PCOM appealed.

Issue

Was Dr. Bryant properly notified that the fetus was suffering heart decelerations, and did the plaintiff's expert witness exceed her scope of opinion in her medical report by stating that the plaintiff should have been admitted and the child delivered despite the private physician's instructions to send her home?

Holding

The Superior Court of Pennsylvania found that the jury could find that the hospital's staff was negligent by not reporting the fetal distress of the unborn child to Dr. Bryant and that the plaintiff's expert witness, Dr. Gabrielson, did not exceed her scope of opinion in her medical report.

Reason

Although a resident and intern claimed they had called Dr. Bryant, neither could testify as to the content of their conversation with him. Dr. Bryant testified that he did not recall receiving any telephone calls. He stated that if he had been aware of the decelerated heart rate, he would have ordered delivery of the child. "Since many of the critical events occurred on September 23, the jury could have determined that PCOM's employees' crucial nonfeasance occurred on that date . . . we must assume that the jury drew this inference." *Id.* at 1002.

Dr. Gabrielson, in three written reports and through oral testimony, testified that if the test results had not been reported to Dr. Bryant, such conduct, in her opinion, fell below the required standard of care. PCOM argued that "this new 'failure to override [Dr. Bryant's possible orders to send Rachel home] theory' was not contained in the reports and that they were unfairly surprised by the opinion." *Id.* at 1003. The superior court did not agree. The following is an excerpt from a report, which presents questioning of Dr. Gabrielson by the plaintiff's counsel:

> **3.** Ms. Greer was sent to Osteopathic Hospital on three occasions for non-stress and contraction stress testing. On the second occasion. . .it was noted that the baby's heart rate showed poor variability. . . . Could you explain the significance of this finding with regard to the health and well-being of the fetus?
>
> **A.** The episode of bradycardia observed on September 20 was a very ominous sign and very suggestive of cord compression probably resulting from oligo-hydramnios. This would result in fetal distress with meconium passage and aspiration. It could result in sudden intrauterine death.
>
> **4.** Once the fetal distress was detected, did the hospital act appropriately by sending Ms. Greer home?
>
> **A.** No.
>
> **5.** What measures, if any, should have been taken to ensure the health and well-being of the fetus?
>
> **A.** Ms. Greer should have been admitted and delivered. *Id.* at 1004.

The question of hospital negligence in sending the plaintiff home was within the fair scope of Dr. Gabrielson's oral testimony and written reports. "PCOM's decision to send Rachel home was contemplated and counsel should have anticipated that the 'failure to override theory' was looming." *Id.* at 1004.

Discussion

1. What steps should hospitals take when a patient is faced with life-threatening test results and the attending physician makes a determination to send the patient home?
2. What effect, if any, should such cases have upon the training of students and residents?
3. What action should a nurse take when faced with questionable actions by physicians and residents?
4. What policies and procedures should be in place to address similar issues in other patient care settings (emergency departments and ambulatory care centers)?

3. NEGLIGENCE/NUTRITIONAL CARE

Citation: *Caruso v. Pine Manor Nursing Ctr.*, 538 N.E.2d 722 (Ill. App. Ct. 1989)

Facts

Duty To Care

In Illinois, a nursing facility by statute has a duty to provide its residents with proper nutrition. Under the Nursing Home Care Reform Act (the Act):

> [T]he owner and licensee [of a nursing home] are liable to a resident for any intentional or negligent act or omission of their agents or employees which injured the resident. [Ill. Rev. Stat. 1981, ch. 111 1/2, ¶ 4153-601.] The Act defines neglect as a failure in a facility to provide adequate medical or personal care or maintenance, which failure results in physical or mental injury to a resident or in the deterioration of the resident's condition. [Ill. Rev. Stat. 1981, ch. 111 1/2, ¶ 4151-116, 4151-117.] Personal care and maintenance include providing food and water and assistance with meals necessary to sustain a healthy life. [Ill. Rev. Stat. 1981, ch. 111 1/2, ¶ 4151-116, 4151-120.] *Id.* at 724.

Breach of Duty

The nursing facility maintained no records of the resident's fluid intake and output. A nurse testified that such a record was a required standard nursing facility procedure that should have been followed for a person in the resident's condition but was not. The resident's condition deteriorated after a stay at the facility of six and one-half days. Upon leaving the facility and entering a hospital emergency department, the treating physician diagnosed the resident as suffering from severe dehydration caused by an inadequate intake of fluids. The nursing facility offered no alternative explanation for the resident's dehydrated condition and failed to keep a chart of fluid intake and output as required by the applicable statute.

Injury

As a result of the facility's failure to maintain adequate records, the resident suffered severe dehydration requiring hospital treatment.

Causation

The evidence presented clearly demonstrated that the proximate cause of the resident's dehydration was the nursing facility's failure to administer proper nourishment to him. It was not unreasonable for the jury to conclude that the resident suffered dehydration and that the nursing facility's treatment of him caused the dehydration.

The trial court found that the record supported a finding that a resident had suffered from dehydration as a result of the nursing facility's negligence. The defendant appealed from a jury verdict awarding $65,000 in damages to the plaintiff. The trial court increased this amount to $195,000 (three times the actual damages) pursuant to Section 3-602 of the Nursing Home Reform Act. Ill. Rev. Stat. ch. 111 1/2, ¶ 4153-602 (1987).

Issue

Did the nursing facility resident suffer harm as a result of its negligence?

Holding

The Appellate Court of Illinois upheld the trial court's finding that the resident suffered dehydration.

Reason

The evidence presented clearly demonstrated that the proximate cause of the resident's dehydration was the nursing facility's failure to administer proper nourishment to him. It was not unreasonable for the jury to conclude that the resident suffered dehydration and that the nursing facility's treatment of him caused the dehydration.

Discussion

1. What steps could the nursing facility have taken in order to prevent such occurrences?
2. What record-keeping requirements did the nursing facility fail to follow?
3. What is the importance of timely nutritional screenings and assessments?
4. How does one monitor the appropriateness and effectiveness of nutritional care?
5. What is the mechanism for screening and assessing the nutritional needs of patients in your organization?

4. NEGLIGENCE/STANDARD OF CARE/ INADEQUATE TREATMENT

Citation: *Flores v. Cyborski*, 629 N.E.2d 74 (Ill. App. Ct. 1993)

Facts

The patient was admitted to the hospital after having complained of abdominal and lower back pain. She was given tests, after which she was diagnosed as having a kidney infection and possible pneumonia. A physician was called in to see her and, by phone, ordered diagnostic tests, which included cultures of the blood, sputum, and urine. He visited the patient soon after the phone call, and she stated that she was experiencing chest pain and had a congestive cough. Her white blood count was elevated, which indicated to the physician that she had a possible infection. He ordered more tests to rule out pneumonia. After studying the results of the patient's tests and chest X-rays, the defendant concluded that she had lower-lobe pneumonia, and he prescribed the broad-spectrum antibiotic Keflin. The next day, the patient said she was feeling better, her lungs sounded better, and her temperature had decreased. The defendant continued her on Keflin and added another antibiotic. Two days later, she told the nurses she was experiencing shooting pains, shortness of breath, and had a pulse rate of 180. The nurses did not notify the physician until his patient was in cardiac arrest. She died later that day.

The patient's estate sued the physician for negligence in treating the patient. Dr. Sharp, who was the brother of an associate at the plaintiff's law firm, testified that the defendant had deviated from the standard of care. He stated that the defendant failed to obtain blood gas tests, prescribe an appropriate antibiotic, and prescribe that the antibiotic be administered intravenously. He further testified that the lowering of the patient's temperature was because of the administration of Tylenol, and not due to the patient's improving condition. The defendant's experts stated that the physician had complied with the applicable standard of care and that the death was unexpected and sudden. Her decreased white blood cell count and the data that had been collected from all who had examined her indicated that she was getting better. The jury returned a verdict for the defendant, and the plaintiff appealed.

Issue

Should the court have allowed the testimony about the relationship between the plaintiff's expert and the plaintiff's brother? Did the physicians improperly diagnose the patient and breach the appropriate standard of care, thus causing her death?

Holding

The Appellate Court of Illinois affirmed the verdict for the defendant.

Reason

The court had a right to allow the testimony regarding the relationship between the plaintiff's expert and attorney during cross-examination for impeachment purposes. The physician's testimony may have been colored by his relationship with his brother. The jury was correctly permitted to consider that possibility in order to judge the credibility of the physician as a witness. The issue of whether the nurses' failure to recognize and respond to the change in the patient's condition was the proximate cause of the patient's death was for the jury to decide. Moreover, there was no evidence that the physician caused the patient's suffering and death.

Discussion

1. Take the position of the defense attorney and explain, giving specific reasons, why the physicians did not breach the applicable standard of care.
2. Discuss what additional evidence would have been helpful to the plaintiff's case.
3. What action should the nurse have taken upon discovering a significant change in the patient's condition?
4. Describe those changes in a patient's condition that would trigger a need to notify a patient's attending physician.
5. What educational processes should an organization have in place to prevent similar incidents from reoccurring?

5. NEGLIGENCE/DUTY TO CARE/VISITOR INJURED

Citation: *Lutheran Hosp. of Ind. v. Blaser*, 634 N.E.2d 864 (Ind. Ct. App. 1994)

Facts

The plaintiff crossed the street one evening after visiting her husband in the hospital and was hit by a car as she was walking up the driveway to the hospital parking lot. She was struck from behind when the car was turning into the parking lot exit. The patient and her husband brought a negligence suit against the hospital as a result of the injuries she suffered.

Drivers in general could not determine that the driveway was not an exit until such time as they were alongside it or were in the process of turning into the driveway. Each night three or four cars mistakenly took the exit for an entrance. Outside visual cues actually drew pedestrians to cross the highway midblock in order to enter the lot. Neither security guards nor the parking lot attendants had attempted to dissuade pedestrians from crossing the street midblock. The superior court found that the funneling of pedestrians and vehicular traffic into the exit driveway created a dangerous condition that the hospital should have reasonably foreseen and the court entered judgment for the plaintiffs. The hospital appealed, claiming that although it maintained the driveway it did not have control over the driveway.

Issue

Did the trial court err by finding that the hospital had a duty of care to the plaintiff? Was the jury's $535,000 damage award excessive?

Holding

The Court of Appeals of Indiana held that the accident was sufficiently foreseeable to require the hospital to protect its invitees from such a mishap; the intervening act of the hit-and-run driver in and of itself does not relieve the hospital of its legal responsibility; and the award of $535,000 was not so high as to demonstrate prejudice on the part of the jury.

Reason

The relationship between the hospital and the plaintiff was that of landowner and business invitee. The hospital, therefore, had a legal duty to exercise reasonable care for the plaintiff's protection. The hospital's failure to post adequate safeguards or warnings to pedestrians and automobiles against the use of the exit driveway as an entrance to the parking lot was the proximate cause of the injuries suffered by the plaintiff. Regardless of whether the hit-and-run driver was confused by inadequate signing or poor illumination, the accident was within the hospital's scope of foreseeability. The hospital was aware of how the driveway was used and yet failed to make any effort to correct the dangerous situation.

The hospital created an unsafe condition and risked a car hitting a pedestrian at the parking lot exit. This was exactly what occurred. Because the subsequent negligent act by the hit-and-run driver was foreseeable by the hospital, the original tort-feasor, the intervening act of the negligent driver does not in and of itself relieve the hospital of its legal responsibility.

As to the damage award, the extent of the plaintiff's injuries (e.g., 44 days in the hospital following the accident, multiple fractures, disfigurement, and the inability to care for her husband) was sufficient evidence to support the jury's award.

Discussion

1. Do you think the court erred in its decision? Explain.
2. What is the intervening act described in this case?

6. NEGLIGENCE/STANDARD OF CARE/ INFORMED CONSENT/CAUSATION

Citation: *Riser v. American Medical Intern, Inc.*, 620 So. 2d 372 (La. Ct. App. 1993)

Facts

Four children brought a medical malpractice action against Dr. Lang, a physician who performed a femoral arteriogram on their 69-year-old mother, Mrs. Riser, who subsequently expired 11 days following the procedure. Mrs. Riser had been admitted to De La Ronde Hospital experiencing impaired circulation in her lower arms and hands. The patient had multiple medical diagnoses, including diabetes mellitus, end-stage renal failure, and arteriosclerosis. Her physician, Dr. Sottiurai, ordered bilateral arteriograms in order to determine the cause of the patient's impaired circulation. Because De La Ronde Hospital could not accommodate Dr. Sottiurai's request, Mrs. Riser was transferred to Dr. Lang, a radiologist at St. Jude Hospital. Dr. Lang performed a femoral arteriogram as opposed to the bilateral brachial arteriogram ordered by Dr. Sottiurai. The procedure seemed to go well and the patient was prepared for transfer back to De La Ronde Hospital. However, shortly after the ambulance departed the hospital, the patient suffered a seizure in the ambulance and was returned to St. Jude. Mrs. Riser's condition deteriorated and she expired 11 days later. The plaintiffs claimed in their lawsuit that Mrs. Riser was a poor risk for the procedure. The District Court ruled for the plaintiffs, awarding damages in the amount of $50,000 for Mrs. Riser's pain and suffering and $100,000 to each child. Dr. Lang appealed.

Issue

Was the standard of care breached when the physician performed an unnecessary procedure that had no benefit to the patient? Did the patient consent to the procedure? Was there a causal connection between the arteriogram and the stroke, leading to the patient's death? Were the damages awarded excessive?

Holding

The Court of Appeal of Louisiana held that Dr. Lang breached the standard of care by subjecting the patient to a procedure that would have no practical benefit to the patient, that Dr. Lang failed to obtain informed consent from the patient, and that the damage award was not excessive.

Reason

Testimony revealed that Dr. Lang had breached the standard of care by performing a procedure that he knew or should have known would have had no practical benefit to the patient or her referring physician. " . . . the defendant himself, as well as the expert witnesses in this case, testified that it is a breach of the standard of care for any physician to subject a patient to a particular test or procedure that has any risk of injury, however small, associated with it if that doctor knows or reasonably should know that the procedure will be of no benefit to the patient." *Id.* at 377.

As to informed consent, a reasonably prudent person in the position of Mrs. Riser would have refused to undergo the procedure if he or she had known of the strong possibility of a stroke. Informed consent requires that the physician reveal to the patient all material risks. The patient's consent to an arteriogram was vitiated by Dr. Lang's failure to disclose such a possibility. The consent form itself did not contain express authorization for Dr. Lang to perform the femoral arteriogram. Dr. Sottiurai ordered a brachial arteriogram, not a femoral arteriogram. Mrs. Riser was under the impression that she was about to undergo a brachial arteriogram, not a femoral arteriogram. Two consent forms were signed; neither form authorized the performance of a femoral arteriogram. Mrs. O'Neil, one of Mrs. Riser's daughters, claimed that her mother said following the arteriogram, "Why did you let them do that to me?" *Id.* at 380. Although Dr. Lang claims that he explained the femoral procedure to Mrs. Riser and Mrs. O'Neil, the trial court, faced with this conflicting testimony, chose to believe the plaintiffs. The appeals court found no manifest error in the trial court's decision.

The defendants argued that the plaintiffs had not established a causal connection between the arteriogram and the stroke. There was conflicting testimony between the pathologists who testified at trial as to the cause of the patient's death. The judge chose to believe the pathologist's testimony that it was more probable than not that the stroke resulted from the arteriogram performed by Dr. Lang. The court of appeal noted " . . . we cannot say that he was manifestly erroneous in this decision as it represented a clear choice between the conflicting opinions of two apparently equally qualified experts." *Id.* at 382. The damages awarded were not so shocking or excessively high as to require a review to change the amount of the award.

Discussion

1. Describe what information a patient should be provided prior to undergoing a risky procedure in order for consent to be "informed."
2. Why is it important to obtain consent from a patient prior to proceeding with a risky procedure?

7. NEGLIGENCE/BREACH OF DUTY/PAP SMEAR MISREAD

Citation: *Sander v. Geib, Elston, Frost Prof'l Ass'n.*, 506 N.W.2d 107 (S.D. 1993)

Facts

As part of her regular care, the patient had several gynecological examinations, including Pap tests, in 1977, 1978, 1980, 1984, 1986, and 1987. All Pap tests were performed by her general practitioner, who then submitted them to the Geib Elston Frost Professional Association d.b.a. Clinical Laboratory of the Black Hills (Clinical Laboratory) for evaluation. The laboratory procedure consisted of a clerk assigning each specimen a number when it was received. It would then be screened by a cytotechnologist. If it was determined to be abnormal, it would be marked for review by a pathologist. Out of the Pap tests that were determined to be normal, only 1 in 10 was actually viewed by a pathologist. The pathologist made recommendations based on the classification of the Pap tests. A biopsy would be recommended if the Pap test was determined to be Class IV.

Except for the Pap test in 1987, which showed premalignant cellular changes, all of the patient's other Pap tests were determined to be negative. In 1986, the laboratory made a notation to the patient's physician that "moderate inflammation" was present. The patient's physician, who was treating her with antibiotics for a foot inflammation, thought that the medication would also treat the other inflammation. In September 1987, the patient returned to her physician complaining of pain, erratic periods, and tiredness. After completing a physical, her physician took a Pap test, which he sent to Clinical Laboratory. He also referred her to a gynecologist. The clinical pathologist recommended a biopsy. Biopsies and further physical examinations revealed squamous cell carcinoma that had spread to her pelvic bones or to one-third of her vagina. Her Pap tests were reexamined by Clinical Laboratory, which reported that the 1986 smear showed that malignancy was highly likely. The patient was referred to the University of Minnesota to determine whether she was a viable candidate for radiation treatment. The cancer, however, had spread, and the patient was not considered a candidate for radiation treatment as she had no chance of survival. When the University of Minnesota reviewed all of the available slides, they found cellular changes back to 1984.

The patient sued in 1988, alleging that Clinical Laboratory failed to detect and report cellular changes in her Pap tests in time to prevent the spread of the cancer. Before trial, the patient died. Her husband and sister were substituted as plaintiffs, and the complaint was amended to include a wrongful death action. After trial, a jury awarded $3.7 million in damages, which were reduced to $1 million by the circuit court. The jury found against Clinical Laboratory and the laboratory appealed.

Issue

Was it erroneous for the trial court to submit to the jury the 1988 negligence claim based on the 1984 slide?

Holding

The Supreme Court of South Dakota upheld the jury verdict and restored the $3.7 million damage award.

Reason

The court found that the damage award was not excessive in light of the evidence; the statutory cap on awards does not apply to Clinical Laboratory because it is a medical corporation. The court determined that evidence relating to negligence claims pertaining to Pap tests taken more than two years before filing the action were admissible because the patient had a continuing relationship with Clinical Laboratory as a result of her physician's submitting her Pap tests to the laboratory over a period of time.

Discussion

1. What changes in procedure should Clinical Laboratory take to help ensure that Pap tests are properly classified?
2. How might continuous quality improvement activities improve the laboratory's operations?

8. FAILURE TO RESTRAIN/PATIENT FALL/RADIOLOGY

Citation: *Cockerton v. Mercy Hosp. Med. Ctr.*, 490 N.W.2d 856 (Iowa Ct. App. 1992)

Facts

On June 23, 1987, the plaintiff, Ms. Cockerton, was admitted to the hospital for the purpose of surgery to correct a problem with her open bite. Dr. Maletta, her physician, ordered postsurgical X-rays for her head and face to be taken the next day. The next morning, between 8:00 A.M. and 8:15 A.M., a hospital employee took the plaintiff from her room to the X-ray department by wheelchair. A nurse had assessed her condition as slightly "oozy" and drowsy. She was wearing a urinary catheter. An IV and a nasogastric tube were still in place.

Ms. Alexander, an X-ray technician, took charge of the plaintiff in the X-ray room. It was her third day on the job. After the plaintiff was taken inside the X-ray room, she was transferred from a wheelchair to a portable chair for the X-ray procedure. Upon being moved, the plaintiff complained of nausea, and Ms. Alexander observed that the plaintiff's pupils were dilated. She did not use the restraint straps to secure the plaintiff to the chair when the X-rays were taken. At some point during the X-ray procedure, the plaintiff had a fainting seizure. Ms. Alexander called for help. When Ms. Hewitt, another hospital employee, entered the room, Ms. Alexander was holding the plaintiff in an upright position. She appeared nonresponsive. The plaintiff only remembered being stood up and having a lead jacket thrown across her back and shoulders. Ms. Alexander maintains that the plaintiff did not fall.

At the time the plaintiff left the X-ray room, her level of consciousness was poor. She was brought back to the ward and the nasogastric tube was removed. Dr. Maletta noticed a deflection of the plaintiff's nose, but had difficulty assessing it because of the surgical procedure from the day before. Because the plaintiff had fainted in the X-ray room, Dr. Maletta requested an incident report from the radiology department. The following day, the deflection of the plaintiff's nose was much more evident. Dr. Maletta consulted Dr. Ericson, a specialist, who attempted to correct the deformity. Dr. Ericson observed that it would require a substantial injury to the nose to deflect it to that severity.

The plaintiff instituted proceedings against the hospital, alleging that the negligence of the nurses or X-ray technicians allowed her to fall during the X-ray procedure and subsequently caused injury to her nose. The trial court did not require expert testimony concerning the standard of care given by the X-ray technician. The jury concluded that the hospital was negligent in leaving the plaintiff unattended or failing to restrain her in the X-ray area, which proximately caused her to fall and to be injured. The jury rendered a verdict of $48,370, and the hospital appealed.

Issue

Is expert testimony required where the health provider's lack of care is so obvious as to be within the comprehension of a layman, and to require only common knowledge and experience to understand?

Holding

The Court of Appeals of Iowa held that the patient was not required to present expert testimony on the issue of the hospital's negligence.

Reason

Ordinarily, evidence of negligence in a medical malpractice action must be proven by expert testimony. The court rejected the hospital's argument that the X-ray procedure could not be categorized as routine or ministerial care. The conduct in question was simply the way the X-ray technician handled the plaintiff during the X-ray examination. In arguing for a professional standard, the hospital pointed to the elaborate training requirements for an X-ray technician, as required by the Iowa Administrative Code. However, the fact that an X-ray technician must meet certain requirements under the Iowa Administrative Code does not make all of the technician's conduct professional in nature. The applicable standard requires that of reasonable care.

The X-ray technician testified that during the X-ray, the plaintiff appeared to have a "seizure episode." She also testified that she left the plaintiff unattended for a brief period of time and that she did not use the restraint straps that were attached to the portable X-ray chair. Using the restraint straps would have secured the plaintiff to the portable chair during the X-ray examination.

Dr. Maletta testified that there had been no problems with the septum during surgery, and that he had never had a complication such as the plaintiff's injury occur during surgery. While the plaintiff was in recovery immediately following surgery, Dr. Maletta observed no injuries to her nose. She did not leave her bed until she was taken to the X-ray room that next morning. The plaintiff had a syncopal episode (similar to a seizure) while she was in the X-ray room. Following the X-ray examination, her nose appeared "grotesque" and injured. Taking the evidence in the light most favorable to the plaintiff, the court found that substantial evidence existed to establish a causal connection between the hospital's conduct and the plaintiff's injury.

Discussion

1. Should the radiologist share responsibility for the negligence of the X-ray technician? Explain.
2. What is the difference between ministerial and professional care?

9. *RES IPSA LOQUITUR*/SURGICAL PROCEDURE/ IMPROPER POSITIONING

Citation: *Wick v. Henderson*, 485 N.W.2d 645 (Iowa 1992)

Facts

The plaintiff, Ms. Wick, entered the defendant hospital for gallbladder surgery. Dr. Henderson, an anesthesiologist, was employed by the defendant Medical Anesthesia Associates, PC (MAA). There is no claim or showing that Dr. Henderson was personally present during the plaintiff's surgery. It was attended by Mr. Byrk, a nurse anesthetist who was also employed by MAA. Dr. Henderson was listed on hospital documents by Mr. Byrk as the anesthesiologist for Ms. Wick's surgery.

Ms. Wick had no recollection of being in the operating room or the recovery room. She had pain in her left arm upon awakening. When discharged from the hospital on August 17, 1987, she was told by an anesthesiologist in the hospital that her arm was "stressed" during surgery. According to the plaintiff's evidence, she sustained a permanent injury to the ulnar nerve in her left upper arm.

A malpractice action was filed against the hospital and Dr. Henderson. Ms. Wick sought recovery on theories of specific negligence and *res ipsa loquitur*. There was testimony that the main cause of the ulnar nerve injury during surgery was the mechanical compression of the nerve by improper positioning of the arm. The trial court granted the hospital, Dr. Henderson, and MAA a directed verdict resulting in dismissal of Ms. Wick's case.

Issue

Does the doctrine of *res ipsa loquitur* apply in this case?

Holding

The Supreme Court of Iowa held that the *res ipsa loquitur* doctrine applies.

Reason

The plaintiff must prove two foundational facts in order to invoke the doctrine of *res ipsa loquitur*. First, the defendants had exclusive control and management of the instrument that caused the plaintiff's injury, and second, it was the type of injury that ordinarily would not occur if reasonable care had been used. As to control, it should be enough that the plaintiff can show an injury resulting from an external force applied while she lay unconscious in the hospital. It is within the common knowledge and experience of a layperson to determine that an individual does not enter the hospital for gallbladder surgery and come out of surgery with an ulnar nerve injury to the left arm.

Discussion

1. Describe three examples when *res ipsa loquitur* would apply.
2. What steps should the hospital take to prevent similar incidents?

10. *RES IPSA LOQUITUR*/SURGICAL PROCEDURE/ SCIATIC NERVE INJURY

Citation: *Lacombe v. Dr. Walter Olin Moss Reg'l Hosp.*, 617 So. 2d 612 (La. Ct. App. 1993)

Facts

On May 31, 1988, the plaintiff, Mrs. Lacombe, was admitted to the hospital for surgery. Upon regaining consciousness in the recovery room, the plaintiff began complaining of severe pain in her right buttock, shooting down the back of her right leg. Mrs. Lacombe underwent a computed tomography (CT) scan, a magnetic resonance imaging (MRI), and a myelogram. All tests showed normal results, and back injury was ruled out as a cause of the problem. Mrs. Lacombe was eventually diagnosed with sciatic nerve injury. It is undisputed that the injury is permanent. Mrs. Lacombe filed a medical malpractice claim against the hospital and the physicians involved in the surgery. A medical review panel rendered a decision finding no breach of the standard of care. Mrs. Lacombe filed a medical malpractice suit against the hospital and physicians. By the time of trial, all defendants except the hospital had been dismissed from the litigation. After trial, the trial judge rendered judgment in favor of the plaintiff. The trial judge found that, applying the doctrine of *res ipsa loquitur* to the evidence, the plaintiff had proven her case. Accordingly, he found the hospital responsible under the theory of *respondeat superior* for the negligent conduct of its agents (the personnel who prepared the plaintiff for surgery and the physicians who conducted the operation).

The hospital contended that the trial court incorrectly applied the doctrine of *res ipsa loquitur*. The Louisiana Supreme Court, in *Cangelosi v. Our Lady of Lake Medical Ctr.*, 564 So. 2d 654, 665–666 (La. 1989), outlined the proper application of the doctrine of *res ipsa loquitur* in a medical malpractice case as follows:

> Negligence on the part of the defendant may be proved by circumstantial evidence alone when that evidence establishes, more probably than not, that the injury was of a kind which ordinarily does not occur in the absence of negligence, that the conduct of the plaintiff or of a third person was sufficiently eliminated by the evidence as a more probable cause of the injury, and that the indicated negligence was within the scope of the defendant's duty to the plaintiff. Although the fact that an accident has occurred does not alone raise a presumption of the defendant's negligence, the doctrine of *res ipsa loquitur* permits the inference of negligence on the part of the defendant from the circumstances surrounding the injury.
>
> In order to utilize the doctrine of *res ipsa loquitur*, the plaintiff must establish a foundation of facts on which the doctrine may be applied. The injury must be of the type which does not ordinarily occur in the absence of negligence. In other words, "the event must be such that in light of ordinary experience it gives rise to an inference that someone must have been negligent." The basis on which this conclusion is drawn is usually knowledge common to the community as a whole, although in cases such as medical malpractice, expert testimony may be used to establish this principle. The plaintiff does not have to eliminate all other possible causes or inferences, but must present evidence which indicates at least a probability that the injury would not have occurred without negligence.

The facts established by the plaintiff must also reasonably permit the jury to discount other possible causes and to conclude it was more likely than not that the defendant's negligence caused the injury. The Fourteenth Judicial District awarded damages to Mrs. Lacombe, and the hospital appealed.

Issue

Did the fact that the patient went into the hospital without sciatic nerve injury and came out with it warrant an inference of *res ipsa loquitur*?

Holding

The Court of Appeals of Louisiana held that the evidence warranted an inference of *res ipsa loquitur*.

Reason

Expert testimony established that the plaintiff was suffering from a sciatic nerve injury and that the injury was permanent. Experts on both sides agreed that sciatic nerve injury was not a known risk of this surgery. The testimony indicated that the plaintiff went into the hospital without the injury and came out with it. The various experts expressed three theories as to the cause of the injury: (1) her position during surgery put pressure on the nerve, (2) the nerve was nicked or caught in a suture during surgery, or (3) either immediately prior to or after surgery, an injection of medication was made directly into the nerve. The actual cause of the nerve injury, however, could not be established. After reviewing the record, the court agreed with the trial court that the evidence warranted an inference that negligence on the part of the defendant caused the injury. Additionally, none of the theories put forward as to the cause of the injury negated the inference.

Discussion

1. Discuss the circumstances under which negligence may be proved by circumstantial evidence.
2. Describe the elements that must be established in order for a case to move forward on the basis of *res ipsa loquitur*.

11. DEFAMATION/PERFORMANCE APPRAISAL/ STATEMENTS NOT LIBELOUS

Citation: *Schauer v. Memorial Care Sys.*, 856 S.W.2d 437 (Tex. Ct. App. 1993)

Facts

On January 9, 1989, the plaintiff, Ms. Schauer, had applied for and was given a supervisory position at Memorial Hospital's new catheterization laboratory. In March 1989, she received an employment appraisal for the period June 1988 through December 1988. At that time, Ms. Schauer's performance was rated by her supervisor as commendable in two categories and fair in eight categories with an overall rating of "fair." Although Ms. Schauer had not lost her job as a result of the appraisal, she brought an action against the hospital and her former supervisor for libel and emotional distress as a result of the appraisal. The hospital moved for summary judgment on the grounds that the employment appraisal was not defamatory as a matter of law; the hospital had qualified privilege to write the performance appraisal; and the claim for emotional distress did not reach the level of severity required for a claim for intentional infliction of emotional distress. The trial court granted the hospital's motion for summary judgment, and Ms. Schauer appealed.

Issue

Did the plaintiff state a claim for defamation and the intentional infliction of emotional distress?

Holding

The Court of Appeals of Texas held that the statements contained in the performance appraisal were not libelous and the appraisal was subject to qualified privilege. Moreover, the hospital's conduct and the statements contained in the appraisal did not support the claim for intentional infliction of emotional distress.

Reason

To sustain her claim of defamation, Ms. Schauer had to show that the hospital published her appraisal in a defamatory manner that injured her reputation in some manner. A statement can be unpleasant and objectionable to the plaintiff without being defamatory. The hospital argued that the statements contained in the appraisal were truthful, permissible expressions of opinion, and not capable of a defamatory meaning. The appraisal was prepared by Ms. Schauer's supervisor as part of her supervisory duties. The appraisal was not published outside the hospital and was prepared in compliance with the hospital policy for all employees. Ms. Schauer disputed her overall rating of fair as being libelous. "Clearly, this is a statement of her supervisor's opinion and is not defamatory as a matter of law." *Id.* at 447.

In her performance appraisal, Ms. Schauer objected to the statement, "Ms. Schauer was not sensitive to employee relations." *Id.* at 447. Ms. Schauer conceded in her deposition that there were a number of interpersonal problems in

the catheterization laboratory and that she did not get along with everyone. The court found that given these admissions the statement was not defamatory.

As to the plaintiff's claim of emotional distress, the plaintiff failed to show that the hospital acted intentionally and recklessly. The *Restatement of Torts, Second*, § 46 (1977) provides:

> Liability has been found only where the conduct has been so outrageous in character, and so extreme in degree, as to go beyond all possible bounds of decency, and to be regarded as atrocious, and utterly intolerable in a civilized community. . . . The liability clearly does not extend to mere insults, indignities, threats, annoyances, petty oppressions, or other trivialities. Complete emotional tranquility is seldom attainable in this world, and some degree of transient and trivial emotional distress is part of the price of living among people. The law intervenes only where the distress is so severe that no reasonable man could be expected to endure it. . . .

Discussion

1. Under what circumstances might the trial court have denied the defendant's motion for summary judgment?
2. Why do supervisors often find it difficult to prepare written performance appraisals?
3. What should be included in a management training program to assist managers in preparing fair and objective performance appraisals?
4. What steps can an organization take to ensure the competence of its staff?
5. What measures can an organization take to improve the competence of its staff?
6. Why is it important that the qualifications of a particular position be commensurate with defined job responsibilities?
7. Should there be a correlation between the job description and performance evaluation? Explain.
8. What mechanisms should the governing body have in place for ensuring that performance evaluations are conducted on a timely basis?
9. What summary information should be included in competency reports to the organization's governing body?

12. DEFAMATION/SLANDER

Citation: *Chowdhry v. North Las Vegas Hosp., Inc.*, 851 P.2d 459 (Nev. 1993)

Facts

On October 2, 1985, a young woman entered the emergency department of the North Las Vegas Hospital complaining of chest pain and shortness of breath. She was seen by Dr. Lapica, the emergency physician on duty. Dr. Lapica diagnosed the patient as suffering from a possible pneumohemothorax, which required the placement of a chest tube to drain accumulated fluids. Dr. Lapica contacted Dr. Chowdhry, a physician who had recently performed surgery on the young woman and who was also the on-call thoracic surgeon at the hospital, and informed Dr. Chowdhry that his services were required at the hospital. The record revealed that Dr. Chowdhry refused to return to the hospital to treat the patient because he had recently left there, and would only treat her if she were transferred to University Medical Center (UMC). Dr. Chowdhry testified that he could not return to the hospital because of a conflicting emergency at UMC.

Dr. Lapica then contacted the hospital's chief of staff, Dr. Wilchins, and told him that Dr. Chowdhry refused to come to the hospital and attend to the patient. Both physicians concluded that if the patient could be safely transported to UMC, the transfer should be effected so she could be treated by Dr. Chowdhry.

Dr. Lapica contacted the emergency department physician at UMC, explained the nature and basis of the problem, and received permission to transfer the patient. The patient was ultimately transported to UMC. Dr. Lapica and Ms. Crow, the supervising nurse at the hospital, prepared incident reports detailing the events and submitted them to the hospital administrator, Mr. Moore.

On October 3, 1985, Mr. Moore informed Dr. Silver, UMC's chief of surgery, that Dr. Chowdhry had refused to come to the hospital emergency department to treat the patient. The matter was directed to the hospital's surgery committee, which recommended summary suspension of Dr. Chowdhry's staff privileges.

On November 1, 1985, in response to Dr. Chowdhry's request, a hearing was held before the medical executive committee. As a result of the hearing, Dr. Chowdhry's staff privileges were reinstated, but a reprimand was placed in his file for jeopardizing himself, the patient, and the hospital. The hospital denied Dr. Chowdhry's subsequent request to have the reprimand expunged from his record, thus prompting Dr. Chowdhry to file an action against the hospital, Dr. Silver, Mr. Moore, Dr. Wilchins, and Dr. Lapica.

Dr. Chowdhry's complaint alleged theories of liability based upon negligence, breach of contract, conspiracy, defamation, and negligent and intentional infliction of emotional distress. The district court concluded that Dr. Chowdhry had no reasonable basis for bringing the action and awarded $209,376 in attorney's fees and $69,835 in costs to the hospital, Dr. Silver, Mr. Moore, and Dr. Wilchins. Dr. Lapica was awarded $47,566 in attorney's fees and $9,428 in costs. Dr. Chowdhry appealed.

Issue

Did the district court err in: (1) dismissing the claims of defamation, punitive damage, and infliction of emotional distress, and (2) awarding respondent attorney's fees? Did the appellant abandon his patient?

Holding

The Supreme Court of Nevada held that the statements accusing Dr. Chowdhry of abandoning his patient were not, in context, capable of a defamatory construction. Moreover, the surgeon had reasonable grounds for his action and thus was not liable for statutory attorney fees, even though he did not prevail.

Reason

Dr. Chowdhry's emotional distress claims are premised upon respondents' accusations of patient abandonment. Dr. Chowdhry testified that as a result, "he was very upset" and could not sleep. Insomnia and general physical or emotional discomfort are insufficient to satisfy the physical impact requirement for emotional distress. Thus, Dr. Chowdhry failed, as a matter of law, to present sufficient evidence to sustain verdicts for negligent or intentional infliction of emotional distress.

In order to establish a prima facie case of defamation, a plaintiff must prove: (1) a false and defamatory statement by defendant concerning the plaintiff, (2) an unprivileged publication to a third person, (3) fault amounting to at least negligence, and (4) actual or presumed damages. Whether a statement is capable of a defamatory construction is a question of law. The actual statements made by the various respondents were not that Dr. Chowdhry "abandoned" his patient but that he "failed to respond" or "would not come" to the hospital to treat his patient. Although these statements cannot themselves be deemed defamatory, the court recognized that "words do not exist in isolation." The record reflected that the statements were made by the respondents to hospital personnel and other interested parties (e.g., the patient's mother), in the context of reporting what was reasonably perceived to be Dr. Chowdhry's refusal to treat the patient at the hospital. The statements attributable to the respondents, taken in context, are not reasonably capable of a defamatory construction.

Dr. Chowdhry, however, had reasonable grounds upon which to bring this action. Thus, the award of attorney's fees was reversed.

Discussion

1. Explain what a plaintiff must prove in order to establish an action for defamation.
2. How does libel differ from slander?

13. DEFAMATION/LIBEL

Citation: *Staheli v. Smith*, 548 So. 2d 1299 (Miss. 1989)

Facts

The plaintiff, Mr. Staheli, a college professor, brought a defamation action against Mr. Smith, the college dean. The plaintiff alleged that he was defamed by the dean's written recommendations, which prevented him from obtaining tenure and a pay raise. Mr. Staheli also alleged that Mr. Smith's recommendations damaged his reputation. Every administrator after Mr. Smith recommended against tenure for the plaintiff and the chancellor denied tenure. All of the administrators agreed that the tenure review process was purely subjective. Mr. Staheli eventually appealed to the faculty senate, which, after reviewing his file, recommended tenure. However, the chancellor again denied tenure. The circuit court granted summary judgment for Mr. Smith, and the plaintiff appealed.

Issue

Did the plaintiff bring his action on a timely basis or was the action barred from proceeding because of the statute of limitations? Did the statements made by the dean constitute qualified privilege?

Holding

The Supreme Court of Mississippi ruled that the summary judgment was appropriate. Although the statute of limitations had not tolled, the statements made were protected by qualified privilege.

Reason

As a general rule, the two-year statute of limitations begins to run in a defamation action when publication of the libelous statement is made to a third party. There is, however, an exception to this rule that provides that the statute begins to run when a plaintiff knew, or within reasonable

diligence should have discovered, that he or she had been defamed. Mr. Staheli claims that he did not have knowledge of the defamatory statements until faculty members told him in May of 1984. Mr. Staheli filed his complaint on May 17, 1984.

The record did not establish that the college dean published his statements outside of those having legitimate and direct interest in the tenure procedure. There was no evidence in the record that Mr. Smith stated a falsehood. Evidence in the record was indisputable as to the fact that tenure recommendations are subjective in nature. Mr. Smith could not be considered to have exceeded his scope of authority and responsibility in making his recommendation against tenure.

"When qualified privilege is established, statements or written communications are not actionable as slanderous or libelous absent bad faith or malice if the communications are limited to those persons who have a legitimate and direct interest in the subject matter." *Benson v. Hall*, 339 So. 2d 570, 573 (Miss. 1973).

In the instant case, there was no publication of the dean's statements "outside the circle" of those with legitimate interest in the tenure decision-making process. Involvement of the faculty senate was brought about because of the plaintiff's appeal.

Discussion

1. Under what circumstances would an action for defamation be granted?
2. Do you agree with the court's decision? Explain.

14. FALSE IMPRISONMENT/PHYSICIAN

Citation: *Desai v. SSM Health Care*, 865 S.W.2d 833 (Mo. Ct. App. 1993)

Facts

The plaintiff, Dr. Desai, brought suit against a hospital and security guards for false imprisonment, battery, and malicious prosecution.

On October 24, 1989, Dr. Desai was walking across the parking lot of the hospital. The parking lot was apparently a shortcut to the St. Louis University Medical School's Institute of Molecular Virology where Dr. Desai worked as part of his graduate studies. He was stopped by two security guards, Mr. Mealey and Mr. Windam, and was asked to show his identification. Dr. Desai said he was a doctor and that he did not have his identification with him. Following an argument, the two security guards grabbed Dr. Desai's arms and Mr. Windam slammed Dr. Desai's head against the trunk of a car. After handcuffing him, the security guards escorted Dr. Desai back to the security office where they were joined by the security guard supervisor. The handcuffs were eventually removed after the security guards received verification that Dr. Desai was affiliated with the Institute of Molecular Virology and confirmation from a nurse supervisor that he was a physician. Shortly thereafter, the St. Louis University campus police arrived. One of the officers asked Dr. Desai to apologize to Mr. Mealey. Dr. Desai refused and said that he wanted the St. Louis City police called, as he wanted to file an official complaint because he had been assaulted by Mr. Windam. At the request of the security guards, Dr. Desai was re-handcuffed and arrested by the St. Louis police for trespassing. The security guards later admitted that they had Dr. Desai arrested in order to avoid getting themselves into trouble. He was not released from jail until noon the following day. While in jail he suffered headaches and seizures.

The defendants moved to have the malicious prosecution count dismissed, and the motion was granted. At the trial, the defendants' motion to dismiss the plaintiff's claim for punitive damages was dismissed. The jury returned a verdict totaling $75,000 in damages for the false imprisonment claim and found in favor of the defendants on the battery claim. The trial court sustained the defendants' motions for judgment notwithstanding the verdict and for directed verdict that had been submitted by the defendants during the time of the trial. The plaintiff appealed.

Issue

Did the plaintiff meet his burden of establishing his case by substantial evidence?

Holding

The Missouri Court of Appeals held that the evidence supported a finding that the security guards falsely imprisoned the physician, and that the physician was entitled to punitive damages on the false imprisonment claim.

Reason

The defendants' own testimony provided the jury with sufficient evidence to establish that the plaintiff had been held against his will. The testimony reads as follows:

Q [Plaintiff's attorney]: So it was verified [Desai] was, in fact, a doctor at St. Louis University?

A [Defendant Windam]: Yes.

Q: And someone took the handcuffs off him to let him go; is that correct?

A: Yes.

Q: Who did that?

A: Officer Mealey.

Q: Were the cuffs subsequently put back on him?

A: Yes, they were.

Q: Why was that?

A: Because Dr. Desai had said, stated that I had assaulted him and he pointed directly to me.

Q: So once he did that, did you direct that he be recuffed?

A: Yes, I did.

Q: What did you say and to whom?

A: I told Officer Mealey to place him under arrest for trespassing.

Q: Why did you do that? . . .

A: To have a report on the incident.

* * * *

Q: Well, are you saying the only reason you wanted to do it was to affect a police report?

A: Yes.

Q: Did you realize the police report can be made out without someone being arrested?

A: No.

* * * *

Q: You didn't want to get in trouble, did you?

A: Right?

Q: That's why you did it, isn't it?

A: Basically, yes. *Id.* at 837.

* * * *

This testimony supported a finding that the arrest was self-serving and resulted in the false imprisonment of Dr. Desai.

As to punitive damages, the arrest by the security guards was reckless and showed indifference to the rights of the plaintiff. The trial court erred in dismissing the punitive damages count as to the false imprisonment claim and, therefore, prevented it from being submitted to the jury.

Discussion

1. What elements are necessary in order to establish that one has been falsely imprisoned?

2. What process should health care organizations implement to help prevent such events from occurring?

15. FRAUD/CONCEALMENT OF PATIENT INFORMATION

Citation: *Robinson v. Shah*, 936 P.2d 784 (Kans. App. 1997)

Facts

The plaintiff was a longtime patient of defendant, Dr. Shah, and placed her physical well-being in the hands of that physician from 1975 to 1986. During that time, the defendant treated the plaintiff for various gynecological disorders. On November 9, 1983, the defendant performed a total abdominal hysterectomy and bilateral salpingo-oophorectomy on the plaintiff. Approximately one week following surgery the plaintiff was discharged from the hospital and was assured that there were no complications or potential problems that might arise as a result of the surgery. On the day after the plaintiff was discharged from the hospital, she began to experience abdominal distress. She consulted the defendant about these symptoms, and the defendant ordered X-rays to be taken of the plaintiff's kidneys, ureter, and bladder in an effort to explain her discomfort.

The X-rays were taken at St. Joseph Memorial Hospital and were read and interpreted by Dr. Cavanaugh, presumably a radiologist associated with that facility. Dr. Cavanaugh was of the opinion, after reading the X-rays, that they showed the presence of surgical sponges that had been left in the plaintiff's abdomen after surgery. Dr. Cavanaugh called the defendant and reported the findings of the X-rays and, in addition, sent the defendant a copy of a written report that also reflected those findings.

The defendant fraudulently concealed from the plaintiff the findings of these X-rays. Instead of being truthful, the defendant intentionally lied to the plaintiff and told her the X-rays were negative and that there were no apparent or unusual complications from the recent abdominal surgery, and she assured the plaintiff that she did not require further treatment. At no time did the defendant reveal to the plaintiff the fact that she had left surgical sponges in the plaintiff's abdomen after the most recent surgery.

Over the next several years, the plaintiff continued to see the defendant for gynecological checkups. She continued to experience abdominal pain and discomfort. Dr. Shah, however, continued to conceal from the plaintiff the existence of the surgical sponges left in the plaintiff's abdomen. The plaintiff ceased seeing Dr. Shah as her physician in 1986. However, she consulted other physicians and continued to experience frequent pain and discomfort in her abdomen, as well as intestinal, urological, and gynecological problems. Although the plaintiff brought her complaints to the attention of other physicians, no one was able to diagnose the source of her problems.

In 1993, one of the physicians attending to the plaintiff's problems diagnosed a pelvic mass, which he felt could be causing some discomfort. The plaintiff underwent pelvic sonograms and X-rays, which revealed the existence of retained surgical sponges. The plaintiff contends the defendant, from and after November 18, 1983, had actual knowledge of the presence of retained surgical sponges in her abdomen and well knew the potential of future complications that could arise from this condition. The plaintiff contends that despite this knowledge, Dr. Shah fraudulently concealed the existence of this condition from her.

The trial court found that the plaintiff was unable to discover the fact that Dr. Shah had negligently left surgical sponges in her abdomen and that this fact was fraudulently concealed from the plaintiff, who did not discover the defendant's fraud until August 11, 1993.

Issue

Is there a cause of action for fraud? Was the cause of action timely filed?

Holding

The appeals court held that where a patient has a cause of action against a physician for malpractice and has been misled by the intentional and knowing lies of the physician to the extent the patient, in reliance on the fraudulent misrepresentation, permits the statute of limitations to bar his or her action, the patient can maintain an action for fraud against the physician, not on account of the original negligence or malpractice, but rather because of the fraudulent actions of the physician that deceived the patient with the consequence that the time bar ran against the original action.

Reason

The defendant left surgical sponges in the plaintiff's abdomen and knew she had done so no later than November 18, 1983. Despite such knowledge, the defendant fraudulently concealed the existence of the retained sponges from the plaintiff and lied to her about the nature of her condition. It was not until August 11, 1993, that the plaintiff knew or could have known what the defendant had done.

All of the related statutes of limitations and statutes of repose had expired. The plaintiff was without a remedy, and the defendant was home free unless an exception exists to preserve her causes of action against the defendant. If no such exception exists, the defendant will be rewarded for her fraud in concealing from the plaintiff that surgical sponges had been left in her abdomen. Over 10 years had passed since the defendant's act of fraudulent concealment. The trial court held that all of the plaintiff's potential legal remedies against the defendant had been outlawed by the statute of limitations. This decision is a direct result of the defendant's fraudulent concealment of the plaintiff's condition. The defendant now seeks to use the statute of limitations as a shield from the consequences of her negligence and her fraud.

The plaintiff's causes of action against the defendant are based on medical malpractice and fraud. It is obvious from a reading of the statutes that each cause of action must be brought within 2 years of its accrual and that the medical malpractice statute of repose is 4 years, whereas the fraud statute of repose is 10 years. It does not require great legal insight to realize that the plaintiff is dead in the water unless the fraudulent conduct on the part of the defendant either tolled or somehow extended the periods of limitations.

Is There a Cause of Action for Fraud?

The broad outlines of fraud are said to include any cunning, deception, or artifice used, in violation of legal or equitable duty, to circumvent, cheat, or deceive another. The forms it may assume and the means by which it may be practiced are as multifarious as human ingenuity can devise, and the courts consider it unwise or impossible to formulate an exact, definite, and all-inclusive definition of the action. It is synonymous with, or closely allied to, other terms indicating positive and intentional wrongdoing, but is distinguishable from mistake and negligence. Actual fraud is an intentional fraud, and the intent to deceive is an essential element of the action. Constructive fraud, however, is a breach of a legal or equitable duty that, irrespective of moral guilt, the law declares fraudulent because of its tendency to deceive others or violate a confidence, and neither actual dishonesty of purpose nor intent to deceive is necessary.

It is beyond question that the defendant's lies to the plaintiff were made to deceive her and conceal the defendant's negligence. The defendant had a legal and an equitable duty to tell the plaintiff the truth. This duty was breached. The plaintiff alleges that the breach of this duty by the defendant caused the plaintiff to lose a valuable cause of action and suffer 10 years of needless pain and discomfort.

We think it is important to note that the defendant in this case is not alleged to have been either mistaken or negligent in her failure to disclose the truth to her patient. She is accused of deceit and lies amounting to positive and intentional wrongdoing. Not every concealment of the truth is actionable. However, when such concealment violates a legal or equitable duty, it becomes actionable and fraudulent.

In order to prove fraud, the following facts must be shown:

1. an untrue statement known to be untrue by the party making it and made with the intent to deceive
2. justifiable reliance by the victim on the truth of the statement
3. damages as a result of that reliance

The plaintiff's petition was found to have set forth sufficient allegations to state a cause of action for actual fraud against the defendant. The appeals court refused to recognize any distinction between the fraud that separates the victim from his or her money and the fraud that deprives a victim of a cause of action for malpractice. The defendant argues, however, that one cannot have a fraud cause of action against a physician. The premise for this argument is that when a physician defrauds a patient out of a cause of action for malpractice, it is not fraud, it is simply more malpractice. Thus, according to the defendant, the physician may hide behind his or her fraudulent conduct and enjoy the benefits of that fraud because it is not fraud, it is malpractice.

The plaintiff seeks to recover damages caused by the fraudulent loss of her cause of action for malpractice. This is not a case that involves the failure to diagnose a condition shown by the X-ray report. This is a case where the defendant lied to the plaintiff.

The plaintiff in count II is not complaining about negligence, incompetence, or unauthorized treatment. She is complaining about being lied to and misled by someone she trusted and by someone who was obligated to tell her the truth. It should not matter if that someone is a physician, lawyer, banker, or magazine salesman. The appeals court rejected the notion that physicians are not answerable for fraud as are the other members of our society.

The obligation to tell the truth to people who depend on you to do so is not an exclusive obligation of a physician. It is an obligation shared with fiduciaries, with bankers, with lawyers, with shoe salesmen, and with myriad other members of our society. The appeals court rejected the notion that because a physician has an obligation to tell his or her patients the truth that any suit against a physician for violating that duty can only be one for malpractice and not for fraud.

There is no logic and no justice in a conclusion that when a physician misleads someone, it is malpractice, but when a banker does so, it is fraud. The duty to speak honestly to those who trust you and to not engage in fraud or deception are duties shared by the medical profession with myriad members of our society. Physicians are not immune from the consequences of their fraudulent conduct.

The appeals court found that where a patient has a cause of action against a physician for malpractice and has been misled by the intentional and knowing lies of the physician to the extent the patient, in reliance on the fraudulent misrepresentation, permits the statute of limitations to bar his or her action, the patient can maintain an action for fraud against the physician, not on account of the original negligence or malpractice but on account of the fraudulent actions of the physician that deceived the patient with the consequence that the time bar ran against the original action.

Was the Action Timely Filed?

Having held that the plaintiff has set forth a valid cause of action for fraud against the defendant, the next question is whether the cause of action was timely filed. Kansas law [K.S.A. 60-513(a)(3)] establishes a limitation of 2 years within which to bring an action for relief on the grounds of fraud. It goes on to provide that such a cause of action shall not be "deemed to have accrued until the fraud is discovered." In this case, the cause of action was filed within 2 years of the discovery of fraud. However, 60-513(b) goes on to provide that "in no event shall an action be commenced more than 10 years beyond the time of the act giving rise to the cause of action."

The action in this case was filed more than 10 years after the fraud was perpetrated. The question is whether the statute of repose was also tolled by the defendant's concealment of the cause of action. It is a relatively simple matter to conclude that the running of the statute of limitations is tolled by concealment of the fraud.

Accordingly, in the event the plaintiff is able to prove that she was prevented from discovering that she had a cause of action against the defendant for her negligence in leaving surgical sponges in the plaintiff's abdomen by the defendant's own fraudulent conduct and misrepresentation, then, in that event, the defendant will be equitably estopped from raising the defenses of the statutes of limitations or the statutes of repose.

Whether or not a defendant will be estopped from raising certain defenses can only be decided on a case-by-case basis. This is one of the cases in which the doctrine is appropriately applied. The appeals court believed that the application of the doctrine of equitable estoppel is required in cases of this nature to prevent physicians from benefiting from their own fraudulent misrepresentation and to avoid any inference that the law would encourage and reward such behavior. To hold that a physician may successfully blunt a malpractice cause of action by fraudulently misrepresenting facts to a patient would be to encourage such fraudulent behavior. The ap-

peals court did not believe that the law can or should be so manipulated, and its decision was to ensure that this will not happen. The decision of the trial court that the plaintiff's causes of action were barred by the statute of limitations and/or the statute of repose was reversed, and the matter was remanded for a trial on the merits consistent with this opinion.

Discussion

1. Is there a cause of action for fraud? Why?
2. Do you agree that the cause of action was filed on a timely basis? Discuss.

16. PRODUCTS LIABILITY/DRUG/NO LIABILITY

Citation: *Cooper v. Sams*, 628 So. 2d 1181 (La. Ct. App. 1993)

Facts

The patient was a 21-year-old male who had sickle cell anemia since childhood. He was admitted to St. Francis Cabrini Hospital on April 11, 1985, with a fever and rash not apparently related to his sickle cell disease. It was thought that he had either an infection or an allergic reaction to an antacid. His condition worsened and he began to exhibit symptoms of sickle cell pain crisis, for which he was administered fluids and a variety of blood products. The patient was also experiencing abdominal pain and vomiting, which was suggestive of gallbladder disease.

On April 22, 1985, his gallbladder was removed and a liver biopsy was taken. On April 23, 1985, while on a ventilator in the hospital's intensive care unit, the patient suffered seizures. This observation had been recorded in the nurses' notes. In addition, the patient was rejecting an endotracheal tube, leading his physician, Dr. Lewis, to order the nurse to inject him with Sublimaze to further sedate him, which she did. He suffered more seizures and high temperatures over the next two hours and was given Dilantin, a seizure medication. The patient was also administered Dantrium, which caused his temperature to subside after reaching a peak of 108 degrees. Thereafter, he went into a semicomatose state and possibly suffered a stroke. Permanent brain damage resulted, which affected his cognitive functioning. He went from an independent working college student to a dependent, nonfunctioning young man with no memory.

The mother brought a medical malpractice action and products liability suit against a physician and both Taylor Pharmaceutical Company and Janssen Pharmaceutica, Inc., manufacturers of the medication Sublimaze. The plaintiff also sued the Louisiana Patient's Compensation Fund (Fund) for all damages in excess of $100,000. The Fund filed third-party damages against the manufacturers.

The trial court found in his favor against the treating physicians, but granted summary judgment in favor of the drug companies, finding no issue of material fact on whether the Sublimaze had an inherent defect that caused the brain damage. In regard to damages, the jury returned a verdict in the amounts of:

1. Bodily injury, pain, suffering, and mental anguish	$285,000.00
2. Permanent disability	570,000.00
3. Economic loss	
a. Past lost wages	67,175.00
b. Loss of future earning capacity	261,250.00
4. Loss of consortium for Sara Cooper	75,000.00
5. Past medical expenses	146,490.00
6. Future medical care and related benefits	1,187,500.00

Id. at 883.

"La. R.S. 40:1299.42(B) provides that the total amount recoverable for malpractice claims for injuries to or death of a patient, exclusive of future medical care and related benefits as provided in R.S. 40:1299.43, shall not exceed $500,000.00, plus interest and costs." *Id.* at 883.

The plaintiff and the Fund appealed.

Issue

Was the patient's brain damage caused by the hospital's negligence in delaying treatment for the patient's high temperature? Was the medication Sublimaze inherently defective, thus causing the patient's brain damage?

Holding

The Court of Appeal of Louisiana affirmed the negligence verdict in favor of the plaintiff and found that the trial judge had appropriately granted summary judgment in favor of the drug manufacturers.

Reason

The evidence presented at trial demonstrated that the patient suffered high temperatures and subsequent brain damage. Although the cause of the fever was guessed at by

the experts, it was never narrowed to one cause, and the jury found that the hospital's failure to control it caused the patient's brain damage.

The pharmaceutical company presented expert evidence demonstrating that Sublimaze was a commonly used anesthetic and that it had been given successfully to over 400,000 patients. It was not known to cause seizures or any of the other symptoms that had been experienced by the patient. Therefore, there was a material issue of fact. The plaintiff failed to show that the Sublimaze administered was defective or that it was the cause of the patient's brain damage.

Discussion

1. Examine the steps that might have been taken to treat the patient in a timely and more effective fashion.
2. What are the necessary elements that must be proven in a products liability case?

17. PRODUCTS LIABILITY/DEFECTIVE SYRINGE

Citation: *Cotita v. Pharma-Plast, U.S.A., Inc.*, 974 F.2d 598 (5th Cir. 1992)

Facts

While providing nursing services to an acquired immune deficiency syndrome (AIDS) patient, Mr. Cotita, a registered nurse, was stuck by a syringe manufactured by the defendant-appellee, Pharma-Plast, U.S.A., Inc. The syringe, although still in its sterile packaging, was missing the protective cap that normally covers the tip of the needle. This improper packaging allowed the needle to pierce its sterile plastic covering and penetrate the protective gloves that Mr. Cotita was wearing. Because of the presence of the patient's blood on his gloves at the time of the needle stick, Mr. Cotita feared that he had been exposed to the human immunodeficiency virus (HIV). Subsequent tests revealed that he was not HIV-positive; nevertheless, he sued Pharma-Plast, seeking damages for mental anguish stemming from his fear of contracting AIDS.

Pharma-Plast admitted defective packaging, and the district court granted summary judgment in Mr. Cotita's favor on the issue of the defective state of the syringe. The issue of damages was specifically reserved for trial. Pharma-Plast moved for leave to amend its answer to assert the defense of Mr. Cotita's negligence. With the trial set for the following month, the district court denied this motion. Later, the trial in this matter was continued. Thereafter, Pharma-Plast resubmitted its motion for leave to amend, which was granted over Mr.

Cotita's objection. Mr. Cotita also objected to the introduction of evidence concerning his negligence, contending that the issue of fault was closed by the court's previous entry of summary judgment on the issue of Pharma-Plast's liability as the manufacturer of the defectively packaged syringe.

The damage issue was tried before a jury that returned a verdict for $150,000 in Mr. Cotita's favor. This amount was reduced by 30 percent, a figure that the jury found reflected his negligence. Mr. Cotita maintained that the issue of his negligence should not have been considered by the jury, nor used to reduce the amount of his award.

Issue

Did the district court err in allowing Pharma-Plast to amend its answer to assert the nurse's negligence?

Holding

The United States Court of Appeals for the Fifth Circuit found no error in the district court's application of comparative fault.

Reason

"Whether to apply comparative fault is a question of law, freely reviewable on appeal." *Cates v. Sears, Roebuck & Co.*, 928 F.2d 679, 683 (5th Cir. 1991). The Louisiana Supreme Court addressed the interplay between comparative fault and products liability in *Bell v. Jet Wheel Blast*, 462 So. 2d 166 (La. 1985). From *Bell*, a two-pronged test has been distilled to ascertain whether comparative fault should be used to reduce a plaintiff's award in a products liability action. First, would the reduction of the award realistically provide an incentive for user care? If this query is answered affirmatively, a court must then ask whether the application of comparative fault would drastically undermine the manufacturer's incentive to make a safe product. If this latter question is answered affirmatively, "Louisiana law prohibits the application of comparative fault." *Id.* at 600.

Pharma-Plast presented evidence that the procedures used by the nurse were in violation of the universal precautions and procedures that are standard in the health care field. The district court here was entitled to determine that the application of comparative fault would ultimately encourage workers in the health care field to follow the established procedures for handling syringes.

The actions of Mr. Cotita in his use of the defective syringe were properly considered in evaluating the damages awarded. The damage phase of the proceeding was separate and apart from the previously decided liability phase. As the court in *Nicholas v. Homelite Corp.* stated, "Comparative fault provides an episodic postmanufacturer reduction in the final economic assessment against the manufacturer based on the user's actions, without regard to the prior actions and responsibilities of the manufacturer." 780 F.2d at 1153.

Discussion

1. Do you agree with the court's reasoning? Explain.
2. What procedures has your organization implemented in order to reduce the likelihood of exposing staff, visitors, and patients to infectious diseases?

18. PRODUCTS LIABILITY/SYRINGE CAP/ LIABILITY NOT ESTABLISHED

Citation: *Seimon v. Becton Dickinson & Co.*, 632 N.E.2d 603 (Ohio Ct. App. 1993)

Facts

On August 17, 1989, the nurse was employed by the hospital as the assistant director of nursing in charge of patient education. As a part of her duties, she was instructing an outpatient on the proper procedure for self-injecting insulin. The patient injected herself, capped the needle, and handed it to the nurse. Upon receiving the syringe from the patient, the nurse's right index finger was punctured by the needle. The needle had penetrated the side of the cap that covered the needle. The nurse performed first aid on herself and reported to the emergency department of the hospital. The nurse, upset that she was exposed to HIV, sought counseling to cope with her fears that she had contracted a deadly, incurable disease.

The nurse brought a product liability action against the syringe manufacturer. She alleged that she feared that she had been infected with HIV. The Court of Common Pleas granted the syringe manufacturer's motion for summary judgment, and the nurse appealed.

Issue

Did the nurse show that a defective needle cap was the cause of her emotional distress?

Holding

The Court of Appeals of Ohio held that the nurse failed to show that the defective needle cap was the proximate cause of her emotional distress as she failed to produce any evidence that she was, in fact, exposed to HIV.

Reason

The nurse had the burden to support the products liability claim by showing that the manufacturer breached its duty to provide needle caps that would protect her from injury. The manufacturer attached a copy of the nurse expert's report to the motion for summary judgment, which supported the nurse's claims. This expert's report was uncontested by the manufacturer. The manufacturer did not contest that the needle puncture caused physical injury, but did, in essence, contest that the defective needle cap was the proximate cause of the emotional suffering. The nurse failed to produce any evidence that she was, in fact, exposed to HIV. The court found that absent some showing that the defective cap was the proximate cause of the nurse's emotional distress, the nurse could not recover.

Discussion

1. What evidence would the nurse need to establish negligence by the manufacturer?
2. What are the elements of negligence that a plaintiff must establish in a products liability case?

19. PRODUCTS LIABILITY/VENTILATOR DESIGN

Citation: *Piper v. Bear Med. Sys., Inc.*, 883 P.2d 407 (Ariz. App. Div. 1 1993)

Facts

After undergoing surgery for the removal of two malignant lung tumors, Mrs. Piper developed adult respiratory distress syndrome. She was placed on the Bear 2 Adult Volume Ventilator ("Bear 2") to assist her breathing. Approximately 10 days after Mrs. Piper was placed on the Bear 2, a nurse accidentally knocked off the expiratory arm causing the ventilator alarms to sound. The nurse attempted to reassemble the parts and sought the help of another nurse because no respiratory therapist was on duty at the time. One of the nurses inverted the one-way check valve on the ventilator when reassembling and the alarms on the Bear 2 continued to sound.

The proper procedure in this situation is to disconnect the patient from the ventilator and use other medical equipment to manually assist breathing. However, Mrs. Piper was not removed from the ventilator for several minutes, during which the inverted check valve permitted her to inhale but prevented her from exhaling. Because the check valve was inverted, the pressure increased in Mrs. Piper's chest, preventing blood from returning to the heart or circulating to the brain, which in turn caused serious, neurological damage.

After this incident, Mrs. Piper's condition steadily deteriorated. With her family's consent, she was eventually taken off the ventilator and died shortly afterward. The surviving spouse filed a wrongful death action against several defendants, including Bear.

It was common for respiratory therapists to modify the expiratory arm by adding parts including the addition of bacterial filters. This was a common and well-known practice in the respiratory therapy industry, and Bear knew its ventilators were being modified. The respiratory therapist who added the filter to Mrs. Piper's ventilator testified that, prior to installing the filter, he called the sales company that represented Bear. He inquired whether filters were being used on ventilators and was told that they were recommended. Peter Holm, a respiratory therapist who had been a Bear consultant, testified that the use of bacterial filters began in the late 1970s and became much more prevalent by 1985.

Dr. Robert B. Spooner, an expert in safety testing medical equipment, testified that the use of bacterial filters in breathing machines, specifically Bear ventilators, was common by 1985 when Mrs. Piper was placed on the Bear 2. He stated that it was reasonable that bacterial filters would be used to improve the care of patients both in preventing exhalation of bacteria into the hospital room and in removing additional moisture in the flow tube to improve the accuracy of measurement of exhaled breath by the flow sensor. In Dr. Spooner's opinion, manufacturers of medical equipment have a responsibility to anticipate such improvements involving their products.

Issue

Was there sufficient testimony from which a jury could find that the addition of the bacterial filter to the Bear 2 was reasonably foreseeable?

Holding

The Court of Appeals held that testimonial evidence was sufficient evidence from which the jury could find that the addition of a bacterial filter to the ventilator was reasonably foreseeable. The design of the ventilator was defective and unreasonably dangerous, and, therefore, a contributing factor to the patient's death.

Reason

A case of strict products liability is established if the:

1. product is defective and unreasonably dangerous
2. defective condition existed at the time product left defendant's control

3. defective condition is the proximate cause of the plaintiff's injuries

At the time the Bear 1 was manufactured, a committee of the American National Standards Institute (ANSI) had promulgated standard Z79.7-1976 for the manufacturing of ventilators. The committee, composed of physicians, respiratory therapists, ventilator manufacturers, and representatives of the Food and Drug Administration, created uniform standards for breathing machines "to insure that machines designed for this purpose shall be safe and reliably effective. . . ." Although ANSI's standards were not mandatory, they were considered authoritative and were followed by the Food and Drug Administration and most ventilator manufacturers.

Section 2.10.9 of Z79.7-1976 required that if an expired gas outlet, such as a one-way check valve, was fitted to a ventilator, "it shall be designed in such a way that it cannot easily be connected to either 22-, 15-, or 30mm cones or sockets. . . ." The purpose of this requirement was to prevent reversal of the expired gas outlet by mistake or misassembly. Despite this requirement, the Bear 2 one-way check valve was made with a 22mm fitting.

Dr. Spooner testified that the easiest way to bring the check valve into compliance was to flare out the end "like the bell on a trumpet," so that no other connections could be made to it. In his opinion, the Bear 2 was defective and unreasonably dangerous at the time it was manufactured.

Discussion

1. If you were conducting a root cause analysis, what would you consider the underlying cause(s) as to why this unfortunate event occurred?
2. Discuss what action(s) you would take to prevent future occurrences.

II

Criminal Aspects of Health Care

1. MISDEMEANOR CHARGES/SUSPENSION OF LICENSE

Citation: *Everett v. Georgia Bd. of Dentistry*, 441 S.E.2d 6 (Ga. 1994)

Facts

The plaintiff, Dr. Everett, had been arrested on misdemeanor charges for possession of marijuana, exhibiting pornography to minors, contributing to the delinquency of minors, and sexual battery. As a result of the charges, the Georgia Board of Dentistry suspended the dentist's license to practice dentistry pending further proceedings. Dr. Everett brought an action challenging the board's decision to suspend his license based on his arrest. He sought injunctive relief based on statutory and constitutional violations allegedly committed by the board. He claimed that he was not given the opportunity to be heard prior to suspension of his license. The trial court denied Dr. Everett's request for an injunction, and he appealed.

Issue

Was the trial court's decision not to grant Dr. Everett an injunction a violation of due process in that it did not require a hearing prior to suspending Dr. Everett's license to practice dentistry?

Holding

The Supreme Court of Georgia held that due process did not require a hearing prior to the board's suspension of Dr. Everett's license. Moreover, Dr. Everett's claim of statutory and constitutional violations was not preserved for appellate review.

Reason

Due process did not require a hearing prior to the suspension of Dr. Everett's license where the board found that public health, safety, or welfare required emergency action. Such action was based on the arrest warrant issued to Dr. Everett for sexual offenses allegedly committed against children at the same location where the physician practiced dentistry. The suspension of Dr. Everett's license did not have to be predicated on his conviction of criminal offenses. Discipline was authorized based on: "... any unprofessional, immoral, unethical, deceptive, or deleterious conduct or practice harmful to the public, which conduct or practice materially affects the fitness of the licensee or applicant to practice dentistry, or [is] of a nature likely to jeopardize the interest of the public, which conduct or practice need not have resulted in actual injury to any person or be directly related to the practice of dentistry but shows that the licensee of applicant has committed any act or omission which is indicative of bad moral character or trustworthiness. . . ." The court found that the charges against Dr. Everett fall within these parameters.

Discussion

1. What criteria is the Board of Dentistry allowed to use in order to revoke a dentist's license without giving the dentist notice or the opportunity to be heard before the revocation?

2. What is meant by due process?

2. MISDEMEANOR/PATIENT NEGLECT

Citation: *State v. Cunningham*, 493 N.W.2d 884 (Iowa Ct. App. 1992)

Facts

The defendant, the owner and administrator of a residential care facility, housed 30 to 37 mentally ill, mentally retarded, and elderly residents. The Iowa Department of Inspections and Appeals conducts routine inspections of health care facilities. All inspections are unannounced and deficiency statements are sent to the administrator of the facility surveyed.

Various surveys were conducted at the defendant's facility between October 1989 and May 1990. All of the surveys except for one resulted in a $50 daily fine assessed against the defendant for violations of the regulations. On August 16, 1990, a grand jury filed an indictment charging the defendant with several counts of wanton neglect of a resident in violation of Iowa Code section 726.7 (1989), which provides "A person commits wanton neglect of a resident of a health care facility when the person knowingly acts in a manner likely to be injurious to the physical, mental, or moral welfare of a resident of a health care facility. . . . Wanton neglect of a resident of a health care facility is a serious misdemeanor."

The district court held that the defendant had knowledge of the dangerous conditions that existed in the health care facility but willfully and consciously refused to provide or exercise adequate supervision to remedy or attempt to remedy the dangerous conditions. The residents were exposed to physical dangers, unhealthy and unsanitary physical conditions, and were grossly deprived of much needed medical care and personal attention. The conditions were likely to and did cause injury to the physical and mental well-being of the facility's residents. The defendant was found guilty on five counts of wanton neglect. The district court sentenced the defendant to one year in jail for each of the five counts, to run concurrently. The district court suspended all but two days of the defendant's sentence and ordered him to pay $200 for each count, plus a surcharge and costs, and to perform community service. A motion for a new trial was denied, and the defendant appealed.

Issue

Was there sufficient evidence to convict the defendant of the charges?

Holding

The Court of Appeals of Iowa held that there was substantial evidence to support a finding that the defendant was responsible for not properly maintaining the nursing facility, which led to prosecution for wanton neglect of the facility's residents.

Reason

Substantial evidence means evidence that would convince a rational fact finder that the defendant was guilty beyond a reasonable doubt. The defendant was found guilty of knowingly acting in a manner likely to be injurious to the physical or mental welfare of the facility's residents by creating, directing, or maintaining the following five hazardous conditions and unsafe practices:

1. There were fire hazards and circumstances that impeded safety from fire.
   - cigarette stubs found in a cardboard box
   - burn holes found in patient clothing
   - burn holes found in furniture
   - cigarette burns noted in nonsmoking areas
   - a rusted fire door that was bent and would not close or latch
   - exposed electrical wiring
2. The facility was not properly maintained.
   - broken glass in patients' rooms
   - excessively hot water in faucets
   - dried feces on public bathroom walls and grab bars
   - insufficient towels and linens
   - dead and live cockroaches and worms in the food preparation area
   - debris, bugs, and grease throughout the facility
   - no soap available in the kitchen
   - at one point only one bar of soap and one container of shampoo found in the entire facility
   - entire facility in a general state of disrepair
3. Dietary facilities were unsanitary and inadequate to meet the dietary needs of the residents.
   - an ordered no concentrated sweets diet for a diabetic patient not followed, subjecting him to life-threatening blood sugar levels
4. There were inadequate staffing patterns and supervision in the facility.
   - no funds spent on employee training (only one of three kitchen employees was properly trained)
   - defendant did not spend the minimum amount of time at the facility, as required by administrative standards

5. Improper dosages of medications were administered to the residents.
   - distributing an ongoing overdose of heart medication to one resident
   - failure to administer medication, resulting in one resident suffering a seizure
   - failure to treat residents' skin lesions and herpes *Id.* at 887–888

The defendant argued that he did not "create" the unsafe conditions at the facility. The court of appeals disagreed. The statute does not require that the defendant create the conditions at the facility to sustain a conviction. The defendant was the administrator of the facility and responsible for the conditions that existed. The defendant also argued that some of the deficiencies cited had been corrected. The statute, however, does not require failure or refusal to remedy the found conditions in order to sustain a conviction.

Discussion

1. The lessons in this case are numerous. As a classroom activity, in groups of three to five, brainstorm the numerous ramifications.
2. Was the sentencing of the court adequate? Explain.

3. CRIMINAL/SEXUAL OFFENSE/REVOCATION OF LICENSE/NURSE

Citation: *Gilpin v. Board of Nursing*, 837 P.2d 1342 (Mont. 1992)

Facts

From 1980 through 1990, the defendant was a registered nurse. His license lapsed at the end of 1990. In 1987, he was convicted of two counts of sexual assault on 11- and 12-year-old girls. After having been sentenced to consecutive terms of four years in prison on each count, the Montana Board of Nursing began a disciplinary proceeding against him involving his license. A hearing examiner heard the case, which was presented on an agreed statement of facts. His license was revoked when the board affirmed the hearing examiner's findings. The defendant then appealed to the district court, which, after hearing both parties' arguments, affirmed the board's decision to revoke the nurse's license. Thereafter, the nurse appealed to the Supreme Court of Montana.

Issue

Did the board have jurisdiction to revoke a nursing license that had expired before they revoked it? Did the revocation take place without a proper hearing? Did the board properly consider criteria for licensure of criminal offenders when they revoked the nurse's license?

Holding

The decision of the board and district court was affirmed, and the license was revoked, although not on a permanent basis.

Reason

The statute that regulates the licensing provisions for nurses in Montana (S 37-8-431(3) MCA) gives the board the power to reinstate a license for three years after it lapses. Therefore, the court determined that the Board retains jurisdiction over a lapsed nursing license for three years after the nurse failed to renew it.

On the issue of whether the nurse had a fair hearing, the material facts of the case were stipulated to, and at the hearing itself, the nurse gave his arguments against the findings of the examiner. Thus, the court found the nurse was not entitled to any further hearings other than what he had.

Finally, regarding the issue surrounding whether the board properly considered the criteria for the licensure of criminals in revoking the nursing license, the court found that the policy of the state and the intent of the legislature are to protect the public health, safety, and welfare of its citizens. Although a license may not be revoked solely on the basis of a prior criminal conviction, when the conviction is one that relates to the public health, welfare, and safety as it applies to the occupation for which the license is sought, the licensing agency may deny or revoke the license, if the agency finds that the applicant has not been rehabilitated to the point that would warrant public trust. Here, the crimes of sexual assault upon young girls were sufficient to revoke the license. Because the practice of nursing brings the nurse into close physical contact with patients, the conviction of sexual assault makes a person unfit to practice nursing. The board properly considered the criteria for licensing criminal defendants.

Discussion

1. What criteria should a board of nursing take into consideration when deciding whether to revoke the license of a nurse convicted of a crime?
2. What procedures should health care organizations take in order to prevent similar offenses from occurring in their facilities?

4. CRIMINAL/SEXUAL CONDUCT/12-YEAR SENTENCE

Citation: *State v. Poole*, 499 N.W.2d 31 (Minn. 1993)

Facts

A physician was convicted of 16 counts of third- and fourth-degree criminal sexual conduct committed against 11 female patients. He was sentenced to 18 years (6 consecutive terms), and he appealed. Although the court of appeals affirmed the decision of the trial court, it did reduce his aggregate sentence from 18 to 12 years (3 consecutive terms). All of the patients complained that the sexual abuse took place during the course of the bimanual part of the physical examination. They testified that part of the examination took 10 to 20 minutes. They had not been given a gown or sheet to cover themselves, and the physician remained in the room with them alone while they dressed. An obstetrical and gynecological practitioner at the University of Minnesota Hospital testified that the entire pelvic examination usually only takes two to three minutes, and that there was no medical reason for any physician to touch a patient in the way this doctor did.

On appeal to the Minnesota Supreme Court, the physician argued that the evidence obtained as a result of the search warrant should not have been allowed into evidence.

Issue

Did the trial court properly deny the physician's motion to suppress evidence seized pursuant to a search warrant?

Holding

The evidence obtained as a result of the search warrant was properly admitted into evidence.

Reason

The warrant was not too broad, and was supported by probable cause. The description of the items sought was as specific as the circumstances and nature of the activity charged allowed. The investigators did not even know the total number of victims, and because of the nature of the charges, it was not likely that all of the victims would have come forward on their own. The records sought involved the privacy of the patients, not the physician, who had no standing to object. The papers and records seized were reviewed in camera by the judge in order to protect the privacy rights of the patients.

Discussion

1. Why was the evidence gathered as a result of the search warrant reviewed in camera by the judge?
2. Was the holding of the courts too harsh? Explain.

5. DRUGS/INVALID PRESCRIPTIONS/ INADEQUATE RECORD KEEPING

Citation: *United States v. Veal*, 23 F.3d 985 (6th Cir. 1994)

Facts

In October 1990, United States Drug Enforcement Administration (DEA) investigators received reports from drug wholesalers that the defendant, Mr. Veal, was making inordinately large purchases of Doriden and Tylenol 4. Doriden, a sleeping medication, and Tylenol 4, a pain medication containing codeine, are Schedule III controlled substances. These drugs have a heroin-like effect when ingested in combination. The combination is commonly referred to in the illegal drug market as "fours and doors." Although a registered pharmacist pays anywhere from four to seven cents a pill of either variety, a single dose of the "fours and doors" combination costs about $20 on the street.

On October 5, 1990, DEA investigators went to the defendant's pharmacy to serve him with a notice of intent to inspect his records, prescriptions, and inventory. The defendant agreed that the agents could perform the inspection four days later, at which time he said he would turn over his records. When the agents returned on October 9, 1990, the defendant asked them whether they would be removing the records. The officers answered that the records would be seized only if they were found to contain incriminating evidence. The defendant responded, "So you'll take my records." The officers reiterated that they would only take the records if they were incriminating; the defendant then withdrew his consent to the search, and the officers left the premises. The officers subsequently obtained a search warrant pursuant to which they went through the defendant's pharmacy records. They discovered significant discrepancies between his controlled substance purchases and quantities accounted for. The records also revealed that the defendant had filled numerous phony prescriptions for Doriden and Tylenol 4. Some of the prescriptions bore the name of a fictitious physician, and others bore the names of actual physicians who testified at trial that they had not, in fact, written the prescriptions.

The defendant was tried on a 13-count indictment, one count of which was eventually withdrawn by the government. The jury returned a verdict of guilty on six counts and not guilty on the remaining counts. A motion for acquittal or a new trial was denied, and the defendant appealed.

Issue

Did the evidence support a determination that the defendant had distributed controlled substances illegally by filling invalid prescriptions? Did the defendant pharmacist maintain inadequate record keeping regarding controlled substances?

Holding

The Court of Appeals for the Sixth Circuit held that the evidence supported a conviction for distribution and possession, and evidence supported conviction on record-keeping charges.

Reason

The defendant contended that the evidence produced at trial was insufficient to support a conviction on any of the charges on which the jury found him guilty. The defendant did not dispute at trial that he had filled invalid prescriptions. He asserted, however, that he did not know they were invalid. There was ample evidence to support a finding that the fraudulent character of the prescriptions should have been obvious to him. The government showed that several prescriptions were issued by a fictitious physician, that several of the prescriptions were facially invalid, and that phone calls to the physicians named on the forged prescriptions would have uncovered the forgeries. Several experts testified about the well-known combination of "fours and doors" and stated that any reasonable pharmacist should have been suspicious of prescriptions calling for that combination. A pharmacist acting in good faith would have called to verify the prescriptions, according to the government's evidence, and the defendant did not do so. The jury was not required to accept this evidence, of course, but it was entitled to do so.

The evidence against the defendant was also sufficient to support the finding of guilt on the charges of inadequate record keeping. In order to convict Mr. Veal on these charges, the government was required to show only that the defendant had not kept a "complete and accurate record of each [con-

trolled] substance manufactured, received, sold, delivered, or otherwise disposed of by him," as required by 21 U.S.C. §§ 827(a)(3) and 843(a)(4)(A). The evidence introduced at trial included the results of an extensive audit that tended to show that the defendant had failed to account for significant quantities of the controlled substances he handled. The audit assumed the validity of all of the distributions documented by the defendant, and it demonstrated that the defendant had failed to account for 951 Doriden tablets (9 percent of his total purchases of Doriden during the audit period), nearly 1,600 Tylenol 4 tablets (19 percent of his total purchases of Tylenol 4 during the audit period), and 3,227 Tylenol 3 tablets (21 percent of his total Tylenol 3 purchases). The government was not required to prove that the missing tablets were dispensed illegally; what actually happened to those substances had no bearing on the record-keeping charges.

Discussion

1. When a pharmacist is charged with filling invalid prescriptions, what must be proven to sustain a conviction?
2. What are the causes for the wide variety of billing scams committed across the nation?
3. Do you think that the use of generic medications increases or decreases the likelihood of such scams? Explain.

6. DRUGS/ILLEGAL DISTRIBUTION/SUFFICIENCY OF EVIDENCE

Citation: *United States v. Neighbors*, 23 F.3d 306 (10th Cir. 1994)

Facts

The defendant pharmacist, Mr. Neighbors, was convicted in the United States District Court of various drug offenses, and he appealed. He was charged with knowingly and intentionally possessing, with the intent to distribute and illegally dispense, Dilaudid, a Schedule II controlled substance, in violation of 21 U.S.C. § 841 (a)(1) (1988). A jury convicted the defendant on a 45-count indictment, and he was sentenced to 78 months imprisonment on each of the first 15 counts, as well as on counts 44 and 45, and 28 months imprisonment on counts 16 through 43, all to be served concurrently. The defendant appealed his conviction and sentence.

Morton Comprehensive Health Services, Inc. (Morton) of Tulsa, Oklahoma, is a charitable, tax-exempt community health organization that receives funding in the form of grants from the federal government. Morton is composed of a medical clinic, a pharmacy located therein, and a homeless clinic operated by Morton on the premises of the Salvation Army. For 10 years the defendant was the chief pharmacist at Morton clinic pharmacy, continuing until he resigned in March 1991 as the ostensible result of his dissatisfaction with his rate of pay.

The government's theory of the case was that for a number of years the defendant ordered various drugs, including Dilaudid and Valium, from Bergen-Brunswig, a drug supplier, and that thereafter the defendant possessed and converted the Valium and Dilaudid for his own purposes. The government's evidence was largely circumstantial, i.e., there were no "eyewitnesses" and the defendant, when questioned by FBI agents, did not "confess" to any criminal act. However, there was evidence that showed rather conclusively and dramatically that Bergen-Brunswig delivered Valium and Dilaudid to Morton pharmacy that greatly exceeded the Valium or Dilaudid dispensed by the pharmacy.

Much of the testimony involved the audits of the records of Morton pharmacy made by three separate investigative agencies. The FBI went through all of the prescriptions filled at the pharmacy from December 29, 1989, to April 2, 1991, a total of some 24,900 prescriptions. Agent Josh Nixon of the FBI testified that because the prescriptions were numbered sequentially, he and his assistants were able to physically locate and account for all but four prescriptions during that time. The audits revealed that no prescriptions were filled by Morton pharmacy for Dilaudid tablets during the relevant time period, and that although a few prescriptions were found for Valium tablets, those prescriptions contained a pharmacy notation indicating that they had been filled with the generic equivalent of Valium-Diazepam. The audits also revealed that, during this same time period, January 1, 1990, to March 31, 1991, Morton pharmacy had ordered and received some 6,500 4-milligram tablets of Dilaudid and over 135,000 5- and 10-milligram Valium tablets from Bergen-Brunswig.

Other than the defendant, who was the only full-time pharmacist, there were three part-time pharmacists working at Morton. According to their testimony, Morton pharmacy never kept a stock supply of either Valium tablets or Dilaudid tablets during the relevant time period. The government introduced inventory documents that supported the part-time pharmacists' assertion that Dilaudid and Valium tablets were not stocked at Morton. Under Oklahoma state law, Morton pharmacy was required to submit a yearly inventory of controlled substances to state authorities. One such inventory dated July 12, 1990, which was signed by the defendant, indicated that Morton pharmacy did not have any Dilaudid in stock. The defendant cosigned an inventory when he left Morton that also indicated that Morton had no stock supply

of Valium tablets or Dilaudid. Additionally, Ms. Myers, who took over as chief pharmacist when the defendant resigned, performed an inventory of Morton's stock medications. She found no Dilaudid and no Valium tablets.

Issue

Was there sufficient evidence presented to support a conviction of the defendant?

Holding

The United States Court of Appeals for the Tenth Circuit held that the evidence was sufficient to support a conviction.

Reason

The record was convincing that the verdicts of the jury on all 45 counts were amply supported. The government's evidence, though basically circumstantial in nature, was, to the court, most convincing. The defendant's conviction was affirmed on all counts. In *United States v. Notch*, 939 F.2d 895, 898 (10th Cir. 1991), the court found that even though so-called direct evidence may be lacking, a criminal conviction can be sustained "solely on circumstantial evidence." And in *United States v. Smith*, 788 F.2d 663, 669 (10th Cir. 1986), the court opined that circumstantial evidence is entitled to the same weight as that given to direct evidence in determining the sufficiency of the evidence to support a guilty verdict. *Id.* at 310.

Discussion

1. What circumstantial evidence was used against the defendant at trial?
2. What is the difference between direct and circumstantial evidence?

7. FILING FALSE MEDICAID CLAIMS/PHYSICIAN

Citation: *Travers v. Shalala*, 20 F.3d 993 (9th Cir. 1994)

Facts

Dr. Travers was accused of filing a false Medicaid claim that resulted in overpayment for services in violation of Utah Code. The physician pled "no contest" to the charge. He agreed to pay restitution, investigation costs, and a penalty. The plea provided that if Dr. Travers failed to make payment within 60 days, the Utah court would accept his no contest plea and proceed with prosecution. If payment was properly received, the court would allow him to withdraw his no contest plea and dismiss the charges with prejudice. Dr. Travers made timely payment as required under the agreement and the criminal charges were dismissed. The Secretary of Health and Human Services determined that Dr. Travers had been convicted of a criminal offense under the Medicaid and Medicare programs. The Medicaid program requires a mandatory exclusion from participation in the Medicaid program for a period of five years. Dr. Travers brought an action against the Secretary of Health and Human Services for her decision to exclude him from participation in the Medicare and Medicaid programs. An administrative judge of a Health and Human Services Appeals Board and the United States District Court upheld the five-year exclusion, and Dr. Travers appealed.

Issue

Was Dr. Travers properly excluded from participation in the Medicare and Medicaid programs?

Holding

The United States Court of Appeals for the Tenth Circuit held that there was substantial evidence in the record to support the Appeals Board determination that the state criminal proceeding against Dr. Travers resulted in a "conviction" of a program-related offense mandating exclusion of his participation in the Medicare and Medicaid programs for a period of five years.

Reason

The Social Security Act mandates that the Inspector General of the Department of Health and Human Services exclude providers from participation in the Medicare and Medicaid programs for a period of five years when they have been convicted of a criminal offense related to the delivery of care or service under the Medicare or Medicaid programs. Congress broadened the definition of "conviction" to include first offender, deferred adjudication, or other programs where judgment of conviction has been withheld:

> (1) when a judgment of conviction has been entered against [an] individual or entity by a Federal, State, or local court, regardless of whether there is

an appeal pending or whether the judgment of conviction or other record relating to criminal conduct has been expunged; (2) when there has been a finding of guilt against [an] individual or entity by a Federal, State, or local court; (3) when a plea of guilty or nolo contendere by [an] individual or entity has been accepted by a Federal, State, or local court; or (4) when [an] individual or entity has entered into participation in a first offender, deferred adjudication, or other arrangement or program where judgment of conviction has been withheld. 42 U.S.C. § 1320a-7(I).

Dr. Travers argued that his conviction, which was withheld under state law, had no bearing on what constituted a "conviction" under federal law. Dr. Travers' participation in a first offender, deferred adjudication, or other arrangement or program where judgment of conviction has been withheld falls within the meaning of "conviction" as described above. "Travers was not at liberty to withdraw his plea and proceed to trial upon his failure to comply with the plea agreement. On the contrary, had he failed to comply, the court would have accepted his no contest plea and proceeded to set the matter for imposition of sentence." *Id.* at 997.

Discussion

1. Does a state agreement not to prosecute a case bar federal action?
2. What is a no contest plea?

8. FALSE MEDICAID CLAIMS/DENTIST/ EVIDENCE

Citation: *People v. Williamson*, 517 N.W.2d 846 (Mich. Ct. App. 1994)

Facts

The defendant, a dentist, was convicted before the circuit court for falsely certifying and filing Medicaid claims. Seven of the defendant's convictions arose from instances where he billed the Medicaid program for taking a full set of X-rays when he actually took less. The defendant contended that § 7 of the Medicaid False Claim Act is unconstitutionally vague because the definition of what constitutes a false Medicaid claim is found in the Medicaid provider manual, the contents of which were not promulgated as rules in accordance with the Administrative Procedures Act.

Issue

Was § 7 of the Medicaid False Claim Act unconstitutionally vague? Was evidence of instances where the defendant submitted such claims admissible? Did the trial court err when it allowed evidence of double billing by the defendant?

Holding

The Supreme Court of Michigan held that § 7 of the Medicaid False Claim Act was not unconstitutionally vague. Evidence that the defendant had submitted Medicaid claims for full sets of X-rays when only partial sets were taken was admissible. However, evidence that the defendant billed both Medicaid and a patient's private insurer for the same procedure was inadmissible.

Reason

The defendant conceded that he had constructive knowledge of guidelines setting forth the appropriate method of billing the Medicaid program for procedures he performed. The provider manual seized from his dental office stated that billing for a full set of X-rays is only appropriate for a minimum of 16 films. This guideline is unambiguous and put the defendant on notice that taking less than 16 films should not be billed as a full series of dental films. The defendant was on notice that he must conform with the guidelines set forth in the Medicaid provider's manual and that deviation from the billing practices set forth in the manual would constitute a false claim.

As to similar instances of submitting false claims, the argument is without merit. The evidence was offered for the purpose of showing absence of mistake regarding what had been considered a full series of X-rays. Such evidence was relevant and had probative value. Evidence that the defendant billed both Medicaid and the patient's private insurer for the same procedure was inadmissible because the defendant was charged with filing a false claim. As a general rule, evidence that tends to show the commission of other criminal acts by a defendant is not admissible to prove guilt of the charged offense. Evidence of double billing in this case was not "so blended or connected with the crime of which the defendant is accused that proof of one incidentally involves the other or explains the circumstances of the crime." *People v. Delgado*, 404 Mich. 76-83, 273 N.W.2d 395 (1978).

Discussion

1. Why was the evidence of double billing entered in error?

2. Was the evidence of doubling billing so prejudicial to the defendant that it could have affected the outcome of the case?

9. FRAUD/FILING OF FALSE INSTRUMENTS

Citation: *People v. Evans*, 605 N.Y.S.2d 287 (N.Y. App. Div. 1993)

Facts

Between 1985 and 1990, the defendant, Mr. Evans, and her partner engaged in a complicated and sophisticated scheme to defraud the Medicaid system in excess of $500,000. In essence, they used various fictitious corporations and payees to bill Medicaid for services, such as the reading of sonograms by a specialist, when they knew such services had not been provided. The defendant argued that she misunderstood the Medicaid regulations. When claims were rejected under one code she would merely resubmit the claim under another code.

The Bronx County Supreme Court jury found the defendant guilty of grand larceny in the second and third degrees, and 20 counts of offering a false instrument for filing in the first degree. The defendant appealed.

Issue

Did the filing of false Medicaid claims for services the physician knew were not provided constitute a false instrument for filing? Was evidence of billing Medicaid twice for the same service, forging physicians' signatures, billing for services never performed, and billing for readings of sonograms by specialists who had never read them admissible in the prosecution for conspiracy to commit grand larceny?

Holding

The New York Supreme Court, Appellate Division, upheld the convictions, finding that the filing of documents to support fraudulent Medicaid claims with regard to services not provided constitutes the offering of a false instrument for filing. The court further found the other fraudulent acts were admissible as evidence to prove the conspiracy to commit grand larceny.

Reason

The court rejected the defendant's argument that, at her trial, the government offered evidence of additional fraudulent acts, such as double billings and forgeries. The court found that the evidence was merely further evidence of the crimes charged.

Discussion

1. Is health care fraud of significant concern to regulatory agencies? Explain.
2. What steps should organizations take to reduce the frequency of health care fraud?
3. What role should health care compliance officers play in reducing the frequency of health care fraud?

10. FRAUDULENT BILLING PRACTICES

Citation: *United States v. Brown*, 988 F.2d 658 (6th Cir. 1993)

Facts

In *United States v. Brown*, approximately 25 percent of the defendants-appellants' (Browns) income came from treating individuals covered by three federal health care programs: Medicare, Railroad Retirement Board (RRB), and Civilian Health and Medical Program of the Uniformed Services (CHAMPUS). There had been an investigation of the Browns' overcharging the federal government for several years. On June 1, 1992, the United States sought a temporary restraining order without notice to the Browns pursuant to 18 U.S.C. § 1345 and the court's general equitable powers. The complaint accused the Browns of false-claims fraud in violation of 18 U.S.C. § 1341 in connection with the following billing practices: "(1) billing for unperformed medical services, (2) performing and billing for medically unnecessary tests and services, (3) double billing for medical services, including the practices of 'unbundling' and 'fragmentation,' whereby services billed together for a set price are also billed again separately at an additional and substantially higher price, and (4) 'upcoding,' or billing for a more expensive service than that which is actually provided to the patients. The United States supported its allegations with 10 sworn 'declarations' from insurance-carrier employees, ex-employees, and ex-patients of the Browns, as well as a variety of statistical and documentary evidence." *Id.* at 559. On June 2, 1992, the district court issued a temporary restraining order that: "(1) enjoined the Browns from making or conspiring to make false or fraudulent Medicare, RRB, and CHAMPUS reimbursement claims, (2) ordered the Browns to preserve financial and accounting records, which detailed the disposition of payments from the federal programs, (3) froze the

Browns' funds held at any financial institution, excepting an allowed withdrawal not to exceed $10,000 per month for business expenses. . . ." *Id.* at 660. The Browns contend that 18 U.S.C. § 1345, as amended in 1990, limits the district court's ability to freeze assets to cases involving banking-law violations. In 1990, in the wake of the multibillion-dollar savings and loan debacle, Congress amended 18 U.S.C. § 1345 as part of the Crime Control Act of 1990. The United States maintains that the court is empowered to attach funds through 18 U.S.C. § 1345(b) and under the equitable power of the district court. Specifically, it relies on the language granting the court the authority "to take such other action, as is warranted to prevent a continuing and substantial injury to the United States . . ." 18 U.S.C. § 1345(b). The Browns contend that the 1990 amendment limited the ability of the courts to freeze assets to only those cases involving banking-law violations. After studying earlier and later versions of the statute, legislative history, and various cases, the United States Court of Appeals concluded that the amendment in 1990 did not change the district court's ability to freeze assets. A district court had the authority to freeze assets that were the "fruits of the fraud" under the pre-1990 version of § 1345. Congress did not alter the district court's authority when it added language regarding banking-law violations to continue to be within the scope of 18 U.S.C. § 1345 after the statute was amended in 1990. The district court may only freeze assets that might be forfeitable to the United States in the event that fraud is established at trial. The district court froze all of the Browns' funds held at any financial institution except for an allowed withdrawal of $10,000 per month for business expenses. In doing so, the district court failed to distinguish between the proceeds from the alleged Medicare fraud and untainted funds from the Browns' business.

Issue

What medical/legal issues can you identify in this case?

Holding

What decision would you make?

Reason

What was the reasoning of your finding?

Discussion

Develop a discussion question.

11. FRAUDULENT BILLING PRACTICES/LICENSE REVOCATION

Citation: *Llewellyn v. Board of Chiropractic Exam'rs*, 850 P.2d 411 (Or. Ct. App. 1993)

Facts

The State Board of Chiropractic Examiners revoked a chiropractor's license based on findings of insurance fraud and unethical conduct. The chiropractor sent bills to insurance companies for chiropractic services that he purportedly provided to insured patients. In fact, he did not provide any service to those patients, because they failed to keep their appointments. The chiropractor instructed his staff to bill for a service that would likely have been provided if the patients had kept their appointments. In response to the insurance company's requests for documentation to support those bills, he produced chart notes indicating the patient had received treatment when, in fact, there was no treatment rendered. The chiropractor repeatedly engaged in conduct with an intent to deceive the insurance companies and to induce them to make payments that they would not otherwise have made.

The board revoked the chiropractor's license on two independent grounds, either one of which it said would warrant revocation of his license. After the board determined that the chiropractor obtained fees through fraud, the chiropractor sought review.

Issue

Was the board's finding of fraud supported by substantial evidence?

Holding

The Court of Appeals of Oregon held that substantial evidence supported the board's order.

Reason

The chiropractor's argument does not merit extended discussion. The evidence against him was extensive and persuasive.

Discussion

1. Do you agree that there was sufficient evidence to support the board's decision to revoke the chiropractor's license? Explain.

2. Do you think the licenses of health professionals who commit insurance frauds should be permanently revoked? Explain.

12. MURDER/PATIENTS INJECTED WITH LIDOCAINE

Citation: *People v. Diaz*, 834 P.2d 1171 (Cal. 1992)

Facts

The defendant, a registered nurse, was working on the night shift at a community hospital. In 3 1/2 weeks, 13 patients on that shift had seizures, cardiac arrest, and respiratory arrest. Nine died. The unit closed, and the defendant went to work at another hospital. Within three days, a patient died after exhibiting the same symptoms while the defendant was on duty. The defendant was arrested and tried for 12 counts of murder.

The testimony revealed that the defendant had injected the patients with massive doses of lidocaine (a rhythm controlling drug). Evidence showed that the defendant had assisted the patients before they exhibited seizures, giving her the opportunity to administer the drug; she was observed acting strangely on the nights of the deaths; high concentrations of lidocaine were found in the patient's syringes and in the hospital. Moreover, lidocaine syringes and vials were discovered in the defendant's home.

The pretrial investigation revealed that 26 other patients had died at the defendant's first hospital while under the nurse's care. All had the same symptoms. The defendant, who waived her right to trial by jury, was found guilty of 12 counts of murder. The nurse appealed the judgment of death.

Issue

Did the expert testimony support the finding that an overdose of lidocaine caused the patients' deaths? Did the evidence prove that the defendant had the opportunity to give patients overdoses of lidocaine?

Holding

The Supreme Court of California upheld the convictions.

Reason

The expert testimony about the levels of lidocaine in the patients' tissue, coupled with the nurses' testimony concerning the symptoms prior to the deaths, confirmed that the patients died from overdoses given to them by the defendant. Also, the evidence proved that the defendant murdered 12 patients. Testimony showed that the defendant was the only nurse on duty the night each patient was poisoned, other nurses were there on only some of the nights, and only the defendant had the opportunity to administer the fatal doses.

Discussion

1. Examine how the evidence showed, when there were no eyewitnesses, that the defendant was the one who killed the 12 patients.
2. What is the difference between preponderance of evidence and evidence beyond a reasonable doubt?

13. GRAND LARCENY/PSYCHIATRIST/LICENSE REVOKED

Citation: *Surpris v. State of N.Y. Admin. Review Bd.*, 610 N.Y.S.2d 373 (N.Y. App. Div. 1994)

Facts

A psychiatrist was convicted of grand larceny in the third degree upon a plea of guilty and his admission that between February 1, 1988, and September 12, 1988, he submitted false Medicaid claims for which he was reimbursed $39,320. The psychiatrist was charged with professional misconduct. Following a hearing before a committee of the State Board for Professional Conduct, his license to practice medicine was revoked. The psychiatrist sought review of the revocation of his license, contending that the penalty was excessive. He also claimed that the hearing committee was arbitrary and capricious for not allowing him to present 34 New York City Human Resources Administration referral forms as evidence of the economic condition of patients who had come to him and the type of treatment they had received.

Issue

Were the referral forms improperly withheld from the hearing committee? Was the revocation of the psychiatrist's license to practice medicine excessive?

Holding

The Supreme Court of New York, Appellate Division, held that the referral forms were properly excluded from the

hearing before the committee of the State Board for Professional Medical Conduct. Moreover, the psychiatrist's submission of false Medicaid claims warranted revocation of his license to practice medicine.

Reason

The court agreed with the state that the referral forms had little relevance to the issue of the mitigation of the penalty revoking the psychiatrist's license. As to the issue of the penalty imposed for the psychiatrist's submission of over 1,600 claims for psychiatric services that were never rendered, the evidence provided ample justification for revocation of the psychiatrist's license to practice medicine.

Discussion

1. Was the revocation of the psychiatrist's license excessive?
2. What is meant by "professional misconduct"?

14. CRIMINAL TRESPASS/EMPLOYEE INJURY

Citation: *Mundy v. Department of Health and Human Resources*, 609 So. 2d 909 (La. Ct. App. 1992)

Facts

The plaintiff was a licensed practical nurse who worked for 11 years for the Department of Health and Human Resources at Charity Hospital. In November 1986, she arrived for work on the evening shift at 11:17 P.M. As she approached the elevators, which were also used by the general public, she noticed that the two guards who were usually stationed at that location were not there. She entered the elevator to go to the 11th floor, and a man jumped in as the doors were closing. He pressed the second floor button, but when the elevator stopped at that floor, he pulled a knife and attacked the plaintiff. Thinking that the alarm would frighten her attacker and alert someone, she pressed the emergency button, but it was not operating. She was then stabbed repeatedly before her attacker fell out of the elevator.

The trial court found the hospital negligent in the maintenance and operation of the premises, and awarded her $125,000.

Issue

Did the hospital breach its duty to take reasonable care for the safety of its employees?

Holding

Judgment of the trial court was reversed in favor of the defendant hospital.

Reason

Security personnel routinely patrolled the floors of the hospital during shift changes and after visiting hours were over. Moreover, at times they would escort people from the building. Escort services were also provided for employees leaving the building at night, but not entering it. The hospital police captain testified that he had no knowledge of criminal acts having been committed near the elevators. When he learned that incidents had taken place near the emergency department, he always posted a guard there.

There was no duty to protect the plaintiff as she came into the hospital. Further, the risk of harm was not related to her employment, nor was it any greater to her than to the general public. At the time and place of her attack, she was not under the supervision and control of her employer. Even if the hospital owed a general duty to provide security for the general public, there was no showing that the hospital was negligent in its security operations. There was no evidence that the hospital knew or should have known that the elevators posed an unreasonable risk of harm to anyone, thereby imposing a duty to provide security guards at the elevators on a permanent basis. There was no legal duty to foresee the attack and as a result, provide security measures to prevent it.

Discussion

1. When an employee is the victim of a criminal act committed on hospital property, what does the employee have to prove in order to establish negligence?
2. What action should an organization take when it becomes aware of significant security hazards on its property?

15. PATIENT ABUSE/PHYSICAL

Citation: *State v. Houle*, 642 A.2d 1178 (Vt. 1994)

Facts

The defendant, a licensed practical nurse, had criminal charges brought against her stemming from her treatment of a stroke patient. It was alleged that she had slapped the patient's legs repeatedly and shackled him to his bed at the wrists and ankles. By the time of trial, the patient had died of causes unrelated to the charged conduct. During the trial, the state presented the testimony of eyewitnesses, including the patient's wife, hospital employees, and an investigator from the Office of the Attorney General. The defendant did not deny that she had restrained the patient, but claimed that her actions were necessary for the patient's protection, as well as her own, and that her actions were neither assaultive nor cruel. The defendant produced the testimony of another nurse who was familiar with the patient's medical condition and his need for restraint. This nurse was also used to impeach the credibility of one of the state's witnesses.

The defendant's first claim was that the trial court improperly admitted, over objection, evidence that the patient gave consistent accounts of the incidents underlying the charges to Ms. Herrick, a hospital employee. The defendant contended that the testimony was not relevant.

Issue

Was the evidence that the patient gave consistent accounts of the incidents underlying the charges to the defendant relevant and admissible in prosecution of the defendant?

Holding

The Supreme Court of Vermont held that the evidence that the victim gave consistent accounts of the incidents underlying the charges to the defendant was relevant and admissible.

Reason

The patient's awareness of what happened to him was relevant to the state's case because the trial court, in its instruction to the jury, defined cruelty as "intentional and malicious infliction of physical or emotional pain or suffering upon a person." By showing that the patient was aware of what had happened to him, the state allowed the jury to infer that he had suffered physical or emotional pain. The state presented a witness who was present when the incident occurred and who was able to describe the acts of abuse in detail. The credibility of this eyewitness testimony, and not what the patient's testimony would have been, was the focus of the trial.

Discussion

1. Why was the evidence admissible at trial?

2. At what point does the application of restraints become a cruelty?

16. REVOCATION OF LICENSE/PHYSICIAN/ SEXUAL ABUSE

Citation: *Rudell v. Commissioner of Health*, 604 N.Y.S.2d 646 (N.Y. App. Div. 1993)

Facts

The petitioner, a physician, was found guilty of professional misconduct after a hearing conducted by a Committee on Professional Conduct of the State Board for Professional Medical Conduct. The professional misconduct charge was based on the alleged sexual abuse of a patient during physical examination and an alleged false statement on his employment application.

The committee recommended the revocation of the physician's license. He appealed to the Administrative Review Board, which sustained the committee's findings. The petitioner then began an Article 78 proceeding, pursuant to N.Y. Public Health Law § 230-c(4)(5), to review the decision of the administrative board. Public Health Law § 230-c(4) proscribes that judicial review is limited to determining whether the board's "determination was made in violation of lawful procedure, was affected by an error of law, or was arbitrary and capricious or an abuse of discretion." The petitioner asserted that the judgment rendered by the board should be annulled, because the committee relied upon legally incompetent and nonprobative evidence, drew impermissible inferences, and allowed evidence of a taped conversation between a patient and petitioner that was unduly prejudicial.

During the hearing, when the committee sought to learn the possibility of the testimony that had been given by the patient concerning the position where the physician stood during the examination, the petitioner's attorney invited the committee into the doctor's examination room. At the time of the visit, the examining table was positioned so that there were only several inches between the foot and the wall. When a committee member pushed the head of the table against the opposite wall, the space was adequate for an adult male to stand and bend over. This corroborated the patient's testimony that the table fit against the wall at the head, but there was space at the end of the table. Petitioner argued that the visit and the moving of the table were improper. He claimed further that the patient's testimony was of little probative value since she could not see what he was doing.

The committee also considered the testimony of the patient's roommate regarding the patient's statements about the physician's conduct and a tape recording of a telephone conversation between the physician and the patient after the incident.

Issue

Should the decision of the Administrative Review Board be affirmed?

Holding

The New York Supreme Court, Appellate Division, affirmed the decision of the Administrative Review Board.

Reason

The court rejected the petitioner's claim that the visit and moving of the table were improper, because the petitioner's attorney invited the committee, and the physician was present during the visit. He did not object to the moving of the table, and he could have questioned and rebutted the evidence that resulted from the viewing. The court further held that there was no prejudice caused by the allowing of the evidence of the taped phone conversation, because the equivocal responses had probative value and did not reveal anything that the patient did not testify to at the hearing. Finally, the court found the decision to revoke the physician's license justified, in light of the serious nature of the offense of sexual abuse.

Discussion

1. Explain how the physician could have prevented the visit to his examination room by the disciplinary committee.
2. What steps should physicians take when conducting history and physical examinations to reduce the opportunity for sexual misconduct?

17. SEXUAL ABUSE/REVOCATION OF LICENSE

Citation: *Nghiem v. State*, 869 P.2d 1086 (Wash. Ct. App. 1994)

Facts

On October 26, 1989, the Washington State Medical Disciplinary Board charged a physician with unprofessional conduct. The board alleged that the physician had asked inappropriate sexual questions of four of his patients. It also alleged that the physician had inappropriate sexual contact with three of the patients. On December 15 and 16, 1989, the board held a hearing regarding these allegations, at which time three patients described their allegations of sexual abuse by the physician. Prior to the hearing, the physician was evaluated by a psychologist who concluded in a prehearing report that the physician was at a significant risk for similar conduct with other patients. The physician presented a number of witnesses who testified as to his good character and reputation in the community. Among the witnesses was a psychologist who testified that the physician admitted to asking sexually oriented questions but denied any sexual contact. As a result of the physician's admission to asking sexually oriented questions, the psychologist testified that the physician "did not exercise good judgment" and that if the allegations were true and the physician's denial false, then "he's not fit to practice" medicine. *Id.* at 1089.

Following the hearing, the board concluded that the physician had engaged in professional misconduct as described within the meaning of RCW.18.130.180(1) and (24), which provide in part "The following conduct, acts or conditions constitute unprofessional conduct for any license holder or applicant under the jurisdiction of this chapter: (1) The commission of any act involving moral turpitude. . . . (24) Abuse of a client or patient or sexual conduct with a client or patient."

The board revoked the physician's license to practice medicine for 10 years. Reinstatement of his license after that period of time was contingent upon his successful completion of a rehabilitation program.

An appeal was taken to the superior court and the board's findings were upheld. A further appeal was then taken to the court of appeals.

Issue

Was there substantial evidence to support the board's findings? Did the board have the authority to condition the return of the physician's license based on successfully completing a rehabilitation program after the 10-year revocation had run?

Holding

The Court of Appeals of Washington held that the board's findings that the physician had engaged in sexually inappropriate behavior toward patients was supported by the evidence, and his actions constituted professional misconduct. The board did not exceed its authority by ordering that revocation of the physician's license last at least 10 years, or by conditioning reinstatement on proof of rehabilitation.

Reason

Substantial evidence is "evidence in sufficient quantum to persuade a fair-minded person of the truth of the declared premises." *Olmstead v. Department of Health*, 61 Wash. App. 888, 893; 812 P.2d 527 (1986). *Id.* at 1090. The board's findings were based on substantial evidence where the physician engaged in sexually inappropriate physical examinations and inappropriate sexual questioning of his patients.

The 10-year revocation of the physician's license and its return contingent upon the physician's successful completion of a rehabilitation program was permissible based on state statute.

> RCW 18.130.160 states in part: Upon a finding that a license holder or applicant has committed unprofessional conduct . . . the disciplinary authority may issue an order providing for one or any combination of the following: (1) Revocation of the license. . . . RCW 18.130.150 states in part: A person whose license has been suspended or revoked under this chapter may petition the disciplining authority for reinstatement after an interval as determined by the disciplining authority in the order. *Id.* at 1091.

Discussion

1. Assuming you were the plaintiff's attorney in a similar case, how would you defend your client?
2. Do you agree that sexually oriented questions by a practitioner to a patient are sufficient reason to remove the practitioner's license?

III

Contracts

1. BREACH OF CONTRACT/INJUNCTIVE RELIEF

Citation: *Sarah Bush Lincoln Health Ctr. v. Perket*, 605 N.E.2d 613 (Ill. App. Ct. 1992)

Facts

The plaintiff, a hospital, sued its former director of physical medicine and rehabilitation to enforce a restrictive covenant in the employment contract precluding the director from accepting similar employment in the same county within one year of termination of employment.

On April 27, 1992, the plaintiff filed a complaint against the defendant seeking preliminary and permanent injunctive relief to uphold the covenant. The plaintiff also filed a motion for the preliminary injunction requested in the complaint. On May 15, 1992, the defendant filed a motion to dismiss the plaintiff's motion for the preliminary injunction and the complaint. On or about February 27, 1991, the parties to the complaint had entered into a contract whereby the defendant was employed as plaintiff's director of physical medicine. The contract provided that:

> During your employment and for a period of one year thereafter, you agree that you shall not, directly or indirectly, invest in, own, manage, operate, control, be employed by, participate in, or be connected in any manner with the ownership, management, operation or control of any person, firm, or corporation engaged in competition with Hospital in providing health services or facilities within Coles County including the provision of services in

a private office, without prior written consent of the Hospital. . . . *Id.* at 615.

On or about September 6, 1991, following the termination, the defendant engaged in the business of providing physical medicine and rehabilitation services in Coles County. The plaintiff argued that unless the defendant was enjoined, the hospital would suffer irreparable injury. The circuit court granted the hospital's motion for preliminary injunction. Complaining that the hospital made no sufficient showing that the defendant was in breach of the covenant, the defendant appealed.

Issue

Was the hospital entitled to a preliminary injunction to enforce the restrictive covenant in the employment contract?

Holding

The Appellate Court of Illinois held that the grant of the preliminary injunction was proper.

Reason

The appellate court determined that the allegation that the defendant was engaging in the business of providing physical medicine and rehabilitation service in Coles County was sufficient. The court also found that the plaintiff's allegation of damages was sufficient. In a similar case, *Cockerill v.*

Wilson, 51 Ill.2d 179, 281 N.E.2d 648 (Ill. App. Ct. 1972), the *Cockerill* Court stated:

> In considering this issue we must consider that the interest plaintiff sought to protect by the covenant was his interest in his clients. (*House of Vision, Inc. v. Hiyane* (1967), 37 Ill.2d 32, [225 N.E.2d 21].) In bringing the defendant into the association plaintiff was thereby bringing him in contact with a clientele which plaintiff had established over a period of years. Plaintiff was naturally interested in protecting his clients from being taken over by defendant as a result of these contacts. *Id.* at 651.

Discussion

1. Do you consider the hospital's contract with the employee too restrictive? Explain.
2. Was the threat of competition real or imagined?

2. EXCLUSIVE CONTRACT/RADIOLOGIST

Citation: *Dutta v. St. Francis Reg'l Med. Ctr.*, 850 P.2d 928 (Kan. Ct. App. 1993)

Facts

On July 1, 1987, Dr. Dutta, a radiologist, began working in the radiology department of the hospital as an employee of Dr. Krause, the medical director of the hospital's radiology department. On August 5, 1988, the hospital terminated Dr. Krause's employment as medical director but encouraged Dr. Dutta to remain with the hospital. On August 8, 1988, Dr. Dutta and the hospital entered into a written employment contract with a primary term of 90 days. The contract provided that if a new medical director had not been hired by the hospital within the 90-day period, the agreement was to be automatically extended for a second 90-day period.

Following a period of recruitment and interviews, the hospital offered Dr. Tan the position. Dr. Tan and the hospital executed a contract making him the medical director of the radiology department. The contract granted Dr. Tan the right "to provide radiation oncology services on an exclusive basis subject to the exception of allowing Dr. Dutta to continue her practice of radiation oncology at the hospital." On April 24, 1989, the hospital notified Dr. Dutta that the 90-day contract had expired and Dr. Tan was appointed as the new medical director. The letter provided in part:

> It is our intent at this time to establish an exclusive contract with Dr. Donald C-S Tan for medical direction and radiation therapy at SFRMC. Your medical staff privileges to practice radiation therapy at SFRMC will not be affected by this action. You will be allowed to maintain your current office space for radiation oncology activities; however, you should make alternative arrangements for your billing and collection activities. *Id.* at 931.

Dr. Dutta and Dr. Tan then practiced independently of each other in the same facility. On October 13, 1989, Dr. Tan became unhappy with this arrangement and requested exclusive privileges, stating he could not continue as medical director without exclusivity. On February, 2, 1990, an exclusive contract was authorized by the hospital. Dr. Dutta was notified that she would no longer be permitted to provide radiation therapy services at the hospital after May 1, 1990. By letter, Dr. Dutta twice requested a hearing on the hospital's decision to revoke her right to use hospital facilities. Both requests were denied.

Dr. Dutta sued the hospital for breach of employment contract after the hospital had entered into an exclusive agreement with Dr. Tan, thereby denying Dr. Dutta the use of the hospital's radiology department and equipment. Dr. Dutta presented evidence about the purpose of the requirement in her contract with the hospital that provided that the new medical director be mutually acceptable to both parties. A hospital administrator testified that the hospital and Dr. Dutta included the phrase "mutually acceptable" in the contract because "[w]e both agreed that we wanted the person being recruited to be compatible with Dr. Dutta." *Id.* at 932.

Issue

Was the language "mutually acceptable" in paragraph four of the employment contract between the hospital and Dr. Dutta ambiguous?

Holding

The Court of Appeals of Kansas held that substantial evidence supported the jury's verdict that the hospital breached its written employment contract with Dr. Dutta by hiring a medical director who was not mutually acceptable to both the hospital and Dr. Dutta.

Reason

The language in the contract is ambiguous if the words in the contract are subject to two or more possible meanings. The determination of whether a contract is ambiguous is a question of law. Paragraphs four and five of the hospital's employment agreement with Dr. Dutta, dated August 8, 1988, read as follows:

> 4. During the term of this Agreement the Medical Center shall be actively recruiting for a full-time Medical Director for the Radiation Therapy department or a one-half time radiation therapist. Dr. Dutta shall be involved in the interviewing process. The person selected for either of the above positions shall be mutually acceptable to the Medical Center and Dr. Dutta. Dr. Dutta may discuss potential business arrangements with each individual interviewed.
> 5. Once the full-time Medical Director or part-time radiation therapist is selected, Dr. Dutta will, in good faith, attempt to reach a satisfactory business arrangement with the selected individual. *Id.* at 936.

The jury would be justified in finding that Dr. Dutta could have rejected Dr. Tan on the basis that he failed to enter into a business agreement, if there was evidence to support that point of view. The testimony of Dr. Dutta, the hospital administrator, and the attorney who represented Dr. Dutta in contract negotiations, when viewed in the light most favorable to Dr. Dutta, provides a factual basis for the jury to find the phrase "mutually acceptable" in the contract was intended by Dr. Dutta to ensure that the hospital would select a medical director who indicated a willingness to form a partnership or otherwise acceptable business relationship.

Discussion

1. What protective elements should each party to an employment contract negotiate?
2. What are the elements necessary to make a contract valid?

3. ANTITRUST ACTION/ANESTHESIOLOGISTS AND HOSPITAL/NURSE ANESTHETISTS

Citation: *Oltz v. St. Peter's Community Hosp.*, 19 F.3d 1312 (9th Cir. 1994)

Facts

Mr. Oltz, a nurse anesthetist, brought an antitrust action against physician anesthesiologists and St. Peter's Community Hospital after he was terminated. Mr. Oltz had a billing agreement with the hospital, which provided 84 percent of

the surgical services in the rural community that
The anesthesiologists did not like competing with ᴜ̆ᴇ nurse anesthetist's lower fees and, as a result, entered into an exclusive contract with the hospital on April 29, 1980, in order to squeeze the nurse anesthetist out of the market. This resulted in cancellation of the nurse anesthetist's contract with the hospital. Mr. Oltz was faced with a decision to either work for the anesthesiology group or leave the community and find another job. He and his wife decided to leave the community. Mr. Oltz found a job two months later working for the University of Iowa. He filed a suit against the anesthesiologists and hospital for violation of the Sherman Antitrust Act, 15 U.S.C. § 1. The anesthesiologists settled for $462,500 before trial.

The case against the hospital proceeded to trial. The jury found that the hospital had conspired with the anesthesiologists and awarded the plaintiff $212,182 in lost income up to November 5, 1986, the date of the trial, and $209,649 in future damages. The trial judge considered the damage award to be excessive and ordered a new trial. The hospital appealed on the issue of "liability" and Mr. Oltz appealed the order for a new trial based on excessive "damages."

The trial court's judgment on liability was affirmed, as well as its order for a new trial on damages. The hospital moved the court to exclude all damages after June 26, 1982, which was the date that the hospital had renegotiated its exclusive contract with the anesthesiology group. The court decided that Mr. Oltz failed to prove that the renegotiated contract also violated antitrust laws, thus ruling that Mr. Oltz was not entitled to damages after June 26, 1982. Because Mr. Oltz conceded that he could not prove damages greater than those offset by his settlement with the physicians, his claim for damages against the hospital was disposed of by summary judgment.

The judge who presided over Mr. Oltz's request for attorney fees restricted the amount that he could claim. Because Mr. Oltz had been denied damages from the hospital, the judge refused to award attorney fees or costs for work performed after the 1986 liability trial.

Issue

Was Mr. Oltz entitled to seek recovery for all damages resulting from destruction of his business after June 26, 1982?

Holding

The United States Court of Appeals for the Ninth Circuit held that Mr. Oltz was entitled to seek recovery for all damages.

Reason

Mr. Oltz had introduced evidence that the initial exclusive contract violated the antitrust laws and that such violation destroyed his practice. "Because the initial conspiracy destroyed his practice, Oltz is entitled to seek recovery for all damages resulting from the destruction of his business in Helena. . . . The legality of any subsequent agreements between the conspirators is irrelevant, because the April 29, 1980 contract severed the lifeline to Oltz's thriving practice in Helena." *Id.* at 1314.

Discussion

1. What should parties to a contract be aware of when negotiating exclusive contracts?
2. What remedies are available when one party breaches a contract by refusing to perform an agreed upon service?

4. INSURANCE DENIAL/PREEXISTING CONDITION

Citation: *Truett v. Community Mut. Ins. Co.*, 633 N.E.2d 617 (Ohio Ct. App. 1993)

Facts

Mr. Truett brought an action against the insurer to recover medical expenses. In June of 1991, Mr. Truett was treated for migraine headaches. As of August 1, 1991, Mr. Truett was covered under an employee benefit plan through a group health insurance contract with Community Mutual Insurance Co. On August 29, 1991, Mr. Truett was hospitalized for dizziness, vomiting, and weakness on his left side. After extensive testing, Dr. Moorthy diagnosed Mr. Truett as suffering from a complicated migraine. Mr. Truett sought reimbursement for medical expenses he incurred during the course of his illness.

Community Mutual concluded on January 20, 1992, that Mr. Truett's medical expenses were not covered because the expenses were for the care of a preexisting condition. Under the insurance policy, conditions that existed prior to the effective date of the policy were not covered if health problems related to the conditions were manifested after the effective date. Mr. Truett challenged this assessment to a Community Mutual appeals board. Dr. Morrow was recruited by Community Mutual to provide an expert assessment of Mr. Truett's case. The Community Mutual appeals board found that Mr. Truett's condition was preexisting because he had been treated in June 1991 for migraine

headaches. Therefore, Community Mutual denied his coverage for his expenses.

On September 1, 1992, the Truetts filed a complaint against Community Mutual to recover Mr. Truett's medical expenses. The Court of Common Pleas entered summary judgment for Community Mutual, and Mr. Truett appealed.

Issue

Was the insurer's denial of coverage arbitrary or capricious?

Holding

The Court of Appeals of Ohio held that the insurer's denial of coverage was not arbitrary or capricious.

Reason

The appeals board had all of Mr. Truett's medical records from before and after the incident in question. It obtained Dr. Morrow's expert opinion that the complicated migraine was a continuation from Mr. Truett's previous bouts with normal migraines. The appeals board and Dr. Morrow relied on medical evidence in making their decisions and neither overlooked nor ignored relevant information. Thus, the decision was not arbitrary or capricious.

Discussion

1. Why was the insurer's denial of coverage neither arbitrary nor capricious?
2. Under what circumstances does the law give a person a right not to perform under a contract?

5. NONCOMPETITION CLAUSE NOT OVERLY RESTRICTIVE

Citation: *Dominy v. National Emergency Servs.*, 451 S.E.2d 472 (Ga. App. 1994)

Facts

The appellee, National Emergency Services (NES), assigned appellant, Dr. Dale Dominy, to the emergency department at Memorial Hospital and Manor (MHM) in Bainbridge, Georgia, where he was working in 1987 when that hospital terminated its contract with NES and contracted with another provider, Coastal Emergency Services, for emergency department physicians. Dr. Dominy continued to perform emergency medical services at MHM under contract with Coastal until 1989.

The contract provided: "The period of this Agreement shall be for one (1) year from the date hereof, automatically renewable for a like period upon each expiration thereof . . ." The only reasonable construction of this provision was that the parties intended to contract for Dr. Dominy's employment for automatically renewable one-year terms upon the mutual assent of the parties. The fact that the agreement did not set out mechanics by which mutual assent may be communicated does not invalidate the contract. *Id.* at 474.

Dr. Dominy challenged the contract's noncompetition clause as overly restrictive. The covenant in this case provides, in pertinent part: "for a period of two (2) years after the termination of this agreement . . . Physician shall not directly or indirectly solicit a contract to perform nor perform nor have any ownership or financial interest in any corporation, partnership, or other entity soliciting or contracting to perform emergency medical service *for any medical institution at which Physician has performed the same or similar services under this Agreement or any prior Agreement between Physician and Corporation. Id.* at 474.

Dr. Dominy also maintained that the contract's $10,000 liquidated damages provision constitutes an unenforceable penalty. "[A] contract provision will be treated as one for liquidated damages only if all of the following questions are answered affirmatively: First, was the injury caused by the breach difficult or impossible of accurate estimation; second, did the parties intend to provide for damages rather than a penalty; and third, was the stipulated sum a reasonable pre-estimation of the probable loss from the breach. In determining whether a designated sum that is to be paid to one party in the event that the other breaches the contract is a penalty, we must ascertain whether it was inserted for the purpose of deterring the party from breaching the contract, and of penalizing him in the event he should do so, or whether it was a sum which the parties in good faith agreed upon as representing those damages which would ensue if the contract should be breached." *Id.* at 474.

Issue

Was the contract's noncompetition clause overly restrictive? Was the liquidated damages provision of $10,000 in relation to the noncompetition clause enforceable?

Holding

The Court of Appeals held that (1) the noncompetition clause was not overly restrictive, and (2) the liquidated damages provision of $10,000 in relation to the noncompetition clause was enforceable.

Reason

The record reveals no attempt by either party to terminate the contract, and it is undisputed that Dr. Dominy received payment for his services at MHM and other benefits from NES consistent with the agreement until the hospital terminated its contract with NES. By their conduct, the parties assented to each of the contract's yearly renewals. Accordingly, the trial court properly granted summary judgment to NES.

As to the contract's noncompetition clause, this restriction only prohibits Dr. Dominy from performing emergency medical services in Memorial Hospital and Manor in Bainbridge, Georgia, where he worked pursuant to a contract with NES, and from having an ownership or financial interest in an entity contracting to provide emergency medical services to that one hospital. He is not precluded from all practice of medicine, with staff privileges at MHM, nor is he prohibited from providing emergency medical services, directly or under contract to a provider of such services, to other hospitals in the immediate vicinity. The court found that such a restriction is reasonably limited in duration and territorial effect while it protects NES's interest in preventing Dr. Dominy from becoming its competitor immediately after termination of its contract with MHM.

At the time the parties entered into contract, they limited NES's consequential damages to $10,000 for any breach of the following noncompetition provisions: whether Dr. Dominy forms a competing corporation to provide physicians to a hospital, or individually performs emergency medical services for a hospital where he had worked under contract with NES. According to NES, $10,000 represents the estimated cost of locating and verifying the credentials of a replacement for the breaching party rather than merely reassigning him to another client hospital in continuation of his contract with NES.

The contract entitles NES to liquidated damages "in addition to any and all remedies available to Corporation under any and all other agreements, and under this Agreement. . . ." Retention of the right to seek injunctive relief and other remedies for other breaches of the contract does not render the liquidated damages provision a penalty. Accordingly, the provision for liquidated damages is enforceable.

Discussion

1. Was the contract's noncompetitive clause overly restrictive? Why?
2. Was the $10,000 liquidated damages provision in relation to the noncompetition clause enforceable? Why?

IV

Civil Procedure and Trial Practice

1. SUMMONS/IMPROPER SERVICE

Citation: *Collins v. Park,* 621 A.2d 996 (Pa. Super. Ct. 1993)

Facts

In this medical malpractice action, the trial court dismissed a complaint against Dr. Park because of improper service upon him. The plaintiff, Mr. Collins, appealed.

On March 13, 1989, the plaintiff commenced the present action by writ of summons issued. On March 14, 1989, the sheriff attempted to serve the writ on Dr. Park by leaving a copy with the receptionist at the hospital. On February 22, 1988, however, Dr. Park had terminated his relationship with the hospital, and he did not thereafter maintain an office or place of business at the hospital.

Issue

Was the sheriff's attempt at service of the writ of summons upon Dr. Park in a medical malpractice action by leaving a copy with the receptionist at the hospital defective?

Holding

The Superior Court of Pennsylvania held that the sheriff's attempt at service of the writ of summons upon the physician by leaving a copy with the receptionist at the hospital was defective, as Dr. Park did not have a proprietary interest in the hospital and, at the time of service, was no longer affiliated with the hospital. The service of a complaint by leaving a copy with the nurse at the intensive care unit was inadequate to confer jurisdiction over him.

Reason

The rule applicable to service in this case is Pa. R.C.P. 402, which provides as follows:

> RULE 402. MANNER OF SERVICE. ACCEPTANCE OF SERVICE
> (a) Original process may be served (1) by handing a copy to the defendant; or (2) by handing a copy (i) at the residence of the defendant to an adult member of the family with whom he resides; but if no adult member of the family is found, then to an adult person in charge of such residence; or (ii) at the residence of the defendant to the clerk or manager of the hotel, inn, apartment house, boarding house or other place of lodging at which he resides; or (iii) at any office or usual place of business of the defendant to his agent or to the person for the time being in charge thereof.

The plaintiff's attempted service of the writ of summons was defective. Because Dr. Park was not affiliated with the hospital at which service was attempted, it seems clear that the hospital cannot be deemed his "office" or "usual place of business." A copy of the complaint was left with a nurse at the intensive care unit of the hospital, where Dr. Park was then a patient. The intensive care unit of a hospital, however, cannot be deemed the patient's place of residence, nor can it be said that the patient resides there. Dr. Park did not voluntarily leave his place of residence to establish a new residence at the hospital.

Discussion

1. What is the proper procedure for serving a summons in your state?
2. What is the difference between a summons and a complaint?
3. Why was the service of the summons determined to be improper?

2. SUMMARY JUDGMENT PRECLUDED/FAILURE TO DIAGNOSE AND TREAT

Citation: *Gerner v. Long Island Jewish Hillside Med. Ctr.*, 609 N.Y.S.2d 898 (N.Y. App. Div. 1994)

Facts

On March 8, 1971, the plaintiff gave birth to her infant son at the defendant medical center. Dr. Geller, a private physician, entered the picture six hours later as attending pediatrician with resident privileges. On March 11, 1971, Dr. Geller, having noted and confirmed a slightly jaundiced condition, ordered phototherapy. After three days of such treatment and monitoring, the child's bilirubin count fell to a normal level, and Dr. Geller ordered the patient discharged. Dr. Geller continued to treat the child over the next four years. The child today is brain damaged, with permanent neurological dysfunction.

The plaintiff alleged medical malpractice on the part of both the medical center and the private attending physician for failing to diagnose and treat the jaundice in a timely manner. Following examinations before trial, the medical center's motion for summary judgment was granted. The plaintiff and Dr. Geller appealed.

Issue

Were there questions of fact as to whether there were indications in the first six hours after the infant's birth, before the private attending pediatrician entered the picture, that should have alerted the hospital delivery and nursery staff of possible hyperbilirubinemia, precluding summary judgment for the hospital?

Holding

The New York Supreme Court, Appellate Division, held that questions of fact precluded summary judgment for the hospital.

Reason

Two factual issues were left unresolved. The first is whether there were indications, in the first six hours after birth, that should have alerted the hospital delivery and nursery staff of possible hyperbilirubinemia. According to the hospital's expert, one such overlooked indicator was a blood incompatibility between the mother and child. Since the hospital acted alone as the plaintiff's medical practitioner over those first six hours, it would have to bear sole responsibility for any malpractice committed during that period.

The second issue is whether the medical center should be exempt from sharing any responsibility for malpractice over the course of the next six days (until the infant's discharge) by reason of the fact that, for the balance of that period, the infant was technically under the care of a private attending physician. A number of allegations are raised as to negligence attributed solely to hospital staff during that period. For example, notes of attending nurses at the nursery failed to record any jaundiced condition, or any reference to color, until the third day after birth, despite the parents' complaints to hospital personnel about the baby's yellowish complexion. Additionally, Dr. Geller ordered a complete blood count and bilirubin test on the morning of March 11, as soon as he learned of the first recorded observation by a nurse of a jaundiced appearance. Test results, which showed a moderately elevated bilirubin count, were not reported by the laboratory until 10 hours after the blood sample was drawn, and it took another 3 hours before Dr. Geller's order for phototherapy was carried out. An issue is thus raised as to whether the 13-hour delay in commencement of the treatment had any permanent effect. Normally, a hospital is shielded from liability for the negligence of a private attending physician practicing at its facility. However, a myriad of cases hold that a hospital may be held concurrently liable with a private practitioner for the independent negligence of the former's medical staff. During pretrial discovery, the hospital failed to dispel allegations of its own negligence concurrent with Dr. Geller's attendance to the patient. Because the court's function on a motion for summary judgment is to identify just such triable issues of fact, the hospital's motion should have been denied.

Discussion

1. If this case were tried in your state, would the statute of limitations time bar the lawsuit?
2. What is the importance of documentation as it relates to this case?
3. What is the importance of assessment and reassessment as it relates to patient care in general?

4. Why did the hospital bear sole responsibility for malpractice in this case?
5. What information management system(s) might the hospital design to help prevent such occurrences in the future?

3. SUMMARY JUDGMENT/TERMINATION OF RADIOLOGIST

Citation: *Byrd v. Hall*, 847 S.W.2d 208 (Tenn. 1993)

Facts

On October 27, 1988, the record revealed that the plaintiff, a former head of the hospital's radiology department, filed a suit alleging that the defendant physicians had tortiously interfered with his employment at the hospital. The plaintiff alleged that he was terminated from his position as head of the radiology department as a result of the defendants' intentional and malicious interference with his employment by exerting influence over the hospital's administration through their use of economic pressures and by interfering with employee performance evaluations.

In October 1989, the defendants served interrogatories upon the plaintiff seeking to discover the details supporting the allegations contained in the complaint. The interrogatories were never answered by the plaintiff and the defendants never filed a motion to compel.

On November 27, 1990, the defendants filed a motion for summary judgment on the basis that the complaint failed to state a cause of action. The plaintiff filed his affidavit in opposition to the motion on the day the motion was argued. The trial court granted the defendants' motion for summary judgment. The court of appeals affirmed, and the plaintiff appealed.

The plaintiff's affidavit, in pertinent part, states, "That he believes that his discharge was in retaliation for his refusal to violate medical procedures and Tennessee law, for his scheduling of technicians employed by Scott County Hospital which the Defendants also employed privately, and not for the reasons stated in his termination notice." *Id.* at 217.

Issue

Is there a genuine issue of material fact that warrants a trial, thus precluding summary judgment for the physicians?

Holding

The Supreme Court of Tennessee held that there were genuine issues of material fact, precluding summary judgment for the physicians.

Reason

Summary judgment statutes were adopted in various forms by some states, including Tennessee, in the 1800s. Tennessee eventually adopted summary judgment in its present form, Tenn.R.Civ.P.56, by order of the Supreme Court in 1970. According to Rule 56.03, summary judgment is to be granted if the "pleadings, depositions, answers to interrogatories, and admissions on file, together with the affidavits, if any, show that there is not a genuine issue as to any material fact and that the moving party is entitled to a judgment as a matter of law."

The cases construing Tenn.R.Civ.P.56 make clear that the summary judgment process is designed to provide a quick, inexpensive means of concluding cases upon issues as to which there is not a genuine dispute regarding material facts. The summary judgment procedure was implemented to enable the courts to pierce the pleadings to determine whether the case justifies the time and expense of a trial. On the other hand, the procedure is clearly not designed to serve as a substitute for the trial of genuine and material factual matters. The cases make clear that the party seeking summary judgment must carry the burden of persuading the court that no genuine and material factual issues exist and that it is, therefore, entitled to judgment as a matter of law. Once it is shown by the moving party that there is no genuine issue of material fact, the nonmoving party must then demonstrate, by affidavits or discovery materials, that there is a genuine, material fact dispute to warrant a trial.

The issues necessary for evaluating a summary judgment motion are: (1) whether a *factual* dispute exists, (2) whether the disputed fact is *material* to the outcome of the case, and (3) whether the disputed fact creates a "genuine" issue for trial. *Id.* at 214. A disputed fact is material if it must be decided in order to resolve the substantive claim or defense at which the motion is directed. When a material fact is in dispute creating a genuine issue, when the credibility of witnesses is an integral part of the factual proof, or when evidence must be weighed, a trial is necessary because such issues are not appropriately resolved on the basis of affidavits. The plaintiff is not required to prove his entire case by a preponderance of evidence at the summary judgment stage. He need only raise genuine issues of material fact.

Discussion

1. Why did the courts adopt the concept of summary judgment?
2. What issues must a court review to evaluate the appropriateness of a motion for summary judgment?

4. STANDARD OF CARE/COVERING PHYSICIAN

Citation: *West v. Adelmann*, 630 N.E.2d 846 (Ill. Ct. App. 1993)

Facts

On February 28, 1985, the plaintiff fell from an all-terrain vehicle and was taken to the medical center where he was found to have fractured his left leg in three places. Dr. Woiteshek initially treated the plaintiff on February 28 by placing a pin in his lower leg, casting the lower portion, and placing the plaintiff in traction to align the fractured thigh bone. Dr. Adelmann practiced with Dr. Woiteshek in Adelmann-Woiteshek Orthopedic Surgeons, SC, a medical partnership, and made hospital visits to the plaintiff, apparently in rotation with Dr. Woiteshek, on March 3, 5, 7, 10, 11, and 13. Dr. Adelmann also cared for the plaintiff from March 15 through 18 when Dr. Woiteshek was on vacation.

On March 15, 1985, Dr. Adelmann noticed a motor palsy (loss of nerve strength) in the plaintiff's left leg and padded the cast at the top to alleviate the problem. On March 17, 1985, the plaintiff complained of pain in his ankle, which Dr. Adelmann initially relieved by adjusting the plaintiff's foot inside the cast. On March 18, 1985, when pain persisted in the heel area, Dr. Adelmann found a blister there and treated it at 1:00 A.M. by cutting a "window" in the cast, repadding the area, and taping the cutout section into its original position.

On March 18, 1985, Dr. Adelmann discovered through new X-rays that there had been a shortening of the leg since the X-rays that were apparently taken two days earlier. There was a shortening of both the lower and upper portions of the leg by approximately 1 inch. That evening, Dr. Adelmann informed the plaintiff's parents what the X-rays revealed and urged them to allow him to recast the leg as soon as possible, including changing the pin, in order to avoid any further damage. The plaintiff's mother immediately consulted with physicians at another hospital and the plaintiff was moved there that night, without any further treatment being administered by Dr. Adelmann.

The plaintiff's expert witness, Dr. Yoslow, an orthopaedic surgeon, testified that the plaintiff's condition required a pin change and a cast change within two or three days of the initial treatment and that Dr. Woiteshek deviated from the accepted standards of orthopaedic surgery when he failed to take such action. Dr. Yoslow stated that the injuries caused by the failure to change the pin and cast included an infection under the cast, a blister on the left heel, shortening of the tibia and femur, and a peroneal nerve palsy. Dr. Yoslow initially had no criticism of Dr. Adelmann's care;

however, his opinion was based on an assumption that Dr. Adelmann was covering (or "marking time") for Dr. Woiteshek when he saw the plaintiff on alternate days and supervised the plaintiff's treatment during Dr. Woiteshek's vacation.

The trial court granting summary judgment for Dr. Adelmann, stated: "I think what's missing is Dr. Adelmann saying he took over the treatment for the plaintiff." The plaintiff contended that summary judgment was improperly granted by the trial court because the court focused on whether Dr. Adelmann made a specific declaration that he had taken over the plaintiff's care from Dr. Woiteshek and not whether Dr. Adelmann's actions allowed a reasonable inference that Dr. Adelmann and the plaintiff enjoyed a physician–patient relationship, thus creating a duty of care for Dr. Adelmann. The plaintiff appealed.

Issue

Did an issue of material fact exist as to whether the surgeon, who was a partner of the original treating surgeon, through his actions in treating and caring for the patient, establish a primary physician–patient relationship for purposes of a medical malpractice action?

Holding

The Appellate Court of Illinois held that there was a genuine issue of material fact as to whether the primary physician–patient relationship existed, thus precluding summary judgment.

Reason

Whether a physician–patient relationship exists depends on the facts and circumstances of each case and is for the trier of fact to determine. A fair reading of Dr. Yoslow's deposition clearly establishes that he believed that if Dr. Adelmann did have a duty to treat the plaintiff after March 15, then he deviated from the applicable standard of care. The court found that the plaintiff clearly established evidence, which raises a question as to whether Dr. Adelmann, through his actions in treating and caring for the plaintiff, established a primary physician–patient relationship. The evidence disclosed that Dr. Adelmann checked on the plaintiff every other day while he was in the hospital, approximately half of the time. The plaintiff sought Dr. Adelmann's assistance when he was in pain and accepted Dr. Adelmann's care of him.

The court expressed its curiosity about the varying responsibilities of a physician who is apparently in charge of a patient's treatment and a physician who "marks time" by checking in on that physician's patient on alternating days. The court, while not sure of the meaning of "marking time," stated, "we certainly would not want our children or spouses to be under the care of a physician who is merely marking time." *Id.* at 850.

Discussion

1. What is necessary in order to establish a physician–patient relationship?
2. From a legal point of view, when does a physician–patient relationship end?
3. From both ethical and legal points of view, what steps would you take to terminate your professional relationship with a patient?

5. STANDARD OF CARE/RADIOLOGIST/ MISINTERPRETATION OF DIAGNOSTIC TESTS

Citation: *Matney v. Lowe,* 444 S.E.2d 730 (W. Va. 1994)

Facts

In 1987, Mr. Matney suffered a back injury in a mine accident. On September 7, 1988, Mr. Matney underwent a spinal fusion surgery performed by Dr. Lowe. On September 11, 1988, the nursing staff noted that Mr. Matney had a temperature of 101.4 degrees. Dr. Pace, a hospital resident, examined Mr. Matney and noted that he complained of some pleuritic right chest and shoulder pain. A chest X-ray and VQ scan were examined by Dr. Dransfeld, a radiologist.

On September 12, Dr. Dransfeld reported that the VQ scan had a "low probability for pulmonary embolus. The chest X-ray showed vaguely defined areas of infiltration through the lung bases, suggesting an inflammatory etiology." *Id.* at 731. Pneumonia was diagnosed, and Mr. Matney was treated with intravenous antibiotics.

A follow-up chest X-ray was performed on September 14, which showed "minimal clearing of the haziness at the right base with residual infiltrate and/or pleural fluid in that region." *Id.* at 731. On September 16, although Dr. Pace noted that Mr. Matney's temperature had been 101.4 degrees the previous midnight and he had an elevated white blood cell count, he discharged Mr. Matney. On September 17, Mr. Matney died at home. The medical examiner determined that the cause of death was a massive pulmonary thromboembolism. Dr. Lowe, who had not settled, was the only defendant remaining in the trial. The evidence was adduced by the

plaintiff from two expert witnesses, Dr. Lincoln and Dr. Maxfield. Dr. Lincoln, an orthopaedic surgeon, testified that Dr. Lowe had fallen below the standard of care in the treatment of Mr. Matney. Dr. Maxfield also testified that Dr. Lowe had fallen below the standard of care. However, he also testified that Dr. Dransfeld had fallen below the standard of care in his interpretation of the VQ scan. According to Dr. Maxfield, the VQ scan should not have been interpreted by Dr. Dransfeld as determining a low probability for pulmonary emboli. He contended that the VQ scan should have been interpreted as indeterminant, which would probably have changed Dr. Lowe's response. Dr. Lowe's attorneys argued that Dr. Lowe acted on Dr. Dransfeld's duty to interpret the VQ scan and that, consequently, Dr. Lowe was not liable for Mr. Matney's death.

Issue

Did the evidence support the jury's finding that Dr. Lowe was not negligent?

Holding

The Supreme Court of Appeals of West Virginia held that the evidence supported the jury's finding that Dr. Lowe was not negligent.

Reason

There is more than enough evidence in the record that would support the jury's finding that Dr. Lowe was not negligent. The testimony of Mr. Matney's own expert, Dr. Maxfield, pointed out that Dr. Lowe had relied on the radiologist's erroneous interpretation of the VQ scan. Thus, the jury verdict was not contrary to the weight of the evidence.

Discussion

1. Do you agree with the court's decision? Explain.
2. What is your reaction to the resident's (Dr. Pace) decision to discharge the patient when he knew that the patient had an elevated white blood count and a temperature of 101.4 degrees?
3. How might collaboration among the various practitioners involved in the care of the patient have resulted in a better outcome?

6. *RES IPSA LOQUITUR*/EXPERT TESTIMONY NOT NECESSARY

Citation: *Graham v. Thompson*, 854 S.W.2d 797 (Mo. Ct. App. 1993)

Facts

This suit involves a claim for medical malpractice based on the doctrine of *res ipsa loquitur*. The trial court granted summary judgment in favor of Dr. Thompson, a plastic surgeon. Ms. Graham, one of the named appellants, suffered a severe cut to the top of her right foot. She was taken to the hospital to receive an operation to repair nerve and tendon damage. Dr. Thompson performed the operation, during which the patient was unconscious. After the operation, Dr. Thompson put a plaster of Paris cast over a splint meant to immobilize the foot. The cast went almost to the top of her calf. When Ms. Graham woke up, she immediately began complaining of pain in her upper right calf in an area just under the cast. She had no problems with her calf prior to this surgery on her foot. Hospital personnel unwrapped the cast and, on Dr. Thompson's orders, washed off the surgical area with an antiseptic, then medicated the painful area (some four inches long and three inches wide), which showed blisters. The personnel applied a new splint and cast. Ms. Graham went home and the next day felt pain in the same spot. The blisters appeared larger, and Dr. Thompson's office personnel advised her to double her pain medication. A day or two later, she went to the doctor's office and was treated for burns, later diagnosed as third-degree burns, which created several spots of dead flesh on her calf. These burns formed the basis of her medical malpractice suit. The hospital was dismissed from the suit, leaving Dr. Thompson as the only defendant. No one seemed to know the cause of the burns.

The circuit court granted summary judgment for the plastic surgeon on the grounds that the plaintiff failed to provide expert medical testimony to support her claim and that the *res ipsa loquitur* doctrine did not apply.

Issue

Could a layperson, as matter of common knowledge, conclude that third-degree burns on the upper back of a patient's right calf were unusual and would not result if due care had been used in performing surgery on top of the patient's right foot so as to bring a case within the *res ipsa loquitur* doctrine?

Holding

The Missouri Court of Appeals held that a layperson, as matter of common knowledge, could conclude that injuries to the calf were so unusual and would not result if due care had been used in the operation so as to bring the case within the *res ipsa loquitur* doctrine.

Reason

"Specifically, to invoke *res ipsa loquitur*, a party must show the occurrence resulting in injury ordinarily does not happen when due care is exercised by the party in control, the instrumentalities involved are under the care and management of the defendant, and the defendant possesses either superior knowledge or means of obtaining information about the cause of the occurrence." *Hasemeier v. Smith*, 361 S.W.2d 697, 799 (Mo. 1962). The plaintiff awoke from an operation with what turned out to be third-degree burns on the back of her calf. She was not negligent. She had no way of knowing whether the burns came from the operation itself or the application of the cast. What can be said was the injury was not a typical occurrence or was not the result of a necessary risk to the type of foot operation performed on her. Laypersons, as a matter of common knowledge, could conclude the injuries were so unusual and would not result if due care had been used.

Discussion

1. What must a plaintiff show in order to move a case forward on the basis of *res ipsa loquitur*?
2. Why was expert testimony not necessary in this case?

7. EXPERT TESTIMONY/DENTIST

Citation: *Smith v. O'Neal*, 850 S.W.2d 797 (Tex. Ct. App. 1993)

Facts

On July 16, 1984, Dr. Smith, a general practice dentist, initially examined Ms. O'Neal. She testified that she informed Dr. Smith she had pain on her lower right side and wanted cosmetic work performed on her teeth. Dr. Smith and Ms. O'Neal discussed a plan for comprehensive treatment, including root canal and fillings.

On July 26, 1984, Dr. Smith told Ms. O'Neal that tooth number 14, an upper left molar, should be extracted. She advised Dr. Smith that another dentist had warned her in 1982 that tooth number 14 should not be pulled because it was embedded in the sinus. Dr. Smith responded that all of her top teeth were in the sinus and that extraction was no problem. Ms. O'Neal relented to Dr. Smith's judgment and tooth number 14 was extracted. Complications developed in the extraction process resulting in an oral antral perforation of the sinus cavity wall. Four days after the extraction, Dr. Smith began root canal work, even though the antral opening wound was not healed. In performing these additional procedures, Dr. Smith used both high and low speed drills, capable of flinging bacteria and other debris about the mouth. Three weeks after the extraction, a tissue mass developed in the tooth socket. The patient was referred to Dr. Herbert, an oral surgeon.

Dr. Herbert testified that the degree of infection inhibited proper healing and closure of the extraction site. After several more months, in January 1985, Ms. O'Neal was referred to Dr. Berman, an ear, nose, and throat specialist. Because of the continual deterioration, Dr. Berman performed an operation known as a Coldwell-Luc procedure. This surgical procedure sealed the extraction site. The surgery required hospitalization and a four- to six-week recuperation period.

Ms. O'Neal brought a malpractice action against the dentist. The trial court entered judgment in favor of Ms. O'Neal. The dentist appealed, arguing that the evidence was factually insufficient to support the judgment.

Dr. Miedzinski, an expert witness for the appellee, testified that Dr. Smith was negligent for not referring the patient to an oral surgeon for the necessary extraction, because of the known risks of roots embedded in the sinus floor. Dr. Smith was also negligent for not referring the patient to a specialist when the antral perforation first occurred and later by not referring her to a specialist when the oroantral fistula and the infection manifested itself. Dr. Smith's expert witness also testified that it is good medical practice to refer a patient to an oral surgeon or other specialist when complications arise from a sinus molar extraction.

Issue

Was the expert's testimony sufficient to support the verdict?

Holding

The Court of Appeals of Texas held that the expert's testimony was sufficient to support the verdict.

Reason

The dentist's expert testimony was found sufficient to support a jury finding that the defendant was negligent in the treatment of his patient. The expert testified that the defendant was negligent by extracting the upper left molar without first attempting endodontic treatment to save the tooth. The patient was not experiencing pain on the left side of her mouth and the tooth did not present an emergency.

Discussion

1. Was expert testimony necessary in order to establish the defendant's negligence? Explain.
2. What lessons are apparent as to the importance of a patient's prior physical and dental history?
3. What weight do you believe a practitioner should give to a consultant's opinion?

8. EXPERT TESTIMONY/NURSE/ADMISSIBILITY

Citation: *Morris v. Children's Hosp. Med. Ctr.*, 597 N.E. 2d 1110 (Ohio Ct. App. 1991)

Facts

The plaintiffs alleged in their complaint that Melissa Morris, while hospitalized at Children's Hospital Medical Center, suffered a laceration to her arm as a result of treatment administered by the defendants and their agents that fell below the accepted standard of care. Mrs. Morris alleged from personal observation that the laceration to her daughter's arm was caused by the jagged edges of a plastic cup that had been split and placed on her arm to guard the intravenous site. A nurse, in her affidavit, who stated her qualifications as an expert, expressed her opinion that the practice of placing a split plastic cup over an intravenous site as a guard constituted a breach of the standard of nursing care.

Issue

Did the complaint state a claim in ordinary negligence under the doctrine of *respondeat superior*? Was the registered nurse competent to give expert testimony on liability issues?

Holding

The Court of Appeals of Ohio held that the complaint stated a claim in ordinary negligence on the theory of *respondeat superior*. The nurse was competent to give expert testimony on liability issues.

Reason

A physician or hospital may be held liable under the doctrine of *respondeat superior*. An allegation of negligence against an individual whose occupation is not among those enumerated in Ohio statutes or within the common law definition of malpractice does not present a claim for malpractice. The plaintiffs alleged that Melissa's injury was caused by the negligence of the defendants and their agents. In the course of discovery, the evidence supported an allegation of negligence on the part of the nursing staff.

Expert testimony is not essential to state a claim in ordinary negligence. Such testimony is, however, admissible in evidence if the witness is qualified as an expert and the expert's specialized knowledge will aid the trier of fact in understanding the evidence. The registered nurse, by affidavit, attested to her qualifications and her familiarity with the standards of nursing care and expressed her opinion that the practice alleged to have caused the child's injury was not in conformity with the accepted standards of nursing care.

Discussion

1. What are the criteria that a court utilizes to determine an individual's competency to testify as an expert?
2. What is the importance of competence assessments and skills checklists as they relate to this case?

9. DISCOVERY/PLAINTIFF'S RELATIONSHIP WITH EXPERT WITNESS

Citation: *Bliss v. Brodsky*, 604 So. 2d 923 (Fla. Dist. Ct. App. 1992)

Facts

Physicians sought discovery from Ms. Rieback, a nurse consultant retained by the personal representative of the estate of the deceased in a medical malpractice action. The consultant was retained by the plaintiff for the presuit investigation process required by section 766.203, Florida Statutes (1991). Ms. Rieback owned and operated Medical Ad-

visors, Inc. She also did business through an entity named Rieback Medical-Legal Consultants. Through her businesses, she assists in locating and hiring expert witnesses for both presuit investigation and trial preparation. Defense counsel sought to depose Ms. Rieback and attempted to subpoena certain documents for the purpose of obtaining information regarding her financial arrangements with her physician expert, Dr. Hammerman, and her financial arrangements with the plaintiff. The subpoena requested the following documents:

- all bills received from Kenneth Hammerman for the period 1986 through present
- documents reflecting the case names and attorneys for all cases in which Medical Advisors consulted with Kenneth Hammerman
- all promotional articles, advertisements, or brochures describing the services provided by Medical Advisors, Inc., including, but not limited to, services in providing expert witnesses
- all reports prepared by Kenneth Hammerman in the above case
- all contracts with Kenneth Hammerman
- all bills for services provided by either Medical Advisors, Inc., or Kenneth Hammerman relating to the above case *Id.* at 924

The circuit court issued an order permitting discovery, and the personal representative petitioned for a writ of certiorari.

Issue

Were the physicians entitled to discovery of the financial arrangements between the consultant and her expert witness, as well as her financial arrangements with the plaintiff?

Holding

The Florida District Court of Appeal held that the trial court properly ruled that defense counsel may inquire into certain matters pertaining to Ms. Rieback's businesses and to the procurement of the services of Dr. Hammerman as an expert for use at trial.

Reason

The business relationship is appropriate discovery because it is reasonably calculated to lead to the discovery of relevant and admissible evidence concerning the physician's bias.

Discussion

1. Regardless of the court's decision in this action, do you agree that the defendants should be entitled to discovery of the financial arrangements between the plaintiff's consultant and her expert witness, as well as to her financial arrangements with the plaintiff? Explain.

10. NURSE MALPRACTICE/EXPERT WITNESS

Citation: *Tye v. Wilson*, 430 S.E.2d 129 (Ga. Ct. App. 1993)

Facts

The plaintiff, the husband of the decedent, sued the hospital, treating physicians, and a registered nurse for medical malpractice he claimed caused his wife's death after she was treated for a hysterectomy and anterior repair. After surgery, the patient began to bleed internally and suffered hypovolemic shock. The plaintiff alleged that the doctors failed to stop the bleeding and did not properly sedate his wife while she was recovering.

Because she was not sedated, she accidentally dislodged her endotracheal tube, causing her death. The nurse filed a motion to dismiss, claiming that the affidavit setting forth a negligent act by her was prepared by a physician who she said was not competent to testify that she was negligent. The trial court rejected her motion, but allowed her to file an interlocutory appeal.

Issue

Will the affidavit of a medical doctor concerning the standard of care in treating a patient be sufficient to support a malpractice claim against a nurse?

Holding

The Court of Appeals of Georgia held that the affidavit of a medical doctor relating to the standard of care in treating and monitoring an intubated patient was sufficient to support a malpractice claim against a nurse.

Reason

The expert stated that he was familiar with the standard of care acceptable to the medical profession generally. The court found that was enough to include the nursing profession. The medical doctor's opinion was that the patient's injury was caused by the negligent application and control of a patient's tourniquet during her operation. There was nothing to suggest that the physicians and nurses are trained differently with regard to treating intubated patients.

Discussion

1. Do you agree with the court's determination that there is nothing to suggest that the physicians and nurses are trained differently with regard to treating intubated patients? Explain.
2. Should nurses be permitted to testify as to the standard of care required of physicians who treat intubated patients?
3. Under what conditions can a physician testify as an expert regarding the proper standard of care to be followed by a nurse?

11. DEMONSTRATIVE EVIDENCE/PATHOLOGY SLIDES

Citation: *O'Leyar v. Callender*, 843 P.2d 304 (Mont. 1992)

Facts

The patient brought a medical malpractice action against the physician who performed laser surgery that caused anal stenosis and fecal incontinence. The patient is a woman with hidradenitis suppurativa (HS), a disease of the apocrine glands. Dr. Callender performed laser surgery on the patient to remove areas of HS infection. The night before surgery, as instructed by the physician, the patient used a magic marker to mark the places in her groin area where she could feel HS. There was a dispute concerning whether the physician excised the area that the patient marked or a larger area. The pathologist made slides of the tissue removed from the patient shortly after the laser procedure and issued a pathology report concerning the tissue slides. The plaintiff's counsel asked the pathologist to take photographs of the slides for use at trial. Defense counsel stated that he learned about the letter and photographs of the slides during a deposition on October 21, 1991. The patient's use of those photographs became an issue in chambers during the course of the trial. The trial court entered judgment for the patient, and the physician appealed.

Issue

Did the trial court err in admitting photographs of pathology slides that had not been available to the physician's expert during his deposition?

Holding

The Supreme Court of Montana held that the trial court properly admitted the photographs of the pathology slides.

Reason

By Dr. Callender's counsel's own admission, the photos were known and available to the defense at least 15 days before trial. Even if it took defense counsel a week to prepare copies of the photographs, the pictures would have been available to the defense 15 days before trial.

Discussion

1. What precautionary measures should the surgeon and hospital take to ensure that the surgical procedure performed conforms to the surgical procedures the patient consented to?
2. Do you agree that the photographs should be allowed into evidence? Explain.
3. Under what circumstances do you think the photographs should not be permitted into evidence?

12. CONTRIBUTORY NEGLIGENCE/FAILURE TO TAKE MEDICATIONS

Citation: *Blades v. Franklin Gen. Hosp.*, 604 N.Y.S.2d 590 (N.Y. App. Div. 1993)

Facts

The plaintiff had breast reduction surgery on September 9, 1986. Although she developed an infection, her physician did not discover it while she was in the hospital, causing it to go untreated. Upon her discharge from the hospital on September 13, the plaintiff was given antibiotics and was instructed to take them four times a day.

Five days later, her physician noted drainage from her right breast. He gave the patient more antibiotics, and told her to wash the area with warm soapy water and change the dressings. Two days later, the plaintiff was readmitted to the hospital through the emergency department, where it was noted that her right breast was tender and swollen. There was also evidence of a large amount of drainage. Once the plaintiff had been admitted, her dressing was changed. The hospital's admittance form contained information that she had begun oral antibiotics two days earlier. The infection caused scarring and deformity, and the patient sued. After trial, the jury found 75 percent fault by the physician, and 25 percent by the plaintiff. The court set aside the 25 percent, and denied the physician's motion to add an affirmative defense of culpability by the plaintiff.

Issue

Was it proven at trial that the plaintiff failed to follow her physician's instructions and therefore contributed to her own breast injury?

Holding

The New York Supreme Court, Appellate Division, upheld the trial court's decision to set aside the jury's finding of 25 percent fault on the part of the plaintiff, and its denial of the physician's motion to add the affirmative defense of contributory negligence.

Reason

There was no evidence offered at trial that the plaintiff contributed to her injuries. In fact, it was the judge who first brought the subject up by asking if the physician wanted contributory negligence charged to the jury. Further, it was the court who asked the physician's expert if failure to take the prescribed antibiotics could have contributed to the breast injury. The expert stated that, "It's hard to say." *Id.* at 591. The physician's other expert, an infectious disease specialist, testified that it couldn't be determined if warm water soaks would help heal as deep an infection as the plaintiff had contracted. Moreover, there was no evidence presented that the plaintiff did not follow the instructions she had been given.

Discussion

1. What specifically would the physician have had to prove in order for the defense of contributory negligence to succeed against the plaintiff? Explain.
2. How could patient education have helped prevent this lawsuit?

13. STATUTE OF LIMITATIONS/ECT TREATMENTS

Citation: *McNall v. Summers*, 30 Cal. Rptr. 2d 914 (Cal. Ct. App. 1994)

Facts

The plaintiff, a registered nurse, was being treated for depression by her psychiatrist, Dr. Hall. The plaintiff was seen in the summer 1979 by Dr. Summers, who was filling in for Dr. Hall. Rather than resuming with Dr. Hall, the plaintiff continued to see Dr. Summers through July 1982. Soon after their relationship began, Dr. Summers recommended that the plaintiff undergo electroconvulsive therapy (ECT) to overcome her depression. A second physician, Dr. Pitts, was consulted. Dr. Pitts concurred with the recommendation for ECT, witnessed the plaintiff's informed consent, and was involved in the plaintiff's ECT treatments. The plaintiff was administered a total of 26 ECT treatments over a period of five months. The plaintiff complained to Dr. Summers about her loss of memory. He said it would return in four to six months. Dr. Summers also gave her an article he had coauthored that stated: "Memory deficits and confusional states are said to be characteristic side effects of electroconvulsive therapy." He generally assured her that her memory problem would go away.

In November 1986, the plaintiff consulted with a neuropsychologist, who concluded that the plaintiff had suffered an injury to the left side of her brain, implicating the frontal and temporal regions. She was referred to Dr. Cummings, a neurologist. He ordered a magnetic resonance imaging (MRI) test, which revealed a "probable old left frontal cortical infarct." He concluded that the plaintiff had suffered an embolic stroke.

In June 1989, Dr. Cummings ordered a single photon emission computed tomography (SPECT) for brain imaging to determine the nature of any functional injury. The SPECT showed a well-established stroke and Dr. Cummings found that the plaintiff's memory impairment was related to this injury and that the injury had occurred sometime during the ECT treatments.

On September 24, 1990, a bifurcated jury trial was commenced. After the parties concluded the introduction of evidence in the first phase of the trial, which was directed to the issue of the statute of limitations, Dr. Summers and Dr. Pitts moved for a directed verdict on the ECT claim, claiming it was time barred. The trial court concluded the ECT claim was barred by the statute of limitations and granted the motion for a directed verdict. The plaintiff contended there was sufficient evidence for the jury to find that her claim for injury due to negligent administration of the ECT treatments was filed in a timely manner.

Issue

Was the plaintiff's suit time barred?

Holding

The court of appeal held that the appellant's continuous and serious loss of memory following ECT treatments was an injury triggering the California three-year statute of limitations on malpractice claims.

Reason

The court determined that review of the directed verdict requires analysis and application of the Code of Civil Procedure, § 340.5, which governs the time limitations for filing medical malpractice actions. The statute provides that "[i]n no event shall the time for commencement of legal action exceed three years." Although the appellant acknowledged her long-term awareness of her memory loss and its correlation to the ECT treatments, she argued that because she was totally unaware she sustained a stroke until it was diagnosed by Dr. Cummings in November 1986, that the statute should not have tolled. The appellant contended that she could not have discovered that she suffered an embolic stroke or that it was caused by the ECT until it was medically diagnosed. Not only did the appellant's onset of complaints immediately follow the ECT, but both she and her physician associated the symptom with that specific treatment. There was nothing hidden about her injury. The appellant fully recognized she was continuously experiencing harmful lapses in memory adversely affecting her professional and personal life. It is uncontroverted that the appellant knew she was damaged in some way by the ECT treatments. That is sufficient to trigger the three-year period provided for in § 340.5.

The appellant's early complaints in 1980 demonstrated the appellant was aware she had experienced manifest injury and appreciable harm, which she directly associated with her ECT treatments. By her own testimony, she "had reason to believe in March of 1984 and before March of 1984 that in fact ECT had caused [her] memory problems." *Id.* at 919. The appellant's serious and continuous loss of memory constitutes "injury" for the purpose of triggering the three-year period even if the appellant did not, or arguably could not, discover the actual organic injury causing the loss of memory or discern the negligent conduct of her doctors. The statutory tolling provisions of fraud and intentional concealment were neither pleaded nor proven and provide no relief to the appellant.

Discussion

1. Do you agree with the court's decision? Explain.
2. What legal and ethical issues arise when a consulting physician stands to benefit financially by recommending a patient for treatment and then performing the recommended treatment?

14. STATUTE OF LIMITATIONS/MISDIAGNOSIS/ RADIOLOGIST

Citation: *Stone v. Radiology Servs., P.A.*, 426 S.E.2d 663 (Ga. Ct. App. 1992)

Facts

The patient, Mr. Stone, and his wife filed malpractice and loss of consortium claims against radiologists and a neurologist, alleging that the physicians misdiagnosed and failed to treat his brain tumor. The defendant physicians and the professional associations that employed them had misdiagnosed Mr. Stone's condition by failing to recognize that a computed tomography (CT) scan of Mr. Stone's brain taken in September 1985 "showed a tumor on [Mr. Stone's] brain."

Mr. Stone had been experiencing severe headaches for many years, but a May 1983 brain scan had revealed no abnormalities. On September 30, 1985, Mr. Stone went to Radiology Services, at which time a CT scan of his brain was performed. Physician employees reviewed the CT film and signed a radiological report, which set forth that the scan had revealed no areas of abnormal density and concluded with the diagnostic impression that the described changes were consistent with cerebellar atrophy.

In early December 1988, an MRI scan of Mr. Stone's brain was taken by one of its employee physicians. The scan has advantages over other scans because it is more sensitive and reveals slightly different angles to physicians' view. The scan revealed that Mr. Stone was suffering from an astrocytoma (type of tumor) in his brain, rather than from changes consistent with cerebellar atrophy.

The superior court entered summary judgment for physician defendants based on a statute of limitations defense, and the plaintiffs appealed.

Issue

When did the statute of limitations begin to toll?

Holding

The court of appeals held that any injury suffered by the patient as a result of the radiologists' misdiagnosis of the brain tumor occurred, for limitations purposes, at the time of misdiagnosis.

Reason

The critical issue is: When did Mr. Stone's injury occur? In most misdiagnosis cases, "the injury begins immediately upon the misdiagnosis due to the pain, suffering or economic loss sustained by the patient from the time of the misdiagnosis until the medical problem is properly diagnosed itself is the injury and not the subsequent discovery of the proper diagnosis." *Id.* at 665.

There was no error in the trial court's determination that Mr. Stone's suit filed in December 1990 was barred by the statute of limitations.

Discussion

1. Do you agree with the court's ruling that from a statute of limitations point of view, the misdiagnosis itself is the injury and not the subsequent discovery of the proper diagnosis? Explain.
2. What is the importance of the statute of limitations from both the plaintiff and defendant perspectives?

15. STATUTE OF LIMITATIONS/MISDIAGNOSIS/ AIDS

Citation: *Bramer v. Dotson*, 437 S.E.2d (W. Va. 1993)

Facts

On March 23 and 24, 1988, the plaintiff, Mr. Bramer, was seen by Dr. Dotson for a physical examination. Prior to his appointment, the patient had been suffering from diarrhea and weight loss. Following examination by Dr. Dotson, Mr. Bramer was diagnosed with Crohn's disease. Dr. Dotson prescribed medications for the diarrhea.

On May 24, 1988, Mr. Bramer's diarrhea did not subside so he returned to Dr. Dotson for further evaluation. A blood specimen was drawn and sent to SmithKline Laboratories for testing for human immunodeficiency virus (HIV). In early June, the laboratory informed Dr. Dotson that Mr. Bramer tested positive for HIV.

On June 13, 1988, Dr. Dotson informed the patient that he had acquired immune deficiency syndrome (AIDS). Mr. Bramer, not believing that his symptoms mimicked those of an individual with AIDS, was retested for HIV. On three separate occasions (July 1, 1988, July 15, 1988, and July 22, 1988) involving two separate laboratories, he tested negative for the virus. In September 1990, Mr. Bramer later filed a lawsuit against Dr. Dotson and SmithKline for the negligent interpretation and reporting of his blood samples as being HIV-positive.

The circuit court, upon agreement of all parties to the lawsuit, agreed to the following certified question for review by the Supreme Court of Appeals of West Virginia: Did the plaintiff state a claim upon which relief could be granted in alleging that the defendants caused him to suffer major depression? The circuit court ruled yes.

Issue

Did the plaintiff state a claim upon which relief could be granted?

Holding

The Supreme Court of Appeals of West Virginia ruled that the plaintiff had stated a claim for the negligent infliction of emotional distress.

Reason

The supreme court found that, "Given the well known fact that AIDS had replaced cancer as the most feared disease in America and, as defendant SmithKline candidly acknowledges, a diagnosis of AIDS is a death sentence, conventional wisdom mandates that fear of AIDS triggers genuine—not spurious—claims of emotional distress. Accordingly, the first certified question was correctly answered by the circuit court. . . ." *Id.* at 775.

Discussion

1. Based solely on the facts presented above, what provisions should the physician have made for reassessment of the patient's condition?
2. What instructions should the physician have provided to the patient for continuing care?

16. STATUTE OF LIMITATIONS/ACTION NOT TIME BARRED/FOREIGN OBJECT LEFT IN PATIENT

Citation: *Williams v. Kilgore*, 618 So. 2d 51 (Miss. 1992)

Facts

A patient, Mrs. Williams, brought a medical malpractice suit against defendant physicians, Dr. Kilgore and Dr. Berrong, based on injuries she allegedly sustained from a biopsy needle fragment that had been left in her left iliac wing.

On March 31, 1964, Mrs. Williams had been admitted to the University Medical Center for treatment of metastatic malignant melanoma on her left groin. On April 6, 1964, a bone marrow biopsy was performed by an unknown resident. The needle broke during the procedure and a fragment had lodged in the patient. She was told that the needle would be removed the following day, when surgery was to be performed to remove a melanoma from her groin. The operating surgeons, Dr. Peede and Dr. Kilgore, were informed of the presence of the needle fragment prior to surgery. A notation by Dr. Peede stated that the needle fragment had been removed. Dr. Berrong was a radiology resident at the time of the surgery who was assigned the responsibility of studying the results of the surgery.

Although the needle fragment had not been removed, the patient remained asymptomatic until she was hospitalized for back pain in September 1985. During her hospitalization, the patient learned that the needle fragment was still in her lower back.

On October 7, 1985, the needle fragment was finally removed. The physician's discharge report suggested that there was a probable linkage between the needle fragment and recurrent strep infections that Mrs. Williams had been experiencing. Although the patient's treating physicians had known as early as 1972 that the needle fragment had not been removed, there was no evidence that Mrs. Williams was aware of this fact.

Summonses served on Dr. Kilgore and Dr. Berrong were returned. The whereabouts of Dr. Peede were unknown. The defendant physicians argued that the statute of limitations had tolled under Mississippi Code, thus barring the case from proceeding to trial. The circuit court entered a judgment for the physicians, and the plaintiff appealed.

Issue

Was the plaintiff's malpractice action time barred?

Holding

The Supreme Court of Mississippi held that the plaintiff's action was not time barred and was, therefore, remanded for trial.

Reason

A patient's cause for action begins to accrue and the statute of limitations begins to run when the patient can reasonably be held to have knowledge of the disease or injury. "In this instance, Mrs. Williams began to experience infections and back pain in 1985. Moreover, this is the date she discovered that the needle was causing her problems, never having been informed previously that the needle from the 1964 biopsy procedure remained lodged within her." *Id.* at 54. "As we (Mississippi Supreme Court) stated in *Gentry v. Wallace*, 606 So. 2d 1117, 1122 (1992), '[t]his Court views statutes of repose with disfavor, and if the statute is ambiguous, we place upon it a construction which favors preservation of the plaintiff's cause of action.' We find therefore that Mrs. Williams properly filed her complaint in this case within two years of that time, thus conforming with the statute of limitations for medical malpractice. . . ." *Id.* at 55.

Discussion

1. Under what circumstances would the plaintiff's action have been time barred?
2. What is your impression of Dr. Peede's claim that the needle fragment had been removed?
3. What is the efficacy of X-rays following the alleged removal of the needle fragment?

17. STATUTE OF LIMITATIONS/NOT TIME BARRED

Citation: *Follett v. Davis*, 636 N.E.2d 1282 (Ind. Ct. App. 1994)

Facts

The superior court, in a medical malpractice action, entered summary judgment for the physician and clinic on the grounds that the statute of limitations had tolled, and the patient appealed.

In 1987, the plaintiff, Ms. Follett, had her first office visit with Dr. Davis. In the spring of 1988, Ms. Follett discovered a lump in her right breast and made an appointment to see Dr. Davis. The clinic had no record of her appointment. The clinic's employees directed her to radiology for a mammogram. Ms. Follett was not offered an examination by Dr. Davis or any other physician at the clinic. In addition, she was not scheduled for a physician's examination as a follow-up to the mammogram. A technician examined Ms. Follett's breast and confirmed the presence of a lump in her right breast. After the mammogram, clinic employees told her that she would hear from Dr. Davis if there was any problem with her mammogram.

The radiologist explained in his deposition that the mammogram was not normal. Dr. Davis received and reviewed the mammogram report and considered it to be negative for malignancy. He did not know of the new breast lump because none of the clinic employees had informed him about it. The clinic, including Dr. Davis, never contacted Ms. Follett about her lump or the mammogram. On April 6, 1990, Ms. Follett called the clinic and was told that there was nothing to worry about unless she heard from Dr. Davis. On September 24, 1990, Ms. Follett returned to the clinic after she had developed pain associated with that same lump. A mammogram performed on that day gave results consistent with cancer. Three days later, Dr. Davis made an appointment for Ms. Follett with a clinic surgeon for a biopsy and treatment. She kept her appointment with the surgeon. Nevertheless, this was her last visit with the clinic, as she subsequently transferred her care to other physicians.

In October 1990, the biopsy confirmed the diagnosis of cancer. In August 1992, Ms. Follett filed her complaint with the Department of Insurance.

Issue

When did the statute of limitations begin to run?

Holding

The Court of Appeals of Indiana held that the doctrine of continuing wrong was applicable so that the period of limitations did not begin to run until the patient's last visit to the clinic.

Reason

Ms. Follett claimed the wrong she suffered was a continuing wrong. The doctrine of continuing wrong is simply a legal concept used to define when an act, omission, or neglect took place. The statutory period of limitations begins to run at the end of the continuing wrongful act. The evidence shows that, after she had found a lump in her breast, she went to Dr. Davis, her regular obstetrician/gynecologist, and the clinic for aid. Dr. Davis and the clinic, through the clinic's employees and agents, undertook to treat her ailment. That undertaking ended only when the clinic's surgeon performed the biopsy and therefore was continuous in nature. When the sole claim of medical malpractice is a failure to diagnose, the omission cannot as a matter of law extend beyond the time the physician rendered a diagnosis. When Ms. Follett last visited Dr. Davis on September 24, 1990, and last visited the clinic on September 27, 1990, the evidence most favorable to her demonstrated that, had clinic procedures been followed, Dr. Davis or another doctor at the clinic would have had occasion to diagnose her problem before either of those dates. On August 20, 1992, Ms. Follett timely filed her proposed complaint within two years of the last visits to Dr. Davis and the clinic.

Discussion

1. What are the pros and cons as to when the statute of limitations should reasonably begin to run?
2. Do you think all of the 50 states should agree as to when the statute of limitations should begin to toll?
3. What are the communications issues involved in this case?

18. STATUTE OF LIMITATIONS/CLAIM FOR MALPRACTICE NOT MADE

Citation: *J.B. v. Sacred Heart Hosp. of Pensacola*, 635 So. 2d 945 (Fla. 1994)

Facts

J.B., his wife, and their three minor children filed suit in Florida District Court against a hospital based on the following facts:

V. That on [or] about April 17, 1989, Sacred Heart hospital was requested by their medical staff to arrange transportation for L.B., a diagnosed AIDS patient, to another treatment facility in Alabama.

VI. That the social services for the hospital were unable to arrange ambulance transport and so took it upon themselves to contact L.B.'s brother in Mississippi, namely J.B., requesting that he come to the hospital and provide the transportation.

VII. J.B., having visited L.B. at the hospital when he was first admitted, was under the impression that his brother's diagnosis was Lyme disease. He had not been notified that there was a change in diagnosis after his visit.

VIII. The patient, L.B., was released from the hospital with excessive fever and a heparin lock in his arm to the plaintiff, J.B., a layman providing a service without the benefit of training in the field of medical treatment and transport.

X. The complainant could not provide adequate care for the transferee in an emergency situation, as he was the operator of the vehicle.

XI. That during the trip, L.B. began to thrash about and accidentally dislodged the dressing to his heparin lock causing J.B. to reach over while driving in an attempt to prevent the lock from coming out of L.B.'s arm. In doing so, J.B. came in contact with fluid around the lock site. J.B.'s hand had multiple nicks and cuts due to a recent fishing trip. *Id.* at 947.

The complaint alleged that the hospital was negligent in arranging for J.B. to transport L.B. in that it knew of L.B.'s condition, the level of care that would be required in transporting him, and the risk involved. J.B. alleged that because he contracted the AIDS virus, his wife was exposed to it through him and his children have suffered a loss of relationship with him. The Florida District Court ruled that J.B.'s complaint stated a claim for medical malpractice and was thus subject to the presuit notice and screening procedures set out in Chapter 766, Florida Statutes (1989). Because J.B. did not follow those procedures, the court dismissed the complaint. On appeal, the Florida Circuit Court declined to rule on J.B.'s claim, concluding that the issues are appropriate for resolution by the Supreme Court of Florida.

Issue

Was the claim of the patient's brother a claim for medical malpractice, and therefore subject to a two-year statute of limitations?

Holding

The Supreme Court of Florida answered that the claim was not a claim for medical malpractice for purposes of the two-year statute of limitations or presuit notice and screening requirements.

Reason

Chapter 95, Florida Statutes (1989), sets a two-year limitation period for medical malpractice actions. J.B.'s injury arose solely through the hospital's use of him as a transporter. Accordingly, this suit is not a medical malpractice action and the two-year statute of limitations is inapplicable. According to the allegations in J.B.'s complaint, the hospital was negligent in using J.B. as a transporter. The complaint does not allege that the hospital was negligent in any way in the rendering of, or the failure to render, medical care or services to J.B. Accordingly, the complaint does not state a medical malpractice claim for Chapter 766 purposes, and the notice and presuit screening requirements are inapplicable.

Discussion

1. Why was the claim made by the plaintiff not an action in malpractice?
2. Do you agree with the court's decision?
3. What precautions should the hospital have taken to help prevent the patient's brother from contracting the virus?
4. What is the importance of patient-family education as it relates to this case?
5. What are the confidentiality issues in cases of this nature?
6. Were the transfer arrangements for the patient appropriate?

19. STATUTE OF LIMITATIONS/FOLLOW-UP CARE ALLEGED LACKING

Citation: *Strong v. University of S.C. Sch. of Med.*, 447 S.E.2d 850 (S.C. 1994)

Facts

The plaintiff underwent four surgical eye procedures that were performed by Dr. Ferguson, an employee of the medical school. The plaintiff became blind after his third surgery on May 11, 1989. Dr. Martin, a colleague of Dr. Ferguson, who had assisted Dr. Ferguson during the May 11 surgery, noted in the patient's medical record that the plaintiff became blind because of poor follow-up care. The plaintiff contacted an attorney sometime thereafter. The plaintiff's medical records were received by his attorney in February 1991 and an action was filed in May 1991. The defendants filed a motion for summary judgment claiming that the two-year statute of limitations had tolled. The circuit court granted

summary judgment for the medical school, and the plaintiff appealed. The plaintiff contended that due to his educational background and blindness, the statute of limitations should not have begun to run until such time as his attorney reviewed the medical records. The plaintiff also alleged that the medical school fraudulently concealed the physician's negligence.

Issue

When did the statute of limitations begin to toll? Should the patient's educational status and blindness bar the action from tolling until the plaintiff's attorney reviewed the record? Did Dr. Ferguson commit fraud by attempting to conceal the alleged poor follow-up and treatment?

Holding

The Supreme Court of South Carolina held that the cause of action accrued at the latest when the physician noted in the medical record that the plaintiff's blindness was due to poor follow-up care. There was no evidence that the medical school had attempted to conceal Dr. Martin's notes regarding poor follow-up care.

Reason

Under the discovery rule in South Carolina, an action accrues when an injury is discovered or "reasonably ought to have been discovered." S.C. Code Ann. § 15-3-545. The tolling of the statute is not contingent on when the advice of counsel is sought or a full-blown theory of recovery is developed. In making his claim, the plaintiff argued that because of his educational background and blindness, the statute of limitations should not have begun to run until such time as his attorney reviewed the medical records. The court found that the plaintiff's cause of injury was readily discoverable "by a person of common knowledge" when Dr. Martin had noted in his medical record that his blindness was due to poor follow-up care. *Id.* at 852.

As to the claim that the medical school fraudulently concealed the physician's negligence, "The practically universal rule is that deliberate acts of deception by a defendant calculated to conceal from a potential plaintiff that he has a cause of action, thereby inducing him to postpone institution of suit will be held to toll the statute." D. W. Louisell and H. Williams, Medical Malpractice ¶ 13.03 p. 13–67 (1993). The supreme court found that there were no allegations or circumstances created by the medical school to prevent the plaintiff from discovering the facts.

Discussion

1. What are the merits of the patient's argument that his educational background and blindness should have prevented the statute from tolling until such time as his attorney reviewed the medical records? Was the circuit court and supreme court too harsh in their decision?
2. Do you think the plaintiff's attorney was negligent in the handling of the suit? Explain.
3. Do you agree with the court's ruling? Explain.
4. Based on the facts of this case as presented, what are the issues you would have as a defendant? What issues would you have as the plaintiff?

20. STATUTE OF LIMITATIONS/CHEMICAL EXPOSURE

Citation: *Goyette v. Mallinckrodt, Inc.*, 612 N.Y.S.2d 474 (N.Y. App. Div. 1994)

Facts

A former laboratory aide brought actions against a chemical manufacturer for wrongful exposure to toxic substances. The Supreme Court denied the defendants' motions for summary judgment, and they appealed. The Supreme Court, Appellate Division, held that the action was time barred. From 1966 to 1969, the plaintiff was employed by third-party defendant, Sterling Drug Inc., as a laboratory aide in the toxicology department where she was exposed to the chemicals xylene, formalin/formaldehyde, and benzene. In 1969, the plaintiff left Sterling to work in a hospital laboratory. In 1971, the plaintiff returned to Sterling and worked in the histology lab where she was exposed to xylene, formalin/formaldehyde, benzene, acetone, and methyl alcohol. From 1975 to 1979, the plaintiff worked in Sterling's autopsy room, where she was exposed to the aforesaid chemicals as well as sodium cyanide. In 1979, the plaintiff was transferred to Sterling's clinical chemistry laboratory, where she continued to be exposed to the aforesaid chemicals. In 1981, the plaintiff began experiencing numbness, a burning sensation in her face, fatigue, and respiratory difficulties, the result of which she sought medical attention. In August 1984, the plaintiff left Sterling, and in September of that year she was diagnosed as having an immunological disorder induced by exposure to petrochemicals. In July 1987, the plaintiff commenced this action against, among others, defendants Mallinckrodt, Inc. and Fisher Scientific Company, the manufacturers of the allegedly damaging chemicals. Mallinckrodt commenced a third-party action against Sterling. After issue was joined and discovery conducted, Sterling moved and

Mallinckrodt and Fisher cross-moved for summary judgment on the grounds that the plaintiff's action was time barred. The New York Supreme Court denied the motions and these appeals ensued. The New York Supreme Court, Appellate Division, reversed and granted the defendants' motions for summary judgment. Contrary to the plaintiff's contention, a cause of action for wrongful exposure to a toxic substance accrues upon the *initial* exposure to the substance, not the *last* exposure. As noted previously, the plaintiff initially was exposed to five of the six chemicals complained of beginning in 1971 and was exposed to the sixth substance beginning in 1975. Accordingly, the three-year statute of limitations commenced to run no later than 1975 and expired in 1978, nearly a decade before commencement of this action. The plaintiff contends, however, and the New York Supreme Court found, that his action is governed by the discovery rule of CPLR 214-c for claims based on exposure to toxic substances. The New York Supreme Court, Appellate Division, disagreed. Although it is true that CPLR 214-c provides that, in exposure cases, the three-year statute of limitations begins to run from the earlier of "the date of discovery of the injury by the plaintiff or from the date when through the exercise of reasonable diligence such injury should have been discovered by the plaintiff" (CPLR 214-c[2]) that provision is expressly inapplicable to any acts before July 1, 1986, or omissions that caused an injury that was discovered or could have been discovered prior to that date and for which an action would have been time barred because the applicable period of limitation had expired before that date. The plaintiff's exposure occurred prior to July 1, 1986, and the plaintiff discovered her injuries prior to that date. Additionally, the then-applicable statute of limitations expired sometime in 1978. Because all three criteria of CPLR 214-c(6) have been met, the three-year statute of limitations governing the plaintiff's claim is measured not from the date of discovery, but rather from the date of injury. Accordingly, this action is time barred and the motions for summary judgment should have been granted.

Issue

What medical and legal issues can you identify in this case?

Holding

What decision would you make?

Reason

What was the reasoning of your finding?

Discussion

Develop a discussion question.

21. COMPLAINT TIME BARRED/FAILURE TO TIMELY NOTIFY PATIENT OF TEST RESULTS

Citation: *Turner v. Nama*, 689 N.E.2d 303 (Ill. App. 1997)

Facts

In 1982, Laura Nelson, plaintiff, began seeing Prabhavthi G. Nama, defendant, who specializes in obstetrics and gynecology. On September 18, 1990, the defendant performed a Pap test on Laura. Some time after September 25, 1990, the plaintiff's estate claims that the defendant received Laura's Pap test results, which indicated a class four carcinoma.

On December 14, 1993, after being diagnosed with cervical cancer by another physician, Laura returned to the defendant for a second opinion. The plaintiff alleges that it was at this visit that the defendant first told Laura of the results from the September 1990 test. The plaintiff alleges that Laura suffered a stroke on January 31, 1995, and that this caused Laura to be under legal disability from that date until she died from progressive metastatic cervical cancer on March 16, 1995.

Claiming that Laura was under the defendant's care from 1982 until December 1993, the plaintiff alleges that the defendant had a continuing duty to ensure that Laura was notified of the test results. According to the complaint, the defendant breached this duty by failing to notify Laura of the results from September 18, 1990, to December 1993 by telephone or by means that would confirm receipt, such as, but not limited to, registered letter or telegram with signature. The plaintiff attached to the complaint an unverified letter from an expert opining that such duty continued for at least a year and that the defendant's attempts to contact Laura and her relatives should have been carefully documented. The plaintiff claimed that the defendant's failure to notify Laura of the diagnosis was the proximate cause of her developing progressive metastatic cervical cancer, which ultimately caused her death.

The plaintiff asserts that although the defendant's records reflect that a letter was sent to Laura regarding the abnormal test results on September 18, 1990, Laura did not learn of the letter until December 14, 1993, when the defendant informed Laura that a letter was sent. According to the complaint, defendant was negligent in failing to follow up after the letter to ensure that Laura knew of the Pap test results, in failing to ensure that Laura was informed of the results from November 1, 1990, and continuing every month and a half until May 1991, and in failing to contact Laura when Laura did not return for either a six-month or yearly check-up.

The estate filed a medical malpractice claim against the defendant alleging that the defendant failed to notify Laura that her Pap test was positive for carcinoma. The trial court granted defendant's motion to dismiss on the basis that plaintiff's complaint was not filed within the statute of repose period set forth in section 13-212(a) of the Limitations Act [735 ILCS 5/13-212(a) (West 1996)].

Issue

Was the action timely filed within the medical malpractice statute of repose?

Holding

The appeals court affirmed the decision of the circuit court finding that the plaintiff's complaint is time barred because the defendant's failure to notify the decedent of her diagnosis, which was the act or omission triggering the running of the statute of repose, occurred more than four years before the plaintiff's filing date.

Reason

Medical malpractice actions in Illinois must be filed within the statute of limitation periods mandated in section 13-212(a) of the Limitations Act [735 ILCS 5/13-212(a) (West 1996)].

Section 13-212(a) is bifurcated, providing both a statute of limitations and a statute of repose. Providing the statute of limitations and incorporating the "discovery rule," the first part of section 13-212(a) states that "no action for damages for injury or death against any [physician], . . . arising out of patient care shall be brought more than 2 years after the date on which the claimant knew, or through the use of reasonable diligence should have known, . . . of the existence of the injury or death for which damages are sought."

The focus in this case, however, is the repose period. The second part of section 13-212(a) provides that "in no event shall [a medical malpractice] action be brought more than 4 years after the date on which occurred the act or omission or occurrence alleged in such action to have been the cause of such injury or death." The distinction between the repose period and the limitations period is that the repose period is triggered by the defendant's wrongful act or omission that causes the injury, whereas the limitations period is triggered by the patient's discovery of the injury. The period of repose effectuates a different policy than the period of limitations; it is intended to terminate the possibility of liability after a defined period of time, regardless of a potential plaintiff's lack of knowledge of his cause of action. Although the statute of repose causes harsh consequences in some cases, the legislature intended to curtail the "long tail" exposure to medical malpractice claims brought about by the advent of the discovery rule by placing an outer time limit within which a malpractice action must be commenced.

The statute of repose is triggered by determining when the defendant's act or omission causing injury occurred. The plaintiff alleges that the defendant's failure to notify began on November 1, 1990, and continued every month and a half until May 1991. In addition, plaintiff avers that defendant failed to notify Laura of the results when Laura returned for neither a six-month check-up nor a yearly check-up. In its brief, the plaintiff argued that the obligation continued until the defendant successfully notified Laura of the results. Despite these assertions, the appeals court found as a matter of law that the defendant's failure to notify Laura triggered the statute of repose no later than late November 1990.

Once a health care provider receives unfavorable test results, it is obligated to timely inform the patient of the results. If the provider is a physician, the physician can delegate this task or do it directly. Nonetheless, the obligation is imposed and continues until the provider exhausts all reasonable means available, including but not limited to a letter, telephone, and any correspondence that would indicate receipt.

Considering the obligation that defendant is charged with, the defendant should and could have satisfied the obligation to notify within, at the very most, a two-month period. When the defendant received the results in late September, defendant should have exhausted, as soon as possible, all reasonable means to notify Laura of the results. This could have included mailing one or two letters, phoning Laura and her relatives, and sending a letter by certified mail. The appeals court concluded that the defendant's omission giving rise to the injury occurred no later than at the end of a two-month period in which defendant could have and should have, but failed to, notify Laura of the unfavorable results. Consequently, the plaintiff's filing date remains more than four months beyond the running of the statute of repose.

Although an obligation to notify might continue, to conclude that an omission of notification reoccurs into perpetuity would contravene the General Assembly's intent behind promulgating the statute of repose. Although the statute of repose creates harsh results in some cases, the court's role is to give effect to the statute in question—regardless of the result. The four-year outer limit of the statute of repose was designed and enacted specifically to curtail the "long tail" exposure to medical malpractice claims brought about by the advent of the discovery rule and to terminate the possibility of liability after a defined period of time. The statute of

repose is only excepted by fraudulent concealment and postponed by an ongoing course of continuous negligent medical treatment. Finding that neither of these applied to the allegations in this case, the appeals court concluded that the trial court properly dismissed the plaintiff's action for being barred by the statute of repose.

Discussion

1. In what way does the "statute of limitations" and "statute of repose" differ?
2. Do you agree that the cause of action in this case should have been time barred? Discuss your answer.
3. What is the purpose of terminating the possibility of liability after a defined period of time?
4. What is the meaning of "long tail" exposure to medical malpractice claims?

22. NURSE'S NEGLIGENCE/QUALIFIED IMMUNITY REJECTED

Citation: *Sullivan v. Sumrall by Ritchey*, 618 So. 2d 1274 (Miss. 1993)

Facts

On April 26, 1988, the patient was admitted to the hospital suffering from a severe headache. Her physician ordered a CT scan for the following morning and prescribed Demerol and Dramamine to alleviate pain. Referring to the patient's medical chart, the nurse stated in her deposition that the patient had received injections of Demerol and Dramamine at 6:45 P.M. and 10:00 P.M. on April 26th. The nurse checked on the patient at 11:00 P.M. The patient's temperature and blood pressure were taken at midnight. Her blood pressure was recorded at 90/60, down from 160/80 at 8:00 P.M. At 12:25 A.M., 2 hours and 25 minutes after her last medication, the nurse administered another injection of Demerol and Dramamine because the patient was still complaining of pain. Although hospital rules require consultation with a patient's admitting physician when there is a question regarding the administration of medication, the nurse stated that she did not call the physician before administering another injection.

At 4:00 A.M. when the nurse made an hourly check of the patient, she discovered that the patient was not breathing. She issued a Code 99 (an emergency signal for a patient in acute distress). An emergency department physician responded and revived the patient. The patient was diagnosed as having suffered "respiratory arrest, with what appears to be hypoxic brain injury." Her CT scans revealed no bleeding, but other tests "revealed [a] grossly abnormal EEG with diffuse and severe slowing." *Id.* at 1275. The patient was transferred to a nursing facility where she apparently remained in a coma at the time of trial.

On October 21, 1988, the patient's daughter and husband filed a complaint against the hospital, alleging that the hospital had been negligent in monitoring and medicating the patient, in failing to notify a physician when her vital signs became irregular, in failing to properly assess her condition and intervene, and in failing to exercise reasonable care. Later, the complaint was amended to include the nurse.

On January 24, 1990, the defendant nurse filed a motion for summary judgment. She asserted that as a matter of law, she was shielded from liability under the qualified immunity afforded public officials engaged in their performance of discretionary functions. The circuit court denied the motion and the nurse appealed.

Issue

Is a nurse employed by a county hospital shielded by public official qualified immunity from a medical negligence action brought against her individually?

Holding

The Supreme Court of Mississippi held that an employee of a county hospital enjoys no qualified immunity.

Reason

There is no qualified immunity for any public hospital employees making treatment decisions. Discretion exercised by medical personnel in making treatment decisions is not the sort of individual judgment sought to be protected by the qualified immunity bestowed upon public officials. In a recent decision, the Supreme Court of Mississippi announced that: "we hold that common law qualified public official immunity will be restricted to its designed purpose. Accordingly, it will not be extended to decisions that involve only individual medical treatment. Those decisions will be judged on the same standards as if made by private providers." *Womble v. Singing River Hosp.*, 618 So. 2d 1252, 1265 (Miss. 1993).

Discussion

1. Do you agree that the nurse should not be shielded from liability on the basis that she is a public official? Explain.

2. What assessment and reassessment issues do you see in this case?
3. Should the dramatic change in the patient's blood pressure have signaled a need to notify the attending physician of the patient's change in health status? Explain.
4. Was the nurse practicing medicine when she administered the second injection without contacting the attending physician?

23. GOOD SAMARITAN STATUTE/APPLICABLE TO CERTAIN EMERGENCY DEPARTMENT PHYSICIANS

Citation: *Deal v. Kearney*, 851 P.2d 1353 (Alaska 1993)

Facts

On September 16, 1984, after the plaintiff, Mr. Kearney, suffered a life-threatening injury, he was taken by ambulance to the emergency department of Kodiak Island Hospital (KIH). When he arrived at 3:45 P.M., he was examined by the on-call emergency department physician, Dr. Creelman, a family practitioner. Dr. Creelman determined that a surgical consultation was necessary and he called Dr. Deal, a surgeon with staff privileges at the hospital. After ordering certain tests, Dr. Deal was of the opinion that Mr. Kearney could not survive a transfer to Anchorage. Dr. Deal then performed emergency surgery that lasted 9 to 10 hours, ending the following morning.

The plaintiff was eventually transferred to Anchorage. His condition worsened and he suffered loss of circulation and tissue death in both legs. The plaintiff alleged that the hospital was negligent in failing to properly evacuate him to Anchorage.

On October 2, 1989, Lutheran Hospitals and Home Society of America (LHHS) and Mr. Kearney entered into a settlement agreement whereby LHHS paid $510,000 to Mr. Kearney. At the same time, LHHS and Mr. Kearney released LHHS, Dr. Deal, and other health care providers from liability. In return, LHHS assigned to Mr. Kearney its rights to indemnity, equitable subrogation, and contribution against Dr. Deal.

On November 1, 1989, Mr. Kearney, as assignee of the rights of LHHS, brought the present action against Dr. Deal, alleging that LHHS had rights of indemnity, contribution, or subrogation against Dr. Deal arising from Dr. Deal's negligent acts or omissions in the care given Mr. Kearney. Dr. Deal moved for summary judgment on two grounds. First, Dr. Deal argued that the assignment of LHHS's claims to Mr.

Kearney was invalid. Second, he claimed to be immune from suit under the Good Samaritan statute.

The trial court denied Dr. Deal's motion for summary judgment, ruling that the claims brought against him were properly assigned to Mr. Kearney, and that the Good Samaritan statute was not applicable to Dr. Deal because he was acting under a preexisting duty to render the emergency care provided Mr. Kearney. Dr. Deal petitioned for review, and his petition was granted.

The superior court held that the immunity provided by the Good Samaritan statute is unavailable to physicians with a preexisting duty to respond to emergency situations. The court concluded that Dr. Deal was under a preexisting duty in the instant case by virtue of his contract with KIH, the duty being part of the consideration that Dr. Deal gave to KIH in exchange for staff privileges at the hospital. The court further found that the Good Samaritan statute did not apply to Dr. Deal in any event, because the actions allegedly constituting malpractice occurred during the follow-up care and treatment given Mr. Kearney after surgery. By then, the court reasoned, Dr. Deal had become Mr. Kearney's treating physician, and was no longer responding to an emergency situation.

Issue

Does the Good Samaritan statute extend immunity to physicians who have a preexisting duty to render emergency care?

Holding

The Supreme Court of Alaska held that the Good Samaritan statute does not extend immunity to physicians who have preexisting duty to render emergency care.

Reason

The Alaska Statute 09.65.090(a) states, "A person at a hospital or any other location who renders emergency care or emergency counseling to an injured, ill, or emotionally distraught person who reasonably appears to be in immediate need of emergency aid in order to avoid serious harm or death is not liable for civil damages as a result of an act or omission in rendering emergency aid."

The legislature clearly intended this provision to encourage health care providers, including medical professionals, to administer emergency medical care, whether in a hospital or not, to persons who are not their patients by immunizing them from civil liability. The legislative history favors Mr.

Kearney's position. The 1976 version of the Good Samaritan statute was based on recommendations of the Medical Malpractice Insurance Commission (Commission). The report of the Commission dated October 1, 1975, included the following recommendation: "Medical professionals should be immune from liability to a person who is not his patient for administering emergency medical care where the giving of immediate aid appears to be the only alternative to death or serious bodily injury or harm." *Id.* at 1357.

The clear inference of this recommendation is that those with a preexisting duty would not be covered by the statute. Courts in other cases have held that physicians were entitled to claim immunity under a Good Samaritan statute where they provided emergency medical care in a hospital that was not part of the doctor's express or customary hospital function and therefore did not have a preexisting duty to treat the patients [e.g., *McKenna v. Cedars of Lebanon Hosp., Inc.*, 93 Cal. 3d 282, 155 Cal. Rptr. 631 (Cal. 1979); *Matts v. Homsi*, 308 N.W.2d 284 (Mich. Ct. App. 1981); *see generally* 68 A.L.R. 4th 323-26].

In summary, the trial court was correct in holding that the Alaska Good Samaritan statute does not extend immunity to physicians who have a preexisting duty to render emergency care.

Discussion

1. Do you agree with the Alaska Statute 09.65.090(a), which provides that a person at a hospital or any other location who renders emergency care or emergency counseling to an injured, ill, or emotionally distraught person who reasonably appears to be in immediate need of emergency aid in order to avoid serious harm or death is not liable for civil damages as a result of an act or omission in rendering emergency aid?
2. What other options might have been available to care for this patient?
3. Do you get the impression that this is a no-win case for the defendants? Explain.

24. JOINT LIABILITY/WRONG PATIENT/RIGHT PROCEDURE

Citation: *Meena v. Wilburn*, 603 So. 2d 866 (Miss. 1992)

Facts

In 1987, the plaintiff, a custodian, was cleaning when she bumped her right leg and injured it. The injury was a "nick" that developed into an ulcer because of poor blood circulation. Due to the plaintiff's diabetic condition, the ulcer did not heal. She visited her physician, who referred her to Dr. Maples, a vascular surgeon. Dr. Maples performed surgery. The surgery was a success and, according to Dr. Maples, the plaintiff was "doing acceptably well." *Id.* at 867.

Two days following surgery, Dr. Meena was at the hospital covering for one of his partners, Dr. Petro, who had asked him to remove the staples from one of his patients, 65-year-old Ms. Slaughter. Ms. Slaughter shared a semi-private room with the plaintiff. Dr. Meena testified that he went and picked up Ms. Slaughter's chart at the nurse's desk and asked one of the nurses as to which bed Ms. Slaughter was in. Dr. Meena claimed that he was led to believe that she was in the bed next to the window. He picked up the chart and asked Ms. Greer, a nurse, to accompany him to the plaintiff's room. Shortly thereafter, Dr. Meena received an emergency call at the nursing station. He said that he asked Ms. Greer to take the staples out, because he had to respond to an emergency call at another hospital. *Id.* at 868. Ms. Greer "conceded during her testimony that, before removing staples from a patient, a nurse 'should read the chart, be familiar with the chart, look at the patient's arm band and compare the arm band to the chart'—all of which she failed to do. Greer rationalized her failure: '[W]hen the doctor I work for is standing at the foot of a patient's bed, I would have no doubt—no reason to doubt what he tells me to do.'" *Id.*

Ms. Greer began to remove the plaintiff's staples. She soon realized that there was a problem. The plaintiff's "skin split 'wide' open—revealing the 'scubcu' or layer of fat under the skin." *Id.* Ms. Greer stopped the procedure and left the room to check the medical records maintained at the nursing station. She realized that she had removed staples from the wrong patient. At that point, she encountered Dr. Maples and explained to him what had happened. Dr. Maples immediately restapled the skin.

Following discharge, the plaintiff's health began to falter and she developed a fever of 101 degrees. The tissue where the staples had been removed had become infected. Dr. Evans ultimately readmitted her to the hospital; she remained there for approximately 22 days—during which time she underwent more surgery and received intensive care for the infection. The plaintiff testified that she continued to experience pain upon being discharged from the hospital in May 1988. Her condition gradually improved and, presumably, she had recovered completely with the exception of some scarring and skin "indention."

In June 1988, a complaint was filed against Dr. Meena and Ms. Greer. After four days of trial, the jury returned a verdict against Dr. Meena and assessed damages in the amount of $125,000. The jury declined to hold the nurse liable for the plaintiff's injuries. Dr. Meena filed motions for a judgment notwithstanding the verdict, new trial, or *remittitur*—all of

which the judge denied. Dr. Meena appealed in November 1990.

Issue

Was the jury's exoneration of the nurse, who removed the surgical staples, grounds for a new trial on the issue of physician's liability?

Holding

The Supreme Court of Mississippi held that the jury's exoneration of Ms. Greer was not grounds for a new trial on the issue of physician's liability.

Reason

Dr. Meena contends that the supreme court should reverse and remand the case for a new trial because "the jury was bound to return a verdict against both defendants, inasmuch as the defendants [were sued] as joint tort-feasors." *Id.* at 71.

The plaintiff argued that the supreme court has often held that it would not reverse a case simply because one joint tort-feasor was deemed liable and the other was exonerated. Two relevant cases are as follows:

> In *Golden Flake Snack Foods v. Thornton*, 548 So. 2d 382 (Miss. 1989). . . . This court left the verdict intact and explained: Mississippi's law on joint and several liability is such that the instant case need not be reversed for the failure to include the defendant Hope Thornton in the verdict. One may recognize that misery wants company, but this court does not have to assign company to those in misery. The jury had the prerogative of including or not including Hope Thornton in the verdict; after a review, they did not. This court is loath to find fault, certainly not intentional fault with 12 men and women tried and true. *Id.* at 383–384.
>
> In *Capital Transport Co. v. McDuff*, 319 So. 2d 658, 660-61 (Miss. 1975), the court held that "For some time it has been the established law in this state that a case will not be reversed simply because a master is held liable where the servant is exonerated. . . ."

The supreme court, under authority of its previous holdings in *Golden Flake* and *Capital Transport*, held that Dr. Meena's contention that the jury improperly returned a verdict against him but not the nurse was rejected.

Discussion

1. Do you agree with the court's decision? Explain.
2. Should liability have been apportioned between the nurse and physician?
3. What are the issues in this case that are applicable to all health care providers?

25. INDEPENDENT CONTRACTOR/HOSPITAL NOT LIABLE

Citation: *Sarivola v. Brookdale Hosp. and Med. Ctr.*, 612 N.Y.S.2d 151 (N.Y. App. Div. 1994)

Facts

This is a malpractice case where the plaintiff seeks to impose liability on the defendant hospital for treatment provided by a radiologist who was not an employee of the hospital but maintained an office there. The plaintiff failed to submit an affidavit setting forth who she believed was responsible for her treatment. The evidence indicated that she was referred to the radiologist by another physician. The radiologist alleged that he specifically advised the plaintiff that he was a private physician, unaffiliated with the hospital. There was no evidence of independent acts of malpractice committed by the hospital's technicians who operated the radiation equipment. There was no evidence or expert testimony that the physician's orders were so radically different from accepted practice that the technicians should have questioned them or not carried them out.

Issue

When treatment is rendered by a private attending physician, not an employee of the hospital, can the hospital, as a general rule, be liable for acts of malpractice that are committed in carrying out the independent physician's orders?

Holding

The New York Supreme Court, Appellate Division, held that the plaintiff could not recover from the hospital.

Reason

When treatment is rendered by a private attending physician, not in the employ of a hospital, the general rule is that the hospital is not liable for acts of malpractice that are committed in carrying out the independent physician's orders. However, a hospital may be held vicariously liable, based on the principle of agency by estoppel, for the acts of an independent physician, where the physician was provided by the hospital or was otherwise acting on the hospital's behalf, and the patient reasonably believed that the physician was acting at the hospital's behest. Because the plaintiff did not seek treatment from the hospital directly, and the hospital did not send the plaintiff to the radiologist, the estoppel theory was not available to the plaintiff. Nor, given the totality of the circumstances here, could the plaintiff have reasonably believed that the physician was employed by the hospital, because it is quite common for independent physicians to utilize hospital office facilities.

Discussion

1. Under what circumstances can a hospital be liable for the negligent acts of a private practicing physician?
2. From a contractual point of view, what are the differences between an employed physician and a private independent contractor?

26. DAMAGES/MODIFIED

Citation: *Doe v. McNulty*, 630 So. 2d 825 (La. Ct. App. 1993)

Facts

The plaintiff, Jane Doe, had been exposed to HIV as the result of sexual contact. The plaintiff consulted her defendant physicians but they failed to diagnose her condition as being positive for either HIV or AIDS. The disease had weakened her immune system and she had developed pneumocystis carinii pneumonia (PCP) and was admitted to a hospital.

The patient was eventually diagnosed with AIDS. The patient's infectious disease expert, Dr. Hill, claimed that proper diagnosis in August, prior to her acute episode, would have provided greater opportunity for improved long-term treatment. Dr. Hill stated that the patient would not have contracted PCP for another year and this would have added another year to her life expectancy and ability to work. The defendants admitted that they negligently failed to timely diagnose the patient's condition.

The defendants' expert witness, Dr. Lutz, testified from his review of the patient's medical record that the patient's diagnosis could not have been determined based on the symptoms as described in the record. Dr. Lutz had never examined the patient and based his determination on the documentation contained in the medical record. Dr. Lutz did, however, agree that if the patient's immune system had not been totally destroyed, preventive treatment could have resulted in a longer life span.

The civil district court entered judgment on a jury verdict of $700,000 in general damages, which included pain and suffering, mental anguish, disability, and the loss of the enjoyment of life, and $314,000 for medical and special damages. The defendant appealed.

Issue

Did the defendant's failure to timely diagnose the plaintiff's condition cause her to lose one year of life? Did the jury commit obvious error in awarding $700,000 in general damages and $314,000 in medical damages?

Holding

The Court of Appeal of Louisiana held that the evidence supported the jury's finding of causation and the award of $700,000 was not excessive. The medical expense award totaling $314,000 could, however, be reduced to $72,337.62. The court found that it was unable to correlate from the evidence as to what expenses had accrued from September 1992 to the date of the trial as being caused by the defendants' negligence.

Reason

The medical defendants agreed that they negligently failed to timely diagnose the patient's condition. The plaintiff's expert witness testified repeatedly "that within the 'reasonable medical probability' standard and the 'more likely than not' standard, if the plaintiff had been properly diagnosed and treated no later than August 18, 1990, which was the date the medical defendants should have diagnosed and treated her, she would have not contracted pneumocystis carinii pneumonia." *Id.* at 826. She would have worked, as well as lived, for another year. As to the amount of the award, the Louisiana Supreme Court, in a number of cases (e.g., *Rossell v. ESCO*, 549 So. 2d 840 [La. 1989]), established the standards for appellate review of general damages awards as follows: "The discretion vested in the trier of fact is 'great,' and even vast, so that an appellate court should rarely disturb an award of general damages." *Id.* at 827–828.

Discussion

1. On what basis should a physician determine the appropriateness of his or her patient's specific clinical needs (e.g., medical history)?
2. When does the physician–patient relationship terminate? Does it terminate at the moment of discharge? Explain.

27. DAMAGES/FAILURE TO TREAT/$16 MILLION NOT EXCESSIVE

Citation: *Callahan v. Cardinal Glennon Hosp.*, 863 S.W.2d 852 (Mo. 1993)

Facts

A medical malpractice action was brought against the employer of a physician, alleging that the physician's failure to properly treat an abscess some three weeks after an infant received a live polio vaccine resulted in suppression of the infant's immune system and the infant's contraction of paralytic polio. The jury in the circuit court returned a $16 million verdict in favor of the plaintiffs, and the defendant appealed. The case was transferred from the court of appeals to the supreme court.

Issue

Was the $16 million verdict excessive and did the trial court err in denying a new trial based on the alleged excessive verdict?

Holding

The Missouri Supreme Court held that there was no basis for a new trial on the grounds of excessiveness of the verdict.

Reason

There is no formula for determining the excessiveness of a verdict. Each case must be decided on its own facts to determine what is fair and reasonable. A jury is in the best position to make such a determination. The trial judge could have set aside the verdict if a determination was made that passion and prejudice brought about an excessive verdict.

The size of the verdict alone does not establish passion and prejudice. The appellant failed to establish that the verdict was: (1) glaringly unwarranted and (2) based on prejudice and passion. Compensation of a plaintiff is based on such factors as the age of the patient, the nature and extent of injury, diminished earnings capacity, economic condition, and awards in comparable cases. "Furthermore, a jury is 'entitled to consider such intangibles' which 'do not lend themselves to precise calculation,' such as past and future pain, suffering, effect on lifestyle, embarrassment, humiliation, and economic loss." *Kenton v. Hyatt Hotels Corp.*, 693 S.W.2d at 98 (Mo. 1985). The supreme court found no error that would substantiate passion or prejudice. Based on this issue, there was no basis for a new trial.

Discussion

1. Do you consider the verdict of $16 million to be excessive?
2. What factors should be taken into account when determining the amount of damages to be awarded a plaintiff?

28. DAMAGES/BLOOD TRANSFUSION/NOT EXCESSIVE

Citation: *Dodson v. Community Blood Ctr.*, 633 So. 2d 252 (La. Ct. App. 1993)

Facts

The Patients' Compensation Fund (PCF) appealed from an order of the trial court, which awarded damages to a patient who contracted hepatitis following blood transfusion.

Mr. Dodson was scheduled to undergo surgery at a medical center. In anticipation of the surgery and out of fear of contracting AIDS through blood transfusions from unknown donors, he arranged to have three known donors donate blood earmarked for his use should transfusion be required.

After surgery, Mr. Dodson was transfused with two pints of blood. However, the blood used was not the blood obtained from Mr. Dodson's voluntary donors. The blood had been taken from the hospital's general inventory, which had been obtained from the Community Blood Center. Mr. Dodson subsequently learned that as a result of the transfusions, he had been infected with what at the time was called non-A non-B hepatitis. It is now referred to as hepatitis C.

Issue

Was the award of $325,000 in general damages to the patient excessive?

Holding

The Court of Appeal of Louisiana held that the award of damages was not excessive.

Reason

The PCF contended the trial court erred in assessing general damages. The plaintiffs were awarded the sum of $325,000 in general damages. PCF alleges that the sum of $150,000 in general damages is the maximum to which the plaintiffs are entitled, thus quantum should be reduced accordingly. A review of the record revealed that Mr. Dodson contracted non-A and non-B hepatitis through the blood transfusions received. Based on tests prior to trial, the chronic hepatitis was either resolved or quiescent. The plaintiff had a good prognosis; however, this prognosis was not guaranteed. There remained a chance that the chronic hepatitis may become active in the future.

In reasons for judgment, the trial court found that Mr. Dodson was a credible witness. He did not exaggerate his symptoms, fears, or worries about his condition. The court believed Mr. Dodson when he said he felt like a leper and feared infecting his wife, child, and friends with the disease. The trial court arrived at what it determined to be an appropriate award for general damages. After careful review of the record and in light of the vast discretion of the trial court to assess general damages, the court found that there was no abuse of discretion.

Discussion

1. Under what circumstances will an appellate court overturn the decision of a lower court?
2. What are the proper procedures for handling blood and blood products in this case?

29. DAMAGES/NOT EXCESSIVE

Citation: *NKC Hosps., Inc. v. Anthony*, 849 S.W.2d 564 (Ky. Ct. App. 1993)

Facts

The decedent was in her first pregnancy under the primary care of Dr. Hawkins, her personal physician and an obstetrician. Mrs. Anthony was in good health, 26 years of age, employed, and about 30 weeks along in her non-eventful pregnancy.

On September 5, 1989, Mrs. Anthony was taken by her husband to the emergency department. She was experiencing nausea, vomiting, and abdominal pain, and because of her pregnancy, she was referred to the hospital's obstetrical unit. In the obstetrical unit, Mrs. Anthony came under the immediate care of Ms. Moore, a nurse, who performed an assessment.

Dr. Hawkins was called later that evening. He issued several orders, including an IV start, blood work, urinalysis, and an antinausea prescription. Later that night, a second call was made to Dr. Hawkins, giving her the test results and informing her that the patient was in extreme pain. Believing Mrs. Anthony had a urinary tract infection, antibiotics were ordered along with an order for her discharge from the hospital.

That same night a third call was made to Dr. Hawkins because of the pain Mrs. Anthony was experiencing, as observed by Ms. Moore. Mr. Anthony also talked with Dr. Hawkins about his wife's pain. Ms. Moore became concerned about Dr. Hawkins' discharge order. Although aware of Ms. Moore's evaluation, Dr. Hawkins prescribed morphine sulfate but was unrelenting in her order of discharge.

At approximately 2:00 A.M., Dr. Love, the resident physician on duty, did not see or examine the patient, although a prescription for the morphine was ordered and administered pursuant to the telephoned directions of Dr. Hawkins. It is not clear from the record, but it is assumed the morphine prescription was written by Dr. Love. It was administered to Mrs. Anthony. Mrs. Anthony rested comfortably for several hours, but awakened in pain again. At 6:00 A.M., the patient was discharged in that condition.

During trial testimony, Ms. Hale, a nursing supervisor, admitted that it was a deviation from the standard of nursing care to discharge a patient in significant pain. Ms. Moore, who was always concerned with the patient's pain, had grave reservations about her discharge in that condition. She suggested that Dr. Love examine Mrs. Anthony. She even consulted her supervisor, Nurse Hale. The major allegation of the hospital's negligence in this case is the undisputed fact that at no time, prior to her discharge, was Mrs. Anthony ever clinically seen or examined by a physician.

At approximately 10:00 A.M., Mrs. Anthony was readmitted to the hospital. Upon readmission, Dr. Hawkins began personal supervision of her patient. It was determined that Mrs. Anthony had a serious respiratory problem. The next day the patient was transferred to the hospital's intensive care unit.

The following day, the baby was delivered by Caesarean section. It was belatedly determined at that time that Mrs. Anthony's condition was caused by a perforation of the appendix at the large bowel, a condition not detected by anyone at the hospital during Mrs. Anthony's first admission. Almost three weeks later, while still in Norton Hospital, Mrs. Anthony died of acute adult respiratory distress syndrome (ARDS), a complication resulting from the delay in the diagnosis and treatment of her appendicitis.

A medical negligence judgment was brought against the hospital. At trial, Dr. Fields, an expert witness for the estate of Mrs. Anthony, board certified in obstetrics and gynecology, testified in no uncompromising terms that the hospital deviated from the standard of care. Pertinent testimony of Dr. Fields is as follows:

> *Question*: Had Margaret [Anthony] received care at Norton's Hospital which was within, which would have been within the standard of care, what would have been the outcome?
> *Answer:* She would have had a prompt appendectomy performed following ruling out of various other conditions, such as kidney infection, and the appendix would have been removed, the antibiotic therapy instituted promptly in the intravenous fashion, her dehydrated state would have been corrected, she would never have suffered the pulmonary complication known as acute adult respiratory distress syndrome.
> *Question:* Within a degree of medical probability, sir, would she be alive today?
> *Answer:* Yes.
> *Question:* Was the discharge of Margaret Anthony from the hospital on the early morning hours of September 6, 1989, a deviation from the standard of care for the hospital?
> *Answer:* Yes, sir. *Id.* at 566.

Dr. Fields' testimony tagged Norton Hospital with negligence as its actions were ". . . below the standard of care for any institution . . ." the reason being as follows:

> Every patient who presents herself to the labor and delivery area, the emergency room, or any area of the hospital, would be seen by a physician before anything is undertaken, and certainly before she is allowed to leave the institution. Furthermore, to provide the patient with medication in the form of a prescription without the physician ever seeing the patient is below any standard I'm acquainted with. *Id.* at 567.

The jury was instructed on the comparative negligence of Dr. Hawkins and the hospital. An award of $2,265,923.70 was returned with an apportionment of causation attributable to Dr. Hawkins as 65 percent and the hospital as 35 percent. The hospital argued that the trial court erred in failing to grant its motions for directed verdict and for judgment notwithstanding the verdict because of the lack of substantial causation in linking the negligence of the hospital to Mrs. Anthony's death.

Issue

Was the negligence of the hospital superseded by the negligence of the patient's primary care physician, and was the award excessive?

Holding

The Court of Appeals of Kentucky held that negligence of the hospital was not superseded by the negligence of the patient's primary care physician, and the award for 20 days of pain and suffering prior to the patient's death was not excessive.

Reason

The hospital's negligence is based on acts of omission, by failing to check Mrs. Anthony's lungs or to have her examined by a physician, and on positive acts of negligence, such as discharging her in pain. The hospital certainly should have foreseen the injury to Mrs. Anthony because its own staff was questioning the judgments of Dr. Hawkins, while at the same time failing to follow through with the standard of care required of it. All qualified health care providers, within the range of care for the patient, were under a duty to exercise their senses and intelligence to investigate and inspect for potential dangers to her. They did not. Their voluntary ignorance of her condition will grant no relief because voluntary ignorance is negligence. The defense that the hospital's nurses were only following a "chain of command" by doing what Dr. Hawkins ordered is not persuasive. The nurses were not the agents of Dr. Hawkins. All involved had their independent duty to Mrs. Anthony.

The court concluded that § 442 B. of the *Restatement of Torts, Second* satisfies our inquiry whether to hold the hospital liable. It states:

> Where the negligent conduct of the actor [here, the hospital] creates or increases the risk of a particular harm and is a substantial factor in causing that

harm, the fact that the harm is brought about through the intervention of another force [here, Dr. Hawkins] does not relieve the actor of liability, except where the harm is intentionally caused by a third person and is not within the scope of the risk created by the actor's conduct.

The evidence was of a woman conscious of her last days on earth, swollen beyond recognition, tubes exiting almost every orifice of her body, in severe pain, and who deteriorated to the point where she could not verbally communicate with loved ones. Among the last things she did was write out instructions about the care for her newborn child. The trial court, when confronted with a motion for a new trial under CR 59.01(d) on excessive damages, must evaluate the award mirrored against the facts. It is said, if the trial judge does not blush, the award is not excessive. No question, the award was monumental but so was the injury. Clearly, the relationship between the award and the injury in this case is not bizarre. The factual basis supporting the award convinces us there was no error or abuse of discretion in the denial of a new trial on this ground.

Discussion

1. Was Dr. Hawkins' "telephone" assessment of the patient appropriate?
2. How would you apportion negligence among the attending physician, resident, obstetrical nurse, nursing supervisor, and hospital?
3. What are the lessons that should be learned from this case?
4. What educational issues are apparent?

30. DAMAGES/FUTURE LEGAL SERVICES

Citation: *Brownsville-Valley Med. Ctr. v. Gamez*, 871 S.W.2d 781 (Tex. Ct. App. 1994)

Facts

A medical center appealed from an order of the 107th District Court awarding attorney *ad litem* fees in connection with settlement of a medical malpractice case brought on behalf of an infant who was in a vegetative state. The medical center challenged five-sixths of a $40,000 attorney *ad litem* fee awarded to Mr. Gamez.

Diana Diaz (three years of age) and her parents sued the medical center and Dr. Lopez for alleged wrongful acts that left Diana in a vegetative state, requiring constant medical supervision for the remainder of her life. Before trial, the parties negotiated a settlement agreement in which the defendants would create a trust on behalf of Diana with a lump sum of $614,389.27 to provide for Diana's future medical needs. Mr. Gamez, who was appointed attorney *ad litem* on January 16, 1992, after settlement negotiations were complete, approved the settlement agreement on Diana's behalf.

From Diana's award, the plaintiffs' attorneys deducted one-third as attorneys' fees. The defendants agreed that the hospital would pay five-sixths and the doctor would pay one-sixth of the court costs, including *ad litem* fees. The court then awarded Mr. Gamez $40,000 in attorney *ad litem* fees. The appellant argued in the hearing on motion for a new trial that Mr. Gamez's continued involvement with the Diaz case would only duplicate the bank trustee's duties. The trial court denied the appellant's motion for a new trial, but, on its own motion, modified the judgment to order the attorney *ad litem* to perform the following duties: (1) to oversee the trust agreement for Diana, (2) to file a total update of the child's trust with the district clerk every six months, and (3) to maintain an updated and accurate accounting of the trust to explain trust expenditures to Diana and her parents.

The medical center argued that the trial court erred as a matter of law when it awarded future attorney *ad litem* fees, even though both Mr. Garza and Mr. Skaggs, attorneys for the defendants, indicated to the trial court that they anticipated that Mr. Gamez's attorney *ad litem* fee would include future legal services.

Issue

Can an attorney *ad litem* recover for future legal services when the trial court has specifically assigned future duties regarding the same lawsuit?

Holding

The Texas Court of Appeals held that attorney *ad litem* may recover for future legal services when the trial court has specifically assigned future duties regarding the same lawsuit.

Reason

The court held that an attorney *ad litem* may recover for future legal services when the trial court has specifically assigned future duties regarding the same lawsuit. Mr. Gamez and Mr. Rhodes, the plaintiff's attorneys, had indicated that Mr. Gamez would remain intimately involved with Diana's trust. Mr. Gamez had provided the court a copy of a letter

from him to the bank trustee, stating that he intended to remain active in the affairs of the trust.

Discussion

1. Do you agree with the court's findings? Explain.
2. What is the purpose of the trust for Diana?
3. Do trusts have any effect on reducing malpractice costs for defendants? Explain.

31. DAMAGES/PAIN AND SUFFERING/NOT EXCESSIVE

Citation: *In re Medical Review Panel of Cl. of Englert,* 605 So. 2d 1349 (La. 1992)

Facts

The physician appealed from judgment of the trial court entered in favor of the patient in a malpractice action. The court of appeals affirmed the finding of liability but reduced damages.

This malpractice action was brought by Ms. Englert, individually and on behalf of her minor child, Kortnei, against Dr. Chin. The trial court, after a bench trial, found that the defendant physician breached the applicable standard of care in failing to timely diagnose a tumor in the child's head, and awarded damages totaling $225,000. On appeal by the defendant, the court of appeal in an unpublished opinion affirmed the finding of liability but reduced the amount of damages to $10,000, concluding that the only adverse effect of the failure to diagnose the tumor six months earlier was continued headaches and vomiting for the six-month period and perhaps some mental anguish.

The plaintiff argued that the evidence supported a finding that the child was taken to the physician with complaints of headaches more than a year and a half prior to the time that he referred her to a specialist and the tumor was diagnosed. The plaintiff further argued that the evidence supported a finding that had surgery to remove the tumor been performed sooner, the entire tumor could have been removed and the risk of future recurrence would have been reduced, thereby justifying the damage award made by the trial court.

The court of appeal summarized the facts and resolved the liability issue as follows: "In February 1986, when Kortnei was seven years of age, the plaintiff took her to Dr. Chin, her pediatrician, with the complaint of headaches over a long period of time. He ordered a CT scan, which revealed a brain tumor. On February 7, surgery was performed and the tumor was removed except for a portion of it which was located on the brain stem. The tumor was benign and was described as a very slow growing tumor which took years to develop before causing symptoms. The possibility exists that the portion of the tumor at the brain stem will grow in the future, but there was no indication of growth at the time of the trial in August 1990."

The child started vomiting with the headaches sometime before February 1986. The plaintiff testified that she regularly reported this to Dr. Chin. "Plaintiff's testimony was flatly contradicted by Dr. Chin's. He said he was never told about these headaches until February 1986. He said if she had complained it would have been recorded in his records. The trial court resolved the conflict in favor of plaintiff and we are bound by this resolution for appellate purposes."

The court of appeal based its reduction in the amount of damages on the following findings:

Nothing in the record even suggests that Kortnei's condition was aggravated in any way by the delay in diagnosis which is the only fault attributable to Dr. Chin.

The only damages sustained by the child as a result of the tardy diagnosis were a six-month period of headaches, some vomiting, and perhaps some mental anguish for not knowing the nature of the problem six months sooner. An award of $10,000 is the most that could be awarded in the range of discretion. *Id.* at 1350–1351.

Issue

Was an award of $100,000 for pain and suffering based on the physician's delay in diagnosing brain tumor excessive?

Holding

The supreme court held that the award for pain and suffering of $100,000 was excessive to the extent that it exceeded $50,000.

Reason

The court concluded that it stands to reason that the new and additional growth of the tumor during the six-month period, which necessarily forms part of the residual that could not be removed, increased the risk of future recurrence to some extent. The reduction in the amount of the award by the court of appeal does not take into account this element of damage. The severity of the pain and suffering endured by the child during the six-month period was somewhat under-

stated by the court of appeal. The child is entitled to be compensated not only for the pain and suffering she endured during the six-month period, but also for the increased risk, although perhaps somewhat minimal, and its accompanying mental anxiety resulting from the delay in diagnosis and surgery. The court of appeal judgment was amended to increase the award from $10,000 to $50,000.

Discussion

1. Discuss your view of the dissenting judge's opinion that: "In view of the fact that the medical malpractice resulted in the child's worsened condition, the greater difficulty in removal of the tumor, and the child's more gloomy prognosis, I cannot agree that the trial court abused its discretion in assessing damages to the extent found by the majority."
2. What risks do defendants take when they appeal the amount of an award granted to the plaintiff?

32. LOSS OF CHANCE OF RECOVERY

Citation: *Delaney v. Cade*, 873 P.2d 175 (Kan. 1994)

Facts

The plaintiff's (Ms. Delaney) car collided with another automobile. As a result of the accident, she suffered numerous injuries. An ambulance transported her to the hospital. Ms. Delaney complained of chest pain. Dr. Cade, a member of the hospital's staff and the physician on call, began treating her. The plaintiff alleged Dr. Cade commenced suturing the lacerations on her knees without performing a physical examination, ordering X-rays, or starting an IV. After two hours at Memorial Hospital, Dr. Cade transferred her to Central Kansas Medical Center (CKMC). Ms. Delaney alleged she had feeling and movement in her legs when she left Memorial Hospital but had lost that feeling by the time she arrived at CKMC.

At the medical center, a physician performed an aortogram that showed the plaintiff had a transected aorta that had thrombosed. The physician operated on the plaintiff to repair the transected aorta. The plaintiff claimed that as a result of the thrombosed aorta she was permanently paralyzed. She contended Dr. Cade's treatment and his delay in transferring her to a facility that was equipped to treat her injuries deprived her of a significant chance to better recover from her permanent injuries. The plaintiff supported her claims with the deposition testimony of three expert witnesses.

These experts agreed the thrombosis of her aorta caused the plaintiff's paralysis.

> The defendants contend Dr. Harrison was the only witness to testify regarding any loss of chance the plaintiff may have suffered. In his deposition testimony, Dr. Harrison explained 10 percent of patients with thoracic aortic injuries like Ms. Delaney's will suffer permanent paralysis regardless of how the injury is managed. If the plaintiff was in that 10 percent, she would have been a paraplegic no matter how much time passed between the accident and surgery. In addition, Dr. Harrison testified he had no way of determining whether the plaintiff was in that 10 percent or in the other 90 percent. However, Dr. Harrison did state that the plaintiff's risk of cord injury was increased 5 to 10 percent by the prolonged period of shock that she suffered prior to surgery. *Id.* at 178.

The trial court granted partial summary judgment for Dr. Cade, holding Kansas did not recognize the doctrine of significant chance of recovery. Ms. Delaney appealed.

Issue

Does Kansas recognize a cause of action for loss of chance of recovery?

Holding

The Supreme Court of Kansas held that Kansas recognizes a medical malpractice cause of action for loss of chance of recovery.

Reason

"The loss of chance doctrine serves to fairly compensate the plaintiff for the tortious deprivation of an opportunity to live longer or recover from a physical injury or condition inflicted by the defendant's wrongful act or omission. In the medical malpractice context, lost chance endeavors to allow a plaintiff to recover for the diminished chances of surviving or recovering from a disease or malady which results from the health care defendant's malpractice." Keith, *Loss of Chance: A Modern Proportional Approach to Damages in Texas*, 44 Baylor L.Rev. 759, 760 (1992).

The trial court made a determination that Kansas would not recognize such a cause of action in a loss of better recovery case even though it had recognized it in loss of chance for survival cases. The Supreme Court of Kansas found no support for the trial court's position. Although several jurisdictions have refused to recognize such a cause of action in either type of case, the court found no jurisdiction that has applied the theory to one type of case and denied it in the other. As noted by the plaintiff in her brief: "There is certainly nothing in that . . . rationale to justify leaving the season open on persons who suffer paralysis, organ loss, or other serious injury short of death while protecting only those who do not survive the negligence." *Id.* at 183. The court found that the fact that most cases have involved death of the patient and that damages may be difficult to resolve in a loss of a better recovery case, this should not be grounds to refuse to recognize the doctrine when medical malpractice has substantially reduced a person's chance of a better recovery.

In conclusion, the court found: "(1) Kansas does recognize a cause of action for the lost chance for a better recovery due to medical malpractice; (2) to withstand summary judgment, a plaintiff must show that the lost chance for a better recovery was a substantial loss of chance as opposed to a theoretical or de minimis loss; (3) the resulting injury or lessened degree of recovery suffered by the plaintiff as the result of the malpractice must be substantial; and (4) the finder of fact shall calculate the monetary recovery on the basis of the proportional damage approach." *Id.* at 187.

The court felt compelled to express a caveat. "In adopting and applying the loss of chance theory to medical malpractice cases, it must always be kept in mind that the practice of medicine and the furnishing of appropriate health care is not an exact science. In many, if not most, instances there is more than one acceptable approach to treatment, and the fact that one doctor selects one method as opposed to another does not in and of itself mean that one method is better than or preferable to another. For every treatment there are undoubtedly other doctors who might have performed or used a different one. The courts should use extreme caution in second-guessing the methods used by medical care providers, particularly in an area as nebulous as the loss of a chance for a better or more satisfactory recovery." *Id.* at 187.

Discussion

1. Discuss the loss of chance of recovery and the concept of loss of chance of better recovery.
2. What was lacking in the assessment of the patient's immediate needs?
3. What can be done to lessen the likelihood of injuries of this nature?
4. What is the importance of collaboration among caregivers in the treatment of patients in the emergency department setting?

33. EVIDENCE/VERDICT AGAINST THE WEIGHT

Citation: *Agustin v. Beth Israel Hosp.*, 586 N.Y.S.2d 252 (N.Y. App. Div. 1992)

Facts

The plaintiff brought a medical malpractice action to recover damages arising from the fatal injuries suffered by his wife as the result of surgery for a degenerative disc disorder in 1985. The evidence adduced at trial revealed that during the surgery, the instrument used by the surgeon, Dr. Noh, severed three of the decedent's major blood vessels, causing internal bleeding from which she ultimately died. The evidence also revealed that during the operation, the decedent suffered a precipitous drop in blood pressure, which, although potentially indicative of internal bleeding, was not reported to Dr. Noh by the primary anesthesiologist, Dr. Thiagarjah, or by his assistant. Immediately following surgery, the decedent was taken to a recovery room while Dr. Noh went to a nearby room to write his postoperative report. The record is unclear as to when Dr. Noh was summoned and when he ultimately arrived in the recovery room, but it was before 2:10 P.M. when he was recorded as present. After Dr. Noh arrived, further tests were administered, but emergency surgery was not commenced until 3:00 P.M. The surgery was not successful, and the decedent died at 3:51 P.M. Expert testimony convincingly demonstrated that had the surgery been commenced sooner, the chances of decedent's recovery would have been substantially enhanced.

Issue

Was the jury's finding that Dr. Noh was not liable in cutting three of the decedent's major blood vessels during surgery against the weight of the evidence?

Holding

The New York Supreme Court, Appellate Division, held that the jury's finding was against the weight of the evidence.

Reason

The supreme court agreed with the trial court that the jury's finding that Dr. Noh was not liable was against the weight of the evidence and that a new trial was therefore required on the issue of whether Dr. Noh committed medical malpractice that was a proximate cause of the decedent's death. A court should find a verdict to be against the weight of the evidence and set it aside when it finds that "the jury could not have reached its verdict on any fair interpretation of the evidence" (*Yalkut v. City of New York*, 162 A.D.2d 185, 188, 557 N.Y.S.2d 3). Here, the expert testimony overwhelmingly demonstrated that the surgery involved herein did not involve a legitimate risk of the disastrous outcome (the severance of the aorta, vena cava, and iliac artery).

Discussion

1. Why did the supreme court agree with the trial court's finding?

34. BLOOD TRANSFUSION/HEPATITIS/IMPLIED WARRANTY

Citation: *Raskin v. Community Blood Ctrs. of S. Florida, Inc.*, 699 So. 2d 1014 (1997)

Facts

Appellant, Betty Raskin, was hospitalized at Boca Raton Community Hospital in December 1991. While at the hospital, she was transfused with five units of whole blood supplied by appellee, Community Blood Centers of South Florida, Inc. In April 1992, the appellant was readmitted to the hospital, where it was determined she had contracted viral hepatitis B. The treating physicians made entries in the hospital records indicating the transfused blood was the source of the virus. Appellants alleged breach of implied warranty under section 672.316(5), Florida Statutes (1989). The statute provided:

> (5) The procurement, processing, storage, distribution, or use of whole blood, plasma, blood products, and blood derivatives for the purpose of injecting or transfusing the same, or any of them, into the human body for any purpose whatsoever is declared to be the rendering of a service by any person participating therein and does not constitute a sale, whether or not any consideration is given therefor; and the implied warranties of merchantability and fitness for a particular purpose are not applicable as to a defect that cannot be detected or removed by a reasonable use of scientific procedures or techniques. Fla. Stat. § 672.316(5) (1989).

It was appellants' position that their obligation was to show the defect could "be detected or removed by a reasonable use of scientific procedures or techniques." The record plainly showed this to be an issue of fact. Appellants had introduced evidence supporting causation.

Issue

Was it necessary for the appellants to show the appellee was negligent in its testing?

Holding

The appeals court held that it was not necessary for the appellants to show the appellee was negligent in its testing. On remand, the trial court was directed to permit the appellants to amend their cause of action for implied warranty.

Reason

The Florida Supreme Court has held that Florida law prior to the enactment of § 672.316(5) was that blood suppliers were strictly liable for defects in blood, under breach of implied warranties, even when the defect was undetectable. Section 672.316(5) was clearly an effort by the legislature to limit implied warranty actions against blood suppliers.

The only limitation on implied warranty cause of actions specified and plainly pronounced in § 672.316(5) is that they "are not applicable as to a defect that cannot be detected or removed by a reasonable use of scientific procedures or techniques." The statute does not specify or state that the plaintiff must allege and prove negligence of the blood supplier in performing the scientific procedures or techniques. Such requirement in the statute would not make sense because the plaintiff in an implied warranty action would have the same burden as the plaintiff in a negligence action.

Application of § 672.316(5), Florida Statutes, provides that a plaintiff may maintain an action for damages on the grounds of breach of implied warranty of fitness or merchantability only if he alleges and proves that the defect of which he complains is detectable or removable by the use of reasonable scientific procedures or techniques.

Discussion

1. Why must a defect be detectable in order for a suit to be filed on the basis of implied warranty?
2. If the appellants could show that the appellee was negligent in its testing of blood for hepatitis, could liability be established for negligent conduct? Discuss.

35. GOOD SAMARITAN STATUTE/IN-HOSPITAL EMERGENCY/IMMUNITY

Citation: *Hirpa v. IHC Hosps., Inc.*, 948 P.2d 785 (Utah 1997)

Facts

Ms. Wordoffa was admitted to Logan Regional Hospital in active labor prior to the birth of her third child. Shortly after the arrival of her personal obstetrician, Dr. Mortenson, Ms. Wordoffa became unresponsive and her hands began to spasm. Dr. Mortenson immediately delivered the baby using forceps and then, after finding that Ms. Wordoffa had no heartbeat or respiration, called a "Code Blue" that was broadcast over the hospital intercom.

The hospital's medical director, Dr. Daines, a specialist in internal medicine, cardiology, and emergency medicine, heard and responded to the Code Blue. Upon arriving at the delivery room, he was asked to "take over" Ms. Wordoffa's care, which he did. He subsequently directed the other members of the response team and made decisions regarding Ms. Wordoffa's care. Seventeen minutes after the arrival of the response team, Dr. Daines declared Ms. Wordoffa dead.

Mr. Hirpa, the surviving spouse of Ms. Wordoffa, individually and as the natural parent and guardian of Ms. Wordoffa's children, filed suit in the United States Court for the District of Utah. Mr. Hirpa alleged negligence on the part of five defendants: IHC Hospitals d.b.a. Logan Regional Hospital; Dr. Daines; Dr. Mortenson; the Logan Women's Clinic, which employed Dr. Mortenson; and Dr. Bienz, to whom the decedent had been referred by Dr. Mortenson early in her pregnancy for treatment of rheumatoid arthritis.

Dr. Daines had moved for summary judgment on the grounds that he was immune from liability for negligence in his treatment of Ms. Wordoffa. He contended that he was acting as a volunteer and was therefore protected by Utah Code Ann. § 58-12-23, Utah's Good Samaritan Act. The State filed a memorandum asserting that the statute should be liberally construed to include emergencies occurring in a hospital setting in order to promote the public policy of encouraging physicians who happen to be in the hospital and are available to provide assistance but that the statute should not be applied to immunize a physician with a preexisting duty to render aid. Thereafter, the trial court denied Dr. Daines's motion, ruling that the statute is constitutional and applies in a hospital setting but that "whether" Dr. Daines had a preexisting duty is a legal question.

Following further discovery, Dr. Daines renewed his motion for summary judgment, asserting that he had no preexisting duty to Ms. Wordoffa as a matter of law. IHC joined Dr. Daines's motion, arguing that it could have no vicarious liability for Dr. Daines's actions if he was immune from liability. The trial court ruled that Dr. Daines had no preexisting duty to Ms. Wordoffa as a matter of law and was therefore immune from liability under the Good Samaritan Act and that IHC could not be liable on a *respondeat superior* theory or otherwise.

Plaintiff appealed from the trial court's grant of summary judgment to the United States Court of Appeals for the Tenth Circuit. After reviewing the issues presented, that court concluded that (1) the Good Samaritan Act is silent as to whether it applies to emergencies occurring in hospital settings; (2) there are no Utah appellate decisions construing the statute; and (3) other state court decisions construing statutes that are silent as to whether they apply in a hospital setting reach inconsistent results. The Tenth Circuit certified questions as to the interpretation of § 58-12-23 and the Utah Constitution to the State of Utah Supreme Court as it appeared that its interpretations may be dispositive in this case. The question discussed here concerns the interpretation of § 58-12-23.

Issue

Whether physicians employed by a hospital and responding to in-hospital emergency situations are entitled to immunity under Utah Code Ann. § 58-12-23 (1996) (the Good Samaritan Statute).

Holding

Utah Code Ann. § 58-12-23 affords immunity to a physician rendering emergency medical care at the scene of an emergency occurring in a hospital, if the physician is under no preexisting duty to do so.

Reason

Utah's Good Samaritan Act, covering licensed medical providers, states "No person licensed under this chapter . . . who in good faith renders emergency care at the scene of the emergency, shall be liable for any civil damages as a result of any acts or omissions by such person in rendering the emergency care" Utah Code Ann. § 58-12-23 (1996).

Plaintiff contends that the term "emergency" in the phrase "emergency care at the scene of an emergency" is unclear and that therefore no "plain meaning" exists. On this basis, plaintiff argues that the statutory definition of emergency contained in § 78-11-22, a Good Samaritan act for lay persons, should be incorporated into the provisions of § 58-12-23.

The court found this argument to be without merit. The term "emergency" is not unclear or ambiguous. "Emergency" is defined as an "unexpected situation or occurrence that demands immediate attention." *American Heritage Dictionary* 232 (2d Coll. ed. 1983). This definition, synonymous with the common understanding of the term, gives courts adequate guidance to decide which factual scenarios qualify as emergencies and therefore fall within the coverage of the statute.

The court believed that even if the term "emergency" in § 58-12-23 were unclear and § 78-11-22's definition of emergency were incorporated into the statute, that § 78-11-22's definition of emergency includes the facts presented by this case. That section defines "emergency" as "an unexpected occurrence involving injury, threat of injury, or illness to a person or the public, including motor vehicle accidents, disasters, actual or threatened discharges, removal, or disposal of hazardous materials, and other accidents or events of a similar nature." The plaintiff contended that "an emergency arising at a hospital during a medical procedure is not an emergency event similar in nature to motor vehicle accidents, disasters or discharges of hazardous materials." However, the plaintiff focused on the terms "motor vehicle accidents, disasters" and "discharges of hazardous materials," forgetting that these are merely examples of situations "included" within the broader definition of emergency. The facts of this case would appear to fall within the broader definition of "an unexpected occurrence involving injury . . . or illness." Even if the court had believed it necessary to incorporate § 78-11-22's definition, it is broad enough that it would not significantly alter the dictionary definition of emergency adopted above.

The plaintiff maintained that the background of Good Samaritan acts and public policy considerations support exclusion of emergency care provided by physicians at emergencies arising in a hospital setting. The court disagreed. Applying the Utah Good Samaritan Act in this case actually furthers the purpose and intent of the legislation.

At common law, there is no affirmative duty to rescue. However, the common law recognizes that once a person chooses to rescue another, he or she is held to a duty of due care.

Good Samaritan statutes encourage licensed providers, whose training and expertise may be beneficial in preserving human life but who have no duty to aid, to respond to emergencies whenever and wherever they arise. A patient in a hospital may need emergency care from a volunteer provider as much as any other emergency victim. In addition, it seems arbitrary to subject a volunteer provider who responds to an emergency, although not obligated to do so, to liability merely because his or her volunteer acts occurred in a hospital. Thus, § 58-12-23 applies without regard to location.

The court's reasoning necessarily compels the result that § 58-12-23 does not apply in a situation involving a preexisting duty to render aid. In that case, no additional encouragement to the provider is needed because he or she already has a duty to respond to the emergency situation. The purpose of encouraging volunteerism would not be furthered because the responding provider could not be considered a volunteer. Rather, he or she would be compelled by a legal duty to act.

If the physician had a particular employment duty to aid the patient at the hospital, then he or she had a duty to the patient to begin with; and in such a case that physician does not need a special inducement to offer aid, the aid offered is not "voluntary" in the sense of a Good Samaritan, and public policy would be ill served if he or she were relieved of the usual physician's duty of care and given immunity in such a case.

Such a duty may arise in a variety of ways. Courts or juries deciding whether a duty existed in a particular case may consider whether the physician was "on call" or otherwise contractually obligated to respond, whether hospital rules required that the physician respond, whether a physician–patient relationship existed, whether employment by the hospital created a duty, or whether a duty was created by the practice or custom of the physician responding to similar emergencies.

Discussion

1. Under what circumstances would a physician be immune from liability under Utah's Good Samaritan Statute when assisting in an in-hospital emergency?
2. Under what circumstances would a physician "not" be immune from liability under Utah's Good Samaritan Statute when assisting in an in-hospital emergency?
3. Should a physician who has been assigned on-call duty in a hospital's emergency department be covered under Good Samaritan statutes? Discuss when coverage under such statutes would be "appropriate" and when it would be "inappropriate."

36. SUMMARY JUDGMENT FOR DEFENDANTS/ APPROPRIATE

Citation: *Taylor v. McCullough-Hyde Mem'l*, 688 N.E.2d 1078 (Ohio App. 1996)

Facts

On March 9, 1992, Theresa Taylor was admitted to the emergency department of McCullough-Hyde Memorial Hospital in Oxford, Ohio, after complaining of chest pain and was subsequently discharged. On March 10, 1992, Ms. Taylor saw Dr. Hunt for further testing and returned home.

Later that same day, Ms. Taylor returned to the emergency department of McCullough-Hyde with complaints of acute abdominal pain. During this visit, Ms. Taylor was treated by Dr. Durbin, who discharged her after reviewing the results of several tests. On March 11, 1992, Dr. Hunt admitted Ms. Taylor to the intensive care unit at McCullough-Hyde. On March 12, 1992, Ms. Taylor was transferred to Christ Hospital in Cincinnati, where she underwent surgery to correct a hemorrhaging aneurysm in her lower abdomen.

Appellants filed a medical malpractice action against Dr. Hunt and Dr. Durbin arising out of the alleged negligent care and treatment of Ms. Taylor. The complaint alleged that Dr. Hunt's and Dr. Durbin's failure to diagnose Ms. Taylor's condition proximately resulted in harm to appellants.

Following the deposition of appellants' expert, Dr. LeWitt, Dr. Hunt and Dr. Durbin filed separate motions for summary judgment on the ground that appellants had failed to present any evidence that would support a finding that the alleged negligence of Dr. Hunt and Dr. Durbin proximately caused Ms. Taylor any harm. The trial court granted the motions for summary judgment and Ms. Taylor appealed.

Issue

Did the trial court commit reversible error in granting the defendants, Dr. Durbin and Dr. Hunt, summary judgment? Did the trial court commit reversible error in granting the defendant, Dr. Hunt, assessing costs and ordering costs, fees, and expenses in the sum of $2,899.30?

Holding

The appeals court found that the trial court did not err in granting summary judgment in favor of Dr. Hunt and Dr. Durbin. In addition, the trial court did not abuse its discretion in awarding attorney fees.

Reason

In the appellants' first issue, the appellants asserted that the trial court erred in granting summary judgment to appellees on the issue of damages because, appellants claim, they presented expert testimony that established damages with reasonable probability. The trial court concluded that appellants failed to produce sufficient evidence that appellees deviated from accepted standard of medical care and that the deviation, if any, was the proximate cause of appellants' alleged harm.

Summary judgment is appropriately rendered when (1) no genuine issue as to any material fact remains to be litigated; (2) the moving party is entitled to judgment as a matter of law; and (3) it appears from the evidence that reasonable minds can come to but one conclusion, and viewing such evidence most strongly in favor of the party against whom the motion for summary judgment is made, that conclusion is adverse to that party.

In order to establish a cognizable claim of medical malpractice, a plaintiff must show the existence of a standard of care within the medical community, breach of that standard of care by the defendant, and proximate cause between the medical negligence and the injury sustained. In addressing the issue of proximate cause, a plaintiff in a malpractice case must prove that defendant's negligence, in probability, proximately caused the death. It is well settled in medical malpractice cases that expert medical testimony is necessary to establish the causal connection between the negligence and the injury whenever the relationship is beyond the common knowledge and understanding of the jury.

The record discloses that Dr. LeWitt was the appellants' sole expert witness. When testifying in his deposition, Dr. LeWitt stated that he had no opinion regarding the care provided to Ms. Taylor, or as to any causal connection between that care and any resulting harm. Dr. LeWitt further testified that he was unable to state with reasonable medical probability whether the outcome would have been any different had Ms. Taylor been hospitalized sooner.

The record revealed that appellants failed to present sufficient evidence that Dr. Hunt and Dr. Durbin deviated from the standard of care or that any such deviation proximately caused any legally recognized injury to appellants. The appeals court concluded that the trial court did not err in granting summary judgment in favor of Dr. Hunt and Dr. Durbin.

As to the appellants' second issue, the appellants contended that the trial court erred in assessing certain costs and expenses incurred by Dr. Hunt associated with Dr. LeWitt's deposition. The costs and expenses that the trial court ordered included attorney fees and court reporter deposition expenses, as well as airfare, car rental, parking fees, mileage, and meal allowances incurred by Dr. Hunt's counsel in traveling to Pennsylvania for the deposition.

Both an assessment of costs and an award of attorney fees were found to be within the sound discretion of the trial court and would not be overturned on appeal absent an abuse of discretion. An abuse of discretion implies that a court's attitude is unreasonable, arbitrary, or unconscionable.

The general rule in Ohio is that a prevailing party may not recover attorney fees as part of the costs of litigation in the absence of statutory authorization. An exception to this general rule permits an award of attorney fees when the party against whom the fees are taxed is found to have acted in bad faith.

The trial court determined that the attorney fees ordered could have been avoided if appellants had told Dr. Hunt that Dr. LeWitt had no opinion regarding Dr. Hunt's actions. Thus, the trial court found that an award of attorney fees incurred by Dr. Hunt to have his counsel attend Dr. LeWitt's deposition was warranted under a bad-faith theory. The appeals court found that the trial court did not abuse its discretion in awarding attorney fees.

The appellants contended that the trial court abused its discretion in awarding deposition expenses as costs. Civ.R. 54(D) states: "Costs. Except when express provision therefor is made either in a statute or in these rules, costs shall be allowed to the prevailing party unless the court otherwise directs."

To be taxable as a cost under Civ.R. 54(D), an expense must be grounded in statute. The statutory basis for taxing the expense of the services of a court reporter at a deposition and the production of a transcript as a cost under Civ.R. 54(D) is R.C. 2319.27. No statutory authority exists for the reimbursement of travel expenses. Accordingly, the appeals court concluded that the court reporter services and resulting transcript fee connected with Dr. LeWitt's deposition may be taxed as costs under Civ.R. 54(D). The trial court did, however, abuse its discretion in ordering an assessment of Dr. Hunt's travel expenses against appellants.

Based on the record, the appeals court modified the trial court's order assessing costs, fees, and expenses against appellants by reducing the amount awarded to $2,053.15.

Discussion

1. Describe how the plaintiff–appellant's expert witness affected the outcome of this case.
2. In general, what actions should hospital emergency departments take to improve patient outcomes?

37. CLASS ACTION/FOOD POISONING

Citation: *Connerwood Healthcare, Inc. v. Estate of Herron,* 683 N.E.2d 1322 (Ind. App. 1997)

Facts

In June 1995, approximately 70 people at the Connerwood residential nursing facility developed symptoms of food poisoning. Thirty-four residents tested positive for salmonella, and 3 died during the outbreak. The estate of one of the residents who died from the alleged salmonella infection filed suit against Connerwood and requested that the case be maintained as a class action. The complaint alleged that Connerwood's negligence caused injury to the residents.

The trial court issued the following findings: (1) In June 1995 there occurred an outbreak of salmonella poisoning at the facility, as evidenced by the Indiana State Health Report; (2) up to 70 residents and employees were affected; (3) the poisoning resulted in physical illness and several deaths; and (4) given the older age and infirm physical condition of many of the residents, certification of this case as a class action would be appropriate in order to fairly and adequately protect the interests of this class. The court concluded that the plaintiffs had satisfied Indiana Trial Rule 23 and conditionally certified the matter as a class action. Connerwood appealed and argued that the claim failed to meet the requirements of class action certification.

Issue

Did the trial court abuse its discretion when it conditionally certified the case as a class action?

Holding

The court of appeals held that the trial court did not abuse its discretion when it conditionally certified the case as a class action.

Reason

The determination of whether an action is maintainable as a class action is committed to the sound discretion of the trial court. The appeals court reviewed the trial court's ruling by employing an abuse of discretion standard. The appeals court neither reweighed evidence nor judged witness credibility. In determining the propriety of class action certification, the trial court must determine whether the class meets the prerequisites of Indiana Trial Rule 23, generally known as numerosity, commonality, typicality, and adequacy of representation.

Connerwood argued that the plaintiff did not meet the numerosity requirement because only 34 people tested positive for salmonella. The Indiana State Department of Health

had reported that 70 people became ill after having been served scrambled eggs. The actual number of persons affected is irrelevant; the real inquiry under the rule is whether joinder would be impractical. The inquiry requires the court to consider judicial economy and the ability of the class members to institute individual suits. The court found that given the age and physical condition of the residents affected by the food poisoning, certification was appropriate and not impractical in order to fairly and adequately protect the interests of this class. Although the number of class members is small, they would have been unable to protect their interests and pursue remedies on an individual basis.

The commonality requirement is satisfied if the individual claims are derived from a common course of conduct. The plaintiff claimed that the negligent use and preparation of nonpasteurized egg products caused the food poisoning. The court concluded that this constitutes a common course of conduct and therefore satisfies the commonality requirement.

Typicality focuses on the desired characteristics of the class representative. Connerwood argued that the plaintiff's claim for wrongful death is shared by only two other residents, while the claims of the other residents are based on common law negligence. Connerwood also argued that the derivative claims of the plaintiff are different in kind and degree from those of other class members. It is not required that all plaintiffs' claims in a class action be identical. The element is satisfied if the representative claims are neither in conflict with or antagonistic to the class as a whole. The cause of action in this case rests on the single course of Connerwood's alleged negligent behavior; therefore, the court concluded that the evidence supports findings of typicality.

The court also determined that class action treatment is a superior method of adjudication in this case. The potential class members are elderly, medically compromised, and may be incapable of exercising their own rights. Both state and federal courts have determined that class action treatment is appropriate for a mass tort such as food poisoning.

Discussion

1. Why did the appeals court uphold the findings of the trial court?
2. Do you agree with the court's holding? Explain.

V

Corporate Liability

1. MEDICAL STAFF PRIVILEGES/NEGLIGENCE

Citation: *Candler Gen. Hosp., Inc. v. Persaud*, 442 S.E.2d 775 (Ga. Ct. App. 1994)

Facts

On or about February 15, 1990, Ms. Persaud was referred to Dr. Freeman for consultation and treatment of infected gallstones. Dr. Freeman recommended that Ms. Persaud undergo a laparoscopic laser cholecystectomy.

On February 16, 1990, Dr. Freeman requested and was granted temporary privileges to perform the procedure. He submitted a certificate of completion of a laparoscopic laser cholecystectomy workshop, which he took on February 10, 1990. The cholecystectomy was performed by Dr. Freeman, who was assisted by Dr. Thomas, on February 20, 1990.

A complaint by the administrator of the patient's estate, supported by an expert's affidavit, alleged that the cholecystectomy was negligently performed, as a result of which the patient bled to death. The complaint charged the hospital with negligence in permitting Dr. Freeman, assisted by Dr. Thomas, to perform the procedure on the decedent without having instituted any standards, training requirements, protocols, or otherwise instituted any method for judging the qualifications of a surgeon to perform the procedure. The complaint also alleged that the hospital knew or reasonably should have known that it did not have a credentialing process that could have assured the hospital of the physicians' education, training, and ability to perform the procedure.

The trial court denied the hospital's motion for summary judgment on the ground that the plaintiffs' evidence was sufficient to raise a question of fact regarding whether a surgical permit should have been issued by the hospital to Dr. Freeman. The hospital appealed.

Issue

Was there a material issue of fact as to whether the hospital was negligent in granting the specific privileges requested by Dr. Freeman?

Holding

The Court of Appeals of Georgia held that there was a material issue of fact as to whether the hospital was negligent in granting the specific privileges requested, thus precluding summary judgment.

Reason

The hospital argued that there is no cause of action against a hospital based solely on the issuance of a surgical permit for a specific procedure to an independent surgeon already duly and properly appointed to its active surgical staff. The plaintiff in *Joiner v. Mitchell County Hosp. Auth.,* 125 Ga. Ct. App. 1, 2(1), 186 S.E.2d 307 (1971), *aff'd*, 229 Ga. 140, 189 S.E.2d 412 (1972), "who had brought her husband into the hospital for emergency treatment, alleged that the negligence of the treating physician who was on the staff of the hospital resulted in her husband's death. She also sought to hold the hospital liable, not under the doctrine of *respondeat superior* or principal and agent, but rather upon the doctrine of independent negligence, in permitting the alleged negligent physician to practice his profession in the hospital when his incompetency was known. 229 Ga. at 141, 189 S.E.2d 412. *Joiner* identified negligence as failing to investigate and require satisfactory proof of the physician's qualifications and as failing to exercise care in determining his professional competency." *Id.* at 777.

The court of appeals found that the question "in this case is whether this authority recognized by the Supreme Court in *Joiner* gives rise to a duty which the hospital owes to a patient when: (1) the patient rather than the hospital selected the independent staff surgeon to perform the procedure at issue, and (2) the hospital was allegedly negligent, not in its appointment or retention of the surgeon on its staff, but rather in its grant to him of privileges to practice a procedure which he allegedly was not qualified to perform." *Id.* at 777.

The court interpreted *Joiner* as authority to support the proposition that a hospital has a direct and independent responsibility to its patients to take reasonable steps to ensure that staff physicians using hospital facilities are qualified for privileges granted. The hospital owed a duty to the plaintiffs' decedent to act in good faith and with reasonable care to ensure that the surgeon was qualified to practice the procedure that he was granted privileges to perform. While there was no evidence of Dr. Freeman's curtailment or denial of staff privileges at other hospitals, the hospital did not dispute that there was a material issue of fact on the question of whether it was negligent in its granting of the staff privileges requested.

Discussion

1. Do you agree that the hospital was negligent in the granting of the privileges requested by Dr. Freeman?
2. If the patient had suffered no injuries, do you think the plaintiffs could have recovered any monetary damages?
3. What credentialing issues are evident in this case?

2. VICARIOUS LIABILITY

Citation: *Citron v. Northern Dutchess Hosp.*, 603 N.Y.S.2d 639 (N.Y. App. Div. 1993)

Facts

A deceased patient's husband instituted an action against Northern Dutchess Hospital for negligence, asserting that it failed to have blood products available for his wife who suffered a ruptured uterus. The patient, 26 weeks pregnant, had complained to her obstetrician about back pain, cramps, and nausea. She was told to go to the hospital's emergency department. It was determined by personnel there that she was suffering from intra-abdominal bleeding. While undergoing surgery performed by her obstetrician, it was learned that her uterus had ruptured. Four hours following surgery, she died of anoxia due to loss of one-half of her total blood. Other than with her obstetrician, she had no physician–patient relationship with any of the emergency department physicians. The trial court jury found in favor of the plaintiff, and the hospital appealed.

Issue

Can a hospital be held vicariously liable for an independent physician's negligent acts, if the patient enters the emergency department and seeks treatment from the hospital, and not a specific physician?

Holding

The New York Supreme Court, Appellate Division, upheld the trial court's decision, finding that the hospital was vicariously liable for the acts of its emergency department physicians, which included treating the deceased without having the necessary blood products available.

Reason

Although neither the patient nor her husband asked for a specific physician once she was admitted to the emergency department, the court found that she "could properly assume that the treating doctors and staff of the hospital were acting on behalf of the hospital. . . ." *Id.* at 641. Expert testimony had revealed that the failure to provide the decedent with proper blood products was a major factor in her death. The court further held that it was a deviation from accepted practice for the hospital not to have platelets on hand or "available within one hour." *Id.* at 639.

Discussion

1. What steps should the hospital take to prevent further incidents of this nature?
2. What issues do you see as to the assessment and reassessment of the patient's needs?

3. *RESPONDEAT SUPERIOR*/RADIOLOGIST/ HOSPITAL NOT LIABLE

Citation: *Hoffman v. Moore Reg'l Hosp., Inc.*, 441 S.E.2d 567 (N.C. Ct. App. 1994)

Facts

Mrs. Hoffman was admitted to the hospital by Dr. Neal, her attending physician, with an order for a renal arteriogram. The hospital informed Dr. Neal that he could not order the procedure because he did not have staff privileges at the hospital. Therefore, Dr. Neal made arrangements with Dr. Daughtridge to order the procedure. After her admission, Mrs. Hoffman was presented with a consent form for the procedure. The consent listed five radiologists on the form but did not specify which radiologist would perform the procedure. The list of radiologists was composed of members of the Pinehurst radiology group. The group determined which radiologist would cover the hospital each day. Dr. Lina was assigned to perform Mrs. Hoffman's procedure. Following the renal arteriogram, Dr. Lina determined that an angioplasty was necessary. Because of complications during the procedure, Mrs. Hoffman had to be transferred to University Medical Center. Her condition deteriorated during the following year and she eventually died. Mr. Hoffman then sought to hold the hospital liable for the negligence of the radiologist under the theory of *respondeat superior*. The trial court granted partial summary judgment against the hospital, dismissing the claim that the hospital was liable under the theory of *respondeat superior*.

Issue

Was the hospital liable for the malpractice of Dr. Lina under the theory of *respondeat superior*?

Holding

The Court of Appeals of North Carolina held that the hospital was not liable for the negligence of Dr. Lina under the theory of *respondeat superior*.

Reason

The court of appeals held that Dr. Lina was not an employee of the hospital. He was not subject to supervision or control by the hospital. There was no evidence that Mrs. Hoffman would have sought treatment elsewhere if she had known for a fact that Dr. Lina was not an employee.

Discussion

1. Under what conditions could the hospital have been liable for Dr. Lina's alleged negligence?
2. Can the patient recover damages from the radiologist who performed the radiologic procedure?
3. Can the patient recover damages from the Pinehurst radiology group?

4. EMERGENCY MEDICAL TECHNICIAN NEGLIGENCE/HOSPITAL NOT LIABLE

Citation: *Riffe v. Vereb Ambulance Serv., Inc.*, 650 A.2d 1076 (Pa. Super. 1994)

Facts

Sonja L. Riffe and Robert B. Anderson, coadministrators of the estate of Steven D. Anderson, deceased, take this appeal from the Order of April 20, 1994, denying plaintiffs' motion to remove "compulsory nonsuit," in which the trial court, after reviewing the papers submitted by both the plaintiff and the defendant, determined that there was no evidence of liability against the defendant–hospital. The underlying wrongful death action was filed by appellants on March 27, 1992, against Vereb Ambulance Service, St. Francis Hospital, and Valerie Custozzo. The complaint alleged that on March 30, 1990, defendant Custozzo, an emergency medical technician employed by Vereb Ambulance Service, while responding to an emergency call regarding Steven Anderson, began administering to Mr. Anderson the drug lidocaine, as ordered over the telephone by the medical command physician at defendant hospital. While en route to the hospital, Mr. Anderson was administered an amount of lidocaine 44 times the normal dosage. Consequently, normal heart function was not restored and Mr. Anderson was pronounced dead at the hospital shortly thereafter.

Issue

Can the emergency medical technician's negligence be imputed to the hospital?

Holding

The Superior Court held that the liability of medical technicians could not be imputed to the hospital, and action against the hospital based on the theory of vicarious liability was barred by earlier settlement by the ambulance company and technician.

Reason

The trial court noted the practical impossibility of the hospital carrying ultimate responsibility for the quality of care and treatment given patients by Emergency Medical Services (EMS). This is propounded proportionately in relation to the density of the population, numbers of hospitals, and number of EMS services. It becomes obvious that the focus of training and monitoring of such services must lie with the EMS regional and local councils pursuant to and subject to regulations promulgated by the Department of Health. While hospitals, as facilities, participate in the overall operation of EMS services, the hospital command facility derives its function from the law and regulations relating to the operation of EMS. The networking of EMS and command facilities is such that they have a common interrelated function that is apart from the administration of the hospitals to which they are attached. Because EMS may be involved with several hospitals depending on specialization, and even allowing for patients' directions, a hospital's legal responsibility for the operation of any given EMS becomes too tenuous. The Superior Court found no error by the trial court in determining that no liability could be imputed on the part of St. Francis Hospital.

Discussion

1. Do you agree with the court's decision? Why?
2. What effect might a finding for the plaintiffs have on hospital-based EMS services?
3. What might the decision of the court have been if the ambulance was owned and operated by the hospital and the ambulance technicians were employees of the hospital?

5. CREDENTIALING PHYSICIANS

Citation: *Corrigan v. Methodist Hosp.*, 869 F. Supp. 1208 (E.D. Pa. 1994)

Facts

The plaintiff first sought medical treatment for back pain from the defendant physicians, Dr. Davne and Dr. Myers.

After several months of treatment for this condition, Dr. Davne and Dr. Myers purportedly represented to Ms. Corrigan that surgery was the only available option to improve her condition. Ms. Corrigan was admitted to defendant Methodist and underwent lumbar fusion surgery.

Following her discharge, Ms. Corrigan continued to be followed by Dr. Davne and Dr. Myers, who prescribed various narcotic medications to relieve the continued intractable pain in her back and legs, muscle spasms, and cramping. These symptoms apparently failed to abate and, in fact, grew worse with time. Ms. Corrigan consulted Dr. Kotopka, Dr. Esterhai, and Dr. Cheatal at the Hospital of the University of Pennsylvania. After several clinical examinations and tests, including magnetic resonance imaging (MRI), she was diagnosed as suffering from a thoracic meningiomal tumor.

Ms. Corrigan filed a lawsuit alleging that Methodist violated the doctrine of corporate negligence in that Methodist negligently permitted use of the Acromed VSP plate and pedicle screw system and negligently extended staff privileges to Dr. Davne and Dr. Myers. In addition, the complaint alleges that the defendant physicians and Methodist Hospital failed to obtain her informed consent for the lumbar fusion surgery in that she was not advised that they planned to use VSP screws in the surgery; there was a risk of screw failure that could lead to an increase in pain, suffering, and disability; and the use of the VSP screws in the spine was still considered investigational for use in lumbar fusion procedures. The complaint alleged that all defendants were negligent in failing to appropriately diagnose and treat Ms. Corrigan's meningiomal tumor with the result that she was forced to suffer unnecessary surgery and pain. The defendants filed a motion for summary judgment.

Issue

Do the pleadings, depositions, answers to interrogatories, and admissions on file, together with the affidavits, show a genuine issue of material fact?

Holding

The district court held that material fact issues existed as to the patient's claims regarding the hospital's liability for use of screws in surgery, for credentialing physicians, and for failing to obtain the patient's informed consent.

Reason

Many of Ms. Corrigan's claims are based on the theory of corporate negligence. Corporate negligence is a doctrine under which the hospital is liable if it fails to uphold the proper standard of care owed the patient, which is to ensure the patient's safety and well-being while at the hospital. Hospitals in general have a duty to

1. Use reasonable care in the maintenance of safe and adequate facilities and equipment.
2. Select and retain only competent physicians.
3. Oversee all persons who practice medicine within its walls as to patient care.
4. Formulate, adopt, and enforce adequate rules and policies to ensure quality care for the patients.

Methodist argued that the VSP screws have not caused Ms. Corrigan any harm; therefore, she has no claim for negligence. In addition, it asserts that Ms. Corrigan must establish, through expert testimony, the connection between the hospital's conduct and the resulting harm complained of in order to prove corporate negligence. The court concluded that Ms. Corrigan has shown a cognizable injury. Ms. Corrigan's experts, including Dr. Alexander and Dr. Kaufman, have opined that Methodist's inadequate policies and practices made it possible for Dr. Davne and Dr. Myers to use the VSP screws on her spine, and therefore suffer the alleged injuries. This is sufficient to show causation. There is a genuine issue of material fact as to whether Methodist's alleged negligence is causally connected to the alleged injuries.

Methodist asserts that there is no evidence to support Ms. Corrigan's negligent credentialing claim. It bases this argument on the theory that Ms. Corrigan's expert on this issue, Dr. Kaufman, improperly relied on privileged peer review material to form his opinion. Methodist informed the court that it would be filing a motion to strike Dr. Kaufman's expert opinion, but had not done so at the time of the court's opinion. Beyond the peer review argument, Methodist presented no legal argument to support its motion for summary judgment. No evidence was presented to show that Dr. Davne and Dr. Myers were properly credentialed.

In contrast, Ms. Corrigan's expert, Dr. Kaufman, opines that Methodist Hospital failed in its duty to Ms. Corrigan by granting privileges to Dr. Davne and Dr. Myers. He apparently based this opinion on both the allegedly privileged quarterly staff meeting minutes of September 19, 1991, and the fact that Dr. Davne had previous medical malpractice suits brought against him.

The court did not rule on whether or not Dr. Kaufman could rely on the quarterly minutes for his opinion. The court drew inferences finding that credentialing physicians with knowledge of, or failure to learn of, their malpractice history could be negligent. This finding was sufficient to raise a genuine issue of material fact as to whether Methodist negligently credentialed Dr. Davne and Dr. Myers. The defendant's motion for summary judgment on this claim was denied.

Discussion

1. What information should be requested from a physician who is seeking specific privileges to perform a new procedure?
2. What should an organization be concerned with when credentialing physicians?
3. Who should be involved in the credentialing process?

6. ANESTHESIA CARE/CORPORATE NEGLIGENCE

Citation: *Denton Reg'l Med. Ctr. v. LaCroix*, 947 S.W.2d 941 (Tex. Ct. App. 1997)

Facts

In the early morning of January 25, 1991, appellees Mr. and Ms. LaCroix went to the Women's Pavilion of appellant Denton Regional Medical Center (the hospital; DRMA) for the birth of their first child, Lawryn. Ms. LaCroix was admitted to the hospital under the care of her obstetrician, Dr. Dulemba. The Women's Pavilion, which opened in 1986, provided 24-hour anesthesia care.

Ms. LaCroix underwent a C-section. Mr. LaCroix was in the operating room for the C-section. Before the C-section began, Ms. LaCroix complained several times of breathing difficulty. When Dr. McGehee, the pediatrician who was going to treat the infant after she was delivered, arrived in the operating room, he noticed that Ms. LaCroix appeared to be in respiratory distress and heard her say, "I can't breathe." Dr. McGehee asked Ms. Blankenship if Ms. LaCroix was okay, and she responded that Ms. LaCroix was just nervous. Mr. LaCroix testified that soon after that, Ms. LaCroix's eyes "got big" and she whispered again to him that she could not breathe. Mr. LaCroix shouted, "She can't breathe. Somebody please help my wife." Ms. Blankenship asked that Mr. LaCroix be removed from the operating room because Ms. LaCroix was having what appeared to her to be a seizure. Mr. LaCroix was escorted out of the operating room.

The nurse, Ms. Blankenship, could not establish an airway with an airbag and mask because Ms. LaCroix's teeth were clenched shut from the seizure. She told one of the nurses: "Get one of the anesthesiologists here now!" Dr. Green, who was in his car, was paged. When he received the page, he immediately drove to the Women's Pavilion. Dr. Dulemba was already making the C-section incision when the seizure occurred, and he told Ms. Blankenship that Ms. LaCroix's blood was dark, as opposed to oxygenated blood, which is bright red. When Lawryn was delivered, she was not breathing, and Dr. McGehee had to resuscitate her.

Meanwhile, to intubate Ms. LaCroix to establish an airway for her, Ms. Blankenship had to paralyze her, using the drug Anectine, and put her to sleep, using sodium pentothal, a general anesthetic. She was then able to intubate Ms. LaCroix, but it was an esophageal intubation, rather than tracheal. After Dr. Dulemba, who was still working inside Ms. LaCroix's abdomen, pointed out that he thought that the intubation was esophageal, Ms. Blankenship removed the tube and successfully intubated Ms. LaCroix.

While Dr. Dulemba was closing the C-section incisions, Ms. LaCroix's blood pressure and pulse dropped, and Ms. Blankenship gave her ephedrine to try to raise her blood pressure. Ms. LaCroix then became asystole—she went into full cardiac arrest and her heart stopped beating. A physician and nurse from the hospital's emergency department had responded to a code for assistance and came into the operating room. Dr. McGehee testified that the emergency department physician said that he did not know how to resuscitate pregnant women and left without providing any medical care. Dr. Dulemba and a nurse began cardiopulmonary resuscitation (CPR) on Ms. LaCroix, and Dr. McGehee, once he was finished treating Lawryn, took control of the code and directed nurses to give Ms. LaCroix atropine and epinephrine to resuscitate her. Ms. LaCroix's heart resumed beating after one dose of epinephrine.

Dr. Pourzan, who was doing a procedure in the hospital's main operating room, was told about the code, got someone to take over his case, and rushed to the Women's Pavilion. He arrived after Ms. LaCroix had been resuscitated and took over Ms. LaCroix's care from Dr. McGehee. Dr. Green also arrived after Ms. LaCroix had been resuscitated. Although Ms. LaCroix was resuscitated, she had suffered irreversible brain injury caused by hypoxia (deprivation of oxygen to the brain). She was comatose for 3 days and hospitalized for a total of 13 days. Ms. LaCroix was then transferred to Epic's Flow Rehab Hospital (Epic) for rehabilitation, where she stayed for 50 days. Because of her brain injury, Ms. LaCroix has a full scale IQ of 76, which places her on the borderline of intellectual functioning, and she is totally and permanently disabled from independent living.

Ms. Blankenship and Dr. Hafiz settled with the LaCroixes by paying $500,000 and $750,000, respectively, for a total settlement of $1.25 million. Dr. Hafiz was the Denton Anesthesiology Associates, PA (DAA) anesthesiologist on call for the Women's Pavilion on the day of Ms. LaCroix's incident.

The trial court entered a judgment against the hospital and for the LaCroixes, awarding the LaCroixes approximately $8.8 million in damages after applying the $1.25 million settlement credit.

Issue

Was the evidence legally and factually sufficient to hold the hospital liable for medical negligence under a theory of direct corporate liability, notwithstanding the jury's failure to find that the treating physicians and nurse were negligent?

Holding

The evidence was legally and factually sufficient to hold the hospital liable for medical negligence under a theory of direct corporate liability, notwithstanding the jury's failure to find that the treating physicians and nurse were negligent. The evidence established that the hospital owed a duty to the plaintiff's decedent to have an anesthesiologist provide or supervise all of her anesthesia medical care, including having an anesthesiologist personally present or immediately available in the operating suite, and that the hospital's breach of this duty had proximately caused her brain damage.

Reason

Mr. LaCroix testified that from the point that the LaCroixes arrived at the hospital, they never were informed that Ms. LaCroix's anesthesia would be administered by a nurse anesthetist or that Ms. Hill or Ms. Blankenship were nurse anesthetists, not anesthesiologists. All along, Mr. LaCroix thought that Ms. Blankenship was a physician. Ms. Blankenship admitted that she never told the LaCroixes that she was a nurse anesthetist and was not a physician. It was undisputed that Ms. LaCroix was never seen by an anesthesiologist until she had suffered brain damage. It was also undisputed, and even agreed to by all the defendants, that the LaCroixes had a right to know that Ms. LaCroix was going to be receiving anesthesia care from a certified registered nurse anesthetist (CRNA) and not from an anesthesiologist. Finally, it was undisputed that no physician ever countersigned in Ms. LaCroix's medical chart any of the medical treatments that were signed by Ms. Blankenship. The hospital's policies and procedures required that the CRNA's supervising physician sign for the CRNA. Around 1:30 P.M., Dr. Dulemba decided that a C-section was warranted because of an occasionally low fetal pulse and Ms. LaCroix's slow cervical dilation. While the C-section was an emergency in that it was unscheduled, it was not a "stat" emergency C-section that had to be done immediately. On her own and without a physician's order, Ms. Blankenship discontinued the Marcaine and began Ms. LaCroix on Nesacaine, a C-section epidural anesthetic, in her labor room. Ms. Blankenship gave Ms. LaCroix a total of 20 cc of Nesacaine.

Ms. Blankenship testified that she cannot administer anesthesia without the medical direction of a physician and that she administered anesthesia and other drugs to Ms. LaCroix under Dr. Dulemba's medical direction and supervision. Dr. Dulemba testified that he did not give Ms. Blankenship medical direction for her anesthesia care of Ms. LaCroix, that he did not supervise Ms. Blankenship, and that he would never supervise a CRNA because he is not qualified to do so.

The evidence showed that the practice of anesthesia is a specialized practice of medicine by a physician—an anesthesiologist. An anesthesiologist is also trained in the practice of taking care of a patient just as any other physician is trained. An anesthesiologist is the most highly trained person who practices anesthesia. A CRNA is a registered nurse who has additionally completed a two-year study in nurse anesthesia and has been certified by the American Association of Nurse Anesthetists. Nurse anesthetists may administer anesthesia, but only under the medical direction or supervision of a physician.

By virtue of a May 31, 1990, contract with the hospital, DAA was the exclusive anesthesia provider for the Women's Pavilion. The contract, which had a term of three years, was a renewal of DAA's prior exclusive contract with the hospital. The contract required DAA to provide "qualified coverage" (supervision and back-up of all CRNAs employed by DAA) in the Women's Pavilion 24 hours per day, 7 days per week, including weekends and holidays.

In determining the standard of care, the hospital's internal bylaws, policies, and procedures, as well as the standards of the Joint Commission on Accreditation of Health Care Organizations (Joint Commission) can be utilized in determining the required standard of care. These factors alone, however, do not determine the governing standard of care.

The Joint Commission's *Accreditation Manual for Hospitals* is basically a document that addresses a "standard" and "characteristics" of the expected elements of hospitalwide policies, departmental policies and procedures, and those of the medical staff as might be expressed in medical staff bylaws, rules and regulations, or policy. Such policy and procedure manuals are hospital specific and can be viewed as setting the standard of care for that institution.

The hospital's anesthesia department had written policies and procedures governing anesthesia care at the hospital. The anesthesia department policies and procedures provided that a CRNA could provide "anesthetic patient care only under the direct and personal supervision of a physician." Supervision of CRNAs was defined as:

Anesthesia direction, management or instruction by one who is physically present or immediately available in the operating suite. An anesthesiologist having such an obligation should not personally be administering another concurrent anesthetic. If the physician is to render only a portion of the anesthesia care, either through supervision or otherwise, the arrangement must be clearly explained to and understood by the patient. Patient deception, whether deliberate or not, is unethical.

The responsible anesthesiologist must perform a preanesthetic evaluation and preparation in which the anesthesiologist:

1. Reviews the chart.
2. Interviews the patient to:
   - Discuss medical history including anesthetic experiences and drug therapy.
   - Perform any examinations that would provide information that might assist in decisions regarding risk and management.
3. Orders test and medications essential to the conduct of anesthesia.
4. Obtains consultations as necessary.
5. Records impressions on the preanesthesia summary along with brief discussion of planned anesthesia management, techniques, and ASA patient classification.
6. CRNAs will document the visit and discuss the evaluation of their patients with the supervising anesthesiologist or the operating physician; the discussion will be documented by the anesthesiologist or the operating physician by signing (with the nurse anesthetist) the preanesthetic summary.

When the LaCroixes arrived at the Women's Pavilion with Ms. LaCroix in labor, they were presented with and signed an anesthesia consent form that had the names of Dr. Green, Dr. Pourzan, and Dr. Hafiz preprinted on it. None of the physicians knew that the hospital was doing the anesthesia consent for patients at the Women's Pavilion in that manner. Ms. LaCroix never received a preanesthetic evaluation by an anesthesiologist, and no anesthesiologist ever explained the anesthesia consent to the LaCroixes.

The LaCroixes contend that the evidence is sufficient to establish that the hospital owed a duty to Ms. LaCroix to have an anesthesiologist provide or supervise all of Ms. LaCroix's anesthesia medical care, including having an anesthesiologist personally present or immediately available in the operating suite, and that the hospital's breach of this duty proximately caused Ms. LaCroix's brain damage. The hospital's anesthesia department policies and procedures required that an anesthesiologist perform the preanesthesia evaluation, that an anesthesiologist discuss with the patient the anesthesia plan, and that an anesthesiologist supervise a CRNA by being "physically present or immediately available in the operating suite." Also, an operating surgeon who requested a CRNA could supervise the CRNA and would be responsible for the CRNA.

The hospital, which opened the Women's Pavilion in 1986, initially entered into an exclusive contract with DAA to provide anesthesia care for the Women's Pavilion. The May 31, 1990, contract was a renewal of DAA's initial exclusive contract with the hospital. Mr. Ciulla was in charge of the DAA contract, which was drafted by Epic's legal department. According to Mr. Ciulla, he renewed the contract in conjunction with the hospital's medical staff.

Mr. Ciulla admitted that before he renewed the contract with DAA, he had been warned by anesthesiologists who practiced at the hospital that DAA's CRNAs were not being properly supervised in the Women's Pavilion. Both Dr. Mickey Via, chairman of the hospital's anesthesiology department in 1991, and Mr. Ciulla testified that Dr. Via and other anesthesiologists had complained to Mr. Ciulla about the lack of proper CRNA supervision in the Women's Pavilion. Dr. Via said that in renewing the contract with DAA, Mr. Ciulla did nothing to address the complaints that had been made.

According to Mr. Ciulla, he renewed the contract in conjunction with the hospital's medical staff. According to Dr. Via, the hospital's medical executive committee recommended to Mr. Ciulla that he not renew DAA's contract and that he seek another anesthesia group for the Women's Pavilion, but the hospital's board of directors renewed the contract anyway.

Four months before the LaCroixes went to the hospital to have their baby, Dr. Via wrote a memo (dated September 10, 1990) to Ciulla complaining that DAA's CRNAs in the Women's Pavilion were still not being supervised by DAA's anesthesiologists.

Dr. Via wrote a memo describing the dissatisfaction of the staff anesthesiologists who voiced concern regarding the medical supervision, or lack thereof, of nurse anesthetists (CRNA) administering anesthetics at DRMC.

Administrators at DRMC not only have failed to heed these concerns but seemingly have promoted the practice by their inaction and the contractual arrangements in the Women's Pavilion. It has be-

come apparent that the contracted anesthesiologists frequently are not present in that facility while anesthetics are being provided by nurse employees. This practice recently has been estimated to occur between 50 and 75 percent of the time. Additionally, nurse employees of Denton Anesthesia Associates on several occasions have provided anesthetics in the main operating room of DRMC without supervision by their employers.

Dr. Lloyd Redick, a Duke University medical professor of anesthesiology and associate professor of obstetrics, testified that Ms. LaCroix's brain damage was caused by a "high block" that resulted from being given too high a dosage of Nesacaine and that her respiratory distress was not recognized and treated quickly enough. Dr. Temple shared this opinion. Both physicians opined that if an anesthesiologist had supervised the administration of Ms. LaCroix's anesthesia, the high block would not have occurred, or would have been recognized and treated more promptly, and that the hospital's failure to have an anesthesiologist present and performing, or directly supervising, Ms. LaCroix's anesthesia care was a direct cause of her brain damage. Dr. McGehee also testified that Ms. LaCroix "failed to receive the proper treatment" and that her situation "should have been prevented." The hospital and Dr. Green and Dr. Pourzan presented several expert witnesses who testified that Ms. LaCroix had an unpredictable "anaphylactic" reaction (a severe allergic reaction) to the Nesacaine and that the presence of an anesthesiologist would not have affected the outcome because the anaphylactic reaction that caused Ms. LaCroix's cardiopulmonary arrest could not have been prevented.

However, Dr. Redick and Dr. Temple testified that an anesthesiologist would have determined through preanesthesia evaluation that Ms. LaCroix was a high risk patient for airway problems; would have known to allow for Ms. LaCroix's labor epidural sensitivity, blood volume depletion, age, weight, and height; and would have reduced the dosage and thus avoided the hypotensive episode and respiratory distress that caused Ms. LaCroix's hypoxic brain damage.

After reviewing the entire record, the court of appeals held that the evidence was legally and factually sufficient to support a finding that the hospital owed a duty to Ms. LaCroix to have an anesthesiologist provide or supervise all of her anesthesia care and that its breach of this duty was the direct cause of her brain injury. As the testimony reflects, the issues of the duty the hospital owed to Ms. LaCroix and the medical cause of Ms. LaCroix's brain injury were at the center of a classic "battle of the experts," and the jury was free to accept or reject either side's theory, both of which are supported by sufficient evidence.

Discussion

1. Conduct a "root cause analysis" describing the many reasons why this outcome occurred and how similar events can be prevented in the future.
2. Discuss hospital policy issues as they relate to:

- contracts (i.e., approval of, medical staff involvement, supervision of CRNAs)
- competency (i.e., CRNAs, emergency department physicians)
- anesthesia assessments (i.e., preanesthesia, preinduction, and postanesthesia)
- patient consent (i.e., informed consent)
- physician dissatisfaction with anesthesia services
3. What other issues can you identify in this case?

VI

Medical Staff

1. ANESTHESIOLOGIST/STANDARD OF CARE/ EXPERT TESTIMONY NOT REQUIRED

Citation: *Welte v. Bello*, 482 N.W.2d 437 (Iowa 1992)

Facts

On April 26, 1986, Ms. Welte was admitted to the hospital for surgery for the correction of a deviated septum. Approximately three hours before surgery, Ms. Welte conferred with her surgeon about the procedure. She then conferred with her anesthesiologist, Dr. Bello, who informed her that he would be administering sodium pentothal through an IV inserted into a vein in her arm. He told her about the potential risks associated with general anesthesia. Ms. Welte read and signed a written "consent to operate, administration of anesthetics, and rendering other medical services. . . ." The consent form provided: "I consent to the administration of anesthesia to be applied by or under the direction and control of Dr. Bello." Also on the form was the statement that "anesthesia and its complications have been explained and accepted." The consent form was signed by both Ms. Welte and Dr. Bello. *Id.* at 438. After talking with the doctors, Ms. Welte was transferred to a presurgical room. While in this room, a nurse inserted a catheter into the vein of Ms. Welte's right arm. Ms. Welte complained of pain after the IV had been inserted. The nurse checked the IV and concluded that it was properly positioned inside the vein. Dr. Bello began injecting drugs through a port in the IV. Dr. Bello then rechecked the site of the IV and, for the first time, noticed swelling on her arm near the point at which the IV had been inserted. As a consequence of the sodium pentothal infiltration of the tissues surrounding the vein, Ms. Welte sustained first-, second-, and third-degree burns resulting in a large permanent scar.

Ms. Welte and her husband commenced two separate malpractice actions, one against the hospital and another against Dr. Bello. The separate suits were consolidated for trial. Prior to trial, Dr. Bello filed a motion for summary judgment claiming Ms. Welte had failed to retain a qualified expert to testify against him and, therefore, they would be precluded from offering any expert testimony at trial. Ms. Welte argued that the tort claim of failure to obtain an informed consent did not require expert testimony. The trial court concluded that any alleged negligence of the anesthesiologists was not so obvious as to be within the comprehension of a layperson.

Issue

Was expert testimony required to establish a claim against the anesthesiologist?

Holding

The Supreme Court of Iowa held that expert testimony was not required to establish a claim against Dr. Bello.

Reason

Citing *Donovan v. State*, 445 N.W.2d 763 (Iowa 1989), "If a doctor operates on the wrong limb or amputates the wrong limb, a plaintiff would not have to introduce expert testimony to establish that the doctor was negligent. On the other hand, highly technical questions of diagnoses and causation which lie beyond the understanding of a layperson require introduction of expert testimony." The chemical burn to Ms. Welte's arm was caused by sodium pentothal that the anesthesiologist injected into the patient's vein, which then infiltrated or escaped from the vein into the surrounding tissues. The Supreme Court of Iowa found that it was within the common experience of a layperson that such an occurrence in the ordinary course of things would not have occurred if reasonable care had been used. The insertion of a needle into a vein is a common medical procedure. It is a procedure that has become so common that laypersons know certain occurrences would not take place if ordinary care is used. *Id.* at 441. The court concluded that the trial court erred in granting partial summary judgment on the general negligence claim against Dr. Bello. Even if expert evidence were required, the record was sufficient to defeat the summary judgment motion. Dr. Bello's expert, Dr. Maxwell, testified in his deposition that in the usual course of events, an IV instituted for purpose of anesthesia does not infiltrate the surrounding tissue. *Id.* at 442.

Discussion

1. What responsibility might an anesthesiologist have in supervising a nurse's negligence?
2. What mechanism might the hospital implement in order to help prevent such occurrences in the future?

2. PHYSICIAN–PATIENT RELATIONSHIP

Citation: *Roberts v. Hunter*, 426 S.E.2d 797 (S.C. 1993)

Facts

A patient who suffered a stroke after leaving the hospital emergency department sued a neurologist for medical malpractice.

On July 6, 1988, Mr. Roberts struck the left side of his neck when he fell from a scaffold. He went to the hospital emergency department at approximately 4:00 P.M., complaining of pain in his neck and shoulder. He was examined by Dr. Hunter, the emergency department physician. Dr. Hunter found no apparent head injury but did find abrasions on Mr. Roberts' neck. A neurological check indicated that his condition was normal. Dr. Hunter then consulted Dr. Mincey, a vascular surgeon at the hospital. Dr. Hunter informed Dr. Mincey that, because of the location of the injury, he was concerned about the possibility of a carotid artery injury. After examining Mr. Roberts, Dr. Mincey

concluded that a carotid artery injury was unlikely. Mr. Roberts was then sent to have his shoulder and neck X-rayed. When he returned, Mr. Roberts complained of blurred vision, seeing spots in front of his eyes. The neurological exam was repeated and indicated no abnormalities. Dr. Hunter again consulted with Dr. Mincey, who suggested a call to Dr. Hayes, a neurologist. Dr. Hunter then called Dr. Hayes, who was treating patients on another floor in the hospital. Dr. Hayes advised that he would examine Mr. Roberts. However, Mr. Roberts left the hospital approximately 15 to 20 minutes later before Dr. Hayes could examine him.

There was conflict in the testimony concerning Mr. Roberts' discharge from the hospital. Dr. Hunter testified that he emphasized to Mr. Roberts and his wife the serious nature of the injury, advising him that he should remain in the hospital for further evaluation. According to Dr. Hunter, Mr. Roberts refused to wait for Dr. Hayes. He did agree, however, to return to the hospital the following day. Mr. Roberts' wife testified that Dr. Hunter never advised them about the nature or possible severity of the injuries. Rather, they were given the option of remaining in the hospital or returning in the morning. In any event, Mr. Roberts was discharged from the hospital at approximately 7:30 P.M. At approximately 10:00 P.M. he returned to the emergency department with paralysis on the right side of his body. The circuit court directed a verdict for the neurologist, and the Robertses appealed.

Issue

Was Dr. Hayes entitled to a directed verdict?

Holding

The Supreme Court of Iowa held that no physician–patient relationship existed.

Reason

It is undisputed that Dr. Hayes neither examined Mr. Roberts nor reviewed his file. An examination was made impossible by Mr. Roberts' departure from the hospital. Based on these circumstances, it was held that no physician–patient relationship existed. Accordingly, a directed verdict in favor of Dr. Hayes was proper.

Discussion

1. In the emergency department setting, when does a physician–patient relationship begin?

2. At what point in the emergency department setting does the physician–patient relationship terminate?

3. MEDICATIONS/PRESCRIPTIONS/FAILURE TO FOLLOW UP

Citation: *Stilloe v. Contini*, 599 N.Y.S.2d 194 (N.Y. App. Div. 1993)

Facts

The plaintiff suffered from a chronic skin condition, for which he consulted the defendant, an internist. The defendant prescribed the steroid prednisone. The plaintiff sued for negligence, alleging that the defendant failed to properly monitor his dosage, as well as his condition. Further, the plaintiff complained that the defendant did not advise him of the risks or dangers associated with the medication. One of the recognized dangers was glaucoma, which the plaintiff contracted, causing him to become blind.

On October 15, 1982, the defendant began prescribing prednisone in 10-milligram strength every other day for a month at a time. After receiving instructions to return for a year, the plaintiff saw the defendant on March 11, 1983, and January 17, 1984. Over the next five years, the defendant prescribed prednisone without seeing the plaintiff. The dosages increased beyond the prescriptions of 1982. The plaintiff sued within 18 months of the last prescription. The New York Supreme Court dismissed the complaint as being time barred, and the plaintiff appealed.

Issue

Does renewal of a prescription by telephone constitute continuous treatment, thus tolling the statute of limitations?

Holding

The New York Supreme Court, Appellate Division, held that the statute of limitations period for the suit began to run on the date the prescription was last renewed by the physician over the telephone, rather than the earlier date when the physician last saw the patient.

Reason

Pursuant to the doctrine of continuous treatment, the time in which to bring a malpractice action is stayed when the course of treatment, including wrongful acts, has run continuously, and is related to the same original condition or complaint. The defendant admitted that the plaintiff was his patient for the time period, and he elected to treat plaintiff and prescribe medication without insisting on seeing the plaintiff-patient. The court held that there was a continuous relationship and treatment took place on every date that a prescription was renewed.

Discussion

1. Under what circumstances would continuous treatment not have applied?
2. What is the importance of patient education as it relates to medications?
3. What issues do you see as to the physician's assessment of the patient's medication needs?

4. DELAYED DIAGNOSIS

Citation: *Sacks v. Mambu*, 632 A.2d 1333 (Pa. Super. Ct. 1993)

Facts

A medical malpractice action was brought by Mrs. Sacks against Dr. Mambu for failure to make a timely diagnosis of her husband's colon cancer. Mrs. Sacks alleged that Dr. Mambu was negligent in that he failed to properly screen Mr. Sacks for fecal occult blood. (A fecal occult blood test is utilized to determine if there is blood in the colon.) Dr. Mambu treated Mr. Sacks, who presented himself with a complaint of abdominal pains in March 1983. Dr. Mambu determined that Mr. Sacks was suffering from a urinary tract infection and prescribed an antibiotic. In August 1983, Mr. Sacks was hospitalized for removal of his gallbladder. The surgeon on the case did not detect any indication of cancer. Dr. Mambu saw the patient regularly following surgery. Because of complaints of fatigue by the patient, Dr. Mambu ordered blood tests that revealed a normal hemoglobin, the results of which suggested that Mr. Sacks had not been losing blood. However, by late July 1984, Mr. Sacks experienced symptoms of jaundice. Dr. Mambu ordered an ultrasound test and Mr. Sacks was subsequently diagnosed with a tumor of the liver. He was admitted to the hospital and diagnosed with having colon cancer. By the time the cancer was detected, it had invaded the wall of the bowel and had metastasized to the liver. The patient expired in March 1985, seven months following his surgery. The court of common pleas entered judgment on a jury verdict for Dr. Mambu and Mrs. Sacks appealed.

Issue

Was Dr. Mambu negligent in failing to order a fecal occult blood test, and if so, did that failure increase the risk of harm to Mr. Sacks by allowing the cancer to metastasize and therefore to become a substantial factor in causing the patient's death?

Holding

The Superior Court of Pennsylvania, holding for Dr. Mambu, upheld the decision of the trial court.

Reason

The possibility that Mr. Sacks would have died anyway was no defense if Dr. Mambu's negligence had been a substantial factor in reducing Mr. Sack's opportunity for survival because Dr. Mambu would have "effectively cut off any chance that [Sacks] had for survival." *Id.* at 1335. The jury had been instructed to address this concern. Had the jury found "the defendant physician negligent in failing to administer a fecal occult blood test, it was the jury's duty to determine whether the doctor's negligence was a proximate cause of the defendant's death." *Id.* at 1336. Mr. Sacks had an occult blood test administered by his primary care physician, Dr. Weiner, in October 1981. Dr. Mambu did not order a fecal occult blood test when he treated the patient in March 1993. The jury determined that the physician's failure to administer the test had not increased the risk of harm by allowing the cancer to metastasize to the liver before discovery and, therefore, was not a substantial factor in causing the patient's death. Although the presence of blood in the stool may be suggestive of polyps, cancer, and a variety of other diseases, not all polyps and cancers bleed. Physicians are therefore in disagreement as to the efficacy of the test.

Discussion

Patient Assessment

1. Should the physician have performed a more thorough assessment?
2. What might the patient's record from previous providers have revealed?

3. Should the patient have provided a more definitive description of his ailment?
4. Were the data gathered regarding the patient's history adequate?
5. Were the screening processes sufficient, based on the patient's complaints?
6. Should the physician consider routine occult blood screening in future examinations? Explain.
7. What could the patient have done so the disease could have been diagnosed earlier?
8. What other actions might have been taken to avoid the outcome in this case?

Patient Reassessment

1. Was there a need for further physical assessment and follow-up?
2. Was follow-up conducted in a timely fashion?

5. FAILURE TO DIAGNOSE/DELAY IN TREATMENT

Citation: *Tomcik v. Ohio Dept. of Rehabilitation and Correction*, 598 N.E.2d 900 (Ohio Ct. App. 1991)

Facts

This case arises from the events that transpired while the plaintiff was in the custody and control of the defendant, the Department of Rehabilitation and Correction (ORW). The plaintiff alleges that, because of certain acts and omissions, the defendant's employees failed to timely diagnose her breast cancer. The asserted result was that the cancer was allowed to progress to the stage where the plaintiff was unable to utilize less drastic treatment procedures. Instead, the plaintiff was required to have her right breast removed.

The defendant denied any negligence on the part of its employees and claimed that the plaintiff's own negligence caused or contributed to whatever damages she may have sustained. The defendant contended that even if its employees were negligent, the plaintiff's cancer was so far developed when discovered that it would nevertheless have required the removal of her entire breast.

Pursuant to ORW's policy of medically evaluating all new inmates, the plaintiff, on May 26, 1989, was given a medical examination by Dr. Evans. He testified that part of his required physical evaluation included an examination of the plaintiff's breasts. However, he stated that his examination was very cursory.

Issue

Did the delay in providing the plaintiff treatment fall below the medically accepted standard of care?

Holding

The Court of Appeals of Ohio held that the delay in providing the plaintiff treatment fell below the medically acceptable standard of care.

Reason

The court was "appalled" that the physician had characterized his evaluation as a medical examination or to imply that what he described as a "cursory breast examination" should be considered a medically sufficient breast examination. It seems incredible to the court that a physician would deliberately choose not to expend the additional few minutes or seconds to thoroughly palpate the sides of the breasts, which is a standard minimally intrusive cancer detection technique. His admission that he merely "pressed" on plaintiff's breasts, coupled with the additional admission that such acts would not necessarily disclose lumps in the breasts, was substandard medical care. *Id.* at 902.

The day following her physical examination, the plaintiff examined her own breasts. At that time she discovered a lump in her right breast, which she characterized as being about the size of a pea. The plaintiff then sought an additional medical evaluation at the defendant's medical clinic. Testimony indicated that less than half of the inmates who sign the clinic list are actually seen by medical personnel the next day. Also, those not examined on the day for which the list is signed are given no preference in being examined on the following day. In fact, their names are simply deleted from the daily list and their only recourse is to continually sign the list until they are examined.

The preponderance of the evidence indicated that after May 27, 1989, the plaintiff constantly signed the clinic list and listed the reason for the requested treatment; yet, she was not seen by any medical personnel until June 21, 1989. The court concluded that such a delay in obtaining treatment was wholly unwarranted.

On June 21, 1989, the plaintiff was examined by Ms. Ardney, a nurse who noted in her nursing notes that the plaintiff had a "moderate large mass in right breast." Ms. Ardney recognized that the proper procedure was to measure such a mass but she testified that this was impossible because no measuring device was available. The missing measuring device to which she alluded was a simple ruler. The nurse concluded that the plaintiff should be examined again by Dr. Evans.

On June 28, 1989, Dr. Evans again examined the plaintiff. He recorded in the progress notes that the plaintiff had "a mass on her right wrist. Will send her to hospital and give her Benadryl for allergy she has." *Id.* at 904. Dr. Evans meant to write "breast" not "wrist." He again failed to measure the size of the mass on the plaintiff's breast.

The plaintiff was transferred to the Franklin County Prerelease Center (FCPR) on September 28, 1989. On September 30, 1989, the plaintiff was examined by a nurse at FCPR. The nurse recorded that the plaintiff had a "golf ball" size lump in her right breast.

The plaintiff was transported to the hospital on October 27, 1989, where she was treated by Dr. Walker. The plaintiff received a mammogram examination, which indicated that the tumor was probably malignant. This diagnosis was confirmed by a biopsy performed on November 9, 1989. The plaintiff was released from confinement on November 13, 1989.

On November 16, 1989, the plaintiff was examined by Dr. Lidsky, a surgeon. Dr. Lidsky noted the existence of the lump in the plaintiff's breast and determined that the size of the mass was approximately four to five centimeters and somewhat fixed. He performed a modified radical mastectomy upon the plaintiff's right breast, by which nearly all of the plaintiff's right breast was removed.

It was probable that an earlier procedure would have safely and reliably conserved a large part of the plaintiff's right breast. Through the inexcusable delays previously mentioned, the plaintiff lost this option and, instead, was medically required to have the entire breast removed. It was therefore the conclusion of the court that the defendant's negligence was the sole and proximate cause of all of the plaintiff's losses in excess of the basic lumpectomy procedure. The court found the plaintiff's total damages to be $85,000.

Discussion

1. What damages would you have awarded the plaintiff in this particular case?
2. Assuming for the moment that your particular state has a cap of $250,000 on pain and suffering, do you consider the plaintiff's total damages to be adequate compensation?
3. List the pros and cons of a cap on malpractice awards. Consider your list from the perspective of both the plaintiff and the defendant.
4. Do you think monetary awards are a deterrent to quality medical care?

6. WRONG SURGERY

Citation: *Bombagetti v. Amine*, 627 N.E.2d 230 (Ill. App. Ct. 1993)

Facts

In the spring of 1982, the plaintiff, Mr. Bombagetti, a pipe fitter, injured his lower back after his 4-year-old daughter jumped on his back. On November 4, 1982, Mr. Bombagetti suffered severe pain and numbness in his legs and could not move his toes. He saw Dr. Amine and was diagnosed with a herniated disk at the L4-L5 space. Dr. Amine performed a laminectomy on the plaintiff on December 14, 1982.

On December 17, 1982, during a review of the plaintiff's postoperative X-rays, Dr. Amine noted that he had mistakenly removed the disk at L3-L4. The plaintiff testified that after the surgery his condition progressively worsened and he underwent a second surgical operation. Although the plaintiff's pain was relieved, he was unable to lift heavy objects and had limited ability to participate in recreational activities.

Six months following the surgery, in August 1983, the plaintiff noticed a snap in his back while lifting some pipe. A few days later the plaintiff awoke with his back kinked to the left. The plaintiff's expert, Dr. Lorenz, testified that removal of the healthy disk caused the space between L3-L4 to collapse and the vertebrae to shift and settle. Dr. Lorenz also testified that the plaintiff's condition is permanent. Even the defendant's expert witness testified that the removal of the healthy disk made the plaintiff more susceptible to future injuries.

The trial court directed a verdict against the defendant based on the defendant's own admission and that of his expert that he was negligent and that his negligence had caused at least some injury to the patient. The defendant appealed.

Issue

Was any of the plaintiff's pain and suffering proximately caused by the negligent removal of his healthy disk?

Holding

The Appellate Court of Illinois held that, based on the evidence presented at trial and the lack of any contradictory evidence, the trial court properly directed a verdict for the plaintiff. Evidence was sufficient to support a determination that the defendant's negligence had caused the plaintiff's pain and suffering.

Reason

The evidence was sufficient to establish that the pain and suffering experienced by the plaintiff was proximately caused by the defendant's removal of the plaintiff's healthy disk. "Both the plaintiff's expert and defendant's expert testified that the plaintiff's kinking episode was more probably than not caused by removal of the wrong disk. . . . " *Id.* at 232. In addition, the "defendant admitted that the removal of the wrong disk predisposed the patient to future injury." *Id.* at 233. It is "well settled that a tortfeasor is liable for the injuries he causes, even though the injuries consist of the aggravation of a pre-existing condition." *Id.* at 233.

Discussion

1. What steps could the physician have taken to have prevented this unfortunate incident?
2. What changes, if any, should be taken by the hospital in order to reduce the likelihood of such occurrences in the future?

7. FAILURE TO DIAGNOSE

Citation: *Griffett v. Ryan*, 443 S.E.2d 149 (Va. 1994)

Facts

The plaintiff, executrix of the estate of Henry Griffett, filed a wrongful death action against the defendants, Dr. Ryan, Dr. Bridges, and the medical center. The plaintiff alleged that the defendants failed to diagnose her husband's cancer and that such failure was the proximate cause of his death.

On February 5, 1988, Mr. Griffett had been taken to the emergency department with a complaint of abdominal pain. Two emergency department physicians evaluated him and ordered X-rays, including a chest X-ray. Dr. Bridges, a radiologist, reviewed the chest X-ray and noted in his written report that there was an abnormal density present in the upper lobe of Mr. Griffett's right lung. Mr. Griffett was referred to Dr. Ryan, a gastroenterologist, for follow-up care. Dr. Ryan admitted Mr. Griffett to the hospital for a 24-hour period and then discharged him without having reviewed the radiology report of the February 5 chest X-ray.

On March 1, 1988, Mrs. Griffett called Dr. Ryan's office to inform him that her husband continued to experience intermittent pain. A nurse in Dr. Ryan's office suggested that Mr. Griffett go to the hospital emergency department if his pain became persistent.

In November 1989, Mr. Griffett, complaining of pain in his right shoulder, was examined by Dr. Baker. Dr. Baker diagnosed Mr. Griffett's condition as being cancer of the upper lobe of his right lung. The abnormal density on the February 5th chest X-ray was a cancerous tumor that had doubled in size from the time it had been first observed on the February 5th chest X-ray. The tumor was surgically removed in February 1990. However, Mr. Griffett expired in September 1990.

Dr. Muller, an internist, was an expert witness for the plaintiff. He testified that Mr. Griffett would have had a greater likelihood of survival if Dr. Ryan had made an earlier diagnosis in February 1988. The defendants objected to Dr. Muller's testimony, arguing that the plaintiff failed to establish that Dr. Muller was an expert witness capable of testifying as to the proximate cause of Mr. Griffett's alleged shorter life span (the causal relationship between Dr. Ryan's breach of standard and Mr. Griffett's death). The trial court initially overruled the defendants' objection to Dr. Muller's testimony. Following a verdict by the jury for the plaintiff, the trial court ruled that it had erred by allowing Dr. Muller to testify as to causation.

The jury returned a verdict for the plaintiff in the amount of $500,000. On a motion from the defendants, the trial court set aside the verdict, and the plaintiff appealed.

Issue

Was Dr. Muller qualified to testify as the plaintiff's medical expert? Did the plaintiff prove that the defendant's negligence was the proximate cause of Mr. Griffett's death and not just the loss of the mere possibility of survival?

Holding

The Supreme Court of Virginia held that the plaintiff had sufficiently identified Dr. Muller as an expert witness capable of testifying as to the question of causation. Evidence was sufficient to establish that the failure to diagnose lung cancer, in connection with the emergency room visit, was the proximate cause of the patient's death.

Reason

Dr. Muller's qualifications were appropriate for the testimony he was called to give. He received his medical degree from Columbia University and is board certified in internal medicine. He was licensed to practice medicine in Virginia, the District of Columbia, and Maryland. He has been practicing medicine since approximately 1970 and taught medical students at Georgetown University.

Virginia Code § 8.01-581.20 provides that: Any physician who is licensed to practice in Virginia shall be presumed to know the statewide standard of care in the specialty or field of medicine in which he is qualified and certified. This presumption shall also apply to any physician who is licensed in some other state of the United States and meets the educational and examination requirements for licensure in Virginia." The court found that "review of the record reveals that Dr. Muller has demonstrated knowledge of the standards regarding what, if anything, an internist, who is also a gastroenterologist, should do regarding medical information that is contained in a patient's medical record. We do not believe that the duty to review an X-ray contained in a patient's medical record should vary between an internist and a gastroenterologist." *Id.* at 153.

As to the defendants' argument that the plaintiff failed to prove that Dr. Ryan's negligence was the cause of the plaintiff's death, the plaintiff presented evidence that showed Dr. Ryan's negligence destroyed "any substantial possibility" of Mr. Griffett's survival. Dr. Muller had testified that within a reasonable degree of medical certainty "there would have been a high likelihood that [an] operation in 1988 would have resulted in the patient being saved." *Id.* at 152. This finding is consistent with *Blondel v. Hays*, 241 Va. at 474, 403 S.E.2d at 344 (1991), where the court stated that "if a plaintiff's evidence has shown that the defendant's negligence has destroyed any substantial possibility of the patient's survival, then there is sufficient evidence of proximate cause to go to the jury."

Discussion

1. Considering the particular issues in this case, do you consider the internist to be appropriately qualified to testify as an expert witness?
2. Do you think there are certain standards of care required of a gastroenterologist on which an internist would not be qualified to render an opinion? Explain.

8. FAILURE TO PRESCRIBE

Citation: *Shelton v. United States*, 804 F. Supp. 1147 (E.D. Mo. 1992)

Facts

The plaintiff suffered an injury to the tip of his finger on his right hand. In spite of the fact that his finger was bleeding and painful, he walked six blocks to his home and called 911 for help. He told the 911 dispatcher that he had been shot. On his way to the Veterans Affairs (VA) hospital in an ambulance, he told different versions regarding the nature of his injury. He claimed that he had been shot, and then claimed that he had been bitten. Although the plaintiff stated that he had told the admitting room nurse that he had been bitten, she had written on the admission form that he had suffered a "trauma" to his right middle finger.

The patient was examined by the evening emergency department physician, who was a second-year resident. During her training, she had seen and treated gunshot wounds and bites. The plaintiff told her he had been bitten, but would not tell her by whom and under what circumstances. At one point he changed his story and told her he had been shot. Again, he would not give any further information. She examined the wound, irrigated it, and sent the plaintiff for X-rays, which showed a fracture. When she again questioned the plaintiff about the cause of the injury, he again did not answer. The resident explained to the plastic surgeon that the patient had given conflicting stories about the injury. She gave him the results of the X-rays and stated that her conclusion was that the laceration of the finger had been caused by a gunshot wound. The resident determined that since it was a gunshot wound, there was no need to prescribe antibiotics. She told the plaintiff to use ice on his finger for the first 24 hours, then to keep the finger clean and dry. She further told him that he should check his finger and that if he had any drainage or swelling, he should go immediately to the emergency department.

A nurse in the emergency department followed the physician's instructions and cleansed and dressed the finger. The patient was provided with written instructions. For four days, the patient had trouble eating and sleeping because of the pain. He put ice on the hand, but returned to the emergency department after he had taken the bandage off and discovered that his finger was discolored. He told a different emergency department physician that he had been struck on the finger. The physician examined his finger and discovered that it was grossly discolored, swollen, and full of pus. Tests indicated a massive infection and gangrene. His finger was amputated, after which the reports on the amputated portions indicated that the finger had suffered a human bite. He returned only twice for physical therapy, and was thereafter discharged from it. The plaintiff sued.

Issue

Was the second-year resident negligent in not prescribing antibiotics? Was the plaintiff at fault for not following instructions with regard to care of the injury?

Holding

The second-year resident was negligent in failing to prescribe antibiotics, the lack of which contributed to the seriousness of the infection, gangrene, and amputation. The plaintiff was 50 percent at fault for failing to follow instructions.

Reason

Medical testimony indicated that when a patient has a serious injury and tells conflicting stories about the origin of the injury, and the injury has a high potential for infection, the doctor should prescribe antibiotics. Moreover, no medical reason was found for not having had a culture done. Although the doctor indicated that she feared an allergic reaction to any antibiotic, there was nothing in the admission report that reflected an allergy to any antibiotic. Further, she never asked the patient if he had allergies. There was sufficient evidence of causation in that it was shown that if certain things had been properly done, the results that did occur would not have occurred.

The court addressed the issue of comparative negligence. There was evidence that the conduct of both the plaintiff and the defendant contributed to cause the damage. The plaintiff was given oral and written instructions that he failed to follow. In addition, if he had checked the wound earlier, he would have discovered the first signs of infection. He would have also minimized the risk of gangrene, which resulted in the amputation of his finger.

Discussion

1. When a patient comes to the emergency department, what treatment questions and steps should the staff, physician, and nurses take when the injury is of an unknown origin, and the patient gives conflicting stories about it?
2. What routine instructions should emergency department patients be given regarding follow-up care?

9. FAILURE TO REPEAT ANGIOGRAM/ NEUROLOGIST

Citation: *Reed v. Weber*, 615 N.E.2d 253 (Ohio Ct. App. 1992)

Facts

On October 14, 1988, the decedent was admitted to the hospital by his family physician for treatment of a severe headache and hypertension. On October 15, 1988, a computed tomography (CT) scan was performed. On October 17, 1988, Dr. Armitage, who served as consulting neurologist at the request of the decedent's family physician, ordered a cerebral angiogram, which was performed by Dr. Weber, a radiologist. In an affidavit submitted in support of Dr. Weber's motion for summary judgment, Dr. Armitage stated that he reviewed the angiogram with Dr. Weber and that he understood that Dr. Weber had performed only a "three-vessel study" because he "was technically unable to visualize the right vertebral artery after repeated attempts." Dr. Armitage averred that, "[a]s the consulting neurologist, and with the understanding that the right vertebral artery had not been visualized, it was [his] best medical judgment that the angiogram did not need to be repeated during [the decedent's] October 1988 hospitalization." Armitage further asserted that the decision of whether to "repeat" the angiogram was his and not Dr. Weber's and that, in his opinion, "Weber adhered to the standard of care applicable to radiologists under like or similar circumstances when he reviewed the angiogram films and reported the results to [Armitage] as the patient's consulting neurologist." *Id.* at 255.

On October 22, 1988, the decedent was discharged by his family physician. On November 16, 1988, the decedent died of a ruptured berry aneurysm of the right vertebral artery.

The trial court entered summary judgment for Dr. Weber upon its determination that Dr. Armitage's decisions and actions constituted a superseding/intervening cause, relieving Dr. Weber of any alleged liability for the incomplete nature of the angiogram study.

Issue

Did a genuine issue of material fact exist as to whether the neurologist's failure to order a repeat of the incomplete angiogram constitute an intervening cause sufficient to break the causal connection between the radiologist's negligence in performing the angiogram and the patient's death from a cerebral aneurysm?

Holding

The Court of Appeals of Ohio held that a genuine issue of material fact existed as to whether the neurologist's failure to order a repeat of an allegedly inadequate angiogram was sufficient to break the causal connection between the radiologist's negligence and the patient's death.

Reason

There may be more than one proximate cause of an injury. When a defendant's conduct is negligent and the plaintiff's injury is the natural and probable consequence of that conduct, the fact that the negligence of others unites with the negligence of the defendant to cause injury does not relieve the defendant of liability. The test is "whether the original and successive acts may be joined together as a whole, linking each of the actors as to the liability, or whether there is a new and independent act or cause which intervenes and thereby absolves the original negligent actor." *Id.* at 256.

The determination of whether negligent conduct was the proximate cause of an injury or whether an intervening act operated to break the chain of causation presented a question of fact. The decedent's representative submitted in opposition to the motion for summary judgment two affidavits and the deposition of Dr. Grossman, a professor of radiology and section chief of neuroradiology at the Hospital of the University of Pennsylvania. Dr. Grossman therein expressed his opinion that: (1) the aneurysm that caused the decedent's death was present on October 15, 1988, when Dr. Weber performed the angiogram; (2) in cases such as that of the decedent, a four-vessel study was essential; (3) Dr. Weber's performance of the angiogram fell below the requisite standard of care when he failed to visualize adequately all four cerebral vessels and then failed to "redo" the inadequate study; and (4) Dr. Weber's failure to visualize the right vertebral artery prevented detection of the aneurysm and precluded any possibility of remedial action.

Viewing the evidence presented, the court found that there remained a genuine issue of fact that was material to the dispositive issue of whether Dr. Armitage's conduct constituted an intervening cause. Accepting Dr. Grossman's statement of the breadth of Dr. Weber's duty to the decedent in performing the angiogram, the court was precluded from a determination as a matter of law that Dr. Armitage's conduct operated independently to break the causal connection between Dr. Weber's negligence and the decedent's death, when Dr. Weber must be said to share with Dr. Armitage responsibility for the inadequacy of the angiogram. *Id.* at 257.

Discussion

1. What is meant by intervening cause?
2. What discharge planning issues do you see in this case?

10. FAILURE TO TREAT/EMERGENCY DEPARTMENT

Citation: *Reese v. Stroh*, 874 P.2d 200 (Wash. Ct. App. 1994)

Facts

In 1984, the plaintiff was being treated for asthma by Dr. Aprill, who referred him to the defendant, Dr. Stroh. The plaintiff was diagnosed by the defendant as having asthma, chronic obstructive pulmonary disease, and alpha-1-antitrypsin (AAT) deficiency. AAT prevents lung destruction. An AAT deficiency can cause the development of emphysema. When he was first diagnosed in 1985, the drug Prolastin was not available. He was prescribed antibiotics, steroids, and other medications, and was told to stop smoking and to avoid environmental irritants.

In 1989, the plaintiff discovered that his brother, who also had an AAT deficiency, was starting on Prolastin therapy. Prolastin therapy had been introduced into the market in 1987. Expert testimony revealed that an injection of it into the blood raises the blood protein levels enough to prevent patients with an AAT deficiency from developing lung disease. The plaintiff went to see his brother's doctor, who started him on Prolastin in 1990.

The plaintiff then sued Dr. Stroh for failing to prescribe Prolastin, which he claimed worsened his lung function. A pulmonary specialist testified as an expert for the plaintiff, stating, among other things, that Prolastin was being used in 1992 to treat over 2,000 patients, and that it was effective. He further testified that if it had been used on the plaintiff as soon as it became available, it would have reduced the rate of decline by 50 percent. The trial court ruled that his testimony was inadmissible because it lacked the necessary foundation for admittance. The court granted a directed verdict in favor of the defendant, and the plaintiff appealed.

Issue

Was there an adequate foundation laid for the expert's opinion that Prolastin would have improved the plaintiff's condition?

Holding

The Court of Appeals of Washington reversed the trial court and found in favor of the plaintiff.

Reason

When scientific testimony is sought to be offered at trial, it must assist the trier of fact to understand a fact that is in issue. Moreover, the expert's opinion must be based on scientific knowledge, and not on speculation. In this case, the court found that the pulmonary specialist had extensive clinical experience with patients on Prolastin therapy, and that numerous scientific tests had been completed with Prolastin before it had been approved by the Food and Drug Administration. Therefore, the court concluded, the expert's opinion was grounded in scientific knowledge and was reliable. Moreover, the court held, his testimony would assist the trier of fact in determining whether Dr. Stroh's failure to treat the emphysema with Prolastin was negligent. The court determined that it is not necessary to have statistical proof before expert testimony will be allowed, and even controversial theories are admissible so long as the expert's methodologies are sound.

Discussion

1. What are the conditions that must be met before a scientific expert will be allowed to testify about a fact in issue?
2. Is expert testimony required in every case involving malpractice? Explain.

11. NEGLIGENCE/INADEQUATE RECORDS

Citation: *Nehorayoff v. Fernandez*, 594 N.Y.S.2d 863 (N.Y. App. Div. 1993)

Facts

Based on allegations that an obstetrician-gynecologist negligently and incompetently performed abortions on patients, the physician was charged by the New York State Board of Professional Misconduct with six specifications of gross negligence and practicing with gross incompetence. One specification involved practicing gross negligence on more than one occasion and five specifications involved failing to maintain adequate records.

Evidence adduced at a nine-day hearing disclosed that the physician had performed several incomplete abortions that, coupled with substandard monitoring and aftercare, resulted in two extensive emergency surgeries—one that resulted in a total abdominal hysterectomy and one that resulted in death. Expert testimony confirmed that the physician's records were sketchy at best and that he continually failed to follow established protocols (e.g., performing procedures in his office that should have been performed in the hospital because of their high risk factors).

Pursuant to Public Health Law, and upon notification of the charges, the physician's license to practice medicine was suspended for three years, two years of which were to be stayed if the physician entered into a qualified residency program. The Director of Public Health, acting on behalf of the Commissioner of Health, urged that the physician's license be revoked. A review committee of the New York State Board of Regents recommended a three-year stayed suspension. The Board of Regents accepted the modified findings, and based on a "more serious view of the misconduct committed" (*Id.* at 864), revoked the petitioner's license to practice medicine. The physician commenced proceedings for review of the determination.

Issue

Did the physician's negligence in performing abortions and his failure to maintain adequate records justify revocation of his license to practice medicine?

Holding

The New York Supreme Court, Appellate Division, held that the physician's negligence in performing abortions and his failure to maintain adequate records justified revocation of his license to practice medicine.

Reason

Because of the serious and repeated nature of the physician's negligence and life-threatening consequences, the penalty imposed was not irrational or disproportionate to the offense "or to the harm or risk of harm . . . to the public." *Id.* at 865. The physician's petition was dismissed.

Discussion

1. What steps should a health care facility take in order to reduce the risks of harm to patients by incompetent health care professionals?
2. Describe a mechanism or process for handling questionable conduct.
3. What role should legal counsel play in the disciplinary process?
4. What is the value of obtaining counsel from an attorney who specializes in health care law?
5. Why can a decision not to take action be more costly than a decision to take action?
6. What is the potential liability of the administration, governing body, medical staff leadership, and other health care professionals who have the responsibility to act but fail to do so?
7. Is a hospital generally liable for the negligent act of a private independent practitioner that occurs in the practitioner's office? Explain.
8. Describe a scenario in which a hospital might be liable for the negligent act of a physician when the act occurred in an office practice.

12. PHYSICIAN'S NEGLIGENCE NOT SUPERSEDED BY THE HOSPITAL

Citation: *Dent v. Perkins,* 629 So. 2d 1354 (La. Ct. App. 1993)

Facts

In January 1981, the plaintiff, Ms. Dent, began prenatal treatment with Dr. Perkins. On June 26, 1981, the plaintiff notified Dr. Perkins' office that she was experiencing labor pains. She was instructed to go to the hospital. The plaintiff arrived at St. Claude General Hospital at 11:00 A.M., and after examination by an obstetrical nurse, was found to be in labor. The nurse on duty, Ms. Patrick, notified Dr. Perkins at approximately 11:45 A.M. of the plaintiff's condition by telephone. Dr. Perkins was off-call beginning at 12:00 noon and his partner, Dr. Dean, was scheduled to attend to his patients. There was no available room for Ms. Dent in the obstetrical unit. The record indicated the patient was admitted to a nonobstetrical unit on the third floor at approximately 2:30 P.M. At 3:40 P.M., the patient delivered a baby girl with the aid of an obstetrical nurse. No physician was present at the time of delivery. After delivery, the infant was transferred to the intensive care unit at Southern Baptist Hospital and was listed in critical condition. The infant died two days later.

Based on the credibility of witnesses, it was concluded that Dr. Perkins acted below the required standard of care and the jury properly found negligence on his part. The matter was referred to the trial court to determine the question of causation. The jury apportioned responsibility to the extent of 35 percent on the part of Dr. Perkins and 65 percent on the part of the hospital.

The Patient's Compensation Fund appealed, claiming that the jury erred in apportioning fault to Dr. Perkins, and that if he was in fact negligent, the superseding and intervening negligence of the nurses and the hospital staff exonerated Dr. Perkins from liability.

Issue

Were Dr. Perkins' negligent acts and omissions a cause in fact of the plaintiff's damages and suffering and death of the plaintiff's infant child?

Holding

The Court of Appeal of Louisiana held that the physician's negligence in placing the plaintiff on a nonobstetrical unit for an unlimited period of time rendered him 35 percent at fault, and the negligence of the hospital nurses and staff in observation and care of the patient, while rendering the hospital 65 percent at fault, did not supersede the physician's negligence.

Reason

In a medical malpractice claim against a physician, a plaintiff carries a twofold burden of proof. The plaintiff must establish first, by a preponderance of the evidence, that the physician's treatment fell below the ordinary standard of care required of physicians in his or her medical specialty, and second, that a causal relationship was established between the alleged negligent treatment and the injury sustained.

Negligence is actionable only where both a cause in fact and a legal cause of the injury exist. Legal cause requires a proximate relation between the actions of a defendant and the harm that occurs, and such relation must be substantial in character. Based on the evidence, the court did not find that the jury erred in placing responsibility on Dr. Perkins and the hospital nurses and staff.

The physician's claim that the negligence of the hospital nurses and staff was an intervening and superseding cause of the infant's death was rejected. The findings were supported by the record. While Dr. Perkins was negligent in placing the

plaintiff on a nonobstetrical unit for an unlimited period of time, the nurses were negligent in their observation and care of the plaintiff. However, this negligence did not supersede the physician's negligence. The nurses failed to adequately observe and monitor the plaintiff. The patient was left in the emergency department from 11:45 A.M., when she was first admitted to the hospital, until 2:30 P.M., when she was finally brought to the nonobstetrical unit of the hospital. Once the plaintiff was brought to this unit, the nurses on several occasions called the labor and delivery unit asking for an obstetrical nurse to respond to the plaintiff's complaints. When it appeared that the plaintiff was about to deliver, an obstetrical nurse assisted in the delivery. No physician was present at the child's birth. The plaintiff's expert testified that had the plaintiff been in the labor and delivery unit where a physician would have been present during delivery, the child would not have died.

Discussion

1. Do you agree with the court's finding?
2. What changes would you make in hospital procedures?
3. Should emergency department staff (physicians and nurses) be cross-trained in the care of obstetrical patients? Explain.

13. ONCOLOGIST/MISDIAGNOSIS

Citation: *Hiers v. Lemley*, 834 S.W.2d 729 (Mo. 1992)

Facts

Mr. Hiers's survivors sued the oncologist for medical malpractice, alleging that he misdiagnosed the patient as having cancer, treated the patient with chemotherapy even though he knew the diagnosis of cancer was in doubt, and failed to promptly inform the patient upon learning that the diagnosis was in error.

On March 6, 1984, the patient was admitted to the hospital for tests to determine the cause of respiratory problems. Biopsies were performed. Three days later, Dr. Sheffield, a pathologist and director of the hospital's pathology laboratory, issued a report concluding that the patient had interstitial pneumonitis and bronchoalveolar carcinoma. Another pathologist, Dr. Boyce, also examined the biopsy slides with Dr. Sheffield. Dr. Boyce was uncertain of the diagnosis. As a result, a sample was sent to an expert in pulmonary diseases.

Dr. Lemley, an oncologist, also viewed the biopsy slides. He informed the patient that he had cancer and had only three weeks to live. Dr. Lemley recommended chemotherapy. Dr. Lemley's recommendation was based on the pathology report and his own examination of the tissue. Dr. Lemley was aware that a request had been made for an outside opinion. The treatment was followed by extreme nausea, debilitation, loss of weight, loss of hair, and abnormal blood counts.

On March 23, 1984, a North Carolina pathologist issued his report that the tissue indicated only interstitial pneumonitis. On April 1, 1984, Dr. Lemley entered Mr. Hiers's hospital room. According to Mrs. Hiers, Dr. Lemley was very excited and reported, "We just received a report back stating your husband does not have cancer." *Id.* at 730. Approximately two years later Mr. Hiers died of interstitial pneumonitis.

Mrs. Hiers brought a survivor's action for medical malpractice against Dr. Lemley, submitting negligence in three respects:

1. misdiagnosing Mr. Hiers as having cancer
2. treating Mr. Hiers with chemotherapy even though he knew the cancer diagnosis was in doubt
3. failing to promptly inform Mr. Hiers upon learning the diagnosis was in error

After the jury returned a verdict for Dr. Lemley, the circuit court granted the survivors' motion for a new trial.

Issue

Was there a submissible case of negligent treatment?

Holding

The Supreme Court of Missouri held that the survivors made a submissible case of negligent medical treatment.

Reason

The first theory of negligence was that Dr. Lemley made a misdiagnosis that Mr. Hiers had lung cancer. The defendant argued that he made no diagnosis or misdiagnosis of lung cancer. The hospital record includes the following entry dictated by Dr. Lemley:

Patient eventually underwent a right minithoracotomy at which time some confusion was initially encountered as to the etiology of his problem, being either desquamative interstitial pneumonitis vs. bronchoalveolar carcinoma; however, on re-

view of pathology slide preparations, this definitely appears to be bronchoalveolar cell carcinoma.

Impression: On the basis of my interpretation of the pathology slide, I definitely feel this is bronchoalveolar cell type of lung carcinoma. Unfortunately, disease at this point is rather far advanced and the patient has a very poor prognosis. *Id.* at 732.

Dr. Lynch, a specialist in pathology, testified at trial that neither an oncologist nor a general pathologist would have had the expertise to make a proper diagnosis of the patient's condition. He also testified that Dr. Lemley's diagnosis and treatment did not measure up to the standard of care that a careful and reasonable physician would have exercised. Mrs. Hiers and a niece testified that Dr. Lemley told them that Mr. Hiers had cancer and would die in three weeks. Treating these facts as true, it could not be said that there was no evidence that Dr. Lemley negligently misdiagnosed the condition as being cancerous.

Discussion

1. In light of the patient's poor prognosis and apparent questionable diagnosis, was the physician's decision to prescribe chemotherapy premature? Explain.

14. PATHOLOGIST/NEGLIGENCE

Citation: *Suarez Matos v. Ashford Presbyterian Community Hosp.*, 4 F.3d 47 (1st Cir. 1993)

Facts

On October 30, 1989, Ms. Matos became ill while vacationing in Puerto Rico. She went to the Ashford Presbyterian Community Hospital emergency department for treatment. She was examined and admitted to the hospital by Dr. Lopez. A uterine tumor was surgically removed from the patient by Dr. Juncosa the following day. The tumor had been examined by Dr. Carrasco, a pathologist on the hospital's medical staff. (Besides being a member of the hospital's medical staff, Dr. Carrasco had an arrangement whereby he shared in certain hospital profits.) He allegedly reported the tumor as being benign.

At the time of discharge, the patient was given instructions to obtain follow-up care upon her return to New York. For referral purposes, the patient was provided with the names of two physicians from whom she could seek such care. The patient visited a clinic upon her return to New

York. Five months later, the patient experienced further pain and was diagnosed with incurable cancer. It was determined that the nature of her tumor was such that it could have become malignant and, therefore, should have been closely monitored. The patient had not been advised of this possibility. Dr. Carrasco admitted that he knew of the possibility of a malignancy. He testified that Dr. Juncosa was warned of this possibility. In addition, Dr. Carrasco testified that the nature of this tumor was also described on the face of his written pathology report. Contradicting Dr. Carrasco's testimony, Dr. Juncosa testified that he was told by Dr. Lopez that Dr. Carrasco told him that the tumor was benign. A district court jury found the defendant guilty of malpractice and the defendant appealed the finding.

Issue

Was there sufficient evidence to support a finding of negligence on the part of the pathologist, and, if so, was the hospital chargeable with his conduct?

Holding

The United States Court of Appeals for the First Circuit held that the evidence was sufficient to support a finding of negligence on the part of the pathologist.

Reason

Without reviewing further, it is enough to say, although difficult, that the jury could combine Dr. Carrasco's admission that he knew of the possibility of malignancy and Dr. Juncosa's statement that Dr. Carrasco told him the reverse, and thus prevent an ordered judgment for defendants. In other words, the jury could find that Dr. Carrasco admittedly knew that the tumor was dangerous but he did not adequately convey this to the operating doctor so that the vital warning never reached the plaintiff. *Id.* at 50.

The hospital is chargeable due to the fact that Dr. Carrasco had been granted medical staff privileges and also shared in the hospital's profits.

Discussion

1. What mechanism should be in place for communication between the surgeon in an operating room and the pathologist who needs to report his findings on a frozen section to the operating surgeon? Face to face communications? A written report? Intercom? What are the pros and cons of these forms of communications?
2. Why was the hospital also liable for the physician's negligence?

15. PATHOLOGIST/MISDIAGNOSIS/STATUTE OF LIMITATIONS

Citation: *Winder v. Avet*, 613 So. 2d 199 (La. Ct. App. 1992)

Facts

On February 2, 1982, Mr. Winder was admitted to a medical center for testing after experiencing symptoms of jaundice. Dr. Tedesco initially diagnosed Mr. Winder as having obstructive jaundice. Eight days later, Dr. Tedesco performed exploratory surgery after further testing indicated that Mr. Winder might have cancer of the pancreas. During the course of surgery, Dr. Tedesco sent several needle biopsies to Dr. Avet, a pathologist, in order to confirm his suspicions. Dr. Avet examined three frozen sections. Based on the third frozen section, he made a diagnosis of poorly differentiated malignancy. After examining the permanent section, Dr. Avet made a diagnosis of well-differentiated adenocarcinoma. Unfortunately, because the pancreas in Mr. Winder's case was too densely adhered to other vital structures, it could not be removed surgically. Relying on the pathologist's positive identification of cancer, Dr. Tedesco bypassed the bile duct into the intestines to relieve the obstruction. Dr. Tedesco also had Dr. Weatherall, a radiologist, insert radioactive seeds into the pancreas. Often pancreatic cancer victims die within six months of the diagnosis. Although sick much of the time, Mr. Winder lived far beyond conventional expectations.

In November of 1985, Dr. Henry, who began treating Mr. Winder's liver infections in 1983, asked Dr. Avet to review his original diagnosis in light of the fact that Mr. Winder had survived far beyond normal expectations. According to Dr. Henry, Dr. Avet examined the 1982 slides and admitted making a mistake. Specifically, Dr. Henry stated: "He said that . . . [a]fter his re-review that his original diagnosis was a mistaken one and that this was—he said something to the effect, this is something that we taught in pathology, a mistake not to make." *Id.* at 200. At this point, Mr. Winder received treatment for chronic pancreatitis and treatment designed to counter the adverse effect of the radiation treatment, including more surgery. These attempts proved unsuccessful.

On January 14, 1986, Mr. Winder died. Although no autopsy was performed, it was presumed Mr. Winder died primarily from liver failure and infection. The defendants contended that the trial court erred, according to its own written reasons for judgment, in finding that the suit could proceed. The court's written reasons stated:

> The Court finds as a fact that it was not until November of 1985 when Dr. Russell Henry and Dr. Phillip Avet had their discussion that there was any basis upon which the plaintiffs could have had any knowledge to bring a claim. While the cited statute for medical malpractice has a three-year limitation, the Court must grant a reasonable time to an innocent victim who has absolutely no knowledge nor any way of ascertaining the knowledge that there may have been a misdiagnosis by an expert, as is the case by a pathologist, that a person had cancer, and leaves that person as a victim. *Id.* at 201.

Because of Dr. Avet's erroneous diagnosis, Mr. Winder was subjected to continuous treatment for the wrong disease from February 10, 1982, until November of 1985. Between November 2, 1982, and January 14, 1986, Mr. Winder was hospitalized 13 times for treatment of cancer of the pancreas and resultant complications. According to the testimony of Dr. Tedesco, more probably than not, the complications that caused Mr. Winder's death arose from the various treatments used to fight the cancer Mr. Winder did not have. Mr. Winder placed his trust and confidence in these physicians, and until November 1985, Mr. Winder did not possess knowledge, either actual or constructive, that he was the possible victim of medical malpractice.

The district court entered judgment in favor of the surviving spouse and children. The defendant appealed.

Issue

When did the three-year prescriptive period for medical malpractice begin to run? Did the evidence establish that the pathologist misdiagnosed the patient's ailment?

Holding

The Court of Appeal of Louisiana held that misdiagnosis was a continuing tort as to which the 3-year prescriptive period did not begin to run at least until a correct diagnosis and evidence established the pathologist's malpractice in misdiagnosing chronic pancreatitis as pancreatic cancer.

Reason

This is a case of a continuing tort. There was continuous action by Dr. Avet, as described above, that resulted in continuous damage to Mr. Winder—infection and liver failure brought about by the radiation treatment for cancer. The plaintiffs answered the appeal, seeking an increase in the trial court's award. The trial court had awarded the plaintiffs $500,000.

Based on statements made by the trial court in its written reasons for judgment, the plaintiffs contended the trial court made a mistake in drafting the judgment. In essence, plaintiffs contended that the trial court erroneously believed that the total award based on medical malpractice could not exceed $500,000, including medical expenses.

Based on the statements made by the trial court, it is clear the actual judgment did not reflect the trial court's intentions. The judgment of the trial court was revised to award past medical expenses in the amount stipulated by the parties, $154,750.73, in addition to the $500,000 awarded by the trial court.

Discussion

1. How did the court determine when the statute of limitations began to toll?
2. Do you agree with the court's decision? Explain.

16. PSYCHIATRY/DUTY TO CARE/RELEASE OF PATIENT APPROPRIATE

Citation: *Leonard v. State*, 491 N.W.2d 508 (Iowa 1992)

Facts

This suit was filed against the mental hospital (MHI) and state alleging that the hospital's decision to discharge Mr. P., a mentally ill patient, gave rise to a duty of care toward the plaintiff, Mr. L. This duty gave rise to rendering the state and hospital liable for injuries the plaintiff incurred as a result of a beating by the patient after his discharge.

On March 30, 1987, Mr. P. was admitted to MHI hospital following a transfer from another hospital where he had been involuntarily committed at the request of his mother. His diagnosis upon admission at MHI was bipolar affective disorder, manic type, with alcohol dependency and suicidal ideation. He was placed on a special assault and suicide precaution.

From April 14 to 17, following two weeks of lithium therapy for Mr. P.'s bipolar disorder, his condition improved sufficiently to warrant a leave to go home. On April 23, the MHI staff determined that Mr. P. was in fair remission and had reached "maximum inpatient psychiatric benefits." He was discharged from MHI with the recommendation that his commitment be continued on an outpatient basis. The patient returned to his work as a demolition contractor. He hired Mr. L. to work for him. On May 6, 1987, the two spent the day drinking instead of working. They ended up at Mr. P.'s home. Late that evening, apparently without provocation, Mr. P. beat Mr. L. severely about the head and body, locked him in his house, and left him unconscious. Mr. P. was subsequently convicted of kidnapping and attempted murder.

Mr. L. claimed that state physicians at MHI negligently treated and discharged Mr. P., which resulted in Mr. L.'s injury.

Issue

Did the psychiatrist owe a duty of care to Mr. L. for the release of Mr. P. from confinement?

Holding

The Supreme Court of Iowa held that the psychiatrist owed no duty of care to Mr. L. for decisions regarding the treatment and release of Mr. P. from confinement.

Reason

Mr. L. was unacquainted with Mr. P. prior to Mr. P.'s commitment or discharge. No threats were ever voiced against Mr. L. by Mr. P. to the psychiatrist. Nor was there any evidence in the summary judgment record from which a reasonable person could find that Mr. L. belonged to a class of persons more endangered by Mr. P.'s release than the public at large. The court found that the risks to the general public posed by the negligent release of dangerous mental patients would be far outweighed by the disservice to the general public if treating physicians were subject to civil liability for discharge decisions. The Missouri Supreme Court described the consequences this way:

> The treating physicians, in their evaluation of the case, well might believe that [the patient] could be allowed to leave the institution for a prescribed period and that his release on pass might contribute to his treatment and recovery. We do not believe that they should have to function under the threat of civil liability to members of the general public

when making decisions about passes and releases. The plaintiff could undoubtedly find qualified psychiatrists who would testify that the treating physicians exercised negligent judgment, especially when they are fortified by hindsight. The effect would be fairly predictable. The treating physicians would indulge every presumption in favor of further restraint, out of fear of being sued. Such a climate is not in the public interest. *Sherrill v. Wilson*, 653 S.W.2d 661, 664 (Mo. 1983).

It is not only the customary procedure, but the constitutionally and statutorily mandated requirement, to treat even seriously mentally impaired persons in the least restrictive environment medically possible. *B.A.A. v. University of Iowa Hosp.*, 421 N.W.2d 118, 124 (Iowa 1988). The Supreme Court of Iowa was convinced that if a psychiatrist's prognosis were subject to second-guessing by any member of the public who might later be injured by the patient, it could severely chill the physician's capacity for decision making and ultimately threaten the integrity of our civil commitment systems.

Discussion

1. Do you agree with the court's reasoning?
2. What would be the ramifications if the court had found for the plaintiff?

17. VICARIOUS LIABILITY/RADIOLOGIST NOT LIABLE FOR TECHNICIAN'S NEGLIGENCE

Citation: *Oberzan v. Smith*, 869 P.2d 682 (Kan. 1994)

Facts

Mr. Oberzan brought a medical malpractice action against a hospital radiologist for injuries allegedly incurred while being prepared by an X-ray technician for a barium enema. Mr. Oberzan admitted to the following nine facts:

1. The pretrial questionnaire prepared by the plaintiff alleges that Dr. Smith or his X-ray technician perforated plaintiff's rectum during the barium enema procedure.
2. The plaintiff was referred to Dr. Smith by Dr. Jones for the barium enema procedure.
3. The usual procedure for performing barium enemas is that the X-ray technician inserts the enema tip for the barium enema and then gets Dr. Smith to begin the

examination. All patients are in the prone position with the tip in place when Dr. Smith walks into the room.

4. With respect to the plaintiff, when Dr. Smith walked into the room, the plaintiff was already lying in the prone position with the tip already inserted by the technician.
5. In February 1988, Ms. Davis was employed by Maude Norton Hospital as an X-ray technician.
6. As an X-ray technician, Ms. Davis was trained to prep patients for examinations, which would include inserting enema tubes for barium enemas.
7. Ms. Davis inserted the enema tip into the rectum of the plaintiff for the barium enema before Dr. Smith entered the room for the procedure.
8. After Dr. Smith entered the room, the exam began. Immediately after Ms. Davis began injecting the barium, she noticed bleeding at the tip of the rectum.
9. After the procedure was halted, Dr. Smith immediately contacted Dr. Jones to inform him of the bleeding.

Mr. Oberzan claimed the physician was vicariously liable for the employee's negligent conduct.

Issue

Was the radiologist vicariously liable for injuries allegedly sustained by the patient while being prepared by the technician for a barium enema? Does administrative regulation providing for supervision of a hospital's radiology department by a designated medical staff physician create a legal duty for the medical staff physician to personally supervise all activities that occur in the radiology department?

Holding

The Supreme Court of Kansas held that the *respondeat superior* doctrine did not apply to the relationship between the technician employed by the hospital and the radiologist so as to impose vicarious liability on the radiologist. Administrative regulation did not impose a legal duty on the radiologist to personally supervise the enema procedure.

Reason

Ms. Davis was not an employee of Dr. Smith. She was not under his direct supervision and control at the time the injury occurred. Dr. Smith did not select Ms. Davis to perform the insertion of the enema tip; she was assigned by the hospital. Vicarious liability under *respondeat superior* did not impose

liability on Dr. Smith. The master–servant relationship was not established because Dr. Smith was not exercising personal control or supervision over Ms. Davis, a nonemployee, at the time of injury. Mr. Oberzan admitted that "[t]he usual procedure for performing barium enemas is that the X-ray technician inserts the enema tip for the barium enema and then gets Dr. Smith to begin the examination."

Mr. Oberzan argued that Kansas law, K.A.R. 28-34-86(a) ("the radiology department and all patient services rendered therein shall be under the supervision of a designated medical staff physician; wherever possible, this physician shall be attending or consulting radiologist") imposes a duty on radiologists to supervise patient services rendered in a hospital radiology department. However, none of the K.A.R. 28-34-12 subsections require that the preparation of a patient for a barium enema be performed under a physician's direct supervision. The purpose of K.A.R. 28-34-12(c) is to establish an administrative head for the radiology department. Mr. Oberzan cited no authority in support of his position that K.A.R. 28-34-12(c) creates a legal duty for a designated medical staff physician to personally control and supervise all activities that occur in a radiology department. The construction suggested by Mr. Oberzan would create physician liability extending far beyond the intent of the regulation.

Discussion

1. Describe a scenario where the radiologist might have shared liability with the hospital.
2. What is meant by vicarious liability?

18. FAILURE TO DIAGNOSE/STANDARD OF CARE

Citation: *Colbert v. Georgetown Univ.*, 623 A.2d 1244 (D.C. Ct. App. 1993)

Facts

In July 1982, Ms. Colbert felt a lump in her left breast. She went to see her gynecologist, who referred her to an oncologist, Dr. Kirson. Although a mammogram conducted on August 9 revealed no evidence of malignancy, a biopsy established that the lump was cancerous. Dr. Kirson urged Ms. Colbert to have the breast removed by a modified radical mastectomy. Because he was about to go out of town, Dr. Kirson gave her the names of two surgeons at Georgetown University Hospital who could perform the operation.

On August 13, Ms. Colbert and her husband met with Dr. Lee, one of the surgeons recommended by Dr. Kirson and a full-time employee of Georgetown Hospital. At that meeting, Dr. Lee suggested a lumpectomy as an alternative treatment option. He told the Colberts that a lumpectomy was cosmetically more attractive than a mastectomy, and that studies in Europe had shown that, when coupled with radiation treatments afterward, it was as effective as a mastectomy at removing cancerous cells from the body. The Colberts agreed to the lumpectomy and scheduled the procedure with Dr. Lee. Six days later, Dr. Lee performed a lumpectomy on Ms. Colbert's left breast, and at the same time he removed several of her left axillary lymph nodes. When one of the nodes tested positive for cancerous cells, he set up a program of systemic chemotherapy.

On September 7, 1982, Ms. Colbert began receiving chemotherapy treatments under the direction of Dr. Goldberg. Several weeks later, Ms. Colbert felt more lumps in her left breast. She tried at that time to get another appointment with Dr. Lee, but she was unsuccessful, so she brought the lumps to Dr. Goldberg's attention. At first Dr. Goldberg did nothing in response to her concerns.

On September 28, 1982, at her last scheduled chemotherapy session, Dr. Goldberg asked Dr. Byrne to examine the lumps in Ms. Colbert's breast. Dr. Byrne arranged for two biopsies to be performed. The biopsies disclosed the continued presence of cancer in Ms. Colbert's left breast, so Dr. Lee told her that she needed a mastectomy. Dr. Lee performed the mastectomy on Ms. Colbert's left breast.

Ms. Colbert asked Dr. Lee if the delay in performing the mastectomy had caused any increased risk. According to her answer to an interrogatory, Dr. Lee replied that "the delay caused enhanced risk of a very high nature." Shortly after the mastectomy, Dr. Lee met with Mr. Colbert. At that meeting, according to Mr. Colbert's deposition, Dr. Lee stated "that it took him a long time to do the operation because in his entire career he had never seen so much tumor mass." *Id.* at 1247. Dr. Lee also said that Ms. Colbert's chances of survival had decreased from 90 percent to 10 percent, and he admitted to Mr. Colbert that he had done "the wrong operation" in August when he performed the lumpectomy instead of the mastectomy recommended by Dr. Kirson. Mr. Colbert also stated in his deposition that Dr. Lee said he "had forgotten" that a lumpectomy was not the proper procedure for a patient with multicentric disease, such as Ms. Colbert. *Id.* at 1247. On March 7, 1983, Ms. Colbert had a mastectomy performed on her right breast. In August 1986, Ms. Colbert consulted an internist because of low back pain. It was determined that Ms. Colbert's cancer had metastasized to her spine. The Colberts filed their malpractice action in August of 1989. Ms. Colbert died in January of 1992. Mr. Colbert was substituted for his wife as appellant.

Issue

Did the statements of Dr. Lee that he should have performed a mastectomy instead of a lumpectomy demonstrate that the standard of care was breached?

Holding

The District of Columbia Court of Appeals held that an admission and other statements by the physician that he should have performed a mastectomy instead of a lumpectomy established a prima facie case of malpractice.

Reason

Dr. Lee's admission of negligence demonstrated that the standard of care was breached. His statement to Ms. Colbert in October 1982 that the delay in performing a mastectomy caused an "enhanced risk of a very high nature, but that only time would tell," provides evidence of causation. *Id.* at 1253. The admission and other statements of Dr. Lee establish a prima facie case of malpractice. They may not ultimately be enough to convince a jury that malpractice actually occurred, but there can be no doubt that they raise an issue that must be submitted to a jury. As with the evidence of the Colberts' state of mind in discovering the relevant injury, the Colberts' presentation of a prima facie case of malpractice necessitates reversal of the trial court's grant of summary judgment for the defendants.

Discussion

1. Do you agree with the court of appeals decision to reverse the trial court's finding? Explain.
2. What is meant by a prima facie case?
3. What are the case issues apparent in this case?

19. SUPERVISION OF RESIDENTS

Citation: *Mozingo v. Pitt County Mem'l Hosp.*, 415 S.E.2d 341 (N.C. 1992)

Facts

On December 5, 1984, the defendant, Dr. Kazior, began his assignment to provide on-call services for the obstetrics residents who were caring for patients. Dr. Kazior remained at his home, available to take telephone calls from the residents. That evening Dr. Kazior received a telephone call from Dr. Warren, a second-year resident at the hospital, informing him that she had encountered a problem with a delivery. The baby was suffering shoulder dystocia, a condition in which a baby's shoulder becomes wedged in the mother's pelvic cavity during delivery. Dr. Kazior stated that he would be there immediately and left his home for the hospital, which was located approximately two miles away. When Dr. Kazior arrived at the hospital, the delivery of the infant had been completed.

On December 3, 1987, the plaintiffs filed an amended complaint alleging the negligent supervision of the obstetrics residents by Dr. Kazior. The plaintiffs alleged that the infant suffered severe and permanent injuries because of the shoulder dystocia and that Dr. Kazior's negligent supervision of the residents proximately caused these injuries.

In October 1989, the defendant filed a motion for summary judgment supported by four affidavits, the pleadings, and other material obtained during discovery. Three of the affidavits were given by the heads of the departments of obstetrics and gynecology of other teaching hospitals in North Carolina. The affidavits stated that the protocol of their respective medical schools "permitted the attending on-call physicians to afford coverage during the hours of their assignment by either being present in the hospital or, unless a problem is specifically anticipated, by being present at their residence or other specified place and immediately available to a telephone so as to come immediately to the hospital upon request." *Id.* at 343.

The plaintiffs responded with the sworn affidavit of Dr. Dillon, who stated that an on-call supervising physician should call in periodically during his coverage shift. Dr. Kazior had a "responsibility, when he came on call, to find out what obstetrical patients had been admitted to the hospital, their condition, and to formulate a plan of management." *Id.* at 343. According to Dr. Dillon, the mother "was a known gestation diabetic with extreme obesity and no established estimated fetal weight notwithstanding sonography. As such there was a known significant risk of an extremely large baby. Therefore, there were very significant known risk factors for this pregnancy which included a known significant risk factor of shoulder dystocia." *Id.* at 343.

In December 1989, the trial court granted summary judgment for Dr. Kazior, and the plaintiffs filed a notice of appeal. The plaintiffs again filed a notice of appeal with the court of appeals. A divided panel of the court of appeals reversed the trial court's entry of summary judgment. Dr.

Kazior contended that the court of appeals erred in reversing the trial court's grant of summary judgment in his favor.

Issue

Did the physician who agreed to provide on-call supervision of obstetric residents at the hospital owe the patient a duty of reasonable care in supervising residents who actually cared for the patient?

Holding

The Supreme Court of North Carolina held that Dr. Kazior owed patients a duty to reasonably supervise obstetrics residents who provided care. Whether Dr. Kazior breached a duty by merely being available for telephone calls was a fact question.

Reason

Uncontroverted evidence before the trial court tended to show that Dr. Kazior's first contact with the infant and his parents occurred when Dr. Kazior arrived at the hospital after the delivery of the infant on December 5, 1984, in response to the telephone call from Dr. Warren. In a stipulation dated March 28, 1988, Dr. Kazior stated he had "responsibility for supervision of the OB/GYN residents and interns at the time of the birth of Alton Ray Mozingo, Jr." *Id.* at 344. "Stipulations are viewed favorably by the courts because their usage tends to simplify, shorten, or settle litigation as well as save costs to litigants." *Pelham Realty Corp. v. Board of Transp.*, 303 N.C. 424, 430–431, 279 S.E.2d 826, 830 (1981). Based on this stipulation and the uncontested fact that Dr. Kazior knew the residents at the hospital were actually treating patients when he undertook the duty to supervise the residents as an on-call supervising physician, the court concluded that Dr. Kazior owed the patients a duty of reasonable care in supervising the residents. The court also concluded that Dr. Kazior's duty of reasonable care in supervising the residents was not diminished by the fact that his relationship with the plaintiffs did not fit traditional notions of the physician–patient relationship.

Dr. Kazior argued that the affidavits of the chairmen of the three teaching hospitals in North Carolina established that he did not breach the applicable standard of care for on-call supervising physicians. The court found that these affidavits are not as unequivocal as the defendant and the dissent suggest. In these affidavits, each chairman using nearly identical language stated that an on-call supervising physician may take calls at home "unless a problem is specifically anticipated." *Id.* at 346. "According to the defendant's own experts, simply remaining at home and available to take telephone calls is not always an acceptable standard of care for supervision of residents." *Id.*

The plaintiffs introduced the affidavit and deposition of Dr. Dillon, in which he stated that Dr. Kazior did not meet the accepted medical standard for an on-call supervising physician, given the known medical condition of the mother.

Discussion

1. What do you think would be an acceptable method of supervising residents?
2. What are the risks of supervising, diagnosing, and prescribing patient care over the telephone?

20. SURGEON/SUSPENSION OF LICENSE

Citation: *Poulard v. Commissioner of Health*, 608 N.Y.S.2d 726 (N.Y. App. Div. 1994)

Facts

A surgeon instituted an Article 78 proceeding to review a determination by the State Board for Professional Conduct that suspended the surgeon's license to practice medicine for one year.

On November 20, 1987, the record disclosed that a patient was admitted to the hospital and diagnosed as suffering from a Morgagni hernia, a condition in which part of the intestine protrudes into the chest cavity through a defect in the diaphragm. On November 27, the surgeon became involved in the patient's care and participated in the surgery to repair the hernia. During the course of the operation, it became apparent that the original diagnosis had been incorrect. The tissue previously thought to be a section of bowel penetrating the diaphragm was in fact a colonic interposition, i.e., a segment of bowel that had been surgically substituted for the patient's esophagus some years earlier.

In January 1992, the Bureau of Professional Medical Conduct (BPMC) charged the surgeon with misconduct. Specifically, the surgeon was charged with practicing with gross negligence and failing to maintain adequate records. Those charges, which were supported by 25 separate allegations of misconduct, stemmed from the surgeon's care and treatment of the patient, a 28-year-old retarded male. Following the surgeon's disciplinary hearing, the hearing com-

mittee imposed a one-year suspension of petitioner's license to practice medicine, said suspension stayed indefinitely, and a fine of $10,000. The surgeon subsequently commenced a CPLR article 78 proceeding pursuant to Public Health Law § 230-c(5).

Issue

Did the evidence support a finding by the committee that the surgeon had practiced with gross negligence?

Holding

The New York Supreme Court, Appellate Division, held that the evidence supported a finding that the surgeon had practiced with gross negligence.

Reason

The hearing committee's determination of gross negligence was based on findings that the surgeon misinterpreted the patient's X-ray, failed to defer the patient's surgery after being informed of certain abnormal test results, failed to recognize the colonic interposition during the course of the patient's surgery, and rendered deficient postoperative care, as evidenced by the patient's severe weight loss. The appeals court was of the view that the testimony offered by an expert, Dr. Roome, a board-certified surgeon, together with other documentary evidence and, in some instances, the surgeon's admissions, provided the substantial evidence necessary to support the findings made as to each of the sustained allegations.

Discussion

1. What are the implications for health care organizations that fail to adequately conduct peer review activities?
2. Why are physicians often reluctant to take disciplinary action during the peer review process?

21. FAILURE TO READ NURSE'S NOTES/ INFECTION/INADEQUATE NUTRITION

Citation: *Todd v. Sauls*, 647 So. 2d 1366 (La. App. 1994)

Facts

Mr. Todd was admitted to Rapides General Hospital on October 3, 1988, and on October 4, 1988, Dr. Sauls performed bypass surgery. Postoperatively, Mr. Todd sustained a heart attack. During the following days, Mr. Todd did not ambulate well and suffered a weight loss of 19.5 pounds. The medical record indicated that Mr. Todd's sternotomy wound and the midlower left leg incision were reddened and his temperature was 99.6 degrees.

Dr. Sauls, admittedly, did not commonly read the nurses' notes but instead preferred to rely on his own observations of the patient. He indicated in his October 18 notes that there was no drainage. The nurse's notes, however, show that there was drainage at the chest tube site. Contrary to the medical records showing that Mr. Todd had a temperature of 101.2 degrees, Dr. Sauls noted that the patient was afebrile.

On October 19, Dr. Sauls noted that Mr. Todd's wounds were improving and he did not have a fever. Nurses' notes indicated redness at the surgical wounds and a temperature of 100 degrees. No white blood count (WBC) had been ordered. On October 20, nurses' notes again indicate wound redness and a temperature of 100.8 degrees. No wound culture had yet been ordered. Dr. Kamil, one of Mr. Todd's treating physicians, noted that Mr. Todd's nutritional status needed to be seriously confronted and suggested that Dr. Sauls consider supplemental feeding. Despite this, no follow-up to his recommendation appears and the record is void of any action by Dr. Sauls to obtain a nutritional consult. By October 21, Mr. Todd was transferred to the intensive care unit (ICU) because he was gravely ill with profoundly depressed ventricular function.

The nurses' notes on October 22 describe the chest tube site as draining foul smelling bloody purulence. The patient's temperature was recorded to have reached 100.6 degrees. This is the first time that Dr. Sauls had the test tube site cultured. The culture report from the laboratory indicated a staph infection and Mr. Todd was started on antibiotics for treatment of the infection.

At the request of family, Mr. Todd was transferred to St. Luke's Hospital. At St. Luke's, Dr. Leatherman, an internist and invasive cardiologist treated Mr. Todd. Dr. Zeluff, an infectious disease specialist, examined Mr. Todd's surgical wounds and prescribed antibiotic treatment. Upon admission to St. Luke's, each of Mr. Todd's surgical wounds was infected. Despite Mr. Todd's care, he died at St. Luke's on November 2, 1988.

Issue

Did the surgeon breach his duty of care owed to the patient by failing to aggressively treat surgical wound infections, not taking advantage of nurses' observations of infections, and allowing the patient's body weight to rapidly waste away by failing to provide adequate nourishment to the patient following surgery?

Holding

The Court of Appeal of Louisiana held that Dr. Sauls committed medical malpractice when he breached the standard of care he owed to Mr. Todd. His malpractice contributed to Mr. Todd's death where Mr. Todd was effectively ineligible for a heart transplant, which was his only chance of survival, due to infections and malnourishment caused by Dr. Sauls' malpractice. Dr. Sauls' testimony convinced the court that he failed to aggressively treat the surgical wound infections, that he chose not to take advantage of the nurses' observations of infection, and that he allowed Mr. Todd's body weight to waste away, knowing firsthand that extreme vigilance was required because of Mr. Todd's already severely impaired heart. The awards of $4,975 for funeral expenses; $19,533.42 for medical expenses; $150,000 for Mrs. Todd; and $50,000 to each of his seven children for loss of love and affection were appropriate.

Reason

In cases where a patient has died, the plaintiff need not demonstrate "that the patient would have survived if properly treated." Rather, the plaintiff need only prove that the patient had a chance of survival and that his or her chance of survival was lost as a result of the defendant/physician's negligence. The defendant/physician's conduct "must increase the risk of a patient's harm to the extent of being a substantial factor in causing the result but need not be the only cause." Dr. Sauls' medical malpractice exacerbated an already critical condition and deprived Mr. Todd of a chance of survival.

Dr. Leatherman stated that it was the responsibility of the surgeon and cardiologist to pay closer attention to Mr. Todd's nutritional status and to have better managed his weight. He emphasized that wounds cannot heal when a patient is malnourished. Dr. Leatherman opined that Dr. Sauls deviated from the required standard of care he owed to Mr. Todd.

Dr. Zeluff stated that impaired nutritional status depresses the body's immune system and adversely affects the body's ability to heal wounds. In response to a hypothetical fact situation based on Mr. Todd's medical records at Rapides General, Dr. Zeluff opined that Dr. Sauls further deviated from the standard of care by failing to initiate alimentation, parenterally or enterally, by at least October 20.

Dr. Pipkin, an expert cardiac surgeon, corroborated the testimony of Dr. Leatherman and Dr. Zeluff on the negative effect that malnourishment has on the healing process and the body's ability to fight infection. Dr. Pipkin stated that it was Dr. Sauls' responsibility to make certain that Mr. Todd received adequate calories and proteins. After reviewing the records of Mr. Todd, Dr. Pipkin found that there was a general wasting of Mr. Todd in the postoperative period as evidenced by his steady loss of weight. Dr. Pipkin opined that Dr. Sauls deviated from the standard of care owed Mr. Todd both with regard to wound infections and malnourishment.

Discussion

1. What liability might be imputed to the hospital if it had purchased Dr. Sauls' practice and he was an employee of the hospital?
2. Discuss how similar events can be prevented from occurring. Consider first why the event occurred, remembering that there may be more than one why.

22. INFECTION/FAILURE TO READ LABORATORY RESULTS

Citation: *Smith v. U.S. Dept. of Veterans Affairs*, 865 F. Supp. 433 (N.D. Ohio 1994)

Facts

Plaintiff, Mr. Smith, was first diagnosed as having schizophrenia in 1972. He had been admitted to the Veterans Affairs (VA) Hospital psychiatric ward 15 times since 1972. His admissions grew longer and more frequent as time passed. On March 17, 1990, he had been drinking in a bar, got into a fight, and was eventually taken to the VA hospital. Dr. Rizk was assigned as Mr. Smith's attending physician.

On March 19, shortly after his arrival, Mr. Smith developed an acute problem with his respiration and level of consciousness. It was determined that his psychiatric medications were responsible for his condition. Some medications were discontinued and others reduced. An improvement in his condition was noted. By March 23, Mr. Smith began to complain of pain in his shoulders and neck. He attributed the pain to osteoarthritis and over 20 years' service as a letter carrier. His medical record indicated that he had similar complaints in the past.

A rheumatology consultation was requested and carried out on March 29. The rheumatology resident conducted an examination and noted that Mr. Smith reported bilateral shoulder pain increasing with activity as an ongoing problem since 1979. Various tests were ordered, including an erythrocyte sedimentation rate (ESR).

On April 1, Mr. Smith became actively psychotic and was placed in four point leather restraints. By April 3, Mr. Smith was incontinent and complained of shoulder pain. By the

afternoon he was out of restraints, walked to the shower, and bathed himself. Upon returning to his room he claimed he could not get into bed. He was given a pillow and slept on the floor. By morning, Mr. Smith was lying on the floor in urine and complaining of numbness. His failure to move was attributed to his psychosis. By evening, it was noted that Mr. Smith could not lift himself and would not use his hands. On April 5, a medical student noted that Mr. Smith was having difficulty breathing and called a pulmonary consultation. He was noted to be either unwilling or unable to grasp a nurse's hand and continued to complain that his legs would not hold him up.

By the morning of April 6, Mr. Smith was complaining that his neck and back hurt and that he had no feeling in his legs and feet. Later that day a medical student noted that the results of Mr. Smith's ESR were more than twice the normal range and his WBC was 18.1, well above the normal rate. There was a note on the medical record that Mr. Smith had been unable to move his extremities for about five days. A psychiatric resident noted that Mr. Smith had been incontinent for three days and had a fever of 101.1 degrees.

On the morning of April 7, Mr. Smith was taken to University Hospital for magnetic resonance imaging of his neck. Imaging revealed a mass subsequently identified as a spinal epidural abscess. By the time it was excised, it had been pressing on his spinal cord too long for any spinal function below vertebrae 4 and 5 to remain.

Issue

Was the physicians' failure to promptly review the results of the plaintiff's erythrocyte sedimentation rate the proximate cause of his paralysis?

Holding

The District Court held that the negligent failure of physicians to promptly review laboratory tests results was the proximate cause of the plaintiff's quadriplegia.

Reason

Of primary importance was the plaintiff's ESR of 110, the result of which was available by April 2, which was not seen, or at least not noted in the record, until April 6. Although witnesses for both sides purported to disagree, there was little disagreement as to the nature and importance of this test. An elevated ESR generally accounts for one of three problems: infection, cancer, or a connective tissue disorder. Most experts agreed that, at the very least, a repeat ESR should have been ordered. The VA's care of the plaintiff fell below the reasonable standard of care in that nobody read the lab results, which were available on the patient care unit by April 2. The fact that the tests were ordered mandates the immediate review of their results. Although it cannot be known with certainty what would have occurred had the ESR been read and acted upon on April 2, it is certain that the plaintiff would have had a chance to fully recover from his infection. By April 6, the chance was gone.

In light of the absence of notes from Dr. Rizk in plaintiff's chart, it is impossible to know if he was aware of the plaintiff's symptoms. It appears that because of the absence of Dr. Rizk's notes into the plaintiff's chart, Dr. Rizk's care of the plaintiff was negligent. The failure to review the results of the plaintiff's ESR constituted negligence under the relevant standard of care. That failure led to the failure to make an early diagnosis of the plaintiff's epidural abscess, and was itself the proximate cause of his eventual paralysis. Negligent conduct is the proximate cause of an injury if the injury is the natural and probable consequences of negligent conduct. An injury is the natural and probable consequences of negligent conduct if the injury might and should have been foreseen. An injury is foreseeable if a reasonably prudent person under the same or similar circumstances would have anticipated that injury to another was the likely result of his conduct. In light of the fact that a high ESR can manifest itself in a very serious illness, it was foreseeable that ignoring a high ESR would lead to serious injury.

Discussion

1. Discuss the importance of a computerized order entry and reporting system. How might the outcome of this case have been different if lab test panic values were immediately directed to the patient care unit and physician?
2. Discuss the importance of charting. How might the outcome of this case have been different if the plaintiff had been on an acute care medical/surgical unit?

23. NEGLIGENT INJECTION

Citation: *Tesauro v. Perrige*, 650 A.2d 1079 (Pa. Super. 1994)

Facts

In 1984, Ms. Tesauro, appellee, saw Dr. Perrige, appellant, to have a lower left molar removed. A blood clot failed to form and the appellant administered an injection of alcohol near the affected area. The appellee began to experience pain, burning, and numbness at the site of the injection—on the left side of her face. She was diagnosed by several physicians as suffering from muscle spasms caused by a damaged trigeminal nerve. Over a five-year period the appellee was treated by a variety of specialists. In 1989, the plaintiff underwent radical experimental surgery. The surgery corrected the plaintiff's most oppressive symptoms. Although the most painful symptoms have been eliminated, the appellee continues to suffer numbness and burning on the left side of her face. A dental malpractice lawsuit was filed against Dr. Perrige alleging that he was negligent in administering the alcohol injection so close to the trigeminal nerve. The jury returned a verdict in favor of the plaintiffs in the amounts of $2,747,000 to Ms. Tesauro and $593,000 to Mr. Tesauro for loss of consortium. Dr. Perrige, the defendant/appellant, appealed.

Issue

Should a new trial be granted based on the excessiveness of the jury verdict?

Holding

The Superior Court held that the evidence supported the damage awards.

Reason

The decision to grant or not to grant a new trial based on the excessiveness of a jury verdict was found to be within the sound discretion of the trial court. In determining excessiveness, a court should consider:

> (1) the severity of the injury; (2) whether the injury is manifested by objective physical evidence or whether it is only revealed by the subjective testimony; (3) whether the injury is permanent; (4) whether the plaintiff can continue with his or her employment; (5) the size of out-of-pocket expenses; (6) the amount of compensation demanded in the original complaint. *Id.* at 1081.

The Superior Court determined that the severity of the plaintiff's injury in itself would support the compensatory award. The plaintiff spent five years trying to find a cure for her pain. While much recovered, the plaintiff continues to suffer from numbness and burning. Her experience clearly falls into the category of severe injury. The severity of the injury had a huge effect on the marital relationship. The compensation awarded to Mr. Tesauro was, therefore, fair and just.

Discussion

1. If Dr. Perrige's practice was owned by a hospital, under what theory might liability be imputed to the hospital?
2. What are the obvious implications in this case for those hospitals considering the purchase of a professional practice?

24. MISDIAGNOSIS AND DISCIPLINARY ACTION

Citation: *Hamilton v. Baystate Med. Educ. & Research Found.*, 866 F. Supp. 51 (D. Mass. 1994)

Facts

The defendants claim that Dr. Hamilton's performance as a pathologist began to deteriorate and became progressively worse. The first indication of Dr. Hamilton's slip in performance was when he incorrectly labeled a specimen in his pathology report in January 1986. A year later, in January 1987, a customary review of one of his cases revealed a misdiagnosis. In biopsies of a right and left breast, Dr. Hamilton incorrectly diagnosed a tumor in the right breast as benign rather than malignant, and improperly classified the tumor in the left breast. Dr. Sullivan, chairperson of the pathology department, met with Dr. Hamilton. They discussed three more cases in which Dr. Hamilton erred in either the diagnosis or labeling of a specimen. In November 1988, Dr. Hamilton misdiagnosed a sample of breast tissue and concluded that the patient had cancer of the right breast. As a result, the patient underwent an unnecessary mastectomy as well as chemotherapy and radiation treatment.

On January 19, 1989, Dr. Sullivan suggested to Dr. Hamilton that he take some vacation time to determine if he was ill. Dr. Sullivan also suggested to Dr. Hamilton that he should consider resigning. January 19, 1989, was the last day Dr. Hamilton performed his duties at the hospital. At about that time, Dr. Hamilton learned that he had been suffering from Graves disease for roughly the previous three years. Graves disease causes the body's immune system to attack the thyroid gland and can result in the impairment of a person's memory and ability to concentrate. Dr. Haag, Dr. Hamilton's treating physician, characterized his condition as severe and believed the Graves disease was most likely responsible for Dr. Hamilton's slip in performance as a pathologist. Dr. Hamilton then filed for long-term disability benefits.

By late spring of 1989, Dr. Hamilton's thyroid hormone levels were within normal limits and controlled by medication. He sent a letter to Dr. Sullivan indicating that he intended to return to work on September 1, 1989. In this same letter he also stated that he did not view himself as being "cured." Dr. Sullivan denied Dr. Hamilton's request to return to work.

Dr. Sullivan, Dr. Hamilton, and other physicians met at the hospital on September 1, 1989. At this meeting, Dr. Hamilton reiterated his desire to return to work on a part-time basis. Dr. Sullivan once again denied his request, claiming that he was concerned about patient safety. Dr. Hamilton alleges that no one at this meeting told him he was formally discharged.

On September 7, 1989, Dr. Hamilton wrote Dr. Sullivan asking to return to work on September 11, 1989. The following day, Dr. Sullivan phoned Dr. Hamilton. Dr. Hamilton alleged that during this phone conversation Dr. Sullivan did not inform him that he was discharged. Defendants claim that by this time they had effectively discharged Dr. Hamilton.

In September 1989, Dr. Hamilton retained an attorney to negotiate a settlement on his claims against the hospital. Dr. Hamilton denies that he was ever told that he was terminated.

Issue

Was the employer's decision to terminate the plaintiff after he had committed serious medical errors reasonable and did the termination constitute a breach of contract?

Holding

The District Court held that the employer's decision to terminate the plaintiff after he had committed serious medical errors was reasonable and did not constitute breach of contract.

Reason

For three years, Dr. Hamilton suffered from a disease that affected his mental faculties. He committed serious medical errors, made a gross misdiagnosis resulting in an unnecessary mastectomy, and subjected the patient to high levels of needless radiation therapy. It is undisputed that Dr. Hamilton himself told Dr. Sullivan that he did not regard himself as being cured. Although Dr. Hamilton asserts that he received medical clearance from expert medical personnel, he presented no evidence to support the claim that he was capable of returning to work.

All evidence before the court confirmed the reasonableness of the defendants' belief that Dr. Hamilton could not fulfill his obligations under the terms of the employment agreement. Whether Dr. Hamilton could have properly performed his obligations does not matter. Based on the undisputed facts, defendants' belief that Dr. Hamilton's illness substantially and adversely affected his ability to fulfill his obligations was reasonable.

Discussion

1. Discuss why physicians and hospitals seem to be reluctant to take disciplinary action on a timely basis.
2. How might this case have been handled differently?

25. X-RAYS MISREAD/JURY INSTRUCTIONS

Citation: *Bouley v. Reisman*, 645 N.E.2d 708 (1995)

Facts

This is an appeal by the plaintiff, administratrix of the estate of Ms. Bouley, from jury verdicts in favor of Dr. Reisman and Dr. Sitzman, both medical doctors, and Emergency Care, Inc. (ECI). The plaintiff had alleged that the death of Ms. Bouley from advanced lung cancer resulted from the medical negligence of each of the defendants in connection with the care Ms. Bouley received at Malden Hospital. On appeal, the plaintiff raised several issues concerning the judge's rulings on her proposed requests for jury instructions.

On February 16, 1986, Ms. Bouley was involved in an automobile accident. That afternoon she went to the emergency department at the Malden Hospital because she had been experiencing pain in the area of her left ribs, which were injured in the accident. At that time she was seen by the defendant, Dr. Reisman, a specialist in emergency medicine and an employee of ECI.

After Dr. Reisman conducted a physical examination of Ms. Bouley, he ordered X-rays taken of Ms. Bouley's left ribs. She went to the X-ray department where four X-rays were taken: three showing the left ribs at different angles and one a posterior, anterior chest X-ray. She then returned with her X-rays to the emergency department. Because it was Sunday and after 5 P.M. when the X-rays were taken, no radiologist was on duty.

Dr. Reisman read and interpreted the X-rays, including the chest X-ray. He wrote "OK" on the reading form and discharged Ms. Bouley. He made a discharge diagnosis of "contusion left ribs" and wrote that her condition upon discharge was "good." He then referred her X-rays to the radiology department for review by a radiologist the following day.

The defendant, Dr. Sitzman, a radiologist, was on duty the next day. He read all of Ms. Bouley's X-rays that morning. When he read Ms. Bouley's chest X-ray, he saw an indeterminate density in the right upper lobe of her lung. It was Dr. Sitzman's opinion that the density he detected in Ms. Bouley's lung represented a "significant positive finding" that required further investigation. Ms. Bouley was not informed of the presence of the density by either Dr. Reisman or Dr. Sitzman or any other physician at the Malden Hospital. Ten months later at the Lahey Clinic, the density seen by Dr. Sitzman was diagnosed as a malignant lung cancer. Ms. Bouley died from lung cancer on February 19, 1987.

Issue

Should the trial judge have included the plaintiff's request, as to an inference to be drawn against Dr. Sitzman from lack of a written record of a telephone call, in his instructions to the jury?

Holding

The judge had discretion to decide whether or not to include the instruction. The appeals court found no abuse of that discretion, especially where the judge gave detailed instructions to the jury about their role in determining the credibility of witnesses and the inferences that they might draw from the direct and circumstantial evidence presented at the trial.

Reason

Dr. Sitzman testified that when a patient was referred to him by the emergency department, it was his personal practice to report significant positive findings (such as he saw in Ms. Bouley's chest X-ray) both through a written report and through a telephone report to the emergency department. It was his practice not to ask for anyone in particular when he called, but rather to give the information to whoever answered the telephone. It was Dr. Sitzman's impression that his oral report of a significant positive finding would always be written down by the person receiving the telephone call in the emergency department. Dr. Sitzman had no actual memory of making a telephone call concerning the Bouley matter but testified that he thinks it was made because he always telephoned in that situation. The physician, an ECI employee, who was on duty in the emergency department the day that Dr. Sitzman read Ms. Bouley's X-rays, could not remember any such telephone call. If that physician had received a telephone call from Dr. Sitzman, there would have been some notation made in Ms. Bouley's medical record about the contents of the telephone message. No such notation appeared in Ms. Bouley's record.

Plaintiff submitted the following request for an instruction by the judge to the jury:

> If you find that it was required of all personnel in the emergency department at the Malden Hospital on February 16, 1986 to make a written record of any telephone calls made by a radiologist reporting abnormal X-rays and that this written record would be made in the emergency department record of the patient or in an addendum to the patient's emergency department record, you may find from the lack or absence of a written record of such a telephone call in the Lillian Bouley's emergency department records or in the addendum to it, that no such telephone call was ever made by the radiologist in this case.

The judge did not include the instruction in his charge to the jury. The plaintiff renewed her request. The trial judge declined to give the requested instruction, stating "I know it is important. I have chosen not to instruct on the possible inferences and identifying the possible inferences." Ms. Bouley claimed error.

Appellate courts have traditionally accorded the trial judge considerable discretion in framing jury instructions, both in determining the precise phraseology to be used and in determining the appropriate degree of elaboration needed. As a general rule, requests seeking an instruction that a finding of certain specified facts (of which there was some evidence) do or do not warrant or require a particular conclusion may, within an exercise of the judge's discretion, be properly refused.

The evidence that there was no notation in Ms. Bouley's record of Dr. Sitzman's telephone call would not necessarily warrant the jury's drawing the inference that Dr. Sitzman did not make the call. The lack of a notation in Ms. Bouley's record could have meant that (1) Dr. Sitzman did not call; (2) Dr. Sitzman did call but the message he left was not passed on to the emergency department physician; or (3) Dr. Sitzman did call, the message was passed on to a physician, but no notation was made on the record. Therefore, several inferences were possible from the lack of a notation, not just the one that was the subject of the requested instruction.

Further, there was conflicting evidence concerning whether the standard of care expected of a qualified radiologist required a telephone call to the emergency department about the significant positive finding in Ms. Bouley's X-ray. While plaintiff's expert and Dr. Sitzman himself testified that the standard of care required a telephone call, there was evidence from Dr. Sitzman's expert and from Dr. Sitzman (he contradicted his earlier testimony) that the standard of care required only a written report, not an oral report. Consequently, a finding that no phone call was made was not decisive on the issue of Dr. Sitzman's negligence because the jury would still have had to determine whether the standard of care required that he make such a call.

Discussion

1. Do you consider this case a people problem or a systems failure? Why?
2. What safeguards might the hospital and physicians implement to prevent similar occurrences in the future?

26. NONTHERAPEUTIC PRESCRIPTION OF CONTROLLED SUBSTANCES

Citation: *Caldwell v. Department of Prof'l Regulation*, 684 N.E.2d 913 (Ill. App. 1997)

Facts

The Illinois Department of Professional Regulation (Department) filed a 20-count complaint against the plaintiff, Dr. Caldwell. Counts XVII through XX alleged that, between 1984 and 1990, the plaintiff prescribed controlled substances to a patient, Ms. Barnes, for nontherapeutic purposes in violation of the Illinois Medical Practice Act, the Illinois Medical Practice Act of 1987, and the Illinois Controlled Substances Act. In each of these counts, the Department sought that plaintiff's medical license be suspended or revoked or that plaintiff be otherwise disciplined. The plaintiff testified on his own behalf. He stated that he first treated Ms. Barnes in 1984 and continues to treat her through the time of the hearing. Ms. Barnes has suffered from numerous ailments, including hypertension, arthritis, obesity, and a herniated disc in her back. The plaintiff treated Ms. Barnes by conducting physical examinations and prescribing medications. The Department introduced into evidence copies of at least 74 prescriptions plaintiff issued to Ms. Barnes for various painkillers and tranquilizers. The plaintiff identified each of these prescriptions, most of which authorized at least one refill.

The drugs prescribed by the plaintiff were Darvocet N-100, meprobamate, phenobarbital, and Tylenol 4. Darvocet and Tylenol 4 are analgesics used to relieve mild to moderate pain. Meprobamate is a tranquilizer that plaintiff testified can be used as a muscle relaxant. Phenobarbital is a sedative. All of these drugs are controlled substances and are capable of causing dependency.

The plaintiff testified that he believes his treatment of Ms. Barnes was consistent with accepted standards of medical care. The plaintiff never detected any signs that Ms. Barnes was becoming dependent on any of the medications he prescribed.

Dr. Singleton testified as an expert witness on the plaintiff's behalf. Dr. Singleton is board certified in neurology, a field that includes treatment of lower back pain. Dr. Singleton testified that a proper course of treatment for a patient such as Ms. Barnes would include physical therapy and prescriptions for analgesics and muscle relaxants. It would not be improper to prescribe these medications again if the patient continued to experience pain. Under questioning from the hearing officer, Dr. Singleton testified that a patient who seeks numerous prescriptions for Darvocet and Tylenol 4, with refills, in the space of two months may be displaying signs of addiction.

Mr. Barnes, Ms. Barnes' husband, testified that he never consulted the plaintiff as a physician. He also stated that he contacted the plaintiff, complaining that his wife was addicted to pain pills. He asked the plaintiff to help her stop taking the pills, but the prescriptions continued. On April 12, 1990, Mr. Barnes found his wife on the bathroom floor unable to stand because she had taken too many pills. He called the paramedics, who took Ms. Barnes to St. Francis Hospital.

She remained there for four or five days. After her release from the hospital, she continued to see the plaintiff, and the plaintiff continued to prescribe the same drugs for her. Ms. Barnes was still seeing the plaintiff at the time of the hearing.

Dr. Koos testified that he was on duty at St. Francis Hospital when Ms. Barnes was admitted. He ordered tests, which indicated that Ms. Barnes had suffered a drug overdose from ingesting a combination of phenobarbital, meprobamate, and Darvocet. Dr. Czarnecki testified as an expert witness for the Department. Dr. Czarnecki is board certified in both cardiology and internal medicine. Prior to testifying, he reviewed insurance claim forms submitted by the plaintiff for the treatment of Ms. Barnes, the prescriptions plaintiff issued to Ms. Barnes, and some of plaintiff's progress notes concerning Ms. Barnes.

Dr. Czarnecki testified that, in his opinion, the prescriptions did not conform to accepted medical standards. He stated that the prescriptions were excessive in quantity, and many of them were inappropriate for Ms. Barnes's ailments. He testified that all of the drugs prescribed by plaintiff are intended to be for short-term use. A treating physician should use these drugs to alleviate the patient's pain while other treatments are used to address the cause of the pain. Dr. Czarnecki testified that these medications should be used

very cautiously when taken with phenobarbital or meprobamate. He concluded that, in his opinion, the continued prescriptions of Darvocet, Tylenol 4, meprobamate, and phenobarbital served no therapeutic purpose. Also, attempts to refill such prescriptions too soon indicate that the patient may be developing an addiction to the medication, which should cause the patient's physician to stop issuing the prescriptions.

The hearing officer released his report and recommendation finding that Ms. Barnes received prescriptions from plaintiff for Darvocet N-100, meprobamate, phenobarbital, and Tylenol 4 on 122 occasions between February 1986 and September 1990. The report stated that Ms. Barnes was a narcotic-dependent person and that plaintiff continued to prescribe controlled substances when he knew or should have known of her dependency. The hearing officer found that the prescriptions were issued in a nontherapeutic manner with recklessness and disregard for the patient's wellbeing. He further specifically found that all of the witnesses who testified during the hearing, except plaintiff, were credible. Plaintiff's testimony was deemed not credible.

The hearing officer found that the Department had proved counts XVII through XX by clear and convincing evidence. As a result, he recommended that plaintiff's medical license be placed on probation for five years, that his controlled substances license be revoked, and that the plaintiff be fined $20,000. Both the medical disciplinary board and the director adopted the hearing officer's findings of fact and conclusions of law. The Director issued a decision imposing the sanctions recommended by the hearing officer.

The plaintiff filed an action for administrative review. The circuit court affirmed the Department Director's decision. The plaintiff filed a motion for reconsideration that the circuit court denied. Plaintiff filed a notice of appeal.

Issue

Was there ample evidence to support the Director's decision that the physician had recklessly prescribed controlled substances for nontherapeutic purposes without regard for the safety of his patient and in violation of the Medical Practice Act and the Controlled Substances Act?

Holding

There was ample evidence to support a decision that the physician had recklessly prescribed controlled substances for nontherapeutic purposes without regard for the safety of his patient and in violation of the Medical Practice Act and the Controlled Substances Act.

Reason

The prescriptions at issue in this case were written between 1984 and 1990. The Illinois Medical Practice Act was amended in 1987, and, therefore, plaintiff was charged under the Act as it existed both before and after the amendment. Nonetheless, the relevant provisions are substantively the same. The 1987 statute provides:

The Department may revoke, suspend, place on probationary status, or take any other disciplinary action as the Department may deem proper with regard to the license or visiting professor permit of any person issued under this Act to practice medicine, . . . upon any of the following grounds:

* * * *

4. Gross negligence in practice under this Act;

* * * *

17. Prescribing, selling, administering, distributing, giving or self administering any drug classified as a controlled substance (designated product) or narcotic for other than medically accepted therapeutic purposes.

The hearing officer found the Department sustained its burden of proving by clear and convincing evidence that the plaintiff wrote prescriptions in a nontherapeutic manner in reckless disregard for Ms. Barnes' well-being. The Director adopted the hearing officer's finding and sanctioned plaintiff in a manner authorized by the Medical Practice Act.

Upon the plaintiff's action for administrative review, the burden shifted to the plaintiff to show that the Director's decision was against the manifest weight of the evidence. The record in this case contains ample evidence to support the Director's decision that the plaintiff recklessly prescribed controlled substances for nontherapeutic purposes without regard for the safety of his patient and in violation of the Medical Practice Act and the Controlled Substances Act. Every witness who testified, including plaintiff and his own expert, provided such evidence. Plaintiff admitted that he issued these prescriptions. He allowed Ms. Barnes to receive narcotic painkillers, tranquilizers, and sedatives in sufficient quantity and with sufficient regularity that Ms. Barnes was almost never without these drugs for a period of six years. The plaintiff issued these prescriptions, most with at least one authorized refill, despite his admitted knowledge that Ms. Barnes was using the drugs too quickly.

According to Dr. Czarnecki, the plaintiff's treatment of Ms. Barnes failed to conform to accepted medical standards. The drugs he prescribed are highly addictive and intended only for short-term use. Also, narcotic analgesics should only be used in combination with tranquilizers in the exercise of extreme caution. Dr. Czarnecki testified that, under the circumstances, it should have been clear to the plaintiff that Ms. Barnes was developing a dependency on these drugs. Even the plaintiff's own expert witness provided some testimony that supports the Director's decision. Dr. Singleton admitted that circumstances such as those may indicate the patient is developing an addiction.

Discussion

1. Do you agree with the court's decision? Why?
2. What are the implications for physicians who are attempting to control a patient's pain with the use of controlled substances?

VII

Nursing and the Law

1. FAILURE TO MONITOR VITAL SIGNS

Citation: *Porter v. Lima Mem'l Hosp.*, 995 F.2d 629 (6th Cir. 1993)

Facts

A medical malpractice action was filed on behalf of Liesl Fitzenrider, an infant who was injured in an automobile accident and subsequently developed paralysis allegedly because of the physician's and hospital's failure to diagnose a spinal cord injury.

On December 1, 1979, the automobile in which Liesl was traveling spun out of control and she was thrown to the floor of the car. The rescue squad personnel examined the infant and found nothing seriously wrong. A rescue squad member then held Liesl in his arms while she and her mother, Mrs. Porter, were transported to Lima Memorial Hospital (Lima), the hospital nearest to the scene of the accident.

The rescue squad took Liesl to the Lima emergency department, where she lay on a hospital table awaiting examination by Dr. Singh, an emergency department physician. Ms. Ogelsbee, a registered nurse, took Liesl's vital signs and recorded them on the medical chart. She reported them to Dr. Singh, upon his arrival, for examination and treatment. At this point, the only observable sign of injury was a small bruise or hematoma on the right side of Liesl's head. Ms. Ogelsbee also reported this to Dr. Singh, and he then assumed primary responsibility for treating Liesl. Dr. Singh found all of Liesl's extremities functioning normally and ordered several laboratory tests and numerous X-rays. He did not, however, order any spinal X-rays and failed to diagnose spinal instability. Ms. Ogelsbee did not repeat the

vital signs during or after Dr. Singh's examination, claiming that she received no doctor's instruction in this regard. After reviewing the X-rays and laboratory tests, Dr. Singh discharged Liesl and provided her mother with written instructions concerning her head injuries.

After Dr. Singh discharged Liesl, she and her mother remained at the hospital while awaiting a ride home. During a period of more than two hours, Liesl apparently displayed no additional signs of serious injury as observed by her mother. Her mother did report a short period of irregular breathing to one of the nurses at Lima. The nurse examined Liesl, determined that nothing was wrong, and returned Liesl to her mother. Mrs. Porter made no further inquiries; she testified that the nurse told her that "babies just breathe funny." When she reached her home, the mother noted that Liesl's condition was worsening and she then took Liesl to Defiance Hospital, where doctors determined, for the first time, that Liesl's legs were not moving. They ordered numerous X-rays and laboratory tests, and eventually another hospital staff doctor diagnosed a subluxation at her first and second lumbar vertebrae, which resulted in Liesl's paralysis from the waist down. The experts who testified in the trial agreed that Liesl suffered paralysis sometime after Dr. Singh's examination and before her arrival, hours later, at Defiance Hospital.

The experts also appeared to agree that Dr. Singh was the primary person who could have prevented the spinal injury by diagnosing Liesl's unstable spine before it became critically injured. Dr. Singh settled for $2,500,000.

Proximate cause was the crucial issue upon which Lima's asserted liability depended. There was evidence that both Dr. Singh and the Lima nurses breached a duty of care, and this evidence of negligence was sufficient to survive Lima's motion for a new trial. The pertinent question was whether the nurses' conduct proximately caused Liesl's paralysis. The district court, after the mother settled with the physician, denied the hospital's motion for judgment, notwithstanding the verdict in favor of the mother, but ordered a new trial at which the jury found the hospital not liable for the infant's injuries. Both the hospital and the mother appealed.

Issue

Did the Lima nurses' conduct proximately cause the infant's paralysis? Does Ohio law require expert testimony as to causation?

Holding

The United States Court of Appeals for the Sixth Circuit held that the nurses' failure to repeat vital signs was legally insufficient to establish a connection between the failure to repeat vital signs and the eventual paralysis.

Reason

After the accident, Liesl was not immobilized while being transported to Lima. Dr. Singh did not direct that she be immobilized at any time while examining, testing, and treating her, but notes that she was moving her extremities. Liesl demonstrated no signs of paralysis while he was examining her, and this would seem to eliminate any failure of this kind, which may have previously occurred, as a proximate cause of the paralysis. The experts on both sides generally agreed that the Lima nurses had no independent duty, apart from a doctor's instructions, to immobilize the infant.

The plaintiff's expert, Dr. Hall, changed his original, unequivocal opinion that the Lima nurses acted appropriately in the care of Liesl, but he made it clear, nonetheless, that the doctor was the ultimate person responsible from the standpoint of proximate cause:

Q. Now, Doctor [Hall], generally speaking, it's the role and responsibility of the emergency room physician to determine the patient's medical diagnosis and then to order the necessary and appropriate medical treatment, is it not?

A. Yes, it is.

Q. And, Doctor, in this case, where the emergency room doctor did not diagnose any spinal cord injury and discharged the baby after examining and X-raying the infant, you're not criticizing the nurses

for not diagnosing and treating the spinal cord injury, are you?

A. That's correct.

Q. And that's because it was Dr. Singh's role and responsibility to do that, correct?

A. Yes.

Q. And what you're telling the jury is that, in your opinion, it was Dr. Singh who was responsible for treating Liesl's spinal cord injury, or at least he was responsible for ordering Liesl to be immobilized and hospitalized for further care and work up, isn't that the thrust of your testimony in this case?

A. Yes.

Q. So you are not saying that the conduct of the nurses or other hospital personnel caused any permanent harm or injury [to Liesl Fitzenrider], are you?

A. That's correct. *Id.* at 634.

Dr. Aranosian, another of the plaintiff's experts, opined that the Lima nurses should have repeated vital signs. Like Dr. Hall, however, he believed it was Dr. Singh's failure rather than the nurses' failure to repeat vital signs or to immobilize Liesl that proximately caused Liesl's injuries:

Q. Okay. And it's your testimony that Dr. Singh should have ordered Liesl to be immobilized after she arrived at the emergency room, isn't that correct?

A. Yes, sir.

Q. And it's your opinion that as far as responsibility for ordering immobilization in the emergency room in 1979 that would be the duty of the emergency room physician involved in the care of the patient, isn't that true?

A. Yes, sir.

Q. And it's also true—now, generally speaking, I will go on. Now, generally speaking, isn't it the real object and responsibility of the emergency room physician to determine the patient's medical diagnosis and then to order the necessary and appropriate medical treatment?

A. Yes, sir.

Q. And, Doctor, in this case, where the emergency room doctor did not diagnose any spinal cord injury and then discharged the baby after examining and X-raying the infant, you certainly are not criticizing the nurses for not diagnosing and treating the spinal cord injury, are you?

A. Well, that's correct. I mean, the nurse would not make the diagnosis on the child. That's correct.

Q. And that's because it was Dr. Singh's role and responsibility to determine the medical diagnosis and then order the necessary and appropriate medical treatment, isn't that correct?

A. Yes, sir. *Id.* at 634.

Dr. Kiehl's testimony as to vital signs was to the same effect. Still another of the plaintiff's experts, Dr. Kytja Voeller, was even more specific in stating: "I don't think the vital signs had any causal relationship" to the paralysis. *Id.*

Discussion

1. What is the importance of patient assessment and documentation?
2. What is the importance of collaboration between the nurse and physician as it relates to this case?

2. MONITORING PATIENT'S PULSE/NURSE'S NEGLIGENCE

Citation: *Luthart v. Danesh*, 649 N.Y.S.2d (N.Y. App. Div. 1994)

Facts

The executrix of the estate of the deceased brought an action alleging that the hospital nurses were negligent in monitoring the pulse in the decedent's leg. The executrix also alleged that the hospital was negligent for failing to have an ultrasonic stethoscope available. The trial court granted the hospital's motion for summary judgment, and an appeal was taken.

Issue

Were there material issues of fact regarding the alleged negligence of hospital nurses in monitoring the pulse in the decedent's leg and the hospital's alleged negligence in failing to have an ultrasonic stethoscope available?

Holding

The New York Supreme Court, Appellate Division, held that there was a material issue of fact regarding the alleged

negligence of the hospital nurses in monitoring the pulse in the decedent's leg, thus precluding summary judgment for the hospital.

Reason

The facts relied upon by the hospital's expert in rendering his expert medical opinion conflicted with the deposition testimony of the defendants, Rathor and Danesh. Thus, credibility issues were raised concerning the expert's opinion that could not be resolved on a summary judgment motion. There was a factual issue regarding the alleged negligence of the hospital nurses in monitoring the pulse in the decedent's lower left leg. There were also factual issues, raised by conflicting expert opinions, as to whether the hospital was negligent in failing to have a Doppler ultrasonic stethoscope available and whether that failure contributed to the decedent's injury.

Discussion

1. What are the factual differences between *Luthart v. Danesh* and *Porter v. Lima Mem'l Hosp.?*
2. What issues should an organization consider when addressing the assessment and reassessment of a patient?

3. NEGLIGENT INJECTION

Citation: *Nueces v. Long Island College Hosp.*, 609 N.Y.S.2d 592 (N.Y. App. Div. 1994)

Facts

The plaintiff brought an action against the hospital seeking to recover damages resulting from a negligently administered injection. The Supreme Court entered judgment on a jury verdict for the patient and the hospital appealed.

Issue

Was the hospital's agent negligent in administering an injection to the patient's left buttock, proximately causing permanent injuries, supported by the evidence? Was the award of $440,000 for pain and suffering, plus $10,000 for past medical damages, excessive?

Holding

The New York Supreme Court, Appellate Division, held that the evidence supported a finding of liability, and the award of damages was not excessive.

Reason

Contrary to the hospital's contention, a review of the evidence demonstrated that the jury's verdict was supported by sufficient evidence. There existed a rational basis for the jury's findings of negligence on the part of the hospital's agent in the administration of an injection to the plaintiff's left buttock proximately causing her permanent injuries. Since the parties' respective medical experts differed concerning the nature and cause of the plaintiff's injuries, the matter was properly left to the jury.

Discussion

1. What is the importance of assessing and reassessing the skills of professional staff?
2. Develop a skills checklist for new nurses.
3. What is the importance of continuing education?
4. What topics should be included in the orientation of a new employee? Consider employee orientation to both the hospital and the department.

4. NEGLIGENCE/FAILURE TO RESPOND

Citation: *Ard v. East Jefferson Gen. Hosp.*, 636 So. 2d 1042 (La. Ct. App. 1994)

Facts

On May 3, 1984, Mr. Ard, a patient, was admitted to the hospital. His admitting diagnosis was a past history of myocardial infarction, stroke, and unstable angina. On May 8, Mr. Ard subsequently underwent a five-vessel coronary bypass surgery. He was transferred to the intensive care unit following his stay in the recovery room.

Mr. Ard was transferred from the intensive care unit on May 13. Two days later, Mr. Ard had respiratory failure and was transferred to the critical care unit. A bronchoscopy was performed to determine the cause of the respiratory problems.

Mr. Ard was transferred from the critical care unit on May 20. Mrs. Ard testified that the nursing staff did not respond timely to her calls for assistance from 5:30 P.M. to 6:45 P.M.

At approximately 6:45 P.M., Mr. Ard stopped breathing and a code was called. Mr. Ard never regained consciousness and died two days later from respiratory failure and cardiac arrest.

Mrs. Ard, who at the time of trial was 70 years old, testified that on the afternoon of May 20, 1984, she was with her husband. He began feeling nauseous and experiencing shortness of breath. She rang the bell for her husband several times and got no response. Finally, sometime in the evening, someone responded and brought him a tablet. However, his nausea worsened. He also vomited once or twice and was in terrible pain. Mrs. Ard described her husband as reeling from one side of the bed to the other. She was trying to hold him so he would not fall off the bed. She continued to ring for a nurse when she noticed he was having difficulty breathing. She called 10 or 12 times and was told a nurse was not there. She estimated she rang the bell for an hour and 15 minutes to an hour and a half. She told the nurse she rang that he was nauseous and vomiting and she could not hold him down. She also noted he was pale. The last time she called she noticed his eyes were rolled back. She reported he was dying and needed a nurse. Someone finally did respond and called a code. The medical records indicated that on May 20, 1984, between the time of 5:30 P.M. and 6:45 P.M., there was no notation that any nurse or doctor checked on Mr. Ard. Therefore, Mrs. Ard's testimony regarding this time period was consistent with the medical records.

A wrongful death action was brought against the hospital. The district court granted judgment for Mrs. Ard and their only child. The hospital appealed.

Issue

Was the testimony by the plaintiff consistent with notations in the medical record? Was there sufficient evidence in the record to support the district court's conclusion that the nursing staff breached the standard of care in the community? Did the negligence of the nurses lessen the patient's chance of survival? Was the district court's award of general damages in the amount of $50,000 to the surviving spouse and $10,000 to the surviving only child an abuse of discretion?

Holding

The Court of Appeal of Louisiana held that the spouse's testimony that no one responded to her calls for assistance for one hour and 15 minutes was consistent with the medical records. There was ample evidence to support the district court's conclusion that the nursing staff breached its standard of care. There was evidence that the negligence of the nurses lessened the patient's chance of survival. Damages awarded were inadequate.

Reason

Ms. Krebs, an expert in general nursing, determined there were six breaches of the standard of care. She particularly stated that after May 15, 1984, it was obvious to the nurses from the doctors' progress notes that the patient was a high risk for aspiration. This problem was never addressed in the nurses' care plan or in the nurses' notes. It was something that should have been addressed. *Id.* at 1045.

On May 20, 1984, Mr. Ard's assigned nurse was Ms. Florscheim. Ms. Krebs stated that Ms. Florscheim did not do a full assessment of the patient's respiratory and lung status. There was nothing in the record indicating that she performed such an evaluation after he vomited. Ms. Krebs also testified that no total swallowing assessment was made at any time by a nurse. Although Ms. Florscheim testified that she checked on Mr. Ard around 6:00 P.M. on May 20, there was no documentation in the medical record.

Ms. Farris, an expert in intensive care nursing and a registered nurse, testified for the defense. She disagreed with Ms. Krebs that there was a breach of the standard of care. On cross-examination, she admitted that if a patient was in the type of distress described by Mrs. Ard and no nurse checked on him for an hour and 15 minutes, that would fall below the standard of care.

Dr. Preis, a cardiologist; Dr. Iteld, a cardiologist; and Dr. Brach, a pulmonary expert, testified that if Mr. Ard was in the type of distress described by his wife, someone should have responded.

The court concluded that there was ample evidence to support the trial judge's conclusion that the nursing staff breached the standard of care. Dr. Iteld testified that with Mr. Ard's history and with reports of nausea, vomiting, rolling around in bed, and paleness, he would have wanted to be notified by the attending nurse had he been the treating physician. He indicated that he would have transferred Mr. Ard back to intensive care immediately because it looked like he was going to have a respiratory and cardiac arrest. Possibly, had he been transferred to the cardiac unit, his chances of going into a code would have been averted. When asked whether this would be more probable than not, he replied: "This is a very sick gentleman and already had two respiratory problems. . . . *I think he would have had a much better chance of survival in the intensive care unit*" [emphasis added]. *Id.* at 1047.

There was sufficient evidence to show the negligence of the nurses lessened Mr. Ard's chance of survival by his not being transferred to the intensive care unit prior to his being coded. In determining whether there had been an abuse of the discretion of the trial judge, we are guided by the explanation given by the Louisiana Supreme Court in *Youn v. Maritime Overseas Corp.*, 623 So. 2d 1257, 1261 (La. 1993):

> the discretion vested in the trier of fact is "great," and even vast, so that an appellate court should rarely disturb an award of general damages. Reasonable persons frequently disagree about the measure of general damages in a particular case. It is only when the award is, in either direction, beyond that which a reasonable trier of fact could assess for the effects of the particular injury to the particular plaintiff under the particular circumstances that the appellate court should increase or decrease the award.

Mrs. Ard testified that she and her husband had been married for 40 years. She was with him during his hospital stay. Ms. Bond testified that she was close to her father. She stayed with her mother at the hospital for almost the entire time he had been there. She stated she missed him "greatly" and was in shock when his condition worsened. *Id.* at 1047–1048.

The court found an abuse of discretion and raised Mrs. Ard's general damages award from $50,000 to $150,000 and Ms. Bond's general damages award from $10,000 to $50,000.

Discussion

1. What should the reasonable standard of care be in responding to a call for assistance?
2. What are the nursing issues in this case?

5. DELIVERY/NURSE'S NEGLIGENCE

Citation: *Fairfax Hosp. Sys., Inc. v. McCarty*, 419 S.E.2d 621 (Va. 1992)

Facts

On June 3, 1987, at 7:30 A.M., Ms. McCarty, who was pregnant, was admitted to the hospital after a spontaneous rupture of the membranes. Her child was born permanently impaired, both neurologically and developmentally. The plaintiffs asserted that the hospital's labor and delivery nurse violated the standard of care because of her inordinate delay in recognizing fetal distress and in initiating appropriate nursing intervention, including timely notification of the attending physician. Following her admission, Ms. McCarty was taken to the labor room and hospital personnel began to electronically monitor the fetal heart rate and maternal contractions.

At 2:00 P.M., Dr. Burka, an obstetrician-gynecologist who often covered for Dr. Ross (Ms. McCarty's primary care physician), examined Ms. McCarty. Later, Dr. Ross asked Dr. Burka to assume Ms. McCarty's full care.

At 6:00 P.M., Dr. Burka examined Ms. McCarty. At 6:10 P.M., Ms. McClure, employed by the hospital as a labor and delivery nurse, began attending the mother while she was still in the first stage of labor. The mother was Ms. McClure's responsibility until 9:00 P.M. From that time until the birth of the child at 9:17 P.M., Dr. Burka was always in the labor and delivery area of the hospital.

At 7:10 P.M., Dr. Burka next examined the mother and determined that she "had made excellent progress . . . in the active phase of labor." An hour later, the second phase of labor began and lasted until the 9:17 P.M. delivery. The significant events in this case occurred during this 67-minute period. Dr. Burka was in the labor room many times between 8:10 P.M. and 8:25 P.M. He was not in the labor room, but in a nearby physicians' lounge, from 8:25 P.M. until nearly 8:58 P.M.

At 8:27 P.M., the evidence established that the fetus began experiencing trouble.

At 8:29 P.M., a broad-based deceleration of the fetal heart rate began to register on the monitor. The mother began abnormal labor. At 8:37 P.M., the baby was sick and getting sicker, as indicated by the monitor's fetal heart rate tracings. At this point, according to the plaintiffs' expert witness, the applicable standard of care required the nurse to institute certain nursing procedures including "to call for help to get this baby delivered." At that time, according to the witness, the delivery could have taken place in 10 to 12 minutes if the mother had been unhooked from the monitor and moved from the labor room to the delivery room 40 feet away. Dr. Burka was unaware of the heart rate fluctuations during this critical period because he was not in the labor room and none of the remote terminals displaying fetal heart-rate tracings for the labor room was working. *Id.* at 624.

At 8:42 P.M., the fetus had exhausted its oxygen supply and began relying on its emergency reserve, a four-minute back-up system that helps the fetus survive the stress of labor. Four minutes later, damage to the brain began. At 8:51 P.M., delivery became necessary to avoid injury to the baby.

By 8:53 P.M., brain damage had occurred that was outside the limit for birth of a neurologically normal baby.

Between 8:50 P.M. and 9:00 P.M., Ms. McClure went to get Dr. Burka. He may have appeared at the labor room door briefly several minutes before 9:00 P.M. Based on what Ms. McClure told him at the time, Dr. Burka understood there had been a decline in the fetal heart rate and that this deceleration "had just happened." According to Dr. Burka,

who testified as a witness for the plaintiffs, "there was no indication that there was an immediate emergency with the baby from Ms. McClure." Dr. Burka testified that if he had been watching the heart-rate tracings, he "would have moved to deliver Mrs. McCarty shortly before 8:40 P.M." Dr. Burka based this conclusion on the fact that during "the previous 10 minutes there had been a dramatic qualitative change in the fetal heart rate tracing from what had previously transpired." There were "progressively longer, deeper, more widely based heart rate decelerations with maternal contractions and pushing efforts." *Id.* at 624. Dr. Burka first realized the baby was in trouble shortly after 9:00 P.M., when the mother had been transferred to the delivery room.

At birth, the infant was neurologically impaired. The evidence established that the cause of this condition at delivery was a "prolonged episode of relatively severe hypoxia or lack of oxygen" that had occurred from 8:40 P.M. until delivery. According to the evidence, the fetus, which was otherwise normal and healthy, did not receive sufficient oxygen or nutrition because of "placental separation and abruption of the placenta which took away his oxygen supply in part and his ability to be nourished by his mother in part for a period of time before birth." *Id.* The plaintiffs' expert testified that Ms. McClure's failure to "take action or notify the physician delayed delivery and consequently contributed in a causative manner to the eventual outcome for this infant." *Id.*

Issue

Was there a jury issue presented as to whether the nurse's breach of the standard of care required resulted in the injuries sustained?

Holding

The Supreme Court of Virginia held that whether the nurse's breach of duty was the proximate cause of the infant's injuries presented a question for the jury.

Reason

The mere recital of the facts in the light most favorable to the plaintiffs shows there was abundant, credible evidence, which the jury was entitled to accept, establishing that Ms. McClure's breach of the standard of care was a proximate cause of the injuries and damages sustained; no further analysis of the evidence is necessary. It is sufficient to state that a jury issue was presented on the question of whether Ms. McClure's delay in recognizing and reacting to fetal distress, and in performing appropriate nursing intervention, including timely notice to the attending physician, were substantial breaches of the standard of care. It was for the jury to say whether these breaches by the hospital's employee constituted an efficient cause of the losses suffered by the plaintiffs.

Discussion

1. Analyzing the time elements in this case, do you agree with the court's decision? Explain.
2. How would you, as the nurse, defend your actions in this case?

6. NEGLIGENT ASSIGNMENT TO NURSING UNIT/ BIRTH INJURIES

Citation: *St. Paul Med. Ctr. v. Cecil*, 842 S.W.2d 808 (Tex. Ct. App. 1992)

Facts

The plaintiffs, Mr. and Mrs. Cecil, brought a negligence action against the attending physician, nurse, and hospital as a result of their son being born with brain damage caused by hypoxia (a decrease in oxygen).

On January 28, 1983, on or about 11:00 P.M., Mrs. Cecil believed that her water had broken. Mr. Cecil called the attending physician, Dr. Cook. Mr. Cecil was instructed to take his wife to the hospital.

The next day at 12:10 A.M., Mrs. Cecil was taken to the delivery room and the nurse performed a pelvic examination and took vital signs. At approximately 1:30 A.M., at the request of the nurse, a resident was called and asked to perform a speculum examination. The resident determined that the membranes had ruptured and meconium was present. The nurse attached an external electronic fetal monitor to record the heart rate. Two hours later, the resident installed an internal electronic fetal monitor. The resident determined from a printout of the heart rate that the fetus showed severe fetal hypoxia, bradycardia (slow heart rate), and more meconium. The resident instructed the nurse to notify Dr. Cook and prepare Mrs. Cecil for an emergency Caesarean section. After arriving at the hospital, Dr. Cook further delayed the delivery because he wanted an anesthesiologist, even though a nurse anesthetist was on duty and present in the hospital. At 4:57 A.M., the infant was born with severe brain damage caused by prolonged hypoxia.

Dr. Cook settled with the plaintiffs before trial. The jury found that the defendants, the nurse and the hospital, proxi-

mately caused the infant's injuries. The plaintiffs were awarded $25,000 for past physical pain and suffering, $50,000 for future physical pain and suffering, $25,000 for past physical impairment, $50,000 for future physical impairment, $1,200,000 for loss of earnings capacity, $36,688.26 for medical care provided in the past, $30,000 for rehabilitative care required in the future, and $30,000 for future educational expenses. After crediting the $412,808.50 settlement from Dr. Cook, the trial court entered a judgment totaling $1,033,879.76 in favor of the plaintiffs, and the defendants appealed. *Id.* at 811.

The hospital argued that there was insufficient evidence to support the jury's finding that the hospital was negligent independent of the negligent conduct of the other defendants, and no expert testimony was presented at trial as to the standard of care required of the hospital.

Issue

Was expert testimony necessary to establish the standard of care required of the hospital? Was there sufficient evidence presented to support the jury's findings? Was the testimony of the plaintiffs and that of the defendants sufficiently inconsistent to establish that there was no evidence of negligence?

Holding

The Court of Appeals of Texas held that expert testimony was not necessary to establish that the hospital was negligent in assigning the nurse. There was sufficient evidence in the record to support the jury's finding of negligence. The court is not a fact finder, and cannot substitute its judgment for that of the jury.

Reason

As to the standard of care required in this case, it is sufficient to say that "the standard of nonmedical, administrative, ministerial, or routine care at a hospital need not be established by expert testimony because the jury is competent from its own experience to determine and apply such a reasonable-care standard." *Id.* at 812.

The evidence supports the plaintiffs' allegations that the hospital had been independently negligent. The hospital was aware of the nurse's poor performance ratings. Three and one-half months before the negligent act occurred, the hospital rated the nurse's performance as unsatisfactory. She sometimes fell asleep on the job and was reluctant to seek guidance from her supervisors in matters concerning maternal and child-health care, as well as problems in labor and delivery. Despite these concerns, the hospital assigned her to the least supervised shift, the night shift. "Laymen aided by these evaluations and guided by their common sense, could fairly determine whether the hospital was negligent in its supervision and assignment of the nurse." *Id.* at 813.

The defendants argued that because the testimony of Dr. Barden and Dr. Ouellette was inconsistent, their testimony created only a mere suspicion as to causation. Dr. Barden, a specialist in maternal–fetal medicine, testified that the nurse was negligent in failing to render adequate care in monitoring the fetus and detecting his hypoxia, which subjected him to prolonged insult and delayed his delivery. He further stated that application of the electronic fetal monitor by a nurse with proper training would have detected the fetus' condition and would have required his delivery as early as 1:30 A.M. on January 23, 1983. This would have limited injury. Dr. Ouellette, a board-certified pediatric neurologist, testified that in reasonable medical probability, injury occurred at 3:20 A.M. on January 29, 1983, and afterward when the fetus suffered an acute hypoxic insult. In Dr. Ouellette's opinion, the present neurological damage could have been prevented if delivery had occurred prior to 3:20 A.M. The defendants' expert, Dr. Elterman, stated his opinion that it is "very uncommon" for an acute intrapartum event right around the time of birth to cause neurological injury, and that 90 percent of the children who have neurological problems suffer from a preexisting insult. The court of appeals held that there was more than a scintilla of evidence that the negligence of the nurse and the hospital proximately caused the injuries that resulted from the delay in delivery of the fetus.

Discussion

1. Why was the hospital found negligent?
2. Do you agree that there was sufficient evidence to support the jury's findings?
3. Who is the fact finder at trial?

7. IMPROPER PLACEMENT OF A FEEDING TUBE

Citation: *Minster v. Pohl*, 426 S.E.2d 204 (Ga. Ct. App. 1992)

Facts

Mr. Minster, as executor of the estate of Ms. Hattrich, filed a medical malpractice action against the physician, the hospital, and its employee, Ms. Hines, a registered nurse,

alleging improper placement of a feeding tube and failure to diagnose a pneumothorax that eventually led to Ms. Hattrich's death. Ms. Hattrich had been admitted to the hospital for surgery. After surgery was performed, she developed respiratory problems. It became necessary to insert a breathing tube and begin nasogastric feeding. The patient apparently pulled out the tubes, and Ms. Hines reinserted the feeding tube. She then asked Dr. Pohl, an emergency department physician, to view an X-ray to verify that she had properly replaced the tube. Dr. Pohl viewed the X-ray and observed that the tube was incorrectly placed in the decedent's right lung rather than in her stomach. The tube needed to be reinserted. Dr. Pohl made note of his findings in the patient's progress notes. A pneumothorax was later discovered in the patient's right lung, eventually leading to her death. Mr. Minster alleged that Ms. Hines was negligent in failing to properly restrain the patient to prevent her from extubating herself, and in improperly inserting and inadequately verifying the placement of the feeding tube. The hospital's liability was premised upon *respondeat superior*. Mr. Minster also alleged that although Dr. Pohl correctly noted that the feeding tube was improperly placed, he was negligent in failing to recognize and report the development of the pneumothorax that was visible on the X-ray.

An affidavit of Dr. Fowler, proffered in opposition to the motion for summary judgment, provided evidence that a physician–patient relationship was established. Dr. Fowler was familiar with the practice of medicine in emergency departments. It was his opinion that, to a reasonable medical certainty, Dr. Pohl's entry on the patient's progress notes could be interpreted as a direction or instruction to replace the feeding tube. This action, as such, was an affirmative intervention into the patient's care. This would amount to treatment that created a limited physician–patient relationship.

Ms. Case, a registered nurse familiar with the standard of care applicable to the nursing profession, generally stated that she had reviewed copies of the decedent's medical records, and from her review of those records, it was her opinion that Ms. Hines should have restrained the patient in order to prevent her from extubating herself. She stated that Ms. Hines had improperly placed the feeding tube and failed to verify placement of the feeding tube in the patient, and that the improper placement of the feeding tube caused the pneumothorax, which eventually led to the patient's death.

The superior court denied the hospital's and nurse's motions to dismiss the case and granted summary judgment to one physician. The hospital and nurse appealed.

Issue

Did a physician–patient relationship arise out of Dr. Pohl's employment as an emergency department physician at the hospital? Did Ms. Case's affidavit comply with the requirements of the statute?

Holding

The Georgia Court of Appeals held that no physician–patient relationship existed between the patient and the physician, who viewed the patient's X-ray merely out of courtesy to the hospital staff and entered a note in the patient's records. Moreover, Ms. Case's affidavit attached to the complaint complied with the requirements of the statute, even though it did not include the nurse's explicit averment that Ms. Hines' actions violated the applicable standard of care.

Reason

Although Dr. Pohl questionably took action with respect to the decedent, viewing the X-ray and making a notation on her chart, nothing in the record justified the inference that he was acting as her physician. Accordingly, the trial court properly found that no physician–patient relationship existed. In his affidavit proffered in support of the motion for summary judgment, Dr. Pohl claimed that he viewed the X-ray as a courtesy to the staff and not out of any obligation or duty.

The trial court found that creating an exception to the rule for the situation before the court would be detrimental to the health care delivery system, causing competent professionals who happen to be on the hospital premises but have no relationship to the patient to decline out of natural prudence to perform even minimal courtesies as a favor to hospital staff. The court of appeals found this danger to be greater than the risk suggested by the executrix of insulating such physicians from liability, particularly because applying the general rule did not leave the patient without a remedy should she prove negligence on the part of the hospital or its employees in any regard.

The hospital and Ms. Hines maintained that Ms. Case's affidavit was insufficient to satisfy OCGA § 9-11-9.1 because it did not include Ms. Case's explicit averment that Ms. Hines' actions violated the applicable standard of care. The trial court did not agree. The statute does not require that specific language be employed. It requires only that the affidavit set forth specify at least one negligent act or omission claimed to exist and the factual basis for each such claim. Ms. Case's affidavit fulfilled this requirement unequivocally by listing the appropriate actions in each case stating that: (1) Ms. Hines did not take the appropriate actions, (2) the decedent should have been restrained, (3) Ms. Hines improperly placed the feeding tube in the patient,

and (4) Ms. Hines did not properly verify placement of the feeding tube.

Discussion

1. What are the competency issues in this case?
2. What educational processes should an organization have in place for continuous competency improvement?

8. STANDARD OF CARE/NURSING

Citation: *McMillan v. Durant*, 439 S.E.2d (S.C. 1993)

Facts

On February 25, 1985, the patient, Joseph McMillan, was born prematurely. He suffered intercranial bleeding that required the insertion of a shunt to relieve pressure on the brain and prevent brain damage. The patient underwent three shunt revisions by a neurosurgeon over a period of time.

On August 15, 1986, Joseph became ill and three days later was taken to a family pediatrician for care. The child was diagnosed as having contracted an upper respiratory infection. On August 22, following further deterioration in his condition, Joseph was admitted to Tuomey Hospital for intravenous hydration. At approximately 10:55 P.M., while a nurse was checking the IV in a semidark room, Mrs. McMillan mentioned that Joseph did not seem to be acting normally. She said Joseph was not opening his mouth when he was breathing. The nurse observed that Joseph had normal respirations, his color was good, and he was resting comfortably.

Seven minutes later, Joseph was checked again in the darkened room by a nursing supervisor. She noted that Joseph was resting comfortably and left the room. During this time there was no attempt to contact the admitting physician or the physician on call. Several minutes after the nursing supervisor left the room, Mrs. McMillan noted that Joseph had stopped breathing. She contacted the floor nurse and efforts were begun immediately to resuscitate the child.

At 11:15 P.M., the attending physician was contacted and notified that Joseph was not breathing. At 11:30 P.M., Joseph was being resuscitated when his attending physician, Dr. Young, arrived. Dr. Young, in consultation with a neurosurgeon, tapped the shunt and drained off the excess fluid. Two hours later Joseph was transferred by his physician to Columbia Hospital, where he was placed under the care of a neurosurgeon. While at Columbia, it was discovered that Joseph's shunt had become blocked at the abdominal end of the shunt. This placed pressure on his brain causing him to stop breathing. As a result, Joseph suffered permanent brain damage.

At trial, a verdict in the amount of $734,100 was returned against the hospital. The trial judge imposed a statutory cap of $200,000 and the hospital appealed.

Issue

Is it proper to allow a physician expert to provide expert opinion as to the appropriate standard of care required of nurses? Should a local or national standard of care be applied?

Holding

The Supreme Court of South Carolina held that a neurosurgeon could give expert testimony as to the standard of care applicable to nurses, and a national standard of care could be applied as opposed to a local standard.

Reason

The supreme court determined that the fact that the physician was not a nurse would go to the weight of his testimony and not to its admissibility. "As a teacher in the field of nursing, the neurosurgeon here . . . was amply qualified to render an opinion in the field of nursing." *Id.* at 832.

As to the issue of whether a national or local standard of care applies, "in South Carolina, we have adopted a national rather than a local standard of care . . . a South Carolina nurse should be held to the same standard of care as any other health care providers." *Id.* at 833. The "evolution of the law appears to support the adoption of a national standard of care throughout the health care system. Several states have extended their appropriate standard of care for physicians to other health care professionals, including nurses." *Id.* at 832. The Kansas Supreme Court, for example, in *Durflinger v. Artles*, 234 Kan. 484, 673 P.2d 86 (1983), held that the "[r]ules of law governing the duty of physicians and surgeons to their patients apply generally to dentists, and to registered nurses." California, Colorado, and New York also recognize a national standard of care for nurses.

Discussion

1. Do you think that a national standard of care should be applicable to all health care professions? Why?
2. What are the pros and cons of a national standard of care?

9. DRUGS/WRONG DOSAGE

Citation: *Harrison v. Axelrod*, 599 N.Y.S.2d 96 (N.Y. App. Div. 1993)

Facts

A nurse was charged with patient neglect in that she administered the wrong dosage of the drug Haldol to a patient on seven occasions while she was employed at a nursing facility. The patient's physician had prescribed a 0.5 milligram dosage of Haldol. The patient's medication record indicated that the nurse had been administering dosages of 5 milligrams, which were being sent to the patient care unit by the pharmacy. A New York State Department of Health investigator testified that the nurse had admitted that she administered the wrong dosage, and that she was aware of the nursing facility's medication administration policy, "which she breached by failing to check the dosage supplied by the pharmacy against the dosage ordered by the patient's doctor." *Id.* at 97. The nurse denied that she made these admissions to the investigator. The Commissioner of the Department of Health made a determination that the administration of the wrong dosage of Haldol on seven occasions constituted patient neglect. The nurse brought an Article 28 proceeding, requesting a review of the Commissioner's finding.

Issue

Was the evidence sufficient to establish that the nurse had been negligent in the administration of the drug Haldol?

Holding

The New York Supreme Court, Appellate Division, held that the evidence established that the nurse administered the wrong dosage of the prescribed drug Haldol to the nursing facility patient. This was a breach of the nursing facility's medication administration policy and was sufficient to support the determination of patient neglect made by the Commissioner of Health.

Reason

Although the nurse had denied making the admissions to the investigator, "it is well settled that the duty of weighing the evidence and resolving conflicting testimony rests solely with the administrative agency, and that the courts may not weigh the evidence or reject the choice made by the agency. . . ." *Id.* at 97.

Discussion

1. Prior to administering a medication, the nurse should check that she is administering the correct medication in the right dosage. What other protocol should a nurse follow in order to safely administer medication to a patient?
2. What steps can an organization take to reduce its medication error rate?
3. What culpability is there on the part of a pharmacist who delivers the wrong dosage of a medication?
4. What steps can pharmacists take to reduce an organization's medication error rate?

10. REVOCATION OF LICENSE/CODE VIOLATION

Citation: *Henley v. Alabama Bd. of Nursing*, 607 So. 2d 56 (Ala. Civ. App. 1992)

Facts

A registered nurse sought review of a decision of the State Board of Nursing revoking her license. The board filed a complaint against the nurse alleging that she had violated Ala. Code 1975, § 34-21-25 and § 610-X-8-.05(c)(d)(e) of the Alabama Board of Nursing Administrative Code. These provisions allow the revocation of a nursing license if (1) the licensee is found unfit or incompetent because of the use of alcohol or is addicted to the use of habit-forming drugs to such an extent as to render the licensee unsafe or unreliable; (2) the licensee is mentally incompetent; or (3) the licensee is guilty of unprofessional conduct of a character likely to deceive, defraud, or injure the public in matters pertaining to health care. This complaint was filed after the nurse was subjected to a series of arrests beginning in November 1986, when she was arrested and charged with disorderly conduct and public intoxication.

Evidence of the allegations in the board's complaint was received by a hearing officer who recommended revocation of the nurse's license. The hearing officer's findings of fact and conclusions of law were adapted by the board, and the nurse's license was revoked. That decision was appealed to the trial court, which upheld the decision of the board. The nurse appealed *pro se*.

Issue

Did the evidence support revocation of the nurse's license?

Holding

The Alabama Court of Civil Appeals found that the evidence of the nurse's arrests and conviction for disorderly conduct and public intoxication supported revocation of her license, absent evidence from a treating physician regarding her competence.

Reason

Appellate review of administrative actions is limited to determinations of "whether the agency acted within the powers conferred upon it by law and the constitution, whether its decision is supported by substantial evidence, and whether the agency's decision is reasonable and not arbitrary." *Alabama Bd. of Nursing v. Herrick*, 454 So. 2d 1041, 1043 (Ala. Civ. App. 1984). The allegations were that the nurse suffered from alcohol addiction and mental incompetency, which rendered her incompetent to assume all of the responsibilities of the practice of nursing. The record contained substantial evidence supporting those allegations and the nurse presented nothing to sufficiently rebut them.

Discussion

1. What other alternatives might the hospital consider in its disciplinary process?
2. Do you agree with the court's decision? Explain.

11. INTOXICATION/NURSE DISCIPLINED

Citation: *Burns v. Board of Nursing*, 495 N.W.2d 698 (Iowa 1993)

Facts

The Board of Nursing found that a nurse had been habitually intoxicated, in violation of Iowa Code § 147.55(4) (1991). On November 5, 1986, the nurse's supervisor had confronted her about her behavior. The nurse stated that it would not happen again. The nurse was given a verbal warning. It was signed by the nurse and her supervisor.

It did happen again and the nurse experienced increasing absenteeism. The nurse's supervisor noted the odor of alcohol and confronted her about it. The nursing director also had spoken to the nurse by telephone as part of her investigation. She noted that the nurse's speech was slurred and she could scarcely be understood. The nurse denied she had an alcoholism problem. She was compelled to submit to an intake assessment by the hospital's alcohol and drug recovery program. When the nurse called the program developer for an appointment, her slurred words and inappropriate comments convinced the developer that Ms. Burns was intoxicated at the time. Although the nurse did not proceed with the program, as a result of an hour-long initial assessment, the director strongly suspected she had a problem with alcohol abuse.

Therefore, the board placed the nurse's license on probation for three years and ordered her to comply with various conditions during the probationary period. When the nurse sought judicial review of the board's decision, the district court reversed, finding there was not substantial evidence to support the charges. The court remanded the matter to the board with instructions to reinstate the nurse's license without restriction. The board appealed.

Issue

Was there sufficient evidence to support the board's findings placing the nurse's license on probation?

Holding

The Supreme Court of Iowa held that the board's finding that the nurse was habitually intoxicated was supported by substantial evidence.

Reason

The board applied an appropriate definition to the facts. The nursing board should not be required to wait until the habitual intoxication becomes so debilitating that there is immediate danger of harm to patients. The Iowa Code section should be liberally applied so as to protect the public by allowing the nursing board to interfere when harm is imminent, and before it occurs.

Discussion

1. Do you agree with the board's findings? Explain.
2. What are the risks of applying the Iowa Code too conservatively?

12. NURSE PRACTITIONER/COMPARATIVE NEGLIGENCE

Citation: *Adams v. Krueger*, 856 P.2d 864 (Idaho 1993)

Facts

The plaintiff initially went to a physician's office for diagnosis and treatment. Her initial assessment was performed by a nurse practitioner who was employed by the physician. The plaintiff was diagnosed by the nurse practitioner as having genital herpes. The physician prescribed an ointment to help relieve the patient's symptoms. The plaintiff eventually consulted with another physician who advised her that she had a yeast infection, not genital herpes.

The plaintiff and her husband then filed an action against the initial treating physician and his nurse practitioner for their failure to correctly diagnose and treat her condition. The action against the physician was based on his failure to review the nurse practitioner's diagnosis and treatment plan.

The court gave instructions to the jury that the plaintiff would recover nothing if it found the plaintiff more than 50 percent negligent. However, the plaintiff would recover if the plaintiff's negligence was less than 50 percent and the combined negligence of the defendants was greater than 50 percent. The jury found the plaintiff 49 percent negligent, the physician 10 percent negligent, and the nurse practitioner 41 percent negligent.

The trial court found in favor of the plaintiff and the defendants appealed. The court of appeals affirmed and further appeal was made.

Issue

Did the trial court err by imputing the nurse's negligence to the physician by applying the comparative negligence statute in effect at the time the present action arose?

Holding

The Supreme Court of Idaho held that the negligence of the nurse was properly imputed to the physician for purposes of determining comparative negligence.

Reason

The supreme court adhered to the reasoning of the court of appeals where the nurse practitioner and her employer/physician would "stand in relation as master and servant, whereby the negligent acts of the servant, or employee, are imputed to the master, or employer, under the doctrine of *respondeat superior*." *Smith v. Thompson*, 103 Idaho 909, 655 P.2d 116 (Idaho Ct. App. 1982). "Comparative negligence, in and of itself, has not changed these basic principles [of imputed negligence]. When negligence is apportioned in the presence of vicarious liability, the master bears the burden of his servant's negligence. If the master has been partially at fault, the percentage of negligence attributed to his servant is added to the percentage attributed to the master." *Schwartz Comparative Negligence* § 16.1 at 253 (2nd ed. 1986). In the present case, it was undisputed that the physician and nurse practitioner stood in a master–servant relationship and that the nurse acted within the scope of her employment. Consequently, her negligence was properly attributed to her employer/physician. *Id.* at 867.

Discussion

1. Do you agree with the court's decision? Explain.
2. What might the physician/employer do to limit his liability in the future for the negligent acts of his professional employees?
3. If the nurse practitioner has malpractice insurance, can the physician recover any of his losses from her insurance carrier?

13. INADEQUATE STERILIZATION/ALLEGED NURSE'S NEGLIGENCE

Citation: *Howard v. Alexandria Hosp.*, 429 S.E.2d 22 (Va. 1993)

Facts

A patient brought a medical malpractice action against a hospital, seeking damages arising out of an operation performed on her with unsterile instruments. The patient had entered the hospital for surgery to relieve her suffering from carpal tunnel syndrome. During her stay in the recovery room following surgery, the operating surgeon reported to the patient that she had been operated on with unsterile instruments. Allegedly, the nurse in charge of the autoclave used to sterilize the instruments did not properly monitor the sterilization process. Because of the patient's fear of a variety of diseases, she was administered several human immunodeficiency virus (HIV) tests, one of which was taken six months following her discharge from the hospital. The patient was evaluated by an infectious disease specialist and was administered antibiotics intravenously. Following her discharge, the patient was placed on several medications and as a result developed symptoms of pseudomembranous enterocolitis. Testimony was entered that described the patient's symptoms as resulting from the administration of the antibiotics. One expert testified that the patient had reason to be concerned for at least six months following the surgical

procedure because of her risk of being infected with one of a variety of diseases. The hospital argued that the patient suffered no physical injury from the surgical procedure and the instruments utilized during the procedure.

The circuit court, entering summary judgment for the hospital, granted a motion by the hospital to strike the evidence on the grounds that no physical injury had been shown.

Issue

Did the trial court err by sustaining the hospital's motion to strike the evidence and enter summary judgment for the hospital?

Holding

The Supreme Court of Virginia held that the patient had suffered injury resulting from measures taken to avoid infection following discovery of the use of unsterile instrumentation, even though the patient did not sustain any infection from use of the instruments. The case was reversed and remanded for a new trial on all issues.

Reason

Injury can be either physical or mental. It is clear that because of the hospital's use of inadequately sterilized instruments, the plaintiff sustained positive, physical, and mental injury.

> As the direct result of the wrong, the plaintiff's body was invaded by intravenous tubes, needles administering pain shots, and instruments used to withdraw blood. She experienced the physical pain and discomfort of headache, nausea, vomiting, fever, chills and unusual sweating. . . . In sum, to argue that the plaintiff established mere emotional disturbance absent physical injury is to ignore the evidence in this case. . . . *Id.* at 25.

Discussion

1. What is meant by summary judgment?
2. What are the educational issues evident in this case?

14. OPERATING ROOM/SPONGE COUNT/ *RESPONDEAT SUPERIOR*

Citation: *Holger v. Irish*, 851 P.2d 1122 (Or. 1993)

Facts

The decedent's estate sued a surgeon and the hospital that employed the nurses who assisted the surgeon during the operation performed upon the deceased. During the course of performing colon surgery, the surgeon placed laparotomy sponges in the decedent's abdomen. After he had removed the sponges at the end of surgery, the two nurses assisting him counted them and verified that they had all been removed. Two years later, a sponge was discovered in the patient's abdomen. It was removed, and the 92-year-old patient died. The decedent's estate settled with the hospital, and although the estate moved to exclude any mention of the settlement at the trial, the judge informed the jury about the settlement. The estate had also asked the judge to instruct the jury with regard to *respondeat superior*, but the judge would not give those instructions. The jury decided in favor of the defendants, and the decedent's estate appealed. The court of appeals reversed, and the Supreme Court of Oregon reviewed the case.

Issue

Were the operating room nurses agents or employees of the defendants, or were the facts sufficient to show that they were under the defendants' supervision and control, and were they negligent?

Holding

The Supreme Court of Oregon held that: (1) the surgeon was not vicariously liable, as a matter of law, for the negligence of the operating room nurses, (2) the decedent's estate was not entitled to a vicarious liability instruction, and (3) the trial judge should not have mentioned the settlement with the hospital. Thus, the case was remanded for trial.

Reason

There was no evidence presented that the nurses were the defendants' employees, or that they were under the supervision or control of the defendant regarding their counting of the sponges. It was their sole responsibility to count the sponges, while the surgeon was responsible for concentrating on the patient. The nurses had been hired and trained by the hospital, which paid for their services.

The trial court should not have instructed the jury about the settlement with the hospital. The court asserted that it did so because the jury would wonder why the hospital was not mentioned throughout the trial. The supreme court found that the trial court had planted in the minds of the jurors that the decedent's estate had already been compensated for damages, therefore nothing further should have been given.

Discussion

1. What are the elements necessary to prove *respondeat superior* or vicarious liability?
2. Why was the surgeon not liable for the negligent acts of the nurses in the operating room?

15. PATIENT OVERDOSED/FAILURE TO TIMELY FILE NOTICE CLAIM

Citation: *Mitchell v. Bingham Mem'l Hosp.*, 942 P.2d 544 (Idaho 1997)

Facts

Appellant Mrs. Mitchell delivered healthy twin boys at respondent Bingham Memorial Hospital (the hospital) on July 20, 1992. Because of a concern for toxemia, she was placed on magnesium sulfate, which was administered through an IV catheter. Later on July 20, 1992, Mrs. Mitchell was overdosed with the magnesium sulfate. The overdose resulted in respiratory arrest necessitating emergency "code blue" resuscitation procedures followed by the transfer of Mrs. Mitchell to the intensive care unit (ICU) of the hospital, where she remained until discharged on July 23, 1992.

The Mitchells were initially told by hospital personnel that the overdose was a result of the malfunction or defect in the medication infusion machine. Two months later, Mrs. Mitchell's physician told the Mitchells that the machine had been checked out by the factory and was not defective, and that the overdose was a result of the nurse's error, probably in pushing the "flush" switch on the machine, which would have triggered the overdose. Thereafter, the hospital repeatedly billed the Mitchells for the ICU expenses. The Mitchells retained counsel when the hospital credit manager threatened to sue them for the bill. According to the Mitchells' counsel, Mr. Hawkes, he spoke with the hospital administrator, Mr. Peterson, about the Mitchells' claim on January 8 and 13, 1993, and met with him on January 20, 1993, a date chosen by Mr. Peterson. Mr. Hawkes stated in his affidavit that at the January 20, 1993, meeting, he furnished copies of the documents that identified the Mitchells, the hospitalization and charges at issue, and their damages as known at that time. He also stated that Mr. Peterson acknowledged liability for the nursing overdose and the error of the hospital in compounding the problem by making collection demands.

Mr. Peterson allegedly offered to pay all of Mrs. Mitchell's additional medical bills resulting from the overdose, and Mr. Hawkes' legal fees to a certain limit. Mr. Hawkes also stated that Mr. Peterson gave him the name of the hospital's insurance agent, and that he met with the agent for a settlement conference on April 15, 1993. The hospital offered to settle the case for $5,000 in June 1993, which, according to Mr. Hawkes, was not accepted because the Mitchells had not fully ascertained their damages. Mr. Hawkes stated that he and the insurance agent discussed the case over a period of many months in 1993, and that he provided the insurance agent with updated information relative to the damages. Mr. Hawkes stated that the agent raised the notice of tort claim issue for the first time on April 18, 1994.

In a supplemental affidavit, Mr. Hawkes stated that settlement of the claim was discussed in his January 13, 1993, phone conversation with Mr. Peterson, and that Mr. Peterson confirmed an interest in resolving the claim informally and without publicity. Mr. Hawkes also stated that in this conversation, Mr. Peterson "made the promise of acknowledging the hospital's error and a good faith follow-up meeting in giving me the January 20th date to meet."

In his second supplemental affidavit, Mr. Peterson acknowledged that he had a conversation with Mr. Hawkes on January 20, 1993, but that he did not consider this conversation to be a presentation of a claim for specific damages against the hospital. Mr. Peterson further acknowledged that he knew Mrs. Mitchell had an overdose and that she would not have been in the ICU except for the overdose. He stated that he and Mr. Hawkes discussed the hospital's position in pursuing the ICU charges. However, Mr. Peterson denied having ever told Mr. Hawkes to withhold filing a notice of tort claim. In July 1994, the Mitchells filed a Prelitigation Hearing Panel Request with the State Board of Medicine. According to Mr. Hawkes, during those proceedings the hospital admitted that the overdose took place, and only disputed the extent of Mrs. Mitchell's damages. The Mitchells filed their complaint on February 1, 1995. In June 1995, the hospital filed a motion to dismiss claiming that the Mitchells did not file a timely notice of tort claim. The district court treated the motion as one for summary judgment and granted it, ruling that the Mitchells had not complied with the notice requirements of the Idaho Tort Claims Act (ITCA) and that the hospital had not waived the right to assert this defense. The Mitchells thereafter filed a motion for reconsideration, which the district court denied. The Mitchells appealed.

Issue

Did the appellants file a timely complaint? Did the 180-day notice requirement begin to run on the date of Mrs. Mitchell's overdose, or on the date the Mitchells were told that the overdose was due to nursing error?

Holding

The Supreme Court of Idaho held that the 180-day notice requirement began to run on the date of Mrs. Mitchell's overdose, July 20, 1992.

Reason

Following the delivery, Mrs. Mitchell was administered an overdose of magnesium sulfate causing immediate respiratory arrest, the initiation of an emergency "code blue" resuscitation procedure, and her transfer to the ICU unit at the hospital. The district court found, and there is no dispute, that the Mitchells were told of the overdose on that date. The hospital initially suggested that the overdose was caused by a malfunction in the infusion machine. In September 1992, the Mitchells were told that the overdose was not caused by a malfunction in the infusion machine, but rather was caused by a probable nursing error.

The Mitchells were aware of the overdose and respiratory arrest on the day the overdose occurred. The facts available to the Mitchells were sufficient to cause a reasonably prudent person to inquire further into the circumstances surrounding the incident. Even if the cause of the overdose had been because of a malfunctioning infusion machine, and although there may be ultimate shared responsibility with a manufacturer in such a case, the hospital is entitled to timely notice of a potential claim. The 180-day period began to run on July 20, 1992, even though the Mitchells did not know the extent of the injury and Mrs. Mitchell's damages or the extent to which the hospital was responsible. The Mitchells had sufficient information on that day to be aware that they had a potential tort claim against the hospital.

Discussion

1. Do you agree with the court's decision? Why?
2. What role should the hospital's legal counsel have played with regard to this incident?
3. Discuss your opinion of Mr. Peterson's discussions with the plaintiff's counsel.
4. What are the pros and cons of the hospital's continued billing of the patient following discharge?

16. NEGLIGENT INJECTION

Citation: *Pellerin v. Humedicenters, Inc.*, 696 So. 2d 590, 96-1996 (La. App. 1997)

Facts

The plaintiff had gone to the emergency department at Lakeland Medical Center complaining of chest pain on

February 22, 1988. An emergency department physician, Dr. Gruner, examined her and ordered a nurse, Ms. Tangney, to give her an injection consisting of 50 milligrams of Demerol and 25 milligrams of Vistaril. Although Ms. Tangney testified she did not recall giving the injection; she did not deny giving it, and her initials are present in the emergency department record. Ms. Tangney further testified to what she routinely does when administering injections such as the one plaintiff received. Ms. Tangney admitted she failed to record the site and mode of injection in the emergency department records. She said she may have written this information in the nurse's notes, but no such notes were admitted into evidence.

The plaintiff testified she felt pain and a burning sensation in her hip during the injection. According to testimony by Dr. Gruner, a burning sensation upon injection of Vistaril is common. However, the burning persisted afterward and progressively worsened over the next several weeks. The pain spread to an area approximately 10 inches in diameter around the injection site.

The plaintiff further testified she consulted her gynecologist, Dr. Farrell, in April 1988. After examining the area of the injection, he recommended she see a neurologist. He referred her to Dr. Krefft, whom she first saw on April 27. Dr. Krefft found decreased sensation to pin pricks and cold in a two centimeter by four centimeter area at the edge of the plaintiff's hip. He diagnosed her with right cutaneous gluteal neuropathy (improper functioning of a nerve running right under the skin in the right buttock region). Dr. Krefft prescribed a medication for nerve pain. However, plaintiff returned on June 21, complaining of continuing pain despite taking the medication. At that time, Dr. Krefft recommended physical therapy, which was started on June 30 with Mr. Reynolds. According to plaintiff's testimony, the physical therapy involved massages, ultrasound, and use of a TENS unit (an electrical skin stimulator that helps block pain while it is being used).

The plaintiff's next visit to Dr. Krefft occurred on August 3. She reported that she continued having sharp pain in her hip. She had stopped taking the pain medication, but the physical therapy and TENS unit were helping. The numbness in her skin was also improving. At the next visit on August 31, 1988, she said she was using the TENS unit every day and was feeling better.

On October 3, plaintiff saw Dr. Krefft's associate, Dr. Burris. At that time, plaintiff had continuing pain in the right hip that came and went twice a day. Most of the numbness had disappeared, but Dr. Burris found decreased sensation to pin prick, touch, and cold. She recommended that plaintiff start using the pain medication again, continue use of the TENS unit, and return to Dr. Krefft in one month. Plaintiff did not see Dr. Krefft again until the following year. Shortly before returning to him she started physical therapy with Mr.

Macalusa, which lasted from March 30 to May 23, 1989. On April 17, 1989, she saw Dr. Krefft because the TENS unit was irritating her skin and the pain in her hip was still severe. She told him she was going to physical therapy three times a week and was able to sleep most nights. Dr. Krefft recommended she continue use of the pain medication.

Plaintiff returned for her last visit with Dr. Krefft on May 24, 1989, with complaints similar to the previous visit. Dr. Krefft referred her to Dr. Morse, a pain management specialist at the Touro Pain Clinic. Dr. Morse testified that the plaintiff reported she had pain two-thirds to three-quarters of her waking hours. Dr. Morse concluded something had irritated the nerves in the soft tissues below the skin along the thigh and caused some tissue irritation or scarring as well. The plaintiff was treated with medication and physical therapy. The plaintiff brought this medical malpractice action alleging she sustained injuries as a result of an improperly administered injection into her hip.

A medical review panel rendered an opinion in favor of Dr. Gruner, Ms. Tangney, and the hospital, finding no breach of the standard of care. However, at trial in 1996, the jury returned a verdict in favor of plaintiff and against Ms. Tangney and awarded $90,304.68 in damages.

Issue

Did the evidence show that the plaintiff's injury was caused by Ms. Tangney's breaching the standard of care required of nurses?

Holding

The appeals court found that there was sufficient evidence to support a jury finding that Ms. Tangney had breached the applicable standard of care in administering an injection of Vistaril into Ms. Pellerin's hip.

Reason

"To prove medical malpractice, the plaintiff must establish by a preponderance of the evidence: the standard of care, a breach of that standard, causation, and damages." A determination of whether a hospital has breached the duty of care owed to a particular patient depends on the facts and circumstances of the case, and in finding or refusing to find a breach of duty, the fact finder has great discretion. To reverse a fact finder's verdict, the appellate court must find from the record that a reasonable factual basis does not exist for the verdict, and that the record establishes the verdict is manifestly wrong.

Defendants argue that the evidence showed the plaintiff's injury could not have been caused by Ms. Tangney breaching the standard of care required of nurses. They contend that plaintiff's injury was proven to be a complication from a properly administered injection rather than a result of Vistaril being injected in subcutaneous tissue.

Dr. Gruner and Dr. McGarity (plaintiff's expert in pharmacology) testified that Vistaril can cause tissue damage if it is not injected into the muscle. Dr. Krefft testified that the plaintiff had nerve damage. Dr. Krefft testified that damage to the nerve is consistent with damage to subcutaneous tissue, which can occur from injection of Vistaril into that tissue. Dr. Krefft qualified this, however, by stating an injection of anything could cause nerve damage because the needle itself could be responsible. Both Dr. Krefft and Dr. Chugden (a member of the medical review panel and defense expert in emergency department medicine) testified that cutaneous neuropathy is more likely to be caused by the mechanics of injecting a needle than by the drug being injected. Examined in its entirety, however, Dr. Krefft's testimony indicates ambivalence concerning the cause of plaintiff's injuries. When pressed into making a choice between which was more likely, Dr. Krefft testified that either the Vistaril or the needle itself could have caused the nerve damage in this case.

Clearly, the jury was confronted with a great deal of conflicting testimony. Dr. Chugden testified that during administering an injection, hitting a subcutaneous nerve was more likely than missing one, and he believed the needle itself probably caused the nerve damage. Dr. Gruner, on the other hand, testified the chances of hitting a nerve are minimal. Where two permissible views of the evidence exists, the fact finder's choice between them cannot be manifestly erroneous or clearly wrong.

The verdict of the jury is very much supported by the record. Ms. Tangney admitted that she failed to record the site and mode of injection in the emergency department records. According to the testimony of two experts in nursing practice, failing to record this information is below the standard of care for nursing. While these omissions could not have affected the administration of the injection, they tend to indicate that in this instance Ms. Tangney did not follow accepted procedure while performing her job. The nurses' testimony alone would not necessarily be enough to support the jury's decision, but when it is added to the other evidence presented, the jury's verdict cannot be said to be erroneous.

Discussion

1. Discuss the theory upon which the hospital is liable.
2. If the nurse had maintained more accurate records, would she have been excused from liability? Discuss.

17. MEDICATION OVERDOSE/*RES IPSA LOQUITUR*

Citation: *Harder v. Clinton, Inc.*, 948 P.2d 298 (Okla. 1997)

Facts

Ms. Kayser was admitted on July 14, 1992, to the Heritage Care Center (nursing home). On the evening of September 30, 1992, she was transferred to the Clinton Regional Hospital after ingesting an overdose of Tolbutamide, a diabetic medication. There she was diagnosed as having a hypoglycemic coma caused by the lowering of her blood sugar from ingestion of the medication. An intravenous device was inserted in the dorsum area of her right foot to treat the coma. Gangrene later developed in the same foot, which eventually required an above-the-knee amputation.

Ms. Harder, Ms. Kayser's sister, brought a suit against the nursing home, as Ms. Kayser's guardian, for harm caused to Ms. Kayser by an overdose of the wrong prescription administered to her while she was in the Center's care and custody. At the close of Ms. Harder's case, which followed a *res ipsa loquitur* pattern of proof, the trial court, on Heritage's demurrer to the evidence, directed a verdict for the nursing home. The trial court ruled that Ms. Harder's evidence fell short of establishing a negligence claim because her proof failed to show all the requisite foundational elements for *res ipsa loquitur*.

Issue

Did the trial court err when it directed a verdict for the nursing home based on its ruling that Ms. Harder had not satisfied the requirements for a *res ipsa loquitur* submission?

Holding

By the evidence adduced at trial, Ms. Harder met the standards for submission of her claim based on the doctrine of *res ipsa loquitur* pattern of proof. The trial court's judgment on directed verdict was reversed and the cause of action was remanded for further proceedings.

Reason

According to Ms. Harder, a directed verdict was inappropriate because she adduced reasonably supportive evidence to establish the foundation facts for application of the *res ipsa loquitur* pattern of proof. The nursing home counters that Ms. Harder cannot invoke the *res ipsa loquitur* evidentiary process because she failed to establish two foundation facts: (a) the thing causing the injury (the Tolbutamide) was under its exclusive control and (b) but for the negligence in administering an overdose of the wrong medication, the harm of which plaintiff complains would not have occurred.

In order to move the case forward on the basis of *res ipsa loquitur* application, Ms. Harder was required to show that:

1. An overdose of the wrong prescription medication is not usually ingested in the course of administering prescription drugs to residents.
2. The nursing home had exclusive control and management of the instrumentality (prescription drugs) that caused the injury.
3. Evidence shedding light on the harmful event is more accessible to the nursing home than to the plaintiff.
4. The administration of the injurious overdose is the sort of occurrence, which, in the ordinary course of events, would not have happened if one having control of the instrumentality exercised due care.

The foundation facts can be established by expert testimony or by demonstrating that the defendant's substandard conduct falls within the realm of common knowledge. If the showing of any foundation fact requires a degree of knowledge or skill not possessed by the average person, expert testimony must be adduced.

Foundation Fact I—The Injury Does Not Occur in the Ordinary Course of Operations

The first foundation fact requires a showing that the injury—an overdose of the wrong prescription—does not occur in the ordinary course of operations at the nursing home.

Ms. Dixon, a licensed practicing nurse (and a medication clerk at the nursing home), testified that the residents' prescription drugs are stored at the nurses' station. She gave a detailed account of the method used for dispensing prescribed medication to the residents. The nursing home's residents have no access to prescription drugs except when they are administered to them by authorized personnel. When medication is to be administered, the correct dosage is removed from the storage site and placed in a cart that is pushed down the halls. The nurse (or certified medication aide) removes the medication from its container, places it in a cup, and then serves it to the resident. The cart is kept locked while the nurse or aide is administering the medication. Dr. Hays—Ms. Kayser's family physician since 1973 (as well as the nursing home's medical director)—testified

that the administration of the wrong prescription drug in an amount that would cause harm is below the applicable standard of care.

The first *res ipsa loquitur* element is met by the evidence adduced because, under the applicable standard of care, the overdose of a wrong prescription drug would not occur in the ordinary course of operations at the defendant nursing home.

Foundation Fact II—The Nursing Home Has Exclusive Control of the Harm-Dealing Instrumentality

The second *res ipsa loquitur* element is satisfied by proof that the agency or instrumentality causing the injury was under the defendant's exclusive control or management at the time the negligence occurred. Exclusive control is a flexible concept that denotes no more than elimination, within reason, of all explanations for the genesis of the injurious event other than the defendant's negligence—a showing that defendant's negligence probably caused the accident. The nature and degree of control must be such that the reasonable probabilities point to the nursing home and support an inference that it was the negligent party.

The plaintiff established that (1) the offending drug was prescribed medicine, (2) the administration of prescription drugs to the residents is within the control of the defendant, and (3) at the time of the harmful event, the decedent, a nursing home resident, was at the nursing home and subject to the policies that govern there the distribution and administration of prescribed medicine. This constitutes a legally sufficient showing to satisfy the control-element requirement for the *res ipsa loquitur* pattern of proof.

Foundation Fact III—True Explanation for the Harm's Occurrence Is More Accessible to the Nursing Home

The third *res ipsa loquitur* element consists of evidence that the precise cause of the accident is more accessible to the defendant than to the plaintiff.

The nursing home is required to chart and keep in its records extensive data about each resident's health, medical history, physician orders, and overall medical treatment. Its records also contain information about the prescribed medication that is ordered, received, stored on its premises, and administered to its residents.

The evidence adduced clearly demonstrates that information about the circumstances surrounding the administration to Ms. Kayser of excessive dosage of the wrong prescription is more accessible to the nursing home than to Ms. Kayser.

Foundation Fact IV—The Defendant's Negligence

The fourth *res ipsa loquitur* element required Ms. Harder to present reasonably supportive evidence that an overdose of a wrong prescription would not ordinarily occur absent negligence on the part of someone who had the instrumentality in its exclusive control and management. It need not be shown that negligence is the only explanation for the injury, but merely that it is the most probable one. This element is satisfied if, under the facts of the case, common experience indicates that the injury was more likely than not the result of the defendant's negligence.

In light of the circumstances that surround the injurious event, and disregarding the defendant's conflicting evidence, it seems reasonably clear that Ms. Kayser's ingestion of a Tolbutamide overdose would not have taken place in the absence of negligence by the nursing home's responsible staff. The record shows that Ms. Kayser had not been prescribed any diabetes medication while a resident at the nursing home and that she had never been prescribed that type of hypoglycemic drug. It is uncontradicted that Ms. Kayser was at the nursing home when she ingested the prescribed medication. There is no direct evidence that anyone else supplied to her the harm-dealing dosage or that the substance in question was kept in her room (or elsewhere within her control). Neither is there indication that any other cause contributed to the coma. According to Ms. Dixon, the nursing home is responsible for the administration of medication to its residents. As Dr. Hays testified, the administra-

tion of the wrong medication in an amount so excessive as to harm a resident would be below the applicable professional standard of care.

In sum, Ms. Harder's evidence laid before the trial court the requisite *res ipsa loquitur* foundation facts from which the trier may infer that the injury—from an overdose of the wrong prescription—was one that would not ordinarily occur in the course of controlled supervision and administration of prescribed medicine in the absence of negligence on the nursing home's part. Because nothing in the record irrefutably negates any of the critical elements for application of *res ipsa loquitur*, Ms. Harder clearly met her probative initiative by establishing the necessary components for invoking the rule. The responsibility for producing proof that would rebut the inferences favorable to Ms. Harder's legal position was thus shifted to the defendant.

Discussion

1. How would you have argued this case if you were the defendant nursing home?
2. What procedures would you consider implementing in order to reduce the likelihood of similar events from occurring in the future?

VIII

Liability by Department and Health Professional

1. DENTAL HYGIENIST/ADMINISTRATION OF NITROUS OXIDE/INCOMPLETE RECORDS

Citation: *Lowenberg v. Sobol*, 594 N.Y.S.2d 874 (N.Y. App. Div. 1993)

Facts

This case arises from a complaint by a dental hygienist against a former employer, Lowenberg and Lowenberg Corporation. The dental hygienist alleged that the defendant allowed the dental hygienists to administer nitrous oxide to patients. Under state law, dental hygienists may not administer nitrous oxide. The Department of Education's Office of Professional Discipline investigated the complaint by using an undercover investigator. The investigator made an appointment for teeth cleaning. At the time of her appointment, she requested that nitrous oxide be administered. Agreeing to the investigator's request, the dental hygienist administered the nitrous oxide. After the procedure was completed, the investigator paid her bill and left the office. There were no notations in the patient's chart indicating that she had been administered nitrous oxide.

The hearing panel found the dental hygienist guilty of administering nitrous oxide without being properly licensed. In addition, the hearing panel found that the dental hygienist had failed to accurately record on the patient's chart that she had administered nitrous oxide. Lowenberg and Lowenberg were reprimanded and fined $750 each. The petitioners, the dental hygienist and Lowenberg and Lowenberg, commenced proceedings for review of the determination.

Issue

Was there sufficient evidence to support a determination that the petitioners engaged in professional misconduct?

Holding

The New York Supreme Court, Appellate Division, held that the investigator's report provided sufficient evidence to support the hearing panel's determination that the dentist and dental hygienist had committed professional misconduct by permitting an unlicensed individual to administer nitrous oxide.

Reason

The dentist's actual knowledge of the hygienist's illegal conduct is not a prerequisite to a finding of misconduct based on a failure to supervise. There is adequate support in the record to support a finding that the dentist's conduct was such that it could reasonably be said that he permitted the dental hygienist to perform acts that she was not licensed to perform.

Discussion

1. What issues does this case raise for health care organizations that fail to provide properly licensed personnel in patient care settings, as required by law (e.g., the availability of registered nurses on nursing units)?
2. Do you agree that there was sufficient evidence to support a determination of professional misconduct?

2. DENTAL MALPRACTICE/CAUSATION

Citation: *Pasquale v. Miller*, 599 N.Y.S.2d 58 (N.Y. App. Div. 1993)

Facts

The plaintiff, Ms. Pasquale, brought a suit against the defendant, Dr. Miller, for dental malpractice. On March 22, 1986, the plaintiff was treated by Dr. Miller for swollen gums. Dr. Miller removed tissue from her gums and used sutures to control the bleeding. Although it was common practice to prescribe antibiotics prior to or following gum surgery, Dr. Miller did not prescribe antibiotics in either case. The following May, after the plaintiff had experienced a persistent fever, she was diagnosed as having contracted subacute bacterial endocarditis. The plaintiff was treated in the hospital for nearly a month. Dr. Miller claimed that the bacterial infection could have resulted from a number of causes. The trial court, upon a jury verdict, found for the plaintiff.

Issue

Did the plaintiff offer sufficient proof to establish that Dr. Miller's failure to administer antibiotics was the cause of the plaintiff's subacute bacterial endocarditis?

Holding

The New York Supreme Court, Appellate Division, held that the evidence supported a finding of causation.

Reason

Sufficient proof was offered as to causation. "A plaintiff is required to offer sufficient proof from which a reasonable person may conclude that it is more probable than not that the injury was caused by the defendant, and the evidence need not eliminate every other possible cause." *Id.* at 59. The plaintiff's expert witnesses testified that her endocarditis was related to the dental surgery and that one of the risks of not prescribing an antibiotic is that bacteria can flow through the bloodstream to the heart. The jury could and did reject testimony from Dr. Miller that the endocarditis could have been caused by something other than the failure to administer antibiotics prior to or following gum surgery.

Discussion

1. What lessons can be learned from the *Pasquale* case?
2. What should the plan of care for a patient undergoing a surgical procedure include?

3. Could the postoperative complication, endocarditis, have been avoided? If yes, how could the complication have been avoided? If no, why not?

3. NURSE'S AIDE/GROSS NEGLIGENCE/TERMINATION

Citation: *Bowe v. Charleston Area Med. Ctr.*, 428 S.E.2d 773 (W. Va. 1993)

Facts

The plaintiff, a nurse's aide, brought an action against a medical center for retaliatory discharge and breach of contract. The nurse's aide had assisted a patient to the bathroom and placed him on the commode. She left him unattended for about 10 minutes. When she returned, the patient was found lying on the floor in a pool of blood. The patient had apparently hit his head on the sink when he fell.

Following an investigation of the incident, the hospital found that the nurse had been grossly negligent and terminated her employment. The personnel director had authorized the employee's termination because of a provision in the employee handbook that makes gross negligence a dischargeable offense. The nurse's aide claimed she had been terminated in retaliation because of complaints she had made about the lack of patient care on the oncology unit to which she had been assigned. No evidence of her complaints could be substantiated by her head nurse and the employee responsible for patient complaints. In addition, there was no evidence in the employee's personnel file that would indicate that she had filed a grievance over patient care.

Upon jury verdict, the circuit court entered judgment for the plaintiff. The plaintiff was awarded $36,238.17 in lost wages and $15,000 for mental suffering. The circuit court added an additional $5,218.30 in interest, and the medical center appealed.

Issue

Did the evidence establish that the nurse's aide was discharged because of patient neglect? Did the employee handbook give rise to a contractual relationship between the aide and the medical center?

Holding

The Supreme Court of Appeals of West Virginia held that: (1) the evidence established that patient neglect by the plaintiff prompted an investigation that led to her subsequent discharge, and (2) the disclaimer in the employee handbook adequately shielded the employer from any contractual liability based on the employee handbook.

Reason

The evidence showed that the nurse's aide, contrary to the medical center's policy, had assisted a patient in getting on a commode and then left him unattended, resulting in a fall and his subsequent death. Leaving the patient unattended for 10 minutes on the commode was clearly against hospital policy. The nurse's aide failed to establish that her discharge was a retaliatory act or that it contravened some public policy. The evidence presented during the development of the present case substantially cast doubt as to whether the plaintiff had ever actually made any complaints about patient care. *Id.* at 777.

The hospital's disclaimer specifically stated that the employee handbook was not intended to create any contractual rights. Employment was subject to termination at any time by either the employee or employer. The disclaimer in the employee handbook read:

> Because of court decisions in some states, it has become necessary for us to make it clear that this handbook is not part of a contract, and no employee of the Medical Center has any contractual right to the matters set forth in this handbook. In addition, your employment is subject to termination at any time by either you or by the Medical Center. *Id.* at 779.

Discussion

1. What value is there in placing a disclaimer in an employee handbook?
2. Will failure to place a disclaimer in an employee handbook result in the handbook being construed as an unconditional contract with employees?

4. EMERGENCY DEPARTMENT/FAILURE TO ADMIT

Citation: *Roy v. Gupta*, 606 So. 2d 940 (La. Ct. App. 1992)

Facts

The husband and children of Mrs. Roy brought this suit for medical malpractice. The claim was initially against Dr. Gupta, Dr. Garcia, and Humana Hospital. Court-approved

settlements were effected with the two physicians and the hospital with reservation of rights against the Louisiana Patients Compensation Fund (the Fund). A trial was held against the Fund. After a bench trial, judgment was rendered in favor of the plaintiffs for damages, costs, and attorney fees. An appeal by the Fund followed.

On October 31, 1987, Mrs. Roy went to the emergency department of Humana Hospital–Marksville complaining of chest pains. At that time she was 42 years old. She had no prior history of heart disease but was taking medication for hypertension. The attending physician was Dr. Gupta, a physician on independent contract who was moonlighting on weekends for the hospital. Upon examination, Mrs. Roy exhibited normal vital signs. She showed no obvious physical abnormalities. Dr. Gupta performed an electrocardiogram that showed ischemic changes indicating a lack of oxygen to the heart tissue. He applied a transdermal nitroglycerin patch and gave her a prescription for nitroglycerin. After monitoring her progress, he sent her home. Several hours later she returned to the emergency department experiencing more chest pains. She was admitted to the hospital and it was determined that she was having a heart attack. Three days later, Mrs. Roy died of a massive myocardial infarction.

On October 29, 1990, a bench trial was held. The trial court found Dr. Gupta negligent in failing to hospitalize Mrs. Roy or failing to inform her of the serious nature of her situation so that she would agree to hospitalization. The trial court also found that had Mrs. Roy been hospitalized on her first visit, her chances of survival would have been greatly increased.

The Fund asserted that the trial court erred in finding that Dr. Gupta failed to advise Mrs. Roy that she should be hospitalized or point out the potential dangers of not being hospitalized.

Issue

Did Dr. Gupta's discharge of the patient from the emergency department while she had chest pains constitute malpractice? Did the trial court err in finding that the patient's chances of survival would have been greatly increased if she had been admitted to the hospital and given proper treatment?

Holding

The Court of Appeal of Louisiana held that Dr. Gupta was negligent in failing to advise Mrs. Roy that she should be hospitalized for chest pains or point out the potential dangers of not being hospitalized.

Reason

Dr. Caskey and Dr. d'Autremont, two expert witnesses, testified that it is common practice to enter in a patient's record whether a recommendation of hospitalization was made. No such notation was made in Mrs. Roy's chart by Dr. Gupta. All of the medical expert witnesses, except Dr. Kilpatrick, a defense witness, testified that Mrs. Roy should have been admitted. Dr. Kilpatrick testified that such a decision varied greatly among physicians. "In any event the trial court disregarded his testimony because he was too hostile in his responses to be of any assistance." *Id.* at 943.

In his reasons for judgment, it was evident the trial judge was not convinced by Dr. Gupta's explanation of why Mrs. Roy was not hospitalized. He focused on Dr. Gupta's failure to have X-rays taken during the first visit, which might have allowed him to determine whether the ischemic changes were due to her hypertension medication or indicated the beginnings of a heart attack. The relative simplicity of the technique and its obvious availability lent credence to the trial judge's belief that the requisite attention was not paid to Mrs. Roy's complaints. *Id.* at 943–944.

The law does not require proof that proper treatment would have been the difference between Mrs. Roy's dying or living. It only requires proof that proper treatment would have increased her chances of survival. Even though the expert testimony of Dr. d'Autremont was guarded in this area, the inference can be drawn from her testimony that while nothing could ensure Mrs. Roy's survival, admittance on the first visit would have at least increased her chances. This is a difficult area in which to make factual determinations, and the degree of specialization requires the trier of fact to rely heavily on the testimony of the experts. The trial judge was present and able to determine the credibility and sincerity of all who testified. Our review of the record revealed the trial court's finding to be sound and thus no manifest error was committed.

As this case was heard by the bench, determinations of possible breaches of the appropriate standard of care were left to the trial judge. He sat as the trier of fact and made his findings related to negligence based on the evidence and inferences therefrom. In order for the court to upset the factual findings of the trial court, there must exist manifest error.

Discussion

1. Why are emergency departments at high risk for lawsuits?
2. What can be done to reduce the risks?
3. What opportunities for improvement do you see in your emergency department?

5. EMERGENCY DEPARTMENT/OFFER OF PROOF SUFFICIENT

Citation: *Feeney v. New England Med. Ctr., Inc.*, 615 N.E.2d 585 (Mass. App. Ct. 1993)

Facts

The plaintiff, administrator, alleging that the death of his son was caused by medical malpractice, commenced this action against the emergency department physician, the nurse on duty, and the hospital.

On December 1, 1987, at 10:16 P.M., an ambulance team of the Boston Department of Health and Hospitals found 26-year-old Mr. Feeney intoxicated, sitting on a street corner in South Boston. Mr. Feeney admitted to alcohol abuse but denied that he used drugs. He was physically and verbally combative and had trouble walking and speaking intelligibly. His condition interfered with the team's conducting an examination of him. Vital signs were not taken.

At 10:45 P.M. Mr. Feeney was picked up by the ambulance and arrived at the hospital. No observer could doubt that the patient was highly intoxicated with alcohol. The autopsy report in fact revealed an ethyl alcohol blood level of 0.39 percent, a very dangerous condition. A physician or nurse could readily recognize a grave risk to the patient through depression of the respiratory system: "in the short run, the systemic effects [of the ingestion of ethanol] with the potential for the greatest negative outcome involves depression of the respiratory system." *Id.* at 586–587.

The documentation for the period between 10:45 P.M. and 11:30 P.M. was "sparse and contradictory," as stated by Dr. McGoey, one of the experts. *Id.* at 587. The next entry on the emergency department record after 10:45 P.M. is at 11:30 P.M., made when the patient was brought to the examining room. He was then without respiration and cyanotic with his pupils fixed and dilated. On the physician documentation record, in which the emergency department physician wrote out the course of the case to the end, he reported (secondhand) that a nurse returned 20 minutes after 10:45 P.M. and found the patient unresponsive and without respiration.

The record goes on to report that the patient was pronounced dead after about 30 minutes of "code." If (referring to the emergency department record) the nurse returned to the patient at 11:30 P.M., then, inferentially, the patient had not been monitored for 45 minutes. On the other hand, if (referring to the physician documentation record) the patient was seen at 11:05 P.M., there was room for the inference that a lapse of 25 minutes intervened between that visit and the commencement of "code." An expert suggested that the former was the "more probable scenario." On either basis, a gap appears, needing explanation. *Id.* at 587.

A Suffolk County medical tribunal found the administrator's offer of proof insufficient, and entered judgment against the physician, dismissing his complaint. The administrator appealed.

Issue

Was the offer of proof made by the administrator sufficient to support a medical malpractice action against the hospital and the emergency department physician and nurse?

Holding

The Appeals Court of Massachusetts held that the administrator's offer of proof was sufficient to sustain his cause of action.

Reason

The minimum standard of care for nursing required monitoring the respiratory rate of the patient every 15 minutes; this "would more likely have permitted the nursing staff to observe changes in the patient's breathing patterns and/or the onset of respiratory arrest." As to the emergency department physician, he failed to evaluate the patient and to initiate care within the first few minutes of Mr. Feeney's entry into the emergency facility. The emergency physician had an obligation to determine who was waiting for physician care and how critical was the need for that care. Had the standards been maintained, respiratory arrest might have been averted. According to the autopsy report, respiratory arrest was the sole cause of death. *Id.* at 587.

The failure to provide adequate care could be rationally attributed to the staff nurse assigned to the area in which the patient lay, as well as to the physicians in charge. The hospital was implicated on the basis of the acts or omission of its staff.

Discussion

1. Do you agree with the court's finding?

2. What effect, if any, might cases of this sort have on the care being rendered in emergency departments?

6. EMERGENCY DEPARTMENT/EMTALA/ HOSPITAL NEGLIGENCE

Citation: *Ballachino v. Anders*, 811 F. Supp. 121 (W.D. N.Y. 1993)

Facts

The decedent presented himself at a Medicare hospital on May 15, 1990, with complaints of chest pain and repeated episodes of loss of consciousness. The physicians allegedly negligently failed to provide an appropriate medical screening examination and failed to determine whether or not an emergency medical condition existed. The patient's survivor and representative brought an action against the hospital and physicians alleging violations of the Emergency Medical Treatment and Active Labor Act (EMTALA) and medical malpractice. EMTALA requires that a three-part duty on a Medicare provider hospital must provide an appropriate medical screening examination to determine whether an emergency medical condition exists for any individual who presents to the emergency department seeking examination or treatment. If the hospital determines that an emergency medical condition exists, then it must either stabilize the patient or provide for transfer of the patient to a facility capable of meeting the patient's medical needs.

Issue

Was there a right of action against the physicians and was a claim appropriately stated against the hospital?

Holding

The United States District Court for the Western District of New York held that there is no private right of action against the individual physicians under EMTALA. However, the representative's complaint did state a claim against the hospital under EMTALA.

Reason

No private right of action exists against individual physicians under EMTALA. The enforcement provision of

EMTALA is explicitly limited to actions against a Medicare participating hospital. While the physicians were alleged to have acted in concert in rendering professional medical and surgical care and treatment to the decedent while at the hospital, the physicians importantly are nowhere alleged to have provided any "emergency screening examination." The plaintiff clearly alleged that these defendants negligently failed to provide an appropriate medical screening examination and failed to determine whether an emergency medical condition existed for the decedent. The court was faced with the question of whether any emergency screening examination occurred at all. The plaintiff also alleged that the hospital failed in its stabilization and transfer procedures. The district court determined that all of the allegations taken together stated a claim against the hospital under EMTALA.

Discussion

1. Should EMTALA be changed to include physicians? Explain.
2. What is the importance of the screening and assessment procedures that should be in place for emergency department patients?

7. EMERGENCY DEPARTMENT/VOLUNTARY TERMINATION OF TREATMENT

Citation: *Matthews v. DeKalb County Hosp. Auth.*, 440 S.E.2d 743 (Ga. Ct. App. 1994)

Facts

A malpractice action was brought against DeKalb County Hospital Authority arising out of the death of Mrs. Carolyn Matthews, an emergency department patient.

On August 10, 1988, the patient had gone unassisted to the emergency department of the hospital complaining of a burning pain in her upper chest that had radiated down her right side that evening, as well as the previous evening. Upon arriving at the hospital's emergency department at about 11:25 P.M., Mrs. Matthews was triaged by a nurse who took her vital signs, recorded her medical history, and made an assessment of her immediate medical needs. Although slightly elevated, Mrs. Matthews' vital signs were within normal limits. She explained to the triage nurse that after her pain had subsided, she needed to have a bowel movement. The triage nurse classified Mrs. Matthews as a "category two" patient, a nonthreatening condition. It was explained to her that she would have a long wait as the emergency department was very busy. A social services representative had testified

that he had spoken to Mrs. Matthews between six and eight times during her wait in the emergency department. He indicated that she was in no apparent distress during those times that he had spoken to her. Following a four-and-one-half-hour wait, Mrs. Matthews left the emergency department without being treated. The social services representative stated that he told Mrs. Matthews that a treatment room was ready for her and that she would be attended to shortly. Mrs. Matthews said that she had already waited long enough and she was leaving. The social services representative stated that he had pleaded with her to stay but she refused, claiming that she would see her own physician in the morning. Mrs. Matthews went to work the following day without having seen her physician. Mrs. Matthews expired on August 12, 1988. The DeKalb Superior Court granted the hospital's motion for summary judgment, and an appeal was taken.

Issue

Was the patient's subsequent death following her visit to the hospital's emergency department because of the negligence of the hospital?

Holding

The Court of Appeals of Georgia held that the patient's voluntary termination of her relationship with the hospital's emergency department personnel effectively severed any relationship between the hospital's act of classifying the patient as a category two patient who could wait to see a physician and her subsequent death two days later. Accordingly, the hospital could not be held liable for the death of the patient. The court also held that the appeal was frivolous and required the imposition of a $250 penalty.

Reason

In order "to recover damages in a tort action, a plaintiff must prove that the defendant's negligence was both the 'cause in fact' and the 'proximate cause' of the injury. The requirement of proximate cause constitutes a limit on legal liability; it is a policy decision . . . that, for a variety of reasons, e.g., intervening act, the defendant's conduct and the plaintiff's injury are too remote for the law to countenance recovery." *Atlanta Obstetrics, etc., v. Coleman*, 260 Ga. 569, 398 S.E.2d 16 (1990). Mrs. Matthews left the hospital on her own cognizance at a time when the hospital's emergency department physician was about to see her. She went to work the following morning without seeing her own physician, as she had indicated that she would. The elements that a plaintiff must establish in a malpractice case are duty to care, breach of duty, injury, and causation. The fact that Mrs. Matthews voluntarily terminated her relationship with the emergency department personnel at DeKalb General effectively severed any causal relationship that might have existed between DeKalb General's act of classifying Mrs. Matthews as a category two patient and her death. *Id.* at 745. Because the appeal was found to be without any arguable merit, a penalty of $250 was assessed against the appellants.

Discussion

1. What elements must a plaintiff establish in a malpractice case in order to establish liability for negligence?
2. Was there adequate evidence to discredit the plaintiff's claim of causation?
3. What steps might the hospital consider taking in the future in order to reduce the risks of lawsuits similar to those in the Matthews case?
4. What are the inherent risks when utilizing a triage nurse in making the initial assessment and prioritizing emergency department patients based on their presenting complaints?
5. In the emergency department setting, at what point should a physician become involved in assessing a patient's needs? Should the physician perform the initial assessment? Explain.

8. EMTALA/WRONGFUL DEATH

Citation: *Huckaby v. East Ala. Med. Ctr.*, 830 F. Supp. 1399 (M.D. Ala. 1993)

Facts

The plaintiff brought an action against the hospital alleging that the deceased patient, Mrs. Wynn, was transferred from the hospital's emergency department before her condition was stabilized. Mrs. Wynn went to the hospital on September 19, 1990, suffering from a stroke. The complaint alleged that Mrs. Wynn's condition was critical and materially deteriorating. Dr. Wheat, the attending emergency department physician, informed Mrs. Wynn's family that she needed the services of a neurosurgeon, but that the hospital "had problems in the past with getting neurosurgeons to accept patients from us." *Id.* at 1401. Upon the recommendation of Dr. Wheat, Mrs. Wynn was transferred to another hospital where she expired soon after arrival. The plaintiff alleged that Dr. Wheat did not inform the family regarding

the risks of transfer and that the transfer of Mrs. Wynn in an unstable condition was the proximate cause of her death.

Issue

Did the plaintiff have a cause of action under EMTALA?

Holding

The United States District Court for the Middle District of Alabama held that the plaintiff stated a cause of action under EMTALA for which monetary relief could be granted.

Reason

In order for the plaintiff to overcome the defendant's motion to dismiss the case, the plaintiff had to demonstrate that, under EMTALA, Mrs. Wynn (1) went to the defendant's emergency department, (2) was diagnosed with an emergency medical condition, (3) was not provided with adequate screening, and (4) was discharged and transferred to another hospital before her emergency condition was stabilized. The plaintiff met this standard.

Discussion

1. Describe how the court decisions in the above EMTALA cases differ.
2. How might the comments of Dr. Wheat, the emergency department physician, affect the final outcome of this case?

9. EMERGENCY DEPARTMENT/EMTALA/ APPROPRIATE DISCHARGE

Citation: *Holcomb v. Humana Med. Corp.*, 831 F. Supp. 829 (M.D. Ala. 1993)

Facts

The administratrix of the estate of a deceased patient, Mrs. Smith, sued the hospital, alleging a violation of EMTALA. Mrs. Smith had entered the emergency department on May 4, 1990, a week after giving birth, with a complaint of a fever, aching, sore throat, and coughing. Mrs. Smith was examined by both a physician's assistant and a physician. The examination revealed that Mrs. Smith had a temperature of 104.3 degrees, a pulse of 146, respirations of 32, and a blood pressure of 112/64. Diagnostic tests ordered included a white blood cell count, urine analysis, and chest X-ray. After reviewing the results of Mrs. Smith's complaints and medical history, physical examination, and test results, the physician diagnosed the patient as having a viral infection. The physician ordered Tylenol and intravenous (IV) fluids as treatment. Mrs. Smith was maintained in the emergency department overnight. The physician conducted a second physical examination during the night. By morning, Mrs. Smith's vital signs had returned to normal. She was discharged with instructions for bed rest, fluids, and a request to return to the hospital if her condition worsened. After returning home, Mrs. Smith reported that she was feeling better but then took a turn for the worse and was admitted to Jackson Hospital on May 6, 1990. She was diagnosed with endometritis and subsequently died on May 9, 1990.

Issue

Was the patient inappropriately discharged from the emergency department under provisions of EMTALA?

Holding

The United States District Court for the Middle District of Alabama held that there was no violation of EMTALA.

Reason

The patient was appropriately examined and screened. The care rendered was standard for any patient based on the complaints given. In addition, the plaintiff failed to demonstrate that an emergency condition existed at the time the patient was discharged.

Discussion

1. What, if any, measures could have been routinely followed to reduce the likelihood of such occurrences in the future?
2. Generally speaking, describe how pressure from third-party payers, concerned with reducing the length of stay, could contribute to occurrences such as this.

10. PHYSICAL THERAPIST/STANDARD OF CARE

Citation: *Hodo v. General Hosps. of Humana*, 438 S.E.2d 378 (Ga. Ct. App. 1993)

Facts

The plaintiff, a patient, brought an action against General Hospitals of Humana, Inc. (hospital's owners) for injuries sustained while undergoing physical therapy. The patient had gone to Humana for physical therapy on October 7, 1991, to learn how to walk with her prosthesis. While the physical therapist was making an initial assessment of the patient's needs, she fell as she attempted to turn around. Humana argued that the plaintiff failed to attach an expert's affidavit with her complaint, as is required under Georgia statute [OCGA (§§ 9-11-9.1, 9-11-9.1a), 43-33-11]. The trial court entered summary judgment in favor of Humana, and the patient appealed.

Issue

Was the cause of the patient's injuries due to "simple" negligence or "professional" malpractice? Was an affidavit from an expert required to be filed with the complaint?

Holding

The Court of Appeals of Georgia held that the action was for malpractice, requiring the patient to file an expert's affidavit with the complaint.

Reason

Physical therapists are professionals within the meaning of the Georgia statute, which requires the filing of an affidavit of an expert with an action for malpractice. The patient's physical capacity was the determinative factor as to the degree of supervision to be accorded to her during physical therapy. Therefore, the physical therapist's initial assessment and evaluation of the patient's capacity to walk with the prosthesis required the exercise of professional judgment.

Discussion

1. How should the standard of care for a physical therapist be determined?
2. How does the standard of care for a physical therapist differ from that of other health care professionals (e.g., nurse, physician, and pharmacist)?

11. PRIVILEGED COMMUNICATIONS/JOINT COMMISSION REPORTS

Citation: *Humana Hosp. Corp. v. Spears-Petersen*, 867 S.W.2d 858 (Tex. Ct. App. 1993)

Facts

The underlying suit in this petition involved a plaintiff, Ms. Garcia, who was scheduled to undergo an epidural steroid injection but was administered a lumbar epidural steroid injection instead by the defendant, Dr. Garg. The plaintiff sued Dr. Garg on the basis of negligence, lack of informed consent, battery, and fraud. She also sued Humana Corporation for negligence in credentialing, supervising, and monitoring Dr. Garg's clinical privileges. The plaintiff's attorney requested documents from Humana, including reports prepared by the Joint Commission on Accreditation of Healthcare Organizations (Joint Commission).

The Joint Commission is a voluntary organization that surveys various health care organizations for the purpose of accreditation. The organization's governing body consists of members representing such organizations as the American Medical Association, the American College of Physicians, and the American Hospital Association.

Humana objected to releasing Joint Commission reports and filed for a protective order preventing disclosure. The Joint Commission reports contained recommendations describing the hospital's noncompliance with certain of its published standards. Humana argued that the Joint Commission reports are privileged information under Texas statute. Under Texas law, the records and proceedings of a medical committee are considered confidential and are not subject to a court subpoena. The plaintiff argued that the Joint Commission is not a medical committee as defined in the Texas statute. The hospital's chief operating officer, Mr. Williams, testified that the Joint Commission surveys and accredits hospitals across the country. The accreditation is voluntary, and the hospital chooses to have the accreditation survey. During the survey, the Joint Commission looks at certain standards it has developed for hospitals to abide by in maintaining quality care. The hospital's executive committee is charged in its bylaws with keeping abreast of the accreditation process. Humana argued that release of the Joint Commission's recommendations would do more than "chill" the effectiveness of such accreditation—no prudent hospital would discuss or release any information to the Joint Commission knowing that it could be used against it in malpractice suits. *Id.* at 861. Humana argued further that even if the information was privileged, it had already been disclosed to a third party, the hospital, thus waiving its rights to nondisclosure. The trial court denied Humana's motion

for a protective order that, if granted, would have permitted it to withhold from discovery any information pertaining to credentialing, monitoring, or supervision practices of the hospital regarding its physicians. Humana appealed.

Issue

Are accreditation reports prepared by the Joint Commission privileged from discovery?

Holding

The Court of Appeals of Texas held that the accreditation reports were privileged because: (1) the Joint Commission was a "joint committee" as created by statute creating a privilege from discovery for hospital review committee deliberations, (2) the disclosure of the Joint Commission's report to the hospital did not result in waiver of the privilege, and (3) the reports reflected a deliberative process by the Joint Commission and were therefore privileged.

Reason

The purpose of privileged communications is to encourage open and thorough review of a hospital's medical staff and operations of a hospital with the objective of improving the delivery of patient care. The plaintiff argued that the Joint Commission is not a medical committee as defined in the Texas statute. The court of appeals found that:

> the determinative factor is not whether the entity is known as a "committee," or a "commission," or by any other particular term, but whether it is organized for the purposes contemplated by the statute and case law. We think it is clear from the evidence we have detailed that the Joint Commission is a joint committee made up of representatives of various medical organizations and thus fits within the statutory definition. . . . Further, it is organized, as are the various in-house medical committees that indisputably come within the statute, for the laudable purposes of improving patient care. Both the statute and case law recognize that the open, thorough, and uninhibited review that is required for such committees to achieve their purpose can only be realized if the deliberations of the committee remain confidential. *Id.* at 862.

As to the Joint Commission's disclosing its report to the hospital, the "only disclosure . . . was to the hospital as the intended beneficiary of the committee's findings. The only disclosure made to the outside world was the accreditation certificate, which merely declares that the hospital has been awarded accreditation by the Joint Commission." *Id.* at 862.

Discussion

1. How might the Joint Commission's new "public disclosure policy" to make available certain information to the public affect the "privilege" of other information surrounding the accreditation process (e.g., interviews, notes, minutes, and reports)?
2. Does privilege from discovery extend to all documents maintained in the normal course of business?

12. PEER REVIEW/CONFIDENTIALITY

Citation: *McGee v. Bruce Hosp. Sys.*, 439 S.E.2d 257 (S.C. 1993)

Facts

The underlying action in this case involved a medical malpractice wrongful death claim. This matter was before the court pursuant to a circuit court order granting the plaintiffs a motion to compel and instructing the defendant, Bruce Hospital System, to produce the credentialing files and clinical privileges for each of the defendant physicians.

The defendant physicians contend that such documentation is protected by the confidentiality statute, S.C. Code Ann. § 40-71-20 (Supp. 1992), which provides that:

> all proceeding of and all data and information acquired by the committee referred to in § 40-71-10 in the exercise of its duties are confidential. . . . These proceedings and documents are not subject to discovery, subpoena, or introduction into evidence in any civil action except upon appeal from the committee action. *Information, documents, or records which are otherwise available from original sources are not immune from discovery or use in a civil action merely because they were presented during the committee proceedings* [emphasis added] nor shall any complainant or witness before the committee be prevented from testifying in a civil action as to matters of which he has knowledge apart from the committee proceedings or revealing such matters to third persons. *Id.* at 259.

The trial judge found that the materials sought were discoverable.

Issue

Are credentialing files, clinical privileges, and the policies and procedures involved in the evaluation of medical staff immune from discovery under the terms of the confidentiality statute?

Holding

The Supreme Court of South Carolina held that: (1) applications for staff privileges and supporting documents of appropriate training were protected by the confidentiality statute, (2) the confidentiality statute did not preclude discovery of general policies and procedures for staff monitoring, and (3) the patient could discover a listing of clinical privileges either granted or denied by the hospital.

Reason

The overriding public policy of the confidentiality statute is to encourage health care professionals to monitor the competency and professional conduct of their peers in order to safeguard and improve the quality of patient care. The underlying purpose behind the confidentiality statute is not to facilitate the prosecution of civil actions, but to promote complete candor and open discussion among participants in the peer review process. As stated in *Cruger v. Lone*, 599 So. 2d 111 (Fla. 1992):

> [t]he policy of encouraging full candor in peer review proceedings is advanced only if all documents considered by the committee . . . during the peer review or credentialing process are protected. Committee members and those providing information to the committee must be able to operate without fear of reprisal. Similarly, it is essential that doctors seeking hospital privileges disclose all pertinent information to the committee. Physicians who fear that information provided in an application might someday be used against them by a third party will be reluctant to fully detail matters that the committee should consider.

The court found that the public interest in candid professional peer review proceedings should prevail over a litigant's need for information from the most convenient source.

The confidentiality statute does, however, provide that documents otherwise available from the original source do not become privileged merely because they are presented to a medical staff committee.

Section 40-71-20 of the South Carolina statute does not preclude the discovery of the general policies and procedures for staff monitoring. The information contained in the written rules, regulations, policies, and procedures for the medical staff would not compromise the statutory goal of candid evaluation of peers in the medical profession.

The court found that the outcome of the decision-making process is not protected. Permitting discovery of the effect of the committee proceedings does not inhibit open discussion. In the court's view, the confidentiality statute was intended to protect the review process, not to restrict the disclosure of the result of the process. Accordingly, the plaintiffs were entitled to a listing of clinical privileges either granted or denied by the hospital.

Discussion

1. Why is the policy of encouraging full candor by medical staff applicants in peer review proceedings so important?
2. What is the reasoning for the establishment of statutes that protect an organization's peer review information?

13. PEER REVIEW/DISCOVERY/SOURCE DOCUMENTS

Citation: *Freeman v. Piedmont Hosp.*, 444 S.E.2d 796 (Ga. 1994)

Facts

Dr. Freeman, an anesthesiologist, and his professional corporation filed suit against Piedmont Hospital, its administrator, the chairman of the hospital's anesthesiology department (Dr. Butler), and a member of the hospital's credentials committee, alleging defamation and intentional interference with business relations. The basis of the suit was the content of a letter sent by the hospital administrator pursuant to the Composite State Board of Medical Examiners after Dr. Freeman voluntarily resigned from the hospital's medical staff. The letter attributed the physician's resignation, in part, to disparaging reports concerning his performance made by Dr. Butler and another physician to the hospital's credentials committee. The letter indicated that the reporting physicians' actions were based primarily on

concerns expressed by hospital nurses regarding Dr. Freeman's performance. When Dr. Freeman's application to join the staff at another hospital was denied "in view of the present controversy at Piedmont Hospital and the impending investigation by the [Board]," the present action ensued. *Id.* at 797. The trial court denied plaintiffs' motion to compel discovery, and granted the defendants' motion for summary judgment. After reversing the grant of summary judgment to Dr. Butler, the court of appeals upheld the denial of the motion to compel discovery, relying on the privilege against discovery of peer review proceedings contained in OCGA § 31-7-133(a).

Issue

Could the motion to compel discovery be denied in its entirety based on the fact that some of the information sought was privileged from discovery under OCGA § 31-7-133(a), a statute protecting work product, records, and proceedings of a hospital peer review organization?

Holding

The Supreme Court of Georgia granted *certiorari* and held that motion to compel discovery could not be denied in its entirety, even though some materials sought were privileged.

Reason

The statute at issue, OCGA § 31-7-133(a), provides:

> Except in proceedings alleging violation of this article, the proceedings and records of a review organization shall be held in confidence and shall not be subject to discovery or introduction into evidence in any civil action arising out of or otherwise directly related to the matters which are the subject of evaluation and review by such organization; and no person who was in attendance at a meeting of such organization shall be permitted or required to testify in any such civil action as to any evidence of other matters produced or presented during the proceedings of such organization or as to any findings, recommendations, evaluations, opinions, or other actions of such organizations or any members thereof. However, information documents, or records otherwise available from original sources, are not to be construed as immune from

discovery or use in any such civil action merely because they were presented during proceedings of such organization, nor should any person who testifies before such organization or who is a member of such organization be prevented from testifying as to matters within his knowledge; but such witness cannot be asked about his testimony before such organization or about opinions formed by him as a result of the organization hearings.

Enactment of § 31-7-133(a) conferred a privilege from discovery upon a peer review organization's proceedings in order to foster the candor necessary for effective peer review, which is an essential element of providing quality health care services. While the statute precludes a party from discovering the proceedings and records of a peer review organization, the statute authorizes a party to seek from original sources documents that the peer review organization examined, and to examine anyone who appeared before or was a member of the peer review organization, so long as the witness is not asked about the peer review proceedings.

Allowing an allegation of malice to trigger the applicability of the exception to the confidentiality requirement would result in the opportunity for full discovery of peer review material in every such case. The use of a bare allegation of malice is not sufficient to elevate a plaintiff's access to evidence over preserving the candor necessary for effective peer review.

Discussion

1. What are the discovery options available for health care professionals who feel that disparaging reports concerning their performance have been made with malice?
2. What are the circumstances under which privileged information should be open for review?

14. PHARMACY/MISFILLED PRESCRIPTIONS/ INFANT DEATHS

Citation: *State Ex Rel. Stolfa v. Ely*, 875 S.W.2d 579 (Mo. Ct. App. 1994)

Facts

The plaintiffs were the parents of Amy and Ashley Stolfa, who died at birth on March 27, 1990. The plaintiffs claimed that the negligence of Kmart and its pharmacist in mistakenly filling a medication prescription when Deborah, the mother, was 25 weeks pregnant, caused the premature birth and the death of the two infants.

The plaintiffs based their claim against Kmart on two separate grounds: first, on the ground that the pharmacist was negligent in furnishing the wrong drug compound, Ritalin instead of ritodrine hydrochloride, the medication prescribed by the physician; second, on the ground that Kmart was negligent in failing to establish and maintain proper protocol and procedures to ensure that appropriate medications were dispensed to consumers.

The plaintiffs sought, by interrogatories, requests for the production of certain documents. By oral depositions, they sought to discover from Kmart information about earlier lawsuits involving allegations of professional liability, information about training of Kmart's pharmacy staff, and information relating to prior incidents involving negligence in the filling or dispensing of prescriptions in Kmart's pharmacies. The trial judge sustained Kmart's objections to such discovery.

Issue

Was discovery sought by the plaintiffs irrelevant and therefore not reasonably calculated to lead to the discovery of admissible evidence? Did the discovery sought by the plaintiffs invade the attorney–client and work–product privilege? Did an order compelling Kmart to respond to the subject discovery requests impose an extraordinary and unreasonable burden on Kmart?

Holding

The Court of Appeals of Missouri held that the information regarding other claims made against the Kmart pharmacy because of misfilled prescriptions was relevant and hence discoverable. Discovery of that information was not unreasonably oppressive and burdensome. The attorney–client privilege and work–product rule did not defeat the entire discovery request.

Reason

The plaintiffs in this case based their claim not only on the negligence of Kmart's pharmacist, for which Kmart would be liable under the doctrine of *respondeat superior*, but also on Kmart's personal corporate negligence, its protocols, and procedures. These, according to the plaintiffs' postulation, were inadequate to prevent the kind of mischance that occurred. To prove notice to Kmart that its protocols and procedures were inadequate, it would be relevant that other claims had been made against Kmart because of misfilled prescriptions. The discovery sought by plaintiffs was a promising source of evidence that Kmart, from the claims made against it growing out of similar misfeasances by pharmacists in Kmart's employ, had actual or constructive notice of the inadequacy of its protocols and procedures.

Without the discovery of similar earlier claims against Kmart, plaintiffs would be hard put to prove notice to Kmart of the inadequacy of its protocols and procedures, if indeed they were inadequate. The necessity of the discovery for the plaintiffs outweighed the inconvenience to Kmart in supplying it.

The litigation files sought to be discovered contain materials that are protected by attorney–client privilege, and by the work–product rule. Any such materials are, or may be, immune from discovery, Rule 56-01(b)(1); *State ex rel. Mitchell Humphrey & Co. v. Provaznik*, 854 S.W.2d 810, 812 (Mo. App. 1993), but that feature does not defeat the discovery request. Any such privileged materials may be protected by the trial court upon Kmart's motion.

Discussion

1. Do you agree with the court's finding? Explain.
2. Can pharmacists be held individually liable for their negligent acts if their employers are held liable for the same negligent acts?

15. RADIOLOGY/TECHNICIAN NEGLIGENCE

Citation: *Fortney v. Al-Hajj*, 425 S.E.2d 264 (W. Va. 1992)

Facts

Mr. Fortney arrived at the emergency department of Thomas Memorial Hospital on November 23, 1987, believing that he had lodged a piece of chicken in his esophagus. Dr. Breland examined Mr. Fortney in the emergency department and ordered a barium swallow test, a procedure designed to identify foreign objects lodged in the upper gastrointestinal tract. The test is conducted by instructing a patient to drink a radiopaque liquid while X-rays are being taken. The presence of the liquid then delineates any irregularities of the gastrointestinal system. Dr. Breland ordered the test to determine whether the piece of chicken was still lodged in Mr. Fortney's esophagus. At the time Dr. Breland ordered the test, Mr. Fortney was not demonstrating any signs of breathing difficulty that could have indicated a perforation of his esophagus. Mr. Fortney was taken to the radiology depart-

ment for the performance of the test. As Mr. Fortney's expert agreed, it was not the responsibility of Dr. Breland to actually perform the test. As Mr. Fortney attempted to drink the barium, his esophagus filled quickly, and the barium began coming back out of his mouth. The X-ray technician instructed the patient to continue drinking the barium, and the patient then began to gag. All of the witnesses at trial agreed that the gagging in the X-ray department caused a perforation in the patient's esophagus. When Mr. Fortney returned to the emergency department, he was in extreme pain. Dr. Breland contacted a consultant, Dr. Harper, a gastroenterologist. The barium swallow test had indicated the presence of a foreign object lodged where the esophagus joins the stomach and had also shown evidence of a perforation in the patient's esophagus. Dr. Harper suctioned out the barium in Mr. Fortney's esophagus but was unable to remove the chicken.

Dr. Figueroa, a cardiothoracic surgeon, was then consulted. He performed surgery, but no perforation in the esophagus was found. The physicians then concluded that the perforation had resealed itself after allowing the contents of the esophagus to escape into other areas of the body. During Mr. Forney's six-week hospitalization in the intensive care unit, he was treated by Dr. Figueroa and Dr. Al-Hajj.

In December 1988, Mr. Fortney initiated a civil action alleging medical malpractice. Prior to the trial, the hospital settled for $47,000. During the trial, Dr. Breland's counsel attempted to establish the hospital's negligence, based on the difficulties encountered during the performance of the barium swallow. Dr. Breland now contends, however, that the trial court impermissibly limited argument regarding the hospital's negligence and failed to inform the jury of the hospital's settlement with Mr. Fortney. Dr. Breland also asserted on appeal that the trial court erred in permitting a general surgeon, Dr. John Wilson, to testify as an expert regarding the appropriate standard of care required in emergency medicine. Prior to opening statements, the trial court explained the following to the parties:

> Don't get into this thing about pointing the finger at Thomas because they're not in this case. They're not in the case. And the only way I'm going to let them in the case is just by telling the jury that they were in the case and they settled. And the jury can make any inference they want from the evidence that comes in, but I don't want you all arguing that. *Id.* at 268.

During his opening statement, counsel for Dr. Breland, without interruption by the lower court or opposing counsel, stated:

In this case, Dr. Breland sent Mr. Fortney back there to radiology, and everyone is going to agree on everything up until that point. Dr. Breland sent him back there to have him take a couple sips of barium. Dr. Breland did not go back with him to do that. Dr. Breland doesn't administer those tests, and he'll tell you that. He was out there caring for patients in the emergency room. He sent him back to radiology. And then Mr. Fortney can be the only one that can tell us about what happened back there in radiology, and he's going to tell you a horrible story.

People back at Thomas Memorial Hospital back in radiology gave him a sip of barium; kept having him sip more and more and more. He'll tell you that it was coming out of his mouth and going all over his clothes. He'll tell you that he was gagging, and he had a real problem back there in radiology; but remember, Dr. Breland is not giving that test back there. He decided that's the appropriate test, but he sent him back there to have it done by the radiology staff at Thomas Memorial Hospital, and Mr. Fortney is going to be the one that will tell you about what happened back there. *Id.* at 268.

Dr. Breland discussed the hospital's role when he questioned Mr. Fortney himself during cross-examination regarding his experience in the radiology department.

Q: Do you believe the standard of care was breached in administering the barium swallow itself, not in ordering?

A: I believe giving it, *per se*, was below the standard, which I've already stated.

Q: You already stated that?

A: Yes. The order is below the standard; to give it is below the standard, to drown him is below the standard. How meaningful it was, I don't know, but those are certainly bad things to do. *Id.* at 268.

Mr. Fortney contended that had Dr. Breland not ordered a barium swallow, no malpractice action would have been instituted. The proper procedure to identify any blockage would have been, according to Mr. Fortney, a bronchoscopy after a plain chest X-ray.

Issue

Did the trial court impermissibly limit evidence regarding the hospital's negligence and the role such negligence might have played in the patient's injuries? Was the general sur-

geon qualified to provide expert testimony on the issue of the standard of care of a physician rendering assistance to a patient suffering from impacted food blockage in the emergency department?

Holding

The Supreme Court of Appeals of West Virginia held that the trial court did not impermissibly limit evidence regarding the hospital's negligence and the role such negligence might have played in the patient's injuries. Furthermore, the general surgeon was qualified to provide expert testimony as to the standard of care required of a physician rendering assistance to a patient suffering from impacted food blockage.

Reason

Based on the supreme court's review of the record, all of the physicians were provided ample opportunity to explain the negligence of the hospital. The trial court's initial admonishment regarding refraining from pointing the finger at the hospital, when viewed in conjunction with the evidence permitted to be introduced as to the hospital, was perceived by Dr. Breland as an appreciable limitation on the presentation of his defense. Otherwise, an objection (or at least a request for clarification) would have been made, and the appellant would not have proceeded to elicit such evidence and make such an argument.

The salient inquiry was to what extent Dr. Wilson was qualified under West Virginia Code § 55-7B-7 to testify as an expert on the issue of the standard of care required in treating a patient suffering an impacted food blockage. We conclude that Dr. Wilson was qualified to provide expert testimony on the issue of the standard of care of a physician rendering assistance to a patient suffering from an impacted food blockage. Any shortcomings that Dr. Breland believed existed in Dr. Wilson's credentials properly could have been the subject of cross-examination. With regard to whether Dr. Breland deviated from the normal standard of care in his treatment, the following dialogue during Dr. Wilson's testimony was relevant:

Q: Dr. Wilson, I guess maybe the best thing to do after all that is I will go back to my question. Do you have an opinion, based upon a reasonable degree of medical probability, through your experience and training, as you indicated, whether or not Dr. Breland deviated from the normal standard of care in his treatment of Mr. Fortney?

A: I have an opinion.

Q: What is your opinion?

A: I believe that he did. *Id.* at 271.

Discussion

1. What are the pros and cons of an emergency department physician overseeing the barium swallow procedure?
2. What are the competency issues described in this case?
3. What action should the organization take to reduce the likelihood of such occurrences?

16. SAFETY/VISITOR SLIP AND FALL

Citation: *Borota v. University Med. Ctr.*, 861 P.2d 679 (Ariz. Ct. App. 1993)

Facts

The plaintiff, Ms. Borota, a hospital visitor, brought an action against University Medical Center to recover for injuries she suffered as a result of slipping on a puddle of milk in the hospital corridor. Ms. Borota claimed that the spill appeared fresh and that there were several spots of milk on the floor and on the walls. She also noted that the corridor was well lit. The trial court granted summary judgment for the hospital, and Ms. Borota appealed.

Issue

Did the hospital have constructive notice that the spill was in the corridor?

Holding

The Court of Appeals of Arizona held that Ms. Borota did not establish constructive notice that would indicate that the hospital was aware of the spilled milk.

Reason

Although it is the responsibility and duty of a hospital to keep its premises reasonably safe for invitees, the hospital does not ensure their safety. The hospital is not liable for the injuries sustained by Ms. Borota unless she can establish that either the hospital's employees caused the spill and failed to clean it on a timely basis or that the milk was there for such

a long period of time that the hospital had constructive notice that the spill was there and failed to clean it. Ms. Borota failed to show evidence that the milk was spilled by a hospital employee. As to constructive notice, Ms. Borota was unable to show that the hospital was aware of the spill. She testified herself that the spill appeared to be fresh.

Discussion

1. Do you agree with the appellate court's finding? Explain.
2. Under what circumstances might the hospital have been liable for the plaintiff's injuries?

17. EMPLOYEE INJURY/MAINTENANCE CONTRACT/LIABILITY

Citation: *Palka v. Servicemaster Management Servs.*, 634 N.E.2d 189 (N.Y. 1994)

Facts

Servicemaster Management Services contracted in 1987 with Ellis Hospital, at the rate of $91,207 biweekly, to develop and implement a maintenance program for the hospital. Servicemaster's duties included the training, management, and direction of all support service employees, including the maintenance department. There had been preexisting wall-mounted fans that had been inspected for safety prior to Servicemaster taking over. The plaintiff, Ms. Palka, a registered nurse employed by the hospital, was injured when one of the fans fell from the wall onto her. She sued Servicemaster for negligence. The jury rendered a verdict for the plaintiff, and Servicemaster appealed, alleging that they had no duty to her. The appellate division reversed and dismissed the complaint. The nurse then appealed.

Issue

Should Servicemaster be held liable for personal injuries arising from their negligence or failed performance of their contractual obligations to Ellis Hospital?

Holding

The court of appeals reversed the decision of the appellate division, and reinstated the jury verdict for the plaintiff.

Reason

Servicemaster, by its contract with the hospital, assumed a duty to act. Although no specific mention of fan maintenance, including inspection of them, was mentioned in the contract, the director of operations for Servicemaster testified that part of their duties was "to create a clean and safe and clean environment" for employees and patients, to reduce safety hazards, and to engage in "preventative maintenance and casualty control or casualty prevention," which is defined as inspection and checking to see if something needs to be repaired before it falls. He further testified that it was Servicemaster's responsibility to train the hospital employees how and when to perform maintenance on all electrical and mechanical equipment. The duty to be obeyed is defined by the risk reasonably to be perceived. The court analyzed the wrongfulness of Servicemaster's action or inaction, and the nurse's reasonable expectation of the care owed and the basis for her expectation. The court found that all persons, including the nurse, who entered the hospital had a reasonable expectation that someone was in charge of maintenance and inspection of both the premises and the equipment. The contract between Servicemaster and the hospital clearly affected the safety of everyone who came onto the hospital premises. All of those people were entitled to rely on the nonnegligent maintenance service and repair responsibilities. Servicemaster contracted with the hospital to perform certain services and performed those services negligently, which caused Ms. Palka's injury. Ms. Palka was part of a known and identifiable group of hospital employees, patients, and visitors who were to be protected by proper safety and maintenance protocols assumed exclusively by Servicemaster.

Discussion

1. What were Servicemaster's responsibilities under their contract with the hospital?
2. Why was Servicemaster liable for the injuries sustained by the nurse?

18. SAFETY/ROOM DESIGN/PATIENT INJURY

Citation: *Dougay v. Seventh Ward Gen. Hosp.*, 619 So. 2d 1084 (La. Ct. App. 1993)

Facts

The plaintiff, a patient, brought an action against Seventh Ward General Hospital for injuries to her back she alleged were caused by the negligent actions of the hospital and one of its nurses.

On September 21, 1989, the patient had a baby by Caesarean section. That evening, the patient got up to go to the bathroom, but before she did she buzzed the nurse for medication, which the nurse indicated she would bring. While she was using the sink on the wall next to the bathroom, the patient claimed that the nurse entered the room, causing the door through which she entered to hit the bathroom door, knocking the knob into the patient's back, which resulted in a ruptured disc. Both the patient's brother and her husband identified the nurse in court after having given an erroneous description of her. The patient and her husband denied that the patient had any other back problems. All three people claimed that the nurse apologized for hitting her in the back. Although the patient thought the incident had been reported, she reported it to her physician the following morning. She sought medical attention from the time of her discharge through June 1991.

In November 1989, when the plaintiff went to the emergency department complaining of back pain, she was diagnosed after X-rays as having an acute lumbar sacral strain.

In April 1990, a magnetic resonance imaging (MRI) test revealed a bulging disc at L4–L5. In 1991, the patient filed for a protective order from her husband for bruising her left kidney and causing blood in her urine. She also revealed an earlier attack in 1990, which resulted in head, neck, and back injuries.

The nurse had no independent recollection of caring for the patient during her hospitalization. She testified that she did not fill out an incident report, which she would have done if she had hit the patient with the door. There was no indication in her notes that an incident with a door had occurred, or that the patient had complained of back pain. The patient's physician did not remember having been told of the incident by the patient, nor did he have written notes that would have indicated that he had knowledge of the incident. The trial judge found for the plaintiff, and the hospital appealed.

Issue

If objective evidence does not contradict a story that has inconsistencies, should the fact finder's finding, based on credibility, be reversed?

Holding

The Court of Appeal affirmed the trial court's finding for the plaintiff.

Reason

Even though the court of appeal would have dismissed the plaintiff's case because of deficiencies, such as the nurse who allegedly caused the injury denying the incident occurred, it found that the fact finder's holding based on credibility could never be clearly wrong. The bulging disc diagnosis had been made in January 1990. The first reported abuse by her husband had taken place in March 1990. The trial court rejected drawing the conclusion that since the plaintiff lied about having had trauma to her back, other than from the hospital incident, she must have lied about not having had that trauma prior to March 1990. The fact finder had the right to make that determination.

Discussion

1. Describe the inconsistencies in the plaintiff's case that could have led the court of appeals to overturn the verdict.
2. What are the safety issues that the organization should address to reduce the likelihood of similar incidents?

19. FALL AT HOSPITAL ENTRANCE

Citation: *Blitz v. Jefferson Parish Hosp. Serv. Dist.*, 636 So. 2d 1059 (La. Ct. App. 1994)

Facts

The plaintiff, Mrs. Blitz, brought a slip-and-fall suit against a hospital alleging that her fall was caused by loose vinyl stripping in the front entrance of the hospital. Mrs. Blitz was at the hospital to register for cataract surgery that was scheduled for the following day at the hospital. She was wearing flat shoes with wedge heels with a height of approximately one-half inch. The front lobby of the hospital was covered by joined sections of carpeting, except for an area surrounding the centrally located information desk, which has terrazzo flooring. The space between the carpeting and terrazzo was covered by vinyl stripping. Mrs. Blitz testified that as she walked across the lobby her foot got caught in the vinyl stripping. She contends that the vinyl stripping was loose, so that the front of the sole of her shoe was caught between the vinyl stripping and the carpeting. Mrs. Blitz testified that it felt like her foot was caught in a bear trap. *Id.* at 1060. The plaintiff contended further that the vinyl stripping was defectively installed and maintained. Mr. Ehlinger, an expert in architecture, testified that there was an insufficient amount of vinyl adhesive on the underside of the vinyl trim stripping in contact with the top of the terrazzo floor. Mr. Ehlinger concluded that either an inad-

equate amount of adhesive was applied during the original installation or that the efficiency of the adhesive originally applied was unacceptably reduced by chemical action on it from the wax that was applied during frequent maintenance of the terrazzo. *Id* at 1061. "Mr. Ehlinger's findings were corroborated by Gary Paulsen, PhD, of Specter Chem Laboratories, whose spectrographic analysis revealed that the underside of the vinyl stripping contained only sporadic, and clearly insufficient, amounts of adhesive." *Id* at 1061.

The plaintiff filed suit against the hospital and was awarded $80,000 after a bench trial. The hospital service appealed, contending that the finding of liability was erroneous and also that the trial judge erred in refusing to accept several defense witnesses as experts.

Issue

Did the evidence support a finding of liability?

Holding

The Court of Appeal held that the evidence supported a liability determination.

Reason

Hospital witnesses were apparently neither as credible nor as acceptable as the plaintiff's witnesses. The court was reluctant to substitute its findings of fact for those of the trial judge. It suffices to say that the determination of liability was supported by adequate evidence and was not clearly erroneous.

Discussion

1. What safety measures should a hospital take to prevent similar incidents from occurring?
2. Do you agree with the appellate court's findings? Explain.

20. FALL ON HOSPITAL GROUNDS

Citation: *Harkins v. Natchitoches Parish Hosp.*, 696 So. 2d 19, 97-83 (La. App. 1997)

Facts

As a part of its facilities, the hospital has workout equipment located on its rehabilitation unit. Ms. Harkins joined the hospital's good health program, which allowed her to use the equipment. Ms. Harkins worked out at the hospital four or five times per week. She had been a member of the program for more than two months prior to the day of her fall and always parked her automobile in the same area when working out at the hospital. Ms. Harkins would then walk across the grassy median in the parking area going to and from the entrance to the hospital. She was very familiar with the general area where she ultimately fell, as she had crossed it between 72 and 80 times, going into and coming out of the hospital the previous two months.

On June 15, 1994, Ms. Harkins worked out in the hospital for an hour. She left the hospital and walked across the grassy median along the cement driveway, in order to get to her car, where she tripped on a piece of black vinyl garden border material, hidden in the grass, and fell to the ground, seriously injuring herself. Another person helped her to get up and walked her to her car. Ms. Harkins drove herself home. In considerable pain, she then went to see her neighbor, Ms. LeVasser, who brought her back to the hospital for treatment. In the emergency department, Ms. Harkins told a physician and a nurse that she had tripped when stepping over the curb. She was given medicine for the pain, an IV, and X-rays were taken. She was found to have an anterior dislocation of the right shoulder and had to endure a painful procedure to reset her shoulder. Notwithstanding, she was dispatched to Schumpert Medical Center in Shreveport for additional treatment because the emergency department personnel thought her shoulder was not back in place.

Two weeks after the fall, Ms. Harkins went back to the area to see just exactly where the accident happened. She then asked her daughter, Ms. Martin, to take photographs of the grassy median where she had fallen.

Dr. Dean treated Ms. Harkins after the fall. The degenerative changes in her shoulder resulting from her fall required surgery. This was accomplished on November 1, 1994. Dr. Dean noted preexisting degenerative changes in the tendons of her rotator cuff. He opined that Ms. Harkins may have had a partial tear of the rotator cuff, which subsequently tore completely with motion and use by Ms. Harkins after her fall.

Even after the surgery, Ms. Harkins never regained full use of her right shoulder. The physician opined that the surgery might have to be redone but that he did not recommend it at that time. Ms. Harkins does not want to go through the surgery again and she lives with constant pain from her injury.

Prior to her fall, Ms. Harkins was completely independent and able to care for herself and her apartment. Since the fall, she requires assistance in cleaning her apartment and managing her daily life's activities because of the partial loss of use of her right shoulder. This loss of use is permanent, and it continues to be painful to her.

The trial court awarded her $50,000, which included medical expenses of $8,600 and general damages for pain and suffering, past and future disability, and deterioration of her general lifestyle.

Issue

Was there sufficient evidence of negligence to establish liability on the part of the hospital?

Holding

There was sufficient evidence of the hospital's negligence to sustain a finding of its liability for Ms. Harkins' injuries.

Reason

A hospital owes a duty to its visitors to exercise reasonable care commensurate with the particular circumstances. It must prove it acted reasonably to discover and correct a dangerous condition reasonably anticipated in its business activity.

Ms. Harkins was required to prove that she tripped and fell and was injured because of some defect at the hospital's premises, creating a presumption of negligence on the hospital's part. If she met this burden of proof, the hospital had to exculpate itself from that presumption.

Ms. Harkins established that she fell because she tripped on the black vinyl plastic gardening border, which was partially hidden by the grass, on the grassy median leading to the parking lot where she parked her car; that she suffered a dislocated shoulder, which ultimately required surgery; and that she might require additional surgery.

It was then up to the hospital to exculpate itself from this presumption of liability. This it failed to do. It offered no proof to show that it acted with reasonable care under the circumstances, by having a hidden black vinyl gardening border in an area near its entrance that was regularly traversed by persons using the hospital's facilities. The hospital offered no proof that it acted reasonably to discover and correct the potential hazard. Instead, it chose to defend itself by simply contending that Ms. Harkins had made inconsistent statements about the location where she tripped, and attempted to prove that the location of the accident actually occurred at the curb of the median, some 10 feet away from the black vinyl plastic gardening border, based upon Ms. Harkins' statements to the emergency department physician and nurse.

The trial judge listened to all the evidence, made his credibility determinations, and made a finding of fact that

Ms. Harkins tripped on the gardening border on the grassy median. Given all of the evidence, this has a reasonable basis. Especially considering the fact that Ms. Harkins was in substantial pain from a separated shoulder while she was in the emergency department, her making a miscalculation about the exact location of where she tripped is entirely understandable. The appeals court found nothing in the record to indicate manifest error regarding this factual finding. The appeals court agreed with the trial judge that it seemed reasonable to believe that the groundskeeper knew the piece of vinyl border material was present and took no action to remove it or place warning signs that it existed. The failure to either remove the vinyl or place warning signs was a failure to exercise reasonable care and under the theory of negligence. The defendants were, therefore, responsible for the injuries sustained by this plaintiff.

Discussion

1. Should Ms. Harkins bear any responsibility for the injuries she suffered? Explain.
2. Discuss what precautions health care facilities should take in order to prevent similar occurrences.

21. SAFETY/PATIENT FALL FROM EMERGENCY DEPARTMENT GURNEY

Citation: *Hussey v. Montgomery Mem'l Hosp.*, 441 S.E.2d 577 (N.C. Ct. App. 1994)

Facts

On June 14, 1986, Mr. Hussey suffered permanent brain damage when he fell from a gurney at the defendant hospital. He had been ill and was taken to the hospital by his wife. Upon arrival, he was seated on a gurney in the emergency department. The gurney had no side rails. Shortly thereafter, Mr. Hussey fell from the gurney and was rendered unconscious. As a result of the fall, Mr. Hussey suffered severe head injury and was comatose and unresponsive. He experienced continuous seizures. After being treated by a physician in the hospital's emergency department, the physician advised Mrs. Hussey that her husband's condition was caused by swelling in the brain, which was the result of his striking his head on the floor. Mr. Hussey was moved by ambulance to another hospital, where he was diagnosed with a dislocated clavicle, laceration of the skin, and two fractures of the lateral wall of the right orbit. He underwent surgery for the dislocated clavicle.

On June 23, 1986, Mr. Hussey was discharged from the hospital. At the time of discharge, he had significant memory loss and was nervous and depressed.

The plaintiffs alleged that during the 10-day period after the fall and again on July 10, 1986, they questioned Dr. Andrews, the attending physician, as to whether there was any permanent brain damage or injury. On each occasion, Dr. Andrews answered that there was not and would not be any brain damage. Two months after the fall, the plaintiffs consulted with an attorney concerning a possible claim against the defendant hospital, but the plaintiffs decided not to pursue a lawsuit at that time because they feared doing so might impair the plaintiff husband's ability to receive medical treatment.

For the next 3 1/2 years, Mr. Hussey continued to see his medical providers. He was kept on medication for his nerves. No physicians had ever disclosed to the plaintiffs that Mr. Hussey had suffered a brain injury or that he may suffer permanent brain impairment.

By April 1990, Mr. Hussey's behavior became severely erratic and unpredictable to the point that Mrs. Hussey took him to Sandhills Center for Mental Health. Mr. Hussey was examined and transferred to the Dartmouth Clinic. Dr. Lee informed the plaintiffs that the test results indicated "permanent and residual brain impairment." On June 12, 1990, the plaintiffs filed a complaint alleging negligence against the hospital. The hospital filed a motion to dismiss on the grounds that the action was barred by the three-year statute of limitations.

On December 22, 1992, the hospital filed a motion for summary judgment seeking dismissal of the complaint on the grounds that the statute of limitations had tolled. The trial judge granted hospital's motion for summary judgment, and the plaintiffs filed timely notice of appeal.

Issue

Was the action time barred?

Holding

The Court of Appeals held that the action was time barred.

Reason

Where the injury is latent, the claim is held not to accrue until the plaintiff discovers the injury. Where causation of an injury is unknown, the action accrues when both the injury and its cause have been (or should have been) discovered. *Black*, 312 N.C. at 645, 325 S.E.2d at 481-82.

The statute of limitations accrued on June 14, 1986, the date of Mr. Hussey's fall. The head injury was not latent. The court acknowledged that the plaintiffs questioned hospital personnel on occasions immediately after the fall to attempt to ascertain the extent of the plaintiff husband's injuries, and that on those occasions, the plaintiffs were told by hospital personnel that there was not and would not be any brain damage or injury. Nonetheless, Mr. Hussey had a cause of action on the date he fell from the gurney. Upon falling from the gurney, he suffered a severe head injury and was rendered unconscious. A treating physician in the emergency department advised Mr. Hussey's wife that her husband's condition was caused by swelling in the brain. The probable cause of the accident was the hospital's negligence. On the date of the fall, it was apparent that there had been wrongdoing, most likely attributable to the hospital. The ultimate injuries sustained by Mr. Hussey were a direct result of the June 14, 1986, fall caused by the hospital's wrongdoing that occurred on that date.

Discussion

1. What steps might the hospital take in order to help prevent the likelihood of such occurrences?
2. Do you agree that this action should be time barred? Explain.

22. SAFETY/FALL IN PARKING LOT

Citation: *Maynard v. Sisters of Providence*, 866 P.2d 1272 (Wash. Ct. App. 1994)

Facts

Mr. Maynard, a hospital visitor, brought a personal injury suit against the Sisters of Providence, the hospital's operator, arising from a fall in the hospital's parking lot. There was some snow on the ground when Mr. Maynard brought his wife to the hospital for admission on February 16, 1990. During the night, it had snowed an additional three or four inches. The following morning at 6:00 A.M., Mr. Maynard went to the hospital to visit with his wife. It began snowing again and he decided to leave. His car, which was parked in the visitor's lot, had gotten stuck in the snow. Following several unsuccessful attempts to move his car, he decided to return to the hospital for some sand to place under his car's tires for traction. As he was walking toward the hospital, he noted that another individual had also gotten stuck. He stopped to help, and, while pushing the car, he fell and injured his knee.

Mr. Maynard filed a lawsuit in which he alleged that Providence was negligent by failing to properly maintain a safe common area for visitors in allowing the accumulation of ice and snow in the visitor's parking lot, and failing to warn visitors of the hazardous conditions in the parking lot. Mr. Maynard alleged further that Providence was aware of the dangerous conditions in the visitor's parking lot. He alleged that the staff parking lot had been sanded several hours before he left the hospital. The superior court granted Providence's motion for summary judgment, and Mr. Maynard appealed.

Issue

Were there issues of material fact as to whether there was unreasonable risk? Did Providence know of or should it have known of the risk? Did Providence fail to take any remedial measures to correct the hazardous condition?

Holding

The Court of Appeals held that there were reasonable issues precluding summary judgment for Providence.

Reason

Material issues of fact as to all of the elements of Mr. Maynard's claim were satisfied. Providence knew or should have known of the risk and unsafe conditions in the visitor's parking lot, the hospital's operators should have anticipated that visitors would park in the lot and that they would eventually need to return to their cars to return home, and the hospital's operators failed to take remedial action. "Maynard's testimony is unrebutted that the staff's parking lot was sanded between two and three hours before he left the hospital the day of the accident. Providence was plainly aware of the hazardous condition on the day in question and, anticipating some form of harm, exercised precautions with respect to the staff parking lot but not as to the visitor's lot. This also establishes that Providence had the capacity to take some remedial measures." *Id.* at 1275. A jury must determine whether the hospital's operators were negligent and to what extent the fault on the part of Mr. Maynard (comparative negligence) played as to the injuries he sustained.

Discussion

1. Were there any other safety issues that might arise as a result of poor weather conditions?

2. Do you agree that there are triable issues of negligence, thus precluding summary judgment for the defendant?

23. SAFETY/SLIP AND FALL/NURSE

Citation: *Glowacki v. Underwood Mem'l Hosp.*, 636 A.2d 527 (N.J. Super. Ct. App. Div. 1994)

Facts

A pediatric transport nurse, who allegedly suffered a herniated disc in a slip-and-fall accident resulting from the hospital's alleged negligence in design or construction of its loading dock, sued to recover for her injuries. The superior court entered judgment on jury verdict in favor of the nurse, and the hospital appealed.

On August, 20, 1984, the nurse, while employed as a pediatric transport nurse for a hospital, was transporting a critically ill infant from the hospital. An isolette was needed for this purpose. This piece of equipment weighed approximately 200 pounds and was on wheels. Part of the nurse's responsibilities was to wheel it out to the ambulance, lower its wheels and then lift it up, with the help of the ambulance driver, into the ambulance. The ambulance arrived at the hospital at about 11:30 P.M. and drove to the emergency department area where it backed up to the loading platform. The back of the ambulance made contact with hard rubbery pieces that jutted out from a wooden bumper. The bumper was separated from the concrete loading platform by intermittent rubber blocks, which left an open space of approximately three and one-half inches between the bumper and the dock. The nurse stepped from the ambulance directly onto the concrete platform. Although the area was lit, it was not that bright because the lights were yellowish-orange and there were some shadows. At the loading platform, the nurse and the driver began the process of lifting the isolette up into the ambulance. The distance or height to the back of the ambulance appeared to have been approximately one foot. During this process, the nurse's foot became wedged into the space between the wooden bumper and the concrete platform. The space was alleged by the nurse to be as wide as her shoe.

A civil engineer testified at trial as an expert on behalf of the nurse. He distinguished the situation in the instant case because this was a "people-loading," not a "cargo-loading," facility. Because those who used this dock would have to pay more attention to their patients than to their own feet, he opined that it was unsafe to have a hole or gap in the bumper system.

The hospital produced a civil engineer who confirmed that there was no standard in the industry applicable to hospital bumpers. He admitted that any design should consider the nature of traffic going over it. It was his opinion that the system in the instant case did not create an unreasonable hazard of tripping or falling. The hospital's director of plant operations conceded that the hospital was aware of the spaces in the bumper system, but indicated there had never been a report of an incident since it was built.

The court charged the jury on principles of ordinary negligence and the liability of a property owner to business invitees for a dangerous condition on its property. The jury was also charged on contributory negligence and ultimate outcome. The jury returned a verdict finding that an unsafe condition existed on the hospital's platform, that the hospital was negligent, and that the negligence was a proximate cause of the nurse's accident. However, the court also found the nurse negligent. Her negligence was found to be a proximate cause of the accident. Thus, the court found the hospital 85 percent negligent and the nurse 15 percent negligent.

The nurse was unable to return to her former occupation as a result of weight-lifting restrictions placed on her after she herniated her disc. The $908,000 award was not so excessive as to be manifestly unjust, where evidence was presented that the nurse had a remaining life expectancy of over 42 years and remaining work life expectancy of over 26 years, and that the nurse's condition was permanent and prevented her from performing such routine tasks as shopping for herself, doing laundry, cooking, or cleaning.

Issue

Was the lump-sum award of $908,000 in damages to the former pediatric transport nurse excessive?

Holding

The Superior Court of New Jersey, Appellate Division, held that the lump-sum damages award of $908,000 was not so excessive as to constitute a miscarriage of justice.

Reason

The defendant argued that the court erred in denying its motion for a new trial on damages because the verdict of $908,000 constituted a miscarriage of justice, was against the weight of the evidence, and was the result of passion, prejudice, sympathy, or mistake. The appeals court disagreed. A trial judge should not interfere with the quantum of damages assessed by a jury unless it is so disproportionate to the injuries and resulting disabilities as to shock the conscience and to convince the judge that to sustain the award would be manifestly unjust. The nurse's symptomatology from the day following the accident to the date of trial eight years later never changed. Her treating physician's clinical opinion never varied. The defendant's argument that a "low back sprain" is not worth $908,000 ignores the principle that consequential damages in personal injury cases are not gauged by any established predetermined scale. The trial judge correctly charged the jury on the elements of damages demonstrated by the nurse and her experts to be implicated by reason of her substantial permanent injury and disability. The nurse's medical proofs were capable of supporting a jury finding that her back injury was one involving the spine and intervertebral discs and not merely a low back sprain.

Discussion

1. Discuss the statement by the director of plant operations that claimed that although the hospital was aware of the spaces in the bumper system, there had never been a report of an incident since it was built.
2. Do you agree with the findings of the appellate court? Explain.

24. SECURITY/BREACH OF DUTY

Citation: *Hanewinckel v. St. Paul's Property & Liab.*, 611 So. 2d 174 (La. App. 1992)

Facts

The plaintiff, a 52-year-old nurse anesthetist, arrived at the hospital at approximately 5:25 A.M. She began to back into a parking lot space, and before she shut off her engine, a man, approximately 30 years old, jumped into her car and sat in the driver's seat. He began to drive off, and the plaintiff asked him what he was doing. When he said that he was going to rape her, she jumped from the car. Before she could get away, her attacker caught her and started to beat her about the face and head. As he was dragging her, she was fighting him, and an employee pulling into the parking lot saw what was happening and alerted security. They found her car running with the lights on, but could not see her because of the fog. When they searched the area, they found her and rescued her. The assailant fled and was never found. She suffered a broken left wrist, 12 teeth either knocked out or broken, severe bruises on her face, and cuts on her legs and knees. She also suffered mental distress from which she had not recovered.

She sued the owner of the parking lot and the security force for breach of their duty to protect her from a criminal attack committed on the premises. The trial court found that the defendant had a duty to provide reasonable and adequate security in the parking area, and that it had breached this duty, which resulted in injury to the plaintiff. The plaintiff was awarded $733,000, $460,000 of which was for pain and suffering. The defendant appealed.

Issue

Did the hospital have a legal duty to protect the employee from harm? Did the hospital breach a duty by failing to patrol the area, thus causing her injury?

Holding

The Court of Appeals affirmed the decision for the plaintiff, finding that the hospital had breached its duty to the employee by failing to patrol the parking lot.

Reason

The hospital took on the responsibility to maintain the security force for the parking lot. As such, the hospital had assumed liability, giving a warranty that, through employment of a security service, their work would be carried out in a nonnegligent manner. The evidence indicated that other witnesses had seen the attacker in or near the parking lot five hours earlier in the day, yet he had not been spotted by any security personnel. Further, there were not enough people on duty that day to patrol the parking lot properly. If they had been patrolling properly, the court concluded that the criminal would have been discovered and the attack prevented. The purpose of the security force was to protect everyone coming onto the hospital grounds from attack. The court found further that the security force breached its duty by negligently failing to provide adequate security, which should have included random patrolling of all of the areas. Once the attacker was reported to security, nothing other than a brief walk through the lot was done.

Discussion

1. Examine the duty to care and breach of duty with regard to the security force and the attack on and injuries suffered by the nurse.
2. What are the implications of this case for health care organizations?

25. SAFETY/FALL FROM WINDOW

Citation: *Waters Ex Rel. Walton v. Del-Ky, Inc.*, 844 S.W.2d 250 (Tex. Ct. App. 1992)

Facts

Mr. Walton was a patient at the Sunnyvale nursing facility who required constant attention. On October 4, 1987, he fell from a second-floor window of the nursing facility. Mr. Walton was discharged from the nursing facility on October 5, 1987. On October 6, the nursing facility called Ms. Waters, Mr. Walton's sister, and informed her of the incident. On October 10, Mr. Walton expired from his injuries. Mr. Walton's death certificate indicated that he died as the result of multiple blunt force injuries from an accident that occurred at the nursing facility.

Katherine Bates, the executive director of United People for Better Nursing Facilities, said that Ms. Waters did not know that her brother had died or that he had been in a nursing facility.

On October 9, 1989, Ms. Waters sent a notice letter to the nursing facility claiming damages for the negligent care of her brother. Ms. Waters' claim against the nursing facility was filed based on negligence and negligence *per se* under the survivorship statute. Ms. Waters claimed damages on behalf of her brother's estate for medical and funeral expenses, physical pain, suffering, mental anguish, and all other damages sustained by her brother before his death.

The nursing facility moved for summary judgment on all of Ms. Waters' claims based on the two-year statute of limitations. The trial court granted the motion, and the plaintiff appealed.

Texas statute (Tex. Civ. Prac. & Rem. Code Ann. § 71.021 [Vernon 1986]) provides that a decedent's action survives his death. The survivor prosecutes the action on his behalf. The survivorship action is wholly derivative of the decedent's rights. The actionable wrong is that which the decedent suffered before his death.

Ms. Waters alleged she could recover for her brother's estate for medical and funeral expenses, physical pain, suffering, mental anguish, and all other damages he sustained before his death.

Issue

When did the two-year statute of limitations begin to run?

Holding

The Court of Appeals of Texas held that the survivorship action against the nursing facility accrued, for purposes of the two-year statute of limitations for medical liability claims, on the date the patient fell from the second floor of the nursing facility resulting in his death several days later.

Reason

The statute of limitations in § 10.01 of article 4590i provides that except as otherwise provided in the section, it applies to all persons regardless of minority or other legal disability. When the precise date of the tort is known, the statutory two-year period begins on that date. Ms. Waters' negligence claim for her brother's personal injuries resulting from the nursing facility's negligence was a derivative action. Because the negligence action is derivative, Ms. Waters had no more rights than her brother would have had if he had lived. Section 10.01 barred her cause of action for personal injuries suffered because of the facility's negligence on October 4, 1989. The two-year limitations applied unless Ms. Waters had a viable legal reason for tolling the statute.

Ms. Waters contended that the nursing facility fraudulently concealed its negligence and the cause in fact of her brother's injuries. The record did not support Ms. Waters' assertion that the facility had a fixed purpose to conceal the wrong. The summary judgment rule did not provide for a trial by deposition or affidavit. The rule provided a method of summarily ending a case that involved only a question of law and no genuine issue of material fact. The trial court's duty was to determine if there were any fact issues to try, not to weigh the evidence or determine its credibility and try the case on affidavits. The summary judgment evidence showed that if Ms. Waters did not know of Mr. Walton's injuries and their causes on October 11, 1987, she did know about them at least by November 16, 1987, the date when Ms. Bates talked to her about her brother's injuries and the causes of those injuries. Ms. Waters did not give notice until October 9, 1989. Her survivorship action is derivative of her brother's common law action. She discovered his injuries while there was still a reasonable time to sue. She had more than 22 months within which to file suit under the survivorship statute.

Discussion

1. Do you think that a statute of limitations of two years is reasonable in this case? Explain.
2. How would you describe the ethical issues in this case?

26. SAFETY/FIRE/WRONGFUL DEATH

Citation: *Stacy v. Truman Med. Ctr.*, 836 S.W.2d 911 (Mo. 1992)

Facts

The patients' families brought wrongful death actions against a medical center and one of its nurses. The wrongful death actions resulted from a fire in the decedents' room at the medical center. On the day of the fire, Ms. Stacy visited her brother Mr. Stacy. When she arrived, Mr. Stacy, who suffered from head injuries and was not supposed to walk around, was in a chair smoking a cigarette with the permission of one of the nurses. No one told Ms. Stacy not to let him smoke. Because Ms. Stacy did not see an ashtray in the room, she used a juice cup and a plastic soup tray for the ashes.

At approximately 5:00 P.M., a nurse came in and restrained Mr. Stacy in his chair with ties to prevent him from sliding out of the chair. Before Ms. Stacy left, she lit a cigarette, held it to Mr. Stacy's mouth, and extinguished it in the soup tray. When Ms. Stacy left, she believed there were one or two cigarette butts in the soup container. Ms. Stacy testified that she did not think she dumped the soup tray into the wastebasket but that she could have. Shortly after 5:00 P.M., a fire started in a wastebasket in Room 327. There was no smoke detector in the room. Mr. Wheeler was in the bed next to the windows. When Ms. Schreiner, the nurse in charge, discovered the fire, she did not think Mr. Wheeler was in immediate danger. She unsuccessfully tried to untie Mr. Stacy from his restraints. Then she attempted to put out the fire by smothering it with a sheet. When her attempts to extinguish the fire failed, she ran to the door of the room and yelled for help, which alerted nurses Ms. Cominos and Ms. Rodriguez. After calling for help, Ms. Schreiner resumed her attempts to smother the flames with bed linens. Subsequently, she and others grabbed Mr. Stacy by the legs and pulled him and his chair toward the hallway. In the process, Mr. Stacy's restraints burned through, and he slid from the chair to the floor. Ms. Schreiner and her assistants pulled him the remaining few feet out of the room and into the hallway. Ms. Schreiner tried to get back into the room but was prevented by the intense smoke, flames, and heat.

After initially entering Room 327, both Ms. Rodriguez and Ms. Cominos returned to the nurse's station to sound alarms and to call security. Neither attempted to remove Mr. Wheeler from the room. Both ran directly past a fire extinguisher, but neither grabbed it before returning to the room. After Mr. Stacy was removed from the room, Ms. Cominos entered the room with a fire extinguisher and tried to rescue Mr. Wheeler. Because of the intense smoke and heat, however, she was unable to reach Mr. Wheeler. Mr. Wheeler died in the room from smoke inhalation. Mr. Stacy survived for several weeks, then died as a result of complications from infections secondary to burns.

The medical center's policy on December 30, 1986, in case of fire, provided for the removal of a patient from the room and out of immediate danger first. In its fire-training programs, the medical center used the acronym of "RACE" to supply a chronology of steps to take in case of a fire.

R—Rescue or remove the patient first.
A—An alarm should be sounded second.
C—The fire should be contained third.
E—Extinguish the fire last.

The medical center also had a training movie depicting a trash can fire (started by cigarettes) that showed how to pull a patient out of bed by the sheets and drag the patient across the floor at the first recognition of a fire.

The medical center's written smoking policy at the time of the fire stated: "No smoking shall be permitted in the Truman Medical Center Health Care Facility except those areas specifically designated and posted as smoking areas. . . ." Room 327 was not posted as a designated smoking area on the date of the fire. The smoking policy further stated: "In the event violations of this policy are observed, the person violating the policy must be requested to discontinue such violation. This shall be the responsibility of all employees and particularly supervisory and security employees." Ms. Cominos admitted that she was a supervisor and that she violated this portion of the smoking policy on the date of the fire by observing smoking and the use of a juice cup for an ashtray in Room 327.

The circuit court entered judgment in favor of the patients' families. The circuit court later entered judgment notwithstanding the verdict based on the doctrine of sovereign immunity. The court of appeals reversed on the same doctrine.

Issue

Does the evidence sufficiently establish a causal connection between the medical center's negligence and the patients' death?

Holding

The Supreme Court of Missouri held that a causal connection between the medical center's negligence and the patients' death was sufficiently established.

Reason

The medical center owed a duty of reasonable care to all its patients. A hospital's duty is proportionate to the needs of the patient, meaning that the hospital must exercise such care and attention as the patient's condition requires. *Robbins v.*

Jewish Hosp. of St. Louis, 663 S.W.2d 341, 346 (Mo. Ct. App. 1983).

The medical center argued that there was no evidence to causally link the alleged negligence in allowing smoking without an approved ashtray to the death of Mr. Wheeler. On the date of the fire, Ms. Stacy was smoking in Room 327 and was using a juice container and soup container for her ashes. Ms. Cominos knew Ms. Stacy was smoking and that she did not have an ashtray. The medical center's policy concerning ashtrays stated that the ashtrays must be of noncombustible material, safe design, and approved by the hospital. When Ms. Cominos made rounds on the date of the fire, she did not see any ashtray in the room. There was evidence that the fire started in the trash can from discarded smoking materials. The jury was free to believe from the evidence presented that had Ms. Stacy been given a hospital-approved ashtray, she would have discarded her cigarette in a proper ashtray and that the fire would not have occurred.

Liberty's Fire Chief Lehman testified that a smoke detector would have given an earlier warning in this fire and that the fire was burning one to three minutes before Ms. Schreiner initially discovered it. The individual in charge of fire safety training at the medical center, Lieutenant Campbell, testified that he did not use the medical center's fire safety manual in his orientation and training of the nurses. He testified that the hospital policy was to first remove a patient from the room and out of immediate danger in case of fire. Chief Lehman testified that the particular training received by the medical center nurses was below the standard of care and that attempting to put the fire out with linens would also be indicative of a lack of training. The medical center's expert, Fire Captain Gibson, testified that throwing dry sheets on the fire would have added to the problem by fueling the fire. The jury could have found that if the medical center's nurses would have been properly trained, they would have followed their training and prevented Mr. Wheeler's death by removing him from the room, in accordance with their training acronym RACE.

Discussion

1. Do you agree with the court's finding? Explain.
2. What is the importance of continuing education in life safety?
3. What topics should be covered when designing a continuing education program for an organization's staff?

27. BURNS/LAMP NEGLIGENTLY PLACED

Citation: *Rice v. Vandenebossche*, 586 N.Y.S.2d 303 (N.Y. App. Div. 1992)

Facts

The plaintiff alleged that while she was being treated for a laceration to her forehead, Dr. Bhargava negligently placed a lamp dangerously close to her, causing burns to her forehead. The complaint contained one general *ad damnum* clause specifying damages against Dr. Bhargava and the hospital without allocating particular amounts as to each cause of action. Dr. Bhargava and the hospital each moved to dismiss the complaint on the ground that the plaintiff failed to attach a certificate of merit to her complaint. The court denied the motion, reasoning that the cause of action sounded in negligence rather than malpractice.

Issue

Does this case raise an issue of malpractice or negligence?

Holding

The New York Supreme Court, Appellate Division, held that the complaint that alleged that the patient was injured by a lamp being used by the physician while he was treating her sounded in medical malpractice.

Reason

The critical question in determining whether an action sounds in medical malpractice or simple negligence is the nature of the duty to the plaintiff that the defendant is alleged to have breached. When the duty owing to the plaintiff by the defendant arises from the physician–patient relationship or is substantially related to medical treatment, the breach thereof gives rise to an action sounding in medical malpractice as opposed to simple negligence. However, if the conduct complained of may be readily assessed on the basis of common, everyday experience of the trier of facts, and expert testimony is unnecessary for such a review, then the cause of action sounds in negligence. In the instant case, the cause of action against Dr. Bhargava and the hospital clearly alleged that the plaintiff was burned on the forehead by a lamp that was being used while she was being treated by the physician for a forehead laceration. Because the conduct complained of was substantially related to the medical treatment, the cause of action sounded in medical malpractice.

Discussion

1. Do you agree with the court's reasoning? Explain.

2. Why is expert testimony generally not required in cases involving simple negligence?

28. EQUIPMENT/FAILURE TO HAVE

Citation: *Jenkins County Hosp. Auth. v. Landrum*, 426 S.E.2d 572 (Ga. Ct. App. 1992)

Facts

The parents of a minor child brought a medical malpractice action against a physician and hospital on behalf of their child, who suffered injuries during a Caesarean delivery. The parents alleged that the attending physician was negligent in performing a premature Caesarean section without having a proper mechanical ventilator available. The equipment was necessary to alleviate the child's respiratory distress. The parents alleged that the hospital was negligent by not having the necessary equipment available. As required by statute (OCGA § 9-1-9.1), the parents filed an affidavit with their complaint addressing the specific allegations made against the physician. The hospital filed a motion to dismiss on the grounds that the parents failed to comply with the statute, claiming that the affidavit did not address any of the allegations of negligence attributed to the hospital. The superior court denied the hospital's motion to dismiss, and an interlocutory appeal was granted.

Issue

Was an affidavit required?

Holding

The court of appeals held that the affidavit under the statute requiring an affidavit of a competent expert to accompany charges of professional malpractice was not required as to allegations of negligence against the hospital.

Reason

This case is controlled by *Lamb v. Candler Gen. Hosp.*, 262 Ga. 70, 413 S.E.2d 720 (1992). Therefore, an affidavit under OCGA § 9-1-9.1 is not necessary, and the trial court did not err in denying the hospital's motion to dismiss.

Discussion

1. What safety issues are relevant to this case, as well as similar, cases?

2. What are the differences between ordinary negligence and malpractice in relation to this case?

29. EQUIPMENT/IMPROPER USE/MEDISCUS BED

Citation: *Parris v. Uni Med, Inc.*, 861 S.W.2d 694 (Mo. Ct. App. 1993)

Facts

In January 1987, the plaintiff was admitted to St. Francis Hospital for a urinary tract infection. While there, he used a Mediscus (a hospital bed marketer and distributor) bed, which was designed with 21 separate air pockets to prevent decubitus ulcers. In May 1987, the plaintiff was again admitted for what turned out to be a decubitus ulcer. He was put in a Mediscus bed that was set up by a Uni Med employee. It took the employee one and a half hours to set up the bed and make adjustments. Upon discharge on May 31, 1987, the pressure ulcer was only barely apparent.

On June 15, 1987, the plaintiff was readmitted. Before he was placed in the Mediscus bed, it was set up in only five minutes. At the time of the June admission, his pressure ulcer was healing. Four days later, a nurse noted that the ulcer condition had worsened and a new pressure ulcer had formed. The nurse noticed that the dressing on the first sight was touching the metal frame on the bed, thus putting pressure on his sacral area every time he sat. The nurse called Uni Med and a company employee made adjustments to the bed. In spite of observed improvement in the pressure ulcers at the time of discharge, the patient deteriorated to such an extent that surgery was required. Evidence showed that the beds were not monitored regularly and that the nurses were not trained to turn the patients or adjust or regulate the beds.

The plaintiff, a 37-year-old paraplegic, brought an action against Uni Med, Inc. for pressure ulcers he sustained during his hospital stay. The jury found that the inadequate pressure setting on the bed was caused by its being improperly set up, thus causing worsening of the condition of the ulcers, necessitating surgery.

Issue

Did the company employee fail to set up the Mediscus bed properly, thus causing the patient's pressure ulcers and subsequent surgery needed to correct his condition?

Holding

The Court of Appeals of Missouri found that: (1) the hospital bed was not set up properly, (2) the failure to set it up properly caused the patient's pressure ulcers and subsequent surgery, and (3) nurses were properly qualified as experts regarding testimony regarding pressure ulcers.

Reason

Evidence demonstrated that the bed had been hastily set up; continuous pressure of two hours on one area of skin can cause pressure ulcers; and nurses did not change the pressure gauges because they had not been trained properly. The court also found that Uni Med had no monitoring system, and the patient's original pressure ulcer had been healing prior to the hospital visit and then worsened after coming into contact with the bed frame. Further, the court found that the patient developed more ulcers on the sacral area, which were present upon discharge.

Discussion

1. What safeguards should Uni Med have implemented to help prevent this unfortunate event?
2. What is the importance of continuing education programs for individuals operating medical equipment?

30. EQUIPMENT/IMPROPER MAINTENANCE/ CHAIR LIFT

Citation: *Thibodeaux v. Century Mfg. Co.*, 625 So. 2d 351 (La. Ct. App. 1993)

Facts

The plaintiff, Ms. Thibodeaux, a nurse's aide at the Rosewood nursing facility, sued Century Manufacturing Company (Century) after she was injured while operating a Saf-Kary chair lift, which was manufactured by Century. The plaintiff was injured when a Saf-Kary chair fell and smashed her finger when the chair's lifting arm failed. The failure occurred when a patient was being lifted from a whirlpool bath. The plaintiff alleged that Century manufactured a defective chair lift that was the cause of her injuries.

Century argued that the chair lift was not defective in design and that the failure of the chair was caused by air in the Saf-Lift hydraulic system, resulting from the nursing facility's lack of maintenance. The plaintiff's expert witness testified that after inspecting the equipment, he found that the accident was caused by the safety lock failing to prevent the chair from disconnecting from the lift. Century "theorized that this want of maintenance caused the whole lift apparatus, including the chair still connected to the lifting

arm of the lift column, to rapidly descend on Irene's finger." *Id.* at 353. Approximately four months before the accident, a Century-licensed service technician, Deryl Bryant, performed an inspection of the equipment. He found leaks of hydraulic fluid, deteriorating seals and rings, a corroded lift base, and an air-contaminated lifting column. He took the chair lift out of service and recommended that Rosewood not use it until repairs were made to restore it to safe operation. These findings were communicated to Rosewood in writing. Rosewood did not make the repairs. *Id.* at 353. The court, on a jury verdict, found that the sole cause of the accident was due to poor maintenance on the part of the nursing facility. The plaintiff appealed.

Issue

Did the evidence support a finding that Century was negligent in its design of the lifting chair and the failure of its safety lock?

Holding

The Court of Appeal of Louisiana held that the evidence supported the conclusion that the accident was caused by the nursing home's failure to properly maintain the equipment and that the injury was not the result of poor design.

Reason

Virtually all products are subject to wear and tear and therefore need periodic maintenance. The nursing facility had been warned by the manufacturer of the need for repairs on the chair lift. The nursing facility failed to heed that warning.

Discussion

1. What procedures should an organization adopt for the safe and effective use of its medical equipment?
2. Should nonmedical equipment be included in an organization's preventive maintenance program? Explain.

31. EMERGENCY DEPARTMENT/SCREENING AND DISCHARGE APPROPRIATE

Citation: *Marshall v. East Carroll Parish Hosp. Serv. Dist.*, 134 F.3d 319 (5th Cir. 1998)

Facts

Fifteen-year-old Nydia Marshall was brought by ambulance to the East Carroll Parish Hospital Service District's (Hospital) emergency department on October 18, 1994, because she "wouldn't move" while at school after the bell rang. Upon her arrival, hospital personnel took her history and vital signs. She was unable to communicate verbally while at the emergency department, but cooperated when removing her clothing and watched movement of persons coming in and out of the emergency department. She was examined by Dr. Horowitz, who also had several medical tests performed on her.

Dr. Horowitz diagnosed Nydia as having a respiratory infection and discharged her. He informed Nydia's mother, Ms. Marshall, that her daughter's failure to communicate was of unknown etiology, and advised her to continue administering the medications that had been prescribed by the family physician on the previous day and to return to the emergency department if the condition deteriorated. The complaint alleged that, later that same day, Nydia's symptoms continued to worsen, and she was taken to the emergency department at a different hospital, where she was diagnosed as suffering from a cerebrovascular accident consistent with a left middle cerebral artery infarction.

This action claimed that the hospital violated EMTALA, 42 U.S.C. § 1395dd, by failing to provide Nydia with an appropriate medical screening examination and failing to stabilize her condition prior to discharge. The hospital moved for summary judgment and submitted supporting affidavits from Dr. Horowitz and a registered nurse who had participated in Nydia's treatment in the hospital's emergency department.

The district court allowed Ms. Marshall three months in which to conduct discovery necessary to respond to the motion. In opposition to that motion, Ms. Marshall submitted a statement of contested facts and the sworn affidavit of Ms. Middlebrooks, a licensed practical nurse, who had been on duty at the hospital emergency department when Nydia was treated.

The district court granted summary judgment for the hospital on the grounds that no material fact issues were in dispute. Ms. Marshall contends that Ms. Middlebrooks' affidavit created a genuine issue of material fact.

Issue

Did the trial court err in granting summary judgment to the hospital?

Holding

The summary judgment was affirmed.

Reason

Summary judgment "shall be rendered forthwith if the pleadings, depositions, answers to interrogatories, and admissions on file, together with the affidavits, if any, show that there is no genuine issue as to any material fact and that the moving party is entitled to a judgment as a matter of law." Fed. R. Civ. P. 56(c); e.g., *Little v. Liquid Air Corp.*, 37 F.3d 1069, 1075 (5th Cir. 1994).

EMTALA provides in relevant part:

> In the case of a hospital that has a hospital emergency department, if any individual . . . comes to the emergency department and a request is made on the individual's behalf for examination or treatment for a medical condition, the hospital must provide for an appropriate medical screening examination within the capability of the hospital's emergency department, including ancillary services routinely available to the emergency department, to determine whether or not an emergency medical condition . . . exists. 42 U.S.C. § 1395dd(a).

The Act defines an "emergency medical condition," in pertinent part, as

> (A) a medical condition manifesting itself by acute symptoms of sufficient severity (including severe pain) such that the absence of immediate medical attention could reasonably be expected to result in
> (i) placing the health of the individual (or, with respect to a pregnant woman, the health of the woman or her unborn child) in serious jeopardy,
> (ii) serious impairment to bodily functions, or
> (iii) serious dysfunction of any bodily organ or part. . . . 42 U.S.C. § 1395dd(e)(1).

And, if the hospital determines that the individual has an "emergency medical condition," then the hospital must provide either

> (A) within the staff and facilities available at the hospital, for such further medical examination and such treatment as may be required to stabilize the medical condition, or

(B) for transfer of the individual to another medical facility. . . . 42 U.S.C. § 1395dd(b)(1).

Ms. Marshall contends that Ms. Middlebrooks' affidavit demonstrates that hospital personnel knew that Nydia had an emergency medical condition and were very concerned about the cursory examination provided by Dr. Horowitz; that Dr. Horowitz should have performed a fundoscopic examination, cranial nerve testing, motor strength testing, and deep tendon reflex testing; and that Nydia should have been admitted to the hospital for observation of her unexplained altered mental status. In essence, Ms. Marshall is contending that Dr. Horowitz committed malpractice in failing to accurately diagnose an emergency medical condition.

The appeals court agreed with other courts that have interpreted EMTALA that the statute was not intended to be used as a federal malpractice statute, but instead was enacted to prevent "patient dumping," which is the practice of refusing to treat patients who are unable to pay.

Accordingly, an EMTALA "appropriate medical screening examination" is not judged by its proficiency in accurately diagnosing the patient's illness, but rather by whether it was performed equitably in comparison to other patients with similar symptoms. If the hospital provided an appropriate medical screening examination, it is not liable under EMTALA even if the physician who performed the examination made a misdiagnosis that could subject him or her and his or her employer to liability in a medical malpractice action brought under state law. A hospital's failure to diagnose a patient's condition may be actionable under state medical malpractice law, but not under EMTALA. Questions regarding whether a physician or other hospital personnel failed to properly diagnose or treat a patient's condition are best resolved under existing and developing state negligence and medical malpractice theories of recovery. In the absence of any allegation that the defendant departed from its standard emergency department procedures in treating a patient, questions related to a patient's diagnosis remain the exclusive province of local negligence and malpractice law. Therefore, a treating physician's failure to appreciate the extent of the patient's injury or illness, as well as a subsequent failure to order additional diagnostic procedures, may constitute negligence or malpractice, but cannot support an EMTALA claim for inappropriate screening. EMTALA does not impose any duty on a hospital requiring that the screening result in a correct diagnosis.

In order to avoid summary judgment, Ms. Marshall was required to present evidence showing a material fact issue as to whether the hospital provided an EMTALA appropriate medical screening examination. But, an "appropriate medical screening examination" is not defined by EMTALA.

Most of the courts that have interpreted the phrase have defined it as a screening examination that the hospital would have offered to any other patient in a similar condition with similar symptoms. An inappropriate screening examination is one that has a disparate impact on the plaintiff. EMTALA is implicated only when individuals who are perceived to have the same medical condition receive disparate treatment. The essence of this requirement is that there be some screening procedure, and that it be administered evenhandedly. When a hospital does not follow its own standard procedures, the plaintiff(s) must prove that the hospital treated a patient differently from other patients. The Act is not intended to ensure that each emergency department patient obtains a correct diagnosis, but rather to ensure that each is accorded the same level of treatment regularly provided to patients in similar medical circumstances. An appropriate medical screening is interpreted to mean a screening that the hospital would have offered to any paying patient. It is the plaintiff's burden to show that the hospital treated her differently from other patients; a hospital is not required to show that it had a uniform screening procedure.

The affidavits submitted by the hospital as part of its evidence in support of summary judgment both state that Nydia was given an appropriate medical screening examination that would have been performed on any other patient, and that she was not diagnosed as having an emergency medical condition. Ms. Marshall contends that these assertions were refuted by Ms. Middlebrooks' affidavit. In her affidavit, Ms. Middlebrooks stated that she witnessed a disagreement between a nurse and Dr. Horowitz over whether Nydia should be admitted or transferred to another hospital, rather than discharged, and, that during her 14-year employment at the hospital she had seen several other patients with symptoms similar to Nydia's who had all been admitted for observation and further testing and treatment.

The hospital moved to strike portions of Ms. Middlebrooks' affidavit on the grounds that it contained inadmissible hearsay, conjecture, and speculation and was not made on the basis of her personal knowledge. Considering that Ms. Middlebrooks is a licensed practical nurse, not a physician, the appeals court questioned whether she is competent to compare the symptoms and treatment of Nydia to other patients. The appeals court agreed with the district court that the conclusory, unsupported statements in Ms. Middlebrooks' affidavit are insufficient to create a material fact issue as to whether Nydia was denied appropriate medical screening procedures, or the screening procedures provided her were different from those provided other patients with similar symptoms. Ms. Middlebrooks' affidavit contains no description or identification of the other patients who allegedly came to the hospital's emergency department with symptoms similar to those of Nydia's, and provides no details of the kind of treatment those patients were given. It goes without saying that such conclusory, unsupported assertions are insufficient to defeat a motion for summary judgment.

As a result, and in the light of the summary judgment record, because there is no material fact issue as to whether Dr. Horowitz conducted an appropriate medical screening examination or as to his determination that Nydia did not have an emergency medical condition, the hospital was entitled to judgment, as a matter of law, that it did not have a duty under EMTALA to provide further medical treatment, to stabilize her condition prior to discharge, or to transfer her to another facility. A duty to stabilize does not arise unless the hospital has actual knowledge of the individual's unstabilized emergency medical condition. The hospital's duty to stabilize the patient does not arise until the hospital first detects an emergency medical condition. Stabilization

and transfer provisions of EMTALA "are triggered only after a hospital determines that an individual has an emergency medical condition." The hospital has no duty under EMTALA to stabilize a condition that was not ascertained in appropriate screening examination.

Discussion

1. Why was EMTALA not applicable in this case? Discuss your answer.
2. On what foundation should the plaintiff have brought this action? Discuss your answer.
3. Develop a root cause analysis and discuss in detail what actions hospitals might take to reduce the likelihood of similar occurrences in the future.

I X

Information Management and Health Care Records

1. CHARTING BY EXCEPTION/NEGLIGENCE

Citation: *Lama v. Borras*, 16 F.3d 473 (lst Cir. 1994)

Facts

In 1985, the patient, Mr. Lama, was suffering from back pain. Dr. Alfonso, the patient's family physician, provided some treatment but then referred him to Dr. Borras, a neurosurgeon. Dr. Borras concluded that the patient had a herniated disc and scheduled surgery. Prior to surgery Dr. Borras neither prescribed nor enforced a regimen of absolute bed rest, nor did he offer other key components of conservative treatment.

On April 9, 1986, while operating on the patient, Dr. Borras discovered that the patient had an extruded disc and attempted to remove the extruded material. Either because Dr. Borras failed to remove the offending material or because he operated at the wrong level, the patient's original symptoms returned in full force several days after the operation. Dr. Borras concluded that a second operation was necessary to remedy the recurrence.

On May 15, Dr. Borras operated again on the patient. Dr. Borras did not order pre- or postoperative antibiotics. It is unclear whether the second operation was successful in curing the herniated disc. On May 17, a nurse's note indicated that the bandage covering the patient's surgical wound was "very bloody," a symptom which, according to expert testimony, indicates the possibility of infection. On May 18, the patient was experiencing local pain at the site of the incision, another symptom consistent with an infection. On May 19, the bandage was soiled again. A more complete account of the patient's evolving condition was not available

because the hospital instructed nurses to engage in charting by exception, a system whereby nurses did not record qualitative observations for each of the day's three shifts, but instead made such notes only when necessary to chronicle important changes in a patient's condition.

On May 21, Dr. Piazza, an attending physician, diagnosed the patient's problem as discitis—an infection of the space between discs—and responded by initiating antibiotic treatment. Mr. Lama was hospitalized for several additional months while undergoing treatment for the infection.

After moving from Puerto Rico to Florida, Mr. Lama filed a tort action in United States District Court for the District of Puerto Rico. While the plaintiff did not claim that the hospital was vicariously liable for any negligence on the part of Dr. Borras, he alleged that the hospital was itself negligent in two respects: (1) failure to prepare, use, and monitor proper medical records; and (2) failure to provide proper hygiene at the hospital premises.

At the close of the plaintiff's case and at the close of all the evidence, the defendants moved for judgment as a matter of law. After the jury returned a verdict awarding plaintiff $600,000 in compensatory damages, the defendants again sought judgment as a matter of law. The district court ruled that the evidence was legally sufficient to support the jury's findings and an appeal was taken.

Issue

Did the evidence support a jury conclusion that the hospital had been negligent in pursuing a charting by exception policy in the postoperative monitoring of the patient, whereby records were entered in the patient's chart only when neces-

167

sary to chronicle important changes in the patient's condition?

Holding

The United States Court of Appeals for the First Circuit held that the evidence supported a jury conclusion that the hospital had been negligent by maintaining a charting by exception method of recording notes in the patient's record, which involved charting only, when necessary, important changes in the patient's condition.

Reason

The defendants argued that the plaintiff failed to prove a general medical standard governing the need for conservative treatment. The court disagreed. The plaintiff's chief expert witness, Dr. Udvarhelyi, testified that, absent an indication of neurological impairment, the standard practice is for a neurosurgeon to postpone lumbar disc surgery while the patient undergoes conservative treatment, with a period of absolute bed rest as the prime ingredient.

The hospital could not seriously dispute that the plaintiff introduced sufficient evidence on the elements of duty and breach. The hospital did not contest the plaintiff's allegation that a regulation of the Puerto Rico Department of Health, in force in 1986, requires qualitative nurses' notes for each nursing shift. Nor did the hospital dispute the charge that, during the patient's hospital stay, the nurses attending to him did not supply the required notes for every shift but instead followed the hospital's official policy of charting by exception. The sole question, then, was whether there was sufficient evidence for the jury to find that the violation of the regulation was a proximate cause of harm to Mr. Lama.

The hospital questioned the plaintiff's proof of causation in two respects. First, the hospital claimed that the plaintiff did not prove that the charting by exception policy was a proximate cause of the delayed detection of the patient's infection. Second, the hospital argued that there was no causal relationship between the belated diagnosis of the infection and any unnecessary harm suffered. There was evidence from which the jury could have inferred that, as part of the practice of charting by exception, the nurses did not regularly record certain information important to the diagnosis of an infection, such as the changing characteristics of the surgical wound and the patient's complaints of postoperative pain. Indeed, one former nurse at the hospital who attended to the patient in 1986 testified that, under the charting by exception policy, she would not report a patient's pain if she either did not administer any medicine or simply gave the patient an aspirin-type medication (as opposed to a

narcotic). Further, since there was evidence that the patient's hospital records contained some scattered possible signs of infection that, according to Dr. Udvarhelyi, deserved further investigation (e.g., an excessively bloody bandage and local pain at the site of the wound), the jury could have reasonably inferred that the intermittent charting failed to provide the sort of continuous danger signals that would be the most likely to spur early intervention by the physician.

The hospital claimed that even if faulty record keeping was a cause of the delayed diagnosis, the plaintiff failed to demonstrate a link between the timing of the diagnosis and the harm the patient eventually suffered. Drawing all inferences in favor of the plaintiff, it appeared that he acquired a wound infection as early as May 17 (when a nurse noted a "very bloody" bandage) or May 19 (when Mr. Lama complained of pain at the site of the wound). The wound infection then developed into discitis on or about May 20 (when Mr. Lama began experiencing excruciating back pain). While there may have been no way to prevent the initial wound infection, the key question then becomes whether early detection and treatment of the wound infection could have prevented the infection from reaching the disc interspace in the critical period prior to May 20. Dr. Udvarhelyi testified that "time is an extremely important factor" in handling an infection. A 24-hour delay in treatment can make a difference, and a delay of several days "carries a high-risk . . . that the infection will [not be] properly controlled." *Id.* at 481. The jury could have reasonably inferred that the diagnosis and treatment were delayed at least 24 hours (May 19 to 20), and perhaps 72 hours (May 17 to 20). As a result, the jury could have reasonably concluded that the delayed timing of the diagnosis and treatment of the wound infection was a proximate cause of the patient's discitis.

Discussion

1. What is charting by exception?
2. What are the pros and cons of charting by exception?

2. PRIVILEGED INFORMATION/PROTECTED

Citation: *Estate of Hussain v. Gardner*, 624 A.2d 99 (N.J. Super. Ct. App. Div. 1993)

Facts

Discovery was sought regarding the statements given by a physician to the hospital's internal peer review committee (quality assessment committee) in connection with his management and treatment of a patient. In this medical malpractice action, the plaintiff alleged that the defendant physician deviated from accepted medical standards in the care and treatment of the plaintiff's decedent during surgical procedures.

Issue

Were the statements given by the defendant to the hospital's internal peer review committee relating to the management and treatment of the plaintiff discoverable?

Holding

The Superior Court of New Jersey held that the information was protected.

Reason

In *Wylie v. Mills*, 195 N.J. Super. Ct. App. Div. 332, 478 A.2d 1273 (Law Div. 1984), the court adopted the privilege used in several federal jurisdictions that prevents disclosure of confidential, critical evaluative, and/or deliberative material whenever the public interest in confidentiality outweighs an individual's need for full discovery. In applying the privilege to information contained in a corporate report on an accident in which an employee was involved, the court held self-evaluation privilege protected the report from discovery. In reaching this conclusion, the court stressed the importance of self-critical analysis in recognizing past problems and trying to eliminate future problems. Without such protection, candid expressions of opinion or suggestions as to future policy would not be forthcoming due to a fear that these statements may be used against the employer in a subsequent litigation. The standard used for disclosure of confidential investigative records was set forth in *McClain v. College Hosp.*, 99 N.J. 346, 492 A.2d 991 (1985). In that case, the court set forth the following factors, which should be taken into consideration: (1) the extent to which the information may be available from other sources, (2) the degree of harm that the litigant will suffer from its unavailability, and (3) the possible prejudice in the agency's investigation. *Id.* at 351, 492 A.2d 991. The court adopted the holding that the plaintiffs had not made a strong showing of a particularized need that outweighs the public interest in the confidentiality of the quality assessment committee. Because information is available from other sources, the court found that the information sought by the plaintiff was readily discoverable.

Discussion

1. Should statements given by a defendant to a hospital's internal peer review committee be discoverable by a plaintiff? Explain.
2. What was the standard set for the release of information in *McClain v. College Hospital*?

3. PRIVILEGED INFORMATION/INFORMATION FOR APPLICATION PURPOSES NOT PROTECTED FROM DISCOVERY

Citation: *May v. Wood River Township Hosp.*, 629 N.E.2d 170 (Ill. App. Ct. 1994)

Facts

The patient's guardian sued the hospital and physicians, alleging that the hospital was negligent in providing care to the patient and in granting staff privileges to the physician. The circuit court granted the guardian's motion to compel, ordering the hospital to answer certain interrogatories, and the hospital appealed.

The plaintiff filed a 20-count complaint against the following defendants: the hospital, Dr. Marrese, Dr. Lin, Dr. Pan, and the anesthesiology consortium. The plaintiff's complaints d rected against the hospital alleged that it was negligent in providing care to Mr. May, Sr., and that it was negligent in granting staff privileges to Dr. Marrese. The hospital submitted a memorandum of law and an affidavit of the current president in support of its opposition to the interrogatories and in support of its motion. Attached to the affidavit were copies of the hospital's bylaws in force at that time. The affidavit further stated that all documents in his possession concerning the granting of associate staff privileges to Dr. Marrese "are being kept in the course of internal quality control," and that the "granting and reviewing of staff privileges at [the hospital] is done to maintain and improve the quality of patient care." *Id.* at 171. The trial court denied the hospital's motion for a protective order and granted the plaintiff's motion to compel, ordering the hospital to answer all of the plaintiff's interrogatories "regarding any material or information generated by anyone on the hospital's executive committee or from any other source so long as it was information generated or made before the date when Dr. Marrese was granted Associate Staff privileges." *Id.*

The trial court ruled that nothing related to work done, communications between executive committee members during their meetings, or discussions related to Dr. Marrese is protected by the Code of Civil Procedure, nor are the minutes of the committee protected so long as this information existed or was created before the actual decision to grant privileges to Dr. Marrese. The court further stated that no privilege exists under the Code as to a review of a physician's qualification for medical staff privileges before said physician is actually on the hospital's staff.

The plaintiff argued that peer review was not involved in the instant case because the materials sought in discovery concerned actions taken by the executive committee prior to the time Dr. Marrese was granted staff privileges. The hospital urged on appeal, however, that no Illinois case has interpreted the Code as being inapplicable to the credentialing process.

Issue

Was the information held by the hospital generated prior to Dr. Marrese's application for hospital privileges, along with his application for privileges, outside the scope of the Code of Civil Procedure and privileged from discovery?

Holding

The Illinois Appellate Court held that the Code of Civil Procedure did not protect information generated prior to the physician's application for staff privileges or his application for the privileges.

Reason

The information generated prior to Dr. Marrese's application for privileges, as well as his application for privileges, is outside the scope of the Code of Civil Procedure and not privileged. The same is true of a whole host of materials that might be considered by the committee, for example:

1. The fact that staff privileges were granted, denied, or revoked at other hospitals.
2. The fact that licenses to practice medicine were awarded, denied, suspended, or revoked in a given state.
3. The fact that an applicant has been sued or has never been sued for malpractice. *Id.* at 174.

These matters are facts that would exist independent of a peer review process. These facts cannot be privileged simply because a committee devoted to quality control or peer review considered them. That which is nonprivileged cannot be converted to being privileged simply by handing the facts to a committee.

On the other hand, if the committee sought to generate new opinions or information for consideration by the committee, a privilege could attach. For example, if the committee interviewed a colleague of Dr. Marrese's to elicit an opinion on Dr. Marrese's ability as a physician, that opinion could be privileged. If, however, the same opinion had been stated earlier in a deposition in a malpractice case and the committee reviewed the deposition, no privilege could attach to conceal the deposition from the discovery process, nor should the fact that it was considered be immune from discovery.

Discussion

1. Do you agree that information gathered prior to a physician's application for staff privileges should not be privileged from discovery? Explain.
2. Under what circumstances should the information be protected?

4. DISCOVERY/INFECTION CONTROL RECORDS NOT PRIVILEGED

Citation: *Smith v. Lincoln Gen. Hosp.*, 605 So. 2d 1347 (La. 1992)

Facts

The plaintiff, a patient, brought an action against a hospital seeking to recover, *inter alia*, for injuries he sustained as a result of a nosocomial infection he allegedly contracted at the hospital. The plaintiff claimed that his infection was due to an act or omission on the part of the hospital in failing to protect him from such infections. During the discovery phase of the proceedings, the plaintiff filed a motion for production of documents seeking studies done by the hospital regarding the percentage of nosocomial infection rates per patients admitted. The hospital objected to this request and the plaintiff obtained an order to compel the hospital to produce the documents. The court of appeal, on review, reversed the trial court's ruling, determining that statutes rendering hospital records confidential barred the information from disclosure. The plaintiff filed an application for writ of *certiorari* seeking supervisory review.

Issue

Do statutes providing for confidentiality of records of committees of hospitals and other medical organizations intended to provide confidentiality to the records and pro-ceedings of such committees insulate them from discovery because they have come under review of a particular com-mittee?

Holding

The Supreme Court of Louisiana held that the records sought by the plaintiff were not entirely privileged from disclosure.

Reason

The reliance of the court of appeal on La. R.S. 13:3715.3(A) and 44:7(D) was partially misplaced. These provisions were intended to provide confidentiality to the records and pro-ceedings of hospital committees, not to insulate from discov-ery certain facts merely because they have come under the review of any particular committee. Such an interpretation could cause any fact that a hospital chooses to unilaterally characterize as involving information relied on by one of its committees formed to regulate and operate the hospital to be barred from an opposing litigant's discovery regardless of the nature of that information. The plaintiff sought facts relating to nosocomial infection rates in the defendant's hospital. A nosocomial infection is the same malady that gave rise to the plaintiff's injuries. Such facts would be highly relevant to the plaintiff's case or highly likely to lead to such evidence.

When a plaintiff seeks information relevant to his case that is not information regarding the action taken by a committee or its exchange of honest self-critical study but merely factual accountings of otherwise discoverable facts, such information is not protected by any privilege as it does not come within the scope of information entitled to that privilege. This does not mean that the plaintiff is entitled to the entire study, as such study may contain evidence of policy making, remedial action, proposed courses of con-duct, and self-critical analysis that the privilege seeks to protect in order to foster the ability of hospitals to regulate themselves unhindered by outside scrutiny and unconcerned about the possible liability ramifications their discussions might bring about. As such, the trial court must make an *in camera* inspection of such records and determine to what extent they may be discoverable.

Discussion

1. What records or parts thereof should be protected from discovery?

2. Do you agree with the court's decision? Explain.

5. FALSIFICATION OF OFFICE RECORDS

Citation: *Moskovitz v. Mount Sinai Med. Ctr.*, 635 N.E.2d 331 (Ohio 1994)

Facts

The facts giving rise to this appeal involved the conduct of Dr. Figgie, who failed to timely diagnose and treat a malig-nant tumor on Mrs. Moskovitz's left leg and altered certain records to conceal the fact that malpractice had occurred.

In 1978, Mrs. Moskovitz was treated by Dr. Gabelman for a tumor on her left leg. The tumor was removed and found to be benign. In 1984, Dr. Gabelman completely and success-fully removed a second mass. In 1985, Mrs. Moskovitz was referred to Dr. Figgie, an orthopaedic surgeon, for treatment of a degenerative arthritic condition in her knees. In October 1985, Dr. Figgie performed surgery on Mrs. Moskovitz. Mrs. Moskovitz underwent additional knee surgery per-formed by Dr. Figgie in May 1986.

On October 2, 1986, Mrs. Moskovitz visited Dr. Figgie's office, complaining of a lump on her leg. Dr. Figgie did not recommend a biopsy of the lesion. Dr. Figgie had been aware that tumors had been removed from Mrs. Moskovitz's left leg in 1978 and 1984.

On November 3, Mrs. Moskovitz was admitted to Univer-sity Hospitals for a right knee revision. Prior to surgery, Mrs. Moskovitz was examined by Mr. Magas, a registered nurse. Mr. Magas' written report of the examination, signed by Dr. Figgie, noted the existence of a firm nodule measuring one centimeter by one centimeter on Mrs. Moskovitz's left Achilles tendon. Dr. Figgie performed the right knee revision on November 5. Following surgery, Mrs. Moskovitz was exam-ined on Dr. Figgie's behalf by Dr. Balourdas, a resident physician at University Hospitals. A discharge summary prepared by Dr. Balourdas (and signed by Dr. Figgie) noted the existence of a "left Achilles tendon mass, [1] x 1 cm. nodule." The report indicated that the mass had been present for some time.

On November 10, 1987, Dr. Figgie removed the mass. On November 13, the tumor was found to be an epithelioid sarcoma, a rare form of malignant soft-tissue cancer. A bone scan revealed that the cancer had metastasized to Mrs. Moskovitz's shoulder and right femur.

Following the diagnosis of cancer, Mrs. Moskovitz's care was transferred to Dr. Figgie's partner at University Ortho-paedic, Dr. Makley, an orthopaedic surgeon specializing in oncology. Dr. Makley received Dr. Figgie's original office chart, which contained seven pages of notes documenting

Mrs. Moskovitz's course of treatment from 1985 through November 1987. Dr. Makley thereafter referred Mrs. Moskovitz to radiation therapy at University Hospitals. Apparently, in November 1987, without Dr. Figgie's knowledge, Dr. Makley sent a copy of page seven of Dr. Figgie's office notes to the radiation department at University Hospitals.

In December 1987, Dr. Figgie, or someone on his behalf, requested that Dr. Makley return Dr. Figgie's office chart pertaining to the care of Mrs. Moskovitz. In December 1987, Dr. Makley was Mrs. Moskovitz's primary treating physician and Dr. Figgie was no longer directly involved in Mrs. Moskovitz's care and treatment.

Dr. Makley's secretary forwarded the chart to Dr. Figgie's office. Dr. Figgie's secretary then sent a copy of the chart to Dr. Ashenberg, Mrs. Moskovitz's psychologist. The copy was received by Dr. Ashenberg sometime between December 14 and 18, 1987.

In January 1988, Dr. Makley's secretary requested that Dr. Figgie's office return the chart to Dr. Makley. At this time, it was discovered that the original chart had mysteriously vanished. On October 21, 1988, Mrs. Moskovitz filed a complaint for discovery in the Court of Common Pleas seeking to ascertain information relative to a potential claim for medical malpractice. Mrs. Moskovitz died on December 5, 1988, as a result of the cancer. Prior to her death, her testimony was preserved by way of videotaped deposition.

Dr. Makley, in his January 30, 1989, deposition, produced a copy of page seven of Dr. Figgie's office chart. That copy was identical to the copy ultimately recovered by the plaintiff's counsel from the radiation department records at University Hospitals. The copy produced by Dr. Makley contained a typewritten entry dated September 21, 1987, which states: "Mrs. Moskovitz comes in today for her evaluation on the radiographs reviewed with Dr. York. He was not impressed that this [the mass on Moskovitz's left leg] was anything other than a benign problem, perhaps a fibroma. We [Figgie and York] will therefore elect to continue to observe." However, the photostatic copy revealed that a line had been drawn through the sentence "We will therefore elect to continue to observe." The copy further revealed that beneath the entry Dr. Figgie had interlineated a handwritten notation: "As she does not want excisional Bx [biopsy] we will observe." The September 21, 1987, entry was followed by a typewritten entry dated September 24, 1987, which states: "I [Figgie] reviewed the X-rays with Dr. York. I discussed the clinical findings with him. We [Figgie and York] felt this to be benign, most likely a fibroma. He [York] said that we could observe and I concur." At some point, Figgie had also added to the September 24, 1987, entry a handwritten notation, "see above," referring to the September 21, 1987, handwritten notation that Mrs. Moskovitz did not want an excisional biopsy. *Id.* at 336.

Dr. Figgie, at his deposition on March 2, 1989, produced records, including a copy of page seven of his office chart. As his original chart had been lost in December 1987 or January 1988, Dr. Figgie had this copy made from the copy of the chart that had been sent to Dr. Ashenberg in December 1987. The September 21, 1987, entry in the records produced by Dr. Figgie did not contain the statement "We will therefore elect to continue to observe." Apparently, that sentence had been deleted (whited out) on the original office chart from which Dr. Ashenberg's copy (and, in turn, Dr. Figgie's copy) had been made, in a way that left no indication on the copy that the sentence had been removed from the original records. *Id.* at 336.

During his deposition, Dr. Figgie maintained that he did not discover the mass on the left Achilles tendon until February 23, 1987, and that Mrs. Moskovitz had continually refused a workup or biopsy.

During discovery, another copy of page seven of Dr. Figgie's office chart, identical to the copy produced by Dr. Makley during his deposition, was recovered from the radiation department records at University Hospitals. This copy had been received by the radiation department in November 1987, when Mrs. Moskovitz was referred to radiation therapy by Dr. Makley. It became apparent that the final sentence in the September 21, 1987, entry had been deleted from Dr. Figgie's original office chart sometime between November 1987, when the radiation department obtained a copy of the record, and mid-December 1987, when Dr. Ashenberg received a copy of the record from Dr. Figgie's office. Presumably, that alteration occurred in December 1987 while the original chart was in the possession of Dr. Figgie.

Eventually, Dr. Figgie's entire office chart was reconstructed from copies obtained through discovery. The reconstructed chart contains no indication that a workup or biopsy was recommended by Dr. Figgie and refused by Mrs. Moskovitz at any time prior to August 10, 1987.

In her videotaped deposition, Mrs. Moskovitz claimed that she never refused to have the tumor biopsied. The panel found in favor of all defendants participating in that proceeding with the exception of Dr. Figgie. The panel made the following findings regarding Dr. Figgie:

> 3. The evidence supported a finding that plaintiffs' [*sic*] decedent had a very good chance of long-term survival if the tumor was found to be malignant at a time when it was less than one centimeter in size. The evidence supported the fact that the tumor had not grown in size as of May 7, 1987. If Dr. Figgie had performed a biopsy prior to this date, the cancer would not have metastasized and the decedent would have recovered.
>
> 4. Dr. Figgie's office chart, which is the primary reference material in analyzing a physician's con-

duct, is filled with contradictions and inconsistencies.

5. Even if Dr. Figgie was first informed of the growth on February 23, 1987, he still fell below acceptable standards of care because he did not conduct further investigation till [*sic*] X-rays performed in September 1987. All handwritten entries which appear on or prior to September 24, 1987, indicating that a biopsy was recommended or that the decedent refused further work-up were subsequent changes of the records done to justify Dr. Figgie's conduct. The sentence "We will therefore elect to continue to observe" on the September 21, 1987 entry was whited out and the handwritten entry "as she does not want excisional biopsy we will observe" was a subsequent alteration of the records. *Id.* at 338.

The jury believed the decedent had a very good chance of long-term survival if the tumor was found to be malignant before it exceeded one centimeter in size. The trial court entered judgment in accordance with the jury's verdict.

The court of appeals upheld the finding of liability against Dr. Figgie on the wrongful death and survival claims. The court of appeals found that the appellant was not entitled to punitive damages as a matter of law. The court of appeals reversed the judgment of the trial court as to the award of damages and remanded the case for a new trial only on the issue of compensatory damages.

Issue

Is an intentional alteration or destruction of medical records to avoid liability sufficient to show actual malice? Can punitive damages be awarded whether or not the act of altering or destroying records directly causes compensable harm?

Holding

The Supreme Court of Ohio held that the evidence regarding the physician's alteration of the patient's records supported an award of punitive damages, regardless of whether the alteration caused actual harm.

Reason

The jury's award of punitive damages was based on Dr. Figgie's alteration or destruction of medical records. Dr. Figgie's alteration of records was inextricably intertwined with the claims advanced by the appellant for medical malpractice, and the award of compensatory damages on the survival claim formed the necessary predicate for the award of punitive damages based on the alteration of medical records.

The purpose of punitive damages is not to compensate a plaintiff, but to punish and deter certain conduct. If the act of altering and destroying records to avoid liability is to be tolerated in our society, the court could think of no better way to encourage it than to hold that punitive damages were not available in this case. Dr. Figgie's conduct of altering records should not go unpunished. The court warned others to refrain from similar conduct through an award of punitive damages.

Dr. Figgie's alteration of records exhibited a total disregard for the law and the rights of Mrs. Moskovitz and her family. Had the copy of page seven of Dr. Figgie's office chart not been recovered from the radiation department records at University Hospitals, the appellant would have been substantially less likely to succeed in this case. The copy of the chart and other records produced by Dr. Figgie would have tended to exculpate Dr. Figgie for his medical negligence while placing the blame for his failures on Mrs. Moskovitz.

A unanimous panel of arbitrators determined that records were altered with bad motive, and that Dr. Figgie was the responsible party. With all due respect to the court of appeals' majority, the supreme court believed that the appellate court simply substituted its judgment for that of the jury and, thereby, invaded the province of the finder of fact. Further, as the supreme court stated in *Myers v. Garson* (1993) 66 Ohio St. 3d 610, 614, 614 N.E.2d 742, 745, "we have often noted in the past, where the decision in a case turns upon credibility of testimony, and where there exists competent and credible evidence supporting the findings and conclusions of the trial court, deference to such findings and conclusions must be given by the reviewing court."

The court reversed the judgment of the court of appeals on the issue of punitive damages. An intentional alteration or destruction of medical records to avoid liability for medical negligence is sufficient to show actual malice, and punitive damages may be awarded whether or not the act of altering, falsifying, or destroying records directly causes compensable harm.

Discussion

1. Do you consider the evidence sufficiently adequate to establish that the surgeon intentionally altered, falsified, or destroyed the patient's medical records to avoid liability for medical negligence? Explain.

2. If you found it necessary to clarify an entry that you made in a patient's medical record, what procedure would you follow?
3. Is the use of correction fluid the preferred way to clarify your entries?

6. RETENTION OF RECORDS/X-RAYS

Citation: *Rodgers v. St. Mary's Hosp. of Decatur*, 597 N.E.2d 616 (Ill. 1992)

Facts

Mr. Rodgers filed a medical malpractice action in the circuit court of Macon County on May 27, 1986, alleging the wrongful death of his wife, who died at the hospital two days after giving birth to their son. Named as defendants in the medical malpractice action were Mrs. Rodgers' obstetricians, her radiologists, and the hospital.

Mr. Rodgers filed a complaint for damages against the hospital alleging that the hospital breached its statutory duty to preserve for five years all of the X-rays taken of Mrs. Rodgers (*see* Ill. Rev. Stat. 1987, ch. 111 1/2, ¶ 157-11 [X-Ray Retention Act]). He claimed that the X-rays were crucial to proving his case against the obstetricians and radiologist. On April 12, 1988, on motion of the hospital, the circuit court dismissed that complaint without prejudice. Mr. Rodgers amended his complaint and brought a medical malpractice action against the hospital on May 25, 1989, the day after he reached an $800,000 settlement with the obstetricians. In his complaint, Mr. Rodgers alleged that his wife's death was caused by a sigmoid colonic volvulus, and that the condition appeared on an X-ray that the hospital had a duty to preserve. He alleged that the hospital's failure to preserve the X-ray was a breach of its duty arising from the X-Ray Retention Act and from the hospital's internal regulations. Mr. Rodgers asserted that because the hospital failed to preserve the X-ray, he was unable to prove his case against the radiologists. The circuit court entered judgment in favor of the hospital, and Mr. Rodgers appealed.

Issue

Did Mr. Rodgers state a cause of action arising out of the hospital's failure to retain X-rays?

Holding

The Supreme Court of Illinois held that a private cause of action existed under the X-Ray Retention Act, and Mr. Rodgers stated a claim under the Act.

Reason

The X-Ray Retention Act provides that "Hospitals which produce photographs of the human anatomy by the X-ray or roentgen process on the request of licensed physicians for use by them in the diagnosis or treatment of a patient's illness or condition shall retain such photographs or films as part of their regularly maintained records for a period of 5 years. . . ." Ill. Rev. Stat. 1987, ch. 111 1/2, ¶ 157-11.

The hospital argued that the statute is merely an administrative regulation to be enforced exclusively by the Public Health Department. The court disagreed. Nothing in the statute suggests that the legislature intended to limit the available remedies to administrative ones. "The threat of liability is a much more efficient method of enforcing the regulation than requiring the Public Health Department to hire inspectors to monitor the compliance of hospitals with the provisions of the Act." *Id.* at 619.

The hospital also argued that its loss of one X-ray out of a series of six should be considered *de minimus* and not a violation of the statute. The court disagreed, finding that the statute requires that all X-rays be preserved, not just some of them. The court concluded that Mr. Rodgers had stated a cause of action against the hospital for failure to preserve the X-ray for use in litigation. Whether the missing X-ray proximately caused Mr. Rodgers to lose his case against the radiologists and to settle for less than the full amount of the judgment is a question for the trier of fact.

Discussion

1. What records should a hospital maintain?
2. How long should patient records, including X-rays, electrocardiograms (ECGs), etc., be maintained?

7. ALTERATION OF RECORDS

Citation: *Dimora v. Cleveland Clinic Found.*, 683 N.E.2d 1175 (Ohio App. 8 Dist. 1996)

Facts

Plaintiff–appellee Ms. Dimora filed a complaint against defendant–appellant Cleveland Clinic Foundation (the Clinic) alleging that the Clinic negligently provided medical care and treatment for her during her confinement there. Ms. Dimora further claimed punitive damages, alleging that the Clinic and/or its agents and/or employees intentionally falsified her medical records or inaccurately reported her condition to avoid liability for their negligence.

Ms. Dimora, a 79-year-old woman, was admitted on October 18, 1993, as a patient at the Cleveland Clinic. She had difficulty in ambulating and transferring, requiring an attendant while using a walker. Her condition was noted numerous times on her chart. She was evaluated as high risk for falls.

On November 5, 1993, Ms. Dimora was preparing to be discharged from the Clinic. After using the toilet with the assistance of a student nurse, she lost her balance and fell backward. The fall caused a severe bruising to her thorax and resulted in the breaking of five or six ribs. The fall was noted both in the nursing notes and the discharge summary by the attending physician, who examined her subsequent to the fall. Upon examination, Ms. Dimora was "found to have good strength in all four extremities," was "without pain of movement," and had a five centimeter by eight centimeter abrasion on the right posterior thorax. The area was noted to be "non-tender with deep palpitation and there was no evidence of crepitus." Ice and lotion were applied to the abraded area. No X-rays were taken at the Clinic after the fall, and no further treatment was administered by the Clinic. Ms. Dimora's broken ribs were not diagnosed until the following day, when X-rays were taken at Marymount Hospital.

Witnesses, Ms. Dimora's daughter, granddaughter, and caregiver, testified that when they arrived at the hospital to pick up Ms. Dimora, she was crying, complaining of pain, and her side was all red. Ms. Dimora's daughter testified that one of the nurses said that her mother had fallen when she was left alone in the bathroom. The three women each testified that they had difficulty getting Ms. Dimora in and out of the car because she was in so much pain. Both movement and breathing caused her pain for a few weeks. Subsequent to this fall, Ms. Dimora required much more care, and she was unable to enjoy many of her former activities.

The defendant moved for a directed verdict claiming that the plaintiff had failed to demonstrate alteration of the record and malice on the part of the Clinic, asserting, therefore, that the claim for punitive damages must fail. The trial court denied this motion. The jury awarded a verdict in favor of Ms. Dimora in the amount of $25,000 for compensatory damages and $25,000 in punitive damages.

Issue

Did the trial court err in denying the applicant's motion for a directed verdict on the appellee's claim for punitive damages, alleging that the appellee failed to present evidence of alteration of the record or, farther, failed to demonstrate fraud and actual malice? The claim of the appellee for punitive damages alleges that the clinic, through its agents and/or employees, intentionally falsified her medical records

or inaccurately and improperly reported the fall incident to avoid liability for its medical malpractice or negligence.

Holding

The judgment of the trial court was affirmed.

Reason

In a case involving medical malpractice where liability is determined and compensatory damages are awarded, punitive damages pled in connection with the claim for malpractice may be awarded upon a showing of actual malice, defined as: the intentional alteration, falsification, or destruction of medical records by a physician, to avoid liability for his or her medical negligence.

At trial, the testimony presented by witnesses for the appellee indicated that the right side of Ms. Dimora's body was red, bruised, and painful after the fall. Three witnesses testified that Ms. Dimora was crying and in pain approximately 45 minutes after the incident while she was still in the hospital. Testimony was offered that broken ribs would be painful upon deep palpation. Pictures were offered into evidence indicating large areas of bruising on Ms. Dimora's body on the day after the event.

In contrast to the evidence presented by the appellee, the progress note of the examining physician at issue here states in part:

> Pt was in transport between walker and toilet seat according to student nurse. Pt was at walker and lost balance backward. The SN acted by holding the pt from the L side and gradually lowering her to the floor, and called for help. Pt was lifted back into wheelchair. On exam, pt has full use of all 4 extremities with good strength and no pain with movement. A small 5 x 8 cm area on the pts r posterior thorax was slightly scraped. It was not tender to deep palpation's and no crepitus was noted. There were no other lacerations bumps or abrasions noted. Head was traumatic. The abrasion on the thorax was treated with lotion and ice. The pt was smiling and laughing pleasantly during the exam.

Appellant contends that this record accurately reflects the incident. However, the testimony presented by the appellee is in apparent conflict with the description of the incident, the injury, and Ms. Dimora's demeanor. The evidence showed that Ms. Dimora had fallen and broken five or six ribs; yet, upon examination, the physician noted that she was smiling and laughing pleasantly with no pain upon deep palpation of the area. Other testimony indicated that she was in pain and crying. The discrepancy between the written progress notes and the testimony of the witnesses who observed Ms. Dimora was sufficient to raise a question of fact as to the possible falsification of documents by the physician to minimize the nature of the incident and the injury of the patient due to the possible negligence of hospital personnel. The testimony of the witnesses, if believed, would be sufficient to show that the physician falsified the record or intentionally reported the incident inaccurately to avoid liability for the negligent care. Such conduct is the type of intentional and deceptive behavior more indicative of actual malice. If such evidence is believed, the jury could award punitive damages. With the proper caution exercised in instructing the jury as to when punitive damages are proper, the issue of punitive damages should have been submitted to the jury.

The trial court properly determined that reasonable minds could differ on the issue of whether the progress notes and the discharge notes were falsified or inaccurately reported to avoid liability for the medical malpractice or negligence of hospital personnel. Therefore, the trial court did not err when it denied the appellant's motions for directed verdicts on the appellee's claims for negligence and for punitive damages.

Discussion

1. Do you agree with the court's finding? Why?
2. What would you have done differently if you were the hospital? Nurse? Physician?

8. REFERENCE LETTER/PRIVILEGED INFORMATION

Citation: *Stricklin v. Becan*, 689 N.E.2d 328 (Ill. App. 4 Dist. 1997)

Facts

In 1996, the plaintiff filed a medical malpractice claim against the defendant, Dr. Becan. Doctor's Hospital, Ltd. (hospital) was named as a respondent in discovery. During the course of discovery, the plaintiff requested any document prepared by a person other than a member of the respondent's medical staff that is critical of or complains about the performance or competence of Dr. Becan. The hospital objected, initially, on the basis of relevance.

The plaintiff subsequently filed a motion to compel the hospital to produce a reference letter. The hospital objected stating that the document is privileged from disclosure under sections 8-2101 and 8-2102 of the Medical Studies Act (Act) [735 ILCS 5/8-2101, 8-2102 (West 1996)]. The hospital

specifically identified the existence of a September 12, 1994, letter from Dr. Ambrose claiming it was a reference letter, which was generated at the request of the Doctor's Hospital Credentialing Committee and was, therefore, privileged. The hospital offered the court an option of making the letter available for an *in camera* inspection.

In a subsequent docket entry, the trial court, after reviewing the authority cited by both sides, found no privilege existed and granted the plaintiff's motion to compel production of the letter. The court did not take the hospital up on its offer to examine the document *in camera*.

The hospital then filed a motion to supplement the record with the affidavit of Ms. Senger and moved the court to reconsider its prior order requiring production. The affidavit of Ms. Senger stated that she was the risk manager of the hospital, had personal knowledge of the files concerning Dr. Becan's application for appointment to the medical staff, and had personal knowledge of the documents kept regarding the credentialing process at the hospital.

Ms. Senger averred that the files contained a July 19, 1994, letter from Doctor's Hospital to a hospital in New Jersey requesting an evaluation of Dr. Becan for the credentialing committee. The file also contained a response to that letter from a Dr. Ambrose. The affidavit concluded that the letter clearly indicates that it is in response to the correspondence received from Doctor's Hospital on behalf of the hospital's credentialing committee. The hospital argued the document was privileged because it was produced at the request of the credentialing committee for use in determining whether permanent privileges should be extended to Dr. Becan, who had been granted temporary privileges at the time he treated the plaintiff.

In a written response, the plaintiff stated, initially, that she had no objection to the defendant's request to supplement the record with the affidavit of Ms. Senger. However, she argued the existence of the affidavit provided no basis for the court to modify its prior decision.

After a hearing, the court granted the motion to supplement but denied the motion to reconsider. Counsel for defendant indicated the hospital would not comply with the turnover order and suggested that it should be found in contempt to test the validity of the ruling by appeal. The trial court then found the hospital in direct civil contempt and imposed a $500 sanction that was stayed pending appeal. The hospital appealed, claiming the document is privileged from discovery under sections 8-2101 and 8-2102 of the Medical Studies Act (Act) [735 ILCS 5/8-2101, 8-2102 (West 1996)].

Issue

Should a hospital's reference letter from a physician, generated at the request of a hospital's credentialing committee, be privileged from discovery?

Holding

The appeals court reversed the order of contempt and sanction with remand to the trial court for the purpose of conducting an *in camera* review of the letter of reference. To the extent the document constitutes a "letter of reference" or "third-party confidential assessment" of Dr. Becan's "professional competence," it is privileged from disclosure. To the extent it relies upon or incorporates other nonprivileged material, that portion of the document was ordered produced to the plaintiff after redacting privileged material.

Reason

On appeal, the plaintiff moved to file supplemental authorities suggesting that the Senger affidavit was not properly before the trial court because it was not attached to the original response to the motion to compel and was only offered with the hospital's motion for reconsideration. The plaintiff, however, waived this argument. Not only did the plaintiff fail to object to consideration of the affidavit, she expressly acquiesced in its being filed when counsel indicated there was no objection to its being considered. The affidavit is, therefore, properly before the court on appeal.

As to the merits of the case, the applicable version of section 8-2101 of the Act provides, in pertinent part:

> Information obtained. All information, interviews, reports, statements, memoranda, recommendations, letters of reference or other third-party confidential assessments of a health care practitioner's professional competence, or other data of the . . . Patient Care Audit Committees, Medical Care Evaluation Committees, Utilization Review Committees, Credential Committees and Executive Committees, or their designees (but not the medical records pertaining to the patient), used in the course of internal quality control or of medical study for the purpose of reducing morbidity or mortality, or for improving patient care or increasing organ and tissue donation, shall be privileged, strictly confidential and shall be used only for medical research, . . . the evaluation and improvement of quality care, or granting, limiting or revoking staff privileges. 735 ILCS 5/8-2101 (West 1996).

Section 8-2102 provides:

> Admissibility as evidence. Such information, records, reports, statements, notes, memoranda, or other data, shall not be admissible as evidence, nor discoverable in any action of any kind in any court or before any tribunal, board, agency or person. The disclosure of any such information or data, whether proper, or improper, shall not waive or have any effect upon its confidentiality, nondiscoverability, or nonadmissibility. 735 ILCS 5/8-2101 (West 1996).

The hospital contended, on the basis of Ms. Senger's affidavit, that the document appears to fall squarely within the protection of the Act because it constitutes a "letter of reference" or a "third-party confidential assessment of a health care practitioner's professional competence." The plaintiff responded that the burden is on the hospital to show the material is privileged and it has failed to do so. The plaintiff argued that documents are privileged only to the extent they are used for "internal quality control or medical study for the purpose of reducing morbidity or mortality, or for improving patient care" and under the hospital's bylaws, a separate quality assurance committee, whose duties do not overlap those of the credentials committee, performs those functions.

In essence, the plaintiff's argument was that granting or limiting staff privileges does not constitute internal quality control at the hospital. The appeals court did not read the language of the statute as narrowly as the plaintiff. The emphasized portion of section 8-2101 of the Act was added by an amendment to the Act in 1994 [Pub. Act 89-393, Section(s) 15, eff. August 20, 1995 (1995 Ill. Laws 4135)]. The appeals court believed the effect of the amendment is to clearly include letters of reference and other third-party confidential personnel assessments within the class of nondiscoverable documents. Section 8-2101 clearly provides that they may be used by credentialing committees for the purpose of determining staff privileges. To the extent the letter is a letter of recommendation or third-party confidential assessment of Dr. Becan's professional competence, used by the credentialing committee, it could be subject to nondisclosure under the Act. The appeals court did agree with the plaintiff, however, that not all documents considered by a credentialing committee are subject to the privilege.

The purpose of the Act is to ensure the effectiveness of professional self-evaluation by members of the medical profession in the interest of improving the quality of health care. The Act is premised on the belief that absent the statutory peer review privilege, physicians would be reluctant to sit on peer review committees and engage in frank evaluations of their colleagues. In *Willing v. St. Joseph Hospital*, 176 Ill. App. 3d 737, 742-43, 126 Ill. Dec. 197, 201-02, 531 N.E.2d 824, 828-29 (1988), the court held that a physician's educational transcripts and applications for appointment to staff, as well as materials regarding the initial privileges granted to the physician and any modifications, including restrictions or revocations, were not privileged under the Act, reasoning that these documents were antecedent or subsequent to the peer review process. In *Roach v. Springfield Clinic*, 157 Ill. 2d 29, 191 Ill. Dec. 1, 623 N.E.2d 246 (1993), the supreme court held that "not all information" that comes into the possession of a hospital staff, even if it is considered by a peer review committee, is barred from discovery. Simply furnishing information to a committee does not create the privilege. It must be information generated during the course of the peer review process. If the information exists in some nonprivileged form, placing it in front of the committee does not transform it into privileged material.

The balance to be struck in determining what is discoverable is described in the case of *May v. Wood River Township Hospital*, 257 Ill. App. 3d 969, 195 Ill. Dec. 862, 629 N.E.2d 170 (1994). There, the court offered the example of a hospital's having come into possession of a newspaper article written two years before the physician applied for privileges that was either complimentary or critical of the physician's competence. The mere fact that the committee considered the article could not reasonably be held to make that nonprivileged article privileged. The court in *May* went on to say:

> On the other hand, if the committee sought to generate new opinions or information for consideration by the committee, a privilege could attach. For example, if the committee interviewed a colleague of [the doctor] to elicit an opinion on [the doctor's] ability as a physician, that opinion could be privileged. If, however, the same opinion had been stated earlier in a deposition in a malpractice case and the committee reviewed the deposition, no privilege could attach to secrete the deposition from the discovery process, nor should the fact that it was considered be immune from discovery. *May*, 257 Ill. App. 3d at 975-76, 195 Ill. Dec. at 866, 629 N.E.2d at 174.

The problem in this case is that the document in question was not before the appeals court as part of the record on appeal and the trial court never took the opportunity to examine it *in camera* even though the hospital offered to produce it for that purpose. The appeals court could not, therefore, determine whether and to what extent privilege may attach. The appeals court reversed the order of contempt and sanction with remand to the trial court for the purpose of conducting an *in camera* review of the communication from Dr. Ambrose to the hospital.

Discussion

1. Should a letter of reference be considered privileged?

2. On what basis should information/documentation *labeled confidential* be considered privileged?

3. Discuss the legal and confidentiality implications from the standpoint of *libel* if letters of reference are considered discoverable.

9. PROGRESS NOTES AND OFFICE RECORDS NOT HEARSAY EVIDENCE

Citation: *Dardeau v. Ardoin*, 703 So. 2d 695, 97-144 (La. App. 1997)

Facts

The plaintiff, Ms. Dardeau, alleges that when she was 28 years old, she came under the care of Dr. Ardoin for routine examinations. She contends that after her first visit with Dr. Ardoin, he recommended and performed radical surgery consisting of a bladder suspension, cystocele repair, rectocele repair, complete hysterectomy, and removal of her ovaries. According to the plaintiff, Dr. Ardoin injured her obturator nerve during the cystocele surgery and that as a result, she has sustained permanent paralysis in her right leg.

The Louisiana Medical Mutual Insurance Company (LAMMICO) contends that when Ms. Dardeau was first seen by Dr. Ardoin, she complained of loss of urine with coughing, sneezing, jumping, and running. The plaintiff related a history of a tubal ligation after the birth of her second child. The plaintiff also complained of painful menstrual periods associated with heaviness in the pelvic region and pain with intercourse. Dr. Ardoin noted a cystocele or herniation of the bladder, a rectocele or herniation of the rectum through the vagina, and some uterine descensus or falling of the uterus. He recommended conservative treatment and advised Ms. Dardeau to return in one month.

According to the defendant, the plaintiff's complaints persisted and Dr. Ardoin recommended diagnostic studies. After review of the diagnostic studies, he suggested surgery to correct the urinary incontinence and to repair the cystocele and rectocele. Dr. Ardoin also recommended a hysterectomy due to the uterine descensus and complaints of dyspareunia or pain with intercourse and dysmenorrhea or painful menstruation. After a discussion of the procedures, the plaintiff executed three consent forms, which were introduced into the record. A second opinion was obtained from Dr. Cantu who agreed with Dr. Ardoin's findings and recommendation for surgery.

After surgery, the plaintiff complained of leg pain. It was determined by the defendant that she suffered from a rare but known complication of injury to the obturator nerve. The record reflects that a medical review panel rendered a unanimous opinion that Dr. Ardoin did not breach the standard of care in his treatment of Ms. Dardeau, and that she had been adequately informed by Dr. Ardoin that serious complications could occur in connection with the surgical procedures. Furthermore, the panel found that Dr. Ardoin recognized the complication early and addressed it appropriately.

The jury concluded that Dr. Ardoin obtained Ms. Dardeau's informed consent prior to surgery; that a reasonable person would have accepted the risk of an obturator nerve injury based upon the medical condition of the plaintiff at the time of the surgery; that Dr. Ardoin was not guilty of substandard conduct constituting malpractice; and that the plaintiff's injury was not caused by any substandard conduct on the part of Dr. Ardoin.

Dr. Ardoin passed away prior to trial. The plaintiff complained in brief that the introduction of progress notes or office chart by Dr. Ardoin constituted hearsay evidence. She argued that LAMMICO defended this case on unauthenticated progress notes claimed to be made by Dr. Ardoin.

Issue

Did the introduction of progress notes or office chart by the physician constitute hearsay evidence?

Holding

The appeals court found no error on the part of the trial court as to the admissibility of the physician's progress notes or office chart and affirmed the jury verdict and the judgment of the trial court.

Reason

The plaintiffs own expert testified that he relied upon Dr. Ardoin's office chart to render his opinion in the case. Ms. Dardeau argues that LAMMICO attempted to introduce Dr. Ardoin's office chart through Ms. Fontenot, Dr. Ardoin's receptionist, who could not provide any of the qualifying circumstances set forth in La. Code Evid. arts. 803 and 804 that ensure the trustworthiness of these records. More specifically, plaintiff argued that Ms. Fontenot did not have personal knowledge of the information contained in the progress notes and had no recollection of anything in the office chart.

A significant portion of Dr. Ardoin's chart was included in the records of Humana Hospital of Ville Platte, which were introduced at trial without objection. Dr. Ardoin's office chart was admissible because it was created during the course of his treatment of the plaintiff and constituted a record maintained in the course of a regularly conducted business activity [La. Code Evid. art. 803(6)]. Dr. Ardoin's receptionist, Ms. Fontenot, testified at trial that the office chart was created in connection with Dr. Ardoin's business, that the entries in the chart were made at the time of treatment, and that the entries were made by Dr. Ardoin who had personal knowledge of the information in the chart. Ms. Fontenot testified that she never saw any chart being altered or falsified by Dr. Ardoin, nor did Dr. Ardoin request that she alter any office chart. No evidence was presented by the plaintiff to indicate that Dr. Ardoin's records were untrustworthy.

Dr. Ardoin's office chart was likewise admissible under La. Code Evid. art. 803(4) relating to statements made for the purpose of medical treatment and diagnosis in connection with treatment. Dr. Ardoin's records, which were made contemporaneously with the history and complaints related by the plaintiff, constitute statements made for the purpose of medical treatment and diagnosis, and thus the office chart falls under the art. 803(4) exception to the hearsay rule.

Discussion

1. What was the appeals court's reasoning for allowing the physician's progress notes and office records to be admissible as evidence?
2. What is the danger of allowing written records admitted into evidence when the author of such records is not available for cross-examination?
3. What is the danger of *not* allowing written records to be admitted into evidence when the author of such records is not available for cross-examination?

10. DISCOVERY/COMMUNICATIONS TO PEER REVIEW COMMITTEE

Citation: *Arlington Mem'l Hosp. Found., Inc. v. Barton*, 952 S.W.2d 927 (Tex. App. 1997)

Facts

Mr. Baird sued Relator Arlington Memorial Hospital Foundation for allowing a single-use item to be reused in his cataract surgery. Mr. Baird filed requests for production and asked for (1) incident reports relating to his care and the cataract machine; (2) telephone logs of calls between the hospital, the interested physicians, and the lab that tested the cataract machine; and (3) correspondence between the parties named in the telephone logs. The hospital objected, claiming that the documents were privileged from discovery as medical peer review documents. After Mr. Baird filed a motion to compel, the hospital submitted the documents for an *in camera* inspection along with an affidavit from the vice president of the hospital, Ms. Harris.

Ms. Harris's affidavit stated that she attends and participates in meetings of the quality management committee of the hospital. She stated she has personal knowledge of the statements made in the affidavit. The affidavit goes on to list all of the peer review committees and the responsibilities of such committees. Ms. Harris then concluded:

> I hereby certify that the documents tendered to the Court by counsel for [the Hospital] constitute confidential documents, communications, and clinical testing done at the behest of the peer review committees of Arlington Memorial Hospital. The documents, communications, and clinical testing constitute proceedings of or communications to the peer review committees of [the Hospital]. The documents, communications, and clinical testing constitute records received, maintained, or developed by the peer review committees of [the Hospital]. The documents, communications, and clinical testing received by the peer review committees of [the Hospital] were created at the behest of the peer review committees of [the Hospital] and were not gratuitously submitted to such peer review committees. The documents, communications, and clinical testing do not constitute routine business or medical records of [the Hospital].

Mr. Baird did not controvert this affidavit in any way or allege that the hospital had waived the privilege. After reviewing the documents *in camera*, the trial court overruled the hospital's objections and ordered the hospital to produce all the documents. The hospital appealed.

Issue

Did the hospital properly plead and prove that the peer review documents were privileged?

Holding

The hospital adequately proved, by affidavit, that the documents were privileged medical peer review documents. Mr. Baird did not raise any controverting evidence. The hospital was entitled to protection from producing those documents.

Reason

No one disputed the fact that medical peer review documents are privileged from discovery under article 4495b unless they are made in the regular course of business. According to the relevant statutes:

> [A]ll proceedings and records of a medical peer review committee are confidential, and all communications made to a medical peer review committee are privileged.

* * * *

> Unless disclosure is required or authorized by law, records or determinations of or communications to a medical peer review committee are not subject to subpoena or discovery and are not admissible as evidence in any civil judicial or administrative proceeding without waiver of the privilege of confidentiality executed in writing by the committee, or a finding that the records were made or maintained on the regular course of Business. [Tex. Rev. Civ. Stat. Ann. art. 4495b, Section(s) 5.06(g), (j) (Vernon Supp. 1997); *see* Tex. Health & Safety Code Ann. Section(s) 161.032(c) (Vernon Supp. 1997); *Irving Healthcare Sys. v. Brooks*, 927 S.W.2d 12, 18 (Tex. 1996) (orig. proceeding) (9-0 decision). Tex. Health & Safety Code Ann. 161.032(a), (c).]

The burden to establish the privilege is on the party seeking to shield information from discovery. The party asserting the privilege has the obligation to prove, by competent evidence, that the privilege applies to the information sought. An affidavit proving the privilege "must necessarily be descriptive enough to be persuasive, but not so descriptive as to provide the very information sought by the opposing party, should the affidavit fall into such party's hands." R. E. Butler, Records and Proceedings of Hospital Committees Privileged Against Discovery, 28 S. Tex. L. Rev. 97, 108 (1987).

Ms. Harris's affidavit, submitted by the hospital, tracked the language of article 4495b. Ms. Harris made her affidavit on personal knowledge and detailed the committees that engage in peer review. She also stated that peer review activity includes "investigation and evaluation of the quality of medical and health care services provided at [the Hospital]." She enumerated Mr. Baird's production requests and stated that the *in camera* documents tendered to the court, which would be responsive to the requests, were "records and proceedings of the peer review committees at [the Hospital]." Ms. Harris also attached to the affidavit the hospital's bylaws, rules, and regulations. Ms. Harris's affidavit sufficiently raised and proved the peer review privilege.

The affidavit, which alleged and proved the privilege, along with the *in camera* submission, shifted the burden to Mr. Baird to either controvert the affidavit, show that the privilege was waived, or that the documents were made in the ordinary course of business. Mr. Baird did none of these things.

Discussion

1. Discuss how the decision in this case is affected (if at all) by the Joint Commission on Accreditation of Healthcare Organizations' Environment of Care Standards requiring that all patient care equipment be regularly scheduled for preventive maintenance.
2. Explain what the plaintiff should have proved in order for the appeals court to have ordered the production of the documents.

X

Patient Consent

1. INFORMED CONSENT/HOSPITAL AND PHYSICIAN RESPONSIBILITY

Citation: *Keel v. St. Elizabeth Med. Ctr., Ky.*, 842 S.W.2d 860 (Ky. 1992)

Facts

A medical malpractice action was filed by a plaintiff, Mr. Keel, who alleged that the hospital performed a medical procedure without his informed consent resulting in medical complications. The plaintiff went to the medical center for a computed tomography (CT) scan, which was to include the injection of a contrast dye material. Prior to the test, he was given no information concerning any risks attendant to the procedure. The dye was injected and the scan was conducted. However, the plaintiff developed a thrombophlebitis at the site of the injection.

The plaintiff argued that recovery may be had upon proof of damages, causation, and lack of informed consent. Moreover, the plaintiff argued that expert medical testimony was not required in order to prove the absence of informed consent. The hospital argued that the question of informed consent, like the question of negligence, must be determined against the standard of practice among members of the medical profession.

The circuit court granted summary judgment to the hospital on the grounds that the plaintiff failed to present expert testimony on the issue. The plaintiff appealed.

Issue

Is expert medical testimony required with respect to risks associated with a CT scan? Did the hospital have a duty to inform the patient as to the risks of the CT scan?

Holding

The Supreme Court of Kentucky held that expert testimony was not required to establish lack of informed consent, and the hospital had a duty to inform the patient of the risks of the procedure. Responsibility did not lie solely with the patient's personal physician. The circuit court's summary judgment for the hospital was reversed and the matter was remanded for further proceedings.

Reason

In most cases, expert medical evidence will likely be a necessary element of a plaintiff's proof in negating informed consent. In view of the special circumstances of this case, the court found it significant that "St. Elizabeth offered Keel *no information whatsoever* concerning any possible hazards of this particular procedure, while at the same time the hospital admits that it routinely questions every patient about to undergo a dye injection as to whether he/she has had any previous reactions to contrast materials. If we are to analogize consent actions to negligence actions, we must also acknowledge that a failure adequately to inform the patient

183

need not be established by expert testimony where the failure is so apparent that laymen may easily recognize it or infer it from evidence within the realm of common knowledge." *Id.* at 862. A juror might reasonably infer from the nontechnical evidence that St. Elizabeth's utter silence as to the risks amounted to an assurance that there were none. The hospital's own questions to patients regarding reactions to the CT scan procedure demonstrated that the hospital recognized the substantial possibility of complications. These inconsistencies are apparent without recourse to expert testimony.

Although not strictly at issue in this case, the court noted, under KRS 304.40-320, the duty to provide informed consent is upon "health care providers"; and KRS 304.40-260 expressly includes hospitals within the definition of that term. The court had no doubt that the duty exists and is breached at peril. *Id.* at 862.

Discussion

1. What procedures should hospitals have in place to ensure that patients are properly informed as to procedures that they are about to undergo?
2. What are the pros and cons of general and specific consent? Which is more effective?
3. What liability, if any, should be imparted to the physician ordering the CT scan? Discuss your answer.

2. INFORMED CONSENT/ALTERNATIVE PROCEDURES

Citation: *Stover v. Surgeons*, 635 A.2d 1047 (Pa. Super. Ct. 1993)

Facts

A patient suffered damage to her heart valves as a result of childhood rheumatic fever. Dr. Ford, one of a group of physicians the patient consulted after her condition had worsened, informed the patient that she needed a heart valve replacement. Testimony from Dr. Ford revealed that he briefly reviewed the details of the surgery with the patient. She indicated that she was told only that mechanical valves outlasted natural tissue valves. She further stated that she was never informed about the risks associated with installing mechanical valves, including the Beall valve that was implanted in her. Thromboemboli, strokes, and the lifelong use of anticoagulants, which are common side effects of valve replacements, were never discussed with her. Dr. Zikria performed the surgery, and could not recall discussing any risks other than clotting risks associated with the implantation. After the surgery, the patient suffered severe, perma-

nent brain damage from multiple episodes of thromboemboli directly caused by the valve implantation. She then sued for lack of informed consent, and the jury returned a verdict for her. The physicians appealed.

Issue

Does the doctrine of informed consent include the selection of a valve to be installed in a patient?

Holding

The Superior Court of Pennsylvania held that the physicians had to discuss alternative prostheses with the patient, where it represented medically recognized alternatives. Evidence that the heart valve actually implanted was no longer in general use at the time of operation was relevant and material to the issue of informed consent.

Reason

Although the physicians argued that the choice of prosthesis should belong to them, the court held that if there are other recognized medically sound alternatives, the patient must be informed about the risks and benefits of them in order to make a sound treatment judgment, including the desire to execute a waiver of consent. The agreement between the physician and the patient is contractual. Therefore, in order for valid consent to occur, there must be a finding that both parties understood the nature of the procedure, including what any possible as well as expected results would be. The consent is not valid if the patient did not understand the operation to be performed, its seriousness, the disease or incapacity, and the possible results. Physicians must disclose risks a reasonable person would consider material to his or her decision of whether to undergo treatment. In the instant case, the physicians failed to inform the patient about the recognized risks of the valve that was implanted.

Finally, the court reasoned that there were alternative valves available that were never discussed with the patient. In order to arrive at an informed decision concerning her treatment, it was material for her to have been told about the alternatives and their risks and benefits.

Discussion

1. What are the elements of informed consent, including the responsibilities of the physician and patient?

2. What are the responsibilities of the hospital in ensuring that informed consent has been obtained from the patient?

3. REFUSAL OF CONSENT/MINOR CHILD

Citation: *Banks v. Medical Univ. of S.C.*, 444 S.E.2d 519 (S.C. 1994)

Facts

The mother of an eight-year-old patient, Phaedra, brought action against physicians and medical university after Phaedra died from pulmonary emboli. The plaintiff alleged wrongful death and survival actions as well as actions for battery, deprivation of liberty interests, breach of duty, and breach of contract. The plaintiff was a Jehovah's Witness, opposed to blood transfusions. She claimed a viable cause of action for battery on the ground that no emergency existed justifying the administration of blood plasma to Phaedra.

On December 8, 1989, the plaintiff took Phaedra to Dr. Read's office. The child was suffering from respiratory distress and intense hip pain. Dr. Read had her transported and admitted to Medical University. Thereafter, she was examined and treated by Dr. Tecklenburg, Dr. Cochran, Dr. Otherson, Dr. Bailey, and Dr. Wright. In seeking to diagnose the source of an infection, the doctors performed exploratory surgery, removed her appendix, administered cardiac resuscitation, and gave her blood transfusions. Tragically, final resuscitative efforts were unsuccessful and Phaedra died. The cause of death was pulmonary emboli, blood clotting in the lungs caused by a protein C blood disorder.

Summary judgment was granted on the battery cause of action. The circuit court granted summary judgment for the physicians on actions for battery, deprivation of liberty interests, and breach of duty. An appeal was taken.

Issue

Did an issue of material fact exist as to whether Phaedra was in a life-threatening situation that would have justified administration of blood transfusions without parental consent?

Holding

The Supreme Court of South Carolina held that there was a fact issue as to whether Phaedra was in a life-threatening situation that would have justified administration of blood transfusions without parental consent, thus precluding summary judgment.

Reason

The plaintiff conceded that she had no authority to withhold necessary medical treatment from her child even if such treatment was contrary to her religious views. However, the plaintiff contended that the transfusions were not necessary and, therefore, her consent was required. The plaintiff presented an issue of material fact as to whether Phaedra was in a life-threatening situation when she presented testimony of an expert witness, Dr. Paolini, to establish that there was no emergency justifying the transfusion of blood to Phaedra. Summary judgment was therefore improperly granted on the battery cause of action.

Discussion

1. Do you agree with the court's decision? Explain.
2. Under what circumstances do you believe the state should interfere with religious beliefs when considering treatment for a minor child (e.g., the administration of blood)?
3. Under what circumstances do you think an adult should have the right to refuse treatment?

4. INFORMED CONSENT/REFUSAL OF BLOOD/ BLOOD ADMINISTERED

Citation: *Matter of Hughes*, 611 A.2d 1148 (N.J. Super. Ct. 1992)

Facts

On May 13, 1991, Mrs. Hughes, a 39-year-old devout Jehovah's Witness, was admitted to the hospital to undergo a hysterectomy. A principal tenet of the Jehovah's Witness faith is the belief that receiving blood or blood products into one's body precludes resurrection and everlasting life after death. At the time of her admission to the hospital, Mrs. Hughes signed forms expressing her desire not to receive any blood or blood products. She also verbally expressed this intention to her treating physician, Dr. Ances. Unanticipated problems arose during surgery that, in Dr. Ances' opinion, required blood transfusions to save Mrs. Hughes' life. Dr. Ances contacted Mr. Hughes, Mrs. Hughes' husband, to discuss the emergency situation and his wife's need for blood. While on the phone, Mr. Hughes, also a Jehovah's Witness, authorized transfusions.

On May 14, 1991, the hospital initiated an emergency hearing before a judge for the purpose of having a temporary guardian appointed for Mrs. Hughes to allow additional transfusions after the surgery. She was unconscious and incapable of expressing her desires at the time.

Dr. Ances testified that Mrs. Hughes, who had been his patient for six weeks, told him that she did not want blood products. He informed her that a time could arise when blood might be needed to save her life. He also told her that, given the procedure and the size of the uterus, it was unlikely that she would need blood during the surgery. Dr. Ances was aware that Mrs. Hughes had signed hospital forms refusing blood. Dr. Ances told the judge that he assumed Mrs. Hughes was aware of the ramifications of refusing the blood and therefore did not specifically discuss them with her. After hearing testimony from Dr. Ances and Mrs. Hughes' family, the judge found that the evidence was unclear as to whether she would want blood or blood products if it meant saving her life. As a result, the judge appointed the hospital's risk manager as temporary guardian for the limited purpose of giving consent to the administration of blood and blood products. The order explicitly extended only until Mrs. Hughes regained consciousness and became competent to make her own decisions. Mrs. Hughes received blood transfusions and recovered. Upon regaining competency, she withdrew the hospital's right to transfuse blood.

Issue

Did the court err in making a temporary emergency decision to appoint a medical guardian?

Holding

The Superior Court of New Jersey held that the judge's decision to appoint a temporary medical guardian for Mrs. Hughes was legally supportable.

Reason

The doctrine of informed consent was developed to protect the right of self-determination in matters of medical treatment. Self-determination encompasses the right to refuse medical treatment and is a right protected by common law as well as by the federal and state constitutional right to privacy. The New Jersey Supreme court has repeatedly addressed the right to decline medical treatment in situations where the patient is opposed to prolonging an otherwise irreversible condition. The distinguishing factor in this case, however, is that the transfusion can preserve a healthy young woman's life, not prolong a painful and imminent death. The Pennsylvania Supreme court affirmed a trial judge's decision to appoint a temporary guardian to consent to blood transfusions when a patient is unconscious. The court reasoned that medical intervention necessary to preserve life requires nothing less than a "fully conscious contemporaneous decision by the patient. . . ." *In re Estate of Darone*, 349 Pa. Super. Ct. 59, 502 A.2d 1271 (1985), *aff'd*, 517 Pa. 3, 534 A.2d 452, 455 (1987). In New Jersey, the decision maker must determine and effectuate, insofar as possible, the decision that the patient would have made if competent. Any information bearing on the person's intent may be an appropriate aid in determining what course of treatment the patient would have wished to pursue.

A subjective standard was held by the Supreme Court of New Jersey to be "applicable in every surrogate-refusal-of-treatment case, regardless of the patient's medical condition of life-expectancy." Under this standard, life-sustaining treatment may be withdrawn or withheld when there is clear and convincing evidence that if the patient were competent, she would decline the treatment. *Id.* at 1152. The present facts indicate that Mrs. Hughes specifically advised Dr. Ances and family members of her desire not to receive blood or blood products. She further directed the hospital and her physician, in writing, to refrain from giving her a transfusion. Yet, some uncertainty remained as to what Mrs. Hughes may have desired had she been competent and understood the gravity of the situation. Mrs. Hughes' statements were made in the context of an impending hysterectomy—a procedure Dr. Ances advised would probably not require a transfusion. At no time did Mrs. Hughes discuss with Dr. Ances the risk of complications during surgery or that she could bleed to death during a routine hysterectomy. Therefore, a doubt existed as to whether Mrs. Hughes had made a fully informed and knowing decision to refuse blood if this meant her death. Any glimmer of uncertainty as to Mrs. Hughes' desires in an emergency situation should be resolved "in favor of preserving life." *In re Conroy*, 98 N.J. at 368, 486 A.2d 1209 (1985).

An approach to reinforce a patient's wishes is to have the patient sign forms prior to medical treatment. These suggested forms should be distinguished from those signed by Mrs. Hughes prior to her surgery. Here, she signed a standard hospital form entitled "Refusal to Permit Blood Transfusion," which used a fill-in-the-blanks type approach. The form stated:

> I request that no blood or blood derivatives be administered to Alice Hughes [typewritten on original form] during the hospitalization. I hereby release the hospital, its personnel, and the attending physi-

cian from any responsibility whatever for unfavorable reactions or any untoward results due to my refusal to permit the use of blood or its derivatives and I fully understand the possible consequences of such refusal on my part. The consequences of this refusal have been explained to me by———.
Id. at 1153.

Mrs. Hughes and a witness signed the form, but there was no indication in the space provided that the consequences of her refusal had been explained to her in the context of this particular operation. These proposed forms must contain an unequivocal statement that under any and all circumstances, blood is not to be used and an acknowledgment that the consequences of the refusal were fully supplied to the patient. The form should fully release the physician, all medical personnel, and the hospital from liability should complications arise from the failure to administer blood, thereby resolving any doubt as to the physician's responsibility to his patient. If a patient refuses to sign such a form, the physician should then decide whether to continue with treatment or aid the patient in finding another physician. *Id.* at 1153.

The court emphasized that this case arose in the context of elective surgery. This was not an emergency situation where the physician and patient did not have time to fully discuss the potential risks of the surgery and the depth of the patient's religious beliefs. A Jehovah's Witness patient has an obligation to make medical preferences unequivocally known to the treating physician, including the course to follow if life-threatening complications should arise. This protects the patient's right to freedom of religion and self-determination, as well as the hospital's obligation to preserve life whenever possible. *Id.*

Discussion

1. Do you agree with the court's finding? Explain.
2. Under what conditions might it be reasonable to administer blood to a Jehovah's Witness?

5. LACK OF INFORMED CONSENT

Citation: *Greynolds v. Kurman*, 632 N.E.2d 946 (Ohio Ct. App. 1993)

Facts

Mr. Greynolds and his wife brought a medical malpractice action against a physician arising from Mr. Greynolds' stroke caused by an angiogram.

On July 29, 1987, Mr. Greynolds suffered from a transient ischemic attack (TIA). A TIA is a sudden loss of neurological function caused by vascular impairment to the brain. As a result of the TIA, Mr. Greynolds had garbled speech and expressive and perceptive aphasia (a medical term used to describe the loss of the power of expression by speech, writing, or signs, or of comprehending spoken or written language). Mr. Greynolds was taken to a hospital's emergency department where he was met by Dr. Litman, a cardiologist. At Dr. Litman's request, he was examined by Dr. Rafecas, a cardiologist. Dr. Rafecas determined that because of Mr. Greynolds' past medical history, which included previous TIAs, he was at a high risk for a stroke, and sought to pinpoint the exact source of vascular insufficiency to the brain.

On August 3, 1987, after receiving the results of noninvasive tests, Dr. Rafecas ordered a cerebral angiogram. The angiogram was performed by Dr. Kurman. Mr. Greynolds suffered a stroke during the procedure that left him severely disabled.

Mr. Greynolds and his wife filed a medical malpractice action against Dr. Rafecas and Dr. Kurman, asserting that Dr. Rafecas had negligently recommended the procedure and that Dr. Kurman had performed the procedure without obtaining the informed consent of the patient.

Dr. Kurman argued that the trial court erred by refusing to enter judgment for him consistent with the answer to jury interrogatory number three:

> *Interrogatory No. 1:* Do you find there was a failure to obtain informed consent?
>
> *Answer:* Yes.
>
> *Interrogatory No. 2:* If you answered Interrogatory No. 1 yes, then state specifically in what manner Dr. Kurman's care fell below the recognized standards of the medical community?
>
> *Answer:* Mr. Greynolds was not in our estimation capable of comprehending the consent form. Therefore, Dr. Kurman should have obtained consent from the next-of-kin, specifically, Mrs. Greynolds.
>
> *Interrogatory No. 3:* If you answered yes to interrogatory No. 1 and you found that Mr. Greynolds did not consent to the procedure, do you find that a reasonable person would have consented to the procedure?
>
> *Answer:* Yes. *Id.* at 949.

Dr. Kurman moved the trial court to grant him a judgment notwithstanding the verdict because the jury's answer to interrogatory number three was inconsistent with the jury's general verdict. The trial court overruled Dr. Kurman's motion and entered judgment for the plaintiffs. Dr. Kurman appealed.

Issue

Was there sufficient evidence to support a judgment for the plaintiffs?

Holding

The Court of Appeals of Ohio held that the evidence was sufficient to support a judgment in favor of the patient and his wife.

Reason

In determining whether a judgment in a civil case is supported by sufficient evidence, the court examines whether the judgment is supported by credible evidence going to all the essential elements of the case. The jury needed to determine that the risks involved in the cerebral angiogram were not disclosed to Mr. Greynolds, that the risks involved in the procedure materialized and caused his stroke, and that a reasonable person in the position of Mr. Greynolds would have decided against having the angiogram had the risks associated with the procedure been disclosed to him. The jury concluded that Mr. Greynolds did not consent to the angiogram because he "was not . . . capable of comprehending the consent form," and further noted that Dr. Kurman should have sought consent from the next of kin, specifically, Mrs. Greynolds. *Id.* at 951. Given the evidence of Mr. Greynolds' condition when he signed the consent forms, his past medical history, and the fact that he was at an increased risk to suffer complications during an angiogram, the court found that there was sufficient evidence to support a finding of lack of informed consent.

Discussion

1. What would constitute informed consent?
2. Who should describe the risks associated with a procedure to the patient?

6. NO CONSENT/WRONG PROCEDURE

Citation: *Marsh v. Crawford Long Hosp.*, 44 S.E.2d 357 (Ga. App. 1994)

Facts

A patient brought an action against a hospital and physician alleging professional negligence, fraud, and conspiracy. The superior court granted summary judgment to the hospital. The patient appealed. The court of appeals held that there was a material issue of fact as to whether the hospital employees breached their duty of care to the patient by allegedly confusing the patient's records regarding which surgical procedure was to be performed on the patient, thus precluding summary judgment for the hospital. In her complaint, Ms. Marsh alleged that she requested and consented to an abdominal liposuction; however, Dr. Bostwick performed an abdominoplasty, a more invasive surgery, which left a scar across her entire abdomen. She also alleged that Dr. Bostwick and the hospital conspired to keep her from discovering their alleged mistake. The nursing assessment form, filled out upon Ms. Marsh's admission to the hospital, indicated that she was scheduled for bilateral mastectomy and liposuction. The intraoperative record indicated that the operative procedure to be performed was an abdominoplasty and a bilateral mastectomy. The intraoperative record also contained a checklist for the verification of the procedure location and acknowledgment of consent. This section of the intraoperative record was not completed. Furthermore, Ms. Marsh maintains that she signed a consent to surgery form on which she handwrote her consent for liposuction because the consent form listed only the bilateral mastectomy procedure. No such consent form is contained in the record. The consent form contained in the record reflects that Ms. Marsh consented to a bilateral mastectomy and an abdominoplasty. She deposed that this consent form was presented to her after the surgery and that she was told to sign it by the physician's assistant. On appeal, Ms. Marsh contends that the trial court erred in granting the hospital's motion for summary judgment "by apparently determining the hospital's nurses had no duty as to Ms. Marsh and that such responsibility fell on the shoulders of Dr. Bostwick." Ms. Marsh's experts and several nurses from the hospital deposed that a patient's chart should be cross-referenced to determine that the appropriate procedure is being performed. Ms. Marsh alleges that the hospital failed to discover the discrepancies in the documents contained in her chart with respect to the procedure to be performed. The hospital argued that the physician is in charge of the operating room and that the hospital's nursing staff is not responsible for mistakes made by the physician regarding what procedure is performed. Dr. Bostwick made the medical determination for an abdominoplasty. However, the hospital's nursing staff never discussed with Ms. Marsh or Dr. Bostwick the discrepancies in Ms. Marsh's records with regard to what procedure was to be performed. The supreme court determined in *Hoffman*, 260 Ga. at 590, 397

S.E.2d 696 (1990) that "[t]here is no transfer of liability [to the physician] for the negligence of an employee in the performance of clerical or administrative tasks not requiring the exercise of medical judgment even though these tasks are related to the treatment of the patient." The trial court in the instant case, therefore, erred in determining that the hospital owed no duty to Ms. Marsh and it is for the jury to determine whether the hospital breached its duty of reasonable care.

Issue

What medical/legal issues can you identify in this case?

Holding

What decision would you make?

Reason

What was the reasoning of your finding?

Discussion

1. Develop a discussion question.

7. INFORMED CONSENT/RISKS

Citation: *Warren v. Schecter*, 67 Cal. Rptr. 2d 573 (Cal. App. 1997)

Facts

Janet Warren was diagnosed as having a stomach ulcer in December 1981. She was initially treated by Dr. Feldman, who referred her to Dr. Schecter, a surgeon. Dr. Schecter sought to perform surgery to remove the portions of the stomach containing the ulcer, which was not healing completely. One of the significant risks of gastric surgery is decreased calcium absorption, leading to early and severe metabolic bone disease (osteoporosis, osteomalacia, or bone pain). Studies have reported that up to 38 percent of patients develop early severe osteoporosis following such surgery. It was Dr. Schecter's role as the surgeon to advise Ms. Warren of the risks of surgery in order to obtain her informed consent. Dr. Schecter did not believe osteoporosis, osteomalacia, and bone pain were risks of the surgery and he did not

discuss those substantial risks with her. Dr. Schecter did advise Ms. Warren that she might experience bowel obstructions. Dr. Schecter also informed Ms. Warren of other risks, including "dumping syndrome," involving nausea, and the slight risk of death from the administering of anesthesia during any operation. Based on the limited risks disclosed to Ms. Warren, she consented to the surgery, which Dr. Schecter performed on September 10, 1982.

The surgery recommended by Dr. Schecter was elective. Ms. Warren had nonsurgical options for her ulcers, namely, to discontinue the use of Advil and aspirin, to cease smoking, and to continue with her ulcer medications. Following the surgery, Ms. Warren developed dumping syndrome, a side effect that occurs in about 1 percent of the patients who undergo this procedure. Warren also developed alkaline reflux gastritis, a condition involving the movement of alkaline fluid back into the stomach.

After Ms. Warren was diagnosed with these complications, she returned to Dr. Schecter, who recommended surgery. The purpose of the second surgery was to relieve the pain and discomfort from the first surgery. The second surgery would enhance the risk of bone disease. However, Dr. Schecter again failed to advise Ms. Warren of the risk of metabolic bone disease.

The first manifestation of bone disease occurred on May 4, 1990, when Ms. Warren fractured her back from the mere act of turning over in bed. Until then, there had been no objective evidence of bone disease and no symptoms. Ms. Warren was taken to emergency at UCLA Hospital, where she was advised she had suffered a fracture of one of the lumbar vertebrae. At that time, she first learned that severe metabolic bone disease was a common side effect of the surgeries she had undergone. Dr. Saleh at UCLA advised Ms. Warren that the surgeries had caused the osteoporosis that had led to the fracture. A bone density scan confirmed that Ms. Warren's bones were soft, brittle, and very breakable, and that she had lost a lot of bone mass. Since the onset of bone disease, Ms. Warren's condition continued to deteriorate.

In January 1991, Ms. Warren filed an action for medical negligence, alleging Dr. Schecter is liable under an informed consent theory for performing surgery without advising her of the risk of bone disease. Ms. Warren claimed that had Dr. Schecter warned her of the risk of metabolic bone disease, she would not have consented to surgery. The jury found on special verdict that: (1) Dr. Schecter did not disclose to Ms. Warren all relevant information that would enable her to make an informed decision regarding surgery, (2) a reasonably prudent person in Ms. Warren's position would not have consented to surgery if adequately informed of all the significant perils, and (3) Dr. Schecter's negligence was a cause of injury to Ms. Warren.

Issue

Was the defendant–physician liable under an informed consent theory for performing surgery without advising the plaintiff of the risk of bone disease?

Holding

The plaintiff was entitled to compensation for all damages proximately resulting from the physician's failure to give full disclosure of the risks of surgery. The patient was entitled to recover not only for the undisclosed complications, but also for the disclosed complications, because she would not have consented to any surgery had the true risk been disclosed, and therefore she would not have suffered those complications.

Reason

There must be a causal relationship between the physician's failure to inform and the injury to the plaintiff. Such causal connection arises only if it is established that had revelation been made, consent to treatment would not have been given. Because at the time of trial the uncommunicated hazard has materialized, it would be surprising if the patient did not claim that had he or she been informed of the dangers, he or she would have declined treatment. "Subjectively" he or she may believe so, with the benefit of hindsight. Thus an "objective test" is preferable: that is, what would a prudent person in the patient's position have decided if adequately informed of all significant perils? The prudent person test for causation was established to protect defendant physicians from the unfairness of having a jury consider the issue of proximate cause with the benefit of hindsight.

A plaintiff meets the burden of establishing a causal relationship between the physician's failure to inform and the injury to the plaintiff by demonstrating that a prudent person in the plaintiff's position would have declined the procedure if adequately informed of the risks. The objective standard, which in effect equates the plaintiff with a reasonable person, is appropriate because it protects the defendant–physician from the self-serving testimony of a plaintiff who inevitably will assert at trial that he or she would have refused the procedure if duly advised of the risk. The objective test required of the plaintiff does not prevent the physician from showing, by way of defense, that even though a reasonably prudent person might not have undergone the procedure if properly informed of the perils, this particular plaintiff still would have consented to the procedure. In sum, it was not Ms. Warren's burden to establish that she would not have consented to the surgery even if adequately in-

formed. Under the objective standard, Ms. Warren only had to prove a prudent person in her position would not have consented if adequately informed of the risks. Dr. Schecter failed to provide Ms. Warren with the risks and benefits of the surgical procedures prior to obtaining her consent for the operations. Ms. Warren testified that she would not have consented to either surgery if duly advised of the risk.

Discussion

1. How much information is sufficient in order for informed consent to be effective?
2. Discuss the implications of the following statement: "Patients are generally persons unlearned in the medical sciences and, therefore, except in rare instances, the knowledge of patient and physician are *not in parity*."

8. NURSES AND INFORMED CONSENT

Citation: *Davis v. Hoffman*, 972 F. Supp. 308 (E.D. Pa. 1997)

Facts

The plaintiff, Ms. Davis, experienced pain in her lower abdomen and consulted Dr. Hoffman. He diagnosed her to be suffering from a fibroid uterus and prescribed a dilation and curettage procedure designed to remove the fibroids. The physician further suggested a laparoscopy and hysteroscopy to search for cancer. The physician's nurse, Ms. Puchini, conducted a presurgical interview with the plaintiff in which she described a video hysteroscopy, a dilation and curettage procedure, a resectoscopic removal of submucous fibroids, a laparoscopy, and a laser myomectomy. The plaintiff claimed that she specifically informed Dr. Hoffman and Ms. Puchini that she did not consent to a hysterectomy. They responded that they would awaken her during the operation to obtain her consent before proceeding to a hysterectomy. At no time did they inform the plaintiff that the physician intended to perform a hysterectomy. The plaintiff underwent a procedure that resulted in a hysterectomy, during which no one awakened her to discuss and explore possible alternatives, or if there was to be a hysterectomy, to first obtain her consent. Claiming that the hysterectomy caused her substantial injuries, the plaintiff brought an action against Dr. Hoffman, Ms. Puchini, and the hospital for lack of informed consent.

Issue

Was the nurse or hospital responsible for informing and obtaining consent from the patient as to the surgical procedures to be performed by the surgeon?

Holding

Responsibility for obtaining informed consent lies with the operating surgeon, not the hospital or nurse.

Reason

In response to the plaintiff's allegation that the hospital committed battery by lack of informed consent to the hysterectomy, the hospital asserted that Pennsylvania law places no duty on a hospital to obtain a patient's consent to an operation. The hospital argued that Pennsylvania courts have applied the doctrine of informed consent only to physicians, not to hospitals.

The plaintiff responded that the hospital gratuitously undertook to obtain her consent prior to the operation. Although the consent form used was authored and printed by the hospital, there was no suggestion in the form that the deficiency in consent was in any way causally inadequate. Rather, any failure is attributed to the omissions in the way the form was completed, or in the way the patient was not informed as to what was to be the next phase of the operation. Thus, the form was causally irrelevant and could not be a basis for finding liability.

Because nurses do not have a duty to obtain informed consent, the plaintiff has not stated a claim for battery by lack of informed consent against Ms. Puchini. Pennsylvania law generally imposes no duty on persons other than surgeons to obtain informed consent before performing surgery. Thus, courts have not imposed the duty on nurses. Persons who assist the primary treating physician have no duty to obtain the patient's informed consent.

Discussion

1. Under what circumstances might a hospital be responsible for ensuring that a patient's informed consent is obtained prior to a medical or surgical intervention (e.g., research protocols, hospital-owned physician practices)?
2. Discuss the circumstances under which a nurse might be responsible for obtaining a patient's informed consent.

9. INFORMED CONSENT/PHYSICIAN'S DUTY TO OBTAIN

Citation: *Mathias v. St. Catherine's Hosp., Inc.*, 569 N.W.2d 330 (Wis. App. 1997)

Facts

Ms. Mathias, a patient of Dr. Witt's at St. Catherine's Hospital, delivered a full-term son by Caesarean on February 2, 1993, while she was under general anesthesia. While in the operating room, Dr. Witt indicated that he needed a particular instrument that would be used in a tubal ligation. The nurses Ms. Snyder and Ms. Perri, employees of St. Catherine's, looked at Ms. Mathias' chart. Ms. Snyder informed Dr. Witt that she did not see a signed consent form for that procedure. In deposition testimony, Ms. Snyder stated that Dr. Witt replied, "Oh, okay."

Dr. Witt performed a tubal ligation. Three days after the procedure had been done, a nurse brought Ms. Mathias a consent form for the procedure. This nurse told Ms. Mathias that the form was "just to close up our records." The nurse testified in her deposition that she signed Ms. Perri's name on that same consent form and backdated it to February 2, 1993, the day the surgery was performed. As the trial court noted in its oral decision granting summary judgment, these actions after the surgery are immaterial to the issue of the hospital's duty to Ms. Mathias. The trial court granted summary judgment dismissing St. Catherine's from their medical malpractice action and from an order denying reconsideration. Mr. and Ms. Mathias appealed the summary judgment contending that the hospital owed a duty to Ms. Mathias to prevent her physician from performing a tubal ligation for which there was no signed consent form.

Issue

Did the hospital owe a duty to Ms. Mathias to prevent her physician from performing a tubal ligation for which there was no consent? Did the trial court err in granting summary judgment to St. Catherine's?

Holding

St. Catherine's fulfilled its duty of ordinary care to Ms. Mathias and therefore is not liable. The trial court's grant of summary judgment was affirmed.

Reason

The law in Wisconsin on informed consent is well settled. In *Scaria v. St. Paul Fire & Marine Ins. Co.*, 68 Wis. 2d 1, 18, 227 N.W.2d 647, 651, 656 (1975), the court held that the duty to advise a patient of the risks of treatment lies with the physician. In that case, a patient became paralyzed from the waist down after a diagnostic test that involved injecting dye into his system. The court was explicit in pointing out that the duty to obtain informed consent lay with the physician, not the hospital.

The duty of the physician to ensure that a patient gives an informed consent to any medical treatment is codified in § 448.30 Wis. Stat., which requires:

> Any physician who treats a patient shall inform the patient about the availability of all alternate, viable medical modes of treatment and about the benefits and risks of these treatments. The physician's duty to inform the patient under this section does not require disclosure of:
>
> 1. information beyond what a reasonably well-qualified physician in a similar medical classification would know
> 2. detailed technical information that in all probability a patient would not understand
> 3. risks apparent or known to the patient
> 4. extremely remote possibilities that might falsely or detrimentally alarm the patient
> 5. information in emergencies where failure to provide treatment would be more harmful to the patient than treatment
> 6. information in cases where the patient is incapable of consenting

This statute is the cornerstone of the hospital's duty in this case. The court noted that the legislature limited the application of the duty to obtain informed consent to the treating physician. While the record is littered with semantic arguments about whether this is a case of nonconsent or lack of informed consent, what the Mathiases seek is to extend the duty of ensuring informed consent to the hospital.

The duty to inform rests with the physician and requires the exercise of delicate medical judgment. A cogent explanation of the reasons for adopting this principle was set out in *Kelly v. Methodist Hosp.*, 444 Pa. Super. 427, 664 A.2d 148, 151 (1995), in which the court held:

> Beyond our conclusion Pennsylvania law does not recognize the cause of action asserted by appellants, we find compelling reasons for not imposing upon hospitals the duty of obtaining informed consent. It is the surgeon and not the hospital who has the education, training and experience necessary to advise each patient of risks associated with the proposed surgery. Likewise, by virtue of his relationship with the patient, the physician is in the best position to know the patient's medical history and to evaluate and explain the risks of a particular operation in light of the particular medical history.

Wisconsin has embodied this principle in § 448.30, which provides specific guidance for physicians to determine what information needs to be revealed while not unduly alarming the patient.

In *Kelley v. Kitahama*, 675 So. 2d 1181 (La. Ct. App. 1996), another case that is instructive, the plaintiff argued that once the hospital "undertook to verify, prior to surgery that informed consent existed," it breached its duty by allowing the surgery to proceed. *See id.* at 1182. This premise was rejected by the court in upholding summary judgment. It held:

> While we agree with Kelley's argument that there are facts at issue in the case as to whether the surgeon verbally provided her with the required information regarding her surgery to which she consented, we do not find that those factual issues are sufficient to defeat the [hospital's] motion for summary judgment. Those facts are not material to the question before us of whether [the hospital] had a duty to ensure informed consent before the surgery. Taking the facts in the light most favorable to Kelley, and assuming that she was not adequately informed prior to her consent to the surgery, we still find no liability in [the hospital] for the alleged failure to adequately inform her. *Id.* at 1183.

The Wisconsin statute, § 448.30, specifies only that a physician obtain informed consent. The legislature could have enumerated other responsible entities had it chosen to do so. It did not. Furthermore, under the plain language of the statute, buttressed by Wisconsin case law and the reasoning of other courts, the appeals court concluded that under the facts of this case summary judgment in favor of St. Catherine's was appropriate.

The Mathiases, however, contend that the nurses had a duty to act under a theory of foreseeability. They argue that "[w]hen one assumes a duty towards another person, one becomes responsible as a participant if the duty is not carried out with reasonable care and caution." According to the Mathiases, "[t]he duty arises when Nurse Perri realizes that the consent form for sterilization is the only form that is not signed, which is a red flag to her, and should have been to any healthcare provider in a modern hospital context."

An act or the omission of an act may form the foundation of a cause of action only when it appears that a duty was owing. At issue here is a determination of what is encompassed by the nurse's duty of ordinary care in this situation. Therefore, having concluded that St. Catherine's did not have a legal duty to ensure that Dr. Witt had obtained informed consent from the patient, the issue presented is whether, under the circumstances of this case, the actions of the nurses conformed to the standard of ordinary care.

The duty to explain the procedure to Ms. Mathias and to obtain her informed consent lay with Dr. Witt. The nurses in the operating room checked Ms. Mathias' medical chart to ascertain whether there were appropriate signed consent forms. Ms. Snyder informed Dr. Witt that a written consent form for the tubal ligation was not in Ms. Mathias' chart. According to Ms. Snyder's deposition, Dr. Witt acknowledged having heard her comment. Although Ms. Mathias' chart did not contain the signed form, that fact alone would not lead a reasonable person to conclude that Dr. Witt was performing a nonconsensual procedure. Based on Dr. Witt's response and the information they had available to them, the nurses had no reason to conclude that the absence of the form was anything more than a clerical error. Ms. Snyder informed Dr. Witt that the chart did not contain a signed consent form; in this instance, neither Ms. Snyder nor Ms. Perri had any duty to take further action.

There were allegations regarding the hospital's obtaining a signed consent form from Ms. Mathias three days after the surgery. This issue was argued extensively in the plaintiffs' affidavits in opposition to the summary judgment motion. Furthermore, evidence of what occurred relating to a consent form after the tubal ligation was performed is immaterial to the legal issue of St. Catherine's duty to Ms. Mathias. The appeals court concurred with the trial court that any evidence as to these actions was merely cumulative.

Discussion

1. Do you agree with the court's finding that the hospital had no legal duty to ensure that Dr. Witt obtain informed consent from Ms. Mathias? Explain.
2. What finding would the Joint Commission on Accreditation of Healthcare Organizations (Joint Commission) make during an accreditation survey if its hospital surveyors found that Ms. Mathias had undergone surgery without informed consent? Should the hospital be penalized by the Joint Commission for the surgeon's failure to obtain informed consent? Explain.
3. What issues do you see in another nurse's decision to sign Ms. Perri's name on the consent form and then backdate it to February 2, 1993?

Legal Reporting Obligations

1. CHILD ABUSE STATUTE/IMMUNITY PROVIDED PSYCHOLOGIST

Citation: *Michaels v. Gordon*, 439 S.E.2d 722 (Ga. Ct. App. 1993)

Facts

As part of an investigation of a report of possible child molestation, the Gwinnett County Department of Family and Children Services placed two children in the temporary custody of a foster family and referred one child, C.J.M., to Dr. Gordon, a licensed psychologist, for evaluation. After two interviews, including a psychological evaluation, Dr. Gordon formed the professional opinion that C.J.M. had been sexually molested. Based in part on statements made by the child, Dr. Gordon further believed that the perpetrator of the suspected molestation was C.J.M.'s father. At a hearing before the juvenile court, the court determined that the evidence adduced did not support a finding that C.J.M. had been abused by his father or that he was at risk at home. Custody was returned to the parents.

C.J.M.'s parents subsequently initiated an action for medical malpractice on behalf of themselves and the two minors. After extensive discovery, Dr. Gordon moved for summary judgment, based in part on a claim of immunity from liability as provided by the child abuse reporting statute, OCGA § 19-7-5. This motion was granted by the trial court and the parents appealed, arguing that the immunity provisions of OCGA § 19-7-5 do not apply to Dr. Gordon because she was not a "mandatory reporter" under that statute. OCGA § 19-7-5(f) provides:

Any person . . . participating in the making of a report . . . or participating in any judicial proceeding or any other proceeding resulting [from such a report of suspected child abuse] shall in so doing be immune from any civil or criminal liability that might otherwise be incurred or imposed, provided such participation pursuant to this Code section . . . is made in good faith. *Any person making a report, whether required by this Code section or not, shall be immune from liability as provided in this subsection* [emphasis added].

Issue

Was the psychologist immune from liability under the child abuse reporting statute? Did the evidence establish that the psychologist acted in bad faith, therefore depriving her of immunity under the child abuse statute?

Holding

The Court of Appeals of Georgia held that the child abuse reporting statute's grant of immunity from liability extended to the psychologist. The evidence did not establish bad faith on the part of the psychologist so as to deprive her of such immunity.

Reason

The statutory language "participating in the making of a report" presupposes the involvement of more than one person and so includes acts beyond the initial communication of suspected child abuse because of a visual inspection of the child, or observed behavior, or the child's statement. The grant of qualified immunity covers every person who, in good faith, participates over time in the making of a report to a child welfare agency.

The parents' evidence of alleged unprofessional acts and omissions committed by Dr. Gordon would authorize a finding that she was negligent or exercised bad judgment in formulating her professional opinion that the child had been sexually abused. However, this proof of mere negligence or bad judgment is not proof that Dr. Gordon refused to fulfill her professional duties, out of some harmful motive, or that she consciously acted for some dishonest purpose. There was no competent evidence that Dr. Gordon acted in bad faith.

Discussion

1. What is immunity?
2. Should immunity extend to the general public?

2. CHILD ABUSE STATUTE/IMMUNITY PROVIDED HOSPITAL AND PHYSICIANS

Citation: *Heinrich v. Conemaugh Valley Mem'l Hosp.*, 8 A.2d 53 (Pa. Super. 1994)

Facts

Molly, a young child, was involved in an accident whereby her walker tipped over, causing her to strike the back of her head on the kitchen floor. On September 27, 1991, appellant Ms. Heinrich noticed that Molly was experiencing some discomfort associated in and around the area of her ears and scheduled an appointment with Dr. Caroff. Dr. Caroff examined Molly, diagnosed her as possibly beginning an ear infection, and prescribed an antibiotic. The next day Ms. Heinrich noticed swelling on and around Molly's left temple, ear, and eye. Because the swelling persisted, she brought Molly to the emergency department of Conemaugh Valley Memorial Hospital. Molly's injury was classified by the triage coordinator as "non-urgent." Dr. George examined Molly and then left. Dr. George returned with Dr. Opila, who also examined Molly. According to the complaint, Dr. George and Dr. Opila observed a non–life-threatening swelling on the left side of the child's head that exhibited no scrapes or abrasions of the skin and arbitrarily concluded that the child suffered a hematoma or bruises to that area of the child's head.

Dr. Opila returned and asked Ms. Heinrich to consent to X-rays of Molly's head, and she consented. Molly was taken for X-rays and was brought back to the emergency department. Ms. Heinrich claims that she could clearly hear a number of nurses at the emergency department desk loudly discussing Molly's condition and treatment and the allegations of abuse and neglect in front of a busy emergency department waiting room. The X-rays were of Molly's entire body and were not limited to X-rays of the child's head to which Ms. Heinrich consented.

Dr. George told Ms. Heinrich that the X-rays were negative, and that he would attempt to contact Dr. Caroff to confirm the results of his examination. Shortly thereafter, Dr. Opila returned and once again began questioning the Ms. Heinrich and the grandparents as to the source of Molly's injury. During this questioning, Dr. Opila gave an opinion that the swelling observed was most consistent with having had a blow in that area of the head. Ms. Heinrich and the grandparents were introduced to Ms. Stock, who identified herself as an employee of the hospital's Department of Social Services. Ms. Stock stated that she had been contacted by Dr. Opila and asked to ascertain how Molly was injured or the source or cause of the swelling. Ms. Stock questioned Ms. Heinrich and the grandparents for approximately 20 minutes. During this time, Dr. George informed Ms. Heinrich and the grandparents that he had spoken with Dr. Caroff, who reported that there had been no swelling on Molly's head when he examined her the day before. Ms. Heinrich responded angrily that she had told him earlier that she had not noticed any swelling prior to the morning of September 28, 1991.

Ms. Stock left and returned shortly thereafter to inform Ms. Heinrich and the grandparents that the physicians wanted to admit Molly in order to observe the head injury for 24 hours. Shortly thereafter, she again began to question Ms. Heinrich and the grandparents. Dr. George entered and informed Ms. Heinrich that he wanted to admit Molly for observation. Ms. Heinrich responded that she wanted Dr. Caroff to examine Molly, or she wanted to take Molly to another hospital because the child had not received any treatment for her swelling since arrival.

Dr. Cole and Dr. Devellen entered the examining room and introduced themselves as family practitioners. They then proceeded to examine Molly. During this time, Dr. Devellen cleaned Molly's ears and observed that her eardrums were slightly red and stated that the swelling was not consistent with a blow to the head because there was no bruising. Ms. Heinrich spoke with Ms. Stouffer by telephone, who introduced herself as a representative of Cambria County Children and Youth Services (CYS). She informed Ms. Heinrich that if she did not admit Molly, CYS would come to the hospital and take custody of the child. Ms. Heinrich informed Ms. Stouffer that she had never refused to admit the child, but had only objected to the fact that the child was not receiving any treatment for the swelling.

Dr. Green, who was covering for Dr. Caroff, examined Molly. He stated that the physicians had diagnosed the swelling as cellulitis from an inner ear infection. On September 30, 1991, Dr. Caroff examined Molly. He informed Ms. Heinrich that he had already contacted CYS in an attempt to resolve any misunderstanding and to correct any misinformation. Dr. Caroff further stated that Dr. Sheridan of Johnstown Pediatrics Association would examine Molly later that day. At approximately 10:00 A.M., a pediatric resident of Johnstown Pediatrics Association examined Molly and reviewed the medical case history with Ms. Heinrich.

On October 1, 1991, Dr. Sheridan and two of his associates examined Molly and further questioned Ms. Heinrich and the grandparents. Dr. Sheridan stated that the fall on her head was the cause of the swelling and diagnosed the child's condition as a subaponeourosis hematoma, caused by a broken blood vessel caused by the fall in the walker. At this time, he directed that Molly was not suffering from an infection. He notified Ms. Heinrich that he was contacting Dr. Caroff concerning Molly's discharge from the hospital. At 5:30 P.M., Ms. Ott, a social worker, spoke with Ms. Heinrich and informed her that she was still under investigation for suspected child abuse. At approximately 6:00 P.M., Molly was discharged from the hospital by authorization of Dr. Caroff. On October 3, 1991, Ms. Heinrich was informed by Ms. Stouffer that the report of suspected child abuse was held to be unfounded, and that she promised to destroy the paperwork as soon as possible.

Ms. Heinrich, in her complaint, asserted that she has been confronted by friends, family members, neighbors, and acquaintances who had independently learned of the above incident and the investigation of suspected child abuse. Ms. Heinrich also asserted that she has suffered from physical manifestations of stress resulting from this incident. She asserted that the actions of the hospital, by and through its employees, representatives, and agents during their dealings and conversations with her, were insulting and outrageous and taken in bad faith and with bad motive, due to their preconceived suspicions, biases, and prejudice based on her economic situation.

A four-count complaint was filed in which causes of action against the hospital for corporate negligence and defamation were alleged, as were causes of action for intentional and negligent infliction of emotional distress. The hospital filed preliminary objections, in which they raised, among other things, immunity from suit under Section 6318 of the Child Protective Services Law. After hearing the argument, the trial court issued an order in which it: (1) dismissed Dr. Cole, Dr. Devellen, and Ms. Ott from the lawsuit because they executed their duties in good faith, and because the second amended complaint failed to provide

specific material facts that would indicate bad faith in order to overcome the statutory presumption of good faith; (2) dismissed the claim of corporate negligence on the basis that the facts alleged in the second complaint were insufficient to constitute a breach of duty, a legal injury, or legal causation; (3) allowed the appellants 20 days to plead more specifically their defamation claim; (4) dismissed the claim for intentional and negligent infliction of emotional distress for failing to state facts that would support extreme and outrageous conduct that rose to and beyond all bounds of decency, and for failing to set forth evidence of any physical or bodily injury; (5) dismissed the claims for punitive damages for failing to state facts that show outrageous behavior on the part of the appellees; and (6) dismissed as defendants the hospital and Dr. Opila, Dr. George, and Ms. Stock under the protection of immunity.

Issue

Did the trial court abuse its discretion or commit an error of law in granting the appellees' preliminary objections to the appellants' seconded amended complaint?

Holding

The superior court held that the appellants failed to overcome statutory presumption of good faith, and thus, the hospital and its agents were immune from liability.

Reason

The purpose of the law is to bring about quick and effective reporting of suspected child abuse so as to serve as a means for providing protective services competently and to prevent further abuse of the children while providing rehabilitative services for them and the parents. To this end, the law requires, under threat of criminal penalty, that health care professionals and others report suspected abuse.

> § 6311. Persons required to report suspected child abuse
> (a) General rule.—Persons who, in the course of their employment, occupation or practice of their profession, come into contact with children shall report or cause a report to be made in accordance with section 6313 (relating to reporting procedure) when they have reason to believe, on the basis of their medical, professional or other training and experience, that a child coming before them in their professional or official capacity is an abused child.

The privileged communication between any professional person required to report and the patient or client of that person shall not apply to situations involving child abuse and shall not constitute grounds for failure to report as required by this chapter.

(b) Enumeration of persons required to report.—Persons required to report under subsection (a) include, but are not limited to, any licensed physician, osteopath, medical examiner, coroner, funeral director, dentist, optometrist, chiropractor, podiatrist, intern, registered nurse, licensed practical nurse, hospital personnel engaged in the admission, examination, care or treatment of persons, a Christian Science practitioner, school administrator, school teacher, school nurse, social services worker, day-care center worker or any other child-care or foster-care worker, mental health professional, peace officer or law enforcement official. 23 Pa. C.S. §§ 6311(a) and (b).

Immunity is clearly provided to those who report under the law:

§ 6318. Immunity from liability
(a) General rule.—A person, hospital, institution, school, facility or agency participating in good faith in the making of a report, cooperating with an investigation or testifying in a proceeding arising out of an instance of suspected child abuse, the taking of photographs or the removal or keeping of a child pursuant to section 6315 (relating to taking child into protective custody) shall have immunity from any civil or criminal liability that might otherwise result by reason of those actions.

(b) Presumption of good faith.—For the purpose of any civil or criminal proceeding, the good faith of a person required to report pursuant to section 6311 (relating to persons required to report suspected child abuse) shall be presumed. 23 Pa. C.S. § 6318.

There is no dispute that all appellees fall within the protection provided under the law. The appellants were afforded three opportunities to amend their complaint so as to assert sufficient specific facts tending to show that the appellees acted in bad faith and thus overcame the statutory presumption. The trial court concluded that the appellants had failed to do so on each occasion. The superior court agreed.

The good faith of the defendant must be judged against an objective standard rather than alleged motives or allegations of maliciousness. The urgency of prompt reporting is stressed throughout the law's provisions. The law does not envision

any prereporting investigation, and, in light of the mandatory reporting procedure and the law's presumption of good faith, the court was unwilling to presume that the failure to conduct such an investigation was in bad faith.

Discussion

1. Do you think the hospital overreacted as to the number of individuals involved in this case? Why?
2. What privacy and confidentiality issues can you identify in this case?

3. FAILURE TO REPORT INCIDENT/EXCLUSION FROM MEDICARE PROGRAM

Citation: *Westin v. Shalala*, 845 F. Supp. 1446 (D. Kan. 1994)

Facts

On December 17, 1984, Ms. Grundmeier, a patient in a nursing facility, was found unconscious and wedged between the mattress and the bedrail in her room. After emergency resuscitation, she was airlifted to a hospital, where she died later that same day.

On November 18, 1985, a grand jury convened and returned an indictment against Ms. Westin in her capacity as the nursing facility's administrator. The indictment charged Ms. Westin with one felony and four misdemeanors.

The Colorado Department of Health, pursuant to the Code of Colorado Regulations at 6 CCR 1011-1 Ch. V § 4.5.4, requires that "accidents and incidents resulting in possible patient injury shall be reported on special report forms. The report shall include date, time, and place of incident; circumstances of the occurrence; signature of witness; time doctor was notified; physician's report; and signature of person making the report. A copy of the report shall be filed in the patient's medical record." Despite these requirements, no incident report was prepared.

On March 13, 1990, upon motion of the district attorney, the court dismissed the case against Ms. Westin. On May 24, 1991, the Inspector General notified Ms. Westin that she was going to be excluded for five years from participation in Medicare and any state health care program because of her conviction of a criminal offense relating to the neglect or abuse of patients. Ms. Westin appealed the Inspector General's decision to the Department of HHS, Departmental Appeals Board (DAB), and an administrative law judge (ALJ) sustained the exclusion imposed. Ms. Westin appealed, and the DAB, Appellate Division, affirmed the ALJ's decision. Ms. Westin then timely appealed the DAB, Appellate Division's, decision.

Issue

Was there sufficient evidence to support the exclusion of Ms. Westin from participating in the Medicare program?

Holding

The United States District Court for the District of Kansas held that there was substantial evidence to support an order excluding Ms. Westin from participation in the Medicare program.

Reason

Ms. Westin argued that there was no evidence that she actually neglected or abused any patient. There is, however, no requirement that the Secretary of HHS demonstrate that actual neglect or abuse of patients occurred, nor is there a requirement that the individual or entity be convicted of an actual offense of patient neglect or abuse. Under Colorado law, Ms. Westin, as an administrator of a nursing home, was required to (1) report all accidents and injuries "resulting in possible patient injury" to the Colorado Department of Health, and (2) file a copy of that report in the patient's medical record. The evidence was clear from the record that the conviction for failing to report the incident occurred while Ms. Grundmeier was a patient at the nursing facility, and that the conviction was connected to the medical services the nursing facility and its employees provided to Ms. Grundmeier. *Id.* at 1452.

Discussion

1. Do you believe the court was too harsh in its decision to exclude the administrator of the nursing facility from participating in the Medicare program for a period of five years? Explain.
2. Why have statutes been enacted that require the reporting of accidents and incidents that result in patient injuries?

4. ACCREDITATION SURVEYS AND STATE ENFORCEMENT OF STANDARDS

Citation: *Evelyn V. v. Kings County Hosp. Ctr.*, 956 F. Supp. 288 (1997)

Facts

The essence of the plaintiffs' claim is that reasonably necessary steps were not taken to ensure that Kings County Hospital complied with established state health standards. The plaintiffs submitted that 42 U.S.C. § 1396a(a)(9) gives them a federal right to such enforcement of state standards. 42 U.S.C. § 1396a(a)(9) states: "A state plan for medical assistance must provide that the State health agency, or other appropriate State medical agency shall be responsible for establishing and maintaining health standards for private or public institutions in which recipients of medical assistance under the plan may receive care or services."

Kings County Hospital Center had a history of noncompliance with health care standards. In January and February 1989, Health and Human Services (HHS) requested that the New York State Department of Health (Department of Health) conduct an allegation survey of the hospital. Based on the survey report, HHS concluded that the hospital was not in compliance with five conditions for participation in Medicare and Medicaid. In April 1989, HHS advised the hospital that a complete Medicare survey would be conducted by the Department of Health, after which the hospital would be expected to submit a plan for correction. HHS warned that if the hospital was unable to achieve compliance with the Medicare conditions, termination action would be pursued.

Before conducting the complete Medicare survey, the Department of Health settled its state enforcement action with the hospital. On April 19, 1989, the hospital agreed to pay a fine and to implement a detailed plan of correction.

In June 1989, the Department of Health conducted the requested survey of the hospital. The hospital was found to be out of compliance with seven conditions for participation in Medicaid and Medicare. Efforts were undertaken by the hospital to correct the cited deficiencies. The Department of Health conducted a follow-up survey in August 1989, and, based on its report, HHS concluded that the hospital had attained compliance with all conditions for participation in Medicare and Medicaid, except those relating to physical environment. HHS accepted the hospital's long-range plan for correction of environment deficiencies. It did, however, advise the hospital that it would no longer be deemed eligible for Medicare and Medicaid participation based on its Joint Commission on Accreditation of Healthcare Organizations (Joint Commission) accreditation. Rather, it would be closely monitored by the Department of Health. Department of Health monitoring reports from September, October, and November 1989 indicate that although the hospital was still experiencing compliance difficulties, significant improvements were being made.

The Department of Health did not conduct, nor does it appear that HHS requested, any comprehensive survey of the hospital in 1990. During that year, the Department of Health investigated 29 specific complaints about the hospital's care and conditions. On-site investigations resulted in the issuance of 11 statements of deficiencies requiring corrections.

From January 7 to January 18, 1991, the Department of Health conducted a federal monitoring survey at the hospital. Based on findings that the hospital was out of compliance with five conditions for participation in Medicare and Medicaid, HHS notified the hospital on March 19, 1991, that its "participation in the Medicare program is being terminated as of May 19, 1991." The hospital was advised that the termination order would be rescinded if it brought itself back to condition-level compliance before the scheduled termination date.

On April 5, 1991, the hospital submitted to the Department of Health a plan of correction and a request for resurvey. The resurvey revealed that although problems had not been completely eliminated, the hospital had managed to achieve condition-level compliance with all federal standards for participation in Medicare and Medicaid except those relating to physical environment. On May 1, 1991, the Department of Health recommended to HHS that the hospital be permitted to continue to participate in the Medicare and Medicaid programs. HHS agreed, and on May 8, 1991, notified the hospital that it was rescinding its previous termination decision. The hospital was warned that because it had not demonstrated the ability to sustain the corrective action outlined in the plan submitted in 1989, the time frames in the current submission would be closely monitored, and the facility would remain under state survey jurisdiction.

A few days later, on May 10, 1991, the Department of Health issued a report finding that the deficiencies noted at the hospital in the January 1991 survey constituted violations of state as well as federal standards. A formal enforcement action was commenced. Negotiations to settle this action were interrupted when the death of a stabbing victim at the hospital raised further questions about the hospital's delivery of care. The Department of Health conducted an investigation into the victim's treatment at the hospital, and in the fall of 1991 cited the hospital for further violations of state health standards.

In October 1991, the Department of Health conducted another federal survey of the hospital and again found several serious departures from federal and state standards. HHS again threatened to terminate the hospital from participation in the Medicare and Medicaid programs, and the Department of Health formally cited the hospital for violations, demanding a plan of correction by November 22, 1991.

The Department of Health resurveyed the hospital in early December 1991 and issued its report to HHS on December 6, 1991. On December 16, 1991, HHS decided once again to rescind its termination of the hospital from the Medicare and Medicaid programs, finding that in the resurvey the hospital had managed to demonstrate condition-level compliance with all requirements except physical environment.

On February 3, 1992, the Department of Health advised the hospital that it was amending the pending state enforcement action to add the deficiencies cited during the October 1991 survey. This action was settled on July 10, 1992. The hospital again agreed to implement a plan of correction. To monitor the hospital's compliance with the plan of correction, the Department of Health was to conduct monitoring visits in October 1992, February 1993, and July 1993. Soon after the October 1991 Department of Health survey, the hospital was surveyed by the Joint Commission to determine whether the hospital should be reaccredited. In January 1992, the Joint Commission notified the hospital that it was recommending against accreditation. The Joint Commission ultimately permitted the hospital to operate with conditional accreditation.

In October 1992, the Department of Health conducted its first monitoring visit of the hospital pursuant to its July 1992 order of settlement with the hospital. The hospital was cited for numerous specific and general violations. The Department of Health demanded that the hospital provide a plan for correction.

In January 1993, the Department of Health conducted a comprehensive state and federal survey of the hospital. Although numerous deficiencies were cited, HHS did not take any action against the hospital. On March 17, 1993, the hospital submitted a plan to the Department of Health to correct the noted deficiencies. Parts of the plan were deemed unacceptable, prompting resubmissions by the hospital in June and July 1993. In July 1993, the Department of Health conducted a monitoring visit of the hospital. Various deficiencies were again noted. In August 1993, the Department of Health accepted the hospital's most recent plan for correction.

In November 1994, the hospital was scheduled to be reviewed by the Joint Commission. Having operated for some time with only conditional accreditation, the hospital understood that it would have to pass the Joint Commission review or lose its accreditation and its status as a Medicare and Medicaid provider. To assist the hospital in preparing for the review, New York City's Health and Hospitals Corporation arranged for a mock survey to be conducted in May 1994. In July 1994, the results were announced: numerous problems still existed. Some changes in management were made and the Health and Hospitals Corporation authorized a one-time allocation of over $1 million to the hospital to address various needs that would be pertinent to the Joint Commission review. These efforts proved successful and the hospital was again accredited by the Joint Commission.

In moving for summary judgment in their favor, the defendants submitted that the plaintiffs failed to state a claim because 42 U.S.C. § 1396a(a)(9) does not confer the right to enforcement of state standards, and even if the court were to find such an enforceable federal right, their actions suffice to satisfy their legal obligations.

As evidence that the state agencies were failing to meet their obligations pursuant to 42 U.S.C. § 1396a(a)(9) with respect to the hospital, the plaintiffs pointed to the various surveys of the hospital over the years revealing noncompliance with health standards. The Department of Health surveyed the hospital to ensure compliance with both federal and state law. 42 U.S.C. § 1395aa(a), expressly referred to in § 1396a(a)(9), provides for the Secretary of HHS to contract with state health agencies to certify those institutions qualifying for Medicaid participation. This law states:

> The Secretary shall make an agreement with any State which is able and willing to do so under which the services of the State health agency or other appropriate State agency (or the appropriate local agencies) will be utilized by him for the purpose of determining whether an institution therein is a hospital or skilled nursing facility, or . . . a home health agency, or . . . a hospice program or . . . a rural health clinic, [or] a rural primary care hospital, . . . or a comprehensive outpatient rehabilitation facility. . . . To the extent that the Secretary finds it appropriate, an institution or agency which such a State (or local) agency certifies is a hospital, skilled nursing facility, rural health clinic, comprehensive outpatient rehabilitation facility, home health agency, or hospice program (as those terms are defined in section 1395x of this title) may be treated as such by the Secretary.

Further, 42 U.S.C. § 1395aa(c) provides for the Secretary of HHS to use state health agencies to conduct surveys of hospitals participating in the Medicaid program. It states:

> The Secretary is authorized to enter into an agreement with any State under which the appropriate State or local agency which performs the certification function described in subsection (a) of this section will survey, on a selective sample basis (or where the Secretary finds that a survey is appropriate because of substantial allegations of the existence of a significant deficiency or deficiencies which would, if found to be present, adversely affect health and safety of patients), hospitals which have an agreement with the Secretary under 1395cc of this title and which are accredited by the Joint Commission on Accreditation of Hospitals. The Secretary shall pay for such services in the manner prescribed in subsection (b) of this section.

42 C.F.R. § 488.26(c)(1) describes the survey process as the means to assess compliance with federal health, safety, and quality standards.

The Secretary of HHS entered into an agreement with the Department of Health to perform the certifications and surveys provided for in these statutes and regulations. It was expressly recognized in the agreement that, in performing its contractual duties, the State acted on behalf of the Secretary.

As a general rule, institutions accredited as hospitals by the Joint Commission are deemed qualified to participate in Medicare and Medicaid. The Secretary of HHS may, however, request a state agency such as the Department of Health to conduct a validation survey to determine whether an accredited hospital does meet Medicare and Medicaid participation standards. The Secretary of HHS may also request that the Department of Health conduct allegation surveys when HHS receives information indicating that a hospital may be out of compliance with the conditions for participation in Medicaid and Medicare, and conduct monitoring surveys to determine if past noted deficiencies have been corrected. Survey reports are submitted to HHS, which makes the final determination as to whether a hospital may continue to participate in the Medicare and Medicaid programs.

Accreditation survey reports constitute recommendations to the Health Care Financing Administration. Based on these recommendations, HHS takes appropriate action. If a survey reveals that a hospital is not in compliance with one or more federal standards, its ability to continue participating in Medicare and Medicaid programs depends on its submission of an acceptable plan of correction for achieving compliance within a reasonable period of time acceptable to the Secretary of HHS. Ordinarily, a deficient hospital is expected to bring itself into compliance with federal conditions within 60 days, but the Secretary of HHS may grant additional time when appropriate. Where noncompliance is acute or persistent, the Secretary of HHS is empowered to terminate a hospital from participation in Medicare and Medicaid programs. The parties agree that such termination would effectively shut down a public hospital because it could not operate without federal funds.

In addition to conducting federally requested surveys, the Department of Health also uses on-site surveys to assess hospitals' compliance with state standards of care. Should deficiencies be detected with respect to these standards, hospitals are required to submit plans of correction, which are reviewed through follow-up surveys. Where appropriate, the Department of Health can commence an enforcement proceeding against a deficient hospital, with possible penalties ranging from a fine to revocation of a hospital's operating certificate and closure.

Issue

Does 42 U.S.C. § 1396a(a)(9) confer on the plaintiffs a federal right enforceable through 42 U.S.C. § 1983 to have the New York State Department of Social Services and the New York State Department of Health take reasonable steps to ensure that hospitals operating as Medicaid providers comply with state standards of operation?

Holding

Because the plaintiffs have no federal right to state enforcement of state standards of health care at hospitals participating in the Medicaid program, summary judgment was granted in favor of the defendants.

Reason

The court had to determine if this case really involved a federal right, as opposed to a claimed violation of federal law. The problem in this case was in deciding precisely what it is Congress mandated in § 1396a(a)(9) for the benefit of Medicaid recipients. Congress requires state Medicaid plans to provide for a state health agency to be responsible for establishing and maintaining health standards for institutions that operate as Medicaid providers. The parties agree that the New York plan provides for the Department of Health to serve this statutory function. They agree that the Department of Health has established standards for state hospitals. Where the parties disagree is in their interpretation of the statute's requirement with respect to maintaining health standards. A thing is "maintained" when it is kept "in a state of repair, efficiency, or validity," when it is "preserve[d] from failure or decline" [*Webster's Third New International Dictionary* 1362 (1986)]. The defendants submitted that the statute thus obligated them to review their health standards and, when necessary, update them to ensure that they remain valid and consistent with current medical practice. The plaintiffs submitted that the statutory obligation is broader— that reasonable efforts must be made to ensure that state hospitals participating in the Medicaid program operate in compliance with established state standards. The court rejected the plaintiffs' construction.

The court noted that, although § 1983 has been used as a vehicle to enforce federal rights embodied in federal regulations as well as statutes, it would be quite remarkable for Congress to federalize a whole body of unspecified state rules and regulations and thereby make the state's enforcement of its own standards a federal right that parties could pursue through private § 1983 actions. The language of § 1396a(a)(9) does not suggest such a sweeping congressional intent. The statute requires simply that a state agency be responsible for establishing and maintaining health standards for participating institutions. An agency can maintain appropriate standards for institutions without having any

enforcement powers over those institutions. Few fields have changed as rapidly in this century as medicine. Surgical procedures, professional training requirements, medication protocols, methods for handling and storing blood, have all evolved considerably, such that standards considered exemplary when § 1396a(a)(9) was first enacted would not be deemed adequate today. Congress wished to ensure that states did not view their § 1396a(a)(9) obligation as static. Rather, they would be expected to maintain, review, and update the health standards they established to ensure that they remained consistent with modern medical practice.

If Congress had wished to mandate enforcement of the state standards, it could easily have expressed this intent by drafting § 1396a(a)(9) to require maintenance of health standards *at* participating institutions, rather than simply *for* participating institutions. As the parties have noted, when the federal government did wish to impose an enforcement obligation on the states with respect to standards for nursing homes, this was plainly expressed. 42 U.S.C. § 1396a(a)(26) requires states to have "medical review teams" conduct "periodic inspections" of such facilities. From 1978 to 1994, 42 C.F.R. § 449.33(5)(iii) required states to review the reports of such medical teams "as they reflect on health and safety requirements and as necessary take appropriate action to achieve compliance or withdraw certification." No such survey or compliance obligation has ever been imposed on states with respect to hospitals.

The plaintiffs submitted that it made no sense that Congress simply wished to require state agencies to promulgate standards and update them from time to time without also contemplating their enforcement. The legislative history reveals that Congress did contemplate local enforcement of state standards, but it did not mandate such enforcement. A senate report indicated that Congress wished to encourage states to improve health care standards while interfering as little as possible in a state's actual articulation or supervision of those standards. Congressional expectations and hopes do not create unambiguous federal rights enforceable through § 1983.

The overall scheme for review of hospitals participating in Medicare and Medicaid is also at odds with the plaintiffs' claim of a federal right to sue state defendants to compel enforcement of state health care standards with respect to hospitals. There is no federal requirement that state agencies ever survey hospitals to assess compliance with their own standards. Instead, the focus of the statute and regulations is on the promulgation and enforcement of federal standards. It is the Secretary of HHS who has sole responsibility for promulgating federal health, safety, and quality standards applicable to hospitals participating in Medicare and Medicaid programs [*see* 42 U.S.C. § 1395x(e)(9)], and who is charged with enforcing these standards by threatening termination.

The focus of this statutory and regulatory scheme on the responsibilities of the Secretary of HHS for the promulgation and enforcement of federal standards of health care necessarily supports the conclusion that a state agency satisfies its § 1396a(a)(9) obligations to "establish and maintain" local standards for health care providers simply by promulgating and then updating these standards. In this way, Congress certainly hoped to encourage better standards of local health care and even their enforcement. Sensitive to differences in regional capabilities, Congress did not create a federal right to any particular state standard or to any level of local enforcement. The core responsibility for ensuring that Medicare and Medicaid providers meet some minimum standard of care remains exclusively with the federal government.

Discussion

1. What was the court's reasoning for not granting the plaintiffs a federal right enforceable through 42 U.S.C. § 1983 to have the New York State Department of Social Services and the New York State Department of Health take reasonable steps to ensure that hospitals operating as Medicaid providers comply with state standards of operation?
2. What are the implications for hospitals that lose their accreditation?

XII

Issues of Procreation

1. ABORTION/STATE IMPOSED RESTRICTIONS

Citation: *Utah Women's Clinic, Inc. v. Leavitt*, 844 F. Supp. 1482 (D. Utah 1994)

Facts

In 1993, the Utah Abortion Act Revision, Senate Bill 60 (S.B. 60; codified at Utah Code Ann. § 76-7-305), was enacted. The legislature closely tailored Senate Bill 60 to those portions of the Pennsylvania law that had already passed constitutional muster in *Planned Parenthood of Southeastern Pennsylvania v. Casey*, 112 S. Ct. 2791, 120 L.E. 2d 674 (1992). Senate Bill 60 provides for informed consent by requiring that certain information be given to the pregnant woman at least 24 hours prior to the performance of an abortion. The law allows for exceptions to this requirement in the event of a medical emergency. Notwithstanding the fact that Senate Bill 60 was modeled after a constitutionally sufficient Pennsylvania law, Utah Women's Clinic filed a 106-page complaint, which could more properly be described as a press release, challenging the constitutionality of the new Utah law. Plaintiffs' counsel asserted that in the instant case, *Planned Parenthood of Southeastern Pennsylvania v. Casey* was not controlling, and that they could prove it. The plaintiffs' case was referred to the magistrate judge, who determined that the 24-hour waiting period does not impose an undue burden on the right to an abortion. Finding that Senate Bill 60 is constitutionally proper, the magistrate judge recommended that the plaintiffs' request for injunctive relief be denied.

Issue

Are the Utah abortion statute's 24-hour waiting period and informed consent requirements facially invalid?

Holding

The United States District Court for the district of Utah held that the Utah abortion statute's 24-hour waiting period and informed consent requirements do not render the statute unconstitutionally vague.

Reason

In 1992, the United States Supreme Court in *Casey* determined that in asserting an interest in protecting fetal life, a state may place some restrictions on previability abortions, so long as those restrictions do not impose an "undue burden" on the woman's right to an abortion. The United States Supreme Court determined that the 24-hour waiting period, the informed consent requirement, and the medical emergency definitions did not unduly burden the right to an abortion and were therefore constitutional. In the instant case, because Senate Bill 60 is less restrictive than the Pennsylvania abortion statute, plaintiffs may not prevail unless they can show material differences between the circumstances of Utah and Pennsylvania. The plaintiffs did not meet this burden. A review of the plaintiffs' complaint in the instant case shows no factual allegations materially different from those already considered by the United States Supreme

Court in *Casey*. Plaintiffs had no case from the beginning. Even if all of the plaintiffs' allegations are accepted as fact, under *Casey*, Senate Bill 60 imposes no undue burden on the right to an abortion when a state passes abortion legislation that is less than or equal to the restrictions imposed by the Pennsylvania law, and where the plaintiffs are unable to allege any effect from the legislation that is more burdensome. *Id.* at 1491.

Under *Casey*, there is no viable legal cause of action. It would be extremely difficult in light of the *Casey* decision, if not impossible, to bring a good faith facial challenge to the constitutionality of Utah's 24-hour waiting period and informed consent requirements. In an emergency situation, there is never a requirement of informed consent or a 24-hour waiting period. The plaintiffs' contention that Senate Bill 60, "when read together with provisions from Utah's 1991 abortion law, does not clearly provide that a woman can obtain an immediate abortion when necessary in a medical emergency" is without merit. *Id.* at 1492. *Plaintiffs' Objections*, at 15. There is no waiting period requirement in the case of a medical emergency.

Section 305(2) states that, prior to performing the abortion, the physician shall inform the woman "of the medical indications supporting his judgment that an abortion is necessary." Such information, which is hardly burdensome or unreasonable, is the only information required to be given, if possible, in the case of a medical emergency. If the medical emergency is such that time does not permit, the physician need not give any information at all.

> The abortion issue is obviously one which invokes strong feelings on both sides. Individuals are free to urge support for their cause through debate, advocacy, and participation in the political process. The subject might also be addressed in the courts so long as there are valid legal issues in dispute. Where, however, a case presents no legitimate legal arguments, the courthouse is not the proper forum. Litigation, or the threat of litigation, should not be used as economic blackmail to strengthen one's hand in the political battle. Unfortunately, the court sees little evidence that this case was filed for any other purpose. *Id.* at 1494.

> Senate Bill 60, the duly enacted law of the people of Utah, has not been enforced for nearly nine months. That will change today. The court hereby adopts the report and recommendation of the magistrate judge, lifts the injunction, and dismisses plaintiffs' case in its entirety with prejudice. *Id.* at 1495.

Discussion

1. Do you agree that individual states should be able to place reasonable restrictions or waiting periods?
2. Who should determine what is reasonable?

2. ABORTION CLINICS/VIOLATION OF INJUNCTION

Citation: *NOW v. Operation Rescue*, 816 F. Supp. 729 (D. D.C. 1993)

Facts

Abortion clinics and others sought enforcement of a revised permanent injunction, entered at 747 F. Supp. 760, precluding antiabortion groups, their leaders, and others from blockading or obstructing access to abortion clinics.

On January 16, 1992, the order required defendants to appear before the court to show cause why each of them should not be cited for contempt for violating and inducing others to violate a July 31, 1990, injunction in the above matter.

On January 22, defendants Mr. Tucci, Mr. Terry, and Mr. Mahoney spoke at a rally. Mr. Tucci was introduced as a leader of Operation Rescue National and spoke about how the group had successfully closed down clinics that day. He also solicited funds for his organization. Mr. Terry said "they needed contributions to keep their work going." The defendant Mr. Gannett had notice in July 1990 of the revised permanent injunction. On January 24, 1992, at a hearing on the matter, Mr. Gannett represented himself *pro se* and admitted that he participated in the Operation Rescue events and intervened at one of the "rescue" blockades. The defendants appeared before the Court at two hearings to show cause why they should not be cited in contempt for violating the court's July 31, 1990, injunction.

Issue

Can antiabortion leaders and groups be fined for violating a permanent injunction barring them from blockading or obstructing access to abortion clinics? Can antiabortion groups be ordered to pay damages to compensate an abortion clinic for property damage resulting from an abortion clinic blockage that violated a permanent injunction?

Holding

The United States District Court for the District of Columbia held that leaders and groups would be fined for violating the injunction. In addition, antiabortion groups are liable to abortion clinics for property damages resulting from blockades.

Reason

At the time the defendants allegedly violated the relevant orders entered, the federal element of jurisdiction was substantial and serious. Blockading of the plaintiffs' premises would also violate District of Columbia trespassing laws (D.C. Code § 22-3102) and public nuisances as well as tortiously interfere with the plaintiffs' professional and business relations. The District of Columbia law claims provide a sufficient basis for retaining federal jurisdiction, enforcing the injunction, protecting the previously established rights of plaintiffs, and vindicating the vital authority of a United States District Court.

The defendants violated those provisions of the injunction "barring all defendants and those acting in concert with them 'from inducing, encouraging, directing, aiding, or abetting others' to trespass on, blockade, or obstruct access to or egress from facilities at which abortions are performed and other medical services are rendered." *Id.* at 734. In blockading the clinics, the defendants violated District of Columbia trespass law, which states, "Any person who, without lawful authority, shall enter, or attempt to enter, any public or private dwelling . . . against the will of the lawful occupant or of the person lawfully in charge thereof . . . shall be guilty of a misdemeanor" (D.C. Code § 22-3102).

The participants in the blockades were under court order not to trespass on the clinics and were ordered by clinic personnel and the police at the time of the blockades to leave the property. Their presence on the property clearly constituted trespass. The July 31, 1990, revised permanent injunction explicitly stated that, in order to coerce compliance, if the terms of the injunction were violated, there would be a "fine to be paid to the medical facility or facilities that are or become the target of the violation." *Id.* at 735. Because of the dual compensatory and coercive nature of civil contempt proceedings, future contempt fines were intended to be payable to the plaintiff clinics "as additional deterrence, and because plaintiffs have demonstrated that defendants' activities cause damage to the blockaded clinics." *Memorandum*, July 31, 1990, at 13. The court has established a schedule of sanctions in order to deter future violations of the revised permanent injunction order. These orders warned defendants that in the event of future violations, sanctions would be imposed.

Discussion

1. What is an injunction?
2. Do you agree with the court's reasoning for enforcing the injunction?
3. Was the court too harsh in rendering fines? Explain.

3. PICKETING ABORTION DOCTORS

Citation: *Murray v. Lawson*, 642 A.2d 338 (N.J. 1994)

Facts

Two physicians brought separate actions to obtain injunctions against antiabortion protesters who had been picketing their residences. The defendant in the *Murray* case discovered the personal address of Dr. Murray and visited the house, where the physician's 14-year-old son answered the door. The defendant told the son to tell his father to stop performing abortions. A month later, the defendant told the police that he and 50 other people were going to picket the physician's home. After being warned about the picketing, Dr. Murray sent his family away. However, he stayed in the house that day, managing, from his home, two of his patients who were in labor. The picketers walked on the sidewalk in front of Dr. Murray's home, carrying posters stating among other things, that he "scars and kills women and their unborn children." They also told neighbors that he was a killer. Dr. Murray filed suit seeking damages and injunctive relief, testifying that the picketing deprived him and his family of their family time, harmed his ability to practice because he had to manage his patients from home, and caused his wife to suffer from nervousness and depression. After the hearing, the medical center where Dr. Murray had performed abortions was burned to the ground. In spite of a telephone bomb threat, police never determined who called in the threat or burned the building. After the bomb threat, the defendant and another picketer protested in front of the Murray house. Dr. Murray called the police, who arrived and told him to stay in the house. He came out, however, and took a swing at the defendant. He was later convicted of assault. The chancery division ordered a permanent injunction prohibiting the defendant and all others from picketing within 300 feet of the Murray home. The defendants appealed, claiming that the injunction impinged upon their freedom of speech. The appellate division affirmed, finding that the injunction set a reasonable time, place, and manner restriction, thereby not violating free speech.

The second physician, Dr. Boffard, performed abortions at a clinic, which had been subjected to protests two years prior to the protests at Dr. Murray's home. In 1990, the protesters appeared at the front of Dr. Boffard's residence. Like the situation in the *Murray* case, the picketers carried signs, some of which read, "Thou Shalt Not Kill." Other signs contained pictures of bloody fetal parts. The demonstrators yelled at the physician's wife that her husband was a murderer. They also told that to a teenage neighbor.

Subsequently, a suit was brought in the chancery division to enjoin the defendants from picketing. The court issued a temporary restraining order prohibiting picketing within 200 feet of the physician's home, from referring to Dr. Boffard as a killer, and from depicting fetuses on posters. The court made the injunction permanent five months later, stopping the picketing within "the immediate vicinity" of Dr. Boffard's home. Again, as in the *Murray* case, the appellate division upheld the injunction. Both cases were appealed to the New Jersey Supreme Court.

Issue

Did the defendants' free speech rights outweigh the plaintiffs' residential privacy interests?

Holding

The New Jersey Supreme Court upheld the injunction in the *Murray* case, but remanded the Boffard injunction for a more precise definition of the spatial scope of the ban, finding that "within the immediate vicinity" was too vague.

Reason

Residential privacy represents a sufficient public policy interest to justify injunctive restrictions. Moreover, the chancery division had the power to enjoin the nonviolent, noncriminal activity of the defendants to protect the plaintiffs' residential privacy. The court determined that the injunctions in both cases were content neutral since they could be justified without referring to the content of the defendants' speech. They prohibited any and all picketing, regardless of the type of speech, within a certain distance of the residences. The court further held that since a state has a significant interest in protecting the residential privacy of its citizens, it is justified in imposing injunctive relief.

Discussion

1. What do you see as the rationale behind a court balancing free speech rights against residential privacy rights in abortion protest cases?
2. Do you agree with the U.S. District Court's decision? Explain.

4. EXCESSIVE FORCE/ABORTION PROTESTERS

Citation: *Forrester v. City of San Diego*, 25 F.3d 804 (9th Cir. 1994)

Facts

In March 1989, the San Diego police became aware that Operation Rescue planned to stage several antiabortion demonstrations in the city. The purpose of the demonstrations was to disrupt operations at the target clinic and ultimately to cause the clinic to cease operations. In each of the three demonstrations at issue, protesters converged on a medical building, blocking entrances, filling stairwells and corridors, and preventing employees and patients from entering.

For each arrest, the officers warned the demonstrators that they would be subjected to pain-compliance measures if they did not move, that such measures would hurt, and that they could reduce the pain by standing up, eliminating the tension on their wrists and arms. The officers then forcibly moved the arrestees by tightening Orcutt police nonchakus (two sticks of wood connected at one end by a cord used to grip a demonstrator's wrist) around their wrists until they stood up and walked. All arrestees complained of varying degrees of injury to their hands and arms, including bruises, a pinched nerve, and one broken wrist. Several subsequently filed suit, claiming that the police violated the Fourth Amendment by using excessive force in executing the arrests. The judge allowed the case to proceed to the jury in order to determine whether any particular uses of force were unconstitutional. After viewing a videotape of the arrests, the jury concluded that none involved excessive force and returned a verdict for the city.

Issue

Did the police officers use excessive force in arresting the demonstrators, in light of the testimony of the officers and demonstrators and the videotape of the arrest?

Holding

The United States Court of Appeals for the Ninth Circuit held that the police did not use excessive force.

Reason

Determining whether the force used to effect a particular seizure is reasonable under the Fourth Amendment requires a careful balancing of the nature and quality of the intrusion on the individual's Fourth Amendment interests against the countervailing governmental interests at stake. The reasonableness inquiry in an excessive force case is an objective one. Are the officer's actions objectively reasonable in light of the facts and circumstances confronting them? *Graham v. Connor*, 490 U.S. at 396-97, 109 S. Ct. at 1872 (1989). There was ample evidence to support the jury's conclusion that the officers acted reasonably in using pain-compliance techniques to arrest the demonstrators. In addition to hearing the testimony of numerous officers and demonstrators, the jury watched the entire videotape of the arrests. As the district court noted, the videotape created an extensive evidentiary record: "thanks to videotaped records of the actual events, plus the testimony of witnesses on both sides, the jury had more than a sufficient amount of evidence presented to them from which they could formulate their verdicts. . . . The extensive use of video scenes of exactly what took place removed much argument and interpretation of the facts themselves." *Id.* at 807.

The police did not threaten or use deadly force and did not deliver physical blows or cuts. The force consisted of physical pressure administered on the demonstrators' limbs in increasing degrees, resulting in pain. The city clearly had a legitimate interest in quickly dispersing and removing the lawbreakers with the least risk of injury to police and others. The arrestees were part of a group of more than 100 protesters operating in an organized and concerted effort to invade private property, obstruct business, and hinder law enforcement. Although many of these crimes were misdemeanors, the city's interest in preventing their widespread occurrence was significant.

Discussion

1. Do you think the police officers used excessive force? Explain.
2. What was the basis for the court's finding?

XIII

Patient Rights and Responsibilities

1. PATIENT'S RIGHT TO REFUSE BLOOD TRANSFUSION

Citation: *Harrell v. St. Mary's Hosp., Inc.*, 678 So. 2d 455 (Fla. Dist. Ct. App. 1996)

Facts

The appellee, St. Mary's Hospital, filed an emergency petition in circuit court regarding the health care of the appellant, Mrs. Harrell. Mrs. Harrell, a Jehovah's Witness, was six months pregnant when physicians discovered a life-threatening blood condition that could rapidly deteriorate and place both her life and the life of the fetus in jeopardy. Because of her religious beliefs, Mrs. Harrell objected to any blood transfusion. After an emergency hearing where the Harrells could not summon an attorney, the court ruled that a blood transfusion could be given to Mrs. Harrell if it was necessary to save the life of the fetus and that after the child was born, a blood transfusion could be given to the child if necessary to save the child's life. However, the child was delivered by Caesarean section and died two days later. No blood transfusion was given to Mrs. Harrell or to the child. As a result, St. Mary's Hospital and the state claim that the appeal of the trial court's order is moot. Because of the hospital's serious misunderstanding about its standing to bring such proceedings, the court addressed the issue of standing as capable of repetition yet evading review.

Issue

Does the medical provider have standing to assert state interests in an attempt to defeat a patient's decision to forgo emergency medical treatment?

Holding

The court concluded that a medical provider does not have standing to assert state interests in a petition to require treatment for its patient. The hospital lacked standing to file the petition.

Reason

Article I, section 23 of the Florida Constitution guarantees that a competent person has the constitutional right to choose or refuse medical treatment, and that right extends to all relevant decisions concerning one's health. In cases where these rights are litigated, a party generally seeks to invoke the power of the state, through the exercise of the court's judicial power, either to enforce the patient's rights or to prevent the patient from exercising those rights. The state has a duty to ensure that a person's wishes regarding medical treatment are respected. That obligation serves to protect the rights of the individual from intrusion by the state unless the state has a compelling interest great enough to override this constitutional right (e.g., protection of innocent third parties). The means to carry out any such compelling state interest must be narrowly tailored in the least intrusive manner possible to safeguard the rights of the individual.

Mrs. Harrell argued that the hospital should not have intervened in her private decision to refuse a blood transfusion. She claimed that the state had never been a party in this action, had not asserted any interest, and that the hospital had no authority to assume the state's responsibilities.

The court concluded that a health care provider must not be forced into the position of having to argue zealously against the wishes of its own patient, seeking deference to the wishes or interests of nonpatients—in this case, the patient's husband, her brothers, the children, and the state itself. Patients do not lose their right to make decisions affecting their lives when they enter into the care of a health care facility. A health care provider's function is to provide medical treatment in accordance with the patient's wishes and best interests, not supervening the wishes of a competent adult. A health care provider must comply with the wishes of a patient to refuse medical treatment unless ordered to do otherwise by a court of competent jurisdiction. A health care provider cannot act on behalf of the state to assert state interests.

In situations like these, health care providers generally have sought judicial intervention to determine their rights and obligations to avoid liability. Health care providers, when terminating life support in accordance with a patient's wishes, are relieved of potential civil and criminal liability as long as they act in good faith, and that no prior court approval of the health care provider's action is required. When a health care provider, acting in good faith, follows the wishes of a competent and informed patient to refuse medical treatment, the health care provider is acting appropriately and cannot be subjected to civil or criminal liability.

Although this procedure absolves the health care facility of any obligation to go to court, the court recognizes the need for the state and interested parties to have the opportunity to seek judicial intervention, if appropriate. A health care provider wishing to override a patient's decision to refuse medical treatment must immediately provide notice to the State Attorney presiding in the circuit where the controversy arises, and to interested third parties known to the health care provider. The extent to which the State Attorney chooses to engage in a legal action, if any, is discretionary based on the law and facts of each case. This procedure should eliminate needless litigation by health care providers while honoring the patient's wishes and giving other interested parties the right to intervene if there is a good faith reason to do so.

The hospital's contention that it had standing to seek judicial intervention to determine its "obligations, duties, and responsibilities" concerning the delivery of medical health care and treatment was rejected. If the hospital wished to override Mrs. Harrell's decision to refuse medical treatment, it was required to immediately provide notice to the State Attorney so that the State Attorney could determine whether it would take legal action to compel the transfusion.

Discussion

1. Describe those circumstances in which a state might have a right to interfere with a patient's decision to forgo emergency care.
2. When considering a person's religious beliefs, should the state have a right to interfere with a mother's decision to refuse a blood transfusion? Why?
3. Should a hospital be able to raise whatever interest the state itself may have in seeking to compel an unwilling patient to undergo a routine, lifesaving medical procedure? Explain.

2. PATIENT'S RIGHT TO SELF-DETERMINATION

Citation: *Stamford Hosp. v. Vega*, 236 Conn. 646, 674 A.2d 821 (Conn. Super. Ct. 1996)

Facts

On August 26, 1994, Ms. Vega was admitted as a patient to the hospital to deliver her first child. That evening, Ms. Vega, a Jehovah's Witness, executed a release requesting that no blood or its derivatives be administered to her during her hospitalization, and relieving the hospital and its personnel of liability for any adverse effects that might result from her refusal to permit the use of blood in her treatment. Ms. Vega's husband also signed the release.

On August 27, 1994, Ms. Vega delivered a healthy baby. Following the delivery, Ms. Vega bled heavily as a result of a retained piece of the placenta. Her obstetrician, Dr. Sood, recommended a dilation and curettage in order to stop the bleeding. Although Ms. Vega agreed to permit Dr. Sood to perform the dilation and curettage, she refused to allow a blood transfusion. Prior to undergoing the procedure, she had signed another release requesting that she be given no transfusions and releasing the hospital from liability. Despite the dilation and curettage, Ms. Vega continued to hemorrhage.

Ms. Vega's physicians tried a number of alternatives to the use of blood, but her condition continued to worsen. Eventually, when she was having difficulty breathing, her physicians placed her on a respirator in the intensive care unit. Ms. Vega and her husband maintained throughout these events that, although she might die without blood transfusions, it was against their religious beliefs to allow the use of blood. Because Dr. Sood and the other physicians involved in Ms. Vega's care believed that it was essential that she receive blood in order to survive, the hospital filed a complaint against Ms. Vega on August 28, 1994, requesting that the court issue an injunction that would permit the hospital to administer blood transfusions to her.

The trial court convened an emergency hearing at the hospital on August 28. Although Ms. Vega's attorney, who was en route to the hospital, had not yet arrived, the court appointed Ms. Vega's husband as her guardian *ad litem* and began hearing testimony. Ms. Vega's physicians testified that they had exhausted all nonblood alternatives and that, with reasonable medical certainty, she would die without blood transfusions. Her husband testified that, on the basis of his religious beliefs as a Jehovah's Witness, he continued to support his wife's decision to refuse transfusions and believed that she would take the same position if she were able to participate in the hearing.

The court, relying on the state's interests in preserving life and protecting innocent third parties, and noting that Ms. Vega's life could be saved by a blood transfusion, granted the hospital's request for an injunction permitting it to administer blood transfusions to her. The court then stayed the order until Ms. Vega's attorney had arrived and had been given an opportunity to present argument and additional evidence. The court reinstated its judgment permitting the hospital to administer blood transfusions to Ms. Vega. Ms. Vega was then given blood transfusions, recovered, and was discharged from the hospital.

Ms. Vega appealed to the Appellate Court from the trial court's judgment. The hospital moved to dismiss the appeal on the ground of mootness, and the Appellate Court granted the hospital's motion.

Ms. Vega argued that if her refusal of blood transfusions interfered with certain state interests, it should be the state itself, not a private hospital, that asserts the state's interests. The hospital responded that, because it was charged with Ms. Vega's care, and because it was required to choose between disregarding either Ms. Vega's wishes or her physicians' recommendations that she receive the transfusions, it had a direct stake in the outcome of the controversy and was a proper party to bring this action.

Issue

1. Was this case moot because the patient recovered and was discharged from the hospital?
2. Did the hospital have standing to challenge Ms. Vega's refusal of lifesaving blood transfusions?
3. Did the issuance of the injunction, followed by the administration of the blood transfusions, violate Ms. Vega's common law right of bodily self-determination?

Holding

The court determined that the case was not moot. Insofar as the hospital's claims are founded on its own interests, rather than those of the state, the court agreed with the hospital that it had standing to bring those claims. The court concluded that, under the circumstances of this case, the hospital's legitimate interest in protecting its patients does not extend that far.

Reason

The hospital later conceded that this case is not moot because it is capable of repetition. Notwithstanding the

hospital's concession and the resulting lack of dispute between the parties, the court considered the issue of mootness.

A challenge to the issuance of an injunction permitting the administration of nonconsensual blood transfusions will virtually always become moot long before appellate litigation can be concluded or initiated. Of necessity, a medically necessary blood transfusion must be accomplished, if at all, as soon as reasonably possible after its need becomes apparent to the patient's health care provider. Once a court order is issued permitting such a transfusion against the patient's will, and the court lifts any stay of that order, as it will inevitably do, it cannot be expected that the health care provider that sought the order will await the outcome of an appeal before complying with the order. Any order that is challenged on appeal is, by its very nature, of such limited duration that it is virtually certain that it will become moot before appellate litigation can be concluded.

The hospital had a legitimate interest in receiving official guidance in resolving the ethical dilemma it faced—whether to practice medicine by trying to save a patient's life despite that patient's refusal to consent to treatment, or to practice medicine in accordance with the patient's wishes and likely watch the patient die, knowing nonetheless that it had the power to save her life. The hospital had conflicting interests, and was in the role not of opposing its patient, but of a party seeking the court's guidance in determining its obligations under the circumstances.

Conferring standing only on the state and denying it to the hospital, in this case, however, would have had the practical effect of requiring the hospital to abandon its own legitimate interests. Such action would have effectively insulated the patient's choice from any official scrutiny because it would have been extremely difficult for the state to initiate judicial proceedings in time to do any good, and even if the state could have done so, it would likely have been unfamiliar both with the medical options available and with the facts and circumstances surrounding the patient's desires. The hospital was the best informed and most feasible candidate, under these circumstances, to set the judicial machinery in motion. The court concluded that, for these reasons, the hospital had standing to challenge Ms. Vega's refusal of blood transfusions.

Ms. Vega claimed that the state's interest in the welfare of her child is not sufficiently compelling as to outweigh her interest in refusing blood transfusions. Ms. Vega maintains that the trial court's injunction, issued at the behest of the hospital, violated her common law right of self-determination, her federal constitutional right to bodily self-determination, her federal constitutional right to free exercise of religion, and her state constitutional right of religious liberty. The court concluded that, under the circumstances of this case, the issuance of the injunction, followed by the administration of the blood transfusions, violated Ms. Vega's common law right of bodily self-determination.

Once the infant was born, Ms. Vega's decision to refuse a blood transfusion posed no risk to the infant's physical health. Ms. Vega's claim centers on her common law right of bodily self-determination. The only question, therefore, is whether the hospital and the trial court were obliged to respect Ms. Vega's decision to refuse blood transfusions, even though her decision would likely have led to her death.

Although the hospital's interests are sufficient to confer standing on it in this case, they are not sufficient to take priority over Ms. Vega's common law right to bodily integrity, even when the assertion of that right threatens her own life. The hospital had no common law right or obligation to thrust unwanted medical care on a patient who, having been sufficiently informed of the consequences, competently and clearly declined that care. The hospital's interests were sufficiently protected by Ms. Vega's informed choice, and neither it nor the trial court was entitled to override that choice. Ms. Vega's common law right of bodily self-determination was entitled to respect and protection. The trial court improperly issued an injunction that permitted the hospital to administer blood transfusions to Ms. Vega.

Discussion

1. Does a hospital have standing to assert the state's *parens patriae* interest in the welfare of a minor child whose adult parent is hospitalized and is refusing allegedly lifesaving medical treatment?
2. Is the state's alleged *parens patriae* interest in the welfare of a minor child whose parent is refusing allegedly lifesaving treatment for religious and medical reasons a compelling state interest that overrides the parent's common law right of bodily self-determination, federal constitutional rights of bodily self-determination and religious free exercise, and state constitutional right of religious liberty?
3. Is the forcible administration of unwanted medical treatment to a competent adult the least restrictive, least intrusive means of protecting the state's alleged *parens patriae* interest in the welfare of that adult's minor child?

3. PATIENT RESPONSIBILITY TO DISCLOSE INFORMATION

Citation: *Oxford v. Upson County Hosp., Inc.*, 438 S.E.2d 171 (Ga. Ct. App. 1993)

Facts

Ms. Oxford brought a lawsuit against the Upson County Hospital and nurses claiming that their medical malpractice caused her injury from a fall in the hospital's bathroom. Ms. Oxford had been admitted to the hospital after having been diagnosed with gastroenteritis and dehydration. Nothing on her chart indicated that she had experienced dizziness. Testimony at the trial indicated that Ms. Oxford had told her nurse that she had to go to the bathroom. Ms. Oxford did not inform the nurse that she felt dizzy. After the nurse escorted her to the bathroom, Ms. Oxford fainted while sitting on the toilet. As she fainted, she hit her head on the bathroom wall.

Two nurse experts testified that it is a patient's responsibility to communicate to the staff any symptoms the patient is experiencing. Ms. Oxford had told her physician prior to her hospitalization about feeling dizzy, but he had not related this information to the hospital's staff.

After a jury verdict for the hospital, Ms. Oxford appealed, arguing that the trial court's jury charges on causation, failure to exercise ordinary care, and comparative negligence were wrong.

Issue

Was there sufficient evidence to warrant the judge's charges to the jury?

Holding

The Georgia Court of Appeals affirmed the jury verdict and found that the judge's charges on the issues had been sufficient.

Reason

The court followed its determination in *Harper*, 196 Ga. Ct. App. 658, 659, 396 S.E.2d 587 (1990), that when a patient fails to disclose all information related to her condition and fails to exercise ordinary care for her safety by seeking medical attention for her worsening condition, a charge of comparative negligence is applicable. In this case, the court did not require that Ms. Oxford diagnose herself, but she should have told the staff about her symptoms so that they could have treated her using their professional judgment.

Discussion

1. What precautions should the admitting physician and nurses take to help prevent similar injuries from occurring in the future?
2. Do you agree with the appellate court's decision?

XIV

Acquired Immune Deficiency Syndrome

1. BLOOD CENTER'S NEGLIGENCE/PROXIMATE CAUSE/HIV INFECTION

Citation: *J.K. & Susie L. Wadley Research Inst. v. Beeson*, 835 S.W.2d 689 (Tex. Ct. App. 1992)

Facts

In January 1983, a blood center knew that blood from homosexual or bisexual males should not be accepted under any circumstances. The blood center's written policy provided that donors who volunteer that they are gay should not be permitted to donate blood.

On April 22, 1983, Dr. Kraus, a cardiologist, discovered that Mr. Beeson, the patient, had severe blockage of two major arteries in his heart and recommended cardiac bypass surgery. During surgery, Mr. Beeson received seven units of blood by transfusion. In May 1987, Mr. Beeson had chest pain and trouble breathing. On June 5, 1987, Mr. Beeson was hospitalized. Dr. Kraus consulted with two specialists in pulmonary medicine about the unusual pneumonia evident in X-rays of Mr. Beeson's lungs. Because there was a possibility that the lung infection was secondary to acquired immune deficiency syndrome (AIDS), Mr. Beeson was tested for the human immunodeficiency virus (HIV). Although Mr. Beeson had not yet been formally diagnosed, physicians started him on therapy for AIDS.

Mr. Beeson was formally diagnosed as HIV-positive. His wife was then tested for HIV, and she learned that she was also HIV-positive. On July 2, 1987, Mr. Beeson expired. On April 21, 1989, the plaintiffs, Mrs. Beeson and her son, filed suit against the blood center alleging that her husband contracted HIV from the transfusion of a unit of blood donated at the blood center on April 19, 1983, by a donor identified at trial as John Doe. The parties stipulated at trial that Mr. Doe was a sexually active homosexual male with multiple sex partners.

The plaintiffs amended their original petition to contend that the blood center's negligence in testing and screening blood donors caused Mrs. Beeson's contraction of HIV. At trial, the jury awarded the plaintiffs $800,000 in damages. Following the trial court's denial of the blood center's motion for judgment notwithstanding the verdict, the blood center filed an appeal. The blood center argued that the trial court erred in denying its motion for judgment notwithstanding the verdict because the evidence of causation was legally insufficient to support the jury verdict.

Issue

Did the evidence support a finding that the blood center's negligence was the proximate cause of Mr. Beeson's contraction of HIV?

Holding

The Court of Appeals of Texas held that the evidence supported a finding that the blood center's negligence in the collection of blood was the proximate cause of Mr. Beeson's HIV infection.

Reason

If there is more than a scintilla of evidence to support the jury's answers to causation, the blood center's no evidence challenge must fail. *Stafford v. Stafford*, 726 S.W.2d 14, 16 (Tex. 1987). The question of causation is a fact question for the jury. The issue of proximate cause includes two essential elements. The first is foreseeability, and the second is cause-in-fact. Both elements must be present and both may be established by direct or circumstantial evidence.

Foreseeability is satisfied by showing that the actor, as a person of ordinary intelligence, should have anticipated the danger to others by its negligent act. Cause-in-fact means that the act or omission was a substantial factor in bringing about the injury and without which no harm would have occurred. *McClure*, 608 S.W.2d at 903.

Mr. Doe testified that he did not know that he was at a high risk for AIDS and that he would never have given blood if he had known that he was at risk for AIDS. This evidence provided some indication that the blood center's screening procedure did not effectively educate donors. The jury could reasonably infer that the blood center's failure to effectively educate Mr. Doe and to ask Mr. Doe specific questions caused him to donate blood rather than to defer. There was more than a scintilla of evidence to support a finding that the blood center, despite its knowledge about the dangers of HIV-contaminated blood, failed to reject gay men, that the blood center's donor screening was inadequate, and that these omissions were substantial factors in causing Mr. and Mrs. Beeson's HIV infections.

The blood center's own technical director admitted that there was "strong evidence" that the blood accepted from Mr. Doe was contaminated with HIV. This statement was based on the fact that Mr. Doe's blood was broken into two components, with red blood cells given to another recipient six months later, and that both Mr. Beeson and the other recipient were subsequently diagnosed as HIV-positive less than six months apart from one another.

Discussion

1. What precautions should the blood center have taken to prevent this unfortunate event?
2. What is meant by foreseeability as it relates to this case?
3. What does cause-in-fact refer to as it relates to this case?

2. PARTIAL DISCLOSURE/PHYSICIAN'S HIV-POSITIVE STATUS

Citation: *Application of Milton S. Hershey Med. Ctr.*, 639 A.2d 159 (Pa. 1993)

Facts

The physician, John Doe, was a resident in obstetrics and gynecology at the Milton S. Hershey Medical Center. In 1991, he cut his hand with a scalpel while he was assisting another physician. Because of the uncertainty that blood had been transferred from Dr. Doe's hand wound to the patient through an open surgical incision, he agreed to have a blood test for HIV. His blood tested positive for HIV and he withdrew himself from participation in further surgical procedures. The date and means by which Dr. Doe contracted HIV could not be determined. The Hershey Medical Center and Harrisburg Hospital, where Dr. Doe also participated in surgery, identified those patients who could be at risk. Hershey identified 279 patients and Harrisburg identified 168 patients who fell into this category. Because the hospital records did not identify those surgeries in which physicians may have accidentally cut themselves, the hospitals filed petitions in the Court of Common Pleas, alleging that there was, under the Confidentiality of HIV-Related Information Act [35 P.S. § 7608(a)(2)], a "compelling need" to disclose information regarding Dr. Doe's condition to those patients who conceivably could have been exposed to HIV. Dr. Doe argued that there was no compelling need to disclose the information and that he was entitled to confidentiality under the Act.

The court issued an order for the selective release of information by providing the name of Dr. Doe to physicians and residents in the Department of Obstetrics and Gynecology, by providing the name of Dr. Doe to physicians with whom he had participated in a surgical procedure or obstetrical care, by providing a letter to the patients at risk describing Dr. Doe as a resident in Obstetrics and Gynecology, and by setting forth the relevant period of such service. The physicians were reminded that they were prohibited under the HIV Act from disclosing Dr. Doe's name. The superior court affirmed the decision of the trial court.

Issue

Was there a compelling need to release selective information regarding Dr. Doe's HIV-positive status as determined by the trial court?

Holding

The Supreme Court of Pennsylvania held that a compelling need existed for at least a partial disclosure of the physician's IIIV status.

Reason

There was no question that Dr. Doe's HIV-positive status fell within the HIV Act's definition of confidential information. There were, however, exceptions within the HIV Act that allowed for disclosure of the information. In this case, there was a compelling reason to allow disclosure of the information. Although a definition of compelling reason is not included in the Act, a balancing analysis needs to be applied. The "court shall weigh the need for disclosure against the privacy interest of the individual and the public interests which may be harmed by disclosure" [35 P.S. § 7608(c)]. All the medical experts who testified agreed that there was some risk to exposure and that some form of notice should be given to the patients at risk. "Even the expert witness presented by Dr. Doe agreed that there was at least some conceivable risk of exposure and that giving a very limited form of notice would not be unreasonable." *Id.* at 162. Failure to notify the patients at risk could result in the spread of the disease to other noninfected individuals through sexual contact and through exposure to other body fluids. Dr. Doe's name was not revealed to the patients, only the fact that a resident physician who participated in their care had tested HIV-positive. "No principle is more deeply embedded in the law than that expressed in the maxim *Salus populi suprema lex,* . . . (the welfare of the people is the supreme law), and a more compelling and consistent application of that principle than the one presented would be quite difficult to conceive." *Id.* at 163.

Discussion

1. What, if any, steps should health care organizations take to reduce the unauthorized access to the medical records of patients who have been diagnosed with HIV?
2. Should the confidentiality of all medical records be treated in the same manner?

X V

End of Life Issues

1. INCOMPETENT PATIENT/REFUSAL TO REMOVE FEEDING TUBE

Citation: *Grace Plaza of Great Neck v. Elbaum*, 623 N.E.2d 513 (N.Y. 1993)

Facts

In September 1986, the plaintiff, Grace Plaza, a long-term care facility, admitted Ms. Elbaum, who had been treated for a stroke by North Shore University Hospital. She was admitted in a persistent vegetative state, necessitating a gastrostomy tube. Her husband informed the nursing home that he wanted them to remove the feeding tube because his wife had told him she wanted to die naturally. When the facility refused to remove the tube, Mr. Elbaum refused to pay for further treatment. When the plaintiff sued to recover the money, Mr. Elbaum was granted summary judgment. The New York Supreme Court, Appellate Division, reversed, and Mr. Elbaum then appealed.

Issue

Does the burden of establishing an incompetent patient's desire to die rest on those asserting that desire? If the provider refuses to abide by the incompetent patient's family's request to suspend treatment, does that suspend the family's obligation to pay?

Holding

The New York Court of Appeals affirmed for the plaintiff.

Reason

If there is a disagreement between the facility and the family of the patient, it is the family who must seek legal determination of the patient's wishes. The defendant did not present any documentary evidence of his wife's intentions. Further, although New York recognizes the right of competent patients to decide what happens to their bodies, including preventing life-sustaining treatment, the patient was incompetent, thus she could not communicate her lack of consent to treatment. Since there were no proxy or living will laws in effect at the time of this case, only the patient had the right to decide what, if any, her course of treatment would be. Families of incompetent patients must establish, by clear and convincing evidence, the patient's wishes regarding continuation of care. In the situation where there is a dispute over the wishes, the provider may refuse to discontinue treatment until the matter is resolved legally. If it continues treatment, it may be paid for services rendered because the refusal to discontinue does not constitute a breach of contract. The request to terminate life support is treated differently than a routine change in treatment. The family of an incompetent patient has the most access to necessary evidence to submit to the court.

Discussion

1. Do you agree with the court's decision? Explain.
2. What role could an ethics committee have played in this scenario?

2. PROLONGING LIFE/WRONGFUL LIVING/NOT ACTIONABLE

Citation: *Anderson v. St. Francis–St. George Hosp.*, 614 N.E.2d 841 (Ohio Ct. App. 1992)

Facts

The administrator of the estate of the deceased patient brought suit against a hospital, alleging battery, negligence, and "wrongful living."

In the administrator's original complaint, he alleged that on May 25, 1988, the deceased, Mr. Winter, was admitted to the hospital with chest pain. After initial treatment in the emergency department, Mr. Winter was given additional care in the hospital's coronary unit. The administrator alleged that Mr. Winter had a discussion with his family and his private physician, Dr. Russo, about the type of treatment that he was to receive while at the hospital. In addition, there was evidence to show that as a result of that discussion, Dr. Russo entered the instruction in the hospital record: "No Code Blue." In his complaint, the administrator claimed that the no code blue entry indicated that Dr. Russo specifically instructed that Mr. Winter not be resuscitated.

During Mr. Winter's subsequent treatment at the hospital, he suffered a ventricular fibrillation. The administrator alleged that, despite Dr. Russo's instructions, a nurse resuscitated Mr. Winter by shocking his heart with an electric current and that the nurse's act of resuscitation constituted a battery. The administrator also maintained that, by keeping Mr. Winter alive, the hospital caused him "great pain, suffering, emotional distress, and disability" as well as medical and other financial expenses.

The Court of Common Pleas granted summary judgment for the hospital, and the administrator appealed.

Issue

Can the prolonging of a patient's life by resuscitating him after he suffered a ventricular fibrillation be considered wrongful living? Can nonconsensual medical treatment that prolongs a person's life be considered a battery for which a plaintiff would be entitled to some relief? Was there a question of fact in defibrillation of the patient, counter to the patient's private physician's instruction not to resuscitate the patient in a code blue situation? Was the hospital or attending nurse negligent by resuscitating the patient, thereby precluding summary judgment on the negligence claim?

Holding

The Court of Appeals of Ohio held that there were questions of fact as to consent and whether the patient's later harms were proximately caused by defibrillation, thus precluding summary judgment on the battery claim. Prolonging of the patient's life was not wrongful living and questions of fact precluded summary judgment on the negligence claim.

Reason

In the appellant's assignment of error, he claims that the decedent's life was prolonged by the defibrillation, but that life "was, for him, not worth living." Appellant coins the name for the cause of action for the life that was forced on decedent by the resuscitation as wrongful living. This rather novel notion has not been addressed directly in Ohio courts. Nonetheless, it is possible to determine that life is not a compensable harm; therefore, there is no cause of action for wrongful living. *Id.* at 845.

The Ohio Supreme Court has referred to the joy of life as an "intangible benefit" that cannot be valued monetarily. *Johnson v. Univ. Hosp. of Cleveland* (1989), 44 Ohio St. 3d 49, 55, 540 N.E.2d 1370, 1375. Damages are not those things that add to life, but those that subtract. Even though a victim must have some legally recognized harm to recover actual damages, nonconsensual medical treatment that prolongs a person's life may still be a battery. Therefore, as in any battery, the plaintiff is entitled to some relief. When, however, the nonconsensual treatment is harmless or beneficial, damages for the wrongful act are nominal only, not actual.

There are, however, questions of fact concerning the possible breach of that duty. There was evidence in the record that indicates that the decedent requested limitations on his care while at the hospital. There was also evidence that the decedent's private physician ordered that the decedent not be resuscitated. Also, there was evidence that either the hospital or the nurse, or both, were negligent in preventing or causing the nonconsensual treatment. Therefore, two issues remain for the trier of fact. First, was the defibrillation precluded by the no code blue instruction? Second, if the defibrillation was within the ambit of the instruction, was either the hospital or the attending nurse negligent by resuscitating the decedent? If the trier of fact determines that either the hospital or the nurse breached a duty to the decedent, just as in battery, the appellant must prove that later harms were proximately caused by the negligent act. In addition, if there were proximately caused harms, the court should allow compensation only for damages that are recognized by Ohio law. In contrast to battery, however, if the court finds negligence, but no compensable harm, it should not allow nominal damages. In this case, genuine issues remained on the question of the defendant's negligence. Therefore, the trial court erred by granting summary judgment on that portion of the case.

The court of appeals affirmed the trial court's judgment dismissing the cause of action for wrongful living. For the issues in both battery and negligence, the case was remanded to the trial court for further proceedings.

Discussion

1. What did the administrator in this lawsuit mean by wrongful living?
2. Do you agree with the court's decision? Explain.

3. RIGHT TO REFUSE TREATMENT/RELIGIOUS GROUNDS

Citation: *Matter of Dubreuil*, 629 So. 2d 819 (Fla. 1993)

Facts

A patient was in the advanced stage of pregnancy when she was admitted through the emergency department of the hospital. At the time of her admission, she signed a standard consent form that included her agreement to have a blood transfusion if necessary. The next day, she was going to have a Caesarean section, but she would not consent to a blood transfusion because of her religious beliefs. During the course of the delivery, after she had lost a significant amount of blood, it was determined that she needed a transfusion to save her life, but she would not give her consent. Her estranged husband was contacted, and upon his arrival at the hospital, he gave his consent for the transfusion. After the first transfusion, physicians determined that she would need more, so they petitioned the circuit court for an emergency declaratory judgment hearing to determine if they could give the transfusion in spite of the patient's lack of consent. Although no testimony was given at the hearing, there was a telephone call advising the court that the patient had just regained consciousness and that she continued to withhold her consent.

The trial court decided to allow the hospital to administer blood as they felt it was necessary. The patient moved for a rehearing, and the circuit court denied it. The patient then sought review by the Florida Supreme Court, arguing that her federal and state constitutional rights of privacy, self-determination, and religious freedom had been denied.

Issue

May a hospital assert state interests in order to defeat a patient's decision to refuse emergency medical treatment? Did the patient's refusal of a blood transfusion constitute abandonment of her minor children, thus giving the state an interest that outweighed her constitutional rights of privacy and religion?

Holding

The district court's decision is quashed.

Reason

A competent person has the right to choose or refuse medical treatment, including all decisions relevant to his or her health. That right merges with the right to refuse a blood transfusion while exercising one's religious beliefs. A health care provider must comply with the patient's wishes unless supported by a court order to do otherwise. Here, the state interest was the protection of the children as innocent third parties. However, in this case there would have been no abandonment, because under Florida law, when there are two living parents, they share equally in the responsibilities of parenting. Had the patient died, her husband would have assumed the care of the children.

Discussion

1. What are the competing rights of the state and patient with regard to refusing blood transfusions because of the patient's religious beliefs?
2. Do you agree with the court's decision? Explain.

4. GUARDIANSHIP/REMOVAL OF LIFE SUPPORT CHALLENGED

Citation: *In re Martin*, 517 N.W.2d 749 (Mich. Ct. App. 1994)

Facts

Mr. Martin sustained debilitating injuries as the result of an automobile accident. He suffered severe subcortical brain damage significantly impairing his physical and cognitive functioning. His injuries left him totally paralyzed on the left side with limited but nonfunctional movement in his right limbs. He could not speak or eat and had no bladder or bowel control. Mr. Martin remained conscious and had some awareness of his surroundings. He could communicate to a very minimal degree through head nods.

The trial court determined that Mr. Martin did not have nor would he ever have the ability to have the requisite capacity to make decisions regarding the withdrawal of life-supporting medical equipment. The evidence demonstrated that Mr. Martin's preference would have been to decline life support equipment given his medical condition and prognosis. The trial court's decision was based on the following four-part test for determining if a person has the requisite capacity to make a decision "whether the person (1) has sufficient mind to reasonably understand the condition, (2) is capable of understanding the nature and effect of the treatment choices, (3) is aware of the consequences associated with those choices, and (4) is able to make an informed choice that is voluntary and not coerced." *Id.* at 751. The trial court also determined that Mrs. Martin, the patient's spouse, was a suitable guardian for him.

Mrs. Martin petitioned to withdraw her husband's life support. Mr. Martin's mother and sister counterpetitioned to have Mrs. Martin removed as the patient's guardian.

Issue

Was there sufficient evidence to support a finding that the patient lacked requisite capacity to make decisions regarding the removal of life-sustaining medical treatment? Was there sufficient evidence to show that the patient had a medical preference to decline life-sustaining medical treatment under circumstances such as those that occurred following his injury? Was Mrs. Martin a suitable individual to represent her husband with respect to making a decision as to withdrawing life-sustaining medical treatment?

Holding

The Michigan Court of Appeals held that the evidence was sufficient to support a finding that the patient lacked capacity to make decisions regarding the withholding or withdrawal of life-sustaining medical treatment. As to the patient's desire not to be placed on life-supporting equipment, there was sufficient evidence to show that the patient had a medical preference to decline medical treatment under circumstances such as those that occurred. There was also sufficient evidence to show that the patient's spouse was a suitable guardian.

Reason

The test for determining if Mr. Martin had the requisite capacity to make a decision regarding the withholding or withdrawal of life-supporting medical treatment was clear and convincing—he did not have sufficient decision-making capacity. The evidence was just as clear that he never would regain sufficient decision-making capacity that would enable him to make such a decision. It was the general consensus of all of the experts that Mr. Martin's condition and cognitive level of functioning would not improve in the future.

Testimony from two of Mr. Martin's friends described statements made by him that he would never want to be maintained in a coma or in a vegetative state. In addition, Mrs. Martin described numerous statements made to her by Mr. Martin prior to the accident that he would not want to be maintained alive given the circumstances described above. The trial court found that Mrs. Martin was "credible, if not the most credible witness the court has heard throughout these proceedings." *Id.* at 753. The court of appeals found no reason to dispute the trial court's finding as to Mrs. Martin's credibility.

Contrary to allegations made by the patient's mother and sister, the evidence was clear that Mrs. Martin's testimony was credible. There was no evidence that Mrs. Martin had anything but her husband's best interest at heart. There were allegations but no evidence of financial considerations or pressure from any other individual that would show that Mrs. Martin's testimony was influenced by other individuals.

Discussion

1. Knowing that the patient had some ability to interact with his environment, discuss the four-part test for determining the patient's ability to make a decision.
2. Do you agree with the court's decision? Explain.
3. Should the concern of the parent and sister have carried more weight in removing custody from Mrs. Martin?
4. What influence do you believe the mother and sister might have had on Mrs. Martin?

5. PENALIZING ASSISTED SUICIDE/STATUTES HELD TO BE CONSTITUTIONAL

Citation: *Quill v. Vacco*, 117 S. Ct. 2293 (1997)

Facts

Plaintiffs–appellants Dr. Quill, Dr. Klagsbrun, and Dr. Grossman challenged the constitutionality of two New York

State statutes penalizing assisted suicide. The physicians contended that each statute is invalid to the extent that it prohibits them from acceding to the requests of terminally ill, mentally competent patients for help in hastening death. In granting summary judgment in favor of defendants–appellees, the district court considered and rejected challenges to the statutes predicated upon the due process and equal protection clauses of the Fourteenth Amendment. The Court of Appeals for the Second Circuit affirmed in part, and reversed in part.

The petitioners were New York public officials, and the respondents were physicians who practiced in New York and three gravely ill patients who died before the case reached the Supreme Court.

Ms. Doe was a 76-year-old retired physical education instructor who was dying of thyroid cancer; Mr. Kingsley was a 48-year-old publishing executive suffering from acquired immunodeficiency syndrome (AIDS); and Mr. Barth was a 28-year-old former fashion editor under treatment for AIDS. Each of these respondents alleged that she or he had been advised and understood that she or he was in the final stages of a terminal illness, and that there was no chance of recovery. Each had sought to hasten death in a certain and humane manner and for that purpose sought necessary medical assistance in the form of medications prescribed by her or his physician, which were to be self-administered.

The physician respondents alleged that they encountered, in the course of their medical practices, mentally competent, terminally ill patients who requested assistance in the voluntary self-termination of life. Many of these patients apparently experienced chronic, intractable pain and/or intolerable suffering and sought to hasten their deaths for those reasons. Mr. Barth was one of the patients who sought the assistance of Dr. Grossman. Each of the physician plaintiffs had alleged that under certain circumstances it would be consistent with the standards of his medical practice to assist in hastening death by prescribing drugs for patients to self-administer for that purpose. The physicians alleged that they were unable to exercise their best professional judgment to prescribe the requested drugs, and the other plaintiffs alleged that they were unable to receive the requested drugs, because of the prohibitions contained in sections 125.15(3) and 120.30 of the New York Penal Law, all respondents being residents of New York. Section 125.15 of the New York Penal Law provides in pertinent part: "A person is guilty of manslaughter in the second degree when . . . He intentionally . . . aids another person to commit suicide." A violation of this provision is classified as a class C felony. *Id.*

Section 120.30 of the New York Penal Law provides: "A person is guilty of promoting a suicide attempt when he intentionally . . . aids another person to attempt suicide." A violation of this provision is classified as a class E felony. *Id.*

Respondents argued that "[t]he Fourteenth Amendment guarantees the liberty of mentally competent, terminally ill adults with no chance of recovery to make decisions about the end of their lives." It also included an allegation that the Fourteenth Amendment guarantees the liberty of physicians to practice medicine consistent with their best professional judgment, including using their skills and powers to facilitate the exercise of the decision of competent, terminally ill adults to hasten inevitable death by prescribing suitable medications for the patient to self-administer for that purpose.

Respondents further urged that the relevant portions of the New York Penal Law deny the patient–plaintiffs and the patients of the physician–plaintiffs the equal protection of the law by denying them the right to choose to hasten inevitable death, while terminally ill persons whose treatment includes life support are able to exercise this choice with necessary medical assistance by directing termination of such treatment.

The respondents requested judgment declaring the New York statutes complained of constitutionally invalid and therefore in violation of 42 U.S.C. § 1983 "as applied to physicians who assist mentally competent, terminally ill adults who choose to hasten inevitable death." Plaintiffs also sought an order permanently enjoining defendants from enforcing the statutes and an award of attorney's fees.

In his supplemental declaration, Dr. Quill declared:

> The removal of a life support system that directly results in the patient's death requires the direct involvement by the doctor, as well as other medical personnel. When such patients are mentally competent, they are consciously choosing death as preferable to life under the circumstances that they are forced to live. Their doctors do a careful clinical assessment, including a full exploration of the patient's prognosis, mental competence to make such decisions, and the treatment alternatives to stopping treatment. It is legally and ethically permitted for physicians to actively assist patients to die who are dependent on life-sustaining treatments. . . . Unfortunately, some dying patients who are in agony that can no longer be relieved, yet are not dependent on life-sustaining treatment, have no such options under current legal restrictions. It seems unfair, discriminatory, and inhumane to deprive some dying patients of such vital choices because of arbitrary elements of their condition which determine whether they are on life-sustaining treatment that can be stopped.

The district court disagreed and concluded "that the type of physician assisted suicide at issue in this case does not involve a fundamental liberty interest protected by the Due Process Clause of the Fourteenth Amendment." *Id.* at 84. The court of appeals for the second circuit reversed. 80 F.3d 716 (1996). It determined that "New York law does not treat equally all competent persons who are in the final stages of fatal illness and wish to hasten their deaths." *Id.* at 727. It further held that the statutes were not rationally related to any legitimate state interest.

Turning to the equal protection issue, the district court identified a reasonable and rational basis for the distinction drawn by New York law between the refusal of treatment at the hands of physicians and physician assisted suicide:

> [I]t is hardly unreasonable or irrational for the State to recognize a difference between allowing nature to take its course, even in the most severe situations, and intentionally using an artificial death-producing device. The State has obvious legitimate interests in preserving life, and in protecting vulnerable persons. The State has the further right to determine how these crucial interests are to be treated when the issue is posed as to whether a physician can assist a patient in committing suicide. *Id.* at 84–85.

Accordingly, the court held "that plaintiffs have not shown a violation of the Equal Protection Clause of the Fourteenth Amendment." *Id.* at 85.

Issue

Do the New York State statutes criminalizing assisted suicide violate the equal protection clause of the Fourteenth Amendment?

Holding

New York's prohibition on assisting suicide does not violate the equal protection clause.

Reason

The Supreme Court found that neither the assisted suicide ban nor the law permitting patients to refuse medical treatment treats anyone differently from anyone else, or draws any distinctions between persons. It explained that there is a distinction between letting a patient die, and making one die. Most legislatures have allowed the former, but have prohibited the latter. The Supreme Court disagreed with the respondents' claim that the distinction is arbitrary and irrational.

In its decision, the Supreme Court determined that New York had valid reasons for distinguishing between refusing treatment and assisting suicide. Those reasons included: prohibiting intentional killing and preserving life; preventing suicide; maintaining the physician's role as his or her patient's healer; protecting vulnerable people from indifference, prejudice, and psychological and financial pressure to end their lives. All of those reasons, the Court decided, constitute valid and important public interests fulfilling the constitutional requirement that a legislative classification bear a rational relation to a legitimate end.

Discussion

1. For what reasons did the Supreme Court disagree with the second circuit and find that New York's statute prohibiting assisted suicide did not violate the equal protection clause?
2. Describe what you think the Supreme Court meant when it stated that there is a difference between letting and making a person die. Cite examples to explain the difference.

6. CONSTITUTIONAL RIGHT TO ASSISTED SUICIDE

Citation: *Kevorkian v. Thompson*, 947 F. Supp. 1152 (1997)

Facts

In this action, plaintiffs Dr. Kevorkian and Ms. Good sought a court order enjoining defendant Mr. Thompson and his successor in the office of Oakland County Prosecutor from prosecuting Dr. Kevorkian for his assisted suicide activities. At the heart of both plaintiffs' amended complaint for declaratory and injunctive relief and their motion for summary judgment is their contention that the statutes and the common law under which Dr. Kevorkian has been prosecuted in the past are unconstitutional, and therefore, any future prosecutions of Dr. Kevorkian will result in the deprivation of their constitutional rights.

The plaintiffs' complaint contained four counts, all of which asked the court for declaratory and injunctive relief. In count I, the plaintiffs asked the court to find that M.C.L. § 750.505 (the Michigan "common law savings statute"), and the Michigan Supreme Court's December 13, 1994, ruling that Dr. Kevorkian may be prosecuted for assisting in a suicide under this statute, is unconstitutionally vague, overbroad, and violates the prohibition against *ex post facto* laws. In count II, the plaintiffs asked the court to declare that mentally competent terminally ill or intractably suffering adults have a liberty interest protected by the Fourteenth Amendment's due process clause to end their suffering by committing suicide and to seek physician aid in doing so. In count III, the plaintiffs sought a declaration that any unwritten common law that afforded patients attached to life support systems the right to terminate life support, but denies a mentally competent, terminally ill, or intractably suffering adult not on life support the right to commit suicide with the assistance of a physician violates the equal protection clause of the Fourteenth Amendment. In count IV, the plaintiffs alleged that should another criminal charge be filed against Dr. Kevorkian and/or Ms. Good under M.C.L. § 750.505, they will be deprived of their Fifth and Fourteenth Amendment liberty interests, and the right to be free of unreasonable seizure under the Fourth and Fourteenth Amendments.

In 1992, the Oakland County Circuit Court entered an order granting Dr. Kevorkian's motion to dismiss two counts of open murder for assisting in the suicides of Ms. Wantz and Ms. Miller in October 1991, on the ground that physician-assisted suicide is not a crime in Michigan. The Oakland County prosecutor appealed that decision to the Michigan Court of Appeals and the appellate court reversed the circuit court's decision.

While the appeal of the Oakland County Circuit Court's 1992 order was pending, on December 15, 1992, the Michigan legislature enacted a statute, M.C.L. § 752.1021, et seq., which took effect on February 25, 1993. That statute established a commission to study voluntary termination of life and created a new crime of "criminal assistance of suicide." Two judges of the Wayne County Circuit Court, in two separate cases, subsequently declared that the criminal provisions of the new statute were unconstitutional. Judge Stephens entered a judgment declaring the new statute unconstitutional in a declaratory judgment action filed by a terminally ill individual, Ms. Hobbins, and seven health care professionals. Judge Stephens also held that individuals have a constitutional right to commit suicide. Judge Kaufman held that in some instances, a person has a constitutional right to commit suicide. Finding that one of Dr. Kevorkian's patients, Mr. O'Keefe, had a constitutional right to commit suicide, Judge Kaufman dismissed the assisted suicide charge against Dr. Kevorkian stemming from his assistance in Mr. O'Keefe's suicide.

The Wayne County prosecutor appealed both cases. The appeals were consolidated and, in 1994, the Michigan Court of Appeals held that the assisted suicide statute, by creating a commission to study issues related to voluntary termination of life, with or without assistance, and specifically criminalized assisted suicide, violated the "one-object" provision of the Michigan constitution. However, the appellate court also found that there is no constitutional right to commit suicide.

The Michigan Supreme Court granted leave to appeal and held that (1) the assisted suicide statute was validly enacted and did not violate the one object clause of the Michigan constitution, (2) the United States Constitution does not prohibit states from imposing criminal penalties for assisting someone in committing suicide, and (3) assisted suicide is a common law crime in Michigan, which may be prosecuted under the common law savings statute, M.C.L. § 750.505. *People v. Kevorkian*, 447 Mich. 436, 527 N.W.2d 714 (1994). Dr. Kevorkian petitioned the United States Supreme Court seeking to overturn the Michigan Supreme Court's decision. The United States Supreme Court denied that petition for *certiorari*.

Meanwhile, following Dr. Kevorkian's assistance with the June 1990 suicide of Ms. Adkins, on February 5, 1991, (that is, before the Wantz/Miller suicides that gave rise to the first charges filed against Dr. Kevorkian) the Oakland County Circuit Court entered an order of permanent injunction, permanently enjoining "Dr. Jack Kevorkian, his agents, and employees, and those in active concert with him . . . from: using, employing, administering, offering, or providing any of his 'suicide machines' or other similar devices, contrivances, or other modalities or drugs (including nonprescription drugs) on, or to, any persons seeking to end a human life, or conducting any acts to help a patient commit suicide regardless of the modality employed." *People v. Kevorkian*, Oakland County Cir. Ct. No. 90-390963-NZ.

In May 1995, after the Michigan Supreme Court issued its ruling finding assisted suicide to be a crime at common law, the Michigan Court of Appeals affirmed the circuit court's imposition of the permanent injunction. *People v. Kevorkian*, 210 Mich. App. 601, 534 N.W.2d 172 (1995). The Michigan Supreme Court denied leave to appeal. *People v. Kevorkian*, 549 N.W.2d 566 (1996). Dr. Kevorkian subsequently petitioned the U.S. Supreme Court for *certiorari*. (See *People v. Kevorkian*, 65 U.S.L.W. 3086.) That petition was pending when this federal action was filed. The petition for *certiorari* was denied on October 15, 1996, after oral argument on the parties' cross-motions for summary judgment in this action was completed. *Kevorkian v. People*, 117 S. Ct. 296, 136 L. Ed. 2d 215 (1996).

Dr. Kevorkian is a well-known advocate of the right to die and the right to physician-assisted suicide. He has previously been prosecuted in Oakland County for his assisted suicide activities, and was acquitted in each instance. He has admitted assisting in numerous suicides both prior to, and after, his last prosecution. Ms. Good is the former president of the Michigan Hemlock Society. According to plaintiffs' amended complaint, Ms. Good suffered from terminal pancreatic cancer. She alleged in this action that if she sought to obtain the assistance of a physician to end her pain and suffering, she faced indictment as a co-conspirator.

Dr. Kevorkian admitted that he helped Ms. Adkins commit suicide by means of his suicide machine, which consists of a frame holding three chemical solutions fed into a common intravenous line controlled by a switch and a timer. Dr. Kevorkian admitted that he inserted the intravenous line needle into Ms. Adkins' arm, but testified that Ms. Adkins activated the switch that turned on the machine.

Dr. Kevorkian placed a mask apparatus on Ms. Miller. The only witness at the preliminary examination who was present at the time said that Ms. Miller opened the gas valve by pulling on a screw driver. The cause of her death was determined to be carbon monoxide poisoning.

The Court used these general descriptions of Dr. Kevorkian's assisted suicide activities as the factual context for its decision in this matter.

Issue

Is there a constitutional right to assisted suicide? Are persons seeking physician assistance with suicide denied equal protection under the law when the law protects the right to reject medical treatment for those on life support, but those not on life support are denied assistance with suicide?

Holding

The Court held that there is no constitutional right to assisted suicide, and the statute barring assisted suicide does not violate the equal protection clause of the Fourteenth Amendment.

Reason

The plaintiffs contended that there is a constitutional right to assisted suicide. The plaintiffs' argument that a mentally competent adult has a protected liberty interest to a physician-assisted suicide under the due process clause of the Fourteenth Amendment was based primarily upon Supreme Court decisions concerning abortion, e.g., *Planned Parenthood v. Casey*, 505 U.S. 833, 112 S. Ct. 2791, 120 L. Ed. 2d 674 (1990), and withdrawal of life support, *Cruzan v. Director, Missouri Dept. of Health*, 497 U.S. 261, 110 S. Ct. 2841, 111 L. Ed. 2d 224 (1990). Thus, the plaintiffs specifically attacked the Michigan Supreme Court's ruling that these cases do not suggest any inclination on the part of the Supreme Court to expand the notion of constitutionally

protected liberty interests to encompass a right to suicide: Such a right is not expressly recognized anywhere in the United States Constitution or in the decisions of the United States Supreme Court and cannot be reasonably inferred.

In resolving these issues, the Supreme Court acknowledged that "the principle that a competent person has a constitutionally protected liberty interest in refusing unwanted medical treatment may be inferred from our prior decisions." 497 U.S. at 277, 110 S. Ct. at 2851. The Court went on, however, to make clear that "determining that a person has a liberty interest under the Due Process Clause does not end our inquiry; 'whether respondent's constitutional rights have been violated must be determined by balancing [her] liberty interests against the relevant state interests.'" *Id.* at 279, 110 S. Ct. at 2851-52.

Although the *Cruzan* Court stopped short of defining a clearly cognizable liberty interest, it assumed the existence of such a constitutional right to terminate unwanted life-sustaining medical treatment in order to reach the specific issue presented in the case, that is, whether Missouri's requirement that evidence of a mentally incompetent patient's wishes as to the withdrawal of life-sustaining medical treatment, expressed while the patient was competent, be established by "clear and convincing evidence" comports with the United States Constitution; "... for purposes of this case, we assume that the United States Constitution would grant a competent person a constitutionally protected right to refuse lifesaving hydration and nutrition." *Id.* at 279, 110 S. Ct. at 2852.

Further, the *Cruzan* court emphasized that if such a liberty interest existed, it would have to be balanced against relevant state interests such as the preservation of life.

With respect to assisted suicide, as the Michigan Supreme Court pointed out, at the time the Fourteenth Amendment was ratified, at least 21 of the 37 then existing states proscribed assisted suicide either by statute or as a common law offense. Presently, 32 jurisdictions have statutes that criminalize assisted suicide. The Model Penal Code also provides penalties for assisted suicide. Model Penal Code §§ 210.5 and 3.07(5).

What was being requested was that judges declare unconstitutional a law that prohibits assistance in taking a viable, self-sustaining life. This struck the Supreme Court as not merely asking courts to venture into uncharted legal territory, but also uncharted moral and ethical territory.

Viewed in this context, it seems particularly critical for the policy branches of government to establish such a right, if one is to be established. Given the historical treatment of suicide and assisted suicide, the Supreme Court was loath to find or create new constitutional rights where none existed before. The Court did not accept the plaintiffs' argument that because the policy branches of government have not acted, the courts must.

The plaintiffs asked the Court to strike down a law adopted by the State of Michigan, through its Supreme Court, in an area that has traditionally been left to the states—the regulation of medical and ethical conduct and the definition of crimes involving the taking of life. The regulation of this area goes to the heart of a state's traditional responsibility to define crimes and make determinations governing general health and welfare issues. Before federal courts invade and preempt this province of the states, it must be shown that there is an overriding federal constitutional interest that dictates such extraordinary action. In this case there has been no showing made of an overriding federal interest that would require displacement of state law.

The Court declined the plaintiffs' request to find a due process liberty interest right in the Constitution that confers constitutionally protected status upon assisted suicide.

The plaintiffs argued that a withdrawal of life-supporting nutrition and hydration is indistinguishable from assisted suicide. They contended that the withdrawal of food, water, and respiration were overt acts, not omissive conduct. They argued that because these acts were overt, there is no rational distinction between them and acts to hasten death by means of assisted suicide. There is a rational basis for distinguishing withdrawal of life support from assisting at a suicide. As the Michigan Supreme Court explained:

[W]hereas suicide involves an affirmative act to end a life, the refusal or cessation of life-sustaining medical treatment simply permits life to run its course, unencumbered by contrived intervention. Put another way, suicide frustrates the natural course by introducing an outside agent to accelerate death, whereas the refusal or withdrawal of life-sustaining medical treatment allows nature to proceed, i.e., death occurs because of he underlying condition. 527 N.W.2d at 728.

The equal protection clause of the Fourteenth Amendment requires only that states treat in a similar manner all individuals who are similarly situated.

Discussion

1. Examine the plaintiffs' arguments for asking the court to decide that prohibiting assisted suicide violates the equal protection clause.
2. For what specific reasons did the court decide there is no constitutional right to assisted suicide?

XVI

Labor Relations/Employment, Discipline, and Discharge

1. UNFAIR LABOR PRACTICES

Citation: *NLRB v. Shelby Mem'l Hosp. Ass'n*, 1 F.3d 550 (7th Cir. 1993)

Facts

The National Labor Relations Board (NLRB) brought an action to enforce its unfair labor practices orders against a nursing facility.

In the early summer of 1990, nurses at the facility began a union drive. The facility unsuccessfully opposed the union. The first case heard by the board arose when, in July 1990, an affiliate of the International Brotherhood of Teamsters and a licensed practical nurse employed by the facility, Ms. Sands, filed charges of unfair labor practices against the facility. The National Labor Relations Act, 29 U.S.C. § 158(a)(1) makes it an unfair labor practice for an employer "to interfere with, restrain, or coerce employees in the exercise of the rights guaranteed in" § 157.

Ms. Welton worked in the facility's dietary department. She attended a union organization meeting on July 5 and signed a union authorization card. At a hearing before the administrative law judge (ALJ), she testified that the day after the meeting her dietary supervisor, Ms. Fisher, took her aside at work and asked whether she or anyone from the dietary department had attended the meeting. Ms. Welton denied any knowledge of the meeting. Before the ALJ, Ms. Fisher denied having any conversation with Ms. Welton about the union meeting. The board found that the questioning of Ms. Welton constituted unlawful interrogation in violation of § 158(a)(1). The board credited Ms. Welton's testimony over that of Ms. Fisher because Ms. Welton was

no longer employed by the facility at the time of the hearing and had nothing to gain by testifying falsely about the incident.

Mr. Hopkins worked as a janitor for the facility. In April 1990, he was laid off as a result of the financial problems the facility was then experiencing. He was rehired in late June. Following his return, Mr. Hopkins attended the meeting on July 5 and signed an authorization card. He testified before the ALJ that, on July 15, five days after the Teamsters Union had filed an election petition, Mr. Carlson, the facility's maintenance supervisor, approached him at work and said "I've got to ask you this question. You can tell me if it's none of my business it you want to. Has [*sic*] any of the nurses or aides harassed you about the union?" *Id.* at 559. Mr. Hopkins said no. The board credited Mr. Hopkins' version of the events, noting that he, like Ms. Welton, was not employed by the facility at the time and had nothing to gain by fabricating his testimony.

On July 18, the facility circulated the following memorandum to all employees: "This is to advise that the NLRB has tentatively set a hearing on Wednesday, July 25th, to decide who can vote in a union election. Our position is supervisors, RNs, and LPNs cannot vote. We will keep you advised." *Id.* at 560.

On July 19, the facility held a mandatory meeting for all registered nurses (RNs), licensed practical nurses (LPNs), and supervisors. The facility's administrator, Mr. Wimer, the facility's attorney, Mr. Yocum, and the chief executive officer, Mr. Colby, of the facility's affiliated hospital, conducted the meeting. Mr. Yocum told the nurses that, in the facility's opinion, all RNs and LPNs were supervisors who could not vote in the upcoming election but must remain loyal to the facility. When asked by Ms. Sands, a union supporter, what he meant by loyalty, Mr. Yocum replied that all RNs and LPNs were prohibited from engaging in union activities. When asked by Ms. Sands why the facility opposed the union, Mr. Yocum responded, "Well, for one thing, they cost too . . . much money . . . [D]o you think those dues come out of thin air?" *Id.* at 560.

The board concluded that the facility, through Mr. Yocum, violated § 158(a)(1) by telling LPNs present at the meeting that they could not vote in the upcoming union election or participate in union activities, and that engaging in such activities could subject them to dismissal.

Issue

Did questioning by supervisors of their subordinates regarding a union meeting constitute an unfair labor practice?

Holding

The United States Court of Appeals for the Seventh Circuit held that the employer's interrogation of nursing facility employees about a union meeting constituted an unfair labor practice.

Reason

On the record as a whole, substantial evidence supported the board's conclusions that the questioning of Ms. Welton and Mr. Hopkins amounted to unlawful interrogation in violation of § 158(a)(1).

Discussion

1. What should be the proper conduct of an organization during an attempt by employees to seek union representation?
2. Do you consider the supervisors' questioning of the employees an unfair labor practice? Explain.

2. EMPLOYMENT AT-WILL/TERMINATION WITHOUT CAUSE

Citation: *Yambor v. St. Vincent Med. Ctr.*, 631 N.E.2d 187 (Ohio Com. Pl. 1993)

Facts

Mr. Yambor, a family counselor, brought a wrongful termination action against St. Vincent Medical Center, its program manager, and program coordinator. Mr. Yambor was hired by St. Vincent as a family counselor in 1984 under an oral agreement. Mr. Yambor understood that so long as he was employed by the medical center, he was to be compensated. He believed he could quit at any time and also assumed that St. Vincent could terminate him at any time. Mr. Yambor acknowledged that, by a letter of March 29, 1991, the medical center advised him that any further failure to perform to standards; any carelessness in areas of documentation or charting; any unscheduled, unexcused, or unauthorized absences; any communication problems or insubordination; or any careless performance would result in his termination. The record showed copies of reports of employee conferences, employee coaching forms, and memoranda reciting his history of discipline at the medical center. He was terminated from employment on July 2, 1991.

Under Ohio law, it is presumed that every employment relationship is "at-will," meaning either party may terminate the relationship at any time for any reason not contrary to law. This presumption of at-will employment can be rebutted if the parties agree that an employee will be discharged only for cause. Mr. Yambor contended that the medical center, by expressing reasons for his termination and by implementing a grievance procedure, represented to him that he could be terminated only for just cause. To this end, he relied on his own assumptions that his termination had to be based on a logical reason. Mr. Yambor argued that disciplinary letters containing complaints over his performance set forth issues of fact that prevented summary judgment.

Issue

Was the family counselor an employee at-will who could be terminated without just cause?

Holding

The court of common pleas held that the counselor was an employee at-will who could be terminated without just cause.

Reason

Mr. Yambor did not come forward with any evidence that the medical center had agreed he would be terminated only for just cause or that he had any basis for this belief. The basis of his claim for breach of oral agreement was the simple fact that he was terminated. Mr. Yambor was not able to specify any policies that were violated. Subjective understandings are insufficient to create material issues of fact.

Discussion

1. What is an at-will employee?
2. Why was Mr. Yambor considered an at-will employee?

3. DISCHARGE/ARBITRARY AND CAPRICIOUS

Citation: *Ward v. Brown,* 22 F.3d 516 (2nd Cir. 1994)

Facts

The plaintiff was a nurse at a Veterans Affairs (VA) Medical Center for nine years. In 1990, he was accused of verbally abusing three patients. The evidence indicated that the two nursing assistants who had reported him had been reprimanded by the nurse after they had left a suicidal patient alone with a razor. Further, it was a matter of record that the nurse was a labor organizer who had filed a number of grievances against his supervisor. He was discharged after a panel conducted an investigation and decided that all three of the charges were substantiated.

After the nurse received a letter of discharge, he requested and was granted a hearing before the department's disciplinary board. The board sustained only one of the charges, but still recommended the plaintiff's discharge for "intentionally teasing, speaking harshly to, threatening and intimidating the patient." *Id.* at 518. The plaintiff brought a suit against the VA, the Secretary of Veterans Affairs, and the director of VA Medical Center. Although the court found that the nurse's conduct constituted patient abuse, it ruled that the medical center's imposition of the penalty of discharge was arbitrary and capricious in light of their policy that was outlined in their manual. Their own policy mandated that the department treat similar offenses with similar penalties, and that they must punish the employees in proportion to the offense committed. The government appealed.

Issue

Was the discharge penalty arbitrary and capricious considering the policy manual and the offense committed?

Holding

The United States Court of Appeals for the Second Circuit held that the penalty of discharge was arbitrary and capricious, and thus had to be vacated.

Reason

Applicable statutes mandated that the board consider punishments that were within the prescribed limitations set by the Secretary of Labor. The penalties varied from a reprimand, to a suspension, to a reduction of pay, and finally to discharge. Further, the board had to recommend a penalty that was appropriate for the offense that was committed. The principle that was necessary to apply was "like penalties for like offenses." The board was found by the court not to have applied that principle. Therefore, it was held that it was arbitrary and capricious for the board not to have considered the applicable statutes. The punishment was inconsistent with that which was imposed on other employees who had committed patient abuse. The policy was required to be considered before recommending a penalty.

Discussion

1. Do you agree with the court of appeals decision? Explain.
2. What was the court referring to when it stated that the board failed to apply the principle "like penalties for like offenses"?

4. DISCHARGE/EQUAL PAY ACT

Citation: *Stevens v. St. Louis Univ. Med. Ctr.,* 83 F. Supp. 737 (E.D. Mo. 1993)

Facts

The plaintiff, a clinical nurse, alleged that she was paid less than a male employee who held a similar position and that she was wrongfully discharged in November 1990 after lodging complaints about such unequal pay. The plaintiff had brought her complaint to the Equal Employment Opportunity Commission (EEOC). The EEOC found that there was no reasonable cause to believe that she had been discriminated against on the basis of sex. The basis on which the medical center assigned various pay levels for clinical nurses included skill, effort, general job responsibilities, working conditions, scope of supervisory responsibilities, complexity of the position, size of the budget managed, and volume of procedures performed. The plaintiff had supervisory responsibility for three employees. Her male counterpart, Mr. Roth, had responsibility for 14 employees in the laboratory. The plaintiff periodically worked in the laboratory. Mr. Roth supervised her work during the times she worked in the laboratory.

Issue

Was the plaintiff discriminated against on the basis of sex and was she wrongfully discharged in retaliation for reporting her complaints to regulatory agencies?

Holding

The United States District Court for the Eastern District of Missouri granted the medical center's motion for summary judgment, dismissing the case.

Reason

The plaintiff's position was not comparable or substantially equal to the position held by the male employee. The Equal Pay Act does not mandate that jobs be identical, rather that they be substantially equal [29 U.S.C.G. § 206(d)]. Employers may differentiate between the sexes based on a seniority system, merit system, a system that measures earnings by quantity or quality of production, or a differential based on any other factor other than sex [29 U.S.C.G. §§ 206(d), (d)(1)].

In the absence of a specific nonretaliation law, a claim for wrongful discharge may be stated only where an employee is terminated for refusal to perform an illegal act or where the employee reported the employer's illegal act. No such allegations were made in this case.

Discussion

1. On what bases are employers prohibited from discharging an employee?
2. What is the employment-at-will doctrine?
3. Do you believe that the employment-at-will common law doctrine is applicable in today's society? Explain.

5. DISCHARGE/BREACH OF CONTRACT

Citation: *Chapman v. University of Mass. Med. Ctr.*, 628 N.E.2d 8 (Mass. 1994)

Facts

The plaintiff, Ms. Chapman, had brought an action against the state university medical center for wrongful discharge in breach of her employment contract. Ms. Chapman was hired as a supervisor of her department in 1978. In 1984, she became the assistant hospital director. She reported directly to Mr. Scarbeau, the chief executive officer. Ms. Chapman was one of four employees who reported directly to Mr. Scarbeau, none of whom had been employed longer than she

had. Ms. Chapman had trained one of three other associates who reported to Mr. Scarbeau, and substituted for the others. She received regular merit raises and had never been criticized. Ms. Chapman's last written contract, which was for the five-year period covering December 10, 1985, through December 9, 1990, provided that the appointments to the professional staff were contingent on the availability of funds. Ms. Chapman was the only person in her job category, and Mr. Scarbeau determined that her position was expendable, although he could have saved it by choosing to lay off other employees. Two months prior to the layoffs, Ms. Chapman had complained to Mr. Scarbeau about the high cost of purchasing radiation equipment. He told her to "mind her own business and she would be spared in the upcoming layoffs." *Id.* at 11. Of the 138 employees laid off, 70 to 80 employees were rehired within a year. Ms. Chapman was not one of them. The superior court held for the plaintiff finding that Mr. Scarbeau violated the medical center's employment contract with the plaintiff by acting in bad faith when he terminated her position.

Issue

Did Mr. Scarbeau act in bad faith by selectively eliminating the plaintiff's position during layoffs, rather than allowing her to bump others in her department?

Holding

The Supreme Judicial Court of Massachusetts affirmed the trial court's decision by finding that Mr. Scarbeau had acted in bad faith.

Reason

The court held that the judge could infer from the proffered testimony that Mr. Scarbeau threatened the plaintiff when she had complained to him about improper equipment bidding and purchasing procedures. He carried out his threat by firing her during layoffs for reasons other than unavailability of funds. The evidence supported the plaintiff's argument that her position was substantially the same as those held by the three associate directors. The plaintiff was qualified to bump others in her department.

Discussion

1. Could the employment-at-will doctrine have been an effective defense for the defendant?

2. Is it possible that the outcome in this case might have been different in another state? What about a different court or a different jury?

6. DISCHARGE/NURSE/PUBLIC POLICY/PATIENT CARE ISSUE

Citation: *Kirk v. Mercy Hosp. Tri-County*, 851 S.W.2d 617 (Mo. Ct. App. 1993)

Facts

The plaintiff was an RN who in 1983 was employed full time as a charge nurse with supervisory duties during her shifts. She reported directly to the hospital's director of nursing. A short time after one of her patients had been admitted to the hospital, the plaintiff diagnosed that the patient was suffering from toxic shock syndrome. Knowing that if left untreated death would result, the plaintiff believed that the physician would immediately order antibiotics. After a period of time had passed without having received those orders from the physician, she discussed the patient's situation with the director of nursing. She was informed by the director to "document, report the facts, and stay out of it." *Id.* at 618.

She further discussed the patient's condition and the lack of orders with the medical chief of staff, who took the appropriate steps. However, the patient still died. After the director was informed by a member of the patient's family that the plaintiff offered to obtain the medical records, and after she was later told that the plaintiff was heard to say that the physician was "paving her way to heaven," the director terminated the plaintiff.

After her termination, the plaintiff received a service letter from the hospital that directed her to refrain from making any further false statements about the hospital and its staff. The trial court entered a summary judgment for the defendant, stating that there were no triable issues of fact, and there was no public policy exception to her at-will termination. Further, the court could not find any law or regulation prohibiting the hospital from discharging her as a nurse. The plaintiff appealed.

Issue

Was there a public policy exception to the Missouri employment-at-will doctrine?

Holding

The Court of Appeals of Missouri reversed the granting of summary judgment and remanded the case for trial, holding that the Nursing Practice Act [§ 335.066.2(5),(6)] provided a clear mandate of public policy that the nurses had a duty to provide the best possible care to patients.

Reason

Public policy clearly mandates that a nurse has an obligation to serve the best interests of patients. Therefore, if the plaintiff refused to follow her supervisor's orders to stay out of a case where the patient was dying from a lack of proper medical treatment, there would be no grounds for her discharge under the public policy exception to the employment-at-will doctrine. She then had a valid action for wrongful discharge. Pursuant to the Nursing Practice Act, the plaintiff risked discipline if she ignored improper treatment of the patient. Her persistence in attempting to get the proper treatment for the patient was her absolute duty. The hospital could not lawfully require that she stay out of a case that would have obvious injurious consequences to the patient. Public policy, as defined in case law, holds that "no one can lawfully do that which tends to be injurious to the public or against the public good." *Boyle v. Vista Eyewear, Inc.*, 700 S.W.2d 859 (Mo. Ct. App. 1985).

Discussion

1. Explain how a public policy would be analyzed and then determined to apply in an employment-at-will case.
2. What was the public policy mandate in this case?

7. RETALIATORY DISCHARGE/PHARMACY TECHNICIAN

Citation: *Dalby v. Sisters of Providence*, 865 P.2d 391 (Or. Ct. App. 1993)

Facts

The plaintiff, Ms. Dalby, a pharmacy technician, brought an action against her former employer for retaliatory discharge and the infliction of emotional distress. Ms. Dalby alleged that in 1989 she was retaliated against for reporting to her supervisor on several occasions that there were inaccuracies in the drug inventory and that record keeping regarding these inaccuracies was in violation of Oregon administrative rules. Ms. Dalby alleged that rather than comply with the regulations, her supervisor retaliated against her because of her insistence that her employer comply with the rules.

Retaliatory actions against Ms. Dalby included accusations of stealing cocaine from the hospital's drug inventory in 1990. In 1991, Ms. Dalby learned that the sheriff's department had been asked to arrest her for stealing the cocaine. The sheriff's department refused to make the arrest. Ms. Dalby also alleged that her supervisor refused to talk to her except for job-related purposes and that hospital attendance policies were rigidly applied against her. As a result of the defendant's actions, Ms. Dalby resigned her position.

Ms. Dalby's former employer argued that the allegations did not demonstrate constructive discharge, which include: "(1) that the employer deliberately created or deliberately maintained the working condition(s), (2) with the intention of forcing the employee to leave the employment, and (3) that the employee left the employment because of the working conditions" [*Bratcher v. Sky Chiefs, Inc.*, 308 Or. 501, 506, 738 P.2d 4 (1989)].

The circuit court dismissed Ms. Dalby's claim, and she appealed.

Issue

Did the plaintiff state a cause of action for wrongful discharge and emotional distress?

Holding

The Court of Appeals of Oregon, assuming the plaintiff's allegation to be true, reversed and remanded the case, holding that the pharmacy technician had stated a cause of action for wrongful discharge and the intentional infliction of emotional distress.

Reason

Ms. Dalby made a good faith report as to the hospital's noncompliance with drug inventory and record keeping requirements required under Oregon regulations. Her report fulfilled an important "societal obligation." An employer may not discharge an employee for making such reports. The conduct of the employer, including false accusations that she had taken cocaine, gave rise to an action for the infliction of emotional distress.

Discussion

1. Regardless of the final disposition of this case by the trial court, what issues remain open for review by management and the governing body?
2. What control mechanisms should be in place to ensure oversight in the drug inventory?

8. DISCHARGE/ARBITRARY AND CAPRICIOUS/ NURSE

Citation: *Ward v. Derwinski*, 837 F. Supp. 517 (W.D. N.Y. 1992)

Facts

The plaintiff, a nurse, was discharged from the Veterans Affairs Medical Center in Canandaigua, New York (VACNY), for verbally abusing a psychiatric patient under his care. The plaintiff had been assigned to a nursing unit with 50 male patients who were hospitalized for chronic conditions, many of which were psychiatric in nature. During the morning of March 31, 1989, the plaintiff spoke with W.J., one of the patients on his floor. The patient had a history of hallucinations and unprovoked attacks on others. W.J. was leaning his head down in front of him. W.J. was giggling and talking to himself. The plaintiff, believing that the patient was hallucinating, called his name twice, but W.J. did not respond. The plaintiff patted W.J. on the shoulder and asked how he was feeling. W.J. responded, "Not good." The plaintiff then asked W.J. "if he felt like fighting." W.J. smiled and said, "Yes." Apparently it was common for the staff to question W.J. about fighting. W.J. was then asked if he would like medication, to which he replied, "Yes." The plaintiff administered Haladol, which was administered to W.J. on an as-needed basis.

Approximately two weeks later, two nurses filed written incident reports alleging that the plaintiff had abused W.J. The nurses claimed that the plaintiff was taunting W.J. and threatened to put him in restraints and "let the other patients at him." *Id.* at 519. The incident was reported to the plaintiff's supervisor, who suggested that they write memos to the medical director to initiate patient abuse charges against the plaintiff. An investigation of the incident by a three-member panel included interviews of nine employees, whose statements were recorded. Upon completion of the investigation, the panel recommended that the plaintiff be discharged. The medical director approved the panel's findings and the proposed discharge. The plaintiff appealed the medical director's decision to a disciplinary board. The board sustained the medical director's decision to discharge the plaintiff for charges of abuse against W.J. The plaintiff appealed to the Secretary of Veterans Affairs, who sustained the medical director's decision. The plaintiff then sought judicial review, alleging that the decision of the board was arbitrary and capricious and not supported by substantial evidence. The plaintiff claimed that "other nurses received less severe penalties for conduct which was much more egregious than the conduct for which he was terminated." *Id.* at 520.

Issue

Was the finding of verbal abuse arbitrary and capricious? Was the discharge penalty for the plaintiff arbitrary and capricious when compared to penalties in other disciplinary cases?

Holding

The United States District Court for the Western District of New York held that the finding by the Secretary of Veterans Affairs that the plaintiff verbally abused the patient was not arbitrary and capricious. The discharge penalty, however, was arbitrary and capricious when compared to penalties imposed in other disciplinary cases. The case was remanded for reconsideration of a penalty consistent with the court's decision.

Reason

The record indicated that the charge of verbal abuse was properly investigated. Nine employees were interviewed under oath. The fact that the board accepted some testimony against the plaintiff was not subject to review by the district court. The district court found that it could not overrule a credibility termination made by those who actually heard the testimony. As to the second issue, the choice of the penalty was largely within the agency's discretion. Although the discharge is permissible, the Veterans Affairs manual recommended that penalties administered be progressively severe before discharge action is initiated, "unless the offense is so serious that it warrants removal action." *Id.* at 523–524. There was no evidence in the record "so serious" as to warrant the plaintiff's discharge. The record contained numerous instances of conduct that were much more severe in nature but did not result in the penalty of discharge. For example:

- A nurse threw a milkshake in a 75-year-old patient's face after he spat medication at her. The nurse was suspended for one day.

- A nurse held down a patient while two other nursing assistants beat him for attempting to leave his area of confinement. The nurse received a 14-day suspension.
- A nurse inflated the retaining balloon and an abdominal feeding tube of a patient in order to facilitate its removal. This was against the hospital policy and procedure. No disciplinary action was taken.

Even more troubling is the indication in the record that plaintiff is the *only* professional nurse disciplined for patient abuse who received the penalty of discharge in the 30-year history of VACNY . . . on this record it is clear, that when compared to the penalties imposed for other instances of verbal and physical patient abuse, plaintiff's penalty is not consistent with VA policy, is extraordinarily severe, and, therefore, arbitrary and capricious. On this record, the determination of an experienced nurse, found to have committed only one instance of verbal patient abuse, is unjustified in fact. *Id.* at 524.

Discussion

1. What alternative disciplinary actions could have been taken?
2. What was the U.S. District Court's reasoning for determining that the discharge penalty was arbitrary and capricious?

9. NATIONAL LABOR RELATIONS ACT/NURSING SUPERVISORS EXEMPT

Citation: *Health Care & Retirement Corp. v. NLRB*, 987 F.2d 1256 (6th Cir. 1993)

Facts

The petitioner operates a nursing facility in Urbana, Ohio. The nursing department was staffed by a director of nursing, an assistant director, 15 RNs and LPNs, and 50 aides. The aides reported directly to the LPNs. From 1988 to 1989, there were continuing disputes between management and employees. After the nursing home administrator refused to meet with three nurses to discuss their complaints, they met with the director and vice president of Health Care and Retirement Corporation, who promised to conduct an investigation. At the completion of the investigation, three nurses were fired and more aides were hired at increased salaries.

The nurses filed a complaint with the NLRB for unfair labor practices. After a hearing, the NLRB found that the nurses were not supervisors, according to the National Labor Relations Act (NLRA), and ordered their reinstatement. The court of appeals, however, found that they were supervisors and not entitled to the NLRA's protection.

Issue

Were the nurses supervisors or employees according to the meaning of the NLRA?

Holding

The nurses were supervisors and not covered under the NLRA. Therefore, the court did not have to address the unfair labor practice claims.

Reason

29 U.S.C.S. 152 (11) of the NLRA defines a supervisor as:

> any individual having authority, in the interest of the employer, to hire, transfer, suspend, lay off, recall, promote, discharge, assign, reward, or discipline other employees, or responsibly direct them, or to adjust their grievances, or effectively to recommend such action, if in connection with the foregoing the exercise of such authority is not of a merely routine or clerical nature, but requires the use of independent judgment.

The nurses failed to establish, by substantive evidence, that they did not serve in a supervisory capacity. Nurse aides reported directly to them, and they had the authority to assign them. It was the LPNs' responsibility to find replacements for the aides if they did not report to work or were late. The LPNs were also responsible for approving lunches and breaks for the aides. An employee was considered a supervisor if any one of the enumerated tasks was performed and if the authority was exercised in the interests of the employer and required independent judgment.

Discussion

1. What would make a nurse a supervisor under the NLRA, resulting in no protection for the nurse under the act?
2. Why did the court determine that the nurses were supervisors?

10. EMPLOYEE HANDBOOK/TERMINATION AT-WILL

Citation: *Frank v. South Suburban Hosp. Found.*, 628 N.E.2d 953 (Ill. App. Ct. 1993)

Facts

The plaintiff, who was hired as a nurse by the South Suburban Hospital Foundation, became the nursing supervisor of the oncology unit when it opened. When she was hired in 1984, she had to attend an orientation meeting, and was told to bring her employee handbook with her. There were other versions of that handbook produced during her employment. In addition, personnel policies and procedures that were distributed were kept by her. The various sections of the handbook, such as the welcome and foreword, described the purpose of the handbook as providing guidelines about the employees' rights and responsibilities. It was also referred to as a "general manual." All units had additional specific operating manuals, policies, procedures, and rules. The discipline section of the handbook outlined five types of disciplinary action that could be taken under certain circumstances. The type of action was dependent on the severity of the offense.

The "Progressive Discipline Operational Practice Standard Procedure" mandated that the supervisor or manager was required to review the facts of the case and the action to be taken with the employee. The employee had to sign the disciplinary action form.

On March 17, 1987, a patient on the plaintiff's unit was experiencing an erratic and accelerated heart rate (170–180 beats per minute). After the completion of a series of tests, Dr. Fanaipour, the patient's physician, ordered intravenous digoxin. The plaintiff, noting from the patient's chart that the patient had been given digoxin in the past, was concerned that the patient might be "digtoxic." She decided to order a digoxin test to determine the level of digoxin in the patient's blood. While awaiting the results of the blood tests, the hospital noted that a staff nurse was preparing to give the patient another injection of digoxin, as ordered by Dr. Mehta, one of the patient's other physicians. The hospital ordered the nurse not to follow the physician's order until the laboratory results were completed. She also massaged the patient to lower his heart rate, which was not to have been done unless the patient was being monitored, which in this case, he was not. When Dr. Mehta arrived and discovered that his orders had not been followed, the nurse supervisor was suspended for three days until an investigation could be conducted. At the end of the three days, she was placed on paid sick leave and then terminated.

The plaintiff filed suit claiming that the hospital's employee handbook created contractual rights giving her employment status that could not be terminated at the will of the hospital. The circuit court granted the hospital's motion for summary judgment based on a finding that the employee handbook did not constitute a clear promise to form an employee contract. The hospital appealed.

Issue

Did the employee handbook and policies provided to the plaintiff at the time of her employment create contractual rights so that she could not be terminated at-will by the hospital?

Holding

The Appellate Court of Illinois held that the handbook did not create contractual rights giving the employee employment status that could not be terminated at the will of the hospital.

Reason

The handbook clearly stated that the type of discipline imposed on an employee would depend on the circumstances and severity of the infraction. It was clear that the employer had the discretion to use progressive discipline or not. The only contract found to exist in this case was that the hospital would abide by the policies and procedures distributed to the employees. The court found that there was no material issue of fact, and thus the employer was entitled to summary judgment.

In order for an employee handbook to constitute a contract, thereby giving enforceable rights to the employee, the following elements must be present:

- The policy must be expressed in language that clearly sets forth a promise that the employee can construe to be an offer.
- The statement must be distributed to the employee, making him or her aware of it as an offer.
- After the employee learns about the offer, he or she must begin or continue to work.

Even if it was determined that a contract existed between the hospital and the plaintiff, the hospital had complete discretion in implementing its progressive disciplinary procedure. The hospital followed its policies and procedures in

this case in that it discharged the plaintiff for a serious breach of hospital practice.

Discussion

1. What are the benefits of an employment contract?
2. Why should employment disclaimers be included in employee handbooks?
3. Is the employment-at-will concept appropriate in today's society?
4. What are the pros and cons of the employment-at-will doctrine?
4. Describe the elements that are necessary for an employee handbook to form a valid contract, granting enforceable rights to an employee.

11. PHYSICIAN'S LOSS OF TITLE CHALLENGED

Citation: *Hanna v. Board of Trustees of N.Y. Univ. Hosp.*, 663 N.Y.S.2d 180 (N.Y. App. Div. 1997)

Facts

The plaintiff physician commenced this action for a mandatory injunction to restore his title of Chief of Pediatric Urology and his blocked operating room time, claiming that his professional privileges at the defendant hospital were improperly withdrawn in violation of Public Health Law 2801-b, which provides that "[i]t shall be an improper practice for the governing body of a hospital to . . . curtail, terminate or diminish in any way a physician's . . . professional privileges in a hospital, without stating the reasons therefore." Professional privileges, also known as hospital privileges or clinical privileges, "are defined as 'permission to provide medical or other patient care services in the granting institution, within well defined limits, based on the individual's professional license and his/her experience, competence, ability and judgment.' [Joint Commission on Accreditation of Healthcare Organizations, *The Accreditation Manual for Hospitals* 53 (1993)]. . . . Physicians must have such privileges in order to use the beds, equipment and support staff within the facility."

Issue

Was the plaintiff's removal from his position as Chief of the Division of Pediatric Urology and the termination of his blocked time in the operating room subject to judicial review under Public Health Law 2801-b?

Holding

The plaintiff's removal from his position as Chief of the Division of Pediatric Urology and the termination of his blocked time in the operating room was not subject to review under Public Health Law 2801-b.

Reason

Because professional privileges in this context are understood to be the ability to admit and treat patients—and this understanding was the reason given by the Public Health Council (the administrative body with expertise regarding staff privileges) for declining to investigate plaintiff's complaint—the plaintiff did not suffer a termination or diminishment of his professional privileges in the hospital, and the complaint should have been found legally insufficient on defendant's pre-answer motion to dismiss. It is well settled that for statutes and regulations requiring special expertise and a knowledge of underlying operational practices, the construction given by the agency responsible for their administration, if not irrational or unreasonable, should be upheld. The Public Health Council's construction of the statute should be accorded due deference and, accordingly, plaintiff's removal from his position as Chief of the Division of Pediatric Urology and the termination of his blocked time in the operating room are not subject to judicial review under Public Health Law 2801-b.

Discussion

1. Discuss a scenario under which the Public Health Council might have agreed to investigate this case.
2. Discuss why clinical privileges are important to physicians.

XVII

Summary Case

The following case never reached the trial stage. This case is presented specifically for classroom review and discussion.

1. INFECTIONS

Citation: *Smith v. Community Med. Ctr.*

Facts

Mrs. Smith was admitted to a 34-bed surgical unit with a diagnosis of thoracic outline syndrome. She was scheduled for surgical removal of the first cervical rib. Upon admission to the community medical center, it was noted that the bed railings had a sufficient buildup of filth that it could have been scraped off with a utility knife. A suction jar, which was attached to the wall at the head of the bed, was filled with body fluids. Blood was splattered on the wall behind the bed. There was one sink, located near Mrs. Smith's bed, in the four-bed room. Surgical residents would enter the room, going from bed to bed examining pre- and postsurgical patients.

A patient in one bed had been admitted for the removal of a leg. She had hidden a thermometer and Tylenol in her pocketbook. The staff was unaware of her hidden stash. She was popping Tylenol because she was fearful her surgery would be canceled because of a fever that she had.

Throughout Mrs. Smith's stay, the room temperature fluctuated between 65 and 90 degrees on any given day. Mrs. Smith's temperature fluctuated between 103 and 106 degrees.

Postoperative nursing care was nonexistent the first 24 hours following surgery. On or about February 24, 1980, a nurse indicated that there were only two registered nurses on duty to care for 27 surgical patients and that it was difficult to render good patient care.

The attending physician failed to seek timely consultations from other specialists until requested to do so by Mrs. Smith's spouse, Mr. Smith. When the specialist, Dr. Berry, eventually did arrive, he stated that drainage tubes should have been inserted much sooner. Dr. Berry was overheard commenting, "I am appalled! Why wasn't I called sooner?"

Antibiotics had to be requested by a friend of the Smith family. Once antibiotics were requested, there was an ongoing failure to have them administered in a timely fashion. On one occasion, Mr. Smith asked a resident to see if the resident could administer Mrs. Smith's antibiotic. The resident responded, "That's not my job." Antibiotics had been ordered to be administered at 9:00 A.M. but were not brought to Mrs. Smith's room until 8:00 P.M. Delays of this nature served only to prolong Mrs. Smith's stay and were detrimental to her health and early recovery. The situation became so frustrating that on two occasions Mr. Smith called Mr. Thompson, the medical center's chief executive officer, in a frantic attempt to obtain his assistance. The calls were never returned. Dr. Plaster was called for assistance and was told that his intervention was necessary because of a lack in the coordination of Mrs. Smith's care.

There was a failure to maintain Mrs. Smith on her antibiotic once it had been prescribed. The IV was pulled out on the night of February 2 at 5:30 A.M. and was not restarted upon discovery. It was later determined that Mrs. Smith should have been maintained on the antibiotic for a longer period of time.

There was also a failure of the residents and interns to follow appropriate safety precautions in changing wound dressings. The spread of infection from one patient to the next was evident. A patient previously discharged from the room was returned to the hospital with an infection. It was only a matter of days until every surgical patient in the room developed an infection. Question remains as to what extent the infection may have spread to other patients on the patient care unit.

The hospital failed to provide Mrs. Smith with any special care, which is considered standard procedure. This information was related to Mr. Smith by a physician who said Mrs. Smith might not make it through the night. Mrs. Smith was discharged with a pocket of fluid between her rib cage and spleen, which was discovered during a sonogram at another hospital following discharge. The pocket of fluid continues to cause pain and discomfort.

Issue

What medical/legal issues can you identify in this case?

Holding

What decision would you make?

Reason

What was the reasoning of your finding?

Discussion

Develop several discussion questions.

Self-Test

Name: _____

Address: _____

_____

Profession: _____

_____

Telephone: _____

I—TORT LAW

1. The mother's premature discharge in *Somoza v. St. Vincent's Hosp.* was due to

   a. the failure of the hospital staff to properly assess the patient prior to discharge
   b. the fact that there was no indication that the patient needed a reassessment
   c. the fact that the patient had a complete history and physical assessment and there was no necessity of further testing
   d. the fact that the physician failed to write a discharge order
   e. the fact that the resident determined that there was no need for further reassessment
   f. a and d above

2. Poor outcomes, such as those described in *Somoza v. St. Vincent's Hosp.*, could be reduced if health care organizations

   a. improved documentation
   b. developed effective department protocols
   c. educated the staff
   d. effectively communicated
   e. a, b, and d above
   f. all of the above

3. *Caruso v. Pine Manor Nursing Ctr.* illustrates the importance of

   a. proper nourishment
   b. monitoring and documenting the intake and output of fluids
   c. taking corrective measures when fluid input and output signal a medical problem
   d. a and c above
   e. a, b, and c above

4. The appellate court in *Flores v. Cyborski* found that when an expert testifies at trial and he has a personal relationship with any of the parties in the case, the jury should be informed of such a relationship because

   a. it might influence how they decide the case
   b. the verdict would always be different if they had known
   c. the jury has a right to know every detail about each witness in a case
   d. that fact affects the credibility of the expert witness, which the jury must determine
   e. such information would never have an effect on the verdict

5. The Supreme Court of Iowa in *Wick v. Henderson* held that the *res ipsa loquitur* doctrine applies because

   a. it is not within the common knowledge and experience of a layperson to determine that an individual does not enter the hospital for gallbladder surgery and come out of surgery with an ulnar nerve injury to the left arm
   b. the defendants had exclusive control and management of the instrument that caused plaintiff's injury
   c. it was the type of injury that ordinarily would not occur if reasonable care had been used
   d. b and c above
   e. a and b above

6. The doctrine of *res ipsa loquitur* will be applied to the evidence in a case when all but one of the following occurs (e.g., *Lacombe v. Dr. Walter Olin Moss Reg'l Hosp.*):

   a. a foundation of facts, on which the doctrine may be applied, must be followed
   b. the injury must be of a type that ordinarily would not occur without negligence
   c. the event must, in light of ordinary experience, give rise to the inference that one is negligent
   d. the plaintiff must eliminate all other inferences and causes
   e. the evidence must show only a probability that the injury would not have occurred without negligence

7. In *Schauer v. Memorial Care Sys.*, the statements contained in performance appraisals are generally considered

   a. open for review by the general public
   b. defamatory statements
   c. libelous
   d. privileged information
   e. none of the above

8. In *Schauer v. Memorial Care Sys.*, performance appraisals should be prepared for all

   a. employees
   b. contracted staff
   c. paid physicians
   d. a and b above
   e. a, b, and c above

9. Even if a defamatory statement was negligently published to a third party (e.g., *Chowdhry v. North Las Vegas Hosp., Inc.*), a lawsuit will not succeed without the plaintiff showing

   a. that the defendant knew what he was repeating was defamatory and he did not apologize
   b. evidence of injury or damages
   c. intent on the part of the defendant
   d. that the plaintiff was upset by the statement in question
   e. that the defendant did not have knowledge the statement was going to be published

10. In *Sander v. Geib, Elston, Frost Prof'l Ass'n*, the statute of limitations will be tolled in a malpractice action only when

   a. there is an ongoing, dependent, and continuing treatment relationship between the plaintiff and the defendant
   b. the plaintiff had return visits to have her condition checked
   c. continuing visits are made to the same physician each time
   d. there would be no prejudice to the defendant
   e. it is a question of fact for the jury

11. In order for a libelous action to be effective in *Staheli v. Smith*, the defendant must show that

   a. the defamatory statement was written
   b. the defamatory statement was published to third persons with legitimate interests in seeing the statement
   c. the defamatory statement was published to persons not having a legitimate interest in seeing the written statement
   d. the action is time barred
   e. a and b above
   f. a, b, and d above

12. The main reason that summary judgment was entered in favor of the drug company in *Cooper v. Sams* was

   a. the company had a reputation for quality products
   b. the patient had not sued them on the correct theory of law
   c. the hospital was more liable than the company
   d. there was no material issue of fact for the court to decide
   e. there was no evidence presented against the company

13. In order to establish that a drug manufacturer is responsible for injuries arising from the use of a drug, the plaintiff in *Cooper v. Sams* must normally establish that

a. a danger exists in the normal use of the drug
b. the danger is not within the knowledge of or obvious to the ordinary user of the drug
c. the manufacturer failed to warn ordinary users of the not so obvious dangers of using the drug
d. there was a failure to adequately warn the prescriber of the drug's inherent dangers
e. all of the above

14. The elements that are necessary in order to establish false imprisonment in *Desai v. SSM Health Care* include

a. causation
b. restraint of an individual against his or her will
c. unlawful detention
d. self-serving restraint
e. b and c above
f. a, b, and c above

15. The preferred form of informed consent in *Riser v. American Medican Intern, Inc.* is a

a. verbal description by the physicians as to the procedure about to be undertaken, including the inherent risks and benefits of the procedure
b. verbal description by the nurse and the physician of the procedure about to be undertaken, including the inherent risks and benefits of the procedure
c. written consent that describes the inherent risks and benefits of the proposed procedure, as well as alternative procedures, if any, that are available
d. written consent and a verbal explanation to the patient regarding the recommended procedure
e. verbal explanation of the proposed procedure, including the inherent risks, benefits, and alternative procedures, as well as a written, signed, dated, and witnessed informed consent

16. Damages were apportioned between the plaintiff and appellee in *Cotita v. Pharma-Plast, U.S.A., Inc.* on the basis of

a. *respondeat superior*
b. independent contractor
c. contributory negligence
d. vicarious liability
e. comparative negligence
f. b and c above

17. The Court of Appeals of Ohio in *Seimon v. Becton Dickinson & Co.* held that the nurse failed to show that the defective needle cap was the proximate cause of her emotional distress because

a. she produced evidence that she was, in fact, exposed to HIV
b. she failed to produce any evidence that she was, in fact, exposed to HIV
c. the defective cap was the proximate cause of the nurse's emotional distress
d. the needle puncture caused physical injury
e. the nurse's right index finger was punctured by the needle
f. a, c, and d above

18. The main cause of Mrs. Piper's death in *Piper v. Bear Med. Sys., Inc.* was

a. bacterial filters were inserted into the Bear ventilator
b. the nurse inverted the one-way check valve on the ventilator
c. Mrs. Piper was not removed from the ventilator and provided with manually assisted breathing
d. the Bear 2 was the wrong equipment to use on Mrs. Piper
e. the design of the ventilator was defective

19. When the physician in *Robinson v. Shah* concealed from the patient that there was a sponge left in her abdomen,

a. he could not be sued because 10 years had passed and the statute of limitations prevented it
b. his actions constituted fraudulent misrepresentation
c. the patient should have discovered it with later X-rays
d. a sponge cannot harm a patient, so it did not matter
e. he had a valid reason to conceal it, so there should not be any sanction

20. Evidence of malpractice in *Cockerton v. Mercy Hosp. Med. Ctr.* is normally proven by

a. hearsay evidence
b. a reasonably prudent person
c. a layperson
d. substantial evidence
e. the court
f. expert testimony

21. Appellate courts in *Cockerton v. Mercy Hosp. Med. Ctr.* generally take evidence in the light most favorable to the

a. appellant
b. nonmovant party
c. appellee
d. movant party

e.   a and b above

f.   b and c above

22. In *Cockerton v. Mercy Hosp. Med. Ctr.*, falls from X-ray tables can be prevented by

a.   establishing appropriate protocols for restraining patients

b.   requiring that new employees be oriented to their job and department

c.   providing continuing education programs

d.   assessing each patient's needs for restraints

e.   a, b, and c above

f.   all of the above

II—CRIMINAL ASPECTS OF HEALTH CARE

1. In *Gilpin v. Board of Nursing*, a nurse's license to practice can be revoked when the nurse has been convicted of a crime that

a.   deals with truth and integrity

b.   impacts on society in general

c.   is based on a sexual act, and the criminal has not been sufficiently rehabilitated so as to enjoy the public trust

d.   deals with patients

e.   was committed on hospital grounds

2. The medical records of a physician's patients, in *State v. Poole*, seized during the course of a search warrant will be allowed into evidence if

a.   the physician gives permission for the records to be used

b.   the search warrant was sufficiently particular given the surrounding circumstances and nature of the crimes charged

c.   the physician is charged with crimes against the patients

d.   the patients have not come forward to charge the physician and the prosecution needs the information from the records to build its case

e.   the physician is employed by a hospital that maintains the records

3. When charging a pharmacist with improper record keeping with regard to the dispensing of narcotics (e.g., *United States v. Veal*), the prosecution does not have to prove that

a.   the defendant maintained an accurate record of controlled substances dispensed by him

b.   the prescriptions were invalid

c.   the missing tablets were dispensed illegally

d.   the defendant's record keeping was inadequate

e.   none of the above

4. The United States Court of Appeals for the 10th Circuit in *United States v. Neighbors* held that the evidence was

a.   sufficient not to support a conviction

b.   convincing so that the verdicts of the jury on all 45 counts were not amply supported

c.   sufficient to support no conviction

d.   inadequate to support a conviction

e.   convincing so that the verdicts of the jury on all 45 counts were amply supported

5. In *Travers v. Shalala*, an arrangement by a state not to prosecute an individual for Medicaid fraud because restitution has been made is

a.   binding on all federal courts

b.   binding on federal agencies

c.   binding on the Secretary of Health and Human Services

d.   a, b, and c above

e.   none of the above

6. The filing of false Medicaid claims, as in *People v. Evans*, constitutes the filing of a false instrument because such activity

a.   is permissible under both the Medicare and Medicaid regulations

b.   is a fraudulent activity

c.   is necessary in order for health care professionals to recoup their expenses for the treatment of Medicaid and Medicare patients

d.   reduces the costs of the Medicaid and Medicare programs

e.   all of the above

7. The chiropractor's argument in *Llewellyn v. Board of Chiropractic Exam'rs* did not merit extended discussion because

a.   he had not committed any fraudulent activities

b.   he was an exemplary employee

c.   the board's findings were not supported by substantial evidence

d. the chiropractor repeatedly engaged in conduct with an intent not to deceive the insurance companies

e. he produced chart notes only on those patients who actually had received treatment

f. none of the above

8. In *Everett v. Georgia Bd. of Dentistry*, pursuant to OCGA § 50-13-18(c)(1), a licensee must be afforded notice and an opportunity to be heard prior to suspension of his license except where

a. an incorrect standard was used to determine whether the license would be revoked

b. injunctive relief is sought

c. public health, safety, or welfare requires it

d. the public petitions for it

e. the board votes unanimously for it

9. Experts are allowed to testify about levels and effects of drugs such as lidocaine because (e.g., *People v. Diaz*)

a. lawyers don't know enough about drugs

b. the average juror does not have sufficient knowledge, so the expert is used to assist jurors as the triers of fact

c. it gives the side with the expert more credibility

d. the average juror has sufficient knowledge, so the expert is used to assist jurors as the triers of fact

e. a and d above

f. a, b, and c above

10. In *Surpris v. State of N.Y., Admin. Review Bd.*, a physician's license can be revoked if he or she

a. engages in submitting false Medicaid claims

b. submits claims for services never rendered

c. engages in double billing to help recover full reimbursement for services rendered

d. a and b above

e. a, b, and c above

11. The Supreme Court of Vermont in *State v. Houle* held that the evidence that the victim gave consistent accounts of the incidents underlying the charges to the nurse was

a. relevant but not admissible

b. the centerpiece of the trial

c. admissible but not relevant

d. relevant and admissible

e. a and c above

f. b and d above

12. In *Rudell v. Commissioner of Health*, the visit to the physician's examination room was determined to be proper because

a. the physician's attorney invited the visit and was present during the visit

b. the patient consented to the visit

c. the disciplinary committee asked to see the room

d. the court ordered the visit

e. a search warrant had been issued

13. In *Mundy v. Department of Health & Human Resources*, the legal duty of a business to take reasonable care to protect its employees and patrons does not extend to

a. criminal acts

b. acts committed where there are no security guards

c. unforeseeable criminal acts committed by third persons

d. foreseeable criminal acts committed by third persons

e. dangerous conditions on the premises

14. In *Nghiem v. State*, reinstatement of a physician's license, revoked because of sexual misconduct, can be contingent on

a. the unsuccessful completion of an appropriate rehabilitation program

b. agreement with the plaintiff's attorney

c. the successful completion of an alcohol rehabilitation program

d. the successful completion of an appropriate rehabilitation program related to the physician's misconduct

e. none of the above

15. The defendant in *State v. Cunningham* was guilty of a misdemeanor because

a. he did not commit wanton neglect of residents of a health care facility because he acted in a manner likely to be injurious to residents

b. he did not create the hazardous conditions

c. he did not refuse to remedy the hazardous conditions

d. he committed wanton neglect of residents of a health care facility because he acted in a manner likely to be injurious to residents

e. c and d above

f. a, b, and c above

III—CONTRACTS

1. The appellate court in *Sarah Bush Lincoln Health Ctr. v. Perket* held that the grant of a preliminary injunction was proper because

   a. the allegation that the defendant was engaging in the business of providing physical medicine and rehabilitation service in Coles County was sufficient
   b. there was insufficient evidence to proceed to trial
   c. the no-competition language contained in the contract was merely boiler plate commentary contained in most well-written contracts
   d. the language contained in the contract, coupled with the allegation in which the defendant was practicing in a geographic area in which she agreed not to practice, was not sufficient evidence to show an agreement of both parties
   e. a and d above
   f. a, c, and d above

2. The evidence in *Dutta v. St. Francis Reg'l Med. Ctr.* supported the jury's verdict that the hospital breached its written employment contract with the plaintiff in that

   a. Dr. Dutta should have been chosen as the medical director of the hospital's radiology department
   b. Dr. Dutta's qualifications to be appointed medical director were equal to or greater than those of Dr. Tan
   c. the hospital hired a medical director who was mutually acceptable to both the hospital and Dr. Dutta
   d. Dr. Tan practiced independently of Dr. Dutta in the same facility
   e. the hospital hired a medical director who was not mutually acceptable to both the hospital and Dr. Dutta

3. Exclusive contracts in *Oltz v. St. Peter's Community Hosp.* are valid if they are constructed to

   a. attract physicians to a particular community or hospital
   b. exclude other practitioners from practicing their profession
   c. eliminate competition
   d. attract specialists when there are no other specialists available in the community
   e. a and d above
   f. all of the above

4. The Court of Appeals of Ohio in *Truett v. Community Mut. Ins. Co.* held that the insurer's denial of coverage was not arbitrary or capricious because

   a. Mr. Truett's expenses were not for the care of a preexisting condition
   b. Mr. Truett's expenses were for the care of a preexisting condition
   c. Mr. Truett was covered under an employee benefit plan through a group health insurance contract with the hospital
   d. under the insurance policy, conditions that existed prior to the effective date of the policy are not covered if health problems related to the conditions were manifested after the effective date
   e. b and d above
   f. a and d above

5. The court in *Dominy v. National Emergency Servs.* held that the noncompetition clause was not overly restrictive because

   a. it did not prevent the physician from performing all practice of medicine
   b. the physician never complained about the contract terms
   c. physicians routinely leave hospitals after they learn everything and then compete with them
   d. the physician helped to write the contract
   e. none of the above

IV—CIVIL PROCEDURE AND TRIAL PRACTICE

1. The Superior Court of Pennsylvania in *Collins v. Park* held that the sheriff's attempt at service of writ of summons upon the physician by leaving a copy with the receptionist at the hospital was

   a. not sufficiently defective to confer jurisdiction
   b. was sufficiently defective
   c. was properly served because the physician was employed by the hospital
   d. was properly served because the physician was not employed by the hospital
   e. none of the above

2. The New York Supreme Court, Appellate Division, in *Gerner v. Long Island Jewish Hillside Med. Ctr.*, held that facts questions precluded summary judgment for the hospital because

a. there were no factual issues left unresolved after the examination before trial
b. the physician properly diagnosed and treated the infant in a timely manner
c. the hospital properly diagnosed and treated the infant in a timely manner
d. factual issues were left unresolved after the examination before trial
e. b and c above
f. b, c, and d above

3. The Supreme Court of Tennessee in *Byrd v. Hall* precluded summary judgment for defendant physicians because

a. there were no genuine issues of material fact
b. the plaintiff did not prove his entire case by a preponderance of the evidence
c. there were genuine issues of material fact
d. no factual dispute existed
e. b and c above

4. The Appellate Court of Illinois in *West v. Adelmann* held that a genuine issue of material fact existed as to whether

a. there was a primary physician–patient relationship
b. the physician was an employee of the hospital
c. the physician was an independent contractor
d. the hospital had failed to establish a physician–patient relationship
e. the hospital had established a physician–patient relationship

5. The Supreme Court of Appeals of West Virginia in *Matney v. Lowe* held that the evidence supported the jury's finding that the physician was not negligent because

a. there was insufficient evidence to support the jury's finding
b. there was more than enough evidence in the record that would not support the jury's finding that Dr. Lowe was not negligent
c. the defendant had relied on the radiologist's erroneous interpretation of the VQ scan
d. there was more than enough evidence in the record that would support the jury's finding that Dr. Lowe was not negligent
e. c and d above
f. b, c, and d above

6. The Missouri Court of Appeals in *Graham v. Thompson* held that a layperson, as a matter of common knowledge, could conclude that injuries to the calf were so unusual and would not result if due care had been used in the operation so as to bring the case within the

a. *res ipsa loquitur* doctrine
b. *respondeat superior* doctrine
c. vicarious liability doctrine
d. independent contractor doctrine
e. borrowed servant doctrine
f. captain of the ship doctrine

7. The Court of Appeals of Texas in *Smith v. O'Neal* held that the expert's testimony was sufficient to support the verdict because

a. the patient was experiencing pain on the left side of her mouth and the tooth did not present an emergency. The expert testified that the defendant was negligent by extracting the upper left molar without first attempting endodontic treatment to save the tooth.
b. the expert testified that the defendant was negligent by extracting the upper left molar without first attempting endodontic treatment to save the tooth. The patient was not experiencing pain on the left side of her mouth and the tooth did not present an emergency.
c. the patient was experiencing pain on the left side of her mouth and the tooth did not present an emergency
d. the expert testified that the defendant was not negligent by extracting the upper left molar without first attempting endodontic treatment to save the tooth
e. a and d above
f. b and d above

8. The nurse in *Morris v. Children's Hosp. Med. Ctr.* was competent to give expert testimony on liability issues because

a. she was qualified as an expert and her specialized knowledge did not aid the trier of fact in understanding the evidence
b. she had specialized knowledge
c. she had specialized training
d. she was qualified as an expert and her specialized knowledge aided the trier of fact in understanding the evidence
e. a and b above
f. b and d above

9. In *Bliss v. Brodsky*, the physicians were entitled to discovery of the financial arrangements between the consultant and her expert witness and her financial arrangements with the plaintiff because

   a. the business relationship cannot reasonably be calculated to lead to the discovery of relevant and admissible evidence concerning the physician's bias
   b. the plaintiff would prefer that such an arrangement be available for discovery
   c. the court has a right to make legislative rulings
   d. the defendant requested it
   e. the business relationship can reasonably be calculated to lead to the discovery of relevant and admissible evidence concerning the physician's bias

10. In the Georgia case *Tye v. Wilson*, the testimony of a physician is permitted in determining the standard of care required of a nurse in the treatment of an intubated patient because

   a. there is nothing to suggest that physicians and nurses are trained differently with regard to treating intubated patients
   b. the standard of care in the treatment of patients is equal for both physicians and nurses regardless of the circumstances
   c. a physician is more qualified to testify as to the standard of care required of a nurse than another nurse
   d. the physician was present and witnessed the nurse's negligence
   e. the physician has testified in other malpractice cases

11. The Supreme Court of Montana in *O'Leyar v. Callender* held that the trial court properly admitted the photographs of the patient's pathology slides because

   a. the photographs were known but not available to the defense
   b. the photographs were available to the defense but they were of such poor quality as to be of little or no probative value
   c. the photographs were available to the plaintiff
   d. the photographs were known and available to the defense at least 15 days before trial
   e. the photographs were not available to the plaintiff
   f. none of the above

12. The physician in *Blades v. Franklin Gen. Hosp.* was found at fault for the breast scarring and deformity of the patient because

   a. he did not call the patient to see that she was following his instructions
   b. he did not see the patient for enough follow-up visits
   c. he initially failed to diagnose the infection
   d. he did not aggressively treat the infection when it was diagnosed
   e. none of the above

13. The Court of Appeal in *McNall v. Summers* held that the appellant's continuous and serious loss of memory following electroconvulsive therapy (ECT) treatments was an injury triggering the California three-year statute of limitations on malpractice claims because

   a. there was nothing hidden about the appellant's injury. The appellant fully recognized she was continuously experiencing harmful lapses in memory adversely affecting her professional and personal life.
   b. there was something hidden about the appellant's injury. The appellant fully recognized she was continuously experiencing harmful lapses in memory adversely affecting her professional and personal life.
   c. there was no serious and continuous loss of memory
   d. the patient's physician gave her an article he had coauthored that stated "memory deficits and confusional states are said to be characteristic side effects of electroconvulsive therapy"
   e. b and d above
   f. a, c, and d above

14. The statute of limitations began to toll in *Stone v. Radiology Servs., P.A.*

   a. when the summons and complaint was filed
   b. when the patient's treatment was completed
   c. upon discovery of the proper diagnosis
   d. when the misdiagnosis was made
   e. c and d above
   f. a and b above

15. If a diagnosis based on blood tests could convey to the patient a feeling of a death sentence (e.g., *Bramer v. Dotson*), before rendering that diagnosis, the practitioner should

   a. reassure the patient as to life expectancy
   b. reorder the tests to confirm the diagnosis
   c. refer the patient for counseling
   d. accept the testing as being accurate
   e. schedule a second appointment six months later to see what other symptoms might develop

16. Prior to discharging a patient from his or her office (e.g., *Bramer v. Dotson*), the physician should provide the patient with

    a. discharge instructions
    b. information on any medications prescribed
    c. follow-up appointments as necessary
    d. referral to a specialist when indicated
    e. all of the above

17. The malpractice action in *Williams v. Kilgore* was not time barred because

    a. the plaintiff's physicians failed to notify her that the needle fragment had not been removed
    b. the plaintiff filed her malpractice action within the statutory time limit of two years from the time of discovering that the needle fragment remained in her
    c. the defendants committed medical malpractice
    d. the defendants had not responded to the plaintiff's initial summons
    e. none of the above

18. In *Follett v. Davis*, the superior court found that the statute of limitations began to run

    a. when the patient made her first visit to the clinic
    b. when the patient made her first visit to the physician
    c. when the patient first discovered the lump on her breast
    d. after the mammogram
    e. following examination by the technician
    f. after the patient's last visit to the clinic

19. The nurse in *Sullivan v. Sumrall by Ritchey*, who was employed by a county hospital, was not shielded by public official qualified immunity from a medical negligence action because

    a. she was a public official
    b. she was a private citizen functioning in the capacity of a public official
    c. she was a private duty nurse
    d. there is no qualified immunity for public hospital employees making treatment decisions
    e. c and d above
    f. none of the above

20. The Good Samaritan law in Alaska (e.g., *Deal v. Kearney*) extends to emergency department physicians

    a. who have a preexisting duty to render emergency care
    b. who are employed by the hospital
    c. who provided contracted services for providing emergency care in hospital emergency departments
    d. who do not have a preexisting duty to render emergency care
    e. a and b above
    f. none of the above

21. The Supreme Court of Mississippi in *Meena v. Wilburn* held that the jury's exoneration of Ms. Greer

    a. was grounds for a new trial on the issue of the physician's liability
    b. should be reversed because a master is held liable and the servant is exonerated
    c. was not grounds for a new trial on the issue of the physician's liability
    d. a and b above
    e. b and c above

22. The New York Supreme Court, Appellate Division, in *Sarivola v. Brookdale Hosp. & Med. Ctr.* (involving treatment of a patient by a private attending physician, not an employee of the hospital), held that the hospital

    a. was not liable for acts of malpractice that were committed in carrying out the independent physician's orders
    b. was liable for acts of malpractice that were committed in carrying out the independent physician's orders
    c. was liable because the physician was provided by the hospital
    d. was liable because the physician was acting on the hospital's behalf
    e. was liable because the plaintiff believed that the physician was employed by the hospital

23. General damages include (e.g., *Doe v. McNulty*)

    a. physical pain
    b. mental anguish
    c. medical expenses
    d. a and b above
    e. a, b, and c above

24. Charting on medical records (e.g., *Doe v. McNulty*) should include the

    a. patient complaints

b. patient history and physical examination
c. tests ordered and results obtained
d. discharge instructions given to the patient
e. all of the above

25. Factors that a jury may consider in awarding damages (e.g., *Callahan v. Cardinal Glennon Hosp.*) include

a. age of the patient
b. sex of the patient
c. extent of injury
d. diminished earnings capacity
e. a, c, and d above
f. all of the above

26. The Court of Appeal of Louisiana in *Dodson v. Community Blood Ctr.* held that the award of damages was not excessive because the plaintiff

a. was a credible witness
b. exaggerated his symptoms, fears, and worries about his condition
c. felt like a leper and feared infecting his wife, child, and friends with the disease
d. contracted non-A and non-B hepatitis through the blood transfusions received
e. a, b, and d above
f. a, c, and d above

27. The Supreme Court of Kansas held in *Delaney v. Cade* that

a. Kansas recognizes a medical malpractice cause of action for the lost chance of a better recovery
b. in adopting and applying the loss of chance theory to medical malpractice cases, it must always be kept in mind that the practice of medicine and the furnishing of appropriate health care is not an exact science. Kansas does not recognize medical malpractice cause of action for the lost chance of a better recovery.
c. for every treatment there are undoubtedly other physicians who might have performed or used a different treatment. The courts should not use extreme caution in second-guessing the methods used by medical care providers, particularly in an area as nebulous as the loss of a chance for a better or more satisfactory recovery.
d. most cases have involved death of the patient and damages may be difficult to resolve in a loss of a chance of a better recovery case. This fact should be grounds to refuse to recognize the doctrine when

medical malpractice has substantially reduced a person's chance of a better recovery.
e. a and c above
f. a, c, and d above

28. In *Raskin v. Community Blood Ctrs. of S. Florida, Inc.*, Florida Statutes provide that a plaintiff may maintain an action for damages on the grounds of breach of implied warranty of fitness or merchantability only if he

a. alleges and proves that the defect of which he complains is not detectable or removable by the use of reasonable scientific procedures or techniques
b. alleges but does not prove that the defect of which he complains is detectable or removable by the use of reasonable scientific procedures or techniques
c. alleges and proves that the defect of which he complains is detectable or removable by the use of reasonable scientific procedures or techniques
d. alleges and proves that the defect of which he complains is detectable or removable by the use of unreasonable scientific procedures or techniques
e. all of the above

29. Utah's Good Samaritan Act affords immunity to a physician rendering emergency medical care at the scene of an emergency occurring in the hospital *(see Hirpa v. IHC Hosps., Inc.)* if

a. the physician is under a preexisting duty to do so
b. the physician is under no preexisting condition to do so
c. the physician is an employee of the hospital
d. the physician is an independent contractor
e. all of the above

30. Expert medical testimony in *Taylor v. McCullough-Hyde Mem'l* was necessary to establish a causal connection between the negligence and the injury whenever the relationship is

a. beyond the common knowledge and understanding of the jury
b. within the common knowledge and understanding of the jury
c. within and beyond the common knowledge and understanding of the expert witness
d. within and beyond the common knowledge and understanding of the court
e. outside the common knowledge of the expert

31. In *Turner v. Nama*, the Illinois statute of repose is only excepted by

a. failure to conceal negligence in the care of the patient

b. postponing patient treatment

c. the statute of limitations

d. fraudulent concealment and postponed by an ongoing course of continuous negligent medical treatment

e. none of the above

V—CORPORATE LIABILITY

1. There was a material issue of fact in *Candler Gen. Hosp., Inc. v. Persaud* as to whether the hospital was negligent in granting the staff the privileges requested because

   a. a hospital has a direct and independent responsibility to its patients to take reasonable steps to ensure that staff physicians using hospital facilities are qualified for privileges granted

   b. the plaintiff sought to hold the hospital liable

   c. there is no evidence of the surgeon's curtailment or denial of staff privileges at other hospitals

   d. the patient, rather than the hospital, selected the independent staff surgeon to perform the procedure at issue

   e. the hospital was negligent in its initial appointment of the physician to the hospital's medical staff

2. Before proceeding with an emergency medical procedure (e.g., *Citron v. Northern Dutchess Hosp.*), the organization should ensure that

   a. the patient has signed the appropriate consent forms

   b. the physician is properly credentialed to perform the procedure he is about to undertake

   c. appropriate blood products are available should they be required during a surgical procedure

   d. the required insurance forms have been completed

   e. appropriate resources are available to perform the proposed surgical or medical procedures

3. In order to better avoid being held vicariously liable for the negligent acts of an independent emergency department physician (e.g., *Citron v. Northern Dutchess Hosp.*), the hospital

   a. should require that the patient request a specific physician

   b. should provide for the proper products for the treatment of the patient by all emergency department physicians

   c. should inform the patients that they disclaim all liability against emergency department physicians

   d. should not allow patients to be admitted through the emergency department

   e. should make emergency department patients sign a release excusing any negligent acts committed on or behalf of the hospital

4. The Court of Appeals of North Carolina in *Hoffman v. Moore Reg'l Hosp., Inc.* held that the hospital was not liable for the negligence of the radiologist under the theory of *respondeat superior* because

   a. he was subject to supervision or control by the hospital

   b. he was not subject to supervision or control by the hospital

   c. he was not subject to supervision of the hospital, but he was subject to its control

   d. the patient could have sought treatment elsewhere

   e. the patient could not have sought treatment elsewhere

5. The emergency medical technician in *Riffe v. Vereb Ambulance Serv., Inc.*, was employed by Vereb Ambulance Service while responding to an emergency call regarding Mr. Anderson, began administering to Mr. Anderson the drug lidocaine, as ordered over the telephone by the medical command physician at defendant hospital. While en route to the hospital, Mr. Anderson was administered an amount of lidocaine 44 times the normal dosage. In a suit involving the hospital, the Court held that

   a. the case was frivolous

   b. action against the hospital based on the theory of vicarious liability was not barred by earlier settlement by the ambulance company and technician

   c. the liability of the hospital could be imputed to the medical technicians

   d. the liability of medical technicians could not be imputed to the hospital, and action against the hospital based on the theory of vicarious liability was barred by earlier settlement by the ambulance company and technician

   e. none of the above

6. Credentialing physicians with knowledge of, or failure to learn of, their malpractice history (e.g., *Corrigan v. Methodist Hosp.*)

   a. is not a credentialing issue

b.   is not considered negligent conduct

c.   can be considered negligent

d.   is not a malpractice issue

e.   gives rise to products liability and fraud

7.   The evidence in *Denton Reg'l Med. Ctr. v. LaCroix* established that the hospital owed a duty to plaintiff's decedent to have an anesthesiologist

a.   provide or supervise most of her anesthesia medical care, including having an anesthesiologist personally present after the patient's discharge from the postanesthesia recovery room

b.   provide or supervise all of her anesthesia medical care, including having an anesthesiologist personally present or immediately available in the operating suite after the surgical procedure had been performed

c.   provide or supervise none of her anesthesia medical care, including having an anesthesiologist personally present or immediately available in the operating suite

d.   provide or supervise all of her anesthesia medical care, including having an anesthesiologist personally present or immediately available in the operating suite, and that the hospital's breach of this duty had proximately caused her brain damage

e.   all of the above

VI—MEDICAL STAFF

1.   The Supreme Court of Iowa held in *Welte v. Bello* that expert testimony

a.   was required to establish a claim against the anesthesiologist

b.   was required to show that anesthesia generally infiltrates surrounding tissue

c.   would be required from a second anesthesiologist in order to establish that both the nurse and anesthesiologist were negligent

d.   was not required to establish a claim against the anesthesiologist

e.   c and d above

2.   The Supreme Court held that no physician–patient relationship existed in *Roberts v. Hunter* because Dr. Hayes

a.   examined the patient but did not review the medical record

b.   did not examine the patient; however, he did review the medical record

c.   reviewed the medical record

d.   examined the patient

e.   neither examined the patient nor reviewed his medical records

3.   A patient is considered to receive continuous treatment (e.g., *Stilloe v. Contini*) when

a.   continuous office visits are made to the physician

b.   the course of treatment is related to the original complaint

c.   at least two physicians treat the same patient for the same ailment

d.   a physician determines that the patient is receiving continuous treatment

e.   none of the above

4.   A patient with a persistent physical complaint that the patient believes has not been accurately diagnosed by the treating physician (e.g., *Sacks v. Mambu*) should

a.   attempt self-diagnosis with the aid of over-the-counter diagnostic tests available at the local pharmacy (e.g., fecal occult blood and pregnancy tests)

b.   seek a second opinion from another physician

c.   attempt to more accurately describe to friends and relatives the physical symptoms that are being experienced

d.   accept the treating physician's diagnosis

e.   none of the above

5.   Malpractice cases can be reduced (e.g., *Sacks v. Mambu*) by

a.   conducting a comprehensive physical assessment based on the patient's needs and presenting complaints

b.   referring the patient to a specialist for evaluation when indicated

c.   ordering diagnostic tests based on efficacy as related to the physician's physical findings

d.   a and c above

e.   a, b, and c above

6.   The assessment of a patient's care needs (e.g., *Sacks v. Mambu*) should be based on data from the patient's

a.   previous health care records

b.   family or significant other

c.   presenting physical complaints

d.   a and c above

e.   a, b, and c above

7. The Court of Claims of Ohio in *Tomcik v. Ohio Dept. of Rehabilitation & Correction* held that the delay in giving inmate treatment fell below medically acceptable standards for provision of medical care because

    a. it is probable that an earlier procedure would not have had any effect on the patient's ultimate treatment. Through the inexcusable delays, the patient lost this option and, instead, was medically required to have the entire breast removed.
    b. the court was "appalled" that Dr. Evans had the audacity to characterize his evaluation as a medical examination
    c. it is probable that an earlier procedure would have safely and reliably conserved a large part of the patient's right breast. Through the inexcusable delays, the patient lost this option and, instead, was medically required to have the entire breast removed.
    d. another physician noted the existence of the lump in the patient's breast and determined that the size of the mass was approximately four to five centimeters and somewhat fixed
    e. the patient was examined by a nurse who noted in her nursing notes that the patient had a moderately large mass in her right breast

8. The patient's suffering in *Bombagetti v. Amine* was attributed to

    a. comparative negligence
    b. contributory negligence
    c. physician malpractice
    d. hospital negligence
    e. negligence on both the part of the hospital and the physician

9. Health care practitioners who accept patients into their practice as a referral from other sources (e.g., physicians, clinics, ambulatory care centers, and hospital emergency departments) should

    a. obtain summary reports from the referral source
    b. obtain the results of diagnostic tests conducted by the referring source
    c. reject all findings of the referring source and conduct a complete history and physical examination and order diagnostic tests as appropriate
    d. a and b above
    e. a, b, and c above

10. The physician in *Shelton v. United States* was held liable for the injury to the patient because

    a. she failed to give antibiotics when there was an obvious chance of infection to the wound site
    b. she never ascertained the origin of the injury
    c. she did not read the treatment instructions to the patient to ensure that he understood them
    d. she did not keep the patient in the hospital to follow up on his care
    e. she did not turn the case over to a specialist

11. An expert's opinion (e.g., *Reese v. Stroh*) must be based on

    a. scientific knowledge
    b. conjecture
    c. speculation
    d. supposition
    e. b, c, and d above

12. Disciplinary action against a health care professional, as in *Nehorayoff v. Fernandez*, is often procrastinated because of

    a. fear of a lawsuit (e.g., defamation action)
    b. inability to obtain cooperation from peers who are aware of a professional's questionable abilities or competence
    c. lack of support from such groups as administration, governing body, medical staff, and nursing administration
    d. fear of backlash from other peers
    e. a and d above
    f. a through d above

13. The Supreme Court of Missouri in *Hiers v. Lemley* held that the survivors made a submissible case of negligent medical treatment because

    a. a specialist in pathology testified at trial that neither an oncologist nor a general pathologist would have the expertise to make a proper diagnosis of the patient's condition
    b. a specialist in pathology testified that an oncologist or a general pathologist would have the expertise necessary to make a proper diagnosis of the patient's condition
    c. another pathologist examined the biopsy slides with Dr. Sheffield and was uncertain of the diagnosis and had them sent to another physician for review
    d. the patient's diagnosis was questionable
    e. a, c, and d above
    f. a through d above

14. A surgeon in the operating room who requests a frozen section of a biopsy (e.g., *Suarez Matos v. Ashford Presbyterian Community Hosp.*) should

  a. verbally confirm with the pathologist his finding prior to proceeding with any radical surgery
  b. require a formal typed written report from the pathologist prior to proceeding with any radical surgery
  c. ideally, verbally confirm via intercom with the pathologist his finding and require, at minimum, a signed and dated handwritten note in the patient's chart describing the pathologist's findings
  d. require the pathologist to report directly to the operating room and describe his findings when radical surgery may be required as a result of the pathological findings
  e. require a verbal report from a laboratory technologist

15. The Court of Appeal of Louisiana in *Winder v. Avet* held that misdiagnosis was a continuing tort as to which the three-year prescriptive period did not begin to run until

  a. the statute of limitations had tolled
  b. evidence did not establish that the pathologist committed malpractice in misdiagnosing chronic pancreatitis as pancreatic cancer
  c. a correct diagnosis and evidence established the pathologist's malpractice in misdiagnosing chronic pancreatitis as pancreatic cancer
  d. the statute of limitations had tolled and a correct diagnosis and evidence established the pathologist's malpractice in misdiagnosing chronic pancreatitis as pancreatic cancer
  e. a, c, and d above
  f. a through d above

16. The Supreme Court of Iowa in *Leonard v. State* held that the psychiatrist owed no duty of care to Mr. L. because

  a. Mr. L. was Mr. P.'s employee
  b. the psychiatrist owed a special duty of care to an individual member of the public for decisions regarding the treatment and release of mentally ill patients from confinement
  c. the psychiatrist's prognosis was subject to second-guessing by any member of the public
  d. the psychiatrist owed no duty of care to an individual member of the public for decisions regarding the treatment and release of mentally ill patients from confinement
  e. a and d above
  f. a through d above

17. The Supreme Court of Kansas in *Oberzan v. Smith* held that a radiologist

  a. could be held liable under the doctrine of *respondeat superior* for the negligent acts of an X-ray technician who was employed by the hospital
  b. could not be held liable under the doctrine of *respondeat superior* for the negligent acts of an X-ray technician who was employed by the hospital
  c. was vicariously responsible for the negligent acts of an X-ray technician who was employed by the hospital
  d. was not vicariously responsible for the negligent acts of an X-ray technician who was employed by the hospital
  e. b and d above
  f. none of the above

18. The District of Columbia Court of Appeals in *Colbert v. Georgetown Univ.* held that the physician should have performed a mastectomy instead of a lumpectomy because

  a. the admissions and other statements of the physician did not establish a *prima facie* case of malpractice
  b. the admission of negligence and other statements of the physician established a *prima facie* case of malpractice
  c. the admissions and other statements of the physician established that the statements had no probative value
  d. the patient's chances of survival had decreased from 90 percent to 10 percent
  e. the patient had received a questionable diagnosis and had a poor prognosis

19. The Supreme Court of North Carolina in *Mozingo v. Pitt County Mem'l Hosp.* held that the on-call physician owed patients a duty to reasonably supervise the obstetrics residents who provided care because

  a. according to the defendant's own experts, simply remaining at home and available to take telephone calls is not always an acceptable standard of care for supervision of residents
  b. according to the defendant's own experts, simply remaining at home and available to take telephone calls is always an acceptable standard of care for supervision of residents
  c. three teaching hospitals established that the defendant did not breach the applicable standard of care for on-call supervising physicians
  d. there was no known significant risk of an extremely large baby

e.   b and d above
f.   a and c above

20. The New York Supreme Court, Appellate Division, in *Poulard v. Commissioner of Health*, held that the surgeon had practiced with gross negligence because

a.   the evidence supported a finding of negligence
b.   the evidence failed to support a finding of negligence
c.   the surgeon interpreted the patient's X-ray
d.   the surgeon deferred the patient's surgery after being informed of certain abnormal test results
e.   the surgeon recognized the colonic interposition during the course of the patient's surgery and rendered efficient postoperative care, as evidenced by the patient's severe weight loss

21. Dr. Sauls' testimony, in *Todd v. Sauls*, convinced the court that he

a.   aggressively treated the surgical wound infections, that he chose not to take advantage of the nurses' observations of infection, and that he allowed Mr. Todd's body weight to waste away, knowing firsthand that extreme vigilance was required because of Mr. Todd's already severely impaired heart
b.   failed to aggressively treat the surgical wound infections, that he chose to take advantage of the nurses' observations of infection, and that he allowed Mr. Todd's body weight to waste away, knowing firsthand that extreme vigilance was required because of Mr. Todd's already severely impaired heart
c.   aggressively treat the surgical wound infections, that he chose not to take advantage of the nurses' observations of infection, and that he allowed Mr. Todd's body weight to waste away, knowing firsthand that extreme vigilance was required because of Mr. Todd's already severely impaired heart
d.   failed to aggressively treat the surgical wound infections, that he chose not to take advantage of the nurses' observations of infection, and that he allowed Mr. Todd's body weight to waste away, knowing firsthand that extreme vigilance was required because of Mr. Todd's already severely impaired heart
e.   aggressively treated the surgical wound infections, that he chose not to take advantage of the nurses' observations of infection, and that he allowed Mr. Todd's body weight to waste away, knowing firsthand that extreme vigilance was required because of Mr. Todd's already severely impaired heart

22. The District Court in *Smith v. U.S. Dept. of Veterans Affairs* held that the negligent failure of physicians to promptly review laboratory tests results was

a.   not the proximate cause of the plaintiff's injury
b.   the proximate cause of the plaintiff's injury
c.   the result of the laboratory technician's negligence
d.   the result of the hospital's negligence
e.   a and c above

23. The decision to grant or not to grant a new trial based on the excessiveness of a jury verdict in *Tesauro v. Perrige* was

a.   within the sound discretion of the trial court and its decision was not upheld
b.   not within the sound discretion of the trial court
c.   within the sound discretion of the trial court and its decision was upheld on appeal
d.   a and c above
e.   none of the above

24. The District Court in *Hamilton v. Baystate Med. Educ. & Research Found.* held that the employer's decision to terminate the plaintiff after he had committed serious medical errors was

a.   not reasonable and did not constitute breach of contract
b.   reasonable and did not constitute breach of contract
c.   reasonable and did constitute breach of contract
d.   not reasonable and did constitute breach of contract
e.   a and d above

25. The appeals court in *Bouley v. Reisman* found no abuse of discretion where the trial judge gave detailed instructions to the jury about their role in determining

a.   the credibility of witnesses and the inferences that they might draw from the direct and circumstantial evidence presented at the trial
b.   the credibility of hearsay evidence
c.   the credibility of the physician's documentation
d.   the credibility of the court's instructions
e.   c and d above

26. The record in *Caldwell v. Department of Prof'l Regulation* contained ample evidence to support the Director's decision that the plaintiff

a.   properly prescribed controlled substances for nontherapeutic purposes

b. recklessly prescribed antibiotics for nontherapeutic purposes without regard for the safety of his patient and in violation of the Medical Practice Act and the Controlled Substances Act

c. prescribed controlled substances for therapeutic purposes with regard for the safety of his patient

d. recklessly prescribed controlled substances for nontherapeutic purposes without regard for the safety of his patient and in violation of the Medical Practice Act and the Controlled Substances Act

e. a and c above

VII—NURSING AND THE LAW

1. The United States Court of Appeals in *Porter v. Lima Mem'l Hosp.* held that the nurse's failure to repeat vital signs was

   a. legally insufficient to establish a causal connection between the failure to repeat vital signs and the patient's eventual paralysis

   b. legally sufficient to establish a causal connection between the failure to repeat vital signs and the patient's eventual paralysis

   c. of significant importance in the treatment of the patient

   d. sufficient to support the claim of negligence

   e. sufficient to support the claim of malpractice

   f. d and e above

2. The New York Supreme Court, Appellate Division, in *Luthart v. Danesh* held that there was

   a. no material issue of fact regarding the alleged negligence of hospital nurses in monitoring the pulse in the decedent's leg, thus precluding summary judgment for the hospital

   b. conflicting expert opinion as to whether the hospital was negligent in failing to have a Doppler ultrasonic stethoscope available and whether that failure contributed to the decedent's injury

   c. a material issue of fact regarding the alleged negligence of hospital nurses in monitoring the pulse in the decedent's leg, thus precluding summary judgment for the hospital

   d. no conflicting expert opinion as to whether the hospital was negligent in failing to have a Doppler ultrasonic stethoscope available and whether that failure contributed to the decedent's injury

   e. b and c above

   f. a and d above

3. The New York Supreme Court, Appellate Division, in *Nueces v. Long Island College Hosp.*, held that the evidence supported a finding of liability, and that the award of damages was not excessive because

   a. there was no rational basis for the jury's findings of negligence on the part of the defendant's agent in the administration of an injection

   b. there existed a rational basis for the jury's findings of negligence on the part of the defendant's agent in the administration of an injection to the plaintiff's left buttock that proximately caused her permanent injuries

   c. the matter was improperly left to the jury to determine

   d. the matter was properly left to the jury to determine

   e. a and d above

   f. b and d above

4. The Court of Appeal of Louisiana in *Ard v. East Jefferson Gen. Hosp.* held that the spouse's testimony that no one responded to her calls for assistance for one hour and 15 minutes was

   a. immaterial as to its significance as evidence

   b. of no probative value

   c. inconsistent with the medical records

   d. consistent with the medical records

   e. inconsequential as to the outcome of the trial

   f. a, b, c, and e above

5. The Supreme Court of Virginia in *Fairfax Hosp. Sys., Inc. v. McCarty* held that whether the nurse's breach of duty was the proximate cause of the infant's injuries

   a. presented a question of fact for the jury

   b. did not present a question of fact for the jury

   c. was not an issue in the case

   d. presented a question of fact for the court to decide

   e. was merely a question of law

6. The hospital's negligence in *St. Paul Med. Ctr. v. Cecil* was because of the

   a. negligence of the attending physician

   b. improper assignment of the nurse to a unit on which she was not competent to serve

   c. the resident's failure to respond to the nurse's call for assistance in a more timely manner

   d. failure of the anesthesiologist to be on duty in the hospital

   e. b and d above

   f. b, c, and d above

7. Malpractice actions filed in cases similar to *St. Paul Med. Ctr. v. Cecil* can be reduced by

    a. scheduling staff to those units in which they are the least knowledgeable
    b. providing in-service education programs to employees in areas other than where they are assigned
    c. assessing the employee's competency level and making assignments according to knowledge and skills level
    d. using skills checklists to determine competency levels
    e. a and b above
    f. c and d above

8. The unfortunate outcome in *St. Paul Med. Ctr. v. Cecil* could have been averted if the medical center had

    a. properly assigned the nurse to a work area that more appropriately matched her skills level
    b. taken a more serious approach to the results of the performance evaluation
    c. provided the employee with in-service education, training, and counseling as to her need for skills improvement in the use of fetal monitoring equipment
    d. discharged the employee
    e. a, b, and c above
    f. a, b, c, and d above

9. No physician–patient relationship in *Minster v. Pohl* existed between the patient and the physician who viewed the patient's X-ray merely out of courtesy to the hospital staff because

    a. there was nothing in the record to justify the inference that the physician was acting as the patient's physician
    b. the record justified the inference that the physician had established a physician–patient relationship by reviewing the X-ray
    c. the record justified the inference that the physician had established a physician–patient relationship by reviewing the X-ray and writing in the patient's medical record
    d. the record justified the inference that the physician had established a physician–patient relationship by writing in the patient's medical record
    e. a and d above

10. A "national" standard of care (e.g., *McMillan v. Durant*) generally applies to

    a. physicians
    b. nurses
    c. dentists
    d. pharmacists
    e. a, b, and c above
    f. a, b, c, and d above

11. The outcome in *McMillan v. Durant* may have been prevented if

    a. lighting was improved in order to properly evaluate the patient's condition
    b. the house physician had been contacted immediately to evaluate the patient's condition
    c. the attending physician had been contacted the following morning to evaluate the patient
    d. a and b above
    e. none of the above
    f. all of the above

12. The Supreme Court of South Carolina in *McMillan v. Durant* held that

    a. a national standard of care could not be applied as opposed to a local standard
    b. a neurosurgeon could not give expert testimony as to the standard of care applicable to nurses
    c. a neurosurgeon could give expert testimony as to the standard of care applicable to nurses
    d. a national standard of care could be applied as opposed to a local standard
    e. c and d above
    f. a and b above

13. If a nurse is unsure or questions the dosage of a medication ordered by a physician (e.g., *Harrison v. Axelrod*), she should

    a. not question the physician's order and administer the medication
    b. refuse to administer the medication and speak to the attending physician in the morning regarding her concerns
    c. administer the medication
    d. contact the attending physician and explain her concerns
    e. contact the attending physician's department chairperson

14. Medications purchased over the counter are generally administered

a. intramuscularly
b. orally
c. subcutaneously
d. rectally
e. intravenously

15. Computer-based ordering of diagnostic tests has the capability of

a. displaying charges
b. improving reporting and feedback to physicians
c. providing early reporting of findings and panic values
d. reducing the number of lost orders
e. reducing costs
f. b, c, d, and e above
g. a through e above

16. Tetracycline should not be given with

a. carrots
b. meats
c. fruits
d. dairy products
e. none of the above

17. Adverse drug reactions can be observed through

a. skin rashes
b. shaking
c. patient complaints
d. tachycardia
e. shortness of breath
f. all of the above
g. none of the above

18. Medication errors are sometimes caused by

a. nurse error
b. physician error
c. pharmacy error
d. manufacturer error
e. a, b, and c above
f. a through d above

19. Medication errors can be reduced by

a. checking the patient's identification band prior to administering medications
b. referring to the patient by name prior to administering any medications

c. reviewing the patient's medical record to note any changes in the patient's medication orders
d. contacting the ordering physician when there are any questions regarding medication orders
e. a, c, and d above
f. a through d above

20. In order for a pharmacy and therapeutics committee to be effective, membership should include an interdisciplinary team consisting of the following professionals:

a. physician, pharmacist, and registered nurse
b. physician, pharmacist, and dietitian
c. physician, nurse, and pharmacist
d. physician, laboratory technologist, pharmacist, dietitian, and registered nurse
e. physician, nurse, and administrator

21. Medication reactions may include:

a. idiosyncratic response
b. reaction to other medications
c. food and drug interactions
d. toxic effects
e. symptoms due to long-term usage
f. all of the above

22. The nurse's license was revoked in *Henley v. Alabama Bd. of Nursing* because

a. she drank alcohol
b. she was abusing drugs
c. her alcohol consumption was not interfering with her work habits
d. the hospital reported the nurse's unprofessional conduct
e. her alcohol consumption was affecting her work habits and posing a threat to patients under her care

23. The Supreme Court of Iowa in *Burns v. Board of Nursing* held that the board's finding, placing the nurse's license on probation for three years for habitual intoxication, was

a. inappropriate
b. not supported by substantial evidence
c. a violation of the Iowa code, which should be liberally applied so as to protect the public by allowing the nursing board to interfere when harm is imminent and before it occurs
d. supported by substantial evidence
e. a violation of the Iowa code, which should not be liberally applied so as to protect the public by allow-

ing the nursing board to interfere when harm is imminent and before it occurs

    f. c and d above

24. An employer physician can be held liable for the negligent acts of his employee nurse practitioner (e.g., *Adams v. Krueger*) under the doctrine of

    a. independent contractor
    b. vicarious liability
    c. *res ipsa loquitur*
    d. fiduciary responsibility
    e. a and b above
    f. none of the above

25. The Supreme Court remanded *Howard v. Alexandria Hosp.* for a new trial because

    a. the patient was evaluated by an infectious disease specialist
    b. the hospital discovered the use of unsterile instrumentation
    c. the patient sustained positive, physical, and mental injury because the hospital used inadequately sterilized instruments
    d. the plaintiff suffered no physical injury from the surgical procedure and the instrumentation utilized during the procedure
    e. the circuit court entered summary judgment for the defendant
    f. none of the above

26. A physician is not held liable for the negligent acts of an assisting nurse (e.g., *Holger v. Irish*) unless

    a. the physician has witnessed the act committed by the nurse
    b. the physician was also negligent
    c. the physician and nurse are named together in the lawsuit
    d. the nurse was not trained properly
    e. the nurse was under the supervision and control of the physician, or was an employee of the physician

27. The Mitchells in *Mitchell v. Bingham Mem'l Hosp.* were initially told by hospital personnel that an overdose was a result of the malfunction or defect in the medication infusion machine. Two months later, Mrs. Mitchell's physician told the Mitchells that the machine had been checked out by the factory and was

    a. defective, and that the overdose was a result of the nurse's error, probably in pushing the "flush" switch

on the machine, which would have triggered the overdose

    b. defective, and that the overdose was not a result of the nurse's error, probably in pushing the "flush" switch on the machine, which would have triggered the overdose
    c. most likely the error of a respiratory therapist, probably in pushing the "flush" switch on the machine, which would have triggered the overdose
    d. not defective, and that the overdose was a result of the nurse's error, probably in pushing the "flush" switch on the machine, which would have triggered the overdose
    e. a result of the physician's error, probably in pushing the "flush" switch on the machine, which would not have triggered the overdose

28. The nurse in *Pellerin v. Humedicenters, Inc.* admitted she failed to record the site and mode of injection in emergency department records. According to the testimony of the two experts in nursing practice, failing to record this information is

    a. below the standard of care for nursing
    b. within the standard of care for nursing
    c. normal nursing practice
    d. the responsibility of the physician
    e. clearly the strict responsibility of the hospital and physician

29. In order to move the case forward on the basis of "*res ipsa* application," the plaintiff in *Harder v. Clinton, Inc.* was required to show that

    a. an overdose of the wrong prescription medication is not usually ingested in the course of administering prescription drugs to residents
    b. the nursing home had exclusive control and management of the instrumentality (prescription drugs) that caused the injury
    c. evidence shedding light on the harmful event is more accessible to the nursing home than to the plaintiff
    d. the administration of the injurious overdose is the sort of occurrence that, in the ordinary course of events, would not have happened if one having control of the instrumentality exercised due care
    e. all of the above

VIII—LIABILITY BY DEPARTMENT AND HEALTH PROFESSIONAL

1. The dentist in *Lowenberg v. Sobol* was found to have engaged in professional misconduct because

a. he permitted his dental assistants to administer nitrous oxide
b. he stood in the doorway while his dental hygienists administered nitrous oxide
c. he permitted his dental hygienists to administer nitrous oxide, which is prohibited under state law
d. he failed to train his dental hygienists in the administration of nitrous oxide
e. he failed to supervise his dental assistants

2. The plan of care for patients scheduled for a surgical procedure (e.g., *Pasquale v. Miller*) should include

a. an assessment describing the patient's need for a surgical procedure
b. a plan for postsurgical care
c. postsurgical procedure monitoring
d. management of postsurgical complications
e. all of the above

3. Which of the following statements is generally considered true?

a. a plaintiff's expert witness is generally considered more credible than the defendant's
b. a defendant's expert witness is generally considered more reliable than the plaintiff's
c. regardless of expert testimony, defendant's or plaintiff's, the proximate cause of a plaintiff's injuries is solely within the purview of the jury to determine and need not take into account expert testimony, especially where such is required because of the highly technical nature of the case
d. when determining causation, the plaintiff is required to offer sufficient evidence from which a reasonable person may conclude that it is more probable than not that an injury was caused by the defendant
e. evidence as to causation should eliminate every other possible cause

4. The plaintiff in *Bowe v. Charleston Area Med. Ctr.* was discharged by her employer because

a. she failed to secure a contract at the time of employment
b. she was negligent in her care of the patient
c. the disclaimer contained in the employee handbook permitted it
d. the medical center retaliated against her
e. she was an at-will employee
f. she filed unjustified grievances against her employer

5. The Court of Appeal of Louisiana in *Roy v. Gupta* held that the emergency department physician was negligent

a. in failing to advise Mrs. Gupta that she should be hospitalized for chest pains
b. in pointing out the potential dangers of not being hospitalized
c. in failing to seek a second opinion
d. in failing to discharge the patient with medication
e. a and b above
f. c and d above

6. Absent any nursing-initiated contact of the emergency physician in *Feeney v. New England Med. Ctr., Inc.*, the court found

a. there was no obligation on the part of the physician to determine who is waiting for care and how critical the need is for that care
b. there was an obligation on the part of the physician to determine who is waiting for physician care and how critical the need is for that care
c. the physician had failed to evaluate the patient within the first few minutes of his entry into the emergency facility and to initiate care
d. the physician was not responsible for evaluating the patient shortly after his arrival to the emergency department
e. a and d above
f. b and c above

7. There is no private right of action against individual physicians under the Emergency Medical Treatment and Active Labor Act (e.g., *Ballachino v. Anders*) because

a. hospitals are more financially secure
b. there are provisions in the act making it applicable to both hospitals and physicians
c. there are provisions in the act that do not apply only to hospitals
d. there is no private right of action against individual physicians under the act
e. none of the above
f. a, c, and d above

8. The elements that a plaintiff must prove in order to establish liability for malpractice (e.g., *Matthews v. DeKalb County Hosp. Auth.*) include

a. duty to care
b. breach of duty
c. injury
d. causation

e. a, b, and d above
f. a, b, c, and d above

9. Plaintiffs bringing a lawsuit based on the Emergency Medical Treatment and Active Labor Act (e.g., *Huckaby v. East Ala. Med. Ctr.*) must establish that

a. the patient had an emergency medical condition
b. the hospital knew of the patient's emergency condition
c. the patient was not properly stabilized prior to discharge or transfer
d. a and c above
e. a, b, and c above

10. An organization with an emergency department (e.g., *Huckaby v. East Ala. Med. Ctr.*) should

a. transfer a patient immediately to another facility if it cannot meet the patient's total care needs
b. stabilize and transfer the care of the patient to an appropriate health care provider that can meet the patient's continuing needs
c. hold the patient for 24 hours pending evaluation and review by the hospital's discharge planner and social worker
d. first develop a written transfer agreement with the organization accepting the patient for care
e. none of the above

11. Regardless of whether a verdict was rendered for the plaintiff or defendant, the fact remains that there was an unfortunate outcome in the case (e.g., *Holcomb v. Humana Med. Corp.*) that would warrant

a. a review by the hospital of its emergency department discharge criteria
b. a review of the hospital criteria for the transfer of patients from the emergency department to an inpatient unit
c. no further review
d. consideration of routine callbacks to patients maintained in the emergency department overnight
e. a, b, and d above

12. Physical therapists are held to the same standard of care (e.g., *Hodo v. General. Hosps. of Humana*) as

a. any reasonably prudent person practicing physical therapy
b. other professional physical therapists practicing physical therapy
c. any nonlicensed layperson

d. a and c above
e. none of the above

13. The Joint Commission on Accreditation of Healthcare Organizations is

a. a voluntary for-profit organization committed to improvement in the quality of care rendered by the nation's health care organizations
b. a governmental organization that establishes standards by which the quality of care rendered by health care organizations can be reviewed for accreditation purposes
c. an organization that provides accreditation services for health care organizations
d. b and c
e. a, b, and c above

14. The Joint Commission on Accreditation of Healthcare Organizations survey process includes

a. a review of the organization's documents
b. interviews with the organization's leaders
c. interviews with selected patients
d. a safety tour of the organization's facilities
e. a public information interview
f. a, b, c, and d above
g. a, b, c, d, and e above

15. Applications for staff privileges and supporting documents of appropriate training in South Carolina (e.g., *McGee v. Bruce Hosp. Sys.*) are protected by the

a. trial court
b. supreme court
c. confidentiality statute
d. U.S. Restricted Disclosure Act
e. defense counsel

16. What information from peer review proceedings do you think might be available for discovery (e.g., *Freeman v. Piedmont Hosp.*)?

a. original source documents
b. the work-product of peer review committees
c. minutes of peer review committees
d. a and b above
e. a, b, and c above

17. The discovery sought by the plaintiffs of Kmart's prior improper filling of prescriptions (e.g., *State Ex Rel. Stolfa v. Ely*) was relevant because

a.   Kmart's pharmacists were not properly licensed
b.   in order to prove notice to Kmart that its protocols and procedures were inadequate, it would be relevant to show that other claims had been made against Kmart because of misfilled prescriptions
c.   the court so ordered
d.   in order to prove notice to Kmart that its protocols and procedures were inadequate, it would not be relevant to show that other claims had been made against Kmart because of misfilled prescriptions
e.   the plaintiff's case hinged on the fact that Kmart seldom filled the correct prescriptions

18. The expert testimony of the surgeon in *Fortney v. Al-Hajj* was allowed because

a.   the surgeon had extensive experience in emergency department procedures
b.   the surgeon lacked experience in emergency department procedures
c.   the surgeon's experience qualified him to testify as to the standard of care required
d.   whether a witness is qualified to state an opinion is a matter that rests within the discretion of the trial court, and its ruling on that point is not ordinarily disturbed unless it clearly appears that the discretion has been abused
e.   a and b above
f.   c and d above

19. If a patient's injuries are because of the negligence of an X-ray technician employed by the hospital (e.g., *Fortney v. Al-Hajj*), the hospital can be held liable for damages on the basis of

a.   independent contractor
b.   comparative negligence
c.   *respondeat superior*
d.   borrowed servant doctrine
e.   captain of the ship doctrine
f.   c and e above

20. A visitor who falls on a liquid spilled on the floor of a hospital corridor (e.g., *Borota v. University Med. Ctr.*) can generally recover damages for injuries sustained if

a.   the hospital was aware of the spill and failed to clean it up
b.   the hospital did not have constructive notice that the spill was present in the corridor
c.   the spill was caused by an employee who walked away from it without attempting to clean it up
d.   a and c above
e.   a, b, and c above

21. Servicemaster (in *Palka v. Servicemaster Management Servs.*) owed a duty to the nurse because

a.   it had a contract with the nurse
b.   it stopped the safety inspections of the wall-mounted fans
c.   the nurse did nothing to cause the fan to fall on her
d.   the hospital had no liability
e.   the nurse was in the class of those who had a right to a reasonable expectation of safe maintenance and inspection of the equipment by Servicemaster

22. The main reason the Court of Appeal of Louisiana (e.g., *Dougay v. Seventh Ward Gen. Hosp.*) affirmed the trial court's finding was

a.   the doors to the bathroom and the patient's room were too close together
b.   the physician did not make note of the incident
c.   the fact finder had a right to base its decision on credibility
d.   the nurse had no independent recollection of caring for the plaintiff
e.   the plaintiff was heard screaming and crying after the knob had hit her

23. The Court of Appeal of Louisiana in *Blitz v. Jefferson Parish Hosp. Serv. Dist.* held that the evidence supported a liability determination because

a.   the hospital had called witnesses who apparently were as credible or as acceptable as the petitioner's witnesses
b.   the determination of liability was not supported by adequate evidence and was clearly erroneous
c.   the hospital had called witnesses who apparently were neither as credible nor as acceptable as the petitioner's witnesses
d.   the court was reluctant to substitute its findings of fact for those of the trial judge
e.   c and d above
f.   a, c, and d above

24. The hospital's motion to dismiss was denied in *Jenkins County Hosp. Auth. v. Landrum* on the basis that

a.   the hospital failed to provide testimony from expert witnesses
b.   the action against the hospital was not accompanied by an affidavit
c.   an affidavit of a competent expert to accompany charges of professional malpractice was not required as to allegations of incompetence against the hospital

d. an affidavit of a competent expert to accompany charges of professional malpractice was required as to allegations of incompetence against the hospital

e. a and b above

f. a, b, and c above

25. *Maynard v. Sisters of Providence* was remanded for trial because

a. the hospital's operators knew or should have known of the safety hazards in the visitors' parking lot

b. the hospital's operators failed to take any remedial action to correct the hazardous conditions in the visitors' lot

c. the hospital's operators should have anticipated that visitors would eventually need to return to the parking lot for their cars

d. a and c above

e. a, b, and c above

26. The Superior Court of New Jersey, Appellate Division, in *Glowacki v. Underwood Mem'l Hosp.* held that the lump-sum damages award of $908,000 was not excessive because

a. the nurse's symptoms never changed from the day following the accident to the date of trial eight years later

b. the treating physician's clinical opinion varied

c. the nurse's medical proofs were capable of supporting a jury finding that her back injury was one involving the spine and intervertebral discs and not merely a low back sprain

d. the treating physician's clinical opinion never varied

e. a, b, and c above

f. a, c, and d above

27. The security force contracted by the hospital (e.g., *Hanewinckel v. St. Paul's Property & Liab.*) was liable for the injury suffered by the plaintiff nurse because

a. it did not provide sufficient security patrol of the parking lot in which the nurse was attacked

b. it specifically stated in its contract that it would prevent third-party assaults

c. the nurse was injured through no fault of her own

d. the parking lot had insufficient lighting

e. the parking lot was the hospital's responsibility

28. The defendant medical center in *Stacy v. Truman Med. Ctr.* violated its smoking policy

a. by allowing smoking without an approved ashtray in Room 327

b. by allowing smoking in a no-smoking area

c. by failing to give adequate fire safety training to its employees concerning removal of patients from the danger of fire

d. by failing to remove the patients from the danger of fire at the first opportunity

e. by failing to have a smoke detector in Room 327

f. all of the above

29. A hospital owes a duty to its visitors to exercise reasonable care to prevent injuries on hospital property. In order to prevent recovery for damages, the hospital had to prove it acted (e.g., *Harkins v. Natchitoches Parish Hosp.*)

a. reasonably to discover and correct a dangerous condition not anticipated in its business activity

b. reasonably to discover and correct a dangerous condition reasonably anticipated in its business activity

c. to discover and correct a dangerous condition reasonably unanticipated in its business activity

d. to prevent injuries by continuing surveillance by the safety officer

e. b and c above

30. The appeals court in *Marshall v. East Carroll Parish Hosp. Serv. Dist.* agreed with other courts that have interpreted the Emergency Medical Treatment and Active Labor Act (42 U.S.C. § 1395dd) that the statute was not intended to be used as a federal malpractice statute, but instead was enacted

a. to prevent "patient dumping," which is the practice of refusing to treat patients who are unable to pay and encourage negligence suits against hospitals

b. to encourage "patient dumping," which is the practice of refusing to treat patients who are unable to pay

c. to prevent "patient dumping," which is the practice of treating patients who are unable to pay

d. to prevent "patient dumping," which is the practice of refusing to treat patients who are unable to pay

e. to legitimize "patient dumping," which is the practice of refusing to treat patients who are unable to pay

f. d and e above

31. In *Parris v. Uni Med, Inc.*, if the distributor had engaged in one of the following acts, it could have avoided liability if it had

a. constructed a better bed
b. trained the nurses how to adjust and change the pressure
c. given the patient warnings about the bed
d. attached an information guide to the bed
e. made available an 800-number hotline

32. In *Thibodeaux v. Century Mfg. Co.*, an organization should ensure that

a. all medical equipment is included in a preventive maintenance program
b. in-service education and training are provided to individuals who will be operating medical equipment
c. continuing education is provided to those individuals operating medical equipment
d. the training and education of employees on the operation of medical equipment is properly documented
e. all of the above

IX—INFORMATION MANAGEMENT AND HEALTH CARE RECORDS

1. The United States Court of Appeals for the 1st Circuit in *Lama v. Borras* held that the evidence

a. failed to support a jury conclusion that the hospital had been negligent by maintaining a charting by exception policy
b. supported a jury conclusion that the hospital had been negligent by maintaining a charting by exception method of recording notes in the patient's record
c. demonstrated that a method of recording notes in the patient's record only when important changes in the patient's condition are evident is the only acceptable method of charting in light of the heavy burden documentation places on the caregivers
d. supported a finding that charting by exception is a necessary evil
e. a, b, and d above
f. none of the above

2. The Superior Court of New Jersey in *Estate of Hussain v. Gardner* held that statements given by a physician to the hospital's internal peer review committee were protected because

a. the information sought by the plaintiff was readily discoverable by the plaintiff

b. the information sought by the plaintiff was not readily discoverable by the plaintiff
c. the plaintiffs made a strong showing of a particularized need that outweighed the public interest in the confidentiality of the quality assessment committee
d. the plaintiffs had not made a strong showing of a particularized need that outweighed the public interest in the confidentiality of the quality assessment committee
e. a and c above
f. a and d above

3. The Appellate Court of Illinois in *May v. Wood River Township Hosp.* held that information gathered prior to a physician's application for staff privileges was

a. not protected
b. protected
c. not subject to disclosure
d. of little value in a malpractice case
e. of little value in a negligence case

4. Statutes providing for confidentiality of records of committees of hospitals and other medical organizations intended to provide confidentiality to the records and proceedings of such committees (e.g., *Smith v. Lincoln Gen. Hosp.*) are

a. entirely privileged information
b. not entirely privileged
c. privileged in totality
d. a relatively benign matter
e. of little if any relevance to a malpractice suit

5. In *Moskovitz v. Mount Sinai Med. Ctr.*, an intentional alteration, falsification, or destruction of medical records to avoid liability was sufficient to show

a. honesty
b. defamation
c. slander
d. malice
e. libel

6. Ideally, patient records should be maintained

a. indefinitely
b. only as long as required by statute
c. as per hospital policy
d. in the physician's office
e. in an organization's medical records department

7. The discrepancy between the written progress notes and the testimony of the witnesses who observed Dimora in *Dimora v. Cleveland Clinic Found.* was sufficient to raise a question of fact as to the possible falsification of documents by the physician

    a. to minimize the nature of the incident and the injury of the patient due to the possible negligence of the plaintiff
    b. to maximize the nature of the incident and the injury of the patient due to the possible negligence of hospital personnel
    c. to minimize the nature of the incident and the injury of the patient due to the possible negligence of hospital personnel
    d. to exaggerate the nature of the incident and the injury of the patient due to the potential negligence of hospital personnel
    e. to downplay the nature of the incident and the injury of the patient due to the inconceivable negligence of hospital personnel

8. The appeals court in *Stricklin v. Becan* found that documents considered by a credentialing committee

    a. included letters of reference and other third-party confidential personnel assessments within the class of nondiscoverable documents (§ 8-2101 clearly provides that they cannot be used by credentialing committees for the purpose of determining staff privileges. To the extent the letter is a letter of recommendation or third-party confidential assessment of Dr. Becan's professional competence, used by the credentialing committee, it could be subject to nondisclosure)
    b. are always subject to the privilege
    c. included letters of reference and other third-party confidential personnel assessments within the class of nondiscoverable documents (§ 8-2101 clearly provides that they may be used by credentialing committees for the purpose of determining staff privileges. To the extent the letter is a letter of recommendation or third-party confidential assessment of Dr. Becan's professional competence, used by the credentialing committee, it could be subject to nondisclosure)
    d. are not always subject to the privilege
    e. c and d above

9. In *Dardeau v. Ardoin*, Dr. Ardoin passed away prior to trial. The plaintiff complains in brief that the introduction of progress notes or office chart by Dr. Ardoin constituted hearsay evidence. She argues that Louisiana Medical Mutual Insurance Company defended this case on unauthenticated progress notes claimed to be made by Dr. Ardoin.

    a. the appeals court found error on the part of the trial court as to the admissibility of the physician's progress notes
    b. the appeals court found no error on the part of the trial court as to the admissibility of the physician's progress notes or office chart and affirmed the jury verdict and the judgment of the trial court
    c. the appeals court found error on the part of the trial court as to the admissibility of the physician's progress notes or office chart and affirmed the jury verdict and the judgment of the trial court
    d. the appeals court reversed the jury verdict and the judgment of the trial court
    e. none of the above

10. The burden to establish privilege, in *Arlington Mem'l Hosp. Found., Inc. v. Barton*, was on the party seeking to shield information from discovery. The party asserting privilege has the obligation

    a. to refute, by competent evidence, that the privilege applies to the information sought
    b. to prove, by incompetent evidence, that the privilege applies to the information sought
    c. to prove, by competent evidence, that the privilege does not apply to the information sought
    d. to prove, by competent evidence, that the privilege applies to the information sought
    e. a and d above

X—PATIENT CONSENT

1. The Supreme Court of Kentucky in *Keel v. St. Elizabeth Med. Ctr., Ky.* held that expert testimony was not required to establish lack of informed consent because

    a. the failure is not so apparent that laymen may not easily recognize it
    b. the failure is so apparent that laymen may not infer it from evidence within the realm of common knowledge
    c. the failure is so apparent that laymen may infer it from evidence within the realm of common knowledge
    d. the failure is so apparent that laymen may easily recognize it or infer it from evidence within the realm of common knowledge
    e. c and d above
    f. b, c, and d above

2. In order to properly obtain a patient's informed consent (e.g., *Stover v. Surgeons*), physicians must discuss with the patient

   a. the risks and benefits of procedures used, and any other medically recognized alternatives
   b. the risks and benefits associated with the procedure that is going to be used
   c. all risks at least twice before surgery
   d. only the details of the surgery to be performed
   e. only the alternative procedures the physician feels most comfortable performing

3. The Supreme Court of South Carolina in *Banks v. Medical Univ. of S.C.* held that there was an issue of fact as to whether blood should have been administered to an eight-year-old child because

   a. the child was in a life-threatening situation
   b. the child was not in a life-threatening situation
   c. evidence had been presented that indicated that the child was in a life-threatening situation
   d. evidence had been presented that indicated that the child had not been in a life-threatening situation
   e. a and c above

4. The Superior Court of New Jersey in *Matter of Hughes* affirmed the judge's decision to appoint a temporary medical guardian for the patient because

   a. this case arose in the context of elective surgery
   b. this case arose in the context of emergency surgery
   c. the patient signed a standard hospital form entitled "Refusal to Permit Blood Transfusion"
   d. some uncertainty remained as to what the patient may have desired had she been competent and understood the gravity of the situation
   e. no uncertainty remained as to what the patient may have desired had she been competent and understood the gravity of the situation

5. The Court of Appeals of Ohio in *Greynolds v. Kurman* held that there was sufficient evidence to support a finding that

   a. there was not a lack of informed consent
   b. adequate consent was given
   c. because of the patient's past medical history and the fact that he was at an increased risk to suffer complications during an angiogram, there was sufficient evidence to support a finding of lack of informed consent

   d. a reasonable person in the position of the patient would have decided to have the angiogram had the risks associated with the procedure been properly disclosed
   e. the evidence presented at trial was not credible

6. The plaintiff in *Warren v. Schecter* was entitled to compensation for all damages proximately resulting from the physician's failure to give full disclosure of the risks of surgery because

   a. the patient was entitled to recover not only for the undisclosed complications but also for the disclosed complications, because she would not have consented to any surgery had the true risk been disclosed, and therefore would not have suffered those complications
   b. there is no obligation of a treating physician to provide to the patient reasonable disclosure of the available choices with respect to proposed therapy and of the dangers inherently and potentially involved in each
   c. the patient was entitled to recover not only for the undisclosed complications but also for the disclosed complications, because she would have consented to any surgery had the true risk been disclosed, and therefore would not have suffered those complications
   d. there is an obligation of a treating physician to provide to the patient reasonable disclosure of the available choices with respect to proposed therapy and of the dangers inherently and potentially involved in each
   e. a and d above
   f. c and d above

7. In response to the plaintiff's allegation in *Davis v. Hoffman* that the hospital committed battery by lack of informed consent to the hysterectomy, the hospital asserted that Pennsylvania law places no duty on a hospital to obtain a patient's consent to an operation. The hospital argued that Pennsylvania courts have applied the doctrine of informed consent only to physicians, not to hospitals.

   a. responsibility for obtaining informed consent lies with the hospital
   b. responsibility for obtaining informed consent lies with the operating surgeon, not the hospital or nurse
   c. responsibility for obtaining informed consent lies with the operating surgeon
   d. responsibility for obtaining informed consent does not lie with the operating surgeon

e. responsibility for obtaining informed consent lies with the operating surgeon and nurse

f. b and d above

8. The law in Wisconsin on informed consent is well settled; the duty to advise a patient of the risks of treatment (*see Mathias v. St. Catherine's Hosp., Inc.*)

a. is the responsibility of the physician

b. lies with the hospital

c. is the responsibility of the nurse because of her frequent contact with the patient

d. is the ultimate responsibility of the patient advocate

e. is the ultimate responsibility of the physician and patient advocate

XI—LEGAL REPORTING OBLIGATIONS

1. The Court of Appeals of Georgia in *Michaels v. Gordon* held that the child abuse reporting statute's grant of immunity from liability

a. did not extend to the psychologist

b. does not extend to psychologists

c. does not cover every person who, in good faith, participates over time in the making of a report to a child welfare agency

d. does cover every person who, in good faith, participates over time in the making of a report to a child welfare agency

e. none of the above

2. Failure of an administrator of a nursing facility to report all accidents and injuries "resulting in possible patient injury" (e.g., *Westin v. Shalala*) can result in

a. an indictment on criminal charges

b. the nursing facility losing its right to participate in the Medicare program

c. charges for neglect

d. a and c above

e. a, b, and c above

3. Under Colorado law, an administrator of a nursing home, is required to (1) report all accidents and injuries "resulting in possible patient injury" to the Colorado Department of Health, and (2) file a copy of that report in the patient's medical record. The evidence was clear from the record in *Westin v. Shalala* that Ms. Westin, as administrator of the nursing home

a. reported an incident that occurred at the nursing facility where she worked

b. failed to report an incident involving Ms. Grundmeier while she was a patient at another facility, and that the conviction was connected to the medical services at that facility and its employees

c. failed to report an incident involving Ms. Grundmeier while she was a patient at the nursing facility

d. failed to report to the patient's attending physician an injury that occurred in the nursing facility

e. b and c above

4. As a general rule, institutions accredited as hospitals by the Joint Commission on Accreditation of Healthcare Organizations are (*see Evelyn V. v. Kings County Hosp. Ctr.*)

a. not deemed qualified to participate in Medicare and Medicaid

b. deemed qualified to participate in Medicare and Medicaid

c. deemed qualified to participate in Medicare and Medicaid so long as the organization has not assumed any long-term care debt

d. deemed qualified to participate in Medicare and Medicaid so long as the organization has participated in surveys by a minimum of three accrediting organizations with deemed status

e. b and d above

XII—ISSUES OF PROCREATION

1. The Utah abortion statute's 24-hour waiting period and informed consent requirements were valid in *Utah Women's Clinic, Inc. v. Leavitt* because

a. the state can place reasonable restrictions or waiting periods

b. Pennsylvania had a similar statute

c. the 24-hour waiting period was an undue burden placed on the patient

d. there were material differences between the Utah and Pennsylvania statutes

e. the case shows factual issues materially different from those already considered in *Casey*

2. The United States District Court for the District of Columbia in *NOW v. Operation Rescue* held that leaders and groups were liable to an abortion clinic for property damages resulting from blockades of the clinics because

a. the defendants did not violate the permanent injunction

b. the defendants violated the permanent injunction

c. the injunction failed to prevent antiabortion groups, their leaders, and others from blockading or obstructing access to abortion clinics

d. there was no actual property damage resulting from the blockades

e. there was property damage resulting from the blockades

3. The main reason that the New Jersey Supreme Court in *Murray v. Lawson* upheld the *Murray* injunction was because

a. Dr. Murray's wife had a nervous breakdown from the protests

b. the defendant called Dr. Murray a murderer

c. the clinic was blown up by the defendant

d. the defendant's freedom of speech was outweighed by the state's interest in protecting residential privacy

e. the state has a right to enforce any injunction for which it finds justification

4. The United States Court of Appeals for the Ninth Circuit in *Forrester v. City of San Diego* held that

a. the police did use excessive force on the demonstrators

b. the police did not use excessive force on the demonstrators

c. the police did not threaten or use deadly force and did not deliver physical blows or cuts. The force consisted of physical pressure administered on the demonstrators' limbs in increasing degrees, resulting in pain.

d. the city clearly did not have a legitimate interest in quickly dispersing and removing the lawbreakers with the least risk of injury to police and others

e. a and d above

f. b and c above

XIII—PATIENT RIGHTS AND RESPONSIBILITIES

1. A medical malpractice action in *Oxford v. Upson County Hosp., Inc.* against the hospital and nurses would have succeeded if

a. a member of the patient's family had assisted her to the bathroom

b. the patient had walked herself to the bathroom without requesting the assistance of a nurse

c. the patient had informed the nurse that she was dizzy and the nurse had walked her to the bathroom and then left her to attend to another patient

d. a and b above

e. none of the above

2. Did the medical provider in *Harrell v. St. Mary's Hosp., Inc.* have standing to assert state interests in an attempt to defeat a patient's decision to forgo emergency medical treatment? The supreme court concluded that the medical provider

a. did not have standing to assert state interests in a petition to require treatment for its patient

b. does have a standing to assert state interests in a petition to require treatment for its patient

c. does have a standing to assert state interests in a petition to require treatment for its patient, so long as there is a valid state interest involved

d. was on shaky grounds for asserting a state interest but would allow the hospital to assert same

e. was on sturdy grounds for asserting a state interest but would allow the hospital to assert same

3. Did Ms. Vega, a Jehovah's Witness, in *Stamford Hosp. v. Vega*, have a right to execute a release requesting that no blood or its derivatives be administered to her during her hospitalization?

a. the hospital's interests were sufficient to take priority over Ms. Vega's common law right to bodily integrity, even when the assertion of that right threatens her own life

b. the hospital had no common law right or obligation to thrust unwanted medical care on a patient who, having been sufficiently informed of the consequences, competently and clearly declined that care

c. the hospital had a common law right or obligation to thrust unwanted medical care on a patient who, having been sufficiently informed of the consequences, competently and clearly declined that care

XIV—ACQUIRED IMMUNE DEFICIENCY SYNDROME

1. The Court of Appeals of Texas in *J.K. & Susie L. Wadley Research Inst. v. Beeson* held that evidence supported a finding that the blood center's negligence in collection of blood was the proximate cause of Mr. Beeson's HIV infection because

a. there was not a scintilla of evidence to support a finding that the blood center, despite its knowledge about the dangers of HIV-contaminated blood, failed to reject gay men

b. the evidence provided some indication that the blood center's screening procedure effectively educated donors

c. the jury could not reasonably infer that the blood center's failure to effectively educate the donor and to ask him specific questions caused him to donate blood rather than to defer

d. there was more than a scintilla of evidence to support a finding that the blood center, despite its knowledge about the dangers of HIV-contaminated blood, failed to reject gay men

e. donor screening was adequate

2. There was a need to disclose the physician's HIV status in the case of *Application of Milton S. Hershey Med. Ctr.* because

a. there is a compelling need to provide, at the very least, limited notice to those who might have been exposed to the virus

b. society in general should know the medical status of all individuals who have been diagnosed with HIV

c. such information is not considered confidential

d. the general public has a compelling need to know the identity of individuals who have been diagnosed with HIV

e. none of the above

XV—END OF LIFE ISSUES

1. The main reason the court held in *Grace Plaza of Great Neck v. Elbaum* that the patient's husband had to pay his wife's nursing facility bills was because

a. the patient was incompetent

b. the husband had signed a promissory note to cover his wife's bills

c. the nursing home had provided the services for which it contracted to perform

d. the defendant acted in bad faith by not paying

e. the defendant did not seek an injunction

2. The Court of Appeals of Ohio held in *Anderson v. St. Francis–St. George Hosp.* that

a. there were no questions of fact as to consent

b. prolonging of the patient's life was not wrongful living

c. questions of fact precluded summary judgment on the claim of negligence

d. there were questions of fact as to consent

e. b, c, and d above

f. a, b, and c above

3. In *Matter of Dubreuil*, a health care provider must comply with a patient's wishes to refuse medical treatment unless

a. the patient obtains a court order

b. the patient is unconscious

c. the patient's wishes are overridden by the patient's family

d. there are minor children involved

e. the patient is in a life-threatening condition

4. The Michigan Court of Appeals held that the evidence in *In Re Martin* was sufficient to support a finding that the patient lacked capacity to make decisions regarding withholding or withdrawal of life-sustaining medical treatment because the patient

a. had sufficient mind to reasonably understand the condition

b. was capable of understanding the nature and effect of the treatment choices

c. was aware of the consequences associated with those choices

d. was unable to make an informed choice that was voluntary and not coerced

e. a, b, and c above

5. Does New York's prohibition on assisting suicide violate the equal protection clause of the Fourteenth Amendment (e.g., *Quill v. Vacco*)?

a. New York's prohibition on assisting suicide does violate the equal protection clause

b. New York's prohibition on assisting suicide does not violate the equal protection clause as long as the physician does not administer the lethal dose of a medication

c. New York's prohibition on assisting suicide does not violate the equal protection clause as long as the patient self-administers the lethal dose of a medication

d. New York's prohibition on assisting suicide does not violate the equal protection clause

e. b, c, and d above

6. Is there a constitutional right to assisted suicide (*see Kevorkian v. Thompson*)?

a. the court held that there was a constitutional right to assisted suicide, and the statute barring assisted suicide does not violate the equal protection clause of the Fourteenth Amendment

b. the court held that there is no constitutional right to assisted suicide, and the statute barring assisted suicide does not violate the equal protection clause of the Fourteenth Amendment

c. the court held that there is no constitutional right to assisted suicide; however, the statute barring assisted suicide does violate the equal protection clause of the Fourteenth Amendment

d. the court held that the case was frivolous and should not have reached the level of the supreme court

e. none of the above

XVI—LABOR RELATIONS/EMPLOYMENT, DISCIPLINE, AND DISCHARGE

1. Questioning by supervisors of their subordinates regarding a union meeting (e.g., *NLRB v. Shelby Mem'l Hosp. Ass'n*)

   a. can constitute an unfair labor practice
   b. is too general an accusation to constitute an unfair labor practice
   c. is a necessary evil
   d. is mandated by the Supreme Court
   e. none of the above

2. An at-will employee (e.g., *Yambor v. St. Vincent Med. Ctr.*)

   a. cannot be terminated by his or her employer without just cause
   b. cannot be terminated without a formal hearing before an organization's governing body
   c. can be terminated without just cause by the employer; in addition, the employee has a right to leave at-will employment
   d. cannot terminate employment without just notification to the employer
   e. a and b above
   f. c and d above

3. The penalty of discharging a nurse for verbal patient abuse in *Ward v. Brown* was arbitrary and capricious because

   a. only physical abuse is punishable by discharge
   b. there was only one incident proven in the nurse's nine-year career

c. it was the other nurse who brought charges, not the patient
d. it was too severe a penalty for the offense
e. the board discharged the nurse without considering the policy manual guidelines

4. In *Stevens v. St. Louis Univ. Med. Ctr.*, an employer may differentiate in pay between the sexes based on a

   a. merit system
   b. seniority system
   c. a system that does not measure earnings by quantity or quality of production
   d. a and b above
   e. a, b, and c above

5. In *Stevens v. St. Louis Univ. Med. Ctr.*, a commonly acceptable reason for differentiating between salaries in the same job category is based on

   a. job title
   b. sex
   c. age
   d. race
   e. position description

6. In the case of *Chapman v. University of Mass. Med. Ctr.*, Mr. Scarbeau acted in bad faith when he laid off Ms. Chapman because

   a. there were adequate funds to keep her
   b. he led her to believe that her position was secure
   c. he could have bumped others
   d. he could have thought of a new position for her
   e. he could have provided her with severance pay

7. A wrongful discharge action in *Kirk v. Mercy Hosp. Tri-County* cannot be pursued successfully by a person who has been an at-will employee, unless there is

   a. a valid reason
   b. a public policy exception
   c. a specific law or regulation by the state
   d. an agreement between the parties to the action
   e. a hearing first

8. In the case of *Dalby v. Sisters of Providence*, the discharge of an employee for reporting incidents required by law

   a. is a legally acceptable practice
   b. can give rise for an action for wrongful discharge
   c. is a societal obligation

d. is acceptable under case law

e. a and c above

f. b, c, and d above

9. In *Ward v. Derwinski*, the nurse was discharged because

a. the nurse was abusive to the patient

b. the nurse administered Haladol to the patient

c. the nurse failed to report the incident to the medical director

d. two other nurses reported the incident

e. none of the above

10. Nursing supervisors are not covered under the National Labor Relations Act in *Health Care & Retirement Corp. v. NLRB* because they

a. report to another individual with supervisory responsibility

b. do not have authority to hire, transfer, suspend, lay off, recall, promote, discharge, assign, reward, or discipline other employees

c. have no administrative responsibility for other staff members

d. have authority to hire, transfer, suspend, lay off, recall, promote, discharge, assign, reward, or discipline other employees

e. do not serve in a supervisory capacity

f. a and e above

11. In the case of *Frank v. South Suburban Hosp. Found.*, an employee cannot be terminated at the will of the employer if

a. the employee did nothing wrong

b. the employee is not given a valid reason for being terminated

c. the employer does not hold a hearing on the infraction

d. there is a valid contract between the employer and employee

e. no progressive discipline procedures were followed

12. Was the plaintiff's removal from his position, in *Hanna v. Board of Trustees of N.Y. Univ. Hosp.*, as Chief of the Division of Pediatric Urology, and the termination of his blocked time in the operating room subject to judicial review under Public Health Law 2801-b?

a. the plaintiff's removal from his position as Chief of the Division of Pediatric Urology, and the termination of his blocked time in the operating room, are subject to judicial review under Public Health Law 2801-b

b. the plaintiff's removal from his position as Chief of the Division of Pediatric Urology, and the termination of his blocked time in the operating room, are not subject to judicial review under Public Health Law 2801-b

c. the plaintiff's removal from his position as Chief of the Division of Pediatric Urology was not subject for review; however, his termination of his blocked time in the operating room, was subject to judicial review under Public Health Law 2801-b

d. the plaintiff's removal from his position as Chief of the Division of Pediatric Urology was subject for review; however, his termination of his blocked time in the operating room was not subject to judicial review under Public Health Law 2801-b

e. c and d above

Answer Sheet

Name: _____   Profession: _____

Address: _____   _____

_____   Telephone: _____

I—TORT LAW

1.	7.	13.	19.
2.	8.	14.	20.
3.	9.	15.	21.
4.	10.	16.	22.
5.	11.	17.	
6.	12.	18.	

II—CRIMINAL ASPECTS OF HEALTH CARE

1.	5.	9.	13.
2.	6.	10.	14.
3.	7.	11.	15.
4.	8.	12.	

III—CONTRACTS

1.	3.	5.
2.	4.	

IV—CIVIL PROCEDURE AND TRIAL PRACTICE

1.	9.	17.	25.
2.	10.	18.	26.
3.	11.	19.	27.
4.	12.	20.	28.
5.	13.	21.	29.
6.	14.	22.	30.
7.	15.	23.	31.
8.	16.	24.	

V—CORPORATE LIABILITY

1.	3.	5.	7.
2.	4.	6.	

VI—MEDICAL STAFF

1.	8.	15.	22.
2.	9.	16.	23.
3.	10.	17.	24.
4.	11.	18.	25.
5.	12.	19.	26.
6.	13.	20.	
7.	14.	21.	

VII—NURSING AND THE LAW

1.	4.	7.	10.
2.	5.	8.	11.
3.	6.	9.	12.

13.	18.	23.	28.
14.	19.	24.	29.
15.	20.	25.	
16.	21.	26.	
17.	22.	27.	

VIII—LIABILITY BY DEPARTMENT AND HEALTH PROFESSIONAL

1.	9.	17.	25.
2.	10.	18.	26.
3.	11.	19.	27.
4.	12.	20.	28.
5.	13.	21.	29.
6.	14.	22.	30.
7.	15.	23.	31.
8.	16.	24.	32.

IX—INFORMATION MANAGEMENT AND HEALTH CARE RECORDS

1.	4.	7.	10.
2.	5.	8.	
3.	6.	9.	

X—PATIENT CONSENT

| 1. | 3. | 5. | 7. |
| 2. | 4. | 6. | 8. |

XI—LEGAL REPORTING OBLIGATIONS

| 1. | 2. | 3. | 4. |

XII—ISSUES OF PROCREATION

| 1. | 2. | 3. | 4. |

XIII—PATIENT RIGHTS AND RESPONSIBILITIES

| 1. | 2. | 3. |

XIV—ACQUIRED IMMUNE DEFICIENCY SYNDROME

1.   2.

XV—END OF LIFE ISSUES

1.   3.   5.

2.   4.   6.

XVI—LABOR RELATIONS/EMPLOYMENT, DISCIPLINE, AND DISCHARGE

1.   4.   7.   10.

2.   5.   8.   11.

3.   6.   9.   12.

Answers

I—TORT LAW

1. a	7. d	13. e	19. b
2. f	8. e	14. e	20. f
3. e	9. b	15. e	21. f
4. d	10. a	16. e	22. e
5. d	11. e	17. b	
6. d	12. d	18. e	

II—CRIMINAL ASPECTS OF HEALTH CARE

1. c	5. e	9. b	13. c
2. b	6. b	10. e	14. d
3. c	7. f	11. f	15. d
4. e	8. c	12. a	

III—CONTRACTS

1. a	3. e	5. a
2. e	4. e	

IV—CIVIL PROCEDURE AND TRIAL PRACTICE

1. b	9. d	17. b	25. e
2. d	10. e	18. f	26. f
3. c	11. a	19. d	27. a
4. a	12. d	20. d	28. c
5. e	13. c	21. c	29. b
6. a	14. a	22. a	30. a
7. b	15. b	23. e	31. d
8. d	16. e	24. e	

V—CORPORATE LIABILITY

1. a	3. b	5. d	7. d
2. e	4. b	6. c	

VI—MEDICAL STAFF

1. d	8. c	15. c	22. b
2. e	9. d	16. d	23. c
3. b	10. a	17. e	24. b
4. b	11. a	18. b	25. a
5. e	12. f	19. a	26. d
6. e	13. e	20. a	
7. c	14. c	21. d	

VII—NURSING AND THE LAW

1. a	4. d	7. f	10. f
2. e	5. a	8. e	11. d
3. f	6. b	9. a	12. e

13. d	18. f	23. f	28. a
14. b	19. f	24. b	29. e
15. f	20. d	25. c	
16. d	21. f	26. e	
17. f	22. e	27. d	

VIII—LIABILITY BY DEPARTMENT AND HEALTH PROFESSIONAL

1. c	9. e	17. b	25. e
2. e	10. b	18. f	26. f
3. d	11. e	19. c	27. a
4. b	12. b	20. d	28. f
5. e	13. d	21. e	29. b
6. e	14. g	22. c	30. d
7. d	15. c	23. e	31. b
8. f	16. a	24. c	32. c

IX—INFORMATION MANAGEMENT AND HEALTH CARE RECORDS

1. b	4. b	7. c	10. d
2. d	5. d	8. e	
3. a	6. a	9. b	

X—PATIENT CONSENT

| 1. e | 3. d | 5. c | 7. f |
| 2. a | 4. d | 6. e | 8. a |

XI—LEGAL REPORTING OBLIGATIONS

| 1. d | 2. e | 3. c | 4. b |

XII—ISSUES OF PROCREATION

| 1. a | 2. b | 3. d | 4. f |

XIII—PATIENT RIGHTS AND RESPONSIBILITIES

| 1. c | 2. a | 3. b |

XIV—ACQUIRED IMMUNE DEFICIENCY SYNDROME

1. d   2. a

XV—END OF LIFE ISSUES

1. c   3. a   5. d

2. e   4. d   6. b

XVI—LABOR RELATIONS/EMPLOYMENT, DISCIPLINE, AND DISCHARGE

1. a   4. d   7. b   10. d

2. c   5. e   8. b   11. d

3. e   6. c   9. a   12. b

Physicians and the Law
Summary Notes

DEFINITION OF NEGLIGENCE
Negligence is the unintentional omission or commission of an act that a reasonably prudent person would or would not do under given circumstances. Negligence by a physician in the performance of his/her duties is referred to as *malpractice*. It can occur when a physician fails to guard against a risk that should have been recognized, when a physician engages in behavior expected to involve unreasonable danger to others, or when a physician has considered the consequences of an act and exercised his/her best possible judgment.

ELEMENTS OF NEGLIGENCE
Plaintiff must show/prove following elements in order to establish liability:
1. *Duty To Use Due Care*—plaintiff must prove a legal obligation exists that requires one to care and safeguard rights of another.
2. *Breach of Duty*—plaintiff must show defendant failed to comply with or adhere to accepted standard of care.
3. *Actual Injury*—plaintiff must show harm or injury. Damages can be either:
   • economic—(e.g., medical expenses and wages)
   • noneconomic—(e.g., pain and suffering)
4. *Causation*—there must be a close and causal connection between defendant's conduct and resulting damages suffered by the plaintiff.
5. *Foreseeability*—it must be established as to whether one of ordinary prudence and intelligence should have anticipated that harm or injury would have resulted from an act or an omission to act. Liability is limited if the injury is not foreseeable.

FORMS OF NEGLIGENCE
1. *Malfeasance*—execution of an unlawful or improper act
2. *Misfeasance*—improper performance of an act
3. *Nonfeasance*—failure to act, when there is a duty to act, as a reasonably prudent person would under similar circumstances

STANDARD OF CARE
The plaintiff must establish that the defendant failed to meet the prevailing standard of care. The standard is based on the expected conduct of accepted medical practice. Most jurisdictions recognize a national standard of care.

Standard of Care Is Based On:
1. *Regulations*—legislative enactments (e.g., good samaritan acts, licensing laws)
2. *Judicial Decisions*
3. *Absence of Legal Definition*—based on
   • age • knowledge • education • training • mental capacity • expert testimony (required when there is a need to explain the customary standard of behavior that is claimed to have been violated)

RESPONDEAT SUPERIOR
A legal doctrine holding an employer liable for the negligence of its employees (also referred to as vicarious liability).
1. *Elements*—in order to transfer liability to the employer, a plaintiff must establish • negligence did occur • tortfeasor is agent or servant of employer • tort was committed within scope of employment
2. *Purpose of Doctrine*—to encourage employer to control the acts and job performance of employees

ABANDONMENT OF PATIENT
The following must be necessary to prove abandonment:
• medical care was unreasonably discontinued • discontinuance against patient's will • physician failed to arrange for patient's future care • foresight indicated discontinuance might result in physical harm to the patient • actual harm was suffered

AGGRAVATION OF PREEXISTING CONDITION
Aggravation through negligence may result in liability for malpractice (liability will be imposed only for additional harm suffered by aggravation).

ANESTHESIOLOGY
• plan for care • assessment of patient prior to induction • informed consent (options and risks) • administration of anesthetics • safety issues (e.g., integrity of equipment) • care of the patient (e.g., physiological monitoring) • maintaining airway • charting • providing sterile environment • maintaining sterile techniques • performing postprocedure assessment

ASSESSMENT OF PATIENT
• bio-psycho-social-spiritual status • care decisions (e.g., diagnostic testing and consultations) • abuse (physical and substance) • nutritional • invasive procedures • preanesthesia • postoperative status • reassessment • documentation • discharge planning

BLOOD TRANSFUSIONS
• assess need, risks, benefits and alternatives
• document on consent form

CARE DECISIONS
• appropriateness • coordination of care/ multidisciplinary treatment plan • ethical issues • patient and family involvement • determining goals • implementation • evaluation and revision

DISCHARGE CARE
• follow up • education • referrals • continuum of care issues

EDUCATION
• patient and family • community resources • diet • medications • follow-up care • medical equipment

EMERGENCY DEPARTMENT
• failure to respond to an emergency department call • failure to triage, assess, and reassess patient needs • delay in treatment • leaving patient unattended • failure to monitor, record, and recognize changes in patient's vital signs • failure to recognize and report signs of abuse or neglect of patient • telephonic medicine a mistake

MEDICAL STAFF PRIVILEGES
• screening process application • physical and mental status • consent for release of information • insurance • state licensure • national practitioner data bank • references • interview process • interview • board action • clinical privileges • continuing education • appeal process • peer review and reappointment • renewal • limiting, suspension, and removal • bylaws, rules, and regulations • house staff supervision

MISDIAGNOSIS
most frequently cited injury event in malpractice suits against physicians • appendicitis • breast cancer • diabetic acidosis • heart failure • perforated bowel • hyperparathyroidism • pregnancy • skull fracture • testicular cancer

DISCHARGE/PREMATURE
• harm to patient likely • need to report

INFECTION CAUSES
• cross-contamination • improper isolation technique • poor aseptic technique • dressing changes • needlesticks

REDUCING RISK OF INFECTION
• require periodic employee physical • practice proper technique • follow policies and procedures • utilize proper attire (e.g., gowns, gloves, boots, and masks)

MEDICAL EQUIPMENT
• lack of training • improper use • defective equipment and alarms • failure to monitor • failure to maintain

MEDICAL RECORDS
Purpose
• communications across disciplines • documentation of patient care • protect legal interests of both patient and health care facility • provide information for education and research

Problems
• failure to record or make entries • incomplete records • inaccurate records • inconsistent/intermittent charting • correcting • distorting • falsifying • fraudulent entries for insurance, reimbursement, and legal purposes • failure to retain records • ambiguous abbreviations • failure to date, time, or sign records • illegible handwriting • unauthorized entries

Charting Reminders
• be accurate • be complete • date entries • be legible • make relevant entries • write with clarity • be concise • do not make defamatory entries • when making corrections do not make erasures • do not use correction fluids • line out mistaken entries • write in correct information • use different colored ink when making corrections (blue or black) • initial and date corrections • do not tamper with the chart • do not make entries in patient's chart without advice of legal counsel if a suit has been threatened • countersign entries by residents • protect records from unauthorized access and entries • release records only to authorized persons • obtain appropriate authorization for release of records

MEDICATION ERRORS AND ISSUES
1. availability
2. ordering
3. preparation
4. administration: • wrong patient • wrong drug • wrong dosage • wrong route • wrong frequency • failure to administer • negligent injection • failure to discontinue • repeated dosage • no prescription • transcription errors • consent for use of experimental drugs • mislabeled • untimely administration • order change • outdated • recalled
5. monitoring

Minimizing Medication Errors
• check chart and verify written orders, correct medication, route, dosage, patient allergies • check the label—do not administer unlabeled medications • identify patient by checking wrist band and talking to the patient • question concerns with nurse or pharmacist • monitor, report, and chart adverse reactions • communicate untoward reactions • follow

procedures for preparation, labeling, storage, and record keeping • use PDR as necessary • follow proper procedures in administering investigational drugs • document medications administered (e.g., dosage, route, time, and initial) • maintain correct policies and procedures on each patient care unit • maintain patient profile on patient unit • computerize record keeping

OBSTETRICS
• highly vulnerable medical specialty • failure to perform a Caesarean section • failure to perform delivery • injury to brachial plexus nerves • joint liability • emergency assistance • nurse assessment • wrongful death of a viable unborn fetus

RADIOLOGY
• judicial notice and X-rays • inadequate X-ray examination • failure to consult with radiologist • failure to read X-rays • failure to notify of X-ray results • incorrect diet

RESTRAINTS
• assess need for restraints • time limit and sign order

SURGERY
1. postoperative care
2. sponge/instrument miscounts
3. infections
4. O.R. suite not adequately cleaned
5. cross-contamination
6. confirm the patient on the O.R. table: • has been properly screened for surgery (with documentation in the patient's record) • is the correct patient • is about to undergo the correct procedure • is properly draped with the correct operative site exposed • has not eaten within the prescribed time period • has signed the appropriate consent forms • is not wearing dentures

Preventing Lawsuits
• practice aseptic technique and maintain sterile environment • ensure patient has not eaten • properly prep patient • ensure appropriate instrumentation is present and sterile • ensure appropriate meds, blood, and blood products are available to complete procedure

TIPS
• avoid criticizing caregivers • prior to rendering care, check patient's chart and note recordings by other caregivers • obtain consultations when needed • maintain confidentiality standards • be a good listener • be empathetic • respect patient privacy • keep patient and family informed • be responsive to patient needs • be observant of changes in patient's condition • be observant of medical equipment connected to the patient, including signs of possible malfunctioning • provide patient/family education • do not guarantee treatment outcome • provide for cross-coverage during days off • maintain timely, complete, and accurate records • do not make

erasures in records • personalize your treatment • do not overextend your practice • provide sufficient time and care to each patient (explain treatment plans and follow-up care to the patient, family, and other caregivers) • avoid telephone-based examinations and prescriptions • do not become careless because you know the patient • request consultations when indicated and refer if necessary • seek advice of counsel should you suspect the possibility of a malpractice claim • perform patient examinations in the presence of another caregiver

REPORTING REQUIREMENTS
• professional • child abuse • elder abuse

INFORMED CONSENT
• a legal concept predicated on the duty of the physician to disclose the information necessary to enable the patient to evaluate a proposed medical or surgical procedure before consenting to it.

Forms
• written: completed, dated, signed, and witnessed • oral • implied

Refusal of Treatment
• obtain written release • if signature refused: note patient's refusal on release form, date it, sign it (both physician and other caregiver), and file it with medical record

Special Consent
• investigational drugs and procedures • invasive procedures (e.g., surgery)

Substituted Judgment
• confirm surrogate rights

Patient Rights
• admission/emergency care • participation in care decisions • complaint resolution process • confidentiality • privacy • discharge • transfer • advance directives/self-determination • refuse treatment • appointment of surrogate decision maker • do not resuscitate orders

Patient Responsibilities
• provide physician with accurate and complete information • abide by rules and regulations of organization • treat others with respect and dignity • make it known whether one comprehends proposed course of action and what is expected of oneself

The preeminent guide to law in health care management entitled *Legal Aspects of Health Care Administration* by George D. Pozgar is available from Aspen Publishers, Inc., 200 Orchard Ridge Drive, Gaithersburg, MD 20878, (800) 638-8437.

Nurses and the Law
Summary Notes

DEFINITION OF NEGLIGENCE
Negligence is the unintentional omission or commission of an act that a reasonably prudent person would or would not do under given circumstances. Negligence by a professional nurse in the performance of his/her duties is referred to as *malpractice*. It can occur when a nurse fails to guard against a risk that should have been recognized, when a nurse engages in behavior expected to involve unreasonable danger to others, or when a nurse has considered the consequences of an act and exercised his/her best possible judgment.

ELEMENTS OF NEGLIGENCE
Plaintiff must show/prove following elements in order to establish liability:
1. *Duty To Use Due Care*—plaintiff must prove a legal obligation exists that requires one to care and safeguard the rights of another.
2. *Breach of Duty*—plaintiff must show defendant failed to comply with or adhere to accepted standard of care.
3. *Actual Injury*—plaintiff must show harm or injury. Damages can be either:
   • economic (e.g., medical expenses and wages)
   • noneconomic (e.g., pain and suffering)
4. *Causation*—there must be a close and causal connection between defendant's conduct and resulting damages suffered by the plaintiff.
5. *Foreseeability*—it must be established as to whether one of ordinary prudence and intelligence should have anticipated that harm or injury would have resulted from an act or an omission to act. Liability is limited if the injury is not foreseeable.

FORMS OF NEGLIGENCE
1. *Malfeasance*—execution of an unlawful or improper act
2. *Misfeasance*—improper performance of an act
3. *Nonfeasance*—failure to act, when there is a duty to act, as a reasonably prudent person would under similar circumstances

STANDARD OF CARE
The plaintiff must establish that the defendant failed to meet the prevailing standard of care. The standard is based on the expected conduct of accepted nursing practice. Most jurisdictions recognize a national standard of care.

Standard of Care Is Based On:
1. *Regulations*—legislative enactments (e.g., good samaritan acts, licensing laws)
2. *Judicial Decisions*
3. *Absence of Legal Definition*—based on
   • age • knowledge • education • training • mental capacity • expert testimony (required when there is a need to explain the customary standard of behavior that is claimed to have been violated)

RESPONDEAT SUPERIOR
Legal doctrine holding an employer liable for the negligence of its employees (also referred to as vicarious liability).
1. *Elements*—in order to transfer liability to the employer, a plaintiff must establish • negligence did occur • tortfeasor/wrongdoer is the agent or servant of the employer • tort was committed within the scope of employment
2. *Purpose of Doctrine*—to encourage employers to control the acts and job performance of employees

BURNS
• food/drinks • heating pads • hot water bottles • showers • baths • surgical instruments • chemical • medical equipment

EMERGENCY DEPARTMENT
• failure to assess and reassess patient needs • improper triage • delay in treatment • leaving patient unattended • failure to monitor, record, and recognize changes in a patient's vital signs • failure to recognize and report signs of abuse

INAPPROPRIATE DISCHARGE
• harm to patient likely • need to report

FAILURE TO FOLLOW INSTRUCTIONS
• policies and procedures of hospital and department • supervisor's • physician's

FAILURE TO RECOGNIZE
• changes in patient's condition • obvious incorrect orders

FAILURE TO REPORT
• changes in patient's condition • professional misconduct

FALLS
• bathroom • beds • wheelchairs • examination tables • spills/wet floors • medications • stairwells • stretchers • chairs • transfers

PREVENTING FALLS
• assess need for restraints (time-limited signed orders) • follow orders • conduct frequent rounds and make observations • utilize bed alarms • display wet floor signs • clean spills promptly • report hazards promptly • make repairs promptly

NURSING PROCEDURES
• failure to follow procedures • failure to track vital signs • improper performance of a procedure • failure to provide adequate inservice • failure to document

INFECTIONS
Causes
• cross-contamination • improper isolation technique • poor aseptic technique during dressing changes • needlesticks

Reducing the Risks of Infection
• require periodic employee physical • practice proper technique • follow policies and procedures • utilize proper attire (e.g., gowns, gloves, boots, and masks)

MEDICAL RECORDS
Purpose
• communication across disciplines • documentation of patient care • protection of legal interests of both patient and health care facility • provision of information for education and research

Problems
• failure to record or make entries • incomplete records • inaccurate records • inconsistent/intermittent charting • correcting • distorting • falsifying • making fraudulent entries for insurance, reimbursement, and legal purposes • unauthorized entries • failure to retain records • ambiguous abbreviations • failure to date, time, or sign records • illegible handwriting

Charting Reminders
• be accurate • be complete • date entries • be legible • make relevant entries • write with clarity • be concise • do not make defamatory entries • when making corrections do not make erasures • do not use correction fluids • line out mistaken entries • write in correct information • use different colored ink when making corrections (blue or black) • initial and date corrections • do not tamper with the chart • do not make entries in a patient's chart without advice of legal counsel if a suit has been threatened • authenticate student entries • report normal and abnormal find-

ings • report patient complaints • protect records from unauthorized access and entries • release records only to authorized persons

OPERATING ROOM
Issues
• sponge/instrument miscounts • O.R. suite not adequately cleaned • cross contamination • confirm that the patient on the O.R. table has been properly identified for surgery (with documentation in the patient's record) • confirm correct patient • confirm patient is about to undergo the correct procedure • confirm patient is properly draped with the correct operative site exposed • confirm patient has not eaten within the prescribed time period • confirm patient has signed the appropriate consent forms • confirm patient is not wearing dentures

Preventing Lawsuits
• practice aseptic technique and maintain sterile environment • ensure patient has not eaten • properly prep patient • ensure appropriate instrumentation is present and sterile • ensure appropriate meds, blood, and blood products are available to complete procedure • protect patient from injury by correctly positioning patient and securing limbs

INCORRECT TELEPHONE ORDERS
• verify physician orders with staff on second phone line • repeat orders to physician

MEDICAL EQUIPMENT
• lack of training • improper use • defective/faulty equipment and alarms • failure to monitor • failure to have backup

MEDICATION ERRORS
• wrong patient • wrong drug • wrong dosage • wrong route (e.g., given intramuscularly v. orally) • wrong frequency • failure to administer • negligent injection • failure to discontinue • repeated dosage • lack of consent for use of experimental drugs • no prescription • transcription errors • untimely administration

Minimizing Medication Errors
• check chart and verify written orders, correct medication, route, dosage, and patient allergies • check the label—do not administer unlabeled medications • identify patient by checking wrist band and

talking to the patient • question concerns with physician or pharmacist • monitor, report, and chart adverse reactions • communicate untoward reactions • follow procedures for preparation, labeling, storage, and record keeping • use PDR as necessary • follow proper procedures in administering investigational drugs • document medications administered, including dosage, route, time, and initial • maintain current policies and procedures on each patient care unit • maintain patient profile on patient unit • computerize record keeping

PREVENTING MEDICAL EQUIPMENT MALFUNCTION
• prompt reporting • preventive maintenance program for all equipment

UNSAFE ENVIRONMENT
• frayed electrical cords • spills • wet floors • clutter • improper placement of equipment

DIETARY
• incorrect diet

OBSTETRICS
• one of the most vulnerable medical specialties

TIPS
1. avoid criticizing caregivers
2. prior to rendering care: • check patient's chart and note changes in physician orders • if orders seem vague or questionable, clarify with physician • ask patient name • verify/check patient wrist band
3. follow a risk management program: • report and investigate incidents promptly • establish prevention programs • identify potential hazardous occurrences and take preemptive action
4. develop a quality improvement program that includes: • planning and designing • measuring • assessing with internal and external databases • improving and redesigning processes
5. keep patient and family informed within hospital policy and medical, legal, and ethical guidelines
6. disseminate information: • poison control • hospital formulary • hospital-sponsored educational programs
7. be observant of changes in patient's condition, vital signs, IVs, etc.
8. be observant of medical equipment connected to the patient, including signs of possible malfunctioning
9. provide patient/family education

REPORTING REQUIREMENTS
• professional (e.g., National Practitioner Data Bank) • child abuse • elder abuse • rape

INFORMED CONSENT
• a legal concept predicated on the duty of the physician to disclose the information necessary to enable the patient to evaluate a proposed medical or surgical procedure before consenting to it.

Forms
• written: completed, dated, signed, and witnessed • oral • implied

Refusal of Treatment
• obtain written release • if signature refused: note patient's refusal on release form, date it, sign it (both physician and other caregiver), and file it with medical record

Special Consent
• investigational drugs and procedures • invasive procedures (e.g., surgery)

Substituted Judgment
• confirm surrogate rights

Patient Rights
• admission/emergency care • participation in care decisions • complaint resolution process • confidentiality • privacy • discharge • transfer • advance directives/self-determination • refuse treatment • appointment of surrogate decision maker • do not resuscitate orders

Patient Responsibilities
• provide physician with accurate and complete information • abide by rules and regulations of organization • treat others with respect and dignity • make it known whether one comprehends proposed course of action and what is expected of oneself

The preeminent guide to law in health care management entitled *Legal Aspects of Health Care Administration* by George D. Pozgar is available from Aspen Publishers, Inc., 200 Orchard Ridge Drive, Gaithersburg, MD 20878, (800) 638-8437.

Pharmacists and the Law
Summary Notes

DEFINITION OF NEGLIGENCE
Negligence is the unintentional omission or commission of an act that a reasonably prudent person would or would not do under given circumstances. Negligence by a pharmacist in the performance of his/her duties is referred to as *malpractice*. It can occur when a pharmacist fails to guard against a risk that should have been recognized, when a pharmacist engages in behavior expected to involve unreasonable danger to others, or when a pharmacist has considered the consequences of an act and exercised his/her best possible judgment.

ELEMENTS OF NEGLIGENCE
Plaintiff must show/prove following four elements in order to establish liability:
1. *Duty To Use Due Care*—plaintiff must prove a legal obligation exists that requires one to care and safeguard rights of another.
2. *Breach of Duty*—plaintiff must show defendant failed to comply with or adhere to accepted standard of care.
3. *Actual Injury*—plaintiff must show harm or injury. Damages can be either:
   • economic (e.g., medical expenses and wages)
   • noneconomic (e.g., pain and suffering)
4. *Causation*—there must be a close and causal connection between defendant's conduct and resulting damages suffered by the plaintiff.

FORESEEABILITY TEST
It must be established as to whether one of ordinary prudence and intelligence should have anticipated that harm or injury would have resulted from an act or an omission to act. Liability is limited if the injury is not foreseeable.

FORMS OF NEGLIGENCE
1. *Malfeasance*—execution of an unlawful or improper act
2. *Misfeasance*—improper performance of an act
3. *Nonfeasance*—failure to act, when there is a duty to act, as a reasonably prudent person would under similar circumstances

STANDARD OF CARE
The plaintiff must establish that the defendant failed to meet the prevailing standard of care. The standard is based on the expected conduct of accepted pharmacy practice.

Standard of Care Is Based On:
1. *Regulation*—legislative enactments (e.g., licensing laws)

2. *Judicial Decisions*
3. *Absence of Legal Definition*—based on
   • age • knowledge • education • training • mental capacity • expert testimony (required when there is a need to explain the customary standard of behavior claimed to have been violated)

RESPONDEAT SUPERIOR
A legal doctrine holding an employer liable for the negligence of its employees (also referred to as vicarious liability).
1. *Elements*—in order to transfer liability to the employer, plaintiff must establish • negligence did occur • tortfeasor is agent or servant of employer • tort was committed within scope of employment
2. *Purpose of Doctrine*—to encourage employer to control the acts and job performance of employees

RECEIVING TELEPHONE ORDERS
• drug/s ordered clearly and correctly • confirm understanding by reading back name of patient, drug, frequency, and dosage ordered

DELIVERY OF WRITTEN ORDERS
• computer order entry • FAX machines • pneumatic tubes

CARE DECISIONS
• appropriateness of medications ordered • multi-disciplinary treatment plan • ethical issues • determining goals • evaluation of effectiveness of medications ordered • recommendations for alternative medications

EMERGENCY DEPARTMENT
• responding to emergency department calls for drug information • identification of drugs • patients on investigational drugs

COMPETENCY
• screening process (e.g. application) • physical and mental status • consent for release of information • insurance • licensure • national practitioner data bank • references • interview process • interview • board action • clinical privileges • continuing education • appeal process • peer review and reappointment • renewal • limiting, suspension, and removal of privileges

INFECTION
Causes
• cross-contamination • poor aseptic technique • needlesticks
Reducing Risks
• require periodic employee physical • practice proper technique • follow policies and procedures • utilize proper attire (e.g., gowns, gloves, boots, and masks)

PHARMACY EQUIPMENT
• training • proper use • equipment maintenance and alarms • failure to monitor • failure to maintain

MEDICAL RECORDS
Purpose
• communications across disciplines • documentation of patient care • protect legal interests of both patient and health care facility • provide information for education and research

Problems
• failure to record or make entries • incomplete records • inaccurate records • inconsistent/intermittent charting • correcting • distorting • falsifying • fraudulent entries for insurance, reimbursement, and legal purposes • failure to retain records • ambiguous abbreviations • failure to date, time, or sign records • illegible handwriting • unauthorized entries

Charting Reminders
• be accurate • be complete • date entries • be legible • make relevant entries • write with clarity • be concise • do not make defamatory entries • when making corrections do not make erasures • do not use correction fluids • line out mistaken entries • write in correct information • use different colored ink when making corrections (blue or black) • initial and date corrections • do not tamper with the chart • do not make entries in patient's chart without advice of legal counsel if suit has been threatened • countersign entries by residents • protect records from unauthorized access and entries • release records only to authorized persons • obtain appropriate authorization for release of records

MEDICATION ERRORS
• failure to order • wrong patient • wrong drug • wrong dosage • wrong route • wrong frequency • missed dose/failure to administer • negligent injection • failure to discontinue • repeated dosage/double dosing • no prescription • transcription errors (e.g., dosing) • no consent (experimental drugs) • mislabeled • untimely administration • order change • outdated • recalled

Minimizing Medication Errors
• education (initial orientation and continuing education) • check chart and verify written orders, correct medication, route, dosage, patient allergies • check label—do not administer unlabeled medications • identify patient by checking wrist band and talking to patient • question concerns

with nurse or pharmacist • monitor, report, and chart adverse reactions • communicate untoward reactions • follow procedures for preparation, labeling, storage, and record keeping • use PDR as necessary • follow proper procedures in administering investigational drugs • document medications administered (e.g., dosage, route, time, and initial) • maintain correct policies and procedures on each patient care unit • maintain patient profile on patient unit • computerize record keeping

FORMULARY
• development (who has input, who approves, how published, how updated) • maintenance (additions, deletions, and substitutions) • mechanism for additions and deletions • nonformulary drugs (how obtained)

ADVERSE DRUG REACTIONS
• unexpected reaction to a drug • mechanism for reporting • tracing/monitoring effect on patient

INVESTIGATIONAL DRUGS
• policy and procedure • obtain informed consent • criteria for study • IRB committee

TIPS
• avoid criticizing caregivers • maintain confidentiality standards • be a good listener • be empathetic • respect patient privacy • keep patient and family informed • be responsive to patient needs • be observant of changes in patient's condition • be observant of medical equipment connected to the patient, including signs of possible malfunction • provide patient/family education • maintain timely, complete, and accurate records

REPORTING REQUIREMENTS
• adverse drug reactions • controlled substances

INFORMED CONSENT
Informed consent is a legal concept predicated on the physician's duty to disclose information necessary to enable the patient to evaluate a proposed medical or surgical procedure or an investigational drug before consenting to it.

Forms
• written: completed, dated, signed, and witnessed • oral • implied

Refusal of Treatment
• obtain written release • if signature refused, note refusal on release form, date

it, sign it (both physician and other caregiver), and file it with medical record

Special Consent Required For:
• investigational drugs and procedures • invasive procedures (e.g., surgery)

Substituted Judgment
• confirm surrogate rights

Patient Rights
• admission/emergency care • participation in care decisions • complaint resolution process • confidentiality • privacy • discharge • transfer • advance directives/self-determination • refuse treatment • appointment of surrogate decision maker • do not resuscitate orders

PHARMACY CHECKLIST
Documents
• policy and procedure (development, review and approval) • licenses • patient medication profiles • patient events reporting and tracking system

Tour
• locked entrance door • drugs mislabeled (unit dose helps prevent mislabeling) • mislabeling by manufacturer • expired drugs • narcotics location and security? • laminar flow hoods (inspection, cleaning) • computerization

Interview
• scope of service • staffing (evening, night, weekend, and on-call coverage) • hours • satellite pharmacies (emergency stock within and outside the pharmacy) • emergency drugs—how obtained • department orientation • skills checklists • in-service education • continuing education • competency reviews • are patient care needs assessed • how is uniform quality assured

Ordering/Prescribing
• credentialing • who can prescribe: physicians, nurse practitioners, physician assistants • mechanism to control • identification of limitations per practitioner • what happens to an order from the time it is initiated • computer/order entry • verbal orders (misheard, misunderstood, mistranscribed)

Patient Profiles
• age, weight, height, diagnoses, allergies • available to whom

Dispensing
• authorization for dispensing • orders for drugs (handling)

Emergency Medications
• availability • dispensing when pharmacy is closed (procedures) • generic substitution • accuracy • mixing IVs after hours

Administration
• confirm identity of patient • ensure appropriate consent forms have been signed

Monitoring
• how information is obtained

Controling
• policy and procedure • dispensing, waste, and returns

Sample Drugs
• controlling • tracking (e.g., register lot numbers with pharmacy) • recalls • on formulary prior to use • which patient receives which lot

Crash Cart Stocking
• security • system for control/process for monitoring • check laryngoscope batteries • check for expired medications

Outpatient Medications
• Teaching

Cost Reduction
• appropriatness of therapy • correlation between knowledge and research, e.g., Zantac v. Tagamet (older patients more side effects), antibiotics, thrombolics: TPA v. streptokinase

Multiple Medications
• protocol for handling • contraindications

Patient/Family Education
• access to community resources on drugs • investigational drugs (informed consent) • role in discharge planning • food-drug interactions • determine whether patient understands instructions

Pharmacy and Therapeutics Committee
• composition (dietitian, lab tech, physician, and pharmacist)

Performance Improvement
• Interdisciplinary meetings • national and local benchmarking—comparing with the best (external databases, literature review, site visits, experts) • kinds of aggregate data available • area of focus (size, complexity of service, measurable characteristics) • success over time

The preeminent guide to law in health care management entitled *Legal Aspects of Health Care Administration* by George D. Pozgar is available from Aspen Publishers, Inc., 200 Orchard Ridge Drive, Gaithersburg, MD 20878, (800) 638-8437.

Assessing the Quality of Care in Health Care Organizations: Self-Evaluation and Redundancy in Systems

SYSTEMS REDUNDANCY

There is a major need in the health care industry to reduce the number of human process errors that are often the "root cause" of poor outcomes. Outcomes need to be predictable. This can occur more frequently if redundant (backup) systems, procedures, and processes are in place for safe and effective patient care. The development of redundant systems will reduce the likelihood of human error. The health care industry should follow the example of other large organizations that respond in a proactive manner. The National Aeronautics and Space Administration (NASA), for example, has numerous redundant systems in place each time a shuttle is flown into space for the safety of the astronauts. Redundancy in systems needs to be in place in hospitals as well, for patient safety. Many hospitals have a variety of redundancy systems to improve patient outcomes. For example, a patient about to undergo surgery would have a variety of clinical tests and assessments prior to undergoing a surgical procedure. There is a necessity to ensure that the right patient is in the right surgical suite and is about to undergo the right procedure on the right body part. The right patient would require appropriate identification of the patient by checking the patient's wristband, identification of the patient by the operating surgeon, staff, and anesthesiologist, and addressing the patient by name prior to induction. Identification of the surgical site should include participation by the patient's marking of the surgical site prior to surgery. Simple procedures, but critical to good outcomes.

It is important to review sentinel events occurring in health care organizations and to conduct root cause analyses, seeking answers as to why a particular outcome occurred and how to prevent similar events from repeating themselves. However, the "how to prevent" an undesirable outcome is as

valuable as the "why" a bad outcome occurred in the first place. More focus on "how" to do it right the first time will lessen the likelihood of having to ask "why" things went wrong.

Redundant systems can improve diagnosis and effective treatment. The questions listed below, although far from exhaustive, are meant to be thought provoking and should lead to deeper inquiry into designing meaningful redundancy in systems.

LEADERSHIP

- What are the organization's mission, vision, and values?
- How has the organization's mission/vision/values changed over time?
- How does the planning process relate to the organization's mission, vision, and values?
- How are the organization's mission, vision, values, and long-range plans communicated throughout the organization and community?
- What is the scope of services provided by the organization?
- How is the scope of services determined?
- How does the leadership effectuate collaboration among the organization's leaders?
- How does the organization plan services for
  - specific patient populations (e.g., indigent patients)?
  - directing and staffing services?
  - coordinating and integrating services?
  - improving services?
- How do the organization's leaders address performance improvement issues?
- What are the characteristics of the governing body?

– What is the composition (community representation) on the governing body?
– What is the size of the board?
– What is the organization's process for orienting and educating new board members?
– What is the organization's process for ongoing education?
– How does one become a member?
– Is there a systems board, single board, or both?
– Is there a community advisory board, and if so, how does one become a member?
– What is the purpose of the community advisory board?
– What is the governing body's process for evaluating/reviewing and improving its effectiveness?
– Is there input from patient focused groups?
• What are the mechanisms used to educate the organization's leadership?
– annual retreats?
– internal and external continuing education programs and seminars?
• How does the governing body assure itself that the organization is delivering quality care?
• How intensely does the governing body probe into the whos, whats, hows, and whys of organizational successes and failures?
• Does the organization practice patient-focused care?
• Does the purchase of cheaper products compromise the quality of patient care?
• How does the leadership evaluate its effectiveness?
• How does the governing body assure and reassure itself that it is doing the right thing?
• Does the governing body conduct a self-assessment?
• How does the organization's leadership know if clinical outcomes are improving?
• What is the organization's mechanism for addressing conflict?
• Has the organization implemented a conflict-of-interest policy?
• How does the governing body assure itself that patient care and clinical outcomes are improving?
• How does the organization assure itself that the same level of care is being delivered across the organization?
• What redundant systems does the organization have in place to improve patient outcomes?
• How does the organization assure itself that the appropriateness of therapy is not based on costs alone?
• Does the organization have a corporate compliance program in place for the prevention of fraud and abuse?
• Does the program provide for a corporate compliance officer?

PLANNING

• What is the organization's planning process/plan for planning?
• Is planning conducted on a collaborative basis?
• How are community needs assessed?
– What is the organization's plan for identifying and addressing community needs?
• How do the organization's leaders and community leaders collaborate to design and prioritize the need for new services?
• How are priorities set?
– Are needs prioritized on a collaborative basis?
– Does prioritizing include administration, trustees, nursing, and medical staff?
– Are power brokers driving their own agenda in prioritizing organizational needs?
• How do services relate to the organization's mission, vision, and values?
• How do services relate to identified needs?
• How does the organization ensure that services are relative to community need?
• How does the organization improve services as a result of patient input?
• Does the organization have a clear strategy and strategic plan that charts the course and direction of the organization in response to the critical health care environment?
• Do planning documents address patient care needs, including needs identified by the medical staff?
• Does the organization obtain patient and family input as to how the organization is meeting the care needs of its patients?
• What is the organization's mechanism for obtaining feedback: satisfaction surveys?
– Are satisfaction surveys used in the planning process?

RESOURCE ALLOCATION

• What processes are in place for the organization to position itself for economic survival?
• What is the mechanism for leadership participation in resource allocation for human resources and capital acquisitions?
• How are priorities set for allocation of financial resources?
• Who has input into setting resource allocation priorities?
• What is the process for defining and approving new services?

- How do department directors participate in the organization's ongoing decision-making processes?
  - for planning?
  - for budgeting?
- What are the organization's parameters for feedback on variance reporting?
- How are funds allocated for
  - orientation, training, and education of staff?
  - patient and family education?
- What is the relationship of patient care services to patient care needs?
- What financial data does the organization provide to its managers?
- What is the organization's process for developing budgets (capital, human resource, and expense)?
- What is the organization's process for approving expenditures?
- What is the organization's methodology for prioritizing budget expenditures?
- What aggregate data are made available to the organization's leadership and managers to support decision-making processes, operations, and performance improvement activities?
- What services does the organization contract out?
- How does the organization ensure effective communications in the delivery of patient care as it relates to
  - language barriers?
  - age-specific barriers?
  - cultural and religious barriers?

PASTORAL CARE SERVICES

- How are the religious and spiritual needs of patients addressed?
- How do patients know such services are available?
- Do organizational policies and procedures address the psychosocial, spiritual, and cultural variables that influence one's understanding and perception of illness?
- How are referrals made by caregivers for spiritual assessment, reassessment, and follow-up?
- What evidence/documentation is placed in a patient's record to indicate that a patient's spiritual needs have been addressed?

PATIENT COMPLAINT PROCESS

- What is the organization's patient complaint process?
- How does the patient know about the process?
- How are complaints addressed in the organization?
- Is the patient informed after his or her complaint is addressed?

PATIENT RIGHTS

- How are advance directives addressed?
  - Are patients queried to determine if they have an advance directive?
  - What happens if the patient has an advance directive? Is a copy placed on the patient's individual record?
  - What happens if the patient has no advance directive? Is the patient given information and an opportunity to execute an advance directive?
- How does the organization address ethical issues?
- Does the organization have a code of ethical behavior?
  - Does this code address admissions, discharge, transfer, billing practices, referrals, and relationships with other health care professionals?
- Does the organization have an ethics committee?
  - What are the functions of the ethics committee?
  - Does committee membership include significant representation from both community and providers?
  - How are the patient and staff educated as to the existence and functions of the ethics committee?
- Are patients provided a statement as to their rights and responsibilities upon admission?
- Do patients have a right to review their medical records?
- How are complaints handled?
- What are the organization's policies and procedures for asking patients and families about organ donations?

HUMAN RESOURCES

- What are the technical skills of the position?
- Is the position applied for a part of the applicant's career path or just another job?
- Does the applicant appear motivated?
- Does the applicant exhibit a sense of excitement about the position?
- Are the applicant's communications skills appropriate for the position applied for?
- How does the organization know that it is adequately staffed?
- What data does the organization collect that indicates the organization is appropriately staffed?
- How does the organization determine the mix, numbers, and qualifications of staff?

- Describe programs in place to promote recruitment, retention, development, and recognition of staff.
- What is the organization's process for verification of licensure?
- Are job descriptions reflective of each staff member's duties and responsibilities?
- What effect has reengineering had on staff?
- Is the organization's reengineering/redesign process nursing or organization specific?
- How does the governing body reassure itself that the competency review process is effective?
- How does the governing body ensure that annual competency evaluations are being performed?
- Do competency reports to the governing body include contracted and other agency staff?
- What mechanisms does the organization have in place to monitor the competency of individuals whose jobs have been reengineered?
- How is the performance of senior management staff evaluated?
- What performance data are collected and used for human resources?
- How does the organization assess the effectiveness and appropriateness of training and education programs?
- How are employees oriented to the culture of the organization?
- How does the organization assess competency?
- How does the competency evaluation relate to the job description?
- Are performance evaluations criteria based?
- How are agency and contracted staff oriented to the organization?
- How are age-specific competencies evaluated?
  - Does the organization utilize a self-testing module (e.g., Erickson's Growth and Development)?
  - Are age-specific criteria applicable to the job classification?
- Describe the organization's general orientation program.
- Does the orientation program provide education relative to
  - mission, vision, and values?
  - review of organizational and department policies and procedures?
  - safety issues?
  - equipment management?
  - the organization's performance improvement process?
- What mechanisms are in place to promote job-related education and advancement goals of staff members?
- How does the organization assess the education and training needs of staff?
- Are volunteers oriented to the organization?
- Are volunteers oriented to the volunteer service?

- Are organized volunteer services provided under the direction of a designated hospital employee or by the establishment of a self-governing auxiliary?

ASSESSMENT OF PATIENT NEEDS

- Is there an interdisciplinary collaborative team that addresses the totality of patient care needs?
- How does the organization ensure that collaboration is effective?
- What is the organization's process for assessing the needs of patients with multisystem breakdown?
- Given an aging population, how do caregivers collaborate in planning a patient's treatment plan (e.g., How are the multiple needs of an 88-year-old patient admitted from a nursing facility with a primary diagnosis of a fractured hip addressed? Assume that the patient also has diagnoses of diabetes, Parkinson's, senility, arthritis, and recent GI bleed.)?
- What is the organization's policy for conducting functional screenings and assessments for
  - medical history and physicals?
  - nursing assessment and reassessments?
  - nutritional screens, assessments, and reassessments?
  - functional screens, assessments, and reassessments?
  - spiritual assessments and reassessments?
  - discharge planning?
- Are second opinions obtained, literature searched, and other resources utilized in search of timely and accurate diagnoses and treatment of patients?

DENTISTRY

- Is conscious sedation administered in any of the organization's dental settings?
- How is dental radiology equipment maintained?
- What is the process for sterilization of dental instruments?
  - Is biological testing conducted?

EMERGENCY DEPARTMENT

- Are patients triaged, assessed, and treated within a reasonable period of time?
- Are all patients assessed and treated by a physician prior to discharge?
- What is the organization's mechanism for obtaining consultations?
- What is the definitive ECG to needle time for the administration of thrombolytics?
- Does the emergency department have an "express care" treatment area?

– What are the criteria for admission and discharge?

– Is response time by physicians on the on-call list timely?

• If admission is necessary, is the designated attending physician responsible for

– accepting the patient as an admission?

– suggesting a specified consulting physician?

– requesting that the emergency department physician hold the patient for further assessment until he or she, the private physician, can assess the patient?

– requesting transfer to a more appropriate facility (e.g., tertiary care)?

• What are the specific competencies required of staff who work in the emergency department?

• Is there a sufficient number, and of staff by discipline, available to care for patients?

• In the event a patient's past admissions are microfilmed, are pertinent sections or specific portions of the previous records readily available as needed?

• Are medical records maintained for each patient treated in the emergency department?

• Are medical records maintained for each patient who meets his or her physician in the emergency department?

• Are copies of the medical records of patients seen in the emergency department sent to each patient's attending physician?

• If a patient has been treated in other settings within the organization (e.g., ambulatory care settings), how are records from those settings accessed?

• What is the process for providing patient education in the emergency department prior to discharge?

• How are patients discharged from the emergency department notified of abnormal lab results?

• What documentation is maintained regarding notification of patients as to test results?

• Who is responsible for follow-up with patients who have abnormal diagnostic tests?

• What are the issues and perceptions identified by patients as to the care being rendered in the emergency department?

• What transfer agreements does the organization have in place to effectuate a timely transfer of a patient in need of an alternate level of care?

• What evaluation tools does the organization utilize to improve the care rendered in the emergency department?

INFORMATION MANAGEMENT

• How does the organization address its information systems needs?

• Does the organization have an interdisciplinary committee structure for assessing and reassessing needs?

– What leaders are represented on the committee?

– What are the functions of the information systems committee?

– Does the committee address satisfaction?

– Does the committee address timeliness of information?

– Does the committee address clinical needs?

– Does the committee address possible systems failures for the year 2000?

• Is there an ongoing process for assessment and reassessment of information needs in the organization?

• What is the methodology for prioritizing needs?

• Has the organization committed appropriate funds for upgrading systems?

• How does the organization maintain systems security and confidentiality?

MEDICAL STAFF

• What are the organization's processes for credentialing physicians and other health care practitioners (e.g., acupuncturists)?

• Is information collected from the National Practitioner Data Bank utilized in the credentialing process?

• How does the organization review and evaluate the competency of the members of the medical staff?

• What mechanism does the organization have in place for ongoing evaluation and reevaluation?

MEDICATION USE

• What is the organization's process for evaluating high-risk, high-volume, and high-cost medications?

• Who is responsible for overseeing the storage and control of medications maintained on patient care units?

• What risk reduction activities does the organization have in place to reduce the likelihood of adverse drug reactions and medication errors?

• What disciplines have been credentialed to prescribe medications (physician's assistants and nurse practitioners)?

• How are controlled substances monitored, inventoried, and wasted (is wasting witnessed and documented)?

• What is the organization's mechanism for monitoring the effect of medications on patients?

MEDICATION ERRORS

• What is the organization's process for monitoring, tracking, and trending medication errors?

- Are medication errors tracked and trended by profession (nurse, pharmacist, and physician)?
  - How is the information gathered utilized to reduce the likelihood of medication errors?
- What are the common causes/trends and patterns for medication errors?
  - Are errors trended by patient unit?
- What processes does the organization have in place to reduce the likelihood of transcription errors?
- What is the frequency of
  - transcription errors?
  - dosing errors (including age-related dosing for neonates, infants, adolescents, adult, and geriatric populations)?
  - administration errors?
  - double dosing?
  - administering medications not ordered?
  - untimely administration of medications?
  - administering a medication to the wrong patient?
  - packaging errors by pharmacy staff?
  - packaging errors by drug manufacturers?
  - errors due to illegible and/or ambiguous handwriting?
- Is consent obtained for the use of investigational drugs and high-risk medications?
- What is the frequency of "missed" doses?
- What educational processes have been implemented to reduce the likelihood of medication errors?

ADVERSE DRUG REACTIONS

- How do reported adverse drug reactions compare with like organizations?
- Is there a mechanism in place for monitoring side effects?
- Is there a mechanism in place for reducing the frequency of adverse drug reactions?

EMERGENCY MEDICATIONS

- How are emergency medications obtained when the pharmacy is closed?
- How are medications obtained that are not included in the hospital's formulary?

INVESTIGATIONAL DRUGS

- Is informed consent obtained from patients prior to the use of investigational drugs?

- Describe the organization's procedure for reviewing and approving research protocols?
- Does the organization have a mechanism in place for approving and overseeing the use of investigational drugs in the organization?
- How are protocols and criteria developed and approved for the use of investigational drugs?

SAMPLE MEDICATIONS

- Does the organization permit the dispensing of sample medications?
- What information is maintained in patient records in the event a sample drug is recalled?
- Does the organization maintain a medication log for tracking the dispensing of sample drugs?
- Does the log include the following pertinent information: medication dispensed; date medication was dispensed; patient name; patient record number; dosage and amounts given; medication control/lot numbers for purposes of recall; expiration date; and physician signature?

MEDICATIONS FROM HOME

- Are patients permitted to self-administer medications (e.g., insulin)?
- Where are the medications stored?
- How is monitoring conducted?

CRASH CARTS

- Who is responsible for stocking medications in crash carts?
- Who is responsible for checking laryngoscope batteries?
- Who is responsible to ensuring that medications have not expired?
- Who is responsible for ensuring the integrity of "crash carts" (e.g., appropriate medications, equipment, and supplies are available when needed)?
- Are logs maintained?
- Does the organization maintain the appropriate equipment on crash carts for treating both children and adults?
- Are staff members appropriately trained in the testing and use of equipment contained in or on the crash cart?
- How are staff members who participate in codes evaluated?
- Do pharmacists attend codes?

– What value might be added if pharmacists attended codes?
• Is there a collaborative approach to reviewing the organization's procedures after a code?
• What mechanisms are in place for reviewing medications administered during a code?

PATIENT/FAMILY EDUCATION

• Is education conducted on a collaborative basis?
  – What is the role of the nurse?
  – What is the role of the pharmacist?
  – What is the role of the physician?
  – How does rehabilitation staff participate in educational processes?
• How is education provided in ambulatory care settings?

MEDICATION USE IMPROVEMENT ACTIVITIES

• How is information on medication monitoring obtained?
• Describe the organization's cost reduction activities and how those activities have affected patient care (e.g., Zantac v. Tagamet; antibiotics; thrombolytics Activase v. streptokinase).
• What is the correlation between knowledge, research, and appropriateness?
• Describe the kinds of aggregate data available for performance improvement activities.

MULTIPLE MEDICATIONS

• What systems does the organization have in place to minimize the likelihood of drug-drug interactions?
• What is the protocol for handling patients on multiple medications?
• What stat lab tests does the organization have in place for patients who have overdosed?

NUTRITION

• Is the organization's mechanism for ordering, preparing, dispensing, administering, and monitoring of parenteral nutrition defined by the medical staff?
• Is the organization's mechanism for ordering, preparing, dispensing, administering, and monitoring of total parenteral nutrition defined by the medical staff?

LABORATORY

• Does laboratory staff participate in the activities of the pharmacy and therapeutics committee?
• Describe the importance of having laboratory representation on the pharmacy and therapeutics committee (e.g., the laboratory provides end data, panic values; monitors therapeutic ranges; checks blood levels for toxicity; determines therapeutic levels; provides lab data vital to evaluating the nutritional status of patients, drugs in—data out information, organism–drug interactions, culture and sensitivity studies, consultative role; evaluates physician ordering practices; etc.).
• Does the laboratory look at test results to discern, review, and evaluate results with clinical presentation and history?
• If test results do not fit the clinical picture or expected outcomes, what happens?
• Are laboratory personnel reviewing test results for drug interactions through testing procedures (e.g., patients can produce antibodies to drugs that can cross-react with laboratory tests)?
• Does communication between the laboratory and pharmacy facilitate the production of more useful data from laboratory tests and allow better utilization of laboratory resources to improve patient care and decrease direct costs to the patient and provider (e.g., documentation of draw times on specimens for therapeutic drug monitoring so that the drug level determined at a known point in time can be related to the specific dose given at a specific time. Without such a relationship in time, interpretation of serum drug levels to drug dosage would be questionable.)?
• What is the importance of having the admitting diagnosis and comments placed on lab slips (e.g., A glucometer ordered with the admitting diagnosis of urosepsis septic shock clues the lab to the fact that the patient may be on antibiotics, which can interfere with tests. A patient in septic shock may have abnormal glucose results on the glucometer. Such results would be followed up with a laboratory glucose to verify glucometer readings.)?
• Describe how the pharmacy, laboratory, and dietary work collaboratively to improve patient care.
• How is monitoring of the various shifts conducted?
• Why should patient assessment include questions of what medications are being administered?

NUTRITIONAL CARE

• How is the diet manual developed and approved?
• How are the criteria for nutritional screens developed and approved?

– Who participates in determining criteria?

– Who performs nutritional screens?

- What is the organization's process for screening and assessing patients at nutritional risk?

  – Is every patient's nutritional status screened?

- Is a physician's order necessary to conduct a full assessment?

- How is the potential for food–drug interactions monitored?

- Who is responsible for modified diet counseling?

- What criteria has the organization established for determining high-risk patients?

- How are patients on special diets monitored to ensure that they have the appropriate food tray?

- How are diet changes monitored?

- Are nutritional assessments conducted on a timely basis?

- How is the appropriateness of diet prescriptions monitored?

- How is the appropriateness and effectiveness of nutritional care monitored?

- How is competency to screen patients assessed?

- Is the patient consulted as part of the screening?

PERFORMANCE IMPROVEMENT (PI)

- What is the organization's process for PI?

- Does the organization have a PI improvement coordinating committee?

- Describe the membership of the committee.

  – Is membership interdisciplinary?

- What is done to educate staff in PI processes?

- What is the organization's methodology for establishing priorities for PI (how are priorities set)?

- How does the organization go about chartering PI teams?

- How has PI improved the health of the community?

- Do PI teams periodically review and revisit the results of their activities?

- How do PI teams go about outcomes measurement?

- What is the organization's methodology for PI?

- How is training and education provided to the staff?

- Describe organizational successes that have come about as a result of PI activities.

- What measurement systems does the organization participate in?

- How does the organization integrate the ambulatory care and other outpatient sites into the organization's PI process?

- What is the organization doing to evaluate the effectiveness and appropriateness of its PI program?

- Is the leadership committed to PI?

– Has commitment and buy-in to PI flowed throughout the organization?

- Are measurement and assessment major components of the PI process?

- Is the organization's leadership committed to the PI process?

- Is consideration given to involving patients and family in the PI process (e.g., focus groups)?

- How does the organization know it is doing well clinically?

- Describe the organization's success in integrating evening/weekend shifts into the PI process?

- What evidence/documentation does the organization have to demonstrate that internal processes are continuously and systematically assessed and improved?

- What is the organization's process for setting priorities?

- How does the organization decide what to review and improve (high-risk, high-volume, problem-prone activities)?

- What is the organization's process for *involvement across disciplines?*

- Does the organization have *collaborative practice teams?*

- How does the organization ensure that all staff participate in PI processes?

- How does the organization identify opportunities for improvement?

- What data does the organization trend for PI activities?

- How does the organization collect data?

- How does the organization measure or validate its successes?

- What clinical databases does the organization have in place for benchmarking?

- What internal and external databases does the organization use for benchmarking?

- What happens when measurement data suggest opportunities for improvement?

- Is intensive assessment conducted when variables of measurement are unacceptable?

- How are data assessed?

- How does the organization assess its success with critical pathways?

- How are PI processes improved?

- What effect has PI had on teamwork?

STERILE SUPPLY

- What is the mandated dress code for decontamination?

- Is decontamination performed elsewhere in the organization (e.g., labor and delivery and emergency department)?

- Are staff members cross-trained for each area?

- How does the organization handle implants?
- Describe the monitoring process of the sterilizers.
- Describe the flow of activities when contaminated instruments are received.
- Is biological testing being conducted and are records being maintained?

SURGICAL PROCEDURES

- Have physicians had the appropriate training and experience in the specialty for which privileges are being sought?
- Is there a listing of which procedures which physician can perform?
- What is the process for credentialing surgeons as to what procedures they can perform?
- Are the credentials of physicians and other professional staff current and organization specific?
- Who ensures that all appropriate assessments have been completed prior to surgery (e.g., history and physical and anesthesia)?
- Does the organization have assessment criteria for emergent and nonemergent surgical cases?
- What patient education is in place prior to surgery?
  - Are patients educated about medical equipment that may be used?
- What is the organization's procedure for ensuring that patients have been informed of the risks, benefits, and alternatives of anesthesia, surgical procedures, and administration of blood or blood products?
- Who is responsible for informing the patient of the risks, benefits, and alternatives to anesthesia, surgical procedures, and the administration of blood or blood products?
- Who verifies that consent forms (e.g., anesthesia, surgical, blood) have been completed and placed on the patient's record)?
- Does the organization have a process by which there is correlation of pathology and imaging findings?
- What is the organization's process for ensuring that it selected the right site and right surgical procedure for the right patient?
- Who is responsible for ensuring that the appropriate equipment, supplies, and staffing are available prior to induction (administration of anesthesia)?
  - Is surgical equipment properly cleaned and stored following each procedure?
  - Is blood stored in the operating room suite?
  - Is blood stored at appropriate temperatures?
  - How are temperatures monitored?

- Is there an alarm system on refrigerators to warn if temperatures fall too low or rise too high?
- Who is responsible for ensuring that each operating room has been properly cleaned prior to the next procedure?
- Do anesthesiologists cover all anesthetizing locations for all procedures?
- Who is responsible for developing and updating the organization's conscious sedation policy?
- Do nurse anesthetists administer conscious sedation and/or general anesthesia?
  - What is the process for credentialing nurse anesthetists?
  - How is competency reviewed?
  - Who monitors their work?
  - Is backup coverage readily available from an anesthesiologist?
  - Are there any limitations as to what forms of anesthesia can be administered?
- Are surgical nurses ACLS certified?
- How are patients monitored?
- Is monitoring the same at all locations?
- Does the organization have a mechanism in place for reviewing and monitoring unplanned returns to the operating suite?
- What are the criteria for discharge from the postanesthesia recovery unit?
- What redundant systems does the organization have in place for electrical failures, equipment breakdown, backup staffing, etc.?
- What processes does the organization have in place to follow up with patients who have postoperative infections?
  - How does the organization identify postoperative infections in day surgery patients?
  - What are the organization's procedures for follow-up on patients who have developed postoperative infections?
  - Is there routine consultative care by an infectious disease specialist when a patient develops a nosocomial infection?
  - How does the organization's infection rate compare with other organizations?
- Does the organization have an ongoing process for improving the outcome of surgical procedures?
- Is there appropriate separation of clean and soiled instrumentation?
- Does the organization perform surgical case reviews 100 percent of the time?
  - When sampling for case review, how are cases selected for review?

REHABILITATION SERVICES

- How are functional screens conducted?
- Is a physician's order necessary for a full assessment?
- If it is determined that a full assessment is necessary, within what time frame must it be completed?
- Who provides patient/family education?
- Does the organization provide for weekend coverage to ensure continuity of care?
- Who conducts the assessment and treatment of occupational performance?
- What skills does the occupational therapist evaluate (e.g., work adjustment, educational, social skills, neuromuscular, cognitive, psychosocial, treatment goals established)?

PATIENT SAFETY

- Does the organization have a designated smoking area?
- Do fire-rated doors
  - have a self-closing device?
  - have a positive latching mechanism?
- Are fire-rated doors smoke tight with vertical gaps no greater than 1/8 inch and undercuts no greater than 3/4 inch?
- Are designated smoking areas appropriately ventilated?
  - Is air exhausted to the outside?
- Are through-the-wall penetrations appropriately sealed to prevent the spread of smoke?
- Is there a clear space 18 inches below sprinkler heads?
- Exit signs
  - Are exit signs clear as to direction of egress?
  - Are exit signs illuminated?
- Do linen and trash chutes have positive latching?
  - Are linen chutes sprinklered on alternating floors?
  - Is the outlet storage room sprinklered?
- How are air handling systems monitored for replacement of air filters?
  - Is there both visual and mechanical monitoring?
- Is there gowning and glove change between patients?
- Are chairs disinfected with germicidal solutions between patients?
- What is the organization's process for disposing of hazardous wastes?
- Are electrical panels secure/locked; labeled; and provided with preventive maintenance?
- Are emergency generators properly tested (50 percent of nameplate rating or 50 percent of connected load, whichever is greater)?
- Are primary and secondary shutoff valves for utility systems labeled?
- Medical gas vacuum:
  - How is air conditioned prior to exhaust (e.g., air wash)?
  - Is the air intake a minimum of 10 feet from nearest air intake?
- Are exit corridors blocked with storage?
- Is there a safety committee?
  - Are safety reports submitted to the governing body?
- Are fire drills conducted?
- Are disaster drills conducted?
- Are fire circuits tested? Are portable fire extinguishers maintained according to appropriate safety codes?
- What precautions are taken for the storage of flammable gases and liquids?
- Have security/safety issues been addressed throughout the organization (e.g., nursery and operating suite)?
  - Have sensitive areas been identified?
  - What security precautions have been taken to protect these areas (e.g., nursery: combination locks, closed circuit TV, security rounds, wristbands alarmed, card alarm, etc.)?
- Are hazardous wastes stored in a safe and secure environment?
- Are hazardous materials inventoried by location?
- Is there a hazardous materials (HAZMAT) response team?
- What hazardous materials and wastes does the organization handle?
- What precautions are taken in handling and storing hazardous materials and wastes?
- How would hazardous spills be handled?
- Are reports of incidents related to spills maintained?
- Does the organization maintain written criteria as to the selection of medical equipment?
- Is equipment tested prior to use?
- Who is responsible for training the "end user"?
- How is equipment testing documented?
  - How are user errors reported?
  - How are programs evaluated?
  - Are there any trends?
  - Are actions taken as appropriate?
  - Are outside maintenance contracts monitored?
- Do medical equipment policies and procedures provide for
  - selecting and acquiring equipment?
  - written criteria to identify, evaluate, and inventory medical equipment?
  - assessing/minimizing clinical and physical risks associated with medical equipment by providing preventive and corrective maintenance services?
  - monitoring and acting on medical equipment hazardous notices and recalls?
  - monitoring and reporting incidents that may have caused or contributed to an injury?

– reporting and investigating equipment management problems?

• Is there is a reliable, adequate emergency power system to provide electricity to all critical areas?

• When testing emergency generators, is the connected load *greater than* 50 percent of the calculated load, or 30 percent of the nameplate rating, or is there an annual load bank test for a minimum of four hours at 80 percent of the nameplate rating?

• Are there current safety policies and procedures for each department?

• How are equipment failures reported?

• How are patients monitored during a total power failure?

• What procedures does the organization follow in the event of loss of water, power, medical gas, heat, and cooling?

RESOURCE CENTER VISIT

• What resources are available to the staff (e.g., Medline)?

• How are needs assessed?

• Are resources available to patients and families?

• In what PI activities does the medical librarian participate?

PATIENT UNIT

• Describe the role of the unit, size, special characteristics, census data, staffing patterns, results of patient satisfaction surveys, etc.

• How are medications stored?

• Where and what hazardous materials are stored, handled, and disposed of?

• What happens if there is a power failure?

• What is the smoking policy?

• Are bathrooms safe; provided with hand rails and call buttons?

• How is patient assessment integrated into the patient's record by the various disciplines?

• How are formulary updates communicated to the staff?

• Describe patient record documentation, including: admission records, history and physicals, anesthesia reports, operative reports, consent, medication records, patient/family education documentation, physician's orders, progress notes, rehabilitative service records, respiratory therapy, test result reporting records (e.g., laboratory, ECG, EEG, imaging reports), nurses' notes, advance directives, restraints, discharge planning, etc.).

• Are there unique safety concerns specific to the unit (e.g., special isolation procedures)?

• Are there age-specific requirements of the unit?

• Describe how patient rights are addressed.

• How are confidentiality issues addressed?

• Are the results of tests available in a timely manner (e.g., laboratory reports, including: routine, stat, panic values)?

• Is there evidence of patient/family education?
    – Is there an assessment of a patient's readiness/willingness, ability, and need to learn?
    – Are patients provided information as to allergies, blood type, etc.?

• What are the security issues specific to the unit?

• What PI activities are conducted on the unit?

• In specialty units such as the intensive care unit and the coronary care unit:
    – Are there monitors in all patient rooms?
    – Is there visual observation of patients at all times?
    – Are there admission criteria to the unit by diagnosis?
    – Are there discharge criteria?
    – Is there a consultation policy?
    – Are there specific triggers to generate a consultation (e.g., infection)?
    – What are the age groups of patients treated on the unit?
    – Are there age-specific criteria in job descriptions or on skills and competency checklists?

PATIENT VISIT

• Greeting: Hello, I'm from the _____. In our process for continuously improving patient care, I would like to ask you a few questions as to your understanding of the care you are receiving.
    – How are you today?
    – What brought you to the hospital?
    – Sounds like you had a bad/good day.
    – Who is your physician?
    – Have your care and treatment been explained to you?
    – Have you had an *opportunity* to ask questions about your care?
    – Did you *understand* the explanation given?
    – Do you believe that the staff has been *responsive* to your needs?
    – Do you feel *comfortable* asking questions?
    – Are you comfortable with your care?
    – Any questions about your care that remain *unanswered?*
    – Have you been to physical therapy?
    – What *activities* do you participate in?

• Education
    – Medication instructions?
    – Diet education?

– Equipment?
– Have the patient and family been involved in treatment planning and education?
• Discharge instructions?

PATIENT AND FAMILY EDUCATION

• How are the learning needs of patients and families addressed?
• How is patient education provided?
• What is the organization's mechanism for documentation on the patient record?
• How are the following issues addressed:
  – medication use?
  – medical equipment use?
  – drug/food interactions?
  – access to community resources?
  – how to obtain further care, if necessary?
  – responsibilities of patient and family?
  – resources available for patient/family education?
• Is the teaching reaching the patient?
  – Does the patient understand the message?
  – What is the likelihood that the patient and family will comply with instructions?
  – How is reinforcement of education conducted?
• Is there an interdisciplinary approach to patient and family education?
• What is the physician's role in patient and family education?
• What are the key factors to assessment and readiness to learn?
• How do you evaluate the effectiveness of patient education resources?
• What resources are available for patient and family education?
• What are your options or opportunities for follow-up and reinforcement of education?

Index